EIGHTEENTH-CENTURY BRITISH AESTHETICS

Edited by
Dabney Townsend
Armstrong Atlantic State University
Savannah, Georgia

Foundations and Frontiers in Aesthetics Series
Series Editors: Colin Martindale and Arnold Berleant

ROUTLEDGE Routledge
Taylor & Francis Group
LONDON AND NEW YORK

First published 1999 by Baywood Publishing Company, Inc.

Published 2018 by Routledge
2 Park Square, Milton Park, Abingdon, Oxon OX14 4RN
52 Vanderbilt Avenue, New York, NY 10017

First issued in paperback 2018

Routledge is an imprint of the Taylor & Francis Group, an informa business

Library of Congress Catalog Number: 97-48317

Library of Congress Cataloging-in-Publication Data

Eighteenth-century Bristish aesthetics / [edited by] Dabney Townsend.
p. cm. -- (Foundations and frontiers in aesthetics series)
Includes bibliographical references and index.
ISBN 0-89503-187-6
1. Aesthetics, British--18th century. I. Townsend, Dabney, 1941- . II. Series.
BH221.G72E34 1999
111'.85'094109033--dc21 97-48317
CIP

ISBN 13: 978-0-415-77233-4 (pbk)
ISBN 13: 978-0-89503-187-7 (hbk)

Preface

This collection brings together a number of hard to find texts dealing with beauty, taste, and related topics in aesthetics and the philosophy of art. It focuses on texts that are of interest to the philosophical study of aesthetics. Thus it omits literary criticism and the theory of painting and music except where they move into philosophy. Such a distinction is artificial, of course, especially in an age where neither philosophy nor literary theory had been segregated into discrete academic fields. Nevertheless, it provides a rough and ready distinction that justifies including writers such as James Harris and Daniel Webb while excluding Pope and the Wartons, who would otherwise be considered more important. I have also opted to include longer selections so that a sustained style and argument can be set forth, even at the expense of omitting some figures.

In choosing and editing this collection of texts, I have been guided by what would be most useful to the student of eighteenth-century British aesthetics or to the scholar who wants a reasonably comprehensive introduction and overview of the subject. These aims are not wholly compatible. Some of the key texts, for example Hume's "Of the Standard of Taste" and Reynolds' "Discourses," are readily available in inexpensive editions. Serious students will have them on their shelf. Yet to omit them here would give a decidedly unbalanced picture of the century. Thus I have elected to include them and others of varying degrees of availability. At the other extreme, there are a number of curiosities such as rhymed essays on taste[1] and Frances Reynolds'[2] curious treatise on the mechanics of beauty that, while they add a bit of esoteric perspective, contribute nothing either philosophically or culturally, though they are hard to come by for those who have an interest in such things. I have reluctantly omitted them in the interests of keeping to a manageable size. Within those limits, I have attempted to provide a representative selection.

A second problem is presented by the texts themselves. The eighteenth-century printed style was ideosyncratic to say the least. Moreover, in the course of the

[1] See, for example, Thomas B. Gilmore, Jr. (ed.), *Early Eighteenth-Century Essays on Taste* (Delmar, New York: Scholars' Facsimiles & Reprints, 1972).

[2] Frances Reynolds, *An Enquiry Concerning the Principles of Taste, and of the Origin of our Ideas of Beauty, &c.* (London: Printed by Baker and Galabin, 1785).

century, the accepted practices of style and printing changed. The predominant practice of capitalizing all nouns faded, as did the extensive use of italics. Spelling also changed. One choice would have been to preserve all textual characteristics. Scholarly fidelity argues for such a choice. It has the disadvantage of exaggerating the choice of edition, however, because consistency would then demand that difficult questions of textual variation and authority be dealt with, issues that are of direct concern only to the most specialized of readers and that are, in any event, often beyond my competence. The eccentricities of typography and excessive concern with minor differences between editions are needlessly off-putting to the reader whose primary interest is in the argument. Thus, I have opted instead to modernize capitals and italics, preserving only those of the latter that clearly are intended for special emphasis. I have also chosen to modernize spelling, though with somewhat more reluctance. A reader quickly becomes used to elided forms of spelling, for example, but there also seems little need to preserve such variations from modern practice. Ease of reading argues for modernization. I have not, however, replaced archaic word-forms with modern equivalents. Thus I have left "shew" for "show," "writ" for "wrote," and "tis" for "it is" as well as "hath," etc. As nearly as possible, I have left anything that would affect the sound or rhythm of the text while choosing the modern spelling when, at most, the alternative would affect the eye. In any instances that might affect the meaning, I have kept the original. Punctuation, which clearly affects the meaning more directly, I have left as it was printed unless it is clearly simply a matter of the printer's style (for example, the practice of repeating quotation marks at the beginning of lines or of varying the length of dashes to fill lines). I have also silently corrected a few obvious misprints, provided that they were truly obvious. Others have been allowed to stand, without the annoyance of scattered *sic*'s or typographical over-printing. The reader should assume that, within the limits of my proof-reading capabilities, oddities are part of the original. Notes that appear in the original have been converted to numbers and repositioned at the end of the reference, but if the text makes a distinction in types of notes, that distinction has been preserved. These are, after all, selections. To be most useful, they must be accessible to as wide an audience as possible while providing a reliable text. The specialist to whom textual variants matter will undoubtedly have to consult the originals or facsimiles of them in any case. I hope that what is presented here will suffice for the kind of philosophical and critical work that this collection is intended to promote.

Acknowledgments

I would like to thank the editors of the Baywood Publishing series, *Foundations and Frontiers in Aesthetics,* Colin Martindale and especially Arnold Berleant for their support and persistence on this project. Arnold has made valuable suggestions about the introductory essay that I have adopted with gratitude. Billie Huges patiently transcribed eighteenth-century texts with their difficult typography, and my colleagues in the Department of Philosophy and Humanities at the University of Texas at Arlington put up with my venting frustrations over problems with one text after the other. I appreciate the help and consideration that I received from everyone.

Contents

Introduction: Aesthetics in the Eighteenth Century 1

CHAPTER 1
John Dryden: "Introduction" to Charles du Fresnoy,
De Arte Graphica (1695) 33

CHAPTER 2
John Dennis: *A Large Account of the Taste in Poetry, and the Causes of the Degeneracy of It* (1702) 55

CHAPTER 3
Anthony Ashley Cooper, Third Earl of Shaftesbury: *Characteristics of Men, Manners, Opionions, Times* (1711) 71

CHAPTER 4
Joseph Addison: *The Spectator* (1712) 107

CHAPTER 5
Francis Hutcheson: *Reflections Upon Laughter* (1725) 137
An Inquiry Into the Original of our Ideas of Beauty and Virtue 150

CHAPTER 6
James Harris: *Three Treatises* (1744) 165

CHAPTER 7
John Baillie: *An Essay on the Sublime* (1744) 191

CHAPTER 8
Samuel Johnson: *The Rambler* (1751) 205

CHAPTER 9
William Hogarth: *Analysis of Beauty, Written with a View of Fixing the Fluctuating Ideas of Taste* (1753) 209

CHAPTER 10
David Hume: *Of the Delicacy of Taste and Passion* (1741) 227
Of the Standard of Taste (1757) 230
Of Tragedy (1757) 242

CHAPTER 11
Edmund Burke: *A Philosophical Enquiry into the Origin of Our Ideas of the Sublime and Beautiful* (1757/1759) 249

CHAPTER 12
Alexander Gerard: *An Essay on Taste* (1759) 279

CHAPTER 13
Joseph Priestley: *A Course of Lectures on Oratory and Criticism* (1759/1777) 297

CHAPTER 14
Daniel Webb: *An Inquiry into the Beauties of Painting and into the Merits of the Most Celebrated Painters, Ancient and Modern* (1760) . . . 303

CHAPTER 15
Henry Home, Lord Kames: *Elements of Criticism* (1762) 309

CHAPTER 16
Sir Joshua Reynolds: *The Idler* (1759) 331
Discourses on Art—Discourse Seven (1776) 337

CHAPTER 17
James Beattie: *Essays on Poetry and Music, as They Affect the Mind* (1762) 355

CHAPTER 18
Hugh Blair: *Lectures on Rhetoric and Belles Lettres* (1783) 373

CHAPTER 19
Archibald Alison: *Essay on the Nature and Principles of Taste* (1790) . . 405

CHAPTER 20
William Gilpin: *Three Essays* (1791) 421

CHAPTER 21
Uvedale Price: *An Essay on the Picturesque as Compared with the Sublime and Beautiful* (1794) 431

CHAPTER 22
Adam Smith: *Of the nature of that Imitation which Takes Place in What are Called the Imitative Arts* (1795) 441

Index 471

Introduction
Aesthetics in the Eighteenth Century

In the eighteenth century, the rise of the philosophic issues that came to form modern aesthetics is a complex movement as one might expect from the broad involvement of critics, artists, philosophers, connoisseurs, and dilettantes of all kinds. It is intimately connected to the new empiricist philosophy of Locke and Newton, but older scholastic modes of expression provide the conceptual framework. Moreover, the terms of the contemporary debates are set by divisions that are different and are understood differently from our modernist understanding of the same issues. We can often detect our own interests, but the contemporary expression of them is couched in terms current to the times. Among the dominant influences in that respect are divisions between classicists and modernists, between rationalist followers of Descartes and/or Leibniz and the followers of Newton and Locke, and between commercially motivated authors and critics and the talented polite learning of the nobility. The central debates are about the relation of poetry to painting and music, the development and judgments of taste, the characteristics of beauty and its uses, and critical issues concerning rules of composition, presentation, and status. The result is a decidedly messy but rich mixture.

1. Aesthetics

One issue of terminology must be dealt with at the beginning to avoid misunderstanding. A. G. Baumgarten coined the word *aesthetics* from the Greek adverb αισθητικος, having to do with perceiving by the senses. Baumgarten used it to mark a distinction between sensible perception and intellectual perception. His task in his aesthetics was to locate sensible experience, and particularly feeling, in the rationalist tradition of Leibniz and Christian Wolff. Baumgarten's strategy was to make a place for feeling both as a first step toward rational knowledge and as a legitimate, though limited, form of knowledge in its own right. Immanuel Kant adopted the word in his critical philosophy and shifted its usage from Baumgarten's narrow reference to felt sensation to any form of pre-theoretical apprehension. The word *aesthetic* did not come into widespread use in Britain until the 1830s, and by then it was being used more broadly than Baumgarten's rationalist project would indicate. Thus to use the word at all with regard to eighteenth-century Britain is anachronistic. It is also misleading because the issues in eighteenth-century British discussions centered on the arts and do not reflect many of the Kantian presuppositions that references to aesthetics now take for granted. Kantian notions of disinterestedness, intuitive sensibility, and the free play of the imagination, as well as relations to art, the beautiful, and the sublime based on an aesthetic attitude appear, if at all, only in tentative ways in the eighteenth century. Even where the word *disinterested* does appear, its context indicates a strong link to anti-Hobbesian moral philosophy, for example.

Nevertheless, it is now taken for granted that, even if the concepts themselves are not present, our understanding of them requires us to look back before their origin to their roots in the philosophy and criticism of the late seventeenth and eighteenth centuries. English and Scottish criticism, belles lettres, and philosophy are much more important to the subsequent history of aesthetics than the academic and near scholastic speculation of Baumgarten and his followers. We find ourselves in the awkward position of having no word that both indicates the subsequent development of aesthetics and is also true to the conceptual structure current in the pre-Kantian discussions in Britain. No neologism has been accepted. Sir William Hamilton would have preferred the coinage *apolaustic* as the umbrella term to refer to the philosophy of taste, the theory of the fine arts, and the science of the beautiful,[1] but it is merely eccentric. We could dispense with a term altogether and refer variously to the controversies, issues, and theories that are of interest to contemporary aesthetics. Yet that loses the significance of bringing them all together. I have chosen, therefore, to live with the anachronism, however misleading, and refer to eighteenth-century British aesthetics even though there is no such thing. In this context, it should be understood as an awkward substitute to avoid periphrastic verbosity.

2. The Ancients and Moderns: Science and Association

Aesthetics in eighteenth-century Britain is not a single, unified movement. It develops in the context of arguments and problems that arise in a variety of situations tangentially related to what we now recognize as philosophical aesthetics. One of those arguments is the ongoing debate within criticism and the arts over the relative priority of classical and modern arts and artists, a debate that is itself a part of a larger argument over the relative merits of modern versus classical learning and culture. The success of scientific and empiricist methodology in the seventeenth and eighteenth centuries was sufficient to produce a widespread public sense of the superiority of modern views of cosmology and physics. Science was still simple enough so that talented amateurs such as Benjamin Franklin and Joseph Priestley could make significant contributions to the study of electricity and chemistry. It also had about it something of popular entertainment. Scientific

[1] According to the OED, *Lectures on Metaphysics*, I, vii, 124.

demonstrations were performed for public audiences, and the collection and exhibition of curiosities was a popular form of display, not unrelated to the development of the museum. Newton acquired the reputation of a secular patron saint, as Pope's epitaph shows:

> Nature and Nature's Laws lay hid in Night;
> God said, Let Newton be! and all was Light.

The foundation of the Royal Society in England and similar groups on the continent, particularly Frederick the Great's sponsorship in Prussia of scientific investigations, institutionalized modern scientific investigation as a new force in learned circles. The best that could be said for classical science was that the moderns built upon the shoulders of giants.

Even that acknowledgment was more an act of cultural piety than of serious influence. As a matter of fact, the new science and mathematics owed very little to classical sources. Instead, it combined the mathematical discoveries of Descartes, Newton, and Leibniz with the rapidly advancing technology that made observation more detailed and the individualism of empiricist philosophy and Rennaissance humanism to completely recast the place of learning and discovery in the human economy. Science was pre-eminently a matter of individual experimentation and exploration. Newton, Boyle, Harvey, and others conducted their own investigations and promoted them as individual achievements. The partisan conflict between the followers of Leibniz and Newton over priority in developing the infinitesimal calculus shows the importance of individual personalities in the development of science.

Science modified the way human psychology was modeled as well. In particular the development of associationism on the model of mechanical causation individualized the view of the mind. What one person thought depended on what that individual had experienced and how a unique set of experiences interacted to produce the ideas that defined a particular person.

Associationist psychology took a number of forms. The basic empiricist scheme laid down by John Locke allows two sources of ideas: sensation or impression, and reflection on the operation of the mind itself. The function of reason is to recognize those ideas and monitor their combination into complex ideas so that the mind is neither deceived by what it apprehends nor misled by its own operations. A fundamental problem for this individualized, empirically formed mind is that minds vary so greatly. An explanation is required to account for why everyone does not know all and only true ideas. Locke introduces the association of ideas at the end of Book II of *An Essay Concerning Human Understanding* in the context of a discussion of madness and error. Association of ideas is essentially negative—something that needs to be controlled. Locke writes,

> Some of our *Ideas* have a natural Correspondence and Connexion one with another: It is the Office and Excellency of our Reason to trace these, and hold them together in that Union and Correspondence which is founded in their peculiar Beings.

> Besides this there is another Connexion of *Ideas* wholly owing to Chance or Custom; *Ideas* that in themselves are not at all of kin, come to be so united in some Mens Minds, that 'tis very hard to separate them, they always keep in company, and the one no sooner at any time comes into the Understanding but 'its Associate appears with it; and if they are more than two which are thus united, the whole gang always inseparable shew themselves together.[2]

He goes on to give several cautionary tales of the evil that can be done by association of ideas if it is not carefully watched in the education and development of the mind. The problem, of course, is that while ideas founded on experience itself are reliable and the powers of the mind, properly exercised, will make only true complexity, association is a matter of chance and individual happenstance.

Nevertheless, association of ideas is too powerful a form of mechanical explanation to be restricted to Locke's essentially negative usage. It reappears vaguely and unsystematically as an adjunct to moral philosophy. John Gay, the cousin of the Poet, appeals to the association of ideas in an essay prefixed to his publication of Archbishop William King's essay on the origin of evil. Gay wants to show that Hutcheson relied too heavily on instinct and some form of innate ideas in his moral philosophy. Gay argues that "our Approbation of Morality, and all Affections whatsoever, are finally resolvable into *Reason*, pointing out *private Happiness*, and are conversant only about things apprehended to be means tending to this end; and that whenever this end is not perceiv'd, they are to be accounted for from the *Association of Ideas*, and may properly be call'd Habits."[3] Gay's account makes virtue and moral sense directly dependent on God's action; Gay wants to exclude any element of innate or instinctive virtue. Thus he accounts for the passions as arising from pleasure and pain and fixed by associations. "The Case is really this. We first perceive or imagine some real Good, i.e. fitness to promote our Happiness in those things which we love and approve of. Hence . . . we annex Pleasure to those things. Hence those things and Pleasures are so ty'd together and associated in our Minds, that one cannot present itself but the other will also occur. And the Association remains ever after that which at first gave them the Connection is quite forgot, or perhaps does not exist, but the contrary."[4] Thus no products of the moral sense are innate or instinctive; we can only acquire them from our own experience or learn them from others. Moreover, association connects ideas and pleasure as well as ideas and other ideas.

From Gay's broadening of the association of ideas to include all of the passions, it is still another step to David Hartley's mechanical theory of the association of ideas that incorporates a Newtonian schema of vibrations and transmission of ideas.

[2] John Locke, *An Essay Concerning Human Understanding*, ed. Peter H. Nidditch (Oxford: Clarendon press, 1975), Book II, Chapter XXXIII, p. 395.

[3] John Gay, *A Dissertation Concerning the Fundamental Principle and Immediate Criteria of Virtue as also the Obligation, and Aprobation of it. With some account of the Orgin of the Passions and Affections* (London: 1731), p. xiv.

[4] *Ibid.*, xxx-xxxi.

Hartley's object is also moral. The second volume of his *Observations on Man* is titled "Observations on the Duty and Expectations of Mankind." But Hartley introduces two major changes from the Lockean model. For Hartley, the association of ideas can actually produce ideas; the vibrations themselves can shift slightly so that new ideas are formed. This might be understood as merely a further complexity, but it allows the mind, through association, to combine and shift ideas so that they are more than merely a complex combination of the simple ideas provided by sense. And the operation is mechanical and involuntary. Instead of being in need of control, it is itself a means to an end. Like Gay, Hartley is prepared to accept that only a directly fortunate divine plan for each individual can lead the moral sense to virtue. Hartley faces the likely objection squarely: "The mechanical Generation of the Pleasures and Pains of the Moral Sense may by some be thought an Objection to the Reasoning here used; but it will appear otherwise, upon due Consideration. For all Things which have evident final Causes, are plainly brought about by mechanical Means; so that we may argue either way, *viz.* either from the mechanical Means, to the Existence of a final Cause, not yet discovered; or from the Existence of a final Cause, to that of a mechanical Means, not yet discovered."[5] Such a mechanical explanation can then be regarded in either of two ways: For the deist, it is working out some predetermined goal. For the Calvinist, it requires the intervention (perhaps to the end of both salvation and damnation) of an inscrutable divine hand.

Hartley's form of association, minus some of the speculative mechanism and theological application, is taken up by Joseph Priestley who uses it as the basis both for his own version of theological explanation and for his rhetorical theories, including a theory of taste. David Hume gives the theory a further twist by distinguishing between the association of ideas and the association of impressions. Impressions are immediate forms of sensation and reflection; association can be appealed to, as it was by Gay, to account for the pleasure and pain that belongs to the passions. But ideas are secondary repetitions of impressions, and association influences the way that ideas are recalled and even how they are perceived through sympathy. Hume develops a complex theory of the passions in Book Two of the *Treatise of Human Nature* that distinguishes between those passions that are immediate and those that require a double object such as possession. In Hume's successors in Scotland, particularly Alexander Gerard and Archibald Alison, association becomes the primary means of explaining aesthetic phenomena such as the perception of grace or beauty.

3. The Ancients and Moderns: Art

Associationist psychology, with its justification of a moral sense, its mechanical speculations, and its rhetorical applications provided a basis for the superiority of

[5] David Hartley, *Observations on Man, His Frame, His Duty, and His Expectations* (London, 1749), II, 338.

modern investigation of the mind and human nature over the psychology of the ancients, particularly Aristotle. This is important because in the arts, the ancients seem to have a much stronger claim. While modern science and cosmology clearly seem even to the most conservative thinkers in the eighteenth century to have won out, it seemed to many in the eighteenth century that the ancients achieved a perfection in the arts that no modern could challenge. This is in part, of course, because the ancients have the advantage of their antiquity: The only ancient texts that we know have stood the test of time that is so often applied as the only way to sort out the error produced by the psychology of individual response. If God alone could assure that a moral sense led to true happiness, and if, according to Calvinist theology, some would lack that final cause, then only time could guide the fickle sense of beauty in the arts. The ancients also have the advantage provided by the fact that education and taste were still formed by classical learning, although that was slowly changing as more middle-class artists and scholars depended less and less on Latin and Greek models. One of the third Earl of Shaftesbury's objections to his grandfather's physician and advisor, John Locke, was that Locke lacked the necessary classical education. The models in the arts remained the acknowledged classics, and the rules derived from them played an important role in shaping eighteenth-century British taste. The desire to emulate the rules of an imagined classical golden age gave weight to the side of the ancients in the arts.

The superiority of the ancients also was promoted by the emerging discoveries and dissemination of classical art works and the speculation that ensued from it. On the continent, J. J. Winckelmann made classical archeology a form of learning, and G. E. Lessing brought critical skill in the arts to bear on classical questions. Their genuine erudition enhanced the prestige of all things classical. It became very desirable not only to imitate classical forms, but also to preserve, restore, collect, and own classical objects. In Britain, Lord Elgin is only the most prominent example of the urge to find, admire and preserve classical artifacts. The same impulse undoubtedly motivated the nationalist desire to discover more native classical sources that led to the Ossian imposture and numerous instances of forgery. If native Britain was to compete with classical Greece and Rome, it was felt that it must have its own classical age with its own epic poets. If they could not be discovered, then they would be invented.

From the standpoint of the development of aesthetic philosophies, the conflicts that arose out of the disputes over the relative priorities of the ancients and moderns shaped the aesthetic questions, therefore. On the one hand, via associationist psychology and an admiration for the achievements of Newtonian science, aesthetic questions were put into empiricist form. On the other hand, in the arts, the authority of classical authors and the achievement of classical artists seemed to place taste and reason on the side of the ancients except in painting, where technical skill in perspective and a lack of ancient examples favored the moderns. This almost intolerable tension shows clearly in the writings of the first half of the century. Shaftesbury tries to balance classical virtue against his own sensibility. Peter Jones argues for the influence of Cicero on Hume's moral and aesthetic thought.[6] And Daniel Webb works within a traditional theory of imitation and continues to defend the ancients, particularly in painting. The problem for Webb is thus how to justify the ancients when modern painting seems superior from the standpoint of technical skill. And the problems posed by the controversy over the relative priority of the ancients and moderns continues to appear well into the time that the combination of association and imagination lead to theories of aesthetic expression.

4. Rationalism and Empiricism

The alliance between Newtonian science and philosophical empiricism is paralleled in another area of fundamental disagreement: the rationalism of Descartes and Leibniz versus not only Locke but the more pragmatic forms of empiricism that Locke's basic principles helped justify. The place of reason as it bears on aesthetic arguments is never a simple choice between reason and experience. Rather it turns on how reason is understood. Reason can be assigned one of two roles: It is either the innate source of principles and rules by which practice should be regulated, or it is a higher-level function that is called upon to order and discipline what experience alone can begin. The latter function is obviously the choice within the empiricist tradition, but it raises serious problems for aesthetic practice.

The problem can be illustrated by considering how secondary qualities are related to the mind. The empiricist tradition widely accepted that qualities such as color and taste are only in the mind and cannot be connected directly to their object. The connection must be made via some form of faculty psychology. If beauty is included among the secondary qualities, it too is not a quality of an object but a quality of the mind's apprehension of the object. Critical and artistic practice, however, indicate otherwise in the case of art. Art is unlike one's color and taste responses in that art is an acquired skill, as Aristotle emphasized and as any eighteenth-century thinker would have accepted. If one begins with experience, that experience must be prior to any formative operations by which one acquires that experience. For the classical theories of beauty, of course, that was not a problem because beauty was understood as a form or order belonging to a higher intellect. Beauty had an ontological status superior to mere physical objects. But for a consistent modern empiricist, a concept of beauty could be based only on some prior sensory experience unless beauty was itself part of the mind's apprehension of its own powers.

That argument leads to rationalism's understanding of the mind, however. The rationalism of the Cartesians and of Leibniz and Spinoza is not opposed to empiricism at a basic level. Both break with classical epistemology. Beauty is not an extra-mental form, nor is the way to beauty through contemplation and participation.

[6] Peter Jones, *Hume's Sentiments: Their Ciceronian and French Context* (Edinburgh: University of Edinburgh Press, 1982).

For the rationalist as much as the empiricist, beauty is a function of individual minds attaining an ordered, psychologically pleasurable form of perception. As the arguments are understood by eighteenth-century thinkers interested in the arts and criticism, both rationalists and empiricists are adherents of the new science. The point of difference lies in how the faculty that grasps beauty is believed to operate. For the rationalist, its function is to deliver clear and distinct ideas. Beauty is thus not sensuous and confused but universal and clear. It abandons the perspectival limitations of the senses and attains a quantitatively larger application than any mere sense perception can claim. As such, beauty belongs not to an object but to the mind's own grasp of what objects confusedly present. The regulative function of reason must be innate, and in order for it to function, the mind's faculty must include some ideational content also, at least in the form of logical, mathematical, and geometrical principles. In the process, art is left behind as one climbs the ladder of the intellect and pulls up the ladder behind one.

While this rationalist picture of beauty overcomes the paradox of artistic production that confronts empiricists, it raises its own kind of problem for art. The sensuous and felt nature of the pleasure provided by art is not, on its face, like the intellectual pleasure of a rationalist's beauty found in clear and distinct ideas. The price for accepting a rationalist construction of an argument for the aesthetic apprehension of beauty is to make the beauty of both art and nature secondary and inferior. It was this failure that led Baumgarten to try to incorporate feeling into the picture as, at least, a useful stage in the mind's apprehension of beauty. If such beauty was, in the last analysis, inferior, it nevertheless might be the most accessible form of perception for most people.

The temptation of this rationalist picture is evident in a number of otherwise empiricist theories of beauty. John Dennis, for example, has his own practical form of the paradox. To be successful, a playwright must appeal to a large public; drama must offer humor, not esoteric wit. The appeal of a play is subjective and thus problematic from the standpoint of producing rules. Therefore, Dennis tries to shift the appeal to a test of time so that the public may be extended sufficiently to account for immediate unpopularity. The good author does not write for "the generality" but for the few who are able to understand. The inconsistency of appealing to humor over wit and yet appealing to an elite audience does not seem to disturb Dennis.

Addison and Hutcheson are more acute thinkers. Addison explicitly appeals to Locke's model (*Spectator* 413). Yet his critical practice based on classical learning, wit, and irony favors an even more elite audience than Dennis's. Francis Hutcheson also explicitly acknowledges Locke's basic outline at the beginning of *An Inquiry into the Original of our Ideas of Beauty and Virtue*. Hutcheson's *Reflections on Laughter* provide another example of the attempt at a philosophical psychology of human nature. They are very much of a piece with Hume's *Treatise*, particularly Book Two. Both Hutcheson and Hume attempt to map the passions as the product of forms of sensory input combined with mental oversight. (Hume is more extreme, however, in limiting that oversight to sentiment itself.) Yet Hutcheson needs some instinctive form of inner sense to correlate uniformity amidst variety with the pleasure provided by the inner senses. That comes close to returning "inner sense" to its rationalist role of mental judge operating on the unruly senses. Hutcheson is no rationalist, but both Gay and Hume reproach him for introducing innate ideas by the back door, and they are not wholly wrong.

Perhaps no one makes a more extensive use of scientific analogies in accounting for taste than Alexander Gerard. The principles of taste are like the principles of mechanics. But Gerard's view of science is over-simple, and he does not consider the problems raised by observation. What, in taste, corresponds to the measurements of force, mass, time and distance? Without those objective measures, the analogy breaks down. His citation of uniformity, simplicity, variety, novelty, and proportion cannot operate in the same way that physical properties do because they are qualitative rather than quantitative. Once again, the empiricist forms of subjectivity need some means of bridging the gap between subjective experience and an authoritative reason. A rationalist can make the subjective qualities themselves into quantitative criteria because a quantity of ideas serves to reduce, though it cannot completely eliminate, confusion just as a multiplicity of perspectives corrects the distortion and limitation of a single point of view. Gerard and those who follow him in multiplying aesthetic predicates and "senses" are impelled by the implicit logic of the rationalist argument.

In contrast to Gerard's overt endorsement of a Newtonian mechanical model for aesthetic epistemology, Edmund Burke starts with the assumption that reason and taste are parallel. In so doing, he goes against the distinction that had grown up within the empiricist tradition that the passions operate differently from reason. Burke is not prepared to follow the sentimentalists in accepting that normative judgments belong to the passions rather than to reason, but his main thrust is that both operate according to common principles. His problem is to supply those principles. Therefore, Burke looks back behind the rationalists to a more formally Aristotelian form of empiricism. Yet the implicit result is the same. He adds the sublime, not in Longinus's merely rhetorical sense, but in a more robustly epistemological sense, to the aesthetic vocabulary of the beautiful. Both beauty and the sublime operate, for Burke, as if they are regulative principles on a par with other essentially rational criteria. One can "know" one's passions by recognizing their aesthetic place. Once this move is accepted, later writers are free to add other such regulative passions. The picturesque ultimately provides a link to an empiricist version of the same aesthetic autonomy provided by Kantian disinterestedness.

To take only one more example, Hugh Blair opts for sense over reason, but he so blurs the lines that one cannot distinguish one from the other. The metaphor of sense, he acknowledges, is based more on the educable palate (improved by exercise as the body is) than on immediate response—on wine tasting more than the distinction of sweet from bitter. Blair also observes that the ancients do not have a word for taste, though he quotes both Cicero and Quintilian as asserting something like taste. Blair's appeal is more explicitly to rhetorical function than the epistemological interests of the other empiricist treatments of beauty cited here, but he is still puzzled by the same paradox that occupies both rationalists and empiricists.

The point of these comparisons is not to blur the lines of difference between rationalists of the Cartesian and Leibnizian persuasion on the one hand and the followers of Locke and Newton on the other, but to emphasize that both are working out a modernist, scientific break with classical forms of aesthetics. Both encounter a problem about aesthetic experience. The rationalist must find some place for it in a system that begins by accepting a view of the mind as essentially a thinking or reasoning machine. The empiricist must find some way to regulate experience by a mind that begins as a blank slate and can only go as far as sensation will take it and thus lacks an innate rational faculty. Put in these schematic terms, the tendency of the British empiricist tradition to slip in elements of their rationalists opponents is obvious. It is ultimately set aside only when a different route is found via the imagination and expression to a romantic and idealist mind that will dominate aesthetics in the nineteenth and twentieth centuries.

5. The Arts and Nature

The kind of disputes over the role of reason that occupy rationalist and empiricist philosophers alike may be central conceptually, but they are by no means the focus of attention for most writers interested in the nature of beauty, the arts, and responses to them. The inherited vocabulary sets the problems more traditionally. P. O. Kristeller argued that the concept of the fine arts is itself a product of an evolving re-orientation of the arts in the eighteenth century.[7] On the one side, the fine arts were not yet completely distinguished from the practical arts. On the other, the arts remained inferior to nature. The function of the artist, therefore, was two-fold. Artists were craftsmen, and their craft required that they know and follow nature.

This seemingly innocent cliché exercised considerable practical power in the formulation of eighteenth-century aesthetic theory. In one respect, it linked artistic practice back to classical models. Classical writers and sculptors were given credit for being much freer of the artificial conventions attributed to medieval artists, and admiration for the Rennaissance was attributed to what was taken to be its successful restoration of classical practices. There was also a reaction against the mannered style of allegory, pastoral, and metaphysical wit. Critics such as Samuel Johnson, in particular, deplored the artificiality of metaphysical poetry and looked to nature as the moral source of poetry.

Yet exactly the same appeal to nature could be made by the more sentimental writers in both moral philosophy and aesthetics—a tradition that Johnson abhorred. The appeal to sentiment was believed to be based on a view of human nature as corrupted only by the excesses of civilization. Shaftesbury's sentimentalism was pilloried by Bishop Berkeley in *Alciphron*, and Hume was lumped together with Rousseau in the mind of his religious opponents. Of course, neither Shaftesbury nor Hume fits the caricatures offered by their opponents. Shaftesbury's view of sentiment requires that it be both corrected and disciplined by a consciousness of the

[7] Paul Oskar Kristeller, "The Modern System of the Arts," *Essays on the History of Aesthetics*, ed. Peter Kivy (Rochester: University of Rochester Press, 1992).

good of the whole and of the individual's place in it. Hume's appeal to sentiment is even more circumscribed. Sentiment must be shaped by the same empirical forces that give us confidence in causation in spite of its equally unprincipled foundations in any rationalist sense of innate or logical principles. The passions may trump any rationalist form of deductive argument, but that is only possible because the passions themselves play a cognitive as well as emotive role. All of this ambiguity is captured by the catch phrase advice to artists to "follow nature."

To artists, in particular, the injunction to follow nature included a command to follow a set of rules that nature provided. Some of this advice was practical. Perspective, for example, had been developed into a quasi-science. Hogarth did a series of engravings illustrating true and false perspective and himself liked to play tricks with the rules of perspective. Similar interest in classical form guided painters. The quest for principles and its relation to the science of human nature therefore casts a different light on the commonplace appeal to nature as the guiding principle. Shaftesbury's method of soliloquy suggests the tension between the individual and the generically human. He presumes a common nature, but it must be discovered by a process of self-examination and self-disclosure. When Reynolds appeals to nature, he should be understood to be appealing to those regularities of the human mind that can be identified and relied upon. That is rather different from a command to "follow nature" that amounts to an appeal to the classical status quo. Nature is the opposite of caprice, changableness, and chance. To follow nature is to rely upon probabilities, as Hume argued, and to avoid the shifting grounds of accidence as Reynolds believed necessary if the painter was to succeed.

6. Rules

Following nature is completely compatible with following rules, therefore. At issue is the nature of the rules. A first step in constructing eighteenth-century aesthetics begins with the craft-like neo-classical quest for these rules and leads inexorably to their abandonment as the early romantic and expressive aesthetic replaces neo-classicism in the course of the century. Rules appear in three related but distinguishable contexts. First, rules are needed by artists to guide their art. Second, rules are needed by the audience to guide their response to art. And finally, rules are needed by critics to judge both works of art themselves and the response of audiences. All three situations are taken for granted in claims about nature and rules, but in fact they change in the course of the eighteenth century.

The nature of rules in all three situations is problematic. One way to regard rules looks back to classical logic. Syllogisms are governed by rules: Given that all men are mortal and that Socrates is a man, it follows by rule that Socrates is mortal. The rules of the schoolmen are thus foundational in the strongest way. The appeal of the ancients and the underlying classical education that was common to neo-classical aesthetics suggests that this sense of 'rule' is not altogether absent. One of the functions of neo-classical rhetoric is to persuade, and the strongest form of persuasion will be logical inferences to which all but the weakest intellects must accede. A good plot, therefore, has the inevitability of a syllogism. The wit of the metaphysical poets likewise depended on the ability of logic to carry a reader beyond what is expected to unexpected but inevitable conclusions. The authority of Aristotle's Poetics gave credence to the establishment of rules for drama that at least are supposed to govern both the response of an audience and the construction of the plot itself.

If the rhetorical force of a syllogism can be understood, then the presence of such rules will determine success. The neo-classical desire for rules is thus intended as a practical guide. In his introduction to Charles du Fresnoy's *De Arte Graphica*, Dryden states clearly what is expected of the philosophy of art at the beginning of the century: the rules of the art, the reasons for appreciation, and the conditions of translating nature into art by imitation. Without these, one might be imposed on by bad works; with them, the direct effects of art are made self-conscious. To achieve this, one needs to formulate the rules and compare the best work. For Dryden, the need for rules follows from the fact that poetry and painting are arts. 'Art' here retains its basic meaning of something made by skill and craft. So if something is an art, there must be means, and hence rules, by which it is made. The fine arts, with their attendant creative mystery, are not yet part of the equation.[8] The kind of rules that Dryden has in mind govern things like the scope of invention, the economy of the plot, and the posture of the characters *vis-a-vis* the audience.

The force of syllogistic rules may be appealing, but it is fundamentally at odds with the empiricist direction that British aesthetics takes under the influence of Locke and Newton. Dryden repeatedly points out that his own plots do not follow such rules. A different sense of 'rule' emerges very soon. Empirical rules have the force of laws of nature if they can be grounded in cause and effect. If not, they still provide inductive guidance. In this sense, 'rule' has a more limited scope. It examines past practice to determine future expected effects. The importance of comparing poetry to painting lies in identifying the common features of both that serve as rules. Thus, though the comparison considers which form is greater, the likeness is more important. Short of the kind of scientific certainty provided by laws of nature, one can still have an expectation of success, and to the practicing artists, that is what is required. Reynolds clearly understands rules in that sense: "What has pleased, and continues to please, is likely to please again: hence are derived the rules of art, and on this immovable foundation they must ever stand."[9]

Since comparison must be based on successful instances if it is to provide sound rules, the production of inductive rules remains conservative. The classical works that are universally acknowledged are the only ones that can be relied on to provide rules. Shaftesbury also looks for rules in nature—proportion, harmony, and numbers are real relations. The problem, of course, is how to relate them to the effects that they are supposed to produce. For, as becomes all too clear, the effects provide the rules for art. Once the effects are taken as constitutive, the kind of rule focuses on the individual members of an audience rather than the universal nature of the rule itself. The Abbé Jean-Baptiste Du Bos laid it down as a rule that only the effect determined the quality of a work: "Since the chief end of poetry and painting is to move us, the

[8] John Dryden, "Introduction to Charles du Fresnoy, *De Arte Graphica*." See p. 33, this volume.

[9] Sir Joshua Reynolds, "Discourse Seven." See p. 337, this volume.

productions of these arts can be valuable only in proportion as they touch and engage us. A work that is exquisitely moving, must be an excellent piece, take it all together. For the same reason, a work which does not move and engage us, is good for nothing." Du Bos influenced Hume directly, and his work was translated into English in 1748 by Thomas Nugent.[10] Thus rules themselves, though intended to provide guidance to the artist and to determine the way an audience should react, come to be grounded in the same subjective responses that they are intended to overcome. The incipient circularity cannot be ignored.

An appeal to science as a source of rules as it is advanced by Gerard, Reynolds, and Kames is in danger of falling into Du Bos' kind of subjectivity, as Hume clearly sees. The principles that are sought cannot be understood to provide *a priori* certainty or Cartesian foundations. They are the kind of empirical laws that, while subject to revision and confirmation, allow a scientist to predict the outcome of experiments. In this case, the field is human nature, and the experiments are practiced by artists in moving the sentiments and passions of their audience. There are varying degrees of confidence in the reliability of such predictions. Everyone agrees that they rest on the common nature shared by all humans. But some, most notably Hume, recognize that the variations are more than science would normally tolerate. Kames and Gerard, on the other hand, are more confident that a standard of taste sufficient to convince everyone is available on the basis of the emergent principles of criticism.

Rules themselves come to require conditions of application. For example, John Dennis lays down three rules for a correct taste for comedy that are necessary both to the writer and the audience: great parts, a generous education, and due application.[11] He interprets the last of these as an ability to enter into the passions of different characters and a detachment from one's own concerns that makes that possible. His condition is thus something like the disinterestedness that will eventually emerge. Along the same lines, Dr. John Baillie adheres to the view that rules govern written forms, but his approach is more philosophically sophisticated than that of Dennis. The manner itself must be defined before rules can be formulated.[12] Rules prove more comforting, therefore, than their application can justify. In many cases, just as an appeal to Nature conceals uncertainty about what that nature is, so an appeal to rules conceals their lack of authority.

Critical correction of the absurdity of rules is common. Samuel Johnson, for example, is only one of the forceful objectors to attempt to make the Aristotelian

[10]Abbé Du Bos, *Réflexions Critiques sur la Poésie et sur la Peinture* (Paris: École nationale supérieure des Beaux-Arts, 1993), p. 276. "Puisque le premier but de la poésie et de la peinture est de nous toucher, les poèmes et les tableaux ne sont de ouvrages qu'à proportion qu'ils nous émeuvent et qu'ils nous attachent. Un ouvrage qui touche beucoup doit être exellent à tout prendre. Par la même raison l'ouvrage qui ne touche point et qui n'attache pas, ne vaut rien." *Critical Reflections on Poetry, Painting and Music*, trans. Thomas Nugent (London: Printed for John Nourse, at the Lamb, opposite Katherine Street in the Strand, 1748), II, 237.

[11]John Dennis, *A Large Account of the Taste in Poetry, and the Causes of the Degeneracy of It.* See p. 55, this volume.

[12]John Baillie, "An Essay on the Sublime." See p. 191, this volume.

dramatic unities more than the most general guides. The most common response to the obvious counterexamples to rules is that it is not the violation of the rules but the overcoming of them by greater beauties that saves dramatists such as Shakespeare from their own flaws. Johnson's ability to ridicule the obvious application of rules and critical formulas shows how deeply clichéd those formulas had become. He sees the hollowness of criticism of painting and imitation of nature. The increasingly ad hoc nature of applying rules gradually so undermines them that they cease to play a significant role in aesthetic theory, though they continue to be acknowledged by a kind of critical piety.

In one area in particular, rules are replaced in the course of the eighteenth century by a greater freedom. As Johnson puts it, "Whatever part of an art can be executed or criticized by rules, that part is no longer the work of genius, which implies excellence out of the reach of rules."[13] Genius is itself a form of *je ne sais quoi,*—"consult the genius of the place in all."[14] It develops from the kind of particular quality that cannot be described but must be experienced to a more theoretically involved alternative to rules as a part of the inductive explanation of how artistic practice is possible and of how that practice is connected to audience expectations. In some ways, the most important theoretical role for rules is that they provide a contrasting principle that can be set aside by genius.

7. Taste

For much of the eighteenth century, the controlling theoretical concept is taste. George Dickie has aptly described the eighteenth century as the century of taste.[15] The origins of the concept, however, pre-date the eighteenth-century uses of it. In classical discussion of art and criticism, taste as such does not appear. The Aristotelian scheme of the senses laid out in *De Anima* gives touch and its near-relative taste (the application of touch to the tongue) a wider scope than might be expected. Sight is placed "above all others" in *Metaphysics A*. Sight is also the most developed sense and leads to imagination.[16] Imagination is directly related to sense and memory by the formation of images. Elsewhere, however, touch is the primary sense. Touch is an unmediated sense; it works by direct contact. It is also the sense without which none of the others is possible.[17] Without touch, one is no longer a sentient being. Touch, in turn, is related to taste. Taste is the subordinate sense to touch because

[13]Sir Joshua Reynolds, "The Idler," No. 76. See p. 331, this volume.

[14]Alexander Pope, "Epistle IV, To Richard Boyle, Earl of Burlington," 1. 57.

[15]George Dickie, *The Century of Taste* (Oxford: Oxford University Press, 1996).

[16]"As sight is the most highly developed sense, the name *phantasia* (imagination) has been formed from *phaso* (light) because it is not possible to see without light." *De Anima* III.3.429a, 589.

[17]"Without touch it is impossible to have any other sense; for every body that has soul in it must, as we have said, be capable of touch. . . . All the other organs of sense, no doubt, perceive by contact, only the contact is mediate: touch alone perceives by immediate contact. . . . Without touch there can be no other sense, and the organ of touch cannot consist of earth or of any other single element." *De Anima,* III.13.435 a-436b, 602. *The Basic Works of Aristotle,* ed. Richard McKeon (New York: Random House, 1941). *De Anima,* trans. J. A. Smith.

taste is impossible without touch.[18] Taste discriminates more accurately than other senses such as smell.[19] So taste is a modification of touch, touch is the most discriminating faculty, and from discrimination comes intelligence. The Aristotelian hierarchy from sense to knowledge has the potential to incorporate each of the senses, including taste, by virtue of its ability to provide images to experience in a discriminating way. Aristotle summed up a classical tradition which, for all of its distrust of individual sense, nevertheless recognized an essential relation between sense and consciousness. The problem with sense and experience was not whether they were necessary, but how they were to be incorporated into judgments. Taste provided an analogy which connected sense and judgment. Sight is the most intellectual sense, but touch is the pre-eminently human sense because, without touch, there is no soul.

Later classical writers, particularly writers on rhetoric, approach the eighteenth-century sense of 'taste,' but they do not develop the metaphor as such. Quintilian and Cicero in particular link response and judgment in ways that suggest the appropriateness of the metaphor of taste, but in a system of the arts that subordinates the productive arts to poetry and poetry to philosophy and contemplation, there is little room for the metaphor to develop. In the Renaissance, however, that context changes. The first appearances of taste as a significant metaphor that combines judgment with the immediacy of a sense occur in the context of Renaissance theorizing about painting. When a painter begins to display a distinctive, individual style and even emphasizes style and individual manner over the subject matter and tradition, taste suggests itself as the appropriate means of response. For example, Georgio Vasari is forced back upon direct experience when he confronts the eccentricity of one work by Jacopo Pontormo: "I am determined, since I myself do not understand it, although I am a painter, to leave all who may see it to form their own judgment, for the reason that I believe that I would drive myself mad with it and would lose myself, even as it appears to me that Jacopo in the period of eleven years that he spent upon it sought to lose himself and all who might see the painting, among all those extraordinary figures."[20] In this context, such individual judgment is not especially positive; it is a form of madness. But it is a relatively short step to a positive version of an individualized response. Federico Zuccaro takes that step when he writes, "Grace is . . . a soft and sweet accompaniment which attracts the eye and contents the taste . . . ; it depends entirely on good judgment and good taste

[18]"What can be tasted is always something that can be touched, and just for that reason it cannot be perceived through an interposed foreign body, for touch means the absence of any intervening body." *De Anima*, II.10. 422a, 575.

[19]"It seems that there is an analogy between smell and taste, and that the species of tastes runs parallel to those of smells—the only difference being that our sense of taste is more discriminating than our sense of smell, because the former is a modification of touch, which reaches in man the maximum of discriminative accuracy." *De Anima*, II.9.421a, 574.

[20]Georgio Vasari, *Lives of Excellent Painters, Sculptors, and Architects*, in *Italian Art, 1500-1600: Sources and Documents*, ed. Robert Klein and Henri Zerner (Englewood Cliffs, New Jersey: Prentice-Hall Inc., 1966), p. 80.

(*gusto*)."[21] At this point, the metaphor of taste explicitly combines judgment and taste.

The origins of the metaphor of taste, therefore, belong to late Rennaissance mannerist painting and theory. The metaphor enters the critical vocabulary of the seventeenth century via the extension of mannerism to other areas of life and the arts. In that context, it provides a prudential piece of advice on how to conform one's own judgment to that of the wider public so that one will be seen as a person of taste. Addison associates taste with the writings of the Spanish mannerist writer, Balthazar Gratian, and defines it as "that faculty of the mind, which distinguishes all the most concealed faults and nicest perfections in writing" and "that faculty of the soul, which discerns the beauties of an author with pleasure, and the imperfections with dislike."[22] Appreciation of the ancients in particular serves as a test whether one has the faculty or not.

Taste is still a questionable faculty at the beginning of the eighteenth century. Shaftesbury rejects innate taste and links taste to criticism. Out of this complex of taste and criticism, eighteenth-century aesthetics arises. The move to taste individualizes judgment and locates it in response. Criticism disciplines taste and provides a means for discrimination. Yet criticism with its rules and taste with its subjectivity are potential antagonists. Eighteenth-century aesthetics can be viewed as a struggle between the two, just as it reflects the struggle between the authority of the ancients and the development of the moderns. Ultimately, subjectivity triumphs, but in doing so, it reduces taste to a mere preference, just as Shaftesbury saw that it would. Alexander Pope regards taste with suspicion in the "Epistle to Burlington":

> "Tis strange, the miser should his cares employ
> To gain those riches he can ne'er enjoy;
> Is it less strange, the prodigal should waste
> His wealth, to purchase what he ne'er can taste?
> . . .
> What brought Sir Visto's ill-got wealth to waste?
> Some daemon whispered, "Visto! have a taste."[23]

The desire to be thought a person of taste leads to all sorts of waste and exaggeration. Yet the metaphor seems firmly established. It combines the immediacy of the sense of taste with the normative elements of liking or disliking, pleasure or pain,

[21]Federico Zucarro (Rome) *Idea de' Pittori, Scultori e Architetti* (1607) cf. Romano Alberti, *Origine e Progresso dell' Academia del Disegno* (1604), p. 59 which contains the minutes of the Academy of Drawing for 1593-94 in which Zucarro is the only speaker. Cited by Anthony Blunt, *Artistic Theory in Italy, 1450-1600* (Oxford: Oxford University press, 1940), p. 146.

[22]Joseph Addison, *The Spectator*, No. 409. See p. 107, this volume.

[23]Pope, ll 1-4; 15-16.

that do not have to be justified by any argument, and in fact cannot be changed without a change in the organ itself.

Shaftesbury in *Advice to an Author* makes it clear that not just any taste will do. There is a right and wrong taste. His rejection of credulity in travel narratives adds another element to the changing picture of taste. Taste must be checked against more basic facts. An element of class is also at work. "True" aristocrats such as Shaftesbury and Burlington do not yield to the vagaries of taste as do newly made peers and the newly rich country squires with their ridiculous collections of eccentricities. Yet taste is at bottom that to which one must appeal because, in the empirical scheme of things, it is the form of direct experience to which all more complex ideas and judgments in the arts must be traced.

8. Sentiment and the Passions

The tradition of sentimentalism in both morals and aesthetics has frequently been misunderstood both in its own time and by later commentators. It appeared to be an abandonment of reason and a surrender to primitive emotion, the triumph of taste over reason. More recent commentary has provided a needed correction. First of all, the passions are never simple emotional indulgence. Those with a classical education would assume the tripartite division of the soul set out in Plato's *Republic*. Reason provides intellectual certainty, and, at the other extreme, bodily appetites surrender to desire and sensation. The passions are a third category. Like the appetites, they provide immediate pleasure and lack reasoned justification. But unlike appetite, the passions have a normative element. They are good (courage, honor) as well as bad (anger, hatred) and they may even be indifferent. For example, although for James Beattie the prevalence of moral sentiments is not a necessary but an empirical fact of human nature, among the facts are "agreeable affections"—Beattie cites joy and hope—that involve neither virtue nor vice.[24] So for those within the tradition that values sentiment, there is a place for a form of taste that combines both normative and affective judgment. Sentiment is not simply pleasant; it is good or bad depending on how it fits into a larger system.

David Hume is the most carefully philosophical defender of sentiment.[25] In "Of the Delicacy of Taste and Passion," Hume distinguishes delicacy of passion from delicacy of taste, though they operate in the same way. But he also uses the Platonic distinction between Passion and appetite: "When a man is possessed of this talent [for controlling delicacy of sentiment], he is more happy by what pleases his taste, than by what gratifies his appetites." The function of delicacy of taste turns out to be to distinguish between good and bad passions: "it [a cultivated taste for the polite arts] rather improves our sensibility for all the tender and agreeable passions; at the same time that it renders the mind incapable of the rougher and more boisterous

[24]James Beattie, *Essays on Poetry and Music, as They Affect the Mind.* See p. 355, this volume.

[25]See Annette Baier, *A Progress of Sentiments* (Cambridge: Harvard University Press, 1993).

emotions."[26] When this view of taste and passion is combined with Hume's extensively worked out reduction of the claims of rationalist argumentation to the status of empirical observation, the result is a view of human nature that incorporates sentiment into the pattern of justification. Hume does not hold, any more than Shaftesbury did, that all sentiment is right because it is pleasant. But by the time Hume has gotten through dismantling the claims of rationalists to be able to establish causal relations and personal identity on the basis of arguments from either direct Cartesian introspection or innately demonstrable premises, it must be acknowledged that reason itself acts only on sentiment and that taste, like moral approbation, is a way of justifying some sentiments and condemning others. Hume does not provide a detailed working out of aesthetic sentiment on a parallel with what he provides for moral sentiment in Book Three of the *Treatise of Human Nature*. We are left with only fragments and hints of how the reconfiguring of reason to depend on beauty and taste would go. Taste, however, clearly has a cognitive role to play.

9. A Standard of Taste

Appeals to taste were already widespread by the time Hume offered his views in the essays, particularly "Of the Standard of Taste." Taste was both defended as a form of polite learning accessible to everyone and reviled as an invitation to vulgar display and immoral subjectivity. By the time Archibald Alison refers to emotions of taste in 1790, a psychological shift had taken place. The passions with their Platonic division of the mind that distinguishes passions from both a rational soul and animal appetites had become a simpler empirical set of emotions resident in the host mind. On that basis, taste becomes only one among many possible emotional reactions and loses its centrality as a cognitive form of sentiment. Aesthetic philosophy shifts its emphasis from the immediacy of emotion to an activity of mind, and the transformation of aesthetic philosophy on the basis of kinds of mental operation brought about by Immanuel Kant's *Critique of Judgment* finally moves the more direct empiricism of Hume and Alison to the margins of the debate.

Before that takes place, however, two issues shape the aesthetics of the mid-eighteenth century. Both have to do with the status of taste. The first is the question whether and how taste can be formed. The metaphor suggests that taste is as immediate and invulnerable to modification as its gustatory counterpart. No amount of argument will convince one that something that tastes bitter is not bitter nor that one should like bitter tastes if one does not. To counter that implication, Edmund Burke denies that taste is a separate faculty, and thus that it is a sense. He gives a much larger role to reason and understanding in forming taste, which incorporates both sensibility and judgment. But Burke's view concedes too much to older forms of reasoning for the tradition in which taste is the central term.

Instead, one finds explanations of taste that point the metaphor itself in a different direction. The preferred analogy is to the development of a palate in wine tasting. While aesthetic taste requires a minimal level of organic input as a necessary

[26]David Hume, "Of the Delicacy of Taste and Passion." See p. 227, this volume.

condition, taste can be refined in the same way that sensory awareness can be made more discriminating. A number of factors are cited as educating taste: comparison, removal of prejudice, and taking account of climate and age. The most important factor, however, is delicacy of taste. Delicacy is at once a given—a function of one's physical make-up like good vision—and something that can be improved by practice. Hume maintains that delicacy of taste can cure delicacy of passion because delicacy of taste is more controllable and provides a more refined and higher pleasure. On the other hand, Priestley worries that too much delicacy may impede enjoyment by making the slightest imperfection in a musical performance painful to the hearer. They agree, however, that delicacy in itself is something to be desired and that it can be improved just as one can develop a better ear for music by a combination of listening and instruction.

The centrality of delicacy makes it important to the other major question about taste, whether there is a standard of taste or not. This question became a common topic of polite philosophizing in the essay tradition of the mid-century. Once taste is acknowledged as an important characteristic for an educated person to cultivate, it becomes equally important to be able to tell good taste from bad taste. In part, this is a prudential question, as Gratian claimed. To the new class of art consumers, to be thought to have good taste was very important. One did not want to appear in public to have liked the wrong things. But taste seemed to offer little ground for a standard. The empirical fact was that opinions varied and controversy could not be settled by asserting one's taste because someone else could counter with an equally vivid and strongly held passion. So if taste was to function, its very advantage—its subjective incorrigibility—was also its disadvantage since one might well find that one had lost status by liking the wrong things.

The need for a standard of taste was also a moral question, however. The link between virtue and aesthetic taste was not to be broken until after Kant's formal separation removed aesthetic intuition from the realm of the practical altogether. For writers who followed Shaftesbury and Hutcheson, taste formed character, and character determined moral sentiment. While in principle it might be possible for someone to have good taste and still be a morally unvirtuous person, in fact the means to form taste and to form character were so connected that to fail in the one was to imply failure in the other. One does not develop good taste without exposing one's opinions to correction by the widest and most disinterested forms of experience, and inevitably that experience will also free one from the selfish forms of hedonism that were still attributed to Hobbes and his followers. So while taste might be acknowledged as of little importance in itself—one of those elements of character that permitted a tolerant diversity and conceded much to personal choice—it was unlikely that a person of taste would not also be a person of sense and benevolence, the characteristics necessary if moral sentiment was to be reliable. This connection easily accommodated the enlightened class awareness of Shaftesbury just as its absence drew the satiric scorn of Pope. For all of its theologically suspect nature, the defense of sentiment could be quite conservative.

The way that Hume separated the need for a standard of taste from the related question of the fact of taste is well known. In the absence of a clear fact of the matter, the judgment that one work is better than another could not be settled by a direct reference to taste. Nor are the kind of principles that inform the education of taste applicable in the difficult cases. Where time is long and difference in quality is great, the inductive appearance of principles, even in the absence of a clear understanding of causal rules, can settle the question. Whoever dislikes Homer is condemned out of his own mouth. But in contemporary cases, nothing like such agreement can be expected. Yet that is where a standard of taste becomes most important because there the prudential and moral risk is greatest. Hume's solution, of course, is to turn to a different question that seems more amenable to factual distinction: the character of the judges. Where that can be determined, true judges can be identified, and then their judgments provide the standard. The principles that Hume refers to in "Of the Standard of Taste" are just those that are used by true judges who in effect become the teachers and guides of others.

Other attempts at a standard were made, however. The most common move was to look for a more easily applied form of induction. Hume's radical revision of the relation of sentiment and reason was too opaque for his contemporaries. They were not prepared to trust sentiment quite so far because they viewed sentiment as one more form of emotion. Instead, they hoped to find rules that corresponded to the rules in science about electricity or gases. There too the microscopic principles were held to be inaccessible, but that did not prevent Robert Boyle from relating pressure and volume for a gas. Alexander Gerard tries for a similar natural philosophy of taste. Mere sentiment is unscientific. But regarded in the light of a common human nature, it can be predicted. Gerard's appeal to reasons or principles against sentiment remains ambiguous, however. He seems to hold both that the principles are like natural laws and that they are the necessary order that corrects the senses. Lord Kames's belief in a standard of taste also depends in large measure on his conviction that there is a common human nature. Thus, part of the interest in a science of human nature rests on the appeal to it to provide standards. Most of those who regard taste as something positive in itself appeal to that assumed common nature as the basis for sorting good from bad taste.

10. Beauty and Aesthetic Pleasure

A continuing concern in eighteenth-century aesthetics is to counter Thomas Hobbes and others who argue for some form of egocentric hedonism. The moral problem raised by the claim that all actions are essentially self-interested and directed toward one's own pleasure has a corresponding aesthetic side. If it can be demonstrated that people have a disinterested pleasure in the arts, then not all pleasure need be self-interested. The same pleasure that one takes in beauty could be felt for benevolent actions. The attempt to identify aesthetic pleasures is another aspect of the psychology of human nature that is important, especially to those sentimentalists who see a relation between aesthetic and moral pleasure.

It is widely held that beauty includes a pleasant emotion in some way. The complication comes in relating beauty and pleasure to the ideational scheme traceable back to Locke. One possibility is that beauty itself is an idea. Hutcheson, for example, refers to beauty as an idea provided by an internal sense. The details of this scheme are more difficult to work out. Sense produces simple ideas, so beauty should be a simple idea itself. On the other hand, beauty does not arise directly from an external sense but only by the intervention of an internal sense whose object is based on a complex comparison of uniformity and variety. Hutcheson is willing to call it a reflexive sense instead of an internal sense. That would seem to indicate that if beauty is representational at all, it must represent a complex idea. The place of pleasure in the idea is equally ambiguous. Beauty is regarded as an emotion or calm passion. As such, it simply is pleasant in the way that other emotions are either pleasant or painful. On the other hand, it seems possible to perceive beauty and yet feel no emotion at all. That we feel pleasure in beauty is a contingent fact of our emotional make-up. We could respond differently. In that case, pleasure is an accompaniment of beauty that supervenes on the idea.

The solutions to these hedonistic puzzles about beauty can take at least three forms. The first understands beauty as a simple idea to which pleasure is somehow necessarily connected. This is the solution most congruent with later views about aesthetic pleasure because it requires aesthetic pleasure as a necessary condition of aesthetic objects. Beauty is a name for an object that is aesthetic, and an object becomes aesthetic if and only if it is accompanied by aesthetic pleasure. An alternative understands an internal sense as allowing complex ideas, on the model of classical accounts of an internal sense that treats it as a form of judgment (e.g., in St. Augustine) and includes pleasure as part of the complex. This view is consistent with the classicism and the psychology of human nature that still looks for an intellectual soul that unites mere sense into perception by the integrating operation of a common sense. The third possibility understands beauty as itself simply a form of pleasure. Beauty is not a representational idea at all. This view leads to a non-cognitive form of aesthetics if it is followed out consistently.

It is too much to expect that a single clear answer will emerge from writers such as Hutcheson and his followers. Both 'idea' and 'beauty' are words that have so many different uses in the eighteenth century that one can expect only a limited consistency. Hume sees the need to distinguish ideas from impressions, for example, but that distinction leads to its own problems about how ideas are related to belief. If ideas are not themselves the direct product of experience, then one is either led back to the problems of integration of ideas and belief found in Aristotle and subsequent Aristotelian forms of epistemology or one must offer some alternative way of validating ideas. Hume's proposal that vivacity alone distinguishes ideas that are believed from those that are merely entertained requires the complex psychological analysis that he attempts in the *Treatise* and that was so widely ignored or misunderstood by his contemporaries.

While aesthetic pleasure as a separate category may seem a plausible solution in the light of nineteenth- and twentieth-century aesthetics, it is at most hinted at in eighteenth-century theories. The issue that dominated eighteenth-century discussions was whether pleasure had to be self-interested. Put that way, the alternatives are self-interested pleasure or a more generic form that permits sympathy and benevolence. All pleasure would conform to one or the other of those possibilities.

One place that this can be illustrated is in the questions that are raised about tragic pleasure. A paradox arises because events that are painful nevertheless are experienced as pleasant when represented in a well-constructed play. If all pleasure is self-interested, one can account for tragic pleasure by the separation of the audience from the events. One's pleasure is essentially a feeling of relief that it is not I, and my pleasure is not implicated in the tragic events. But to those who hold that aesthetic pleasure is a form of sympathy, then to take pleasure in suffering seems paradoxical. Du Bos appeals to mental activity to explain the paradox. A mind occupied, even with tragic events, is more satisfied than a mind with no object. Fontenelle shows that pleasure and pain are similar, so that a painful emotion attenuated by its being fictional is felt as pleasant. Hume, notes, however, that some such emotions are historical, not fictional, so he adds a third factor, the beauty from eloquence and imitation.[27] Burke, on the other hand, focuses on the removal of pain as productive of relative pleasure.

A problem remains, of course. It is not just that people take pleasure in the portrayal of tragic events, either in plays or history. They flock to executions and disasters. The imposition of an aesthetic distance is not sufficient to explain tragic pleasure unless the pleasure itself can be distinguished, and that kind of distinction is not available in eighteenth-century psychology, even as practiced by Hume. In eighteenth-century British aesthetics, a different route is ultimately followed. Rhetorical strategy depends on being able to produce the expected effects, so the problem of tragic pleasure is viewed as one more rhetorical problem by Priestley and Kames, among others. Kames sees this rhetorical strategy as a problem about the combination of ideas, a kind of psychological manipulation based on human nature. While Kames seems merely to be accumulating rhetorical advice, his way of explaining how ideas become pleasant in certain combinations is a significant move toward an expressive aesthetic. It will be taken up by Alison and given more theoretical shape. Thus aesthetic pleasure comes to be viewed as a product of the association of ideas and a mechanics of emotion. Rather than an autonomous form of aesthetic pleasure, all pleasure depends on the combination of simpler ideas that are pleasant in themselves.

The particular combinations that are effective may well be accidental, however. If they are, then no regularity will be discoverable, and thus no rhetorical strategy can be effective. The need to explain aesthetic pleasure thus leads back to either some form of fortunate teleology, or it must be supported by an "experimental" account of the laws of human nature. The former is represented in Addison's treatment of the pleasures of the imagination. Addison's structure is teleological: we are formed so as to take pleasure in that which leads to the ultimate pleasure, God. Everything is ordered to that end if it is natural. The unnatural cannot reproduce itself. Hutcheson also has a fortunate teleology at work. His

[27] David Hume, "Of Tragedy." See p. 242, this volume.

account of laughter takes on aesthetic significance because it tries to show that laughter is not just self-interested relief but a form of human community provided by God. The latter is the goal for Hume, who remains somewhat skeptical about his own success, and for optimistic scientists of human nature such as Priestley and Kames.

11. Imitation

One of the most important sources of aesthetic pleasure links empiricist theories to classical philosophies of art. A continuing theme in eighteenth-century theories of art attributes pleasure to the practice of imitation, and one of the persistent problems for imitation theories in the eighteenth century is how to account for the pleasure that one takes in otherwise unpleasant things. The simple answer is Aristotle's—that we take pleasure in imitation itself. But as Adam Smith noted, that, by itself, cannot account for the fact that painting can imitate unpleasant objects while sculpture cannot. The solution to this puzzle must come from a full theory of imitation. For most of the century, the stock answer to the question, "What is art?" involves imitation, most commonly the imitation of nature. The most common imitation theory is based on Aristotle, both because of the influence of the *Poetics* and because Aristotelian metaphysics continues to exert a strong influence even on those who adhere to the new science.

James Harris develops a thorough-going Aristotelian version of imitation. His first treatise is a straightforward Aristotelian attempt at definition in terms of the four causes. He defines art as "an habitual power in man, of becoming the cause of some effect, according to a system of various and well approved precepts." He then explains these precepts in terms of Aristotle's formal, efficient, material, and final causes, beginning with what is really the formal cause—something caused intentionally and artificially by a person according to some rules. He then goes on to the purpose and means of art. What subject does art operate on? "On a contingent, which is within the reach of the human power to influence." For what reason? "For the sake of some absent good, relative to human life and attainable by man, but superior to his natural and uninstructed faculties." Where does art end? "Either in some energy, or in some work." Harris identifies these as the four causes.[28] Imitation of nature also has a normative element: it produces the best pleasure and the most noble forms. Thus pleasure and the nobility of nature are linked. The imitation of nature produces admiration, and admiration is always pleasant.

A theory of imitation is important in two additional respects. First, it supports the link between pleasure and the new psychology of the mind. Thus Burke, like most others, psychologizes the theory of imitation. Imitation is understood to produce a kind of mental operation, rather than defining a kind of object (as in Plato or Aristotle). That mental operation is the source of the pleasure of art. Second, imitation retains the nominal link to classicism that gives art and its objects status

[28] James Harris, "Three Treatises." See p. 165, this volume.

while opening the way for more concrete explorations of art objects. The century produces some rather acute analyses of the way that particular forms of art work by starting with imitation. Music, however, presents a problem because its imitative function is so limited. Imitation also allows a distinction between art and ordinary objects. Adam Smith's analysis of imitation notices the difference between imitation in ordinary objects, where exactness is a merit, and imitation in painting, where exactness cannot match the original and where the pleasure depends on a difference when the object is otherwise ordinary.

All imitation theory is not Aristotelian, however. If imitation is fundamentally imitation of nature, then Nature is often understood as those essential forms instantiated by natural things. An essentially Platonic view of beauty remains strong. The forms that appear in matter are inevitably compromised. Nature, therefore, is at once the model and a problem. As the model, one can only follow nature. But nature is material and thus incapable of a perfect presentation of the beauty of forms. The role of the painter is to form beauties that are superior to nature. Nature, in this context, is the intermediary between Platonic forms and the mind. The mind, being intellectual in its own nature, is able to accomplish what nature alone cannot. Yet gradually emerging from this very traditional picture is a view of the mind as individual that is at odds with its Platonic model. In neo-Platonism, there is only one mind. For an eighteenth-century artist, each mind competes for superiority.

Platonic imitation has problems of its own as well as presenting a delicate balancing act between the classical and modern views of the mind. For example, Dryden is aware that the standard view of nature as Platonic emblem presents a problem for portrait painting where the image must conform to the sitter, and for tragedy and comedy which both must admit the failings and errors of humans. Idealization may produce greater beauty, but audiences expect more contemporary references. Dryden's own *Absalom and Achitophel* was read by his contemporaries as a defense of the succession of James, Duke of York. Portrait painting in the mode of Reynolds, Gainsborough, and especially Thomas Lawrence might make its obeisance to classical beauty in the pose and background, but the sitter was not just recognizable but naturalized, particularly in portraits of actors, which introduce an additional distance from the reality of form as it is described in the *Republic*. Lawrence's portrait of George III's queen, Charlotte, remained unaccepted by the King because it was deemed not regal enough by the King. Daniel Webb distinguishes mechanical painting from ideal painting, but then he argues for sensibility as the perception of the idea, thus uniting a kind of practical Platonism with sentimentalism. Beauty is treated as a separate quality by Addison, but it is also acknowledged to belong to the eye of the beholder.

12. Beauty

In general, beauty is replaced by taste as the central theoretical term, as we have noted. Beauty becomes a secondary quality of objects or more often a calm passion. It is assimilated to the predominant empirical psychology of the mind, and as such, attention shifts to the mode of reception—either an internal sense or taste or both.

Attempts to relocate beauty in terms of sensation lead in turn to attempts at definition in terms of some necessary or sufficient set of secondary qualities of objects that correlate to human sensory reception. The classical definitions in terms of harmony and proportion are recast into properties or combinations of properties. Hogarth's sensuous line and Hutcheson's uniformity amidst variety are the most widely acknowledged definitions. One thing to note about both of these that helps account for their widespread appearance in other texts is the way that they shift classical definitions. Hogarth's sinuous line looks back to the classical proportion represented by the golden ratio. What in classical terms was a matter of numerical harmony and a reality independent of its instantiation becomes for Hogarth a psychological generalization, a piece of practical knowledge that artists can utilize just as they can utilize knowledge of perspective and of color relations. Hutcheson's formula also recalls the classical qualities of unity and participation. It is no wonder that Hutcheson's followers have difficulty reconciling uniformity amidst variety with Locke's ideas. Beauty never fits comfortably into that scheme.

Treatments of beauty after Hutcheson tend to confuse the classical mode with the new psychology. For example, John Baillie seeks defining characteristics for beauty, and accepts Hutcheson's uniformity amidst variety before he goes on to his own treatment of the sublime, another classical term that is relocated theoretically in the course of the eighteenth century. Kames attributes beauty to regularity, uniformity, proportion, order, and simplicity. His organization is Aristotelian, especially in the search for final causes and utility, but the way that the Aristotelian causal structure continues to be used even when the basic thesis is ideational is interesting. Order is both a natural order implicit in things that makes them beautiful and the rhetorical order that allows language to be manipulated at will. Hugh Blair, who follows Kames rhetorically, lacks originality and never goes into any great depth. He does, however, provide a very clear enumeration of the various characteristics claimed to produce the emotion of beauty. He distinguishes the sublime from looser uses, but is content to leave beauty as a kind of omnibus term covering a number of different kinds

Toward the end of the century, 'beauty,' which tends to be an omnibus term applied to many different secondary qualities, has largely been replaced by more particular quality terms such as 'sublimity' and 'picturesqueness' for which theoretically inclined critics try to give specific characteristics. The result is a further psychologizing of beauty in terms of its causes and consequences. Adam Smith recognizes the role that fashion and expense play in finding some objects beautiful and others less so. He notes that sculptured foliage that would be ordinary in nature is beautiful when done in stone. He then mounts a modest defense of sculptured shrubbery on the grounds that it does not really differ from sculptured marble except in the expense of the materials. One ought, therefore, to find both beautiful, though he does not press the matter, since skill will favor the marble.[29] The Rev. William

[29] Adam Smith, "Of the Nature of that Imitation which Takes Place in What are Called the Imitative Arts." See p. 441, this volume.

Gilpin goes farther by looking for a quasi-scientific explanation. Smoothness corresponds to the ease of the eye moving over the surface, and is thus beautiful.[30] What we observe in these later examples is that even when the description retains Platonic or Aristotelian verbal forms, its logic is that of subjective response. Some things just affect human beings that way, and what one wants to know is how and when the pleasure of beauty will be felt. Gradually, the answer involves breaking the response down more carefully into other feelings. By then, the need for an all-encompassing beauty is largely gone. Even taste divides into a multiplicity of tastes.

The same thing happens, however, to the notion of an internal sense. An internal sense appears most important when beauty is still the final cause. Then internal sense plays the role of reflective unifier. Without an internal sense, uniformity amidst variety could not come together. The emphasis on an analogy of sense conceals to some extent, perhaps even from its advocates, the real function of sense theories. They do not just operate like the external senses. An internal sense only begins after external sensation has been organized and presented by the mind as perception. The function of an internal sense, therefore, is not just to immediately respond to perception; an internal sense must repeat the perceptive act. The unity of internal sense is imposed by the sense but equally is the product of what is sensed. Thus beauty and virtue require an internal sense, but the number of senses is limited to what exists. When Alexander Gerard begins to multiply senses, therefore, he is implicitly acknowledging that an internal sense no longer responds to some higher level organization. All that is left for sense to do is to attach a label to a response. So one finds a sense of novelty and a sense of ridicule as well as the more classical senses of virtue, harmony, beauty, and imitation. Novelty and ridicule depend on the subject. Something that is novel to one person will not be to another.

13. Imagination

Instead of an internal sense, a different kind of faculty, imagination, emerges. Imagination changes its function in the course of the eighteenth century. From a subordinate position in the scheme of simple and complex ideas, it eventually becomes the dominant creative faculty, the specific function of genius, which has also changed from a characteristic of places and people to a creative force.

The imagination is an important element in early eighteenth-century theory, of course. It is a source of pleasure and a major part of the new faculty psychology built on experience. Addison relates imagination primarily to sight. Its function is to provide images from ideas. In that role, imagination is active but limited. It is synonymous with fancy, the ability to combine and recombine ideas at will. While this is a powerful tool, it does not do anything that is not also done by other reflective faculties, such as memory and reason, and these have the larger role because what they do provides truth while imagination or fancy provides only artificial combinations.

[30]William Gilpin, "Three Essays." See p. 421, this volume.

The importance of imagination thus rests on its ability to please and entertain rather than on any central epistemological role. Addison accounts for imagination's ability to provide pleasure in terms of the exercise of the mind. Different degrees of exercise produce different degrees of pleasure. One of the advantages of imagination over understanding is that the understanding requires too violent an exercise of the mind. Imagination is pleasurable just because it provides moderate exercise without too much worry about consequences. When imagination begins to intrude into more serious matters, it works like a disease. Samuel Johnson's philosophical tale, *Rassalas*, illustrates how excess imagination can lead to madness. The good and wise astronomer comes to imagine that he controls the weather and seasons. In one of the more poignant passages in eighteenth-century literature, Imlac observes "Of the uncertainties of our present state, the most dreadful and alarming is the uncertain continuance of reason."[31] Johnson himself feared such an imagination.

Imagination gradually comes to play a different role. Hume attributes to the imagination the ability to represent ideas. The imagination is thus on a par with memory, and because the only difference in ideas is their vivacity, imagination can contribute directly to the process of linking ideas into the kind of expectations and habits that allows sentiment to become a cognitive operation on a par with or superior to reason. As internal sense fragments, much of the role of combining and ordering shifts to the faculty of the imagination. Imagination in that sense would be especially dangerous if it were not controllable. Control comes from the increased attention to the powers of the mind itself, however. Imagination converts painful passions into pleasure, because the force of imagination is always pleasant. A normal mind will be guided by its own sensitive responses to avoid the extremes that it finds painful. The control of the imagination thus comes from a kind of built in governor, one more aspect of the psychologizing of epistemology that is taking place. What was, for Addison, a subordinate explanation of innocent pleasures becomes in its turn a naturally powerful substitute for excessive reliance on reason. A diseased mind, however, will not be able to control its own imaginative faculty, and the tendency of romanticism to run into the abnormal only illustrates how central imagination becomes.

14. Aesthetic Predicates: The Sublime and Picturesque

The place of the imagination in philosophy of art is a function of an expanded awareness of possible responses to art and nature and attempts to systematize them. The two most important are the sublime and the picturesque. Burke's kind of sublimity is anticipated by Addison's description of the great and uncommon as pleasures of the imagination. Addison treats novelty in the same way.[32] We might identify three stages of the sublime. In Longinus, at least as he was understood in the eighteenth century, sublimity is a rhetorical effect connected to a form of passionate

[31]Samuel Johnson, *Rassalas*, Ch. 43; *Rassalas*, ed. Bertrand H. Bronson (New York: Holt, Reinhart and Winston, 1958), p. 595.

[32]Joseph Addison, "The Spectator," No. 412. See p. 107, this volume.

ecstasy. That is, the sublime is a way of lifting the reader out of the ordinary into a more intellectual world. John Baillie's sublime remains essentially that of neo-Platonic participation. The highest form of sublime passion is love, which unites the mind with divinity. Yet in spite of his acceptance of Longinus and Longinian rhetorical rules, Baillie traces the sublime to the mind's expansion and explains that expansion in terms of the extent and vastness of ideas.[33] The second stage frees the sublime from its Platonic roots. Edmund Burke's youthful analysis of the sublime is also classically influenced, but it is Aristotle's analytical structure rather than neo-Platonism that organizes Burke's sublime. Burke not only reduces beauty to a parallel position with the sublime—smallness and smoothness as opposed to greatness and vastness—he grounds the sublime in natural passions. Feminine beauty and masculine sublimity are not just metaphors for Burke; they are real passionate sources, and they are to be interpreted concretely. The final stage of the development of the sublime loses Burke's physiological psychology and retains only his qualitative characterizations. Uvedale Price limits the sublime to a certain kind of response —that produced by mental expansion—and thus reduces the sublime to one among many possible mental forms.

The most important of these additional forms is the picturesque. Price's quest for qualities of the picturesque is curious in the following way. He identifies the effect, then looks for the qualities that produce it. It would seem that the effect is identified before its identifying qualities, therefore, and in fact it is. The only criteria for picturesqueness is a felt quality. Everything else is a kind experimental introspection, a thought experiment carried out to determine when the response in question occurs. When Price settles on roughness and sudden variation joined to irregularity as the causes of picturesqueness, however, he is doing more than just providing an efficient cause.[34] Instead of giving a definition, he is providing a recipe based on experience. His purpose is practical and empirical in the sense that it is the way to achieve the effects desired. By turning to a kind of emotional catalogue, the basis for aesthetics shifts from feeling itself to a variety of separate feelings. The only reason for singling out the picturesque, therefore, has to do with its relation to nature on the one hand and pictures on the other. Exactly the same principles would allow urban manufacturing to be related to pictures when the futurists in the early twentieth century turn their picturesque eye in that direction.

The path followed by the development of the picturesque provides a clear picture of the way that eighteenth-century aesthetics develops. Picturesqueness begins simply as that quality in a scene that would be appropriate for a picture. Addison uses it in that way. However, the social and economic forces in the century impose a distance on picturesque painting. What is at first merely a scene appropriate for painting is modified as the roles reverse. Under the influence of landscape painters, natural scenes are shaped to fit painterly criteria. Landscape gardening

[33]John Baillie, "An Essay on the Sublime." See p. 191, this volume.

[34]Uvedale Price, "An Essay on the Picturesque as Compared with the Sublime and Beautiful." See p. 431, this volume.

becomes an art. At first this is simply another instance of idealizing nature. Smoothness and a tailored form replace the excessive formalism of seventeenth-century landscape gardening. Classical references are incorporated into the garden via grottos and statues. Sweeping drives, waters, and clumps of trees present vistas and replace older buildings. Capability Brown and Humphrey Repton become great improvers of nature. More is at work, however, than merely presenting nature as a stage in which a new landed gentry can play out their social roles.[35] Landscape becomes something to be looked at rather than lived in. The landscape painter must separate himself from the scene. Picturesqueness calls for stronger emotions, but it also imposes distance in a number of ways. The actual economic effect places a distance between vision and real effect.[36] Whole villages may have to be moved or destroyed to create a single composition. A different kind of artificiality than the idealizing classicism of early picturesque scenes emerges. The distance demanded includes a distance in time and lived space. What is wanted is not the smoothness of Brown but the wildness of Salvator Rosa and Claude Lorraine. If it is not to be found at hand, it can be built. A desire for the picturesque inspires purposely-built ruins and rustic scenery. Never mind that such scenes are inconvenient and even destructive. Early exhibitions of taste provoked scorn because of their wastefulness and pretension. The creation of picturesque scenery carried that wastefulness to an extreme. The Rev. William Gilpin was hard pressed to justify his tourist journeys and guides. The very idea of a tourist who came only to look from outside a scene was a middle-class transformation of the earlier notion of a grand tour as an educational experience.

The picturesque provides a psychological bridge between the aesthetics of taste that is still based on imitation and a moral unity of sensibility and virtue and the emerging aesthetic of individual experience that can only be experienced at a distance and under conditions that separate both the artist and the audience from the ordinary world. The picturesque is a denial of that world at the same time that it is an affirmation of the independent value of a particular class of experiences for their own sake. The banditti and poor who appear in picturesque painting are only tolerable as long as a clear separation between art and reality is maintained.[37] The movement to an increasingly individualized psychology in the course of the eighteenth century finds its artistic counterpart in the picturesque movement that eventually develops into an aesthetic of autonomous experience, imagination, and fine art as a form valuable for its own sake.

[35]John Dixon Hunt, *Gardens and the Picturesque: Studies in the History of Landscape Architecture* (Cambridge: MIT Press, 1992), p. 114.

[36]John Barrell, *The Dark Side of Landscape: The Rural Poor in English Painting 1730-1840* (Cambridge: Cambridge University Press, 1980), pp. 134-135.

[37]Barrell, *The Dark Side of Landscape*, 101.

15. Expression

Aesthetic theories based on imitation are replaced by theories based on expression as the aesthetic justification for sensibility at the end of the eighteenth century. The explanatory and theoretical importance of expression is, itself, a direct outgrowth of the increased emphasis on the importance of the imagination, sublimity, and picturesqueness. Imitation theory said "Follow Nature" and provided an aesthetic of construction and transcendent beauty. Expression said, "Look to the mind itself"; the activity of the mind is the source of aesthetic experience just as the experience of the world is the source of ideas. However, expression is psychologically atomistic in a very different way from the psychological atomism of Locke's ideas. Emotion tends to be divorced from knowledge. Adam Smith introduces and discusses directly expression in both painting and music. He defines expression as the effect upon the mind of the work. In painting, that effect arises from the thought of something. It is distinct from the drawing and coloring that are a product of skill. In instrumental music, however, the effect is the necessary result of the melody and harmony. They are not distinct from what the music expresses. This is because the effects of instrumental music as imitation are very limited, but its emotional effects on the mind are nevertheless expressive though different from imitation.[38]

Archibald Alison turns associationist psychology to a different end than it originally served by combining it with a theory of the mind's expressive powers to produce an extensive theory of aesthetic effects and predicates. Earlier associationist psychology served an explanatory function. It either explained the negative effect that interfered with the mind's ability to respond naturally or it explained positively how one mind could by association understand the workings of another. For Alison, however, association is productive in a different way. Our language and emotions work together to provide a kind of experience that the mind itself can relish. The hedonism of earlier aesthetics sought to provide an alternative to a purely hedonistic self-interest by showing how one's deepest self-interest was served by aesthetic pleasure. Alison's hedonism changes self-interest into disinterestedness in order to preserve and promote a form of experience that is independent of one's other concerns. Alison frees aesthetics from its moral connections to virtue—ironically, given his own moral purposes.

Alison's particular form of expressiveness is supplanted by Kant's more powerful transcendental theory. Aesthetics develops along a different line from Alison's form of associationism. But elements of what we might call an expressive naturalism continue to influence British aesthetics through Ruskin and the pre-Raphaelites and into the particularly British versions of post-Kantian idealism. Unlike its idealist continental counterparts in the nineteenth century, British aesthetics retains a direct concern with the way that particular works of art are formed by the imaginative powers of individual artists. Coleridge may take over whole sections of Schelling, and Ruskin may graft his social reforms onto his views of aesthetic education, but

[38]Adam Smith. See p. 441, this volume.

both find the connection between nature and aesthetic expression essential to the creative act.

16. Cultural Forces

One final note needs to be added to complete this sketch of eighteenth-century British aesthetics. None of the theorizing described above takes place in an economic or social vacuum. The idea that aesthetics is distanced from the world is a product of aesthetic movements that are only beginning to take shape by the end of the century. It is enough to merely list some of the interactions of theory, art, and audience to see how powerfully they influence each other. Beginning with Dryden and Dennis, the professional author is transformed from a creature of patronage to an entrepreneur. Patronage does not disappear, of course, but it, like the monarchy itself, becomes decidedly more middle class. New economic forces mean new audiences. Private reading, professional critics, circulating libraries, and serial publications transform literary expectations. The novel itself is a form appropriate to the linear time of the eighteenth-century belief in progress and the voracious public appetite for sensation. Salons and academy exhibitions anticipate the museum culture that is already emerging from the classical collecting impulses of the eighteenth century and the opening of great houses and collections to picturesque tourists such as William Gilpin. It would be naive not to recognize the influence of these institutions and economic forces on the production of art and the corresponding changes in art theory. That is not to say that theory is merely a social consequence of other forces. Quite the contrary. The picturesque is only one example of how theory produces a change in the art world. What we must recognize is that the eighteenth century is at once the root of our modern aesthetic and at the same time so very different from it that we make a serious mistake if we view the century with post-Kantian eyes.

CHAPTER 1

John Dryden*

"Introduction" to Charles du Fresnoy, *De Arte Graphica*

De Arte Graphica
Preface of the Translator, with a Parallel, of Poetry and Painting
1695

It may be reasonably expected, that I should say something on my own behalf, in respect to my present undertaking. First, then, the reader may be pleased to know, that it was not of my own choice that I undertook this work. Many of our most skillful painters and other artists were pleased to recommend this author to me, as one who perfectly understood the rules of painting; who gave the best and most concise instruction for performance, and the surest to inform the judgment of all who loved this noble art: that they who before were rather fond of it, than knowingly admired it, might defend their inclination by their reason; that they might understand those excellencies which they blindly valued, so as not to be farther imposed on by bad pieces, and to know when nature was well imitated by the most able masters. 'Tis true indeed, and they acknowledge it, that beside the rules which are given in this treatise, or which can be given in any other, that to make a perfect judgment of good pictures, and to value them more or less when compared with one another,

---

*John Dryden (1631-1700) was the son of a Northhamptonshire landowner. He attended Westminster school and Trinity College, Cambridge. His family had sided with the commonwealth during the war, but Dryden formed a friendship with the royalist Sir Robert Howard, the younger son of the Earl of Berkshire. Dryden married his sister, Lady Elizabeth Howard and eventually converted to Roman Catholicism. In 1662, he was elected to the Royal society and embarked on a successful career as a playwright. He prospered artistically and politically under the restoration, reaching a position of dominance in literary society. The exile of James II and accession of William III saw a change in Dryden's political fortunes, but his literary career continued largely undiminished until his death.

there is farther required a long conversation with the best pieces, which are not very frequent either in France or England; yet some we have, not only from the hands of Holbein, Rubens, and Van Dyck, (one of them admirable for history-painting, and the other two for portraits,) but of many Flemish masters, and those not inconsiderable, though for design, not equal to the Italians. And of these latter also, we are not unfurnished with some pieces of Raphael, Titian, Correggio, Michael Angelo, and others.

But to return to my own undertaking of this translation, I freely own, that I thought my self uncapable of performing it, either to their satisfaction, or my own credit. Not but that I understood the original Latin, and the French author perhaps as well as most Englishmen; but I was not sufficiently versed in the terms of art; and therefore thought that many of those persons who put this honorable task on me, were more able to perform it themselves, as undoubtedly they were. But they assuring me of their assistance, in correcting my faults where I spoke improperly, I was encouraged to attempt it, that I might not be wanting in what I could, to satisfy the desires of so many gentlemen who were willing to give the world this useful work. They have effectually performed their promise to me; and I have been as careful on my side, to take their advice in all things; so that the reader may assure himself of a tolerable translation: Not elegant, for I proposed not that to my self; but familiar, clear, and instructive. In any of which parts, if I have failed, the fault lies wholly at my door. In this one particular only I must beg the readers pardon. The prose translation of the poem is not free from poetical expressions, and I dare not promise that some of them are not fustian, or at least highly metaphorical; but this being a fault in the first digestion (that is, the original Latin) was not to be remedied in the second (viz.) the translation. And I may confidently say, that whoever had attempted it must have fallen into the same inconvenience; or a much greater, that of a false version.

When I undertook this work, I was already engaged in the translation of Virgil, from whom I have borrowed only two months, and am now returning to that which I ought to understand better. In the mean time I beg the readers pardon, for entertaining him so long with my self: 'Tis an usual part of ill manners in all authors, and almost in all mankind, to trouble others with their business; and I was so sensible of it beforehand, that I had not now committed it, unless some concernments of the readers had been interwoven with my own. But I know not, while I am atoning for one error, if I am not falling into another: for I have been importuned to say something farther of this art; and to make some observations on it in relation to the likeness and agreement which it has with poetry, its sister. But before I proceed, it will not be amiss, if I copy from Bellori (a most ingenious author, yet living) some part of his idea of a painter, which cannot be unpleasing, at least to such who are conversant in the philosophy of Plato. And to avoid tediousness, I will not translate the whole discourse, but take and leave as I find occasion.

> God Almighty, in the fabric of the universe, first contemplated himself, and reflected on his own excellencies; from which he drew, and constituted those first forms, which are called idea's: So that every species which was afterwards

expressed was produced from that first idea, forming that wonderful contexture of all created beings. But the celestial bodies above the moon being incorruptible, and not subject to change, remained for ever fair, and in perpetual order: On the contrary, all things which are sublunary are subject to change, to deformity, and to decay. And though nature always intends a consummate beauty in her productions, yet through the inequality of the matter, the forms are altered; and in particular, human beauty suffers alteration for the worse, as we see to our mortification, in the deformities, and disproportions which are in us. For which reason the artful painter and the sculptor, imitating the divine maker, form to themselves as well as they are able, a model of the superior beauties; and reflecting on them endeavor to correct and amend the common nature; and to represent it as it was first created without fault, either in color or in lineament.

This idea, which we may call the Goddess of painting and of sculpture, descends upon the marble and the cloth, and becomes the original of those arts; and being measured by the compass of the intellect, is it self the measure of the performing hand; and being animated by the imagination, infuses life into the image. The idea of the painter and the sculptor, is undoubtedly that perfect and excellent example of the mind; by imitation of which imagined form, all things are represented which fall under human sight: Such is the definition which is made by Cicero in his book of the orator to Brutus. "As therefore in forms and figures there is somewhat which is excellent and perfect, to which imagined species all things are referred by imitation, which are the objects of sight, in like manner we behold the species of eloquence in our minds, the effigies, or actual image of which we seek in the organs of our hearing. This is likewise confirmed by Proclus in the dialogue of Plato called Timaeus: If, says he, you take a man, as he is made by nature and compared him with another who is the effect of Art; the work of nature will always appear the less beautiful, because art is more accurate than nature." But Zeuxis, who from the choice which he made of five virgins, drew that wonderful picture of Helena, which Cicero in his *Orator* before mentioned, sets before us as the most perfect example of beauty, at the same time admonishes a painter, to contemplate the ideas of the most natural forms; and to make a judicious choice of several bodies, all of them the most elegant which he can find: by which we may plainly understand that he thought it impossible to find in any one body all those perfections which he sought for the accomplishment of a Helena, because nature in any individual person makes nothing that is perfect in all its parts. For this reason Maximus Tyrius also says, that the image which is taken by a painter from several bodies produces a beauty, which 'tis impossible to find in any single natural body, approaching to the perfection of the fairest statues. Thus nature on this account is so much inferior to art, that those artists who propose to themselves only the imitation and likeness of such or such a particular person, without election of those idea's before-mentioned, have often been reproached for that omission: Demetrius was taxed for being too natural; Dionysius was also blamed for drawing men like us, and was commonly called, Ανθρωπόγραφοζ that is, a painter of men. In our times Michael Angelo da Caravaggio, was esteemed too natural. He drew persons as they were; and Bamboccio, and most of the Dutch painters, have drawn the worst likeness. Lysippus of old, upbraided the common sort of sculptors, for making men such as they were found in nature; and boasted of himself that he made them as they ought to be; which is a precept of Aristotle, given as well to poets as to painters. Phidias raised an admiration even to astonishment, in those who beheld his statues, with the forms, which he gave to his Gods and heroes; by imitating the idea rather than nature. And Cicero speaking of him affirms, that figuring Jupiter and Pallas, he did not contemplate any object from whence he took the likeness, but considered in his own mind a great and admirable form of beauty, and according to that image in his soul, he directed the operation of his hand. Seneca also seems to wonder, that Phidias having never beheld either Jove or Pallas, yet could conceived their divine images in his mind. Apollonius Tyanaeus says the same in other words, that the fancy more instructs the painter than the imitation; for the last makes only the things which it sees, but the first makes also the things which it never sees.

Leon Battista Alberti tells us, that we ought not so much to love the likeness as the beauty, and to choose from the fairest bodies severally the fairest parts. Leonardo da Vinci instructs the painter to form this idea to himself: And Raphael, the greatest of all modern masters, writes thus to Castiglione, concerning his Galatea: "To paint a fair one, 'tis necessary for me to see many fair ones; but because there is so great a scarcity of lovely women, I am constrained to make use of one certain idea, which I have formed to my self in my own fancy." Guido Reni sending to Rome his St. Michael which he had painted for the church of the Capuchins, at the same time wrote to Monsignor Massano, who was Maestro di Casa (or steward of the house) to Pope Urban the Eighth, in this manner: "I wish I had the wings of an Angel, to have ascended into paradise, and there to have beheld the forms of those beatified spirits, from which I might have copied my archangel: But not being able to mount so high, it was in vain for me to search his resemblance here below: so that I was forced to make an introspection, into my own mind, and into that idea of beauty, which I have formed in my own imagination. I have likewise created there the contrary idea of deformity and ugliness; but I leave the consideration of it, 'till I paint the devil: and in the mean time shun the very thought of it as much as possibly I can, and am even endeavoring to blot it wholly out of my remembrance."

There was not any lady in all antiquity, who was mistress of so much beauty as was to be found in the Venus of Gnidus, made by Praxiteles, or the Minerva of Athens by Phidias; which was therefore called the beautiful form. Neither is there any man of the present age, equal in the strength, proportion, and knitting of his limbs, to the Hercules of Farnese, made by Glycon: Or any woman who can justly be compared with the Medicean Venus of Cleomenes. And upon this account, the noblest poets and the best orators, when they desired to celebrate any extraordinary beauty, are forced to have recourse to statues and pictures, and to draw their persons and faces into comparison. Ovid endeavoring to express the beauty of Cyllarus, the fairest of the centaurs, celebrates him as next in perfection, to the most admirable statues.

Gratus in ore vigor, cervix, humeriq; manusq;
Pectoraq; Artificum laudatis Proxima Signis.

A pleasing vigor his fair face expressed;
His neck, his hands, his shoulders, and his breast,
Did next in gracefulness and beauty stand,
To breathing figures of the sculptor's hand.

In another place he sets Apelles above Venus.

Si Venerem Cois nunquam pinxisset Apelles,
Mersa sub aequoreis illa lateret Aquis.

thus varied.

> One birth to seas the Cyprian Goddess owed,
> A second birth the painter's art bestowed:
> Less by the seas than by his power was given;
> They made her live, but he advanced to heaven.
>
> The idea of this beauty, is indeed various, according to the several forms which the painter or sculptor would describe; as one in strength, another in magnanimity: and sometimes it consists in cheerfulness, and sometimes in delicacy; and is always diversified by the sex and age.
>
> The beauty of Jove is one, and that of Juno another: Hercules, and Cupid are perfect beauties, though of different kinds; for beauty is only that which makes all things as they are in their proper and perfect nature, which the best painters always choose by contemplating the forms of each. We ought farther to consider, that a picture being the representation of a human action, the painter ought to retain in his mind, the examples of all affections, and passions, as a poet preserves the idea of an angry man, of one who is fearful, sad or merry, and so of all the rest: For 'tis impossible to express that with the hand, which never entered into the imagination. In this manner as I have rudely and briefly shewn you, painters and sculptors, choosing the most elegant natural beauties, perfectionate the idea, and advance their art, even above nature it self, in her individual productions; which is the utmost mastery of human performance.
>
> From hence arises that astonishment, and almost adoration which is paid by the knowing to those divine remainders of Antiquity. From hence Phidias, Lysippus, and other noble sculptors, are still held in veneration; and Appelles, Zeuxis, Protogenes, and other admirable painters, though their works are perished, are and will be eternally admired; who all of them drew after the ideas of perfection, which are the miracles of nature, the providence of the understanding, the exemplars of the mind, the light of the fancy; the sun which from its rising, inspired the statue of Memnon, and the fire which warmed into life the image of Prometheus: 'Tis this which causes the graces, and the loves to take up their habitations in the hardest marble, and to subsist in the emptiness of light, and shadows. But since the idea of eloquence is as far inferior to that of painting, as the force of words is to the sight, I must here break off abruptly, and having conducted the reader as it were to a secret walk, there leave him in the midst of silence to contemplate those ideas; which I have only sketched, and which every man must finish for himself.

In these pompous expressions, or such as these, the Italian has given you his idea of a painter; and though I cannot much commend the style, I must needs say there is somewhat in the matter: Plato himself is accustomed to write loftily, imitating, as the critiques tell us, the manner of Homer; but surely that inimitable poet, had not so much of smoke in his writing, though not less of fire. But in short, this is the present genius of Italy. What Philostratus tells us in the proem of his figures is somewhat plainer; and therefore I will translate it almost word for word.

> He who will rightly govern the art of painting, ought of necessity first to understand human nature. He ought likewise to be endued with a genius to express the signs of their passions whom he represents; and to make the dumb as it were to speak; he must yet further understand what is contained in the constitution of the cheeks, in

> the temperament of the eyes, in the naturalness (if I may so call it) of the eye-brows; and in short whatsoever belongs to the mind and thought. He who thoroughly possesses all these things will obtain the whole: And the hand will exquisitely represent the action of every particular person. If it happen that he be either mad, or angry, melancholic, or cheerful, a sprightly youth, or a languishing lover; in one word, he will be able to paint whatsoever is proportionable to any one. And even in all this there is a sweet error without causing any shame: For the eyes and minds of the beholders being fastened on objects which have no real being, as if they were truly existent, and being induced by them to believe them so, what pleasure is it not capable of giving? the ancients, and other wise men, have written many things concerning the symmetry which is in the art of painting; constituting as it were some certain laws for the proportion of every member, not thinking it possible for a painter to undertake the expression of those motions which are in the mind, without a concurrent harmony in the natural measure: For that which is out of its own kind and measure, is not received from nature, whose motion is always right. On a serious consideration of this matter it will be found, that the art of painting has a wonderful affinity with that of poetry; and that there is betwixt them a certain common imagination. For as the poets introduce the Gods and heroes, and all those things which are either majestical, honest or delightful, in like manner the painters, by the virtue of their out-lines, colors, lights and shadows, represent the same things and persons in their pictures.

Thus, as convoy ships either accompany, or should accompany their merchants till they may prosecute the rest of their voyage without danger, so Philostratus has brought me thus far on my way, and I can now sail on without him. He has begun to speak of the great relation betwixt painting and poetry, and thither the greatest part of this discourse by my promise was directed. I have not engaged my self to any perfect method, neither am I loaded with a full cargo. 'Tis sufficient if I bring a sample of some goods in this voyage. It will be easy for others to add more when the commerce is settled: For a treatise twice as large as this of painting could not contain all that might be said on the parallel of these two sister arts. I will take my rise from Bellori before I proceed to the author of this book.

The business of his preface is to prove, that a learned painter should form to himself an idea of perfect nature. This image he is to set before his mind in all his undertakings, and to draw from thence as from a store-house, the beauties which are to enter into his work; thereby correcting nature from what actually she is in individuals, to what she ought to be, and what she was created. Now as this idea of perfection is of little use in portraits (or the resemblances of particular persons) so neither is it in the characters of comedy, and tragedy; which are never to be made perfect, but always to be drawn with some specks of frailty and deficiency; such as they have been described to us in history, if they were real characters; or such as the poet began to shew them at their first appearance, if they were only fictitious, (or imaginary). The perfection of such stage-characters consists chiefly in their likeness to the deficient faulty nature, which is their original: Only, as 'tis observed more at large hereafter, in such cases there will always be found a better likeness, and a worse; and the better is constantly to be chosen: I mean in tragedy, which represents the figures of the highest form amongst mankind. Thus in portraits, the painter will not take that side of the face which has some notorious blemish in it; but either draw it in profile (as Apelles did Antigonus, who had lost one of his eyes) or else shadow the more imperfect side. For an ingenious flattery is to be allowed to the professors of both arts; so long as the likeness is not destroyed. 'Tis true that all manner of imperfections must not be taken away from the characters, and the reason is, that there may be left some grounds of pity for their misfortunes. We can never be grieved for their miseries who are thoroughly wicked, and have thereby justly called their calamities on themselves. Such men are the natural objects of our hatred, not of our commiseration. If on the other side their characters were wholly perfect (such as for example, the character of a saint or martyr in a play,) his, or her misfortunes, would produce impious thoughts in the beholders: they would accuse the heavens of injustice, and think of leaving a religion, where piety was so ill requited. I say the greater part would be tempted so to do, I say not that they ought: and the consequence is too dangerous for the practice. In this I have accused my self for my own *St. Catherine*, but let truth prevail. Sophocles has taken the just medium in his *Oedipus*. He is somewhat arrogant at his first entrance; and is too inquisitive through the whole tragedy: Yet these imperfections being balanced by great virtues, they hinder not our compassion for his miseries; neither yet can they destroy that horror which the nature of his crimes have excited in us. Such in painting are the warts and moles, which adding a likeness to the face, are not therefore to be omitted: But these produce no loathing in us. But how far to proceed, and where to stop, is left to the judgment of the poet and the painter. In comedy there is somewhat more of the worse likeness to be taken, because that is often to produce laughter; which is occasioned by the sight of some deformity: but for this I refer the reader to Aristotle. 'Tis a sharp manner of instruction for the vulgar who are never well amended, till they are more than sufficiently exposed.

That I may return to the beginning of this remark, concerning perfect ideas, I have only this to say, that the parallel is often true in epic-poetry. The heroes of the poets are to be drawn according to this rule. There is scarce a frailty to be left in the best of them; any more than is to be found in a divine nature: And if Aeneas sometimes weeps, 'tis not in bemoaning his own miseries, but those which his people undergo. If this be an imperfection, the Son of God when he was incarnate shed tears of compassion over Jerusalem: And Lentulus describes him often weeping, but never laughing; so that Virgil is justified even from the holy scriptures. I have but one word more, which for once I will anticipate from the author of this book. Though it must be an idea of perfection, from which both the epic poet, and the history painter draws; yet all perfections are not suitable to all subjects: But every one must be designed according to that perfect beauty which is proper to him. An Apollo must be distinguished from a Jupiter, a Pallas from a Venus: and so in poetry an Aeneas from any other hero: for piety is his chief perfection. Homer's Achilles is a kind of exception to this rule: but then he is not a perfect hero, nor so intended by the poet. All his Gods had somewhat of human imperfection; for which he has been taxed by Plato, as an imitator of what was bad: But Virgil observed his fault, and mended it. Yet Achilles was perfect in the strength of his body, and the vigor of his mind. Had he been less passionate, or less revengeful, the poet well foresaw that Hector had been killed, and Troy taken at the first assault; which had destroyed the beautiful contrivance of his *Iliads*, and the moral of preventing discord amongst confederate princes, which was his principal intention. For the moral (as Bossu observes) is the first business of the poet, as being the ground-work of his instruction. This being formed, he contrives such a design, or fable, as may be most suitable to the moral. After this he begins to think of the persons, whom he is to employ in carrying on his design: and gives them the manners, which are most proper to their several characters. The thoughts and words are the last parts, which give beauty and coloring to the piece.

When I say, that the manners of the hero ought to be good in perfection, I contradict not the Marquess of Normanby's opinion, in that admirable verse, where speaking of a perfect character, he calls it "A faultless monster, which the world ne're knew": For that excellent critique, intended only to speak of dramatic characters, and not of epic.

Thus at least I have shewn, that in the most perfect poem, which is that of Virgil, a perfect idea was required, and followed, and consequently that all succeeding poets ought rather to imitate him, than even Homer.

I will now proceed as I promised, to the author of this book. He tells you almost in the first lines of it, that the chief end of painting is to please the eyes: and 'tis one great end of poetry to please the mind. Thus far the parallel of the arts holds true: with this difference, that the principal end of painting is to please; and the chief design of poetry is to instruct. In this the latter seems to have the advantage of the former; but if we consider the artists themselves on both sides, certainly their aims are the very same: they would both make sure of pleasing, and that in preference to instruction. Next, the means of this pleasures is by deceit. One imposes on the sight, and the other on the understanding. Fiction is of the essence of poetry as well as of painting; there is a resemblance in one, of human bodies, things and actions which are not real, and in the other, of a true story by a fiction. And as all stories are not proper subjects for an epic poem, or a tragedy, so neither are they for a noble picture. The subjects both of the one, and of the other, ought to have nothing of immoral, low, or filthy in them; but this being treated at large in the book it self, I waive it to avoid repetition. Only I must add, that though Catullus, Ovid and others were of another opinion, that the subject of poets, and even their thoughts and expressions might be loose, provided their lives were chaste and holy, yet there are no such licenses permitted in that art any more than in painting, to design and color obscene nudities. *Vita proba est*, is no excuse, for it will scarcely be admitted, that either a poet or a painter can be chaste, who give us the contrary examples in their writings and their pictures. We see nothing of this kind in Virgil: that which comes the nearest to it, is the Adventure of the cave, where Dido and Aeneas were driven by the storm: Yet even there the poet pretends a marriage before the consummation; and Juno her self was present at it. Neither is there any expression in that story, which a Roman matron might not read without a blush. Besides, the poet passes it over as hastily as he can, as if he were afraid of staying in the cave with the two lovers, and of being a witness to their actions. Now I suppose that a painter would not be much commended, who should pick out this cavern from the whole *Aeneids*, when there is not another in the work. He had better leave them in their obscurity, than let in a flash of lightning to clear the natural darkness of the place, by which he must discover himself as much as them. The alter-pieces, and holy decorations of painting, show that art may be applied to better uses, as well as poetry. And amongst many other instances, the Farnesian gallery, painted by Hannibal Carracci, is a sufficient witness yet remaining: the whole work being morally instructive, and particularly the *Hercules Bivium*, which is a perfect triumph of virtue over vice, as 'tis wonderfully well described by the ingenious Bellori.

Hitherto I have only told the reader what ought not to be the subject of a picture or of a poem: what it ought to be on either side; our author tells us: it must in general be great and noble: and in this, the parallel is exactly true. The subject of a poet either in tragedy or in an epic poem is a great action of some illustrious hero. 'Tis the same in painting; not every action, nor every person is considerable enough to enter into the cloth. It must be the anger of an Achilles, the piety of an Aeneas, the sacrifice of an Iphigenia (for heroines as well as heroes are comprehended in the rule;) but the parallel is more complete in tragedy, than in an epic poem. For as a tragedy may be made out of many particular episodes of Homer or of Virgil, so may a noble picture be designed out of this or that particular story in either author. History is also fruitful of designs both for the painter and the tragic poet: Curtius throwing himself into a gulf, and the two Decii sacrificing themselves for the safety of their country, are subjects for tragedy and picture. Such is Scipio restoring the Spanish bride, whom he either loved or may be supposed to love, by which he gained the hearts of a great nation, to interest themselves for Rome against Carthage: These are all but particular pieces in Livy's history; and yet are full complete subjects for the pen and pencil. Now the reason of this is evident. Tragedy and picture are more narrowly circumscribed by the mechanic rules of time and place than the epic poem. The time of this last is left indefinite. 'Tis true, Homer took up only the space of eight and forty days for his *Iliads*; but whether Virgil's action was comprehended in a year or somewhat more, is not determined by Bossu. Homer made the place of his action Troy, and the Grecian camp besieging it. Virgil introduces his Aeneas, sometimes in Sicily, sometimes in Carthage, and other times at Cumae, before he brings him to Laurentum; and even after that, he wanders again to the kingdom of Evander and some parts of Tuscany, before he returns to finish the war by the death of Turnus. But tragedy according to the practice of the ancients, was always confined within the compass of twenty-four hours, and seldom takes up so much time. As for the place of it, it was always one, and that not in a larger sense (as for example, a whole city or two or three several houses in it) but the market or some other public place, common to the chorus and all the actors; which established law of theirs, I have not an opportunity to examine in this place, because I cannot do it without digression from my subject, though it seems too strict at the first appearance because it excludes all secret intrigues, which are the beauties of the modern stage: for nothing can be carried on with privacy, when the chorus is supposed to be always present. But to proceed, I must say this to the advantage of painting, even above tragedy, that what this last represents in the space of many hours, the former shows us in one moment. The action, the passion, and the manners of so many persons as are contained in a picture, are to be discerned at once, in the twinkling of an eye; at least they would be so, if the sight could travel over so many different objects all at once, or the mind could digest them all at the same instant or point of time. Thus in the famous picture of Poussin, which represents the institution of the blessed sacrament, you see our savior and his twelve disciples, all concurring in the same action, after different manners, and in different postures; only the manners of Judas are distinguished from the rest. Here is but one indivisible point of time observed: but one action performed by so many persons, in the one room and at the same table: yet the eye cannot comprehend at once the whole object, nor the mind follow it so fast; 'tis considered at leisure, and seen by intervals. Such are the subjects of noble pictures: and such are only to be undertaken by noble hands.

There are other parts of nature, which are meaner, and yet are the subjects both of painters, and of poets. For to proceed in the parallel, as comedy is a representation of human life, in inferior persons, and low subjects, and by that means creeps into the nature of poetry, and is a kind of juniper, a shrub belonging to the species of cedar, so is the painting of clowns, the representation of a Dutch Kermis, the brutal sport of snick or snee, and a thousand other things of this mean invention, a kind of picture, which belongs to nature, but of the lowest form. Such is a lazar in comparison to a Venus; both are drawn in human figures: they have faces alike, though not like faces.

There is yet a lower sort of poetry and painting, which is out of nature: For a farce is that in poetry, which grotesque is in a picture. The persons, and action of a farce are all unnatural, and the manners false, that is, inconsistent with the characters of mankind. Grotesque-painting is the just resemblance of this; and Horace begins his *Art of Poetry* by describing such a figure, with a man's head, a horse's neck, the wings of a bird, and a fishes tail; parts of different species jumbled together, according to the mad imagination of the dawber; and the end of all this, as he tells you afterward, to cause laughter: A very monster in a Bartholomew-Fair for the mob to gape at for their two-pence. Laughter is indeed the propriety of a man, but just enough to distinguish him from his elder brother, with four legs. 'Tis a kind of bastard-pleasures too, taken in at the eyes of the vulgar gazers, and at the ears of the beastly audience. Church-painters use it to divert the honest countryman at public prayers, and keep his eyes open at a heavy sermon, and farce-scriblers make use of the same noble invention to entertain citizens, country-gentlemen, and Covent-Garden fops. If they are merry, all goes well on the poet's side. The better sort go thither too, but in despair of sense, and the just images of nature, which are the adequate pleasures of the mind. But the author can give the stage no better than what was given him by nature: and the actors must represent such things, as they are capable to perform, and by which both they and the scribbler may get their living. After all, 'tis a good thing to laugh at any rate, and if a straw can tickle a man, 'tis an instrument of happiness. Beasts can weep when they suffer, but they cannot laugh. And as Sir William Davenant observes in his preface to *Gondibert*, 'tis the wisdom of a government to permit plays (he might have added farces) as 'tis the prudence of a carter to put bells upon his horses, to make them carry their burdens cheerfully.

I have already shewn, that one main end of poetry and painting is to please, and have said something of the kinds of both, and of their subjects, in which they bear a great resemblance to each other. I must now consider them, as they are great and noble arts; and as they are arts, they must have rules, which may direct them to their common end.

To all arts and sciences, but more particularly to these, may be applied what Hippocrates says of physic, as I find him cited by an eminent French critic. Medicine has long subsisted in the world. The principles of it are certain, and it has a certain way; by both which there has been found in the course of many ages, an infinite number of things, the experience of which has confirmed its usefulness and goodness. All that is wanting to the perfection of this art, will undoubtedly be found, if able men, and such as are instructed in the ancient rules will make a farther enquiry into it, and endeavor to arrive at that, which is hitherto unknown, by that which is already known. But all who having rejected the ancient rules, and taken the opposite ways, yet boast themselves to be masters of this art, do but deceive others, and are themselves deceived; for that is absolutely impossible.

This is notoriously true in these two arts: for the way to please being to imitate nature; both the poets and the painters, in ancient times, and in the best ages, have studied her: and from the practice of both these arts, the rules have been drawn, by which we are instructed how to please, and to compass that end which they obtained, by following their example. For nature is still the same in all ages, and can never be contrary to her self. Thus from the practice of Aeschylus, Sophocles, and Euripides, Aristotle drew his rules for tragedy; and Philostratus for painting. Thus amongst the moderns, the Italian and French critics by studying the precepts of Aristotle, and Horace, and having the example of the grecian poets before their eyes, have given us the rules of modern tragedy: and thus the critics of the same countries, in the art of painting have given the precepts of perfecting that art.

'Tis true that poetry has one advantage over painting in these last ages, that we have still the remaining examples both of the Greek and Latin poets: whereas the painters have nothing left them from Apelles, Protogenes, Parrhasius, Xeuxis, and the rest, but only the testimonies which are given of their incomparable works. But instead of this, they have some of their best statues, bass-relievo's, columns, obelisques, etc. which were saved out of the common ruin, and are still preserved in Italy: and by well distinguishing what is proper to sculpture, and what to painting, and what is common to them both, they have judiciously repaired that loss. And the great genius of Raphael, and others, having succeeded to the times of barbarism and ignorance, the knowledge of painting is now arrived to a supreme perfection, though the performance of 'tis much declined in the present age. The greatest age for poetry amongst the Romans was certainly that of Augustus Caesar; and yet we are told that painting was then at its lowest ebb, and perhaps sculpture was also declining at the same time. In the rein of Domitian, and some who succeeded him, poetry was but meanly cultivated, but painting eminently flourished. I am not here to give the history of the two arts; how they were both in a manner extinguished, by the irruption of the barbarous nations, and both restored about the times of Leo the Tenth, Charles the Fifth, and Francis the First; though I might observe, that neither

Ariosto, nor any of his contemporary poets ever arrived at the excellency of Raphael, Titian, and the rest in painting. But in revenge at this time, or lately in many countries, poetry is better practiced than her sister-art. To what height the magnificence and encouragement of the present King of France may carry painting and sculpture is uncertain, but by what he has done, before the war in which he is engaged, we may expect what he will do after the happy conclusion of a peace, which is the prayer and wish of all those who have not an interest to prolong the miseries of Europe. For 'tis most certain, as our author amongst others has observed, that reward is the spur of virtue, as well in all good arts, as in all laudable attempts: and emulation which is the other spur, will never be wanting either amongst poets or painters, when particular rewards and prizes are proposed to the best deservers.

But to return from this digression, though it was almost necessary; all the rules of painting are methodically, concisely, and yet clearly delivered in this present treatise which I have translated. Bossu has not given more exact rules for the epic poem, nor Dancier for tragedy in his late excellent translation of Aristotle and his notes upon him, than our Fresnoy has made for painting; with the parallel of which I must resume my discourse, following my author's text, though with more brevity than I intended because Virgil calls me.

The principal and most important parts of painting, is to know what is most beautiful in nature, and most proper for that Art: that which is the most beautiful is the most noble subject: so in poetry, tragedy is more beautiful than comedy; because, as I said, the persons are greater whom the poet instructs, and consequently the instructions of more benefit to mankind: the action is likewise greater and more noble, and thence is derived the greater and more noble pleasure.

To imitate nature well in whatsoever subject, is the perfection of both arts; and that picture and that poem which comes nearest to the resemblance of nature is the best. But it follows not, that what pleases most in either kind is therefore good; but what ought to please. Our depraved appetites, and ignorance of the arts, mislead our judgments, and cause us often to take that for true imitation of nature, which has no resemblances of nature in it. To inform our judgments, and to reform our tastes, rules were invented, that by them we might discern when nature was imitated, and how nearly. I have been forced to recapitulate these things, because mankind is not more liable to deceit, than 'tis willing to continue in a pleasing error strengthened by a long habitude. The imitation of nature is therefore justly constituted as the general, and indeed the only rule of pleasing both in poetry and painting. Aristotle tells us, that imitation pleases, because it affords matter for a reasoner to inquire into the truth or falsehood of imitation, by comparing its likeness or unlikeness with the original: But by this rule, every speculation in nature, whose truth falls under the enquiry of a philosopher, must produce the same delight, which is not true. I should rather assign another reason. Truth is the object of our understanding, as good is of our will: And the understanding can no more be delighted with a lie, than the will can choose an apparent evil. As truth is the end of all our speculations, so the discovery of it is the pleasure of them. And since a true knowledge of nature gives us pleasure, a lively imitation of it, either in poetry or painting, must of necessity produce a much greater: For both these arts as I said before, are not only true imitations of nature, but of the best nature, of that which is wrought up to a nobler pitch. They present us with images more perfect than the life in any individual: and we have the pleasure to see all the scattered beauties of nature united by a happy chemistry, without its deformities or faults. They are imitations of the passions which always move, and therefore consequently please: for without motion there can be no delight; which cannot be considered, but as an active passion. When we view these elevated idea's of nature, the result of that view is admiration, which is always the cause of pleasure.

This foregoing remark, which gives the reason why imitation pleases, was sent me by Mr. Walter Moyle, a most ingenious young gentleman, conversant in all the studies of humanity much above his years. He had also furnished me (according to my request) with all the particular passages in Aristotle and Horace, which are used by them to explain the art of poetry by that of painting: which, if ever I have time to retouch this essay, shall be inserted in their places.

Having thus shewn that imitation pleases, and why it pleases in both these arts, it follows that some rules of imitation are necessary to obtain the end: for without rules there can be no art; any more than there can be a house without a door to conduct you into it.

The principal parts of painting and poetry next follow. Invention is the first part, and absolutely necessary to them both: yet no rule ever was or ever can be given how to compass it. A happy genius is the gift of nature: it depends on the influence of the stars, say the astrologers, on the organs of the body, say the naturalists; 'tis the particular gift of heaven, say the divines, both Christians and heathens. How to improve it, many books can teach us; how to obtain it, none: that nothing can be done without it, all agree.

Tu nihil invitâ dices faciesue Minervâ.

Without invention a painter is but a copier, and a poet but a plagiary of others. Both are allowed sometimes to copy and translate; but as our author tells you, that is not the best part of their reputation. Imitators are but a servile kind of cattle, says the poet; or at best, the keepers of cattle for other men: they have nothing which is properly their own; that is a sufficient mortification for me while I am translating Virgil. But to copy the best author is a kind of praise, if I perform it as I ought; as a copy after Raphael is more to be commended, than an original of any indifferent painter.

Under this head of invention is placed the disposition of the work, (to put all things in a beautiful order and harmony, that the whole may be of a piece). The compositions of the painter should be conformable to the text of ancient authors, to the customs, and the times. And this is exactly the same in poetry; Homer, and Virgil, are to be our guides in the epic; Sophocles, and Euripides, in tragedy: in all things we are to imitate the customs, and the times of those persons and things which we represent: Not to make new rules of the drama, as Lopez de Vega has attempted unsuccessfully to do; but to be content to follow our masters, who understood nature better than we. But if the story which we treat be modern, we are to vary the customs, according to the time and the country where the scene of action lies: for this is still to imitate nature, which is always the same, though in a different dress.

As in the composition of a picture, the painter is to take care that nothing enter into it, which is not proper, or convenient to the subject; so likewise is the poet to reject all incidents which are foreign to his poem, and are naturally no parts of it: they are wenns, and other excrescences, which belong not to the body, but deform it: no person, no incident in the piece, or in the play, but must be of use to carry on the main design. All things else are like six fingers to the hand; when nature which is superfluous in nothing, can do her work with five. A painter must reject all trifling ornaments, so must a poet refuse all tedious, and unnecessary descriptions. A robe which is too heavy, is less an ornament than a burden.

In poetry Horace calls these things, *Versus inopes rerum, nugaeque canorae*; these are also the *lucus & ara Dianae*, which he mentions in the same *Art of Poetry*. But since there must be ornaments both in painting and poetry, if they are not necessary, they must at least be decent: that is, in their due place, and but moderately used. The painter is not to take so much pains about the drapery as about the face, where the principal resemblance lies: neither is the poet who is working up a passion, to make similes which will certainly make it languish. My Montezuma dies with a fine one in his mouth: but it is ambitious and out of season. When there are more figures in a picture than are necessary, or at least ornamental, our author calls them figures to be let: because the picture has no use of them. So I have seen in some modern plays above twenty actors; when the action has not required half the number. In the principal figures of a picture, the painter is to employ the sinews of his art, for in them consists the principal beauty of his work. Our author saves me the comparison with tragedy, for he says that herein he is to imitate the tragic poet, who employs his utmost force in those places wherein consists the height and beauty of the action.

Du Fresnoy, whom I follow, makes design or drawing the second part of painting: But the rules which he gives concerning the posture of the figures, are almost wholly proper to that art; and admit not any comparison, that I know, with poetry. The posture of a poetic figure is, as I conceive, the description of his heroes in the performance of such or such an action: as of Achilles just in the act of killing Hector: or of Aeneas who has Turnus under him. Both the poet and the painter vary the postures according to the action, or passion which they represent of the same person: But all must be great and graceful in them. The same Aeneas must be drawn a suppliant to Dido, with respect in his gestures, and humility in his eyes: But when he is forced in his own defense to kill Lausus, the poet shows him compassionate, and tempering the severity of his looks with a reluctance to the action, which he is going to perform. He has pity on his beauty, and his youth; and is loath to destroy such a masterpiece of nature. He considers Lausus rescuing his father at the hazard of his own life, as an image of himself when he took Anchises on his shoulders, and bore him safe through the rage of the fire, and the opposition of his enemies: And therefore in the posture of a retiring man, who avoids the combat, he stretches out his arm in sign of peace, with his right foot drawn a little back, and his breast bending inward, more like an orator than a soldier; and seems to dissuade the young man from pulling on his destiny, by attempting more than he was able to perform. Take the passage as I have thus translated it.

> Shouts of applause ran ringing through the field,
> To see the son, the vanquish'd father shield:
> All, fir'd with noble emulation, strive;
> And with a storm of darts to distance drive
> The trojan chief; who held at bay, from far
> On his Vulcanian orb, sustain'd the war.
> Aeneas thus o'erwhelm'd on every side,
> Their first Assault undaunted did abide;
> And thus to Lausus, loud with friendly threatning cry'd,
> Why wilt thou rush to certain death, and rage
> In rash attempts beyond thy tender Age,
> Betray'd by pious love?

And afterwards.

> He grieved, he wept; the sight an image brought
> Of his own filial love; a sadly pleasing thought.

But beside the outlines of the posture, the design of the picture comprehends in the next place the forms of faces, which are to be different: and so in a poem, or a play, must the several characters of the persons be distinguished from each other. I knew a poet, whom out of respect I will not name, who being too witty himself, could draw nothing but wits in a comedy of his: even his fools were infected with the disease of their author. They overflowed with smart reparties, and were only distinguished from the intended wits by being called coxcombs; though they deserved not so scandalous a name. Another, who had a great genius for tragedy, following the fury of his natural temper, made every man, and woman too, in his plays stark raging mad: there was not a sober person to be had for love or money. All was tempestuous and blustering; heaven and earth were coming together at every word; a mere hurricane from the beginning to the end, and every actor seemed to be hastening on the day of judgment.

Let every member be made for its own head, says our author; not a withered hand to a young face. So in the persons of a play, whatsoever is said or done by any of them, must be consistent with the manners which the poet has given them distinctly: and even the habits must be proper to the degrees, and humors of the persons, as well as in a picture. He who entered in the first act a young man, like Pericles Prince of Tyre, must not be in danger in the fifth act, of committing incest with his daughter: nor an usurer, without great probability and causes of repentance, be turned into a cutting moorcraft.

I am not satisfied that the comparison betwixt the two arts in the last paragraph is altogether so just as it might have been; but I am sure of this which follows.

The principal figure of the subject must appear in the midst of the picture, under the principal light, to distinguish it from the rest which are only its attendants. Thus in a tragedy or an epic poem, the hero of the piece must be advanced foremost to the view of the reader or spectator; he must out-shine the rest of all the characters; he must appear the prince of them, like the sun in the Copernican system, encompassed with the less noble planets. Because the hero is the center of the main action; all the lines from the circumference tend to him alone: He is the chief object of pity in the drama, and of admiration in the epic poem.

As in a picture, besides the principal figures which compose it, and are placed in the midst of it, there are less groups or knots of figures disposed at proper distances, which are parts of the piece, and seem to carry on the same design in a more inferior manner; so in epic poetry, there are episodes, and a chorus in tragedy, which are members of the action, as growing out of it, not inserted into it. Such in the Ninth Book of the *Aeneids* is the episode of Nisus and Euryalus: the adventure belongs to them alone; they alone are the objects of compassion and admiration; but their business which they carry on, is the general concernment of the Trojan camp, then beleaguered by Turnus and the Latins, as the Christians were lately by the Turks. They were to advertise the chief hero of the distresses of his subjects occasioned by his absence, to crave his succor, and solicit him to hasten his return.

The Grecian tragedy was at first nothing but a chorus of singers; afterwards one actor was introduced, which was the poet himself, who entertained the people with a discourse in verse, betwixt the pauses of the singing. This succeeding with the people, more actors were added to make the variety the greater; and in process of time, the chorus only sung betwixt the acts; and the Coryphaeus, or chief of them, spoke for the rest, as an actor concerned in the business of the play.

Thus tragedy was perfected by degrees; and being arrived at that perfection, the painters might probably take the hint from thence, of adding groups to their pictures. But as a good picture may be without a group; so a good tragedy may subsist without a chorus: notwithstanding any reasons which have been given by Dacier to the contrary.

Monsieur Racine has indeed used it in his *Esther*, but not that he found any necessity of it, as the French critic would insinuate. The chorus at St. Cyr, was only to give the young ladies an occasion of entertaining the king with vocal music, and of commending their own voices. The play it self was never intended for the public stage, nor, without disparagement to the learned author, could possibly have succeeded there; and much less the translation of it here. Mr. Wicherly, when we read it together, was of my opinion in this, or rather I of his; for it becomes me so to speak of so excellent a poet, and so great a judge. But since I am in this place, as Virgil says, *spatiis exclusus iniquis*, that is, shortened in my time, I will give no other reason, than that it is impracticable on our stage. A new theater much more ample and much deeper must be made for that purpose, besides the cost of sometimes forty or fifty habits, which is an expense too large, to be supplied by a company of actors. 'Tis true, I should not be sorry to see a chorus on a theater more than as large and as deep again as ours, built and adorned at a king's charges; and on that condition, and another, which is, that my hands were not bound behind me, as now they are, I should not despair of making such a tragedy, as might be both instructive and delightful, according to the manner of the Grecians.

To make a sketch, or a more perfect model of a picture, is in the language of poets, to draw up the scenery of a play, and the reason is the same for both; to guide the undertaking, and to preserve the remembrance of such things, whose natures are difficult to retain.

To avoid absurdities and incongruities, is the same law established for both arts. The painter is not to paint a cloud at the bottom of a picture, but in the uppermost parts: nor the poet to place what is proper to the end or middle in the beginning of a poem. I might enlarge on this, but there are few poets or painters, who can be supposed to sin so grossly against the laws of nature, and of art. I remember only one play, and for once I will call it by its name, *The Slighted Maid*, where there is nothing in the first act, but what might have been said or done in the fifth; nor any thing in the midst, which might not have been placed as well in the beginning or the end. To express the passions which are seated in the heart, by outward signs, is one great precept of the painters, and very difficult to perform. In poetry, the same passions and motions of the mind are to be expressed; and in this consists the principal difficulty, as well as the excellency of that art. This, says my author, is the gift of Jupiter: and to speak in the same heathen language, we call it the gift of our Apollo: not to be obtained by pains or study, if we are not born to it: For the motions which are studied are never so natural, as those which break out in the height of a real passion. Mr. Otway possessed this part as thoroughly as any of the ancients or moderns. I will not defend every thing in his *Venice Preserved*; but I must bear this testimony to his memory, that passions are truly touched in it, though perhaps there is somewhat to be desired both in the grounds of them, and in the height and elegance of expression; but nature is there, which is the greatest beauty.

"In the passions," says our author, "we must have a very great regard to the quality of the persons who are actually possessed with them." The joy of a monarch for the news of a victory, must not be expressed like the ecstasy of a harlequin on the receipt of a letter from his mistress; this is so much the same in both the arts, that it is no longer a comparison. What he says of face painting, or the portrait of any one particular person (concerning the likeness) is also as applicable to poetry. In the character of an hero, as well as in an inferior figure, there is a better or worse likeness to be taken; the better is a panegyric if it be not false, and the worse is a libel: Sophocles, says Aristotle, always drew men as they ought to be, that is, better than they were; another, whose name I have forgotten, drew them worse than naturally they were. Euripides altered nothing in the character, but made them such as they were represented by history, epic poetry or tradition. Of the three, the draught of Sophocles is most commended by Aristotle. I have followed it in that part of Oedipus, which I writ, though perhaps I have made him too good a man. But my characters of Antony and Cleopatra, though they are favorable to them, have nothing of outrageous panegyric: their passions were their own, and such as were given them by history; only the deformities of them were cast into shadows, that they might be objects of compassion: whereas if I had chosen a noon-day light for them, somewhat must have been discovered, which would rather have moved our hatred than our pity.

The Gothic manner, and the barbarous ornaments, which are to be avoided in a picture, are just the same with those in an ill ordered play. For example, our English tragicomedy must be confessed to be wholly Gothic, notwithstanding the success which it has found upon our theater, and in the *Pastor Fido* of Guarini; even though Corisca and the satyr contribute somewhat to the main action. Neither can I defend my *Spanish Fryar*, as fond as otherwise I am of it, from this imputation: for though the comical parts are diverting, and the serious moving, yet they are of an unnatural mingle. For mirth and gravity destroy each other, and are no more to be allowed for decent, than a gay widow laughing in a mourning habit.

I had almost forgotten one considerable resemblance. Du Fresnoy tells us, "that the figures of the groups, must not be all on a side, that is, with their face and bodies all turned the same way; but must contrast each other by their several positions." Thus in a play, some characters must be raised to oppose others, and to set them off the better, according to the old maxim, *contraria juxta se posita, magis elucescunt*. Thus in *The Scornful Lady*, the usurer is set to confront the prodigal. Thus in my *Tyrannique Love*, the atheist Maximin is opposed to the character of St. Catherine.

I am now come, though with the omission of many likenesses, to the third part of painting, which is called the cromatic or coloring. Expression, and all that belongs to words, is that in a poem, which coloring is in a picture. The colors well chosen in their proper places, together with the lights and shadows which belong to them, lighten the design, and make it pleasing to the eye. The words, the expressions, the tropes and figures, the versification, and all the other elegancies of sound, as cadences, turns of words upon the thought, and many other things which are all parts of expression, perform exactly the same office both in dramatic and epic poetry. Our author calls coloring, *lena sororis*; in plain English, the bawd of her sister, the design or drawing: she clothes, she dresses her up, she paints her, she makes her appear more lovely than naturally she is; she procures for the design, and makes lovers for her: For the design of it self, is only so many naked lines. Thus in poetry, the expression is that which charms the reader, and beautifies the design which is only the out-lines of the fables. 'Tis true, the design must of it self be good; if it be vicious or (in one word) unpleasing, the cost of coloring is thrown away upon it. 'Tis an ugly woman in a rich habit set out with jewels, nothing can become her: But granting the design to be moderately good, 'tis like an excellent complexion with indifferent features; the white and red well mingled on the face, make what was before but passable, appear beautiful *Operum colores* is the very word which Horace uses, to signify words and elegant expressions, of which he himself was so great a master in his odes. Amongst the ancients, Zeuxis was most famous for his coloring; amongst the moderns, Titian and Correggio. Of the two ancient epic poets, who have so far excelled all the moderns, the invention and design were the particular talents of Homer. Virgil must yield to him in both, for the design of the Latin was borrowed from the Grecian: But the *Dictio Virgiliana*, the expression of Virgil, his coloring, was incomparably the better, and in that I have always endeavored to copy him. Most of the pedants I know maintain the contrary, and will have Homer excel even in this part: But of all people, as they are the most ill mannered, so they are the worst judges. Even of words, which are their province, they seldom know more than the grammatical construction, unless they are born with a poetical genius; which is a rare portion amongst them. Yet some I know may stand excepted; and such I honor.

Virgil is so exact in every word, that none can be changed but for a worse: nor any one removed from its place, but the harmony will be altered. He pretends sometimes to trip; but 'tis only to make you think him in danger of a fall, when he is most secure: Like a skillful dancer on the ropes (if you will pardon the meanness of the similitude) who slips willingly and makes a seeming stumble, that you may think him in great hazard of breaking his neck; while at the same time he is only giving you a proof of his dexterity. My late Lord Roscomon was often pleased with this reflection, and with the examples of it in this admirable author.

I have not leisure to run through the whole comparison of lights and shadows with tropes and figures; yet I cannot but take notice of metaphors, which like them have power to lessen or greaten any thing. Strong and glowing colors are the just resemblances of bold metaphors, but both must be judiciously applied; for there is a difference betwixt daring and foolhardiness. Lucan and Statius often ventured them too far, our Virgil never. But the great defect of the *Pharsalia* and the *Thebais* was in the design; if that had been more perfect, we might have forgiven many of their bold strokes in the coloring; or at least excused them: yet some of them are such as Demosthenes or Cicero could not have defended. Virgil, if he could have seen the first verses of the *Sylvae*, would have thought Statius mad in his fustian description of the statue on the brazen horse. But that poet was always in a foam at his setting out, even before the motion of the race had warmed him. The soberness of Virgil, whom he read it seems to little purpose, might have shown him the difference betwixt *Arma virumq; cano*, and *magnanimum aeacidem, formidatamq; tonanti progeniem*. But Virgil knew how to rise by degrees in his expressions: Statius was in his towering heights at the first stretch of his pinions. The description of his running horse just starting in the funeral games for Archemorus, though the verses are wonderfully fine, are the true image of their author:

Stare adeo nescit, pereunt vestigia mille
Ante fugam; absentemq; ferit gravis ungula campum;

which would cost me an hour, if I had the leisure to translate them, there is so much of beauty in the original.

Virgil, as he better knew his colors, so he knew better how and where to place them. In as much haste as I am, I cannot forbear giving one example. 'Tis said of him, that he read the second, fourth and sixth books of his *Aeneids* to Augustus Caesar. In the sixth, (which we are sure he read, because we know Octavia was present, who rewarded him so bountifully for the twenty verses which were made in honor of her deceased son Marcellus) in this Sixth Book, I say, the poet speaking of Misenus the trumpeter, says,

—Quo non praestantior alter,
Aere ciere viros, —

and broke off in the hemistich or midst of the verse: but in the very reading, seized as it were with a divine fury, he made up the latter part of the hemistich, with these following words:

—Martemq; accendere cantu.

How warm, nay how glowing a coloring is this! In the beginning of the verse, the word *Aes*, or brass, was taken for a trumpet, because the instrument was made of that metal, which of it self was fine; but in the latter end, which was made *ex tempore*, you see three metaphors, *martemque,—accendere,—cantu*. Good heavens! How the plain sense is raised by the beauty of the words! But this was happiness, the former might be only judgment: this was the *curiosa felicitas*, which Petronius attributes to Horace; 'tis the pencil thrown luckily full upon the horse's mouth to express the foam which the painter with all his skill could not perform without it. These hits of words a true poet often finds, as I may say, without seeking: but he knows their value when he finds them, and is infinitely pleased. A bad poet may sometimes light on them, but he discerns not a diamond from a Bristol-stone; and would have been of the cocks mind in Aesop, a grain of barley would have pleased him better than the jewel. The lights and shadows which belong to coloring, put me in mind of that verse in Horace, *Hoc amat obscurum, vult hoc sub luce videri*: some parts of a poem require to be amply written, and with all the force and elegance of words: others must be cast into shadows; that is, passed over in silence, or but faintly touched. This belongs wholly to the judgment of the poet and the painter. The most beautiful parts of the picture and the poem must be the most finished, the colors and words most chosen; many things in both which are not deserving of this care, must be shifted off; content with vulgar expressions, and those very short, and left, as in a shadow, to the imagination of the reader.

We have the proverb, *manum de tabulâ,* from the painters; which signifies, to know when to give over, and to lay by the pencil. Both Homer and Virgil practiced this precept wonderfully well, but Virgil the better of the two. Homer knew that when Hector was slain, Troy was as good as already taken; therefore he concludes his action there. For what follows in the funerals of Patroclus, and the redemption of Hector's body, is not (properly speaking) a part of the main action. But Virgil concludes with the death of Turnus: for after that difficulty was removed, Aeneas might marry and establish the trojans when he pleased. This rule I had before my eyes in the conclusion of the *Spanish Fryar*, when the discovery was made, that the king was living, which was the knot of the play untied; the rest is shut up in the compass of some few lines, because nothing then hindered the happiness of Torismond and Leonora. The faults of that drama are in the kind of it, which is tragi-comedy. But it was given to the people; and I never writ any thing for my self but *Antony and Cleopatra*.

This remark I must acknowledge is not so proper for the coloring as the design; but it will hold for both. As the words, etc. are evidently shown to be the clothing of the thought, in the same sense as colors are the clothing of the design, so the painter and the poet ought to judge exactly, when the coloring and expressions are perfect, and then to think their work is truly finished. Apelles said of Protogenes, that he knew not when to give over. A work may be over-wrought as well as under-wrought: too much labor often takes away the spirit by adding to the polishing, so that there remains nothing but a dull correctness, a piece without any considerable faults, but with few beauties; for when the spirits are drawn off, there is nothing but a *caput mortuum*. Statius never thought an expression could be bold enough; and if a bolder could be found he rejected the first. Virgil had judgment enough to know daring was necessary; but he knew the difference betwixt a glowing color and a glaring: as when he compared the shocking of the fleets at Actium to the jostling of islands rent from their foundations, and meeting in the ocean. He knew the comparison was forced beyond nature and raised too high: he therefore softens the metaphor with a *credas*. You would almost believe, that mountains or islands rushed against each other.

> *—credas innare revulsas*
> *Cycladas: aut montes concurrere montibus aequos.*

But here I must break off without finishing the discourse.

Cynthius aurem vellit & admonuit, &c. The things which are behind are of too nice a consideration for an essay, begun and ended in twelve mornings, and perhaps the judges of painting and poetry, when I tell them how short a time it cost me, may make me the same answer, which my late Lord Rochester made to one, who to commend a tragedy, said it was written in three weeks; "How the devil could he be so long about it?" For that poem was infamously bad; and I doubt this parallel is little better; and then the shortness of the time is so far from being a commendation, that 'tis scarcely an excuse. But if I have really drawn a portrait to the knees, or an half length with a tolerable likeness, then I may plead with some justice for my self, that the rest is left to the imagination. Let some better artist provide himself of a deeper canvas, and taking these hints which I have given, set the figure on its legs, and finish it in the invention, design and coloring.

CHAPTER 2

John Dennis*
A Large Account of the Taste in Poetry, and the Causes of the Degeneracy of It
1702

To the Honorable George Granville, Esq;.

Sir,

I know that a great many persons in the world would take it for an affront, to have a play addressed to them, which had been unfortunate in the representation. But you, sir, have discernment enough to be of another opinion; for a poet, who dedicates a play that has not been successful, will, if he takes care of his reputation, choose a powerful patron, who is every way qualified to defend it. One who is generous enough to support whatever he can justly excuse, and who with a piercing eye can reach to his beauties, while others stop at his faults.

When I first communicated the design which I had of altering this comedy of Shakespear, I found that I should have two sorts of people to deal with, who would equally endeavor to obstruct my success. The one believed it to be so admirable, that

*John Dennis (1657-1734) was born in London where his father was a prosperous saddler. He was educated at Harrow and Caius College Cambridge. After leaving college, he toured in France and Italy. He inherited property from his father and uncle that allowed him for a time to move freely in fashionable literary circles, but later had to live by his writing and amassed considerable debt. He was a supporter of the protestant succession and secured the patronage of the Duke of Marlborough for a time. He began to publish poetry in 1692, and his first play was performed in 1697. His success as a playwright was mixed, at best, and his failure to achieve what he considered his due colored his criticism. Dennis is referred to in Pope's *Essay on Criticism,* which initiated a long and often bitter exchange. Dennis also was involved in controversies with Addison and Steele. *The Dictionary of National Biography* describes his last years as "wretched."

nothing ought to be added to it; the others fancied it to be so despicable, that anyone's time would be lost upon it.

That this comedy was not despicable, I guessed for several reasons: First, I knew very well, that it had pleased one of the greatest Queens that ever was in the world, great not only for her wisdom in the arts of government, but for her knowledge of polite learning, and her nice taste of the drama, for such a taste we may be sure she had, by the relish which she had of the ancients. This comedy was written at her command, and by her direction, and she was so eager to see it acted, that she commanded it to be finished in fourteen days; and was afterwards, as tradition tells us, very well pleased at the representation. In the second place, in the reign of King Charles the Second, when people had an admirable taste of comedy, all those men of extraordinary parts, who were the ornaments of that court; as the late Duke of Buckingham, my Lord Normanby, my Lord Dorset, my late Lord Rochester, Sir Charles Sidley, Dr. Frazer, Mr. Savil, Mr. Buckley, were in love with the beauties of this comedy. In the third place, I thought that after so long an acquaintance as I had with the best comic poets, among the ancients and moderns, I might depend in some measure upon my own judgment, and I thought I found here three or four extraordinary characters, that were exactly drawn, and truly comical; and that I saw besides in it some as happy touches as ever were in comedy: Besides I had observed what success the character of Falstaff had had, in the first part of *Harry the Fourth*. And as the Falstaff in the *Merry Wives* is certainly superior to that of the second part of *Harry the Fourth*, so it can hardly be said to be inferior to that of the first.

For in the second part of *Harry the Fourth*, Falstaff does nothing but talk, as indeed he does nothing else in the third and fourth acts of the first part. Whereas in *The Merry Wives*, he every where acts, and that action is more regular, and more in compass than it is in the first part of *Harry the Fourth*. 'Tis true, what he says in *Harry the Fourth* is admirable; but action at last is the business of the stage. The drama is action itself, and it is action alone that is able to excite in any extraordinary manner the curiosity of mankind. What news, is the question now a days every moment, but people by that question demand what is done, and not what is said upon the great stage of the world. In short, I defy any man to name me a play that has ever succeeded without some sort of action or another. But I could if I pleased mention more than one, that has succeeded barely by the force of action, without almost any thing else.

It was for the above-named reasons, that I thought this by no means a despicable comedy. And it was for the reasons which follow, that I believed it not so admirable, but that it might receive improvement. First, I knew very well, that in so short a time as this play was writ, nothing could be done that is perfect. Secondly, I knew very well, that this comedy had never upon revivals had any great successes, and that particularly when it was revived in King Charles the Second's time, the only character that pleased to a height was slender acted by Wintershal. And that though something like this may very well happen to a living author without any just cause, yet that there must be reason for it, when it happens to an author who has a long time been dead, and whose reputation has been long established. And indeed the *Merry Wives of Windsor*, as it has great beauties, so it has strange defects, which though they past at first for the sake of the beauties, yet will come to be less endured as the stage grows more regular. For there are no less than three actions in it that are independent one of another, which divide and distract the minds of an audience, there is more than one insignificant scene, which has nothing to do with any other part of the play, which is enough to obstructs and stifle the action. The style in some places is stiff and forced and affected, whereas the dialogue in comedy ought to be as free as the air. This affectation is particularly remarkable in some part of the first scene between the wives, and in all Ford's part of the first scene between him and Falstaff. This is not said in the least with a design to derogate from Shakespear's merit, who performed more than any one else could have done in so short a time. In the alteration I have endeavored to correct the foresaid errors.

I have made every thing instrumental to Fenton's marriage, and the whole to depend on one common center, which I believe was hardly in the power of every writer to perform. I have added to some of the parts in order to heighten the characters, and make them show the better. I have above all things endeavored to make the dialogue as easy and free as I could. For in comedy, which is an image of common life, every thing which is forced is abominable. In short, I have altered every thing which I disliked, and retained every thing which I or my friends approved of, excepting something of Justice Shallow in the first scene of the play, which I omitted for two reasons, the one was because I could not bring it into the same design with the rest, the second because I knew nobody who would be capable of acting that character, unless those who would be otherwise employed.

Thus, sir, I have endeavored to convey two things by you to the general reader, the one, that this comedy is not so despicable as to be incapable of improvement; the other, that it is not so admirable, as not to stand in need of any. Whether, sir, I have improved it or no I leave it to you to determine, whether the scene between the wives in the first act be altered for the better or the worse, whether that between Falstaff and Ford in the second act is aptly contrived to give occasion to an excellent actor to shew himself; whether that between Falstaff and the wives in the third act be wholly without art, and whether that between Falstaff and Ford in the fourth act, may be said to be truly comical.

But before it comes to that, sir, I who am resolved to have you fully informed before you come to give sentence, and who am ignorant whether you were in town when this play was acted or no, think my self obliged to make you acquainted, that Falstaff's part, which you know to be the principal one of the play, and that on which all the rest depends, was by no means acted to the satisfaction of the audience, upon which several fell from disliking the action to disapproving the play, which will be always very natural upon such occasions, though sometimes not very reasonable, and divers objections were immediately made, which if the play had succeeded, had perhaps never been thought of. I desire that you would give me leave to lay them and their answers before you, and so leave the whole to your impartial decision.

The first is, that the characters in this comedy are very low, and that there is neither much wit, nor love nor gallantry in it. To which I answer first, that though the characters are low they are true and good, that there is as perfect a plot as I was able to build upon another man's foundation; and that the lowness of the characters derogates not a jot from the perfection of the fable; that in all fables all characters are universal and allegorical, and that it signifies nothing to the beauty of the fiction, or the importance of the moral, whether we bring in kings or shepherds, so they are introduced aptly. In the next place, there is humor every where in this comedy. And humor after the plot is what is most valuable in comedy. I desire then, sir, that I may have leave to prove two things: First, that humor is more the business of comedy than wit: And secondly, that humor is more to be found in low characters, than among persons of a higher rank, and consequently that low characters are more proper for comedy than high, and that low comedy is to be preferred to the high. And when I have done this, I desire to speak a word of love and gallantry, of the want of which this play is accused.

First then, humor is the business in comedy, and not wit. The business of a comic poet is to shew his characters and not himself, to make every one of them speak and act, as such a person in such circumstances would probably act and speak. Comedy, is an image of common life, and in life, a man, who has discerning eyes, may find something ridiculous in most people, but something that is witty in very few. And a comic poet may be certain of this, that the grossest touches which are in nature, will please the men of sense, more than the most delicate strokes which are out of it. Now that which is truly ridiculous in any man is chiefly humor, or the effect of humor. 'Tis plain too for the following reasons, that humor is more proper for comedy than wit. First, because it is harder to write, for the writing wit is the effect of the fancy, and the writing humor the work of the judgment. 'Tis observation alone that can qualify a man for it, and observation is the business of the judgment. Now though a fine imagination is to be met with in few, judgment is to be found in fewer. Humor then is harder to be written than wit, and that which in any kind of writing is the hardest to be attained, makes the principal beauty of that kind of writing: But secondly humor is more proper for comedy than wit; because it gives a necessary occasion for action, which wit does not, and action after all is the very life and soul of the theater. Now that humor gives a necessary occasion for action is plain, because humor is passion, as I have shewn in another place,[1] and nothing but action is able to express passion, as nothing but passion can give an occasion for action: But thirdly, humor in comedy is to be preferred to wit, because it distinguishes the characters better. For wit very often destroys and confounds them, whereas humor if it be true and good must always maintain and preserve them, as we shall prove more evidently, when we come to shew that humor is chiefly to be found in low characters, and therefore since humor distinguishes the characters, it must be always agreeable to men of sense, whereas wit must be often shocking and nauseous to them, because it destroys and confounds the characters, which is a fourth reason for giving humor the preference; because it is plain that what is always agreeable in any kind of writing must be preferable to that which is sometimes shocking. But fifthly and lastly, if comedy is poetry, 'tis humor chiefly which makes it so, for that which characteristically distinguishes poetry from prose is passion, as I have proved in

[1] *Advancement and Reformation of Modern Poerty.*

another place,[2] and humor is subordinate passion. You know very well, sir, that what I have said here is exactly agreeable to the sentiments of a great[3] critic, who speaking of comedy tells us.

A fault which often does befall,
Is when the wit of some great poet shall
So overflow, that it be none at all;
That all his fools speak sense, as if possest,
And each by inspiration breaks his jest.
If once the justness of each part be lost;
Well we may laugh, but at the poets cost.

How fine an observation is this, sir? For the different characters in comedy, like the several parts in music, make up the consort of the play, and as soon as one character says any thing which does not belong to it, there is a string which is out of tune, and the harmony of the whole is destroyed. But that noble critic goes on.

That silly thing men call sheer wit avoid,
With which our age so nauseously is cloyed;
Humor is all, wit should be only brought
To turn agreeably some proper thought.

Thus, sir, having shewn that humor is more properly the business of comedy than wit, I come now to shew in the second place, that humor is chiefly to be found in the lower sort of people. For reason in one man is the same with reason in another man, excepting the differences of more or less. But passion and humor, which is a sort of passion, are very different according to their different subjects in their kinds, as well as their degrees. For every man shews his anger and his joy, his peevishness and his jollity a different way from another. Reason is a calm and quiet thing, and has nothing to do with the body, only passion and humor can reach the body, and by the influence which they have upon the voice, and the gestures, sensibly distinguish one character from another. So that 'tis passion and humor (which is subordinate passion), which distinguish man from man. Now the more education a man has, the more he is capable of subduing, or at least of hiding his passions and his humors. And that which we call good breeding, is, or should be nothing else but a habit and custom of doing things, which reason has dictated for the convenience, and ease, and good of society. From which it follows, that among people of condition, there is more resemblance, and a greater appearance of reason. And 'tis among people of the lower sort, that by the means of passion and humor, nature appears so admirably conspicuous in all her charming diversities: Since therefore humor is the chief business in comedy after the fable, and humor is more to be found among those of

[2] *Advancement and Reformation of Modern Poetry.*

[3] Lord Marquess of Normanby.

the lower sort, than among those of a higher rank, it is very plain that low characters are more proper for comedy than high ones, and that low comedy is to be preferred to the high.

Not but that high characters are very good sometimes for the sake of variety, and consequently wit is very good, when it is so writ, that it falls within the compass of the characters which speak it. But by wit here I by no means intend point, the excess of which is always despicable, but such fine observation and fine satire as my Lord Normanby means, and as is to be found in Mr. Wycherley's writings; who since he comes in my way, must have justice done him; and be allowed to be almost the only person, who has given the world a master-piece, in which a great deal of humor is shewn in high characters. But that is not to be done every day; and we are treating here of such comedy as is usually writ. But to return from whence we digressed. As wit in comedy, where it is proper, is very good and diverting, so is gallantry and courtly love, for it is now time to speak a word of them too; but humor is to be preferred before either of them, and for most of the very same reasons, for which it is to be preferred before wit. For humor is harder to write than love; because every body has something of love in him, and is helped in writing it, by the present influence which that passion has upon him; whereas writing humor must be chiefly the effect of his past observation. But secondly, humor distinguishes the character better, and gives an occasion for a greater variety of action. For though the love of one man must be allowed to be very different from the love of another man, yet love is but a single passion, and humor comprehends them all. For to every passion there is a humor which answers to it, which humor is nothing but a less degree of that passion. As for example, anger is a passion, peevishness and moroseness are humors, joy when it is great is a passion, jollity and gayety perhaps may be said to be humors, so that if any man asks for a description of humor, I answer that 'tis the expression of some subordinate passion. But if he asks for a full definition of it, by which we may distinguish humor in one man from humor in another man; I answer that humor is subordinate passion expressed in a particular manner. Fear is a passion, timorousness is a humor. Now since humor comprehends all passions, it must have infinitely more variety than a single passion.

But further, without the *ridiculum* comedy cannot subsist, for the design of comedy is to amend the follies of mankind, by exposing them. But the *ridiculum* is a great deal more to be found in humor, than it is in love. For love is so agreeable in its own nature, that it can never be made to appear ridiculous, unless it is joined with an humor. Besides, humor, if it is well writ, is always both delightful and instructive, it entertains and does good at the same time; whereas love is very often agreeable without being instructive; nay, it very often gives a pernicious pleasure. For after all, it is a very great error in some persons at present, to be so shy of bawdy, and so fond of love. For obscenity cannot be very dangerous because it is rude and shocking; but love is a passion, which is so agreeable to the movements of corrupted nature, that by seeing it lively touched and often represented, an amorous disposition insensibly insinuates itself into the chastest breast. Now as the design of every art is to instruct and delight, it must be the design of comedy; and therefore humor which always both instructs and delights, must be more proper for comedy than love, which sometimes only barely delights, and sometimes is so far from instructing, that it insensibly corrupts an audience.

After all, I was so willing to comply with custom, that this play has more of love in it than the original comedy. But I desire people to consider, that Moliere got a great deal of reputation in France by comedies, in which there is very little or no love, and that by those comedies he very agreeably entertained the finest ladies of the court of France; that Madam de Montausier highly approved of the *Precieuses Ridicules*, though there was not one jot of love in it, that those ladies were too proud to be thought to have souls that were incapable of being pleased with an exact imitation of nature, though that imitation had nothing in it of the business to which they were bred; that those persons who are for nothing but perpetual love in our plays, would do well to consider, whether they do not give others an occasion to think, that this error in them, proceeds either from the narrowness of their capacities, or the corruptness of their desires; that humor, which was a diversion to Queen Elizabeth, and the ladies of the court of France, may not be thought a very improper one, for the most delicate persons of the present age; that Shakespear had little love in the very best of his plays, and Jonson less in his, and yet that this last was one of the best comic poets that ever was in the world; that he was so sensible, that the *ridiculum* was the chief thing in comedy, that he has always in his chief comedies joined his love with humor, and so made it ridiculous.

Another objection is, that several characters of this comedy are obsolete and quite out of date. The matter of fact indeed cannot be denied, and the objection has some force. For if there is any thing resembling in poetry and painting, as the sisters are certainly like, then heroic and tragic poetry may be compared to history painting; and comedy, to drawing after the life. Now the pictures which are done after the life, if they are drawn by masters, will certainly please masters, and all who are able to judge of the boldness and the delicacy of the strokes: But the people who judge only of the resemblance, are most delighted with the pictures of their acquaintance. Thus any characters in comedy, which are finely drawn, will please those who can judge; but a poet to please the generality, must copy the present age. Thus, sir, have I fairly stated the objection in its utmost force; and now I shall answer two things to it, first, that I never made it my chief aim to please the generality, and a little lower shall give my reasons for it. Secondly, that supposing I had, though several of the characters of this play are indeed obsolete, yet that of Falstaff will always be new, and whenever it comes to be acted to the satisfaction of an audience, will infallibly fill the stage better than a great many characters.

These, sir, are the two general objections, but there are two particular ones. The first is, that I have introduced an unnecessary character in the host of The Bull. But I believe, sir, that I have considered of this matter with a little more attention than they who made the objection, and I know, that that character is absolutely necessary for the carrying on the action probably, which in the original play is by no means probable. For it is not likely, that Falstaff would suffer himself to be carried in the basket, as far as Dachet Mead, which is half a mile from Windsor; and it is plain, that they could not carry him, if he made any resistance. Nor is it likely, that he would defer his reflections upon his adventure, till he came back to Windsor. So that the soliloquies which he makes in the fourth act before Ford's entrance, are not designed for himself, but apparently addressed to the audience, which is the greatest fault that can possibly be in the drama.

The last objection is, that the forementioned scene in the fourth act, which is very long, is nothing but a discovery of what the audience had been eye-witnesses of before. But this objection is unreasonable with relation to the original play, and more unreasonable with relation to the altered one. For in the original play, Falstaff makes a relation to Ford not so much of his being put into the buck basket, as of the circumstances which attended it; of what he suffered while he was in it, and upon his coming out of it. And in this lies the excellency of that scene, that it gives an occasion for a great actor to shew himself. For all the while Falstaff is making this relation, Ford at the same time, that in dumb acting, he shews a concern, and a fellow-feeling to the knight, shews a great deal of joy and satisfaction to the audience.

Thus in the original scene Falstaff makes a relation of what had happened to him, since he left the stage last, and that relation must be comical, by reason of the occasion that it gives for an excellent actor to shew himself. But for the altered scene there is something more to be said. For after that Falstaff has raised Ford's joy for the others disappointment, which yet he was forced to screen and shelter from the knight with a dissembled sorrow, Falstaff by making a discovery of something which had not happened, and strangely altering the adventure of Mrs. Page, which he thought himself obliged to do for the sake of his credit, gives his jealous coxcomb a fresh alarm, and throws him into real convulsions.

Thus, sir, have I laid before you the objections and the answers to them, and leave it to you to judge, whether the last are satisfactory, and whether the first had ever been made, if the play had succeeded on the stage; for you know, sir, that plays are like men, the successful are sure to find friends enough, let them be never so worthless, while every maggot will be censuring the conduct of the deserving unfortunate. For so fantastic a composition is man, that though of all the creatures which the sun illuminates, he is at once the vainest and most miserable, at the same time so vain and so miserable, that nature seems to have given him vanity as a support, and a counterbalance for misery; yet he is often so very unthinking, and so foolishly severe against himself, as to affirm that there can be no merit, where there is no success.

Thus fortune enslaves even the souls of men to opinion; but she has never been able to reach yours. You have been so far from thinking the better of others for their enjoying her, that you have yourself refused her favors, and disdained the allurements of a mistress, in whom you would have so many worthless persons your rivals. You look upon things as you see them yourself, and not as the world mistakes them. You know that success can at the best but illustrate merit, and that it never gives it. That good sense like virtue is not always prosperous at first, while folly like vice triumphs. That it is unreasonable to believe that any thing that is writ, should be better for succeeding, any more than any thing that is done. That if an action may succeed because it is base and villainous, a play may well be supposed to take because it is very foolish.

But that as an action that pleases good men, must be in itself good, the play must certainly be well writ, which pleases those who have taste. That as the action which pleases none but villains, must in itself be horribly villainous, the play which satisfies only those persons who are not able to judge, must in itself be extremely ridiculous.

In short, sir, that you might always pass a true judgment on the productions of the mind, you have religiously observed the beautiful directions of a modern critic.[4] From hence it comes that you have neither shown an unjust aversion for the living, nor a fantastic veneration for the dead, that you reject what's trifling in the last, while you esteem what's valuable in the first. That as novelty has no allurements for you, you have no aversion for that, but embrace or reject the works of an author according to their real merit, and the impression which they ought truly to make upon you; and that your decisions are as just and reasonable, and as free from whimsey as they are impartial.

To conclude that a play is good because Mr. Granville is pleased by it, is but a reasonable way of arguing. But to say, that it is good because it pleases the generality of an audience is a very absurd one. For every man has and will have his different pleasure. Wise men will be sure to be pleased with things that are wise, and fools will be inclined to be pleased with things that are foolish. Montaigne was pleased with playing with his cat; but at the same time he does her and himself the justice to believe she thought him an ass for it. Would to heaven that some part of our audiences were but as just as the Frenchman, and some part of our authors but as reasonable as the beast. Before a play can be concluded to be good because it pleases, we ought to consider who are pleased by it, they who understand, or they who do not. They who understand? Alas, they are but few, and are seldom pleased there of late. They who do not? That methinks is odd. Suppose a man should tell an author he never so much as heard of his play, and should the very moment following tell him he liked it. Would he be satisfied with this approbation? would he not be really mortified at it? Now every one who talks like an ass tells the world, though against his will, that he does not understand one word of a play; and is not he who never heard a word of a cause as justly qualified to determine it, as he who never understood a word of it?

'Tis for this reason, sir, that when-ever I write I make it my business to please such men as you are. As very well knowing that whatever is writ has its immediate success from fortune, but its lasting one from art and nature. That the people are always uncertain and fluctuating, and guided by opinion, and not by judgment, that the surest way to arrive at reputation, is to please the knowing few, for that they at last must draw in the multitude, but are never to be drawn in by them.

I have been already tedious, or it would be an easy matter to shew, that they who in all ages have appeared at once good poets and good critics have writ to a few persons, I mean to a few at present. For he who writes to the many at present writes only to them, and his works are sure never to survive their admirers; but he who

[4] St Evremont

writes to the knowing few at present, writes to the race of mankind in all succeeding ages. But I am glad that this is addressed to a gentleman, who needs only be put in mind of this, who is perfectly well acquainted with Horace and Boileau, and who has often read the satires and the epistles of both; and who consequently is able to inform others, that those two celebrated poets directed their writings to the knowing few, and were neither exalted by the approbation, nor dejected by the censure of the rest, and that by such a proceeding they came to please universally: That some of the most agreeable parts of those satires and those epistles, are those in which they laugh at the taste of the vulgar, and that among the vulgar they reckoned not only a great many who were distinguished by their rank from others, but several whom the world called wits and poets; and that they had a greater contempt for those wits and poets, than they had for any sort of people whatever, unless for those who admired them.

Ainsi qu'en sois Auteurs
Notre siecle est fertile en sots admirateurs
Et sans ceux que fournit la ville et la Province
Il en est chez le Duc, Il en est chez le prince
L'ouvrage le plus plat, a chez les courtesans
De tout temps rencontrez des Zeles partisans,
Et pour finir enfin par un trait de Satyre
Un sot trouve toujours un plus sot qui l'admire.[5]

As th' Age produces shoals of scribbling Fools,
'Tis full as fertile in admiring Tools;
Besides whole swarms in Country and in Town,
Versailles has some of Lustre and Renown.
Th' Absurdest Ass that e're made Reader sport,
Has in all times found zealous Friends at Court,
No scribbling Fools so much a Fool can be,
But finds to admire him greater Sots than he.

They were perfectly satisfied that your ill poets, and your would-be-wits have in all ages been the most undiscerning and most injudicious absurd people upon earth even in their own business. That it is not wit, but reason and judgment, which distinguish a man of sense from a fool. That as nothing but reason distinguishes man from beast, he who in his writings frequently shocks reason infallibly shews himself an ass; and that though he may impose upon fools for a time, by a wretched glimmering of fancy, and a contemptible clink of verse, as woodcocks and widgeons are caught by a loud bell and by a greasy light, yet whenever he comes to write in prose, where reason is plainly to appear, he plainly appears to have none.

I could have said a great deal to have shewn, that the most judicious of the ancient Romans, and the modern French have been out of humor with the taste of the people, if I had not writ to a gentleman, who is perfectly satisfied about the matter.

[5] Bouleau, *L'Art Poetique*, Cant. 1.

But now, if Horace was justly out of humor with the taste of the Roman people in the time of Augustus Caesar, I believe no reasonable man will wonder if an English writer is dissatisfied with the taste of the English at this present conjuncture. For you know very well, sir, that let us flatter ourselves as long as we please, there is no manner of comparison between the Roman people and ours. And the English were never sunk so miserably low in their taste, as they are at present. If then the advice that Horace gave in the *Tenth Satire* of the first Book was good at that time, when directed to Roman authors,

> *Neque te ut miretur Turba labores*
> *Contentus paucis lectoribus.*

It certainly must be much better now, when addressed to our English writers. I will not now pretend to determine whether the general taste of England ever was good or no. This we know very well, that several plays have been indifferently received at first, which have succeeded very well afterwards. The only play that ever Mr. Cowley writ, was barbarously treated the first night, as the late Mr. Dryden has more than once informed me, who has told me that he went to see it with the famous Mr. Sprat, now Bishop of Rochester, and that after the play was done, they both made a visit to Mr. Cowley, whom the death of his brother had obliged to keep the house, and that Mr. Cowley received the news of his ill success, not with so much firmness, as might have been expected from so great a man.

But to return from whence I digressed, *She Would If She Could* met with no better usage from the people at first, though at the same time it was esteemed by the men of sense, for the trueness of some of its characters, and the purity and freeness and ease grace of its dialogue. I need not say, that both those plays have been since acted with a general applause; and it would be as needless to shew on the other side, that a thousand plays which were extravagantly applauded at first, are not sunk to the very last degree of contempt.

But, sir, whether the general taste of England ever was good or no, this I think cannot be controverted, that the taste of England for comedy, which ought to be the thing in question now, was certainly much better in the reign of King Charles the Second, than it is at present. For it was then extremely good, and is now excessively bad. The occasion, sir, is fair, and nothing in this sort of criticism could be more curious or more important than to enquire into the causes of this degeneracy of taste. Notwithstanding that I have already detained you too long, I flatter myself so far as to fancy, that the handling a subject so very new, may prove entertaining to you, and therefore I will venture to treat of it.

Give me leave then, sir, to lay down the following maxims, as things that are self-evident, and require no proof.

First, that then there is among any people a good taste for comedy, when a very considerable part of an audience are qualified to judge for themselves and when they who are not qualified to judge for themselves, are influenced by the authority of those who are rightly qualified. Secondly, that then there is among any people a bad taste for comedy, when very few of an audience are qualified to judge for themselves, and when the rest are influenced by the authority of those who are not rightly qualified.

And now having laid down these two maxims, I shall shew as briefly as I can,

First, that in the reign of King Charles the Second, a considerable part of an audience were qualified to judge for themselves, and that they who were not qualified, were influenced by the authority of those who were.

Secondly, that in the present reign a very inconsiderable part of an audience are qualified to judge for themselves, and that the rest are not influenced by the authority of those, who are rightly qualified; but in order to the doing this, it will be requisite to declare what qualifications are necessary for the judging of comedy.

This, I think, sir, need not be disputed, that for the judging of any sort of writings, those talents are in some measure requisite, which were necessary to produce them. As for example, there are two things absolutely required for the succeeding in polemical divinity; the one is a reasonable head, and the second an acquaintance with the scriptures, fathers and councils; and it is plain, that a proportional share of reason, and an acquaintance with the same learning are absolutely necessary to judge of the goodness or badness of such controversies. Now there are three things required for the succeeding in poetry. 1. Great parts. 2. A generous education. 3. A due application.

First, there are required great parts. I suppose, sir, this need not be proved, because it has been sufficiently proved by experience. For whenever a good poet has laid aside poetry for any other employment, he has seldom failed of succeeding in that employment, though it has been of never so great importance; but here by great parts is meant chiefly a lively, and a warm, and a strong imagination, and a solid and piercing judgment; for the production of a reasonable creature, must derive its chief advantage from reason, which gave occasion for that precept of Boileau in the first canto of his *Art of Poetry*.

Aimez donc la Raison que toujours vos Ecrits
Empruntent d'elle seule et leur lustre et leur prix.

But secondly, for the succeeding in comedy, there is required a generous education, which comprehends; 1. Learning. 2. A knowledge of mankind and the world. 1. Learning, for though it may be pretended, that some have succeeded in comedy, without the least knowledge of the learned languages; yet here by learning I mean the knowledge of things, and not that of words, which knowledge is absolutely necessary, because the ultimate end of comedy is to instruct, and to instruct all; and it is impossible that the learned should be instructed by the ignorant. But secondly, a knowledge of the world and of mankind, are necessary for succeeding in comedy. For since comedy is drawing after the life, and a comic poet is obliged to copy the age to which he writes, how should he possibly draw them like, without knowing the persons.

But the third thing requisite for the succeeding in comedy is a due application, and that likewise includes two things, the one of which is leisure, and the other serenity. First, leisure, for poetry is of that dignity, that it requires the whole man.

And never any man writ any thing that was admirable, who had any avocations at the time that he writ it. But secondly, to succeed in comedy requires serenity. For a comic poet is obliged to put off himself, and transform himself into his several characters; to enter into the foibles of his several persons, and all the recesses and secret turns of their minds, and to make their passions, their interests, and their concern his own. Now how should he possibly do this, unless he is absolutely free, and undisturbed by tormenting passions, which bind him, as it were, and if I may use that expression, chain him fast to himself.

But now, as parts, education and application are necessary to succeed in the writing poetry, they are requisite in some degree for the forming a true judgment of it. No man can judge of a beautiful imagination in another, without some degree of it in himself. And as for the judging rightly of any thing without judgment, that is a contradiction in terms. And if philosophy and a knowledge of the world are necessary to a comic poet, for his forming his characters; if an acquaintance with the best authors among the ancients and moderns, be requisite for the attaining the vivacity and grace of the dialogue; why, then for the forming a true judgment of these, the same learning and the same experience are necessary. And lastly, if a poet had need to have his mind free, that he may the more thoroughly enter into the concerns of the theater, and put on the passions and humors of his different characters, so as to make them by turns his own; why the spectator, that he may judge whether the author does this or no, must enter into those passions and humors in some proportionable degree, and consequently ought to have his mind free from all avocations of business, and from all real vexatious passions.

Having premised all this, we shall now come to shew: First, that in the reign of King Charles the Second, a considerable part of an audience had those parts, that education and that application, which were requisite for the judging of poetry, and that they who had not, were influenced by the authority of those who had; and secondly, that in the present reign very few in an audience have the aforementioned qualifications; and that those who have them not, have not the advantage to be influenced by the authority of those who have.

First then, in the reign of King Charles the Second, a considerable part of an audience had those parts, which were requisite for the judging of comedy. And we have shewn above that those parts comprehend principally a fine imagination and a sound judgment. Well, but says an objector; are not the imaginations and judgments of mankind the same that they were then, or is human nature decayed since the reign of Charles the Second? To which I answer, that the capacity of imagining and of judging have been in all ages equal in mankind. But then this is certain, that the faculties of the soul, like the parts of the body, receive nourishment from use, and derive skill as well as they do force and vigor from exercise. Now I leave to any one to judge whether the imaginative faculty of the soul, must be more exercised in a reign of poetry and of pleasure, or in a reign of politicks and of business. Besides, as an artist may have that sort of beauty of imagination, which is sufficient for the succeeding in painting and carving, and may at the same time be not one jot the more qualified for the succeeding in poetry; so a man may have that sort of imagination, which is necessary for the judging of painting and carving, and yet may not be at all capacitated to give his judgment of poetry; and this, if we will believe the testimony of Horace, was the case of the great Alexander.

> *Idem rex tille Poema*
> *Qui tam ridiculum tam care prodigus emit*
> *Edicto vetuit ne quis se praeter Apellen*
> *Pingeret aut aluis Lysippo duceret aera.*
> *Fortis Alexandri vultum simulantia quod si,*
> *Judicium subtile videndis artibus illud,*
> *Ad libros & ad haec Musarum dona vocares*
> *Baeotum in Crasso Juares aere natum.*

We may say the very same thing of judgment, a man may be well qualified to judge of fortifications, or the interest of princes, and yet may show himself to be very weak, when he comes to judge of poetry (not that I think that either a statesman or an engineer is obliged to understand poetry; but he who pretends to judge of any thing which he does not understand is certainly so far weak). So that 'tis education and application, which qualify the imagination and the judgment for the passing a right judgment on poetry; and therefore 'tis time to proceed to the consideration of those two heads.

Secondly, then in the reign of King Charles the Second, a considerable part of an audience had such an education as qualified them to judge of comedy. That reign was a reign of pleasure, even the entertainments of their closet were all delightful. Poetry and eloquence were then their studies, and that human, gay, and sprightly philosophy, which qualified them to relish the only reasonable pleasures which man can have in the world, and those are conversation and dramatic poetry. In their closets they cultivated at once their imaginations and judgments, to make themselves the fitter for conversation, which requires them both. And the conversation of those times was so different from what it is now, that it let them as much into that particular knowledge of mankind, which is requisite for the judging of comedy, as the present conversation removes us from it. The discourse, which now every where turns upon interest, rolled then upon the manners and humors of men. For let us take a little view of the state of the nation, during the reign of that prince, from the year sixty to eighty. They were overjoyed to find themselves delivered from the apprehensions of another civil war, and not only in quiet, but as they thought, in profound security. They were at the same time free from fears and taxes, and by reason of that plenty which overflowed among them, they were in the happiest condition in the world, to attain to that knowledge of mankind, which is requisite for the judging of comedy. For while some were dissolved in the wantonness of ease, and grown careless how they exposed themselves, others were at leisure to observe their frailties; to watch the turns and counterturns of their humors, and trace the windings of them up to their very springs. All the sheer originals in town were known, and in some measure copied. But now the case is vastly different. For all those great and numerous originals are reduced to one single coxcomb, and that is the foolish false politician. For from Westminster to Wapping, go where you will, the conversation turns upon politics. Wherever you go, you find atheists and rakes standing up for the Protestant religion, fellows who never saw a groat in their lives, vehemently maintaining property, and people that are in the Fleet and the King's Bench upon execution for their lives, going together by the ears about the liberty of the subject. There is not the emptiest coxcomb in town, but has got his politic shake and his shrug, and is pretending to wisdom by gestures, while his tongue, the surest index of his soul, declares him a very ass. Go among either the lame or the blind, and you shall find them intercepting the plate fleet, or sending forces into Italy. For all men are alarmed by the present posture of affairs, because all men believe they are concerned, which universal alarm has reduced those characters which were so various before, to a dull uniformity. For great fools, like great wits, require leisure and ease to shew themselves. And as this uniformity of characters has directly done a great deal of harm to comedy, because our poets, for want of originals are forced to bring copies, or else to draw after their own imagination, rather than after the life, so it has hurt it too indirectly, by the harm which it has done to playing. For observation is necessary to our comedians as well as our comic poets. And I verily believe, that the want of originals has been one great cause of the decay of acting. And the decay of this is the cause that when a good comedy does come to be writ, it can never be liked because it can never be acted, for the better a play is acted, the better it is sure to succeed. Now an empty trifling play can better be acted by ill or indifferent actors, than one that is strongly writ in nature, because the last requires masters.

Besides, there are three sorts of people now in our audiences, who have had no education at all; and who were unheard of in the reign of King Charles the Second. A great many younger brothers, gentlemen born, who have been kept at home, by reason of the pressure of the taxes. Several people, who made their fortunes in the late war; and who from a state of obscurity, and perhaps of misery, have risen to a condition of distinction and plenty. I believe that no man will wonder, if these people, who in their original obscurity, could never attain to any higher entertainment than tumbling and vaulting and ladder dancing, and the delightful diversions of jack pudding, should still be in love with their old sports, and encourage these noble pastimes still upon the stage. But a 3d sort of people, who may be said to have had no education at all in relation to us and our plays, is that considerable number of foreigners, which within these last twenty years have been introduced among us; some of whom not being acquainted with our language, and consequently with the sense of our plays, and others disgusted with our extravagant, exorbitant rambles, have been instrumental in introducing sound and show, where the business of the theater does not require it, and particularly a sort of a soft and wanton music, which has used the people to a delight which is independent of reason, a delight that has gone to a very great way towards the enervating and dissolving their minds.

But thirdly, in the reign of King Charles the Second, a considerable part of an audience had that due application, which is requisite for the judging of comedy. They had first of all leisure to attend to it. For that was an age of pleasure, and not of business. They were serene enough to receive its impressions: For they were in ease and plenty. But in the present reign, a great part of the gentlemen have not leisure, because want throws them upon employments, and there are ten times more gentlemen now in business, than there were in King Charles his reign. Nor have they serenity, by reason of a war, in which all are concerned, by reason of the taxes which make them uneasy. By reason that they are attentive to the events of affairs, and too full of great and real events, to receive due impressions from the imaginary ones of the theater. They come to a playhouse full of some business which they have been soliciting, or of some harangue which they are to make the next day; so that they merely come to unbend, and are utterly incapable of duly attending to the just and harmonious symmetry of a beautiful design. Besides, the faction which has been so long in their politicks is got into their pleasures, and they refuse to be delighted with what some people write, not because they really dislike it, but only because others are pleased with it, as if any one should be such a sot to refuse Champaign, because his enemy finds it delicious.

Thus, sir, I have shewn, that in King Charles the Second's time, a considerable part of an audience were qualified to judge for themselves, and that at present a considerable part of our audiences are not qualified for it. But there is an important thing behind, which I have only time to hint at. That they who were not qualified to judge in King Charles his reign, were influenced by the authority of those who were; and that is of the court, which always in a peculiar manner influences the pleasures of the gentry. And some of the most eminent young courtiers had then an admirable taste of comedy, as it must always happen in a court where the prince delights in it. But the court of England at present has other things to mind than to take care of comedy. 'Tis true, there may be several gentlemen in it who are capable of setting others right but neither have they leisure to do it, nor have others time to attend to them.

Thus, sir, have I endeavored to shew the causes of the degeneracy of taste in comedy; which is every day more and more declining. I might perhaps say the same thing concerning tragedy: For, in short, sir, some of the best tragedies which have been writ since Shakespear's time were writ in the reign of Charles the Second. And you are almost the only person alive, who are capable of writing a true tragedy. In that which you have already given us, you took the judicious advice of Horace, and chose a known subject from one of the noblest poems in the world. Your incidents have both art and nature to maintain them, and are as probable as they are surprising: Your characters resembling your sentiments, easy, proper, great, elevated; your expressions strong without constraint, engaging without artifice, charming without wantonness, and majestic without pride. These, sir, together with that noble fire which every where reigns in your writings, are the qualities which make you a poet, and so clearly distinguish you from the common numerous playwrights that pass upon the easy town.

But 'tis high time to have done, for I am not only guilty of a fault myself, but what is worse, making you guilty of a greater. For I am declaring what all the world is sensible of, and you are blushing only at hearing the truth. I am,

Sir,

Your most humble and most obedient servant,

John Dennis

CHAPTER 3

Anthony Ashley Cooper, Third Earl of Shaftesbury*
Characteristics of Men, Manners, Opionions, Times
1711

Advice to an Author

Section III

We are now arrived to that part of our performance where it becomes us to cast our eye back on what has already passed. The observers of method generally make this the place of recapitulation. Other artists have substituted the practice of apology or extenuation. For the anticipating manner of prefatory discourse is too well known to work any surprising effect in the author's behalf, preface being become only another word to signify excuse. Besides that the author is generally the most straitened in that preliminary part which on other accounts is too apt to grow voluminous. He therefore takes the advantage of his corollary or winding-up, and

*Anthony Ashley Cooper, third earl of Shaftesbury (1671-1713) was the grandson of the first earl, who was one of the leading political figures of the restoration, defending the protestant succession and playing an important role in the Glorious Revolution of 1688. The first earl's physician and advisor was John Locke, and Locke guided the education of the earl's grandson. The second earl was largely incapacitated for public life for reasons that remain unclear, and the third earl was eduated to be his grandfather's political successor. He served for a time in parliament, but his real interests were in literature and philosophy. His first published work was a collection of the sermons of Benjamin Whichcote. *An Inquiry Concerning Virtue* was published without his permission in 1699. Shaftesbury's positions in that work on the relation of religion to virtue were too radical for a practical politician, and his association with radical dissenters such as John Toland and Anthony Collins was also suspect. In any event, his health forced him to retire from public life and he settled in Italy where he wrote and served as a patron of the arts. His essays were collected in his *Characteristics*, published in 1711. He was completing revisions on this volume for a new edition at the time of his death in 1713.

ends pathetically by endeavoring in the softest manner to reconcile his reader to those faults which he chooses rather to excuse than to amend.

General practice has made this a necessary part of elegance, hardly to be passed over by any writer. 'Tis the chief stratagem by which he engages in personal conference with his reader, and can talk immoderately of himself with all the seeming modesty of one who is the furthest from any selfish views or conceited thoughts of his own merit. There appears such a peculiar grace and ingenuity in the method of confessing laziness, precipitancy, carelessness, or whatever other vice have been the occasion of the author's deficiency, that it would seem a pity had the work itself been brought to such perfection as to have left no room for the penitent party to enlarge on his own demerits. For from the multiplicity of these he finds subject to ingratiate himself with his reader, who doubtless is not a little raised by this submission of a confessing author, and is ready on these terms, to give him absolution and receive him into his good grace and favor.

In the *galante* world, indeed, we easily find how far a humility of this kind prevails. They who hope to rise by merit are likeliest to be disappointed in their pretensions. The confessing lover, who ascribes all to the bounty of the fair one, meets his reward the sooner for having studied less how to deserve it. For merit is generally thought presumptuous, and supposed to carry with it a certain assurance and ease with which a mistress is not so well contented. The claim of well-deserving seems to derogate from the pure grace and favor of the benefactrice, who then appears to herself most sovereign in power, and likeliest to be obeyed without reserve, when she bestows her bounty where there is least title or pretensions.

Thus a certain adoration of the sex which passes in our age without the least charge of profaneness or idolatry, may, according to vulgar imagination, serve to justify these *galante* votaries in the imitation of the real religious and devout. The method of self-abasement may perhaps be thought the properest to make approaches to the sacred shrines; and the entire resignation of merit, in each case, may be esteemed the only ground of well-deserving. But what we allow to Heaven or to the fair should not, methinks, be made a precedent in favor of the world. Whatever deference is due to that body of men whom we call readers, we may be supposed to treat them with sufficient honor if with thorough diligence and pains we endeavor to render our works perfect, and leave them to judge of the performance as they are able.

However difficult or desperate it may appear in any artist to endeavor to bring perfection into his work, if he has not at least the idea of perfection to give him aim he will be found very defective and mean in his performance. Though his intention be to please the world, he must nevertheless be, in a manner, above it, and fix his eye upon that consummate grace, that beauty of Nature, and that perfection of numbers which the rest of mankind, feeling only by the effect whilst ignorant of the cause, term the *je ne sais quoi*, the unintelligible or the I know not what, and suppose to be a kind of charm or enchantment of which the artist himself can give no account.

But here I find I am tempted to do what I have myself condemned. Hardly can I forbear making some apology for my frequent recourse to the rules of common artists, to the masters of exercise, to the academies of painters, statuaries, and to the rest of the virtuoso tribe. But in this I am so fully satisfied I have reason on my side, that let custom be ever so strong against me, I had rather repair to these inferior schools to search for Truth and Nature than to some other places where higher arts and sciences are professed.

I am persuaded that to be a virtuoso (so far as befits a gentleman) is a higher step towards the becoming a man of virtue and good sense than the being what in this age we call a scholar.[1] For even rude Nature itself, in its primitive simplicity, is a better guide to judgment than improved sophistry and pedantic learning. The "*faciunt, nae, intellegendo, ut nihil intellegant*" will be ever applied by men of discernment and free thought to such logic, such principles, such forms and rudiments of knowledge as are established in certain schools of literature and science. The case is sufficiently understood even by those who are unwilling to confess the truth of it. Effects betray their causes. And the known turn and figure of those understandings, which sprout from nurseries of this kind, give a plain idea of what is judged on this occasion. 'Tis no wonder if after so wrong a ground of education there appears to be such need of redress and amendment from that excellent school which we call the world. The mere amusements of gentlemen are found more improving than the profound researches of pedants; and in the management of our youth we are forced to have recourse to the former, as an antidote against the genius peculiar to the latter. If the formalists of this sort were erected into patentees with a sole commission of authorship, we should undoubtedly see such writing in our days as

[1] It seems indeed somewhat improbable that according to modern erudition, and as science is now distributed, our ingenious and noble youths should obtain the full advantage of a just and liberal education by uniting the scholar-part with that of the real gentleman and man of breeding. Academies for exercises, so useful to the public, and essential in the formation of a genteel and liberal character, are unfortunately neglected. Letters are indeed banished, I know not where, in distant cloisters and unpracticed cells, as our poet has it, confined to the commerce and mean fellowship of bearded boys. The sprightly arts and sciences are severed from philosophy, which consequently must grow dronish, insipid, pedantic, useless, and directly opposite to the real knowledge and practice of the world and mankind. Our youth accordingly seem to have their only chance between two widely different roads: either that of pedantry and school-learning, which lies amidst the dregs and most corrupt part of ancient literature, or that of the fashionable illiterate world, which aims merely at the character of the fine gentleman, and takes up with the foppery of modern languages and foreign wit. The frightful aspect of the former of these roads makes the journey appear desperate and impracticable. Hence that aversion so generally conceived against a learned character, wrong turned, and hideously set out under such difficulties, and in such seeming labyrinths and mysterious forms. As if a Homer or a Xenophon imperfectly learnt, in raw years, might not afterwards, in a riper age, be studied as well in a capital city and amidst the world as at a college or country-town! Or as if a Plutarch, a Tully, or a Horace, could not accompany a young man in his travels, at a court, or (if occasion were) even in a camp! The case is not without precedent. Leisure is found sufficient for other reading of numerous modern translations and worse originals, of Italian or French authors, who are read merely for amusement. The French indeed may boast of some legitimate authors of a just relish, correct, and without any mixture of the affected or spurious kinds: the false tender, or the false sublime; the conceited jingle or the ridiculous point. They are such geniuses as have been formed upon the natural model of the ancients, and willingly own their debt to those great masters. But for the rest, who draw from another fountain, as the Italian authors in particular, they may be reckoned no better than the corrupters of true learning and erudition, and can indeed be relished by those alone whose education has unfortunately denied them the familiarity of the noble ancients, and the practice of a better and more natural taste. See above, p. 186, etc. and Moralists, part i. §1. [Here and elsewhere, when Shaftesbury refers in notes to sections of *Characteristics* not reprinted by the page numbers, the page number given refers to Benjamin Rand's editions of *Characteristics*, (Indianapolis: Bobbs-Merrill, 1964).]

would either wholly wean us from all books in general, or at least from all such as were the product of our own nation under such a subordinate and conforming government.

However this may prove, there can be no kind of writing which relates to men and manners where it is not necessary for the author to understand poetical and moral truth,[2] the beauty of sentiments, the sublime of characters, and carry in his eye the model or exemplar of that natural grace which gives to every action its attractive charm. If he has naturally no eye or ear for these interior numbers, 'tis not likely he should be able to judge better of that exterior portion and symmetry of composition which constitutes a legitimate piece.

Could we once convince ourselves of what is in itself so evident, "That in the very nature of things there must of necessity be the foundation of a right and wrong taste, as well in respect of inward characters and features as of outward person, behaviour, and action," we should be far more ashamed of ignorance and wrong judgment in the former than in the latter of these subjects. Even in the Arts, which are mere imitations of that outward grace and beauty, we not only confess a taste, but make it a part of refined breeding to discover amidst the many false manners and ill styles the true and natural one, which represents the real beauty and Venus of the kind.[3] 'Tis the like moral grace and Venus which, discovering itself in the turns of character and the variety of human affection, is copied by the writing artist. If he knows not this Venus, these graces, nor was ever struck with the beauty, the decorum of this inward kind, he can neither paint advantageously after the life nor in a feigned subject where he has full scope. For never can he, on these terms, represent merit and virtue, or mark deformity and blemish.[4] Never can he with justice and true proportion assign the boundaries of either part, or separate the distant characters. The schemes must be defective and the draughts confused where the standard is weakly established and the measure out of use. Such a designer, who has so little feeling of these proportions, so little consciousness of this excellence or these perfections, will never be found able to describe a perfect character; or, what is more according to art,[5] "express the effect and force of this perfection from the result of various and mixed characters of life."

And thus the sense of inward numbers, the knowledge and practice of the social virtues, and the familiarity and favor of the moral graces, are essential to the character of a deserving artist and just favorite of the Muses. Thus are the Arts and Virtues mutually friends; and thus the science of virtuosi and that of virtue itself become, in a manner, one and the same.

[2] *Supra*, p. 136.

[3] *Supra*, p. 92, etc.; and *Misc.* iii. ch. ii. in the notes.

[4] *Supra*, p. 136.

[5] See *Misc.* v. ch. i. in the notes.

One who aspires to the character of a man of breeding and politeness is careful to form his judgment of arts and sciences upon right models of perfection. If he travels to Rome, he inquires which are the truest pieces of architecture, the best remains of statues, the best paintings of a Raphael or a Caraccio. However antiquated, rough, or dismal they may appear to him at first sight, he resolves to view them over and over, till he has brought himself to relish them, and finds their hidden grace and perfections. He takes particular care to turn his eye from everything which is gaudy, luscious, and of a false taste. Nor is he less careful to turn his ear from every sort of music besides that which is of the best manner and truest harmony.

'Twere to be wished we had the same regard to a right taste in life and manners. What mortal being, once convinced of a difference in inward character, and of a preference due to one kind above another, would not be concerned to make his own the best? If civility and humanity be a taste; if brutality, insolence, riot, be in the same manner a taste, who, if he could reflect, would not choose to form himself on the amiable and agreeable rather than the odious and perverse model? Who would not endeavor to force Nature as well in this respect as in what relates to a taste or judgment in other arts and sciences? For in each place the force on Nature is used only for its redress. If a natural good taste be not already formed in us, why should not we endeavor to form it, and cultivate it till it become natural?

"I like! I fancy! I admire! How? By accident, or as I please? No. But I learn to fancy, to admire, to please, as the subjects themselves are deserving, and can bear me out. Otherwise, I like at this hour but dislike the next. I shall be weary of my pursuit, and, upon experience, find little pleasure in the main,[6] if my choice and judgment in it be from no other rule than that single one, because I please. Grotesque and monstrous figures often please. Cruel spectacles and barbarities are also found to please, and, in some tempers, to please beyond all other subjects. But is this pleasure right? And shall I follow it if it presents? not strive with it, or endeavor to prevent its growth or prevalency in my temper?—How stands the case in a more soft and flattering kind of pleasure?—Effeminacy pleases me. The Indian figures, the Japan work, the enamel strikes my eye. The luscious colors and glossy paint gain upon my fancy. A French or Flemish style is highly liked by me at first sight, and I pursue my liking. But what ensues?—Do I not for ever forfeit my good relish? How is it possible I should thus come to taste the beauties of an Italian master, or of a hand happily formed on nature and the ancients? 'Tis not by wantonness and humor that I

[6] *Supra*, p. 200, and *Moralists*, part ii. §1.

shall attain my end and arrive at the enjoyment I propose. The art itself is severe,[7] the rules rigid. And if I expect the knowledge should come to me by accident, or in play, I shall be grossly deluded, and prove myself, at best, a mock-virtuoso or mere pedant of the kind."

Here therefore we have once again exhibited our moral science in the same method and manner of soliloquy as above. To this correction of humor and formation of a taste our reading, if it be of the right sort, must principally contribute. Whatever company we keep, or however polite and agreeable their characters may be with whom we converse or correspond, if the authors we read are of another kind, we shall find our palate strangely turned their way. We are the unhappier in this respect for being scholars if our studies be ill chosen. Nor can I, for this reason, think it proper to call a man well-read who reads many authors, since he must of necessity have more ill models than good, and be more stuffed with bombast, ill fancy, and wry thought than filled with solid sense and just imagination.

But notwithstanding this hazard of our taste from a multiplicity of reading, we are not, it seems, the least scrupulous in our choice of subject. We read whatever comes next us. What was first put into our hand when we were young, serves us afterwards for serious study and wise research when we are old. We are many of us, indeed, so grave as to continue this exercise of youth through our remaining life. The

[7] Thus Pliny speaking with a masterly judgment of the dignity of the then declining art of painting ("de dignitate artis morientis") shows it to be not only severe in respect of the discipline, style, design, but of the characters and lives of the noble masters; not only in the effect, but even in the very materials of the art, the colors, ornaments, and particular circumstances belonging to the profession. Euphranoris discipulus Antidotus . . . diligentior quam numerosier, et in coloribus serverus. . . . Niciae comparatur, et aliquanto praefertur Athenion Maronites, Glaucionis Corinthii discipulus, et austerior colore, et in austeritate jucundior, ut in ipsa pictura eruditio eluceat. . . . Quod nisi in juventa obiisset, nemo ei compararetur. . . . Pausiae filus et discipulus Aristolaus e severissimis pictoribus fuit. . . . Fuit et nuper gravis ae severus pictor Amulius. . . . Paucis diei horis pingebat, id quodque cum gravitate, quod semper togatus, quamquam in machinis. Pliny, H.N. xxxv. One of the mortal symptoms upon which Pliny pronounces the sure death of this noble art, not long survivor to him, was what belonged in common to all the other perishing arts after the Fall of Liberty: I mean the luxury of the Roman court, and the change of taste and manners naturally consequent to such a change of government and dominion. This excellent, learned, and polite critic represents to us the false taste springing from the court itself, and from that opulence, splendor, and affectation of magnificence and expense proper to the place. Thus in the statuary and architecture then in vogue nothing could be admired beside what was costly in the mere matter or substance of the work. Precious rock, rich metal, glittering stones, and other luscious ware, poisonous to art, came every day more into request, and were imposed as necessary materials on the best masters. 'Twas in favor of these court beauties and gaudy appearances that all good drawing, just design, and truth of work began to be despised. Care was taken to procure from distant parts the most gorgeous splendid colors, of the most costly growth or composition; not such as had been used by Apelles and the great masters, who are justly severe, loyal and faithful to their art. This newer coloring our critic calls the florid kind. The materials were too rich to be furnished by the painter, but were bespoke or furnished at the cost of the person who employed him ("quos dominus pingemi praestat"). The other he calls the austere kind. And thus, says he, "Rerum, non animi pretiis excubatur: The cost, and not the life and art is studied." He shows, on the contrary, what care Apelles took to subdue the florid colors by a darkening varnish: "et cadem res," says he, "nimis floridis coloribus austeritatem occulte daret." And he says just before, of some of the finest pieces of Apelles, "that they were wrought in four colors only." So great and venerable was simplicity held among the ancients, and so certain was the ruin of all true elegance in life or art where this mistress was once quitted or contemned! See Pliny, xxxv. See also above, p. 95, in the notes; and p. 145.

exercising authors of this kind have been above described[8] in the beginning of this treatise. The manner of exercise is called meditation, and is of a sort so solemn and profound, that we dare not so much as thoroughly examine the subject on which we are bid to meditate. This is a sort of task-reading, in which a taste is not permitted. How little soever we take of this diet, 'tis sufficient to give full exercise to our grave humor, and allay the appetite towards further research and solid contemplation. The rest is holiday, diversion, play, and fancy. We reject all rule, as thinking it an injury to our diversions to have regard to truth or nature, without which, however, nothing can be truly agreeable or entertaining, much less instructive or improving. Through a certain surfeit[9] taken in a wrong kind of serious reading, we apply ourselves, with full content, to the most ridiculous. The more remote our pattern is from anything moral or profitable, the more freedom and satisfaction we find in it. We care not how Gothic or barbarous our models are, what ill-designed or monstrous figures we view, or what false proportions we trace or see described in history, romance, or fiction. And thus our eye and ear is lost. Our relish or taste must of necessity grow barbarous, whilst barbarian customs, savage manners, Indian wars, and wonders of the *terra incognita*, employ our leisure hours and are the chief materials to furnish out a library.

These are in our present days what books of chivalry were in those of our forefathers. I know not what faith our valiant ancestors may have had in the stories of their giants, their dragons, and St. Georges. But for our faith indeed, as well as our taste in this other way of reading, I must confess I cannot consider it without astonishment.

It must certainly be something else than incredulity which fashions the taste and judgment of many gentlemen whom we hear censured as atheists, for attempting to philosophize after a newer manner than any known of late. For my own part, I have ever thought this sort of men to be in general more credulous, though after another manner, than the mere vulgar. Besides what I have observed in conversation with the men of this character, I can produce many anathematized authors who, if they want a true Israelitish faith, can make amends by a Chinese or Indian one. If they are short in Syria or the Palestine, they have their full measure in America or Japan. Histories of Incas or Iroquois, written by friars and missionaries, pirates and renegades, sea-captains and trusty travelers, pass for authentic records and are canonical with the virtuosi of this sort. Though Christian miracles may not so well satisfy them, they dwell with the highest contentment on the prodigies of Moorish and Pagan countries. They have far more pleasure in hearing the monstrous accounts of monstrous men and manners than the politest and best narrations of the affairs, the governments, and lives of the wisest and most polished people.

'Tis the same tastes which makes us prefer a Turkish history to a Grecian or a Roman, an Ariosto to a Virgil, and a romance or novel to an Iliad. We have no regard to the character or genius of our author, nor are so far curious as to observe how able

[8] Pp. 109, 110, etc.

[9] *Supra*, pp. 50, 51.

he is in the judgment of facts, or how ingenious in the texture of his lies. For facts unably related, though with the greatest sincerity and good faith, may prove the worst sort of deceit; and mere lies, judiciously composed, can teach us the truth of things beyond any other manner.[10] But to amuse ourselves with such authors as neither know how to lie nor tell truth, discovers a taste which, methinks, one should not be apt to envy. Yet so enchanted we are with the traveling memoirs of any casual adventurer, that be his character or genius what it will, we have no sooner turned over a page or two, than we begin to interest ourselves highly in his affairs. No sooner has he taken shipping at the mouth of the Thames, or sent his baggage before him to Gravesend or Buoy in the Nore, than straight our attention is earnestly taken up. If in order to his more distant travels, he takes some part of Europe in his way, we can with patience hear of inns and ordinaries, passage-boats and ferries, foul and fair weather, with all the particulars of the author's diet, habit of body, his personal dangers and mischances on land and sea. And thus, full of desire and hope, we accompany him till he enters on his great scene of action, and begins by the description of some enormous fish or beast. From monstrous brutes he proceeds to yet more monstrous men. For in this race of authors he is ever completest and of the first rank who is able to speak of things the most unnatural and monstrous.

This humor our old tragic poet[11] seems to have discovered. He hit our taste in giving us a Moorish hero, full-fraught with prodigy, a wondrous story-teller! But for the attentive part, the poet chose to give it to womankind. What passionate reader of travels, or student in the prodigious sciences, can refuse to pity that fair lady, who fell in love with the miraculous Moor? especially considering with what suitable grace such a lover could relate the most monstrous adventures, and satisfy the wondering appetite with the most wondrous tales: Wherein, says the hero-traveller,

[10]The greatest of critics says of the greatest of poet, when he extols him the highest, "that above all others he understood how to lie: δεδίδαχε δὲ μάλιστα Ὅμηρος, καὶ τοὺς ἄλλους ψευδῆ λέξειν ὡς δεῖ. Arist. De Poet. xxiv. See *Misc.* v, ch. i. in the notes.

[11]Shakespere.

> Of antres vast and deserts idle,
> It was my hint to speak . . .;
> And of the Cannibals that each other eat,
> The Anthropophagi and men whose heads
> Do grow beneath their shoulders. This to hear
> Would Desdemona seriously incline.

Seriously, 'twas a woeful tale! unfit, one would think, to win a tender fair one. It is true, the poet sufficiently condemns her fancy, and makes her (poor lady!) pay dearly for it in the end. But why, amongst his Greek names, he should have chosen one which denoted the lady superstitious, I cannot imagine: unless, as poets are sometimes prophets too, he should figuratively, under this dark type, have represented to us that about a hundred years after his time, the fair sex of this island should, by other monstrous tales, be so seduced as to turn their favor chiefly on the persons of the tale-tellers, and change their natural inclination for fair, candid, and courteous knights, into a passion for a mysterious race of black enchanters, such as of old were said to creep into houses, and lead captive silly women.

'Tis certain there is a very great affinity between the passion of superstition and that of tales. The love of strange narrations, and the ardent appetite towards unnatural objects, has a near alliance with the like appetite towards the supernatural kind, such as are called prodigious and of dire omen. For so the mind forebodes on every such unusual sight or hearing. Fate, destiny, or the anger of Heaven seems denoted, and as it were delineated, by the monstrous birth, the horrid fact, or dire event. For this reason the very persons of such relators or tale-tellers, with a small help of dismal habit, suitable countenance and tone, become sacred and tremendous in the eyes of mortals who are thus addicted from their youth. The tender virgins, losing their natural softness, assume this tragic passion, of which they are highly susceptible, especially when a suitable kind of eloquence and action attends the character of the narrator. A thousand Desdemonas are then ready to present themselves, and would frankly resign fathers, relations, countrymen, and country itself, to follow the fortunes of a hero of the black tribe.

But whatever monstrous zeal or superstitious passion the poet might foretell, either in the gentlemen, ladies, or common people of an after age, 'tis certain that as to books the same Moorish fancy, in its plain and literal sense, prevails strongly at this present time. Monsters and monster-lands were never more in request; and we may often see a philosopher, or a wit, run a tale-gathering in those idle deserts as familiarly as the silliest woman or merest boy.

One would imagine that our philosophical writers,[12] who pretend to treat of morals, should far out-do mere poets in recommending virtue, and representing what was fair and amiable in human actions. One would imagine that if they turned their eye towards remote countries (of which they affect so much to speak) they should search for that simplicity of manners and innocence of behaviour which has been often known among mere savages, ere they were corrupted by our commerce, and, by sad example, instructed in all kinds of treachery and inhumanity. 'Twould be of advantage to us to hear the causes of this strange corruption in ourselves, and be made to consider of our deviation from nature, and from that just purity of manners which might be expected, especially from a people so assisted and enlightened by religion. For who would not naturally expect more justice, fidelity, temperance, and honesty from Christians than from Mahometans or mere pagans? But so far are our modern moralists from condemning any unnatural vices or corrupt manners, whether in our own or foreign climates, that they would have vice itself appear as natural as virtue, and from the worst examples would represent to us "that all actions are naturally indifferent; that they have no note or character of good or ill in themselves; but are distinguished by mere fashion, law, or arbitrary decree," Wonderful philosophy! raised from the dregs of an illiterate mean kind, which was ever

[12]Considering what has been so often said on this subject of philosophy, learning, and the sister arts, after the ancient model which has since been so much corrupted, it may not be amiss perhaps to hear the confession of one of the greatest and most learned of moderns upon this head: "Scilicet assensuri isti sunt veteribus sapientibus, poeticam τῆς σεμνοτάτης φιλοσφίας εἶναι σύνναον, severissimae philosophiae contubernalem esse; quos videmus omni cura morum posthabita, quae vera philosophia est, in nescio quibus argumentatiunculis, in nugis sophisticis, in puerilibus argutiolis, λωβοῖς denique ῥηματίοις της διά-λεκτικῆς quod sua jam aetate Euphrades, Themistius conquerebatur, summam sapientiam ponere! Scilicet facundiae Persii virile robur, aut recondita illa eruditio eos capiet, quibus pristinam barbariem mordicus retinere, et in antiqutatis totius ignoratione versari, potius videtur esse ac melius, quam possessionem literarum, olim simili socordia extinctarum, memoria vero patrum magno Dei immortalis beneficio in lucem revocatarum ex alta hominum oblivione, sibi vindicare, et pro sua quemque virili posteris asserere! . . . Scribit vero Arrianus, sapientissimum senem illum Epictetum, impietatis in Deum eos insimulasse, qui in philosophae studiis τὴν ἀπαγγέλτικην δύναμιν sive sermonis curam tanquam rem levem aspernarentur: quoniam quidem, aiebat vir divinus, ἀσεβοῦς ἐστίν ἀνθρώπου τὰς παρὰ τοῦ θεοῦ χάριτας ἀτιμάζειν En Germanum philosophum! En vocem auream! Nec minus memorabile Synesii philosophi praetantissimi vaticinium tristi eventu confirmatum, quod multo ante ab ipso est editum, cum rationem studiorum similiter perverti ab aequalibus suis cerneret. Disputans enim contra eos qui ad sanctissimae theolgiae studia infautiam et sophisticen pro solida eruditione afferent, fatidicam hanc quasi sortem edidit. κίνδυνος, inquit, εiς ἄβυσσόν τίνα φλυαρίας ἐμπεσόντας τούτους διαφθαρῆναι. Periculum est ne ejusmodi homines in abyssum quandam ineptiarum delapsi penitus corrumpantur. Utinam defuisset huic oraculo fides. Sed profecto, depravationi illi, et hujus scientiarum reginae, et omnium aliarum, quae postea accidit, occasionem quidem Gothorum et Alanorum invasiones praebuerunt: at causa illius propior ac vers est, ratio studiorum perversa, et in liberalibus disciplinis prava institutio, ac linguarum simul et universae literaturae melioris ignoratio. . . . Atqui non in cum certe finem viri magui et praecepta et exempla virtutum memoriae commendata ad posteros transmiserunt, ut ad inanem aurium oblectationem, vel jactationem vanam inutilis eruditionis, ea cognosceremus; verum ut suis nos lucubrationibus excitarent ad effodienda et in actum producenda recti honestique semina; quae cum a natura accepissemus, vitiis tamen circumfusa, et tantum non obruta, sic in nostris animis, nisi cultura melior accedat, latent, quasi in altum quendam scrobem penitus defossa. Huc spectant tot illa volumina quae de morali disciplina philosophi confecerunt. Tendit eodem et Graecorum Latinorumque postarum pleraque manus; sed itineribus diversis. Quot sunt enim poetarum genera (sunt autem quamplurina) tot fere diverticula et viarum ambages eo ducentium." Is. Casaub. in Praefatione Commentarii ad Pers. See *Misc.* ii, chs, i. ii., and v. ch. i. in the notes.

despised among the great ancients and rejected by all men of action or sound erudition; but in these ages imperfectly copied from the original, and, with much disadvantage, imitated and assumed in common both by devout and indevout attempters in the moral kind.

Should a writer upon music, addressing himself to the students and lovers of the art, declare to them "that the measure or rule of harmony was caprice or will, humor or fashion," 'tis not very likely he should be heard with great attention or treated with real gravity. For harmony is harmony by nature, let men judge ever so ridiculously of music. So is symmetry and proportion founded still in nature, let men's fancy prove ever so barbarous, or their fashions ever so Gothic in their architecture, sculpture, or whatever other designing art. 'Tis the same case where life and manners are concerned. Virtue has the same fixed standard. The same numbers, harmony, and proportion will have placed in morals, and are discoverable in the characters and affections of mankind; in which are laid the just foundations of an art and science superior to every other of human practice and comprehension.

This, I suppose therefore, is highly necessary that a writer should comprehend. For things are stubborn and will not be as we fancy them, or as the fashion varies, but as they stand in nature. Now whether the writer be poet, philosopher, or of whatever kind, he is in truth no other than a copyist after nature. His style may be differently suited to the different times he lives in, or to the different humor of his age or nation; his manner, his dress, his coloring may vary; but if his drawing be uncorrect or his design contrary to nature, his piece will be found ridiculous when it comes thoroughly to be examined. For Nature will not be mocked. The prepossession against her can never be very lasting. Her decrees and instincts are powerful and her sentiments inbred. She has a strong party abroad, and as strong a one within ourselves; and when any slight is put upon her, she can soon turn the reproach and make large reprisals on the taste and judgment of our antagonists.

Whatever philosopher, critic, or author is convinced of this prerogative of nature, will easily be persuaded to apply himself to the great work of reforming his taste, which he will have reason to suspect, if he be not such a one as has deliberately endeavored to frame it by the just standard of nature. Whether this be his case, he will easily discover by appealing to his memory; for custom and fashion are powerful seducers; and he must of necessity have fought hard against these to have attained that justness of taste which is required in one who pretends to follow nature. But if no such conflict can be called to mind, 'tis a certain token that the party has his taste very little different from the vulgar. And on this account he should instantly betake himself to the wholesome practice recommended in this treatise. He should set afoot the powerfullest faculties of his mind, and assemble the best forces of his wit and judgment, in order to make a formal descent on the territories of the heart; resolving to decline no combat, nor hearken to any terms, till he had pierced into its inmost provinces and reached the seat of empire. No treaties should amuse him; no advantages lead him aside. All other speculations should be suspended, all other mysteries resigned, till this necessary campaign was made and these inward conflicts learnt; by which he would be able to gain at least some tolerable insight into himself and knowledge of his own natural principles.

It may here perhaps be thought that notwithstanding the particular advice we have given in relation to the forming of a taste in natural characters and manners, we are still defective in our performance whilst we are silent on supernatural cases, and bring not into our consideration the manners and characters delivered us in Holy Writ. But this objection will soon vanish when we consider that there can be no rules given by human wit to that which was never humanly conceived, but divinely dictated and inspired.

For this reason 'twould be in vain for any poet or ingenious author to form his characters after the models of our sacred penmen.[13] And whatever certain critics may have advanced concerning the structure of a heroic poem of this kind, I will be bold to prophesy that the success will never be answerable to expectation.

It must be owned that in our sacred history we have both leaders, conquerors, founders of nations, deliverers, and patriots who, even in a human sense, are no way behind the chief of those so much celebrated by the ancients. There is nothing in the story of Aeneas which is not equaled or exceeded by a Joshua or a Moses. But as illustrious as are the acts of these sacred chiefs, 'twould be hard to copy them in just heroic. 'Twould be hard to give to many of them that grateful air which is necessary to render them naturally pleasing to mankind, according to the idea men are universally found to have of heroism and generosity.

Notwithstanding the pious endeavors which, as devout Christians, we may have used in order to separate ourselves from the interests of mere heathens and infidels, notwithstanding the true pains we may have taken to arm our hearts in behalf of a chosen people against their neighboring nations of a false religion and worship, there will be still found such a partiality remaining in us towards creatures of the same make and figure with ourselves, as will hinder us from viewing with satisfaction the punishments inflicted by human hands on such aliens and idolaters.

In mere poetry, and the pieces of wit and literature, there is a liberty of thought and easiness of humor indulged to us in which, perhaps, we are not so well able to contemplate the divine judgments, and see clearly into the justice of those ways which are declared to be so far from our ways and above our highest thoughts or understandings. In such a situation of mind we can hardly endure to see heathen treated as heathen, and the faithful made the executioners of the divine wrath. There is a certain perverse humanity in us which inwardly resists the divine commission, though ever so plainly revealed. The wit of the best poet is not sufficient to reconcile us to the campaign of a Joshua, or the retreat of a Moses by the assistance of an Egyptian loan. Nor will it be possible, by the Muses' art, to make that royal hero appear amiable in human eyes who found such favor in the eye of Heaven. Such are mere human hearts that they can hardly find the least sympathy with that only one which had the character of being after the pattern of the Almighty's.

'Tis apparent, therefore, that the manners, actions, and characters of sacred writ are in no wise the proper subject of other authors than divines themselves. They are matters incomprehensible in philosophy; they are above the pitch of the mere human

[13] *Misc.* v. ch. i. in the notes.

historian, the politician, or the moralist, and are too sacred to be submitted to the poet's fancy when inspired by no other spirit than that of his profane mistresses the Muses.

I should be unwilling to examine rigorously the performance of our great poet,[14] who sung so piously the Fall of Man. The War in Heaven and the catastrophe of that original pair from whom the generations of mankind were propagated are matters so abstrusely revealed, and with such a resemblance of mythology, that they can more easily bear what figurative construction or fantastic turn the poet may think fit to give them. But should he venture farther into the lives and characters of the patriarchs, the holy matrons, heroes and heroines of the chosen seed; should he employ the sacred machine, the exhibitions and interventions of divinity according to Holy Writ to support the action of his piece; he would soon find the weakness of his pretended orthodox Muse, and prove how little those divine patterns were capable of human imitations, or of being raised to any other majesty, or sublime, than that in which they originally appear.

The theology or theogony of the heathens could admit of such different turns and figurative expressions as suited the fancy and judgment of each philosopher or poet. But the purity of our faith will admit of no such variation. The Christian theology, the birth, procedure, generation, and personal distinction of the Divinity, are mysteries only to be determined by the initiated or ordained, to whom the State has assigned the guardianship and promulgation of the divine oracles. It becomes not those who are uninspired from heaven and uncommissioned from earth, to search with curiosity into the original of those holy rites and records by law established. Should we make such an attempt, we should in probability find the less satisfaction the further we presumed to carry our speculations. Having dared once to quit the authority and direction of the law, we should easily be subject to heterodoxy and error when we had no better warrant left us for the authority of our sacred symbols than the integrity, candor, and disinterestedness of their compilers and registers. How great that candor and disinterestedness may have been, we have no other histories to inform us than those of their own licensing or composing. But busy persons, who officiously search into these records, are ready even from hence to draw proofs very disadvantageous to the fame and character of this succession of men. And persons moderately read in these histories are apt to judge no otherwise of the temper of ancient councils than by that of later synods and modern convocations.

When we add to this the melancholy consideration of what disturbances have been raised from the disputes of this kind; what effusion of blood, what devastations of provinces, what shock and ruin of empires have been occasioned by controversies founded on the nicest distinction of an article relating to these mysteries, 'twill be judged vain in any poet or polite author to think of rendering himself agreeable or entertaining whilst he makes such subjects as these to be his theme.

But though the explanation of such deep mysteries and religious duties be allotted as the peculiar province of the sacred order, 'tis presumed, nevertheless, that

[14]Milton.

it may be lawful for other authors to retain their ancient privilege of instructing mankind in a way of pleasure and entertainment. Poets may be allowed their fictions and philosophers their systems. 'Twould go hard with mankind should the patentees for religion be commissioned for all instruction and advice relating to manners or conversation. The stage may be allowed to instruct as well as the pulpit. The way of wit and humor may be serviceable as well as that of gravity and seriousness; and the way of plain reason as well as that of exalted revelation. The main matter is to keep these provinces distinct and settle their just boundaries. And on this account it is that we have endeavored to represent to modern authors the necessity of making this separation justly and in due form.

'Twould be somewhat hard, methinks, if Religion, as by law established,[15] were not allowed the same privilege as Heraldry. 'Tis agreed on all hands that particular persons may design or paint, in their private capacity, after what manner they think fit; but they must blazon only as the public directs. Their lion or bear must be figured as the science appoints, and their supporters and crest must be such as their wise and gallant ancestors have procured for them. No matter whether the shapes of these animals hold just proportion with Nature. No matter though different or contrary forms are joined in one. That which is denied to painters or poets is permitted to heralds. Naturalists may, in their separate and distinct capacity, inquire as they think fit into the real existence and natural truth of things; but they must by no means dispute the authorized forms. Mermaids and griffins were the wonder of our forefathers, and, as such, delivered down to us by the authentic traditions and delineations above mentioned. We ought not so much as to criticize the features or dimensions of a Saracen's face, brought by our conquering ancestors from the holy wars; nor pretend to call in question the figure or size of a dragon, on which the history of our national champion and the establishment of a high order and dignity of the realm depends.

But as worshipful as are the persons of the illustrious heralds, Clarencieux, Garter, and the rest of those eminent sustainers of British honor and antiquity, 'tis to be hoped that in a more civilized age, such as at present we have the good fortune to live in, they will not attempt to strain their privileges to the same height as formerly. Having been reduced by law or settled practice from the power they once enjoyed, they will not, 'tis presumed, in defiance of the magistrate and civil power, erect anew their stages and lists, introduced the manner of civil combat, set us to tilt and tournament, and raise again those defiances and moral frays of which their Order were once the chief managers and promoters.

To conclude: the only method which can justly qualify us for this high privilege of giving advice, is in the first place to receive it ourselves with due submission where the public has vouchsafed to give it us by authority. And if in our private capacity we can have resolution enough to criticize ourselves, and call in question our high imaginations, florid desires, and specious sentiments, according to the manner of soliloquy above prescribed, we shall, by the natural course of things, as

[15] *Misc.* i. ch. ii; v. ch. i.

we grow wiser, prove less conceited, and introduce into our character that modesty, condescension, and just humanity which is essential to the success of all friendly counsel and admonition. And honest home-philosophy must teach us the wholesome practice within ourselves. Polite reading, and converse with mankind of the better sort, will qualify us for what remains.

Miscellaneous Reflections

For our part, we neither care that foreigners should travel to us,[16] nor any of ours should travel into foreign countries. Our best policy and breeding is, it seems, "to look abroad as little as possible, contract our views within the narrowest compass, and despise all knowledge, learning, or manners which are not of a home growth." For hardly will the ancients themselves be regarded by those who have so resolute a contempt of what the politest moderns of any nation besides their own may have advanced in the way of literature, politeness, or philosophy.

This disposition of our countrymen, from whatever causes it may possibly be derived, is, I fear, a very prepossessing circumstance against our author, whose design is to advance something new, or at least something different from what is commonly current in philosophy and morals. To support this design of his he seems intent chiefly on this single point, "to discover how we may to best advantage form within ourselves what in the polite world is called a relish or good taste."

He begins, it is true, as near home as possible, and sends us to the narrowest of all conversations, that of soliloquy or self-discourse. But this correspondence, according to his computation, is wholly impracticable without a previous commerce with the world; and the larger this commerce is, the more practicable and improving the other, he thinks, is likely to prove. The sources of this improving art of self-correspondence he derives from the highest politeness and elegance of ancient

[16]An ill token of our being thoroughly civilized, since in the judgment of the polite and wise this inhospitable disposition was ever reckoned among the principal marks of barbarism. So Strabo, from other preceding authors, κοινὸν μὲν εἶναι τοις βαρβάροις πᾶσιν ἔθος τὴν ξενηλασίαη.

The Ζεὺς Ξένιος of the ancients was one of the solemn characters of divinity: the peculiar attribute of the supreme Deity, benign to mankind, and recommending universal love, mutual kindness, and benignity between the remotest and most unlike of human race. Thus their divine poet, in harmony with their sacred oracles, which were known frequently to confirm this doctrine —

ξεῖν', οὔ μοῖ θέμις ἔστ', ούδ' εἰ κακίων σέθενελθοι,
ξεῖνον ἀτιμῆσαι πρὸς γὰρ Διός ἔισιν ἅπαντες.
ξεῖνοι

Again, —

οὐδέ τις ἄμμι βροτῶν ἐπιμίσγεται ἄλλος
ἀλλ' ὅδε τις δύστηνος ἀλώμενος ἔνθαδ' ἱκάνει
τὸν νῦν χρὴ κομέειν' πρὸς γὰr Διός εισιν ἅπαντες
ξεῖνοι.

And again, —

αφνειὸς βιότοιο, φιλος δ' ἦν ἀνθρώποισι'
πάντας, γὰρ φιλέεσκεν ὁδῷ ἔπι οίκια ναίων.

See also Odyssey, lib. iii, 34, etc., and 67, etc.; lib. iv. 30, etc., and 60.

Such was ancient heathen charity and pious duty towards the whole of mankind, both those of different nations and different worships. See *Inquiry Concerning Virtue*, bk. ii. part ii. §3.

dialogue and debate, in matters of wit, knowledge, and ingenuity. And nothing, according to our author, can so well revive this self-corresponding practice as the same search and study of the highest politeness in modern conversation. For this, we must necessarily be at the pains of going further abroad than the province we call home. And by this account it appears that our author has little hopes of being either relished or comprehended by any other of his countrymen than those who delight in the open and free commerce of the world, and are rejoiced to gather views and receive light from every quarter in order to judge the best of what is perfect, and according to a just standard and true taste in every kind.

It may be proper for us to remark, in favor of our author, that the sort of ridicule or raillery which is apt to fall upon philosophers is of the same kind with that which falls commonly on the virtuosi or refined wits of the age. In this latter general denomination we include the real fine gentlemen, the lovers of art and ingenuity, such as have seen the world, and informed themselves of the manners and customs of the several nations of Europe; searched into their antiquities and records; considered their police, laws, and constitutions; observed the situation, strength, and ornaments of their cities, their principal arts, studies, and amusements; their architecture, sculpture, painting, music, and their taste in poetry, learning, language, and conversation.

Hitherto there can lie no ridicule, nor the least scope for satiric wit or raillery. But when we push this virtuoso character a little further and lead our polished gentleman into more nice researches, when from the view of mankind and their affairs, our speculative genius and minute examiner of Nature's works proceeds with equal or perhaps superior zeal in the contemplation of the insect life, the conveniences, habitations, and economy of a race of shell-fish; when he has erected a cabinet in due form, and made it the real pattern of his mind, replete with the same trash and trumpery of correspondent empty notions and chimerical conceits, he then indeed becomes the subject of sufficient raillery, and is made the jest of common conversations.

A worse thing than this happens commonly to these inferior virtuosi. In seeking so earnestly for rarities they fall in love with rarity for rareness' sake. Now the greatest rarities in the world are monsters. So that the study and relish of these gentlemen, thus assiduously employed, becomes at last in reality monstrous; and their whole delight is found to consist in selecting and contemplating whatever is most monstrous, disagreeing, out of the way, and to the least purpose of anything in Nature.

In philosophy, matters answer exactly to this virtuoso scheme. Let us suppose a man who, having this resolution merely, how to employ his understanding to the best purpose, considers "who or what he is; whence he arose or had his being; to what end he was designed; and to what course of action he is by his natural frame and constitution destined"; should he descend on this account into himself and examine his inward powers and faculties, or should he ascend beyond his own immediate species, city, or community, to discover and recognize his higher polity or community (that common and universal one of which he is born a member), nothing surely of this kind could reasonably draw upon him the least contempt or mockery.

On the contrary, the finest gentleman must after all be considered but as an idiot, who, talking much of the knowledge of the world and mankind, has never so much as thought of the study or knowledge of himself, or of the nature and government of that real public and world from whence he holds his being.

Quid sumus, et quidnam victuri gignimur?[17]

"Where are we? under what roof? or on board what vessel? whither bound? on what business? under whose pilotship, government, or protection?" are questions which every sensible man would naturally ask if he were on a sudden transported into a new scene of life. 'Tis admirable, indeed, to consider, that a man should have been long come into a world, carried his reason and sense about with him, and yet have never seriously asked himself this single question, "where am I? or what?" but, on the contrary, should proceed regularly to every other study and inquiry, postponing this alone, as the least considerable, or leaving the examination of it to others commissioned, as he supposes, to understand and think for him upon this head. To be bubbled, or put upon by any sham advices in this affair, is, it seems, of no consequence. We take care to examine accurately, by our own judgment, the affairs of other people, and the concerns of the world which least belong to us. But what relates more immediately to ourselves, and is our chief self-interest, we charitably leave to others to examine for us, and readily take up with the first comers, on whose honesty and good faith 'tis presumed we may safely rely.

Here, methinks, the ridicule turns more against the philosophy-haters than the virtuosi or philosophers. Whilst philosophy is taken (as in its prime sense it ought) for mastership in life and manners, 'tis like to make no ill figure in the world, whatever impertinencies may reign, or however extravagant the times may prove. But let us view philosophy, like mere virtuosoship, in its usual career, and we shall find the ridicule rising full as strongly against the professors of the higher as the lower kind. Cockle-shell abounds with each. Many things exterior and without ourselves, of no relation to our real interests or to those of society and mankind, are diligently investigated; Nature's remotest operations, deepest mysteries and most difficult phenomena discussed and whimsically explained; hypotheses and fantastic systems erected, a universe anatomized, and by some notable scheme[18] so solved and reduced as to appear an easy knack or secret to those who have the clue. Creation itself can, upon occasion, be exhibited; transmutations, projections, and other philosophical arcana, such as in the corporeal world can accomplish all things; whilst in the intellectual a set frame of metaphysical phrases and distinctions can serve to solve whatever difficulties may be propounded either in logics, ethics, or any real science of whatever kind.

It appears from hence that the defects of philosophy and those of virtuosoship are of the same nature. Nothing can be more dangerous than a wrong choice or

[17]Pers. *Sat.* iii. 67.

[18]*Moralists*, part i. §1.

misapplication in these affairs. But as ridiculous as these studies are rendered by their senseless managers, it appears, however, that each of them are, in their nature, essential to the character of a fine gentleman and man of sense.

To philosophize, in a just signification, is but to carry good-breeding a step higher. For the accomplishment of breeding is, to learn whatever is decent in company or beautiful in arts; and the sum of philosophy is, to learn what is just in society and beautiful in Nature and the order of the world.

'Tis not wit merely, but a temper which must form the well-bred man. In the same manner, 'tis not a head merely, but a heart and resolution which must complete the real philosopher. Both characters aim at what is excellent, aspire to a just taste, and carry in view the model of what is beautiful and becoming. Accordingly, the respective conduct and distinct manners of each party are regulated; the one according to the perfectest ease and good entertainment of company, the other according to the strictest interest of mankind and society; the one according to a man's rank and quality in his private station, the other according to his rank and dignity in Nature.

Whether each of these offices or social parts are in themselves as convenient as becoming, is the great question which must some way be decided. The well-bred man has already decided this in his own case, and declared on the side of what is handsome; for whatever he practices in this kind,[19] he accounts no more than what he owes purely to himself, without regard to any further advantage. The pretender to philosophy, who either knows not how to determine this affair, or if he has determined, knows not how to pursue his point with constancy and firmness, remains in respect of philosophy what a clown or coxcomb is in respect of breeding and behaviour. Thus, according to our author, the taste of beauty and the relish of what is decent, just, and amiable perfects the character of the gentleman and the philosopher. And the study of such a taste or relish will, as we suppose, be ever the great employment and concern of him who covets as well to be wise and good as agreeable and polite.

Quid verum atque decens curo et rogo, et omnis in hoc sum.[20]

Chapter II

Explanation of a taste continued—Riciculers of it—Their wit and sincerity— Application of the taste to affairs of government and politics—Imaginary characters in the State—Young nobility and gentry—Pursuit of beauty—Preparation for philosophy.

By this time, surely I must have proved myself sufficiently engaged in the project and design of our self-discoursing author, whose defense I have undertaken. His pretension, as plainly appears in this third treatise[21] is to recommend morals on the same foot with what in a lower sense is called manners, and to advance

[19] *Wit and Humor*, part iv. §1.

[20] Hor. *Epist.* I. i. 11.

[21] *Treatise* III. part iii. §3.

philosophy (as harsh a subject as it may appear) on the very foundation of what is called agreeable and polite. And 'tis in this method and management that, as his interpreter or paraphrast, I have proposed to imitate and accompany him, as far as my miscellaneous character will permit.

Our joint endeavor, therefore, must appear this: to show "that nothing which is found charming or delightful in the polite world, nothing which is adopted as pleasure or entertainment, of whatever kind, can any way be accounted for, supported, or established, without the pre-establishment or supposition of a certain taste." Now a taste or judgment, 'tis supposed, can hardly come ready formed with us into the world. Whatever principles or materials of this kind we may possibly bring with us, whatever good faculties, senses, or anticipating sensations and imaginations may be of Nature's growth, and arise properly of themselves, without our art, promotion, or assistance, the general idea which is formed of all this management and the clear notion we attain of what is preferable and principal in all these subjects of choice and estimation will not, as I imagine, by any person be taken for innate. Use, practice, and culture must precede the understanding and wit of such an advanced size and growth as this. A legitimate and just taste can neither be begotten, made, conceived, or produced without the antecedent labor and pains of criticism.

For this reason we presume not only to defend the cause of critics, but to declare open war against those indolent supine authors, performers, readers, auditors, actors or spectators who, making their humor alone the rule of what is beautiful and agreeable, and having no account to give of such their humor or odd fancy, reject the criticizing or examining art, by which alone they are able to discover the true beauty and worth of every object.

According to that affected ridicule which these insipid remarkers pretend to throw upon just critics, the enjoyment of all real arts or natural beauty would be entirely lost; even in behaviour and manners we should at this rate become in time as barbarous as in our pleasures and diversions. I would presume it, however, of these critic-haters, that they are not yet so uncivilized or void of all social sense as to maintain "that the most barbarous life or brutish pleasure is as desirable as the most polished or refined."

For my own part, when I have heard sometimes men of reputed ability join in with that effeminate plaintive tone of invective against critics, I have really thought they had it in their fancy to keep down the growing geniuses of the youth, their rivals, by turning them aside from that examination and search, on which all good performance as well as good judgment depends. I have seen many a time a well-bred man, who had himself a real good taste, give way with a malicious complaisance to the humor of a company, where, in favor chiefly of the tender sex, this soft languishing contempt of critics and their labors has been the subject set afoot. "Wretched creatures! (says one) impertinent things, these critics, as ye call them! As if one could not know what was agreeable or pretty without their help. 'Tis fine, indeed, that one should not be allowed to fancy for oneself. Now should a thousand critics tell me that Mr. A_____'s new play was not the wittiest in the world, I would not mind them one bit."

This our real man of wit hears patiently, and adds, perhaps of his own, "that he thinks it truly somewhat hard, in what relates to people's diversion and entertainment, that they should be obliged to choose what pleased others and not themselves." Soon after this he goes himself to the play, finds one of his effeminate companions commending or admiring at a wrong place. He turns to the next person who sits by him, and asks privately, "what he thinks of his companion's relish."

Such is the malice of the world! They who by pains and industry have acquired a real taste in arts, rejoice in their advantage over others, who have either none at all or such as renders them ridiculous. At an auction of books or pictures, you shall hear these gentlemen persuading every one "to bid for what he fancies." But at the same time they would be soundly mortified themselves if, by such as they esteemed good judges, they should be found to have purchased by a wrong fancy or ill taste. The same gentleman who commends his neighbor for ordering his garden or apartment as his humor leads him, takes care his own should be so ordered as the best judgments would advise. Being once a judge himself, or but tolerably knowing in these affairs, his aim is not "to change the being of things, and bring truth and Nature to his humor; but, leaving Nature and truth just as he found them, to accommodate his humor and fancy to their standard." Would he do this in a yet higher case, he might in reality become as wise and great a man as he is already a refined and polished gentleman. By one of these tastes he understands how to lay out his garden, model his house, fancy his equipage, appoint his table; by the other he learns of what value these amusements are in life, and of what importance to a man's freedom, happiness, and self-enjoyment. For if he would try effectually to acquire the real science or taste of life, he would certainly discover "that a right mind and generous affection had more beauty and charm than all other symmetries in the world besides." And "that a grain of honesty and native worth was of more value than all the adventitious ornaments, estates, or preferments; for the sake of which some of the better sort so oft turn knaves, forsaking their principles and quitting their honour and freedom for a mean, timorous, shifting state of gaudy servitude."

A little better taste (were it a very little) in the affair of life itself would, if I mistake not, mend the manners and secure the happiness of some of our noble countrymen, who come with high advantage and a worthy character into the public. But ere they have long engaged in it, their worth unhappily becomes venal. Equipages, titles, precedencies, staffs, ribbons, and other such glittering ware are taken in exchange for inward merit, honor, and a character.

This they may account perhaps a shrewd bargain. But there will be found very untoward abatements in it when the matter comes to be experienced. They may have descended in reality from ever so glorious ancestors, patriots, and sufferers for their nation's liberty and welfare; they may have made their entrance into the world upon this bottom of anticipated fame and honor; they may have been advanced on this account to dignities which they were thought to have deserved. But when induced to change their honest measures, and sacrifice their cause and friends to an imaginary private interest, they will soon find, by experience, that they have lost the relish and taste of life; and for insipid wretched honors of a deceitful kind have unhappily exchanged an amiable and sweet honor, of a sincere and lasting relish and good savor. They may, after this, act farces as they think fit, and hear qualities and virtues assigned to them under the titles of graces, excellencies, honors, and the rest of this mock praise and mimical appellation. They may even with serious looks be told of honor and worth, their principle, and their country; but they know better within themselves, and have occasion to find that after all the world too knows better, and that their few friends and admirers have either a very shallow wit or a very profound hypocrisy.

'Tis not in one party alone that these purchases and sales of honor are carried on. I can represent to myself a noted patriot and reputed pillar of the religious part of our constitution, who having by many and long services and a steady conduct gained the reputation of thorough zeal with his own party, and of sincerity and honor with his very enemies, on a sudden (the time being come that the fullness of his reward was set before him) submits complacently to the proposed bargain, and sells himself for what he is worth, in a vile, detestable old age, to which he has reserved the infamy of betraying both his friends and country.

I can imagine, on the other side, one of the contrary party, a noted friend to liberty in Church and State; an abhorrer of the slavish dependency on courts, and of the narrow principles of bigots. Such a one, after many public services of note, I can see wrought upon, by degrees, to seek court preferment, and this too under a patriot character. But having perhaps tried this way with less success, he is obliged to change his character, and become a royal flatterer, a courtier against his nature; submitting himself and suing, in so much the meaner degree, as his inherent principles are well known at court and to his new adopted party, to whom he feigns himself a proselyte.

The greater the genius or character is of such a person, the greater is his slavery and heavier his load. Better had it been that he had never discovered such a zeal for public good, or signalized himself in that party which can with least grace make sacrifices of national interests to a crown, or to the private will, appetite, or pleasure of a prince. For supposing such a genius as this had been to act his part of courtship in some foreign and absolute court, how much less infamous would his part have proved? how much less lavish, amidst a people who were all slaves? Had he peradventure been one of that forlorn begging troop of gentry extant in Denmark or Sweden, since the time that those nations lost their liberties; had he lived out of a free nation and happily balanced constitution; had he been either conscious of no talent in the affairs of government or of no opportunity to exert any such to the advantage of mankind: where had been the mighty shame, if perhaps he had employed some of his abilities in flattering like others, and paying the necessary homage required for safety's sake and self-preservation, in absolute and despotic governments? The taste, perhaps, in strictness, might still be wrong, even in this hard circumstance; but how inexcusable in a quite contrary one! For let us suppose our courtier not only an Englishman, but of the rank and stem of those old English patriots who were wont to curb the licentiousness of our court, arraign its flatterers, and purge away those poisons from the ear of princes; let us suppose him of a competent fortune and moderate appetites, without any apparent luxury or lavishment in his manners: what shall we, after this, bring in excuse, or as an apology, for such a choice as his? How shall we explain this preposterous relish, this odd preference of subtlety and indirectness to true wisdom, open honesty, and uprightness?

'Tis easier, I confess, to give account of this corruption of taste in some noble youth of a more sumptuous, gay fancy; supposing him born truly great and of honorable descent, with a generous free mind, as well as ample fortune. Even these circumstances themselves may be the very causes perhaps of his being thus ensnared. The elegance of his fancy in outward things may have made him overlook the worth of inward character and proportion: and the love of grandeur and magnificence, wrong turned, may have possessed his imagination over-strongly with such things as frontispieces, parterres, equipages, trim varlets in parti-colored clothes, and others in gentlemen's apparel,—magnanimous exhibitions of honour and generosity! "In town, a palace and suitable furniture! In the country the same, with the addition of such edifices and gardens as were unknown to our ancestors, and are unnatural to such a climate as Great Britain!"

Meanwhile the year runs on, but the year's income answers not its expense. For "which of these articles can be retrenched? Which way take up, after having thus set out?" A princely fancy has begot all this, and a princely slavery and court dependence must maintain it.

The young gentleman is now led into a chase, in which he will have slender capture, though toil sufficient. He is himself taken. Nor will he so easily get out of that labyrinth, to which he chose to commit his steps, rather than to the more direct and plainer paths in which he trod before. "Farewell that generous, proud spirit, which was wont to speak only what it approved, commend only whom it thought worthy, and act only what it thought right! Favorites must be now observed; little engines of power attended on and loathsomely caressed; an honest man dreaded, and every free tongue or pen abhorred as dangerous and reproachful." For till our gentleman is become wholly prostitute and shameless; till he is brought to laugh at public virtue, and the very notion of common good; till he has openly renounced all principles of honour and honesty, he must in good policy avoid those to whom he lies so much exposed, and shun that commerce and familiarity which was once his chief delight.

Such is the sacrifice made to a wrong pride and ignorant self-esteem, by one whose inward character must necessarily, after this manner, become as mean and abject as his outward behaviour insolent and intolerable.

There are another sort of suitors to powers, and traffickers of inward worth and liberty for outward gain, whom one would be naturally drawn to compassionate. They are themselves of a humane, compassionate, and friendly nature, well-wishers to their country and mankind. They could, perhaps, even embrace poverty contentedly rather than submit to anything diminutive either of their inward freedom or national liberty. But what they can bear in their own persons they cannot bring themselves to bear in the persons of such as are to come after them. Here the best and novelest of affections are borne down by the excess of the next best, those of tenderness for relations and near friends.

Such captives as these would disdain, however, to devote themselves to any prince or ministry whose ends were wholly tyrannical and irreconcilable with the true interest of their nation. In other cases of a less degeneracy, they may bow down perhaps in the temple of Rimmon, support the weight of their supine lords, and prop the steps and ruining credit of their corrupt patrons.

This is drudgery sufficient for such honest natures, such as by hard fate alone could have been made dishonest. But as for pride or insolence on the account of their outward advancement and seeming elevation, they are so far from anything resembling it that one may often observe what is very contrary in these fairer characters of men. For though perhaps they were known somewhat rigid and severe before, you see them now grown in reality submissive and obliging. Though in conversation formerly dogmatical and overbearing on the points of State and government, they are now the patientest to hear, the least forward to dictate, and the readiest to embrace any entertaining subject of discourse, rather than that of the public and their own personal advancement.

Nothing is so near virtue as this behaviour; and nothing so remote from it, nothing so sure a token of the most profligate manners, as the contrary. In a free government, 'tis so much the interest of every one in place, who profits by the public, to demean himself with modesty and submission, that to appear immediately the more insolent and haughty on such an advancement is the mark only of a contemptible genius, and of a want of true understanding, even in the narrow sense of interest and private good.

Thus we see, after all, that 'tis not merely what we call principle, but a taste which governs men. They may think for certain, "this is right, or that wrong": they may believe "this a crime, or that a sin; this punishable by man, or that by God": yet if the savor of things lies across to honesty; if the fancy be florid and the appetite high towards the subaltern beauties and lower order of worldly symmetries and proportions, the conduct will infallibly turn this latter way.

Even conscience, I fear, such as is owing to religious discipline, will make but a slight figure where this taste is set amiss. Among the vulgar, perhaps, it may do wonders. A devil and a hell may prevail where a jail and gallows are thought insufficient. But such is the nature of the liberal polished, and refined part of mankind. So far are they from the mere simplicity of babes and sucklings that, instead of applying the notion of a future reward or punishment to their immediate behaviour in society, they are apt much rather, through the whole course of their lives, to show evidently that they look on the pious narrations to be indeed no better than children's tales or the amusement of the mere vulgar:—

> Esse aliquos Manes, et subterranea regna,
>
> . . .
>
> Nec pueri credunt, nisi qui nondum acre lavantur.[22]

[22]Juv. ii. 141-151.

Something before should, methinks, be further thought of in behalf of our generous youths towards the correcting of their taste or relish in the concerns of life. For this at last is what will influence. And in this respect the youth alone are to be regarded. Some hopes there may be still conceived of these. The rest are confirmed and hardened in their way. A middle-aged knave (however devout or orthodox) is but a common wonder; an old one is no wonder at all; but a young one is still (thank heaven!) somewhat extraordinary. And I can never enough admire what was said once by a worthy man at the first appearance of one of these young able prostitutes, "that he even trembled at the sight, to find nature capable of being turned so soon; and that he boded greater calamity to his country from this single example of young villainy than from the practices and arts of all the old knaves in being."

Let us therefore proceed in this view, addressing ourselves to the grown youth of our polite world. Let the appeal be to these whose relish is retrievable, and whose taste may yet be formed in morals, as it seems to be already in exterior manners and behavior.

That there is really a standard of this latter kind will immediately, and on the first view, be acknowledged. The contest is only, "which is right; which the unaffected carriage and just demeanor; and which the affected and false." Scarce is there any one who pretends not to know and to decide what is well-bred and handsome. There are few so affectedly clownish as absolutely to disown good breeding, and renounce the notion of a beauty in outward manners and deportment. With such as these, wherever they should be found, I must confess I could scarce be tempted to bestow the least pains or labor towards convincing them of a beauty in inward sentiments and principles.

Whoever has any impression of what we call gentility or politeness is already so acquainted with the decorum and grace of things that he will readily confess a pleasure and enjoyment in the very survey and contemplation of this kind. Now if in the way of polite pleasure the study and love of beauty be essential, the study and love of symmetry and order, on which beauty depends, must also be essential in the same respect.

'Tis impossible we can advance the least in any relish or taste of outward symmetry and order, without acknowledging that the proportionate and regular state is the truly prosperous and natural in every subject. The same features which make deformity create incommodiousness and disease. And the same shapes and proportions which make beauty afford advantage by adapting to activity and use. Even in the imitative or designing arts (to which our author so often refers) the truth or beauty of every figure or statue is measured from the perfection of Nature in her just adapting of every limb and proportion to the activity, strength, dexterity, life and vigor of the particular species or animal designed.

Thus beauty and truth are plainly joined with the notion of utility and convenience,[23] even in the apprehension of every ingenious artist, the architect,[24] the statuary, or the painter. 'Tis the same in the physician's way. Natural health is the just proportion, truth, and regular course of things in a constitution. 'Tis the inward beauty of the body. And when the harmony and just measures of the rising pulses, the circulating humors, and the moving airs or spirits, are disturbed or lost, deformity enters, and with it, calamity and ruin.

Should not this (one would imagine) be still the same case and hold equally as to the mind? Is there nothing there which tends to disturbance and dissolution? Is there no natural tenor, tone, or order of the passions or affections? No beauty or deformity in this moral kind? Or allowing that there really is, must it not, of consequence, in the same manner imply health or sickliness, prosperity or disaster? Will it not be found in this respect, above all, "that what is beautiful is harmonious and proportionable;[25] what is harmonious and proportionable is true; and what is at once both beautiful and true is, of consequence, agreeable and good?"

[23]*Treatise* II. part iv. §3.

[24]In Graecis operibus nemo sub mutulo denticulos constituit, etc. Quod ergo supra cantherios et templa in veritate debet esse collocatum, id in imaginibus, si infra constitutum fuerit, mendosam habebit operis rationem. Etiamque antiqui non probaverunt, neque instituerunt, etc. Ita quod non potest in veritate fieri, id non putaverunt in imaginibus factum, posse certam rationem habere. Omnia enim certa proprietate et a veris naturae deductis moribus traduxerunt in operum perfectiones: et ea probaverunt quorum explicationes in disputationibus rationem possunt habere veritatis. Itaque ex eis orginibus symmetrias et proportiones uniuscujusque generis constitutas reliquerunt. Vitruvius, iv. 2, whose commentator Philander may be also read on this place. See above, Treatise III, part i., end; part iii. §3. and below, Misc. v. ch. i.

[25]This is the honestum, the pulchrum, τὸ καλόν, on which our author lays the stress of virtue, and the merits of this cause; as well in his other Treatises as in this of *Soliloquy* here commented. This beauty the Roman orator, in his rhetorical way, and in the majesty of style, could express no otherwise than as a mystery. "Honestum igitur id intellgimus, quod tale est, ut, detracta moni utilitate, sine ullis praemiis fructibusve, per seipsum possit jure laudari. Quod quale sit, non tam defintione qua sum usus intelligi potest (quanquam aliquantum potest) quam communi omnium judicio, et optimi cujusque studiis, atque factis; qui permulta ob eam unam causam faciunt, quia decet, quia rectum, quia honestum est; etsi nullum consecuturum emolumentum vident." Our author, on the other side, having little of the orator, and less of the constraint of formality belonging to some graver characters, can be more familiar on this occasion; and accordingly descending without the least scruple into whatever style or humor, he refuses to make the least difficulty or mystery of this matter. He pretends, on this head, to claim the assent not only of orators, poets, and the higher virtuosi, but even of the beaux themselves, and such as go no farther than the dancing-master to seek for grace and beauty. He pretends, we see, to fetch this natural idea from as familiar amusements as dress, equipage, the tiring-room, or toy-shop. And thus in his proper manner of soliloquy or self-discourse, we may imagine him running on, beginning perhaps with some particular scheme or fancied scale of beauty, which according to his philosophy, he strives to erect by distinguishing, sorting, and dividing into things animate, inanimate, and mixed, as thus: —

In the inanimate: beginning from those regular figures and symmetries with which children are delighted, and proceeding gradually to the proportions of architecture and the other arts. The same in respect of sounds and music. From beautiful stones, rocks, minerals, to vegetables, woods, aggregate parts of the world, seas, rivers, mountains, vales. The globe. Celestial bodies and their order. The higher architecture of Nature. Nature herself considered as inanimate and passive.

In the animate: from animals and their several kinds, tempers, sagacities, to men. And from single persons of men, their private characters, understandings, geniuses, dispositions, manners, to public societies, communities or commonwealths. From flocks, herds, and other natural assemblages or groups of living creatures, to human intelligencies and correspondencies, or whatever is higher in the kind. The correspondence, union and harmony of Nature herself, considered as animate and intelligent.

In the mixed: as in a single person (a body and a mind) the union and harmony of this kind, which constitutes the real person; and the friendship, love, or whatever other affection is formed on such an object. A household, a city or nation, with certain lands, buildings, and other appendices or local ornaments which jointly form that agreeable idea of home, family, country.

"And what of this?" says an airy spark, no friend to meditation or deep thought. "What means this catalogue or scale, as you are pleased to call it? Only, sir, to satisfy myself that I am not alone or single in a certain fancy I have of a thing called beauty; that I have almost the whole world for my companions; and that each of us admirers and earnest pursuers of beauty (such as in a manner we all are) if peradventure we take not a certain sagacity along with us, we must err widely, range extravagantly, and run ever upon a false scent. We may (in the sportsman's phrase) have many hares afoot, but shall stick to no real game, nor be fortunate in any capture which may content us.

"See with what ardor and vehemence the young man, neglecting his proper race and fellow-creatures, and forgetting what is decent, handsome, or becoming in human affairs, pursues these species in this common objects of his affection, a horse, a hound, a hawk! What doting on these beauties! What admiration of the kind itself! And of the particular animal, what care, and in a manner idolatry and consecration, when the least beloved is (as often happens) even set apart from use, and only kept to gaze on and feed the enamored fancy with highest delight! See in another youth, not so forgetful of human kind, but remembering it still in a wrong way! a φιλόκαλςos of another sort, a Chaerea. Quam elegans formarum spectator! See as to other beauties, where there is no possession, no enjoyment or reward, but barely seeing and admiring; as in the virtuoso-passion, the love of painting and the designing arts of every kind so often observed. How fares it with our princely genius, our grandee who assembles all these beauties, and within the bounds of his sumptuous palace incloses all these graces of a thousand kinds? What pains! study! science! Behold the disposition and order of these finer sorts of apartments, gardens, villas! The kind of harmony to the eye from the various shapes and colors agreeably mixed and ranged in lines, intercrossing without confusion, and fortunately coincident. A parterre, cypresses, groves, wildernesses. Statues here and there of virtue, fortitude, temperance. Heroes' busts, philosophers' heads, with suitable mottoes and inscriptions. Solemn representations of things deeply natural — caves, grottoes, rocks, urns and obelisks in retired places and disposed at proper distances and points of sight, with all those symmetries which silently express a reigning order, peace, harmony, and beauty! . . . But what is there answerable to this in the minds of the possessors? What possession or propriety is theirs? What constancy or security of enjoyment? What peace, what harmony within?"

Thus our monologist, or self-discussing author, in his usual strain, when incited to the search of Beauty and Decorum by vulgar admiration and the universal acknowledgment of the species in outward things, and in the meaner and subordinate subjects. By this inferior species, it seems, our strict inspector disdains to be allured; and refusing to be captivated by anything less than the superior, original, and genuine kind, he walks at leisure, without emotion, in deep philosophical reserve, through all these pompous scenes; passes unconcernedly by those court pageants, the illustrious and much envied potentates of the place; overlooks the rich, the great, and even the fair, feeling no other astonishment than what is accidentally raised in him by the view of these impostures and of this specious snare. For here he observes those gentlemen chiefly to be caught and fastest held who are the highest ridiculers of such reflections as his own, and who in the very height of this ridicule prove themselves the impotent contemners of a species which, whether they will or not, they ardently pursue, some in a face and certain regular lines or features, others in a palace and apartments, others in an equipage and dress. "O effeminacy, effeminacy! Who would imagine this could be the vice of such as appear no inconsiderable men? But person is a subject of flattery which reaches beyond the bloom of youth. The experienced senator and aged general can in our days dispense with a toilet and take his outward form into a very extraordinary adjustment and regulation. All embellishments are affected, besides the true. And thus, led by example, whilst we run in search of elegancy and neatness, pursuing beauty, and adding, as we imagine, more luster and value to our own person, we grow, in our real character and true self, deformed and monstrous, servile and abject, stooping to the lowest terms of courtship, and sacrificing all internal proportion, all intrinsic and real beauty and worth for the sake of things which carry scarce a shadow of the kind." Supra, *Moralists*, part iii, §2; *Wit and Humor*, part iv. §2; *Advice*, part iii. §3.

Where then is this beauty or harmony to be found? How is this symmetry to be discovered and applied? Is it any other art than that of philosophy or the study of inward numbers and proportions which can exhibit this in life? If no other, who then can possibly have a taste of this kind, without being beholden to philosophy? Who can admire the outward beauties and not recur instantly to the inward, which are the most real and essential, the most naturally affecting, and of the highest pleasure, as well as profit and advantage?

In so short a compass does that learning and knowledge lie on which manners and life depend. 'Tis we ourselves create and form our taste. If we resolve to have it just, 'tis in our power. We may esteem and resolve, approve and disapprove, as we would wish. For who would not rejoice to be always equal and consonant to himself, and have constantly that opinion of things which is natural and proportionable? But who dares search opinion to the bottom, or call in question his early and prepossessing taste? Who is so just to himself as to recall his fancy from the power of fashion and education to that of reason? Could we, however, be thus courageous, we should soon settle in ourselves such an opinion of good as would secure to us an invariable, agreeable, and just taste in life and manners.

Thus have I endeavored to tread in my author's steps, and prepare the reader for the serious and down right philosophy which even in this[26] last commented treatise, our author keeps still as a mystery and dares not formally profess. His pretense has been to advise authors and polish styles, but his aim has been to correct manners and regular lives. He has affected soliloquy, as pretending only to censure himself, but he has taken occasion to bring others into his company and make bold with personages and characters of no inferior rank. He has given scope enough to raillery and humor, and has entrenched very largely on the province of us miscellanarian writers. But the reader is[27] now about to see him in a new aspect, "a formal and professed philosopher, a system-writer, a dogmatist and expounder." *Habes confitentem reum.*

So to his philosophy I commit him. Through, according as my genius at present disposition will permit, I intend still to accompany him at a distance, keep him in sight, and convoy him, the best I am able, through the dangerous seas he is about to pass.

Inquiry Concerning Virtue or Merit

Part II

Section I

When we reflect on any ordinary frame or constitution either of Art or Nature, and consider how hard it is to give the least account of a particular part without a competent knowledge of the whole, we need not wonder to find ourselves at a loss in

[26]Treatise III. (*Advice to an Author*)
[27]Treatise IV. (*The Inquiry*)

many things relating to the constitution and frame of Nature herself. For to what end in Nature many things, even whole species of creatures, refer, or to what purpose they serve, will be hard for any one justly to determine; but to what end the many proportions and various shapes of parts in many creatures actually serve, we are able, by the help of study and observation, to demonstrate with great exactness.

We know that every creature has a private good and interest of his own, which Nature has compelled him to seek, by all the advantages afforded him within the compass of his make. We know that there is in reality a right and a wrong state of every creature, and that his right one is by nature forwarded and by himself affectionately sought. There being therefore in every creature a certain interest or good, there must be also a certain end to which everything in his constitution must naturally refer. To this end if anything, either in his appetites, passions, or affections, be not conducing but the contrary, we must of necessity own it ill to him. And in this manner he is ill with respect to himself, as he certainly is with respect to others of his kind, when any such appetites or passions make him anyway injurious to them. Now, if by the natural constitution of any rational creature, the same irregularities of appetite which make him ill to others, make him ill also to himself, and if the same regularity of affections which causes him to be good in one sense, causes him to be good also in the other, then is that goodness by which he is thus useful to others a real good and advantage to himself. And thus virtue and interest may be found at last to agree.

Of this we shall consider particularly in the latter part of our inquiry. Our first design is to see if we can clearly determine what that quality is to which we give the name of goodness or virtue.

Should a historian or traveler describe to us a certain creature of a more solitary disposition than ever was yet heard of; one who had neither mate nor fellow of any kind, nothing of his own likeness, towards which he stood well-affected or inclined, nor anything without or beyond himself for which he had the least passion or concern; we might be apt to say perhaps, without much hesitation, "that this was doubtless a very melancholy creature, and that in this unsociable and sullen state he was like to have a very disconsolate kind of life." But if we were assured that, notwithstanding all appearances, the creature enjoyed himself extremely, had a great relish of life, and was in nothing wanting to his own good, we might acknowledge, perhaps, "that the creature was no monster, nor absurdly constituted as to himself." But we should hardly, after all, be induced to say of him "that he was a good creature."

However, should it be urged against us "that such as he was, the creature was still perfect in himself, and therefore to be esteemed good; for what had he to do with others?"—in this sense, indeed, we might be forced to acknowledge "that he was a good creature; if he could be understood to be absolute and complete in himself, without any real relation to anything in the universe besides." For should there be anywhere in nature a system of which this living creature was to be considered as a part, then could he nowise be allowed good; whilst he plainly appeared to be such a part as made rather to the harm than good of that system or whole in which he was included.

If therefore in the structure of this or any other animal, there be anything which points beyond himself, and by which he is plainly discovered to have relation to some other being or nature besides his own, then will this animal undoubtedly be esteemed a part of some other system. For instance, if an animal has the proportions of a male, it shows he has relation to a female. And the respective proportions both of the male and female will be allowed, doubtless, to have a joint relation to another existence and order of things beyond themselves. So that the creatures are both of them to be considered as parts of another system, which is that of a particular race or species of living creatures, who have some one common nature, or are provided for by some one order or constitution of things subsisting together, and cooperating towards their conservation and support.

In the same manner, if a whole species of animals contribute to the existence or well-being of some other, then is that whole species, in general, a part only of some other system.

For instance, to the existence of the spider that of the fly is absolutely necessary. The heedless flight, weak frame, and tender body of this latter insect, fits and determines him as much a prey as the rough make, watchfulness, and cunning of the former fits him for rapine and the ensnaring part. The web and wing are suited to each other. And in the structure of each of these animals there is as apparent and perfect a relation to the other as in our own bodies there is a relation of limbs and organs; or as in the branches or leaves of a tree we see a relation of each to the other, and all, in common, to one root and trunk.

In the same manner are flies also necessary to the existence of other creatures, both fowls and fish. And thus are other species or kinds subservient to one another, as being parts of a certain system, and include in one and the same order of beings.

So that there is a system of all animals: an animal-order or economy, according to which the animal affairs are regulated and disposed.

Now, if the whole system of animals, together with that of vegetables, and all other things in this inferior world, be properly comprehended in one system of a globe or earth, and if, again, this globe or earth itself appears to have a real dependence on something still beyond, as, for example, either on its sun, the galaxy, or its fellow-planets, then is it in reality a part only of some other system. And if it be allowed that there is in like manner a system of all things, and a universal nature, there can be no particular being or system which is not either good or ill in that general one of the universe; for if it be insignificant and of no use, it is a fault or imperfection, and consequently ill in the general system.

Therefore if any being be wholly and really ill, it must be ill with respect to the universal system; and then the system of the universe is ill or imperfect. But if the ill of one private system be the good of others; if it makes still to the good of the general system (as when one creature lives by the destruction of another; one thing is generated from the corruption of another; or one planetary system or vortex may swallow up another), then is the ill of that private system no real ill in itself, any more than the pain of breeding teeth is ill in a system or body which is so constituted that, without this occasion of pain, it would suffer worse by being defective.

So that we cannot say of any being that it is wholly and absolutely ill, unless we can positively show and ascertain that what we call ill is nowhere good besides, in any other system, or with respect to any other order or economy whatsoever.

But were there in the world any entire species of animals destructive to every other, it may be justly called an ill species, as being ill in the animal system. And if in any species of animals (as in men, for example) one man is of a nature pernicious to the rest, he is in this respect justly styled an ill man.

We do not, however, say of any one that he is an ill man because he has the plague-spots upon him, or because he has convulsive fits which make him strike and wound such as approach him. Nor do we say on the other side that he is a good man when, having his hands tied up, he is hindered from doing the mischief he designs; or (which is in a manner the same) when he abstains from executing his ill purpose through a fear of some impending punishment, or through the allurement of some exterior reward.

So that in a sensible creature that which is not done through any affection at all makes neither good nor ill in the nature of that creature, who then only is supposed good when the good or ill of the system to which he has relation is the immediate object of some passion or affection moving him.

Since it is therefore by affection merely that a creature is esteemed good or ill, natural or unnatural, our business will be to examine which are the good and natural, and which the ill and unnatural affections.

Section II

In the first place, then, it may be observed that if there be an affection towards any subject considered as private good, which is not really such, but imaginary, this affection, as being superfluous, and detracting from the force of other requisite and good affections, is in itself vicious and ill, even in respect of the private interest or happiness of the creature.

If there can possibly be supposed in a creature such an affection towards self-good as is actually, in its natural degree, conducing to his private interest, and at the same time inconsistent with the public good, this may indeed be called still a vicious affection; and on this supposition a creature[28] cannot really be good and natural in respect of his society or public, without being ill and unnatural towards himself. But if the affection be then only injurious to the society when it is immoderate, and not so when it is moderate, duly tempered and allayed, then is the immoderate degree of the affection truly vicious, but not the moderate. And thus if there be found in any creature a more than ordinary self-concernment or regard to private good, which is inconsistent with the interest of the species or public, this must in every respect be esteemed an ill and vicious affection. And this is what we commonly call selfishness,[29] and disapprove so much in whatever creature we happen to discover it.

[28] *Infra*, bk. ii. part 1; part ii. §3
[29] *Essay on Wit and Humor*, part iii. §3

On the other side, if the affection towards private or self-good, however selfish it may be esteemed, is in reality not only consistent with public good, but in some measure contributing to it; if it be such, perhaps, as for the good of the species in general every individual ought to share; 'tis so far from being ill or blamable in any sense, that it must be acknowledged absolutely necessary to constitute a creature good. For if the want of such an affection as that towards self-preservation be injurious to the species, a creature is ill and unnatural as well through this defect as through the want of any other natural affection. And this no one would doubt to pronounce, if he saw a man who minded not any precipices which lay in his way, nor made any distinction of food, diet, clothing, or whatever else related to his health and being. The same would be averred of one who had a disposition which rendered him averse to any commerce with womankind, and of consequence unfitted him through illness of temper (and not merely through a defect of constitution) for the propagation of his species or kind.

Thus the affection towards self-good may be a good affection or an ill one. For if this private affection be too strong (as when the excessive love of life unfits a creature for any generous act) then is it undoubtedly vicious, and if vicious, the creature who is moved by it is viciously moved, and can never be otherwise than vicious in some degree when moved by that affection. Therefore if through such an earnest and passionate love of life a creature be accidentally induced to do good (as he might be upon the same terms induced to do ill) he is no more a good creature for this good he executes than a man is the more an honest or good man either for pleading a just cause, or fighting in a good one, for the sake merely of his fee or stipend.

Whatsoever therefore is done which happens to be advantageous to the species through an affection merely towards self-good, does not imply any more goodness in the creature than as the affection itself is good. Let him in any particular act ever so well, if at the bottom it be that selfish affection alone which moves him, he is in himself still vicious. Nor can any creature be considered otherwise when the passion towards self-good though ever so moderate, is his real motive in the doing that to which a natural affection for his kind ought by right to have inclined him.

And indeed whatever exterior helps or succors an ill-disposed creature may find to push him on towards the performance of any one good action, there can no goodness arise in him till his temper be so far changed that in the issue he comes in earnest to be led by some immediate affection, directly and not accidentally, to good and against ill.

For instance, if one of those creatures supposed to be by nature tame, gentle, and favorable to mankind, be, contrary to his natural constitution, fierce and savage, we instantly remark the breach of temper, and own the creature to be unnatural and corrupt. If at any time afterwards the same creature, by good fortune or right management, comes to lose his fierceness, and is made tame, gentle, and treatable like other creatures of his kind, 'tis acknowledged that the creature thus restored becomes good and natural. Suppose now that the creature has indeed a tame and gentle carriage, but that it proceeds only from the fear of his keeper, which if set aside, his predominant passion instantly breaks out; then is his gentleness not his real temper, but his true and genuine nature or natural temper remaining just as it was: the creature is still as ill as ever.

Nothing therefore being properly either goodness or illness in a creature, except that is from natural temper, "A good creature is such a one as by the natural temper or bent of his affections is carried primarily and immediately, and not secondarily and accidentally, to good and against ill;" and an ill creature is just the contrary, viz. "One who is wanting in right affections of force enough to carry him directly towards good, and bear him out against ill; or who is carried by other affections directly to ill and against good."

When in general all the affections or passions are suited to the public good, or good of the species, as above mentioned, then is the natural temper entirely good. If, on the contrary, any requisite passion be wanting, or if there be any one supernumerary or weak, or anywise disservicable or contrary to that main end, then is the natural temper, and consequently the creature himself, in some measure corrupt and ill.

There is no need of mentioning either envy, malice, forwardness or other such hateful passions, to show in what manner they are ill, and constitute an ill creature. But it may be necessary perhaps to remark, that even as to kindness and love of the most natural sort (such as that of any creature for its offspring) if it be immoderate and beyond a certain degree it is undoubtedly vicious. For thus over-great tenderness destroys the effects of love, and excessive pity renders us incapable of giving succor. Hence the excess of motherly love is owned to be a vicious fondness; over-great pity, effeminacy and weakness; over-great concern for self-preservation, meanness and cowardice; too little, rashness; and none at all, or that which is contrary (viz. a passion leading to self-destruction), a mad and desperate depravity.

Section III

But to proceed from what is esteemed mere goodness, and lies within the reach and capacity of all sensible creatures, to that which is called virtue or merit, and is allowed to man only.

In a creature capable of forming general notions of things, not only the outward beings which offer themselves to the sense are the objects of the affection, but the very actions themselves, and the affections of pity, kindness, gratitude, and their contraries, being brought into the mind by reflection, becomes objects. So that, by means of this reflected sense, there arises another kind of affection towards those very affections themselves, which have been already felt, and are now become the subject of a new liking or dislike.

The case is the same in the mental or moral subjects as in the ordinary bodies or common subjects of sense. The shapes, motions, colors, and proportions of these latter being presented to our eye, there necessarily results a beauty or deformity,[30]

[30] *The Moralists*, part iii. §2

according to the different measure, arrangement, and disposition of their several parts. So in behavior and actions, when presented to our understanding, there must be found, of necessity, an apparent difference, according to the regularity or irregularity of the subjects.

The mind, which is spectator or auditor of other minds, cannot be without its eye and ear, so as to discern proportion, distinguish sound, and scan each sentiment or thought which comes before it. It can let nothing escape its censure. It feels the soft and harsh, the agreeable and disagreeable in the affections; and finds a foul and fair, a harmonious and a dissonant, as really and truly here as in any musical numbers or in the outward forms or representations of sensible things. Nor can it withhold its admiration and ecstasy, its aversion and scorn, any more in what relates to one than to the other of these subjects. So that to deny the common and natural sense of a sublime and beautiful in things, will appear an affectation merely, to any one who considers duly of this affair.[31]

Now as in the sensible kind of objects the species or images of bodies, colors, and sounds are perpetually moving before our eyes, and acting on our senses even when we sleep; so in the moral and intellectual kind, the forms and images of things are no less active and incumbent on the mind, at all seasons, and even when the real objects themselves are absent.

In these vagrant characters or pictures of manners, which the mind of necessity figures to itself and carries still about with it, the heart cannot possibly remain neutral; but constantly takes part one way or other. However false or corrupt it be within itself, it finds the difference, as to beauty and comeliness, between one heart and another, one turn of affection, one behavior, one sentiment and another; and accordingly, in all disinterested cases, must approve in some measure of what is natural and honest, and disapprove what is dishonest and corrupt.

Thus the several motions, inclinations, passions, dispositions, and consequent carriage and behaviour of creatures in the various parts of life, being in several views or perspectives represented to the mind, which readily discerns the good and ill towards the species or public, there arises a new trial or exercise of the heart, which must either rightly and soundly affect what is just and right, and disaffect what is contrary, or corruptly affect what is ill and disaffect what is worthy and good.

And in this case alone it is we call any creature worthy or virtuous, when it can have the notion of a public interest, and can attain the speculation or science of what is morally good or ill, admirable or blamable, right or wrong. For though we may vulgarly call an ill horse vicious, yet we never say of a good one, nor of any mere beast, idiot, or changeling, through ever so good-natured, that he is worthy or virtuous.

So that if a creature be generous, kind, constant, compassionate, yet if he cannot reflect on what he himself does, or sees others do, so as to take notice of what is worthy or honest, and make that notice or conception of worth and honesty to be an object of his affection, he has not the character of being virtuous; for thus, and no

[31] *Essay on Wit and Humor,* part ii. §2 (end); *Miscellaneous Reflections,* Misc. ii. ch. 1.

otherwise, he is capable of having a sense of right or wrong, a sentiment or judgment of what is done through just, equal, and good affection, or the contrary.

Whatsoever is done through any unequal affection is iniquitous, wicked, and wrong. If the affection be equal, sound, and good, and the subject of the affection such as may with advantage to society be ever in the same manner prosecuted or affected, this must necessarily constitute what we call equity and right in any action. For wrong is not such action as is barely the cause of harm (since at this rate a dutiful son aiming at an enemy, but by mistake or ill chance happening to kill his father, would do a wrong), but when anything is done through insufficient or unequal affection (as when a son shows no concern for the safety of a father; or, where there is need of succor, prefers an indifferent person to him) this is of the nature of wrong.

Neither can any weakness or imperfection in the senses be the occasion of iniquity or wrong; if the object of the mind itself be not at any time absurdly framed, nor any way improper, but suitable, just, and worthy of the opinion and affection applied to it. For if we will suppose a man who, being sound and entire both in his reason and affection, has nevertheless so depraved a constitution or frame of body that the natural objects are, through his organs of sense, as through ill glasses, falsely conveyed and misrepresented, 'twill be soon observed, in such a person's case, that since his failure is not in his principal or leading part, he cannot in himself be esteemed iniquitous or unjust.

'Tis otherwise in what relates to opinion, belief, or speculation. For as the extravagance of judgment or belief is such that in some countries even monkeys, cats, crocodiles, and other vile or destructive animals have been esteemed holy, and worshipped even as deities; should it appear to any one of the religion or belief of those countries that to save such a creature as a cat, preferably to a parent, was right, and that other men who had not the same religious opinion were to be treated as enemies till converted; this would be certainly wrong and wicked in the believer; and every action, grounded on this belief, would be an iniquitous, wicked, and vicious action.

And thus whatsoever causes a misconception or misapprehension of the worth or value of any object, so as to diminish a due, or raise any undue, irregular or unsocial affection, must necessarily be the occasion of wrong. Thus he who affects or loves a man for the sake of something which is reputed honorable, but which is in reality vicious, is himself vicious and ill. The beginnings of this corruption may be noted in many occurrences; as when an ambitious man, by the fame of his high attempts, a conqueror or a pirate by his boasted enterprises, raises in another person an esteem and admiration of that immoral and inhuman character which deserves abhorrence, 'tis then that the hearer becomes corrupt, when he secretly approves the ill he hears. But on the other side, the man who loves and esteems another, as believing him to have that virtue which he has not, but only counterfeits, is not on this account either vicious or corrupt.

A mistake therefore, in fact, being no cause or sign of ill affection, can be no cause of vice. But a mistake of right being the cause of unequal affection, must of necessity be the cause of vicious action in every intelligent or rational being.

But as there are many occasions where the matter of right may even to the most discerning part of mankind appear difficult, and of doubtful decision, 'tis not a slight mistake of this kind which can destroy the character of a virtuous or worthy man. But when, either through superstition or ill custom, there come to be very gross mistakes in the assignment or application of the affection; when the mistakes are either in their nature so gross, or so complicated and frequent, that a creature cannot well live in a natural state, nor with due affections, compatible with human society and civil life; then is the character of virtue forfeited.

And thus we find how far worth and virtue depend on a knowledge of right and wrong, and on a use of reason, sufficient to secure a right application of the affections; that nothing horrid or unnatural, nothing unexemplary, nothing destructive of that natural affection by which the species or society is upheld, may on any account, or through any principle or notion of honor or religion, be at any time affected or prosecuted as a good and proper object of esteem. For such a principle as this must be wholly vicious; and whatsoever is acted upon it can be no other than vice and immorality. And thus if there be anything which teaches men either treachery, ingratitude, or cruelty, by divine warrant or under color and pretense of any present or future good to mankind; if there be anything which teaches men to persecute their friends through love,[32] or to torment captives of war in sport, or to offer human sacrifice, or to torment, macerate, or mangle themselves in a religious zeal before their God, or to commit any sort of barbarity or brutality as amiable or becoming; be it custom which gives applause, or religion which gives a sanction; this is not, nor ever can be, virtue of any kind, or in any sense, but must remain still horrid depravity, notwithstanding any fashion, law, custom or religion which may be ill and vicious itself, but can never alter the eternal measures and immutable independent nature of worth and virtue.

[32] *Letter Concerning Enthusiasm*, §2; *Misc.* ii. ch. iii.

CHAPTER 4

Joseph Addison*
The Spectator
1712

No. 409, 411-421
The Pleasures of the Imagination

No. 409 Thursday, June 19, 1712

———*Musaeo contingens cuncta lepore.*—Lucr.

Gratian very often recommends the fine taste, as the utmost perfection of an accomplished man. As this word arises very often in conversation, I shall endeavor to give some account of it, and to lay down rules how we may know whether we are possessed of it, and how we may acquire that fine taste of writing which is so much talked of among the polite world.

---

*Joseph Addison (1677-1719) was the son of a Wiltshire clergyman. He was educated at Lichfield, Charterhouse, and Queen's College Oxford. He was an accomplished classical scholar, and remained in Oxford on various fellowships where his Latin poems were highly praised. He was favored by Charles Montague, the Earl of Halifax, who made it possible for him to go Italy and France where he was introduced to French literary circles (1699-1703). The change in government on the death of William III left him without political support for a time, but his personality was such that he remained on good terms with both parties. He was a member of the Whig Kitcat Club, and as Whig influence grew, Addison benefited by a number of political appointments. He developed friendships with Swift and Richard Steele and other leaders of the coffee house set. He was elected to Parliament in 1709 and served in the house until his death. He contributed to *The Tatler* when it was begun by Steele, and collaborated on *The Spectator*. His play *Cato* was a success, though it provoked a controversy with John Dennis who probably envied Addison's position. Addison married the widowed Countess of Warwick in 1716, and was appointed Secretary of State in 1717. He retired in 1718 in ill health. His last year was marred by a quarrel with his old friend Steele to whom he had loaned money.

Most languages make use of this metaphor, to express that faculty of the mind, which distinguishes all the most concealed faults and nicest perfections in writing. We may be sure this metaphor would not have been so general in all tongues, had there not been a very great conformity between that mental taste, which is the subject of this paper, and that sensitive taste which gives us a relish of every different flavor that affects the palate. Accordingly we find, there are as many degrees of refinement in the intellectual faculty, as in the sense, which is marked out by this common denomination.

I knew a person who possessed the one in so great a perfection, that after having tasted ten different kinds of tea, he would distinguish, without seeing the color of it, the particular sort which was offered him; and not only so, but any two sorts of them that were mixed together in an equal proportion; nay, he has carried the experiment so far, as upon tasting the composition of three different sorts, to name the parcels from whence the three several ingredients were taken. A man of a fine taste in writing will discern after the same manner, not only the general beauties and imperfections of an author, but discover the several ways of thinking and expressing himself, which diversify him from all other authors, with the several foreign infusions of thought and language, and the particular authors from whom they were borrowed.

After having thus far explained what is generally meant by a fine taste in writing, and shewn the propriety of the metaphor which is used on this occasion, I think I may define it to be that faculty of the soul, which discerns the beauties of an author with pleasure, and the imperfections with dislike. If a man would know whether he is possessed of this faculty, I would have him read over the celebrated works of antiquity, which have stood the test of so many different ages and countries; or those works among the moderns, which have the sanction of the politer part of our contemporaries. If upon the perusal of such writings he does not find himself delighted in an extraordinary manner, or if, upon reading the admired passages in such authors, he finds a coldness and indifference in his thoughts, he ought to conclude, not (as is too usual among tasteless readers) that the author wants those perfections which have been admired in him, but that he himself wants the faculty of discovering them.

He should, in the second place, be very careful to observe, whether he tastes the distinguishing perfections, or, if I may be allowed to call them so, the specific qualities of the author whom he peruses; whether he is particularly pleased with Livy for his manner of telling a story, with Sallust for his entering into those internal principles of action which arise from the characters and manners of the persons he describes, or with Tacitus for his displaying those outward motives of safety and interest, which give birth to the whole series of transactions which he relates.

He may likewise consider, how differently he is affected by the same thought, which presents it self in a great writer, from what he is when he finds it delivered by a person of an ordinary genius. For there is as much difference in apprehending a thought clothed in Cicero's language, and that of a common author, as in seeing an object by the light of a taper, or by the light of the sun.

It is very difficult to lay down rules for the acquirement of such a taste as that I am here speaking of. The faculty must in some degree be born with us, and it very often happens, that those who have other qualities in perfection are wholly void of this. One of the most eminent mathematicians of the age has assured me, that the greatest pleasure he took in reading Virgil, was in the examining Aeneas his voyage by the map; as I question not but many a modern compiler of history would be delighted with a little more in that divine author, than the bare matters of fact.

But notwithstanding this faculty must in some measure be born with us, there are several methods of cultivating and improving it, and without which it will be very uncertain, and of little use to the person that possesses it. The most natural method for this purpose is to be conversant among the writings of the most polite authors. A man who has any relish for fine writing, either discovers new beauties, or receives stronger impressions from the masterly strokes of a great author every time he peruses him. Besides that he naturally wears himself into the same manner of speaking and thinking.

Conversation with men of a polite genius is another method for improving our natural taste. It is impossible for a man of the greatest parts to consider any thing in its whole extent, and in all its variety of lights. Every man, besides those general observations which are to be made upon an author, forms several reflections that are peculiar to his own manner of thinking; so that conversation will naturally furnish us with hints which we did not attend to, and make us enjoy other men's parts and reflections as well as our own. This is the best reason I can give for the observation which several have made, that men of great genius in the same way of writing, seldom rise up singly, but at certain periods of time appear together, and in a body; as they did at Rome in the reign of *Augustus,* and in *Greece* about the age of Socrates. I cannot think that Cornille, Racine, Moliere, Boileau, la Fontaine, Bruyere, Bossu, or the Daciers, would have written so well as they have done, had they not been friends and contemporaries.

It is likewise necessary for a man who would form to himself a finished taste of good writing, to be well versed in the works of the best critics both ancient and modern. I must confess that I could wish there were authors of this kind, who beside the mechanical rules which a man of very little taste may discourse upon, would enter into the very spirit and soul of fine writing, and shew us the several sources of that pleasure which rises in the mind upon the perusal of a noble work. Thus although in poetry it be absolutely necessary that the unities of time, place and action, with other points of the same nature, should be thoroughly explained and understood; there is still something more essential to the art, something that elevates and astonishes the fancy, and gives a greatness of mind to the reader, which few of the critics besides Longinus have considered.

Our general taste in England is for epigram, turns of wit, and forced conceits, which have no manner of influence, either for the bettering or enlarging the mind of him who reads them, and have been carefully avoided by the greatest writers, both among the ancients and moderns. I have endeavored in several of my speculations to banish this gothic taste, which has taken possession among us. I entertained the town for a week together with an essay upon wit, in which I endeavored to detect several of those false kinds which have been admired in the different ages of the world; and at the same time to shew wherein the nature of true wit consists. I afterwards gave an instance of the great force which lies in a natural simplicity of thought to affect the mind of the reader, from such vulgar pieces as have little else besides this single qualification to recommend them. I have likewise examined the works of the greatest poet which our nation or perhaps any other has produced, and particularized most of those rational and manly beauties which give a value to that divine work. I shall next Saturday enter upon an essay on the pleasures of the imagination, which, though it shall consider that subject at large, will perhaps suggest to the reader what it is that gives a beauty to many passages of the finest writers both in prose and verse. As an undertaking of this nature is entirely new, I question not but it will be received with candor.

No. 411. Saturday, June 21, 1712

Avia pieridum peragro loca, nullius ante
Trita solo; juvat integros accedere fonteis,
Atque haurire—————, —Lucr.

Our sight is the most perfect and most delightful of all our senses. It fills the mind with the largest variety of ideas, converses with its objects at the greatest distance, and continues the longest in action without being tired or satiated with its proper enjoyments. The sense of feeling can indeed give us a notion of extension, shape, and all other ideas that enter at the eye, except colors; but at the same time it is very much straightened and confined in its operations, to the number, bulk, and distance of its particular objects. Our sight seems designed to supply all these defects, and may be considered as a more delicate and diffusive kind of touch, that spreads its self over an infinite multitude of bodies, comprehends the largest figures, and brings into our reach some of the most remote parts of the universe.

It is this sense which furnishes the imagination with its ideas; so that by the pleasures of the imagination or fancy (which I shall use promiscuously) I here mean such as arise from visible objects, either when we have them actually in our view, or when we call up their ideas into our minds by paintings statues, descriptions, or any the like occasion. We cannot indeed have a single image in the fancy that did not make its first entrance through the sight; but we have the power of retaining, altering and compounding those images, which we have once received, into all the varieties of picture and vision that are most agreeable to the imagination; for by this faculty a man in a dungeon is capable of entertaining himself with scenes and landscapes more beautiful than any that can be found in the whole compass of nature.

There are few words in the English language which are employed in a more loose and uncircumscribed sense than those of the fancy and the imagination. I therefore thought it necessary to fix and determine the notion of these two words, as I intend to make use of them in the thread of my following speculations, that the reader may conceive rightly what is the subject which I proceed upon. I must therefore desire him to remember, that by the pleasures of the imagination, I mean only such pleasures as arise originally from sight, and that I divide these pleasures into two kinds: My design being first of all to discourse of those primary pleasure of the imagination, which entirely proceed from such objects as are before our eyes; and in the next place to speak of those secondary pleasures of the imagination which flow from the ideas of visible objects, when the objects are not actually before the eye, but are called up into our memories, or formed into agreeable visions of things that are either absent or fictitious.

The pleasures of the imagination, taken in the full extent, are not so gross as those of sense, nor so refined as those of the understanding. The last are, indeed, more preferable, because they are founded on some new knowledge or improvement in the mind of man; yet it must be confessed, that those of the imagination are as great and as transporting as the other. A beautiful prospect delights the soul, as much as a demonstration; and a description in Homer has charmed more readers than a chapter in Aristotle. Besides, the pleasures of the imagination have this advantage, above those of the understanding, that they are more obvious, and more easy to be acquired. It is but opening the eye, and the scene enters. The colors paint themselves on the fancy, with very little attention of thought or application of mind in the beholder. We are struck, we know not how, with the symmetry of any thing we see, and immediately assent to the beauty of an object, without inquiring into the particular causes and occasions of it.

A man of a polite imagination is let into a great many pleasures, that the vulgar are not capable of receiving. He can converse with a picture, and find an agreeable companion in a statue. He meets with a secret refreshment in a description, and often feels a greater satisfaction in the prospect of fields and meadows, than another does in the possession. It gives him, indeed, a kind of property in every thing he sees, and makes the most rude uncultivated parts of nature administer to his pleasures: So that he looks upon the world, as it were, in another light, and discovers in it a multitude of charms, that conceal themselves from the generality of mankind.

There are, indeed, but very few who know how to be idle and innocent, or have a relish of any pleasures that are not criminal; every diversion they take is at the expense of some one virtue or another, and their very first step out of business is into vice or folly. A man should endeavor, therefore, to make the sphere of his innocent pleasures as wide as possible, that he may retire into them with safety, and find in them such a satisfaction as a wise man would not blush to take. Of this nature are those of the imagination, which do not require such a bent of thought as is necessary to our more serious employments, nor, at the same time, suffer the mind to sink into that negligence and remissness, which are apt to accompany our more sensual delights, but, like a gentle exercise to the faculties, awaken them from sloth and idleness, without putting them upon any labor or difficulty.

We might here add, that the pleasure of the fancy are more conducive to health, than those of the understanding, which are worked out by dint of thinking, and attended with too violent a labor of the brain. Delightful scenes, whether in nature, painting, or poetry, have a kindly influence on the body, as well as the mind, and not only serve to clear and brighten the imagination, but are able to disperse grief and melancholy, and to set the animal spirits in pleasing and agreeable motions. For this reason Sir Francis Bacon, in his essay upon health, has not thought it improper to prescribe to his reader a poem or a prospect, where he particularly dissuades him from knotty and subtle disquisitions, and advises him to pursue studies that fill the mind with splendid and illustrious objects, as histories, fables, and contemplations of nature.

I have in this paper, by way of introduction, settled the notion of those pleasures of the imagination which are the subject of my present undertaking and endeavored, by several considerations, to recommend to my reader the pursuit of those pleasures. I shall, in my next paper, examine the several sources from when these pleasures are derived.

No. 412. Monday, June 23, 1712

——*Divisum sic breve fiet opus.*——Mart.

I shall first consider those pleasures of the imagination, which arise from the actual view and survey of outward objects: And these, I think, all proceed from the sight of what is great, uncommon, or beautiful. There may, indeed, be something so terrible or offensive, that the horror or loathsomeness of an object may over-bear the pleasure which results from its greatness, novelty or beauty; but still there will be such a mixture of delight in the very disgust it gives us, as any of these three qualifications are most conspicuous and prevailing.

By greatness, I do not only mean the bulk of any single object, but the largeness of a whole view, considered as one entire piece. Such are the prospects of an open champion country, a vast uncultivated desert, of huge heaps of mountains, high rocks and precipices, or a wide expanse of waters, where we are not struck with the novelty or beauty of the sight, but with that rude kind of magnificence which appears in many of these stupendous works of nature. Our imagination loves to be filled with an object, or to grasp at any thing that is too big for its capacity. We are flung into a pleasing astonishment at such unbounded views, and feel a delightful stillness and amazement in the soul at the apprehension of them. The mind of man naturally hates every thing that looks like a restraint upon it, and is apt to fancy it self under a sort of confinement, when the sight is pent up in a narrow compass, and shortened on every side by the neighborhood of walls or mountains. On the contrary, a spacious horizon is an image of liberty, where the eye has room to range abroad, to expatiate at large on the immensity of its views, and to lose it self amidst the variety of objects that offer themselves to its observation. Such wide and undetermined prospects are as pleasing to the fancy, as the speculations of eternity or infinitude are to the understanding. But if there be a beauty or uncommonness joined with this grandeur, as in a troubled ocean, a heaven adorned with stars and meteors, or a spacious landscape cut out into rivers, woods, rocks, and meadows, the pleasure still grows upon us, as it arises from more than a single principle.

Every thing that is new or uncommon raises a pleasure in the imagination, because it fills the soul with an agreeable surprise, gratifies its curiosity, and gives it an idea of which it was not before possessed. We are indeed so often conversant with one set of objects, and tired out with so many repeated shows of the same things, that whatever is new or uncommon contributes a little to vary human life, and to divert our minds, for a while, with the strangeness of its appearance: It serves us for a kind of refreshment, and takes off from that satiety we are apt to complain of in our usual and ordinary entertainments. It is this that bestows charms on a monster, and makes even the imperfections of nature please us. It is this that recommends variety, where the mind is every instant called off to something new, and the attention not suffered to dwell too long, and waste it self on any particular object. It is this, likewise, that improves what is great or beautiful, and makes it afford the mind a double entertainment. Groves, fields, and meadows, are at any season of the year pleasant to look upon, but never so much as in the opening of the spring, when they are all new and fresh, with their first gloss upon them, and not yet too much accustomed and familiar to the eye. For this reason there is nothing that more enlivens a prospect than rivers, jetteaus, or falls of water, where the scene is perpetually shifting, and entertaining the sight every moment with something that is new. We are quickly tired with looking upon hills and valleys, where every thing continues fixed and settled in the same place and posture, but find our thoughts a little agitated and relieved at the sight of such objects as are ever in motion, and sliding away from beneath the eye of the beholder.

But there is nothing that makes its way more directly to the soul than beauty, which immediately diffuses a secret satisfaction and complacency through the imagination, and gives a finishing to any thing that is great or uncommon. The very first discovery of it strikes the mind with an inward joy, and spreads a cheerfulness and delight through all its faculties. There is not perhaps any real beauty or deformity more in one piece of matter than another, because we might have been so made, that whatsoever now appears loathsome to us, might have shewn it self agreeable; but we find by experience, that there are several modifications of matter which the mind, without any previous consideration, pronounces at first sight beautiful or deformed. Thus we see that every different species of sensible creatures has its different notions of beauty, and that each of them is most affected with the beauties of its own kind. This is no where more remarkable than in birds of the same shape and proportion, where we often see the male determined in his courtship by the single grain or tincture of a feather, and never discovering any charms but in the color of its species.

Scit thalamo servare fidem, sanctasque veretur
Connubii leges; non illum in pectore candor
Sollicitat niveus; neque pravum accendit amorem
Splendida lanugo, vel honesta in vertice crista,
Purpureusve nitor pennarum; ast agmina late
Foeminea explorat cautus, maculasque requirit
Cognatas, paribusque interlita corpora guttis:

Ni faceret, pictis sylvam circum undique monstris
Confusam aspiceres vulgo, partusque biformes,
Et genus ambiguum, & veneris monumenta nefandae,
Hinc merula in nigro se oblectat nigra marito,
Hinc socium lasciva petit philomela canorum,
Agnoscitque pares sonitus, hinc noctua tetram
Canitiem alarum, & glaucos miratur ocellos.
Nempe sibi semper constat, crescitque quotannis
Lucida progenies, castos confessa parentes;
Dum virides inter saltus lucosque sonoros
Vere novo exultat, plumasque decora juventus
Explicat ad solem, patriisque colorbus ardet.

There is a second kind of beauty that we find in the several products of art and nature, which does not work in the imagination with that warmth and violence as the beauty that appears in our proper species, but is apt however to raise in us a secret delight, and a kind of fondness for the places or objects in which we discover it. This consists either in the gaiety or variety of colors, in the symmetry and proportion of parts, in the arrangement and disposition of bodies, or in a just mixture and concurrence of all together. Among these several kinds of beauty the eye takes most delight in colors. We no where meet with a more glorious or pleasing show in nature, than what appears in the heavens at the rising and setting of the sun, which is wholly made up of those different stains of light that shew themselves in clouds of a different situation. For this reason we find the poets, who are always addressing themselves to the imagination, borrowing more of their epithets from colors than from any other topic.

As the fancy delights in every thing that is great, strange, or beautiful, and is still more pleased the more it finds of these perfections in the same object, so it is capable of receiving a new satisfaction by the assistance of another sense. Thus any continued sound, as the music of birds, or a fall of water, awakens every moment the mind of the beholder, and makes him more attentive to the several beauties of the place that lie before him. Thus if there arises a fragrancy of smells or perfumes, they heighten the pleasures of the imagination, and make even the colors and verdure of the landscape appear more agreeable; for the ideas of both senses recommend each other, and are pleasanter together, than when they enter the mind separately: As the different colors of a picture, when they are well disposed, set off one another, and receive an additional beauty from the advantage of their situation.

No. 413 Tuesday, June 24, 1712

———*Causa latet; vis est notissima*———,—Ovid.

Through in yesterday's paper we considered how every thing that is great, new, or beautiful, is apt to affect the imagination with pleasure, we must own that it is impossible for us to assign the necessary cause of this pleasure, because we know neither the nature of an idea, nor the substance of a human soul, which might help us to discover the conformity or disagreeableness of the one to the other; and therefore, for want of such a light, all that we can do in speculations of this kind, is to reflect on those operations of the soul that are most agreeable, and to range, under their proper heads, what is pleasing or displeasing to the mind, without being able to trace out the several necessary and efficient causes from whence the pleasure or displeasure arises.

Final causes lie more bare and open to our observation, as there are often a greater variety that belong to the same effect; and these, though they are not altogether so satisfactory, are generally more useful than the other, as they give us greater occasion of admiring the goodness and wisdom of the first contriver.

One of the final causes of our delight, in any thing that is great, may be this. The supreme author of our being has so formed the soul of man, that nothing but himself can be its last, adequate, and proper happiness. Because, therefore, a great part of our happiness must arise from the contemplation of his being, that he might give our souls a just relish of such a contemplation, he has made them naturally delight in the apprehension of what is great or unlimited. Our admiration, which is a very pleasing motion of the mind, immediately arises at the consideration of any object that takes up a great deal of room in the fancy, and, by consequence, will improve into the highest pitch of astonishment and devotion when we contemplate his nature, that is neither circumscribed by time nor place, nor to be comprehended by the largest capacity of a created being.

He has annexed a secret pleasure to the idea of any thing that is new or uncommon, that he might encourage us in the pursuit after knowledge, and engage us to search into the wonders of his creation; for every new idea brings such a pleasure along with it, as rewards any pains we have taken in its acquisitions, and consequently serves as a motive to put us upon fresh discoveries.

He has made every thing that is beautiful in our own species pleasant, that all creatures might be tempted to multiply their kind, and fill the world with inhabitants; for 'tis very remarkable that wherever nature is crossed in the production of a monster (the result of any unnatural mixture) the breed is incapable of propagating its likeness, and of founding a new order of creatures; so that unless all animals were allured by the beauty of their own species, generation would be at an end, and the earth unpeopled.

In the last place, he has made every thing that is beautiful in all other objects pleasant, or rather has made so many objects appear beautiful, that he might render the whole creation more gay and delightful. He has given almost every thing about us the power of raising an agreeable idea in the imagination: So that it is impossible for us to behold his works with coldness or indifference, and to survey so many beauties without a secret satisfaction and complacency. Things would make but a poor appearance to the eye, if we saw them only in their proper figures and motions. And what reason can we assign for their exciting in us many of those ideas which are different from any thing that exists in the objects themselves, (for such are light and colors) were it not to add supernumerary ornaments to the universe, and make it more agreeable to the imagination? We are every where entertained with pleasing shows and apparitions, we discover imaginary glories in the heavens, and in the earth, and see some of this visionary beauty poured out upon the whole creation; but what a rough unsightly sketch of nature should we be entertained with, did all her coloring disappear, and the several distinctions of light and shade vanish? In short, our souls are at present delightfully lost and bewildered in a pleasing delusion, and we walk about like the enchanted hero in a romance, who sees beautiful castles, woods and meadows; and at the same time hears the warbling of birds, and the purling of streams; but upon the finishing of some secret spell, the fantastic scene breaks up, and the disconsolate knight finds himself on a barren heath, or in a solitary desert. It is not improbable that something like this may be the state of the soul after its first separation, in respect of the images it will receive from matter; though indeed the ideas of colors are so pleasing and beautiful in the imagination, that it is possible the soul will not be deprived of them, but perhaps find them excited by some other occasional cause, as they are at present by the different impressions of the subtle matter on the organ of sight.

I have here supposed that my reader is acquainted with that great modern discovery, which is at present universally acknowledged by all the inquirers into natural philosophy: Namely, that light and color, as apprehended by the imagination, are only ideas in the mind, and not qualities that have any existence in matter. As this is a truth which has been proved incontestably by many modern philosophers, and is indeed one of the finest speculations in that science, if the English reader would see the notion explained at large, he may find it in the eighth chapter of the second book of Mr. Lock's essay on human understanding.

No. 414 Wednesday, June 25, 1712

———*Alterius sic*
Altera poscit opoem res & conjurat amice.——Hor.

If we consider the works of nature and art, as they are qualified to entertain the imagination, we shall find the last very defective, in comparison of the former; for though they may sometimes appear as beautiful or strange, they can have nothing in them of that vastness and immensity, which afford so great as entertainment to the mind of the beholder. The one may be as polite and delicate as the other, but can never shew herself so august and magnificent in the design. There is something more bold and masterly in the rough careless strokes of nature, than in the nice touches and embellishments of art. The beauties of the most stately garden or palace lie in a narrow compass, the imagination immediately runs them over, and requires something else to gratify her; but, in the wide fields of nature, the sight wanders up and down without confinement, and is fed with an infinite variety of images, without any certain stint or number. For this reason we always find the poet in love with a country life, where nature appears in the greatest perfection, and furnishes out all those scenes that are most apt to delight the imagination.

Scriptoum chorus omnis amat nemus & fugit urbes.—Hor.

Hic secura quies, & nescia fallere vita,
Dives opum variarum, hic latis otia fundis,
Speluncae, vivique lacus, hic frigida Tempe,
Mugitusque boum, mollesque sub arbore somni.—Virg.

But though there are several of these wild scenes, that are more delightful than any artificial shows; yet we find the works of nature still more pleasant, the more they resemble those of art: For in this case our pleasure rises from a double principle; from the agreeableness of the objects to the eye, and from their similitude to other objects: We are pleased as well with comparing their beauties, as with surveying them, and can represent them to our minds, either as copies or originals. Hence it is that we take delight in a prospect which is well laid out, and diversified with fields and meadows, woods and rivers; in those accidental landscapes of trees, clouds and cities, that are sometimes found in the veins of marble; in the curious fret-work of rocks and grottos; and, in a word, in any thing that has such a variety or regularity as may seem the effect of design in what we call the works of chance.

If the products of nature rise in value, according as they more or less resemble those of art, we may be sure that artificial works receive a greater advantage from their resemblance of such as are natural; because here the similitude is not only pleasant, but the pattern more perfect. The prettiest landscape I ever saw, was one drawn on the walls of a dark room, which stood opposite on one side to a navigable river, and on the other to a park. The experiment is very common in optics. Here you might discover the waves and fluctuations of the water in strong and proper colors, with the picture of a ship entering at one end, and sailing by degrees through the whole piece. On another there appeared the green shadows of trees waving to and fro with the wind, and herds of deer among them in miniature, leaping about upon the wall. I must confess, the novelty of such a sight may be one occasion of its pleasantness to the imagination, but certainly the chief reason is its near resemblance to nature, as it does not only, like other pictures, give the color and figure, but the motion of the things it represents.

We have before observed, that there is generally in nature something more grand and august, than what we meet with in the curiosities of art. When, therefore, we see this imitated in any measure, it gives us a nobler and more exalted kind of pleasure than what we receive from the nicer and more accurate productions of art. On this account our English gardens are not so entertaining to the fancy as those in France and Italy, where we see a large extent of ground covered over with an agreeable mixture of garden and forest, which represents every where an artificial rudeness, much more charming than that neatness and elegancy which we meet with in those of our own country. It might, indeed, be of ill consequence to the public, as well as unprofitable to private persons, to alienate so much ground from pasturage, and the plow, in many parts of a country that is so well peopled, and cultivated to a far greater advantage. But why may not a whole estate be thrown into a kind of garden by frequent plantations, that may turn as much to the profit, as the pleasure of the owner? A marsh overgrown with willows, or a mountain shaded with oaks, are not only more beautiful, but more beneficial, than when they lie bare and unadorned. Fields of corn make a pleasant prospect, and if the walks were a little taken care of that lie between them, if the natural embroidery of the meadows were helped and improved by some small additions of art, and the several rows of hedges set off by trees and flowers, that the soil was capable of receiving, a man might make a pretty landscape of his own possessions.

Writers, who have given us an account of China, tell us the inhabitants of that country laugh at the plantations of our Europeans, which are laid out by the rule and line; because, they say, any one may place trees in equal rows and uniform figures. They choose rather to shew a genius in works of this nature, and therefore always conceal the art by which they direct themselves. They have a word it seems in their language, by which they express the particular beauty of a plantation that thus strikes the imagination at first sight, without discovering what it is that has so agreeable an effect. Our British gardeners, on the contrary, instead of humoring nature, love to deviate from it as much as possible. Our trees rise in cones, globes, and pyramids. We see the marks of the scissors upon every plant and bush. I do not know whether I am singular in my opinion, but, for my own part, I would rather look upon a tree in all its luxuriancy and diffusion of boughs and branches, than when it is thus cut and trimmed into a mathematical figure; and cannot but fancy that an orchard in flower looks infinitely more delightful than all the little labyrinths of the most finished parterre. But as four great modellers of gardens have their magazines of plants to dispose of, it is very natural for them to tear up all the beautiful plantations of fruit trees, and contrive a plan that may most turn to their own profit, in taking off their evergreens, and the like moveable plants, with which their shops are plentifully stocked.

No. 415 Thursday, June 26, 1712

Adde tot egregias urbes, operumque laborem.—Virg.

Having already shewn how the fancy is affected by the works of nature, and afterwards considered in general both the works of nature and of art, how they mutually assist and complete each other, in forming such scenes and prospects as are most apt to delight the mind of the beholder, I shall in this paper throw together some reflections on that particular art, which has a more immediate tendency, than any other, to produce those primary pleasures of the imagination, which have hitherto been the subject of this discourse. The art I mean is that of architecture, which I shall consider only with regard to the light in which the forgoing speculations have placed it, without entering into those rules and maxims which the great masters of architecture have laid down, and explained at large in numberless treatises upon that subject.

Greatness, in the works of architecture, may be considered as relating to the bulk and body of the structure, or to the manner in which it is built. As for the first, we find the ancients, especially among the eastern nations of the world, infinitely superior to the moderns.

Not to mention the Tower of Babel, of which an old author says, there were the foundations to be seen in his time, which looked like a spacious mountain; what could be more noble than the walls of Babylon, its hanging gardens, and its temple to Jupiter Belus, that rose a mile high by eight several stories, each story a furlong in height, and on the top of which was the Babylonian observatory? I might here, likewise, take notice of the huge rock that was cut into the figure of Semiramis, with the smaller rocks that lay by it in the shape of tributary kings; the prodigious basin, or artificial lake, which took in the whole Euphrates, 'till such time as a new canal was formed for its reception, with the several trenches through which that river was conveyed. I know there are persons who look upon some of these wonders of art as fabulous, but I cannot find any grounds for such a suspicion, unless it be that we have no such works among us at present. There were indeed many greater advantages for building in those times, and in that part of the world, than have been met with ever since. The earth was extremely fruitful. Men lived generally on pasturage, which requires a much smaller number of hands than agriculture: There were few trades to employ the busy part of mankind, and fewer arts and sciences to give work to men of speculative tempers; and what is more than all the rest, the prince was absolute; so that when he went to war, he put himself at the head of a whole people: As we find Semiramis leading her three millions to the field, and yet overpowered by the number of her enemies. 'Tis no wonder, therefore, when she was at peace, and turned her thoughts on building, that she could accomplish so great works, with such a prodigious multitude of laborers: Besides that, in her climate, there was small interruption of frosts and winters, which make the northern workmen lie half the year idle. I might mention too, among the benefits of the climate, what historians say of the earth, that it sweated out a bitumen or natural kind of mortar, which is doubtless the same with that mentioned in holy writ, as contributing to the structure of Babel. "Slime they used instead of mortar."

In Egypt we still see their pyramids, which answer to the descriptions that have been made of them; and I question not but a traveler might find out some remains of the labyrinth that covered a whole province, and had a hundred temples disposed among its several quarters and divisions.

The wall of China is one of these eastern pieces of magnificence, which makes a figure even in the map of the world, although an account of it would have been thought fabulous, were not the wall it self still extant.

We are obliged to devotion for the noblest buildings that have adorned the several countries of the world. It is this which has set men at work on temples and public places of worship, not only that they might, by the magnificence of the building, invite the deity to reside within it, but that such stupendous works might at the same time, open the mind to vast conceptions, and fit it to converse with the divinity of the place. For every thing that is majestic imprints an awfulness and reverence on the mind of the beholder, and strikes in with the natural greatness of the soul.

In the second place we are to consider greatness of manner in architecture, which has such force upon the imagination, that a small building, where it appears, shall give the mind nobler ideas than one of twenty times the bulk, where the manner is ordinary or little. Thus, perhaps, a man would have been more astonished with the majestic air that appeared in one of Lysippus's statues of Alexander, though no bigger than the life, than he might have been with Mount Athos, had it been cut into the figure of the hero, according to the proposal of Phidias, with a river in one hand, and a city in the other.

Let any one reflect on the disposition of mind he finds in himself, at his first entrance into the pantheon at Rome, and how his imagination is filled with something great and amazing; and, at the same time, consider how little, in proportion, he is affected with the inside of a gothic cathedral, though it be five times larger than the other; which can arise from nothing else but the greatness of the manner in the one, and the meanness in the other.

I have seen an observation upon this subject in a French author, which very much pleased me. It is in Monsieur Freart's parallel of the ancient and modern architecture. I shall give it the reader with the same terms of art which he has made use of. "I am observing" (says he) "a thing, which, in my opinion, is very curious, whence it proceeds, that in the same quantity of superficies, the one manner seems great and magnificent, and the other poor and trifling; the reason is fine and uncommon. I say then, that to introduce into architecture this grandeur of manner, we ought so to proceed, that the division of the principal members of the order may consist but of few parts, that they be all great and of a bold and ample *relievo*, and swelling; and that the eye beholding nothing little and mean, the imagination may be more vigorously touched and affected with the work that stands before it. For example: In a cornice, if the *gola* or *cymatium* of the *corona*, the coping, the medallions or *dentelli*, make a noble show by their graceful projections, if we see none of that ordinary confusion which is the result of those little cavities, quarter rounds of the *astragal*, and I know not how many other intermingled particulars, which produce no effect in great and massy works, and which very unprofitably take up place to the prejudice of the principal member, it is most certain that this manner will appear solemn and great; as on the contrary, that will have but a poor and mean effect, where there is a redundancy of those smaller ornaments, which divide and scatter the angels of the sight into such a multitude of rays, so pressed together that the whole will appear but a confusion."

Among all the figures in architecture, there are none that have a greater air than the concave and the convex, and we find in all the ancient and modern architecture, as well in the remote parts of china, as in countries nearer home, that round pillars and vaulted roofs make a great part of those buildings which are designed for pomp and magnificence. The reason I take to be, because in these figures we generally see more of the body, than in those of other kinds. There are, indeed, figures of bodies, where the eye may take in two thirds of the surface; but as in such bodies the sight must split upon several angles, it does not take in one uniform idea, but several ideas of the same kind. Look upon the outside of a dome, your eye half surrounds it; look up into the inside, and at one glance you have all the prospect of it; the entire concavity falls into your eye at once, the sight being as the center that collects and gathers into it the lines of the whole circumference. In a square pillar, the sight often takes in but a fourth part of the surface, and, in a square concave, must move up and down to the different sides, before it is master of all the inward surface. For this reason, the fancy is infinitely more struck with the view of the open air, and skies, that passes through an arch, than what comes through a square, or any other figure. The figure of the rainbow does not contribute less to its magnificence, than the colors to its beauty, as it is very poetically described by the son of Sirach: "Look upon the rainbow, and praise him that made it, very beautiful it is in its brightness, it encompasses the heavens with a glorious circle, and the hands of the most high have bent it."

Having thus spoken of that greatness which affects the mind in architecture, I might next shew the pleasure that rises in the imagination from what appears new and beautiful in this art; but as every beholder has naturally a greater taste of these two perfections in every building which offers it self to his view, than of that which I have hitherto considered, I shall not trouble my reader with any reflections upon it. It is sufficient for my present purpose, to observe, that there is nothing in this whole art which pleases the imagination, but as it is great, uncommon, or beautiful.

No. 416 Friday, June 27, 1712

Quatenus hoc simile est oculis, quod mente videmus.——Lucr.

I at first divided the pleasure of the imagination, into such as arise from objects that are actually before our eyes, or that once entered in at our eyes, and are afterwards called up into the mind either barely by its own operations, or on occasion of something without us, as statues, or descriptions. We have already considered the first division, and shall therefore enter on the other, which for distinction sake, I have called the secondary pleasures of the imagination. When I say the ideas we receive from statues, descriptions, or such like occasions, are the same that were once actually in our view, it must not be understood that we had once seen the very place, action, or person which are carved or described. It is sufficient, that we have seen places, persons, or actions in general, which bear a resemblance, or at least some remote analogy with what we find represented. Since it is in the power of the imagination, when it is once stocked with particular ideas, to enlarge, compound, and vary them at her own pleasure.

Among the different kinds of representation, statuary is the most natural, and shews us something likest the object that is represented. To make use of a common instance, let one who is born blind take an image in his hands, and trace out with his fingers the different furrows and impressions of the chisel, and he will easily conceive how the shape of a man, or beast, may be represented by it; but should he draw his hand over a picture, where all is smooth and uniform, he would never be able to imagine how the several prominencies and depressions of a human body could be shewn on a plain piece of canvas, that has in it no unevenness or irregularity. Description runs yet further from the things it represents than painting; for a picture bears a real resemblance to its original, which letters and syllables are wholly void of. Colors speak all languages, but words are understood only by such a people or nation. For this reason, though men's necessities quickly put them on finding out speech, writing is probably of a later invention than painting; particularly we are told, that in America when the Spaniards first arrived there, expresses were sent to the emperor of Mexico in paint, and the news of his country delineated by the strokes of a pencil, which was a more natural way than that of writing, though at the same time much more imperfect, because it is impossible to draw the little connections of speech, or to give the picture of a conjunction or an adverb. It would be yet more strange, to represent visible objects by sounds that have no ideas annexed to them, and to make something like description in music. Yet it is certain, there may be confused, imperfect notions of this nature raised in the imagination by an artificial composition of notes; and we find that great masters in the art are able, sometimes to set their hearers in the heat and hurry of a battle, to overcast their minds with melancholy scenes and apprehensions of deaths and funerals, or to lull them into pleasing dreams of groves and elisiums.

In all these instances, this secondary pleasure of the imagination proceeds from that action of the mind, which compares the ideas arising from the original objects, with the ideas we receive from the statue, picture, description, or sound that represents them. It is impossible for us to give the necessary reason, why this operation of the mind is attended with so much pleasure, as I have before observed on the same occasion; but we find a great variety of entertainments derived from this single principle: For it is this that not only gives us a relish of statuary, painting and description, but makes us delight in all the actions and arts of mimicry. It is this that makes the several kinds of wit pleasant, which consists, as I have formerly shewn, in the affinity of ideas: And we may add, it is this also that raises the little satisfaction we sometimes find in the different sorts of false wit; whether it consist in the affinity of letters, as an anagram, acrostic; or of syllables, as in doggerel rhymes, echoes; or of words, as in puns, quibbles; or of a whole sentence or poem, to wings, and altars. The final cause, probably of annexing pleasure to this operation of the mind, was to quicken and encourage us in our searches after truth, since the distinguishing one thing from another, and the right discerning betwixt our ideas, depends wholly upon our comparing them together, and observing the congruity or disagreement that appears among the several works of nature.

But I shall here confine my self to those pleasures of the imagination, which proceed from ideas raised by words, because most of the observations that agree with descriptions, are equally applicable to painting and statuary.

Words, when well chosen, have so great a force in them, that a description often gives us more lively ideas than the sight of things themselves. The reader finds a scene drawn in stronger colors, and painted more to the life in his imagination, by the help of words, than by an actual survey of the scene which they describe. In this case the poet seems to get the better of nature; he takes, indeed, the landscape after her, but gives it more vigorous touches, heightens its beauty, and so enlivens the whole piece, that the images which flow from the objects themselves appear weak and faint, in comparison of those that come from the expressions. The reason, probably, may be, because in the survey of any object, we have only so much of it painted on the imagination, as comes in at the eye; but in its description, the poet gives us as free a view of it as he pleases, and discovers to us several parts, that either we did not attend to, or that lay out of our sight when we first beheld it. As we look on any object, our idea of it is, perhaps made up of two or three simple ideas; but when the poet represents it, he may either give us a more complex idea of it, or only raise in us such ideas as are most apt to affect the imagination.

It may be here worth our while to examine, how it comes to pass that several readers, who are all acquainted with the same language, and know the meaning of the words they read, should nevertheless have a different relish of the same descriptions. We find one transported with a passage, which another runs over with coldness and indifference, or finding the representation extremely natural, where another can perceive nothing of likeness and conformity. This different taste must proceed either from the perfection of imagination in one more than in another, or from the different ideas that several readers affix to the same words. For, to have a true relish, and form a right judgment of a description, a man should be born with a good imagination, and must have well weighed the force and energy that lie in the several words of a language, so as to be able to distinguish which are most significant and expressive of their proper ideas, and what additional strength and beauty they are capable of receiving from conjunction with others. The fancy must be warm, to retain the print of those images it has received from outward objects; and the judgment discerning, to know what expressions are most proper to clothe and adorn them to the best advantage. A man who is deficient in either of these respects, though he may receive the general notion of a description, can never see distinctly all its particular beauties: As a person with a weak sight may have the confused prospect of a place that lies before him, without entering into its several parts, or discerning the variety of its colors in their full glory and perfection.

No. 417 — Saturday, June 28, 1712

Quem tu, Melpomene, semel
Nascentem placido lumine videris,
Illum non labor Isthmius
Clarabit pugilem non equus impiger, etc.

Sed quae Tibur aquae fertile perfluunt,
Et spissae nemorum comae
Fingent Acolio carmine nobilem.—Hor.

We may observe, that any single circumstance of what we have formerly seen often raises up a whole scene of imagery, and awakens numberless ideas that before slept in the imagination; such a particular smell or color is able to fill the mind, on a sudden, with the picture of the fields or gardens where we first met with it, and to bring up into view all the variety of images that once attended it. Our imagination takes the hint, and leads us unexpectedly into cities or theaters, plains or meadows. We may further observe, when the fancy thus reflects on the scenes that have past in it formerly, those, which were at first pleasant to behold, appear more so upon reflection, and that the memory heightens the delightfulness of the original. A Cartesian would account for both these instances in the following manner.

The set of ideas which we received from such a prospect or garden, having entered the mind at the same time, have a set of traces belonging to them in the brain, bordering very near upon one another; when, therefore, any one of these ideas arise in the imagination, and consequently dispatches a flow of animal spirits to its proper trace, these spirits, in the violence of their motion, run not only into the trace, to which they were more particularly directed, but into several of those that lie about it. By this means they awaken other ideas of the same set, which immediately determine a new dispatch of spirits, but in the same manner open other neighboring traces, till at last the whole set of them is blown up, and the whole prospect or garden flourishes in the imagination. But because the pleasure we received from these places far surmounted, and overcame the little disagreeableness we found in them, for this reason there was at first a wider passage worn in the pleasure traces, and, on the contrary, so narrow a one in those which belonged to the disagreeable ideas, that they were quickly stopped up, and rendered incapable of receiving any animal spirits, and consequently of exciting any unpleasant ideas in the memory.

It would be in vain to inquire, whether the power of imagining things strongly proceeds from any greater perfection in the soul, or from any nicer texture in the brain of one man than of another. But this is certain, that a noble writer should be born with this faculty in its full strength and vigour, so as to be able to receive lively ideas from outward objects, to retain them long, and to range them together, upon occasion, in such figures and representations as are most likely to hit the fancy of the reader. A poet should take as much pains in forming his imagination, as a philosopher in cultivating his understanding. He must gain a due relish of the works of nature, and be thoroughly conversant in the various scenery of a country life.

When he is stored with country images, if he would go beyond pastoral, and the lower kinds of poetry, he ought to acquaint himself with the pomp and magnificence of courts. He should be very well versed in every thing that is noble and stately in the productions of art, whether it appear in painting or statuary, in the great works of architecture which are in their present glory, or in the ruins of those which flourished in former ages.

Such advantages as these help to open a man's thoughts, and to enlarge his imagination, and will therefore have their influence on all kinds of writing, if the author knows how to make right use of them. And among those of the learned languages who excel in this talent, the most perfect in their several kinds, are perhaps Homer, Virgil, and Ovid. The first strikes the imagination wonderfully with what is great, the second with what is beautiful, and the last with what is strange. Reading the *Iliad* is like traveling through a country uninhabited, where the fancy is entertained with a thousand savage prospects of vast deserts, wide uncultivated marshes, huge forests, mishapen rocks and precipices. On the contrary, the *Aeneid* is like a well ordered garden, where it is impossible to find out any part unadorned, or to cast our eyes upon a single spot, that does not produce some beautiful plant or flower. But when we are in the *Metamorphosis,* we are walking on enchanted ground, and see nothing but scenes of magic lying round us.

Homer is in his province, when he is describing a battle or a multitude, a hero or a god. Virgil is never better pleased, than when he is in his elysium, or copying out an entertaining picture. Homer's epithets generally mark out what is great, Virgil's what is agreeable. Nothing can be more magnificent than the figure Jupiter makes in the first *Iliad,* nor more charming than that of Venus in the first *Aeneid.*

> Ἧ καὶ κυανέῃσιν ἐπ' ὀφρύσι νεῦσε Κρονίων
> Ἀμβρόσιαι δ' ἄρα χαῖται ἐπερρώσαντο ἄνακτος
> Κρατὸς ἀπ' ἀθανάτοιο μέγαν δ' ἐλέλιξεν Ὄλυμπον

> *Dixit, & avertens rosea cervice refulsit;*
> *Ambrosiaeque comae divinum vertice odorem*
> *Spiravere: pedes vestis defluxit ad imos;*
> *Et vera incessu patuit dea*

Homer's persons are most of them god-like and terrible. Virgil has scarce admitted any into his poem, who are not beautiful, and has taken particular care to make his hero so.

> —— *lumenque juventae*
> *Purpureum, & laetos oculis afflavit honores.*

In a word, Homer fills his readers with sublime ideas, and, I believe, has raised the imagination of all the good poets that have come after him. I shall only instance Horace, who immediately takes fire at the first hint of any passage in the *Iliad* or *Odyssey* and always rises above himself, when he has Homer in his view. Virgil has drawn together, into his *Aeneid,* all the pleasing scenes his subject is capable of admitting, and in his *Georgics* has given us a collection of the most delightful landscapes that can be made out of fields and woods, herds of cattle, and swarms of bees.

Ovid, in his *Metamorphosis,* has shewn us how the imagination may be affected by what is strange. He describes a miracle in every story, and always gives us the sight of some new creature at the end of it. His art consists chiefly in well-timing his description, before the first shape is quite worn off, and the new one perfectly finished; so that he every where entertains us with something we never saw before, and shews monster after monster, to the end of the *Metamorphosis.*

If I were to name a poet that is a perfect master in all these arts of working on the imagination, I think Milton may pass for one. And if his *Paradise Lost* falls short of the *Aeneid* or *Iliad* in this respect, it proceeds rather from the fault of the language in which it is written, than from any defect of genius in the author. So divine a poem in English, is like a stately palace, built of brick, where one may see architecture in as great a perfection as in one of marble, though the materials are of a coarser nature. But to consider it only as it regards our present subject. What can be conceived greater than the battle of angels, the majesty of messiah, the stature and behavior of Satan and his peers? What more beautiful than pandemonium, paradise, heaven, angels, Adam and Eve? What more strange, than the creation of the world, the several metamorphoses of the fallen angels, and the surprising adventures their leader meets with in his search after paradise? No other subject could have furnished a poet with scenes so proper to strike the imagination, as no other poet could have painted those scenes in more strong and lively colors.

No. 418 Monday, June 30, 1712

——*Ferat & rubus asper amomum.*—Virg.

The pleasures of these secondary views of the imagination, are of a wider and more universal nature than those it has when joined with sight; for not only what is great, strange or beautiful, but any thing that is disagreeable when looked upon, pleases us in an apt description. Here, therefore, we must inquire after a new principle of pleasure, which is nothing else but the action of the mind, which compares the ideas that arise from words, with the ideas that arise from the objects themselves; and why this operation of the mind is attended with so much pleasure, we have before considered. For this reason therefore, the description of a dunghill is pleasing to the imagination, if the image be represented to our minds by suitable expressions; though, perhaps, this may be more properly called the pleasure of the understanding than of the fancy, because we are not so much delighted with the image that is contained in the description, as with the aptness of the description to excite the image.

But if the description of what is little, common or deformed, be acceptable to the imagination, the description of what is great, surprising or beautiful, is much more so; because here we are not only delighted with comparing the representation with the original, but are highly pleased with the original it self. Most readers, I believe, are more charmed with Milton's description of paradise, than of hell; they are both, perhaps, equally perfect in their kind, but in the one the brimstone and sulfur are not so refreshing to the imagination, as the beds of flowers and the wilderness of sweets in the other.

There is yet another circumstance which recommends a description more than all the rest, and that is, if it represents to us such objects as are apt to raise a secret ferment in the mind of the reader, and to work, with violence, upon his passions. For, in this case, we are at once warmed and enlightened, so that the pleasure becomes more universal, and is several ways qualified to entertain us. Thus, in painting, it is pleasant to look on the picture of any face, where the resemblance is hit, but the pleasure increases, if it be the picture of a face that is beautiful, and is still greater, if the beauty be softened with an air of melancholy or sorrow. The two leading passions which the more serious parts of poetry endeavor to stir up in us, are terror and pity. And here, by the way, one would wonder how it comes to pass, that such passions as are very unpleasant at all other times, are very agreeable when excited by proper descriptions. It is not strange, that we should take delight in such passages as we apt to produce hope, joy, admiration, love, or the like emotions in us, because they never rise in the mind without an inward pleasure which attends them. But how comes it to pass, that we should take delight in being terrified or dejected by a description, when we find so much uneasiness in the fear or grief which we receive from any other occasion?

If we consider, therefore, the nature of this pleasure, we shall find that it does not arise so properly from the description of what is terrible, as from the reflection we make on our selves at the time of reading it. When we look on such hideous objects, we are not a little pleased to think we are in no danger of them. We consider them at the same time, as dreadful and harmless; so that the more frightful appearance they make, the greater is the pleasure we receive from the sense of our own safety. In short, we look upon the terrors of a description, with the same curiosity and satisfaction that we survey a dead monster.

> ———— *Informe cadaver*
> *Protrahitur: nequeunt expleri corda tuendo*
> *Terribliles oculos, voltum, villosaque setis*
> *Pectora semiferi atque extinctos faucibus ignes.*—Virg.

It is for the same reason that we are delighted with the reflecting upon dangers that are past, or in looking on a precipice at a distance, which would fill us with a different kind of horror, if we saw it hanging over our heads.

In the like manner, when we read of torments, wounds, deaths, and the like dismal accidents, our pleasure does not flow so properly from the grief which such melancholy descriptions give us, as from the secret comparison which we make between our selves and the person who suffers. Such representations teach us to set a just value upon our own condition, and make us prize our good fortune, which exempts us from the like calamities. This is, however, such a kind of pleasure as we are not capable of receiving, when we see a person actually lying under the tortures that we meet with in a description; because, in this case, the object presses too close upon our senses, and bears so hard upon us, that it does not give us time or leisure to reflect on our selves. Our thoughts are so intent upon the miseries of the sufferer, that we cannot turn them upon our own happiness. Whereas, on the contrary, we consider the misfortunes we read in history or poetry, either as past, or as fictitious, so that the reflection upon our selves rises in us insensibly, and over-bears the sorrow we conceive for the sufferings of the afflicted.

But because the mind of man requires something more perfect in matter, than what it finds there, and can never meet with any sight in nature which sufficiently answers its highest ideas of pleasantness; or, in other words, because the imagination can fancy to it self things more great, strange, or beautiful, than the eye ever saw, and is still sensible of some defect in what it has seen; on this account it is the part of a poet to humor the imagination in its own notions, by mending and perfecting nature where he describes a reality, and by adding greater beauties than are put together in nature, where he describes a fiction.

He is not obliged to attend her in the slow advances which she makes from one season to another, or to observe her conduct in the successive production of plants and flowers. He may draw into his description all the beauties of the spring and autumn, and make the whole year contribute something to render it the more agreeable. His rose-trees, wood-bines and jessamines may flower together, and his beds be covered at the same time with lilies, violets, and amaranths. His soil is not restrained to any particular set of plants, but is proper either for oaks or myrtles, and adapts it self to the products of every climate. Oranges may grow wild in it; myrrh may be met with in every hedge, and if he thinks it proper to have a grove of spices, he can quickly command sun enough to raise it. If all this will not furnish out an agreeable scene, he can make several new species of flowers, with richer scents and higher colors than any that grow in the gardens of nature. His consorts of birds may be as full and harmonious, and his woods as thick and gloomy as he pleases. He is at no more expense in a long vista, than a short one, and can as easily throw his cascades from a precipice of half a mile high, as from one of twenty yards. He has his choice of the winds, and can turn the course of his rivers in all the variety of meanders, that are most delightful to the reader's imagination. In a word, he has the modeling of nature in his own hands, and may give her what charms he pleases, provided he does not reform her too much, and run into absurdities, by endeavoring to excel.

No. 419 Tuesday, July 1, 1712

——*Mentis gratissimus error.*—Hor.

There is a kind of writing, wherein the poet quite loses sight of nature, and entertains his reader's imagination with the characters and actions of such persons as have many of them no existence, but what he bestows on them. Such are fairies, witches, magicians, demons, and departed spirits. This Mr. Dryden calls the *fairy way of writing*, which is, indeed, more difficult than any other that depends on the poet's fancy, because he has no pattern to follow in it, and must work altogether out of his own invention.

There is a very odd turn of thought required for this sort of writing, and it is impossible for a poet to succeed in it, who has not a particular cast of fancy, and an imagination naturally fruitful and superstitious. Besides this, he ought to be very well versed in legends and fables, antiquated romances, and the traditions of nurses and old women, that he may fall in with our natural prejudices, and humor those notions which we have imbibed in our infancy. For, otherwise, he will be apt to make his fairies talk like people of his own species, and not like other sets of beings, who converse with different objects, and think in a different manner from that of mankind;

Sylvis deducti caveant, me judice, Fauni
Ne velut innati triviis, ac pene forenses,
Aut nimium teneris juventur versibus.—Hor.

I do not say with Mr. Bays in the *Rehearsal*, that spirits must not be confined to speak sense, but it is certain their sense ought to be a little discolored, that it may seem particular, and proper to the person and condition of the speaker.

These descriptions raise a pleasing kind of horror in the mind of the reader, and amuse his imagination with the strangeness and novelty of the persons who are represented in them. They bring up into our memory the stories we have heard in our childhood, and favor those secret terrors and apprehensions to which the mind of man is naturally subject. We are pleased with surveying the different habits and behaviors of foreign countries; how much more must we be delighted and surprised when we are led, as it were, into a new creation, and see the persons and manners of another species? Men of cold fancies, and philosophical dispositions, object to this kind of poetry, that it has not probability enough to affect the imagination. But to this it may be answered, that we are sure, in general, there are many intellectual beings in the world besides our selves, and several species of spirits, who are subject to different laws and economies from those of mankind; when we see, therefore, any of these represented naturally, we cannot look upon the representation as altogether impossible; nay, many are prepossed with such false opinions, as dispose them to believe these particular delusions; at least, we have all heard so many pleasing relations in favor of them, that we do not care for seeing through the falsehood, and willingly give our selves up to so agreeable an imposture.

The ancients have not much of this poetry among them, for, indeed, almost the whole substance of it owes its original to the darkness and superstition of later ages, when pious frauds were made use of to amuse mankind, and frighten them into a sense of their duty. Our forefathers looked upon nature with more reverence and horror, before the world was enlightened by learning and philosophy, and loved to astonish themselves with the apprehensions of witchcraft, prodigies, charms and enchantments. There was not a village in England that had not a ghost in it, the church-yards were all haunted, every large common had a circle of fairies belonging to it, and there was scarce a shepherd to be met with who had not seen a spirit.

Among all the poets of this kind our English are much the best, by what I have yet seen, whether it be that we abound with more stories of this nature, or that the genius of our country is fitter for this sort of poetry. For the English are naturally fanciful, and very often disposed by that gloominess and melancholy of temper, which is so frequent in our nation, to many wild notions and visions, to which others are not so liable.

Among the English, Shakespeare has incomparably excelled all others. That noble extravagance of fancy, which he had in so great perfection, thoroughly qualified him to touch this weak superstitious part of his reader's imagination; and made him capable of succeeding, where he had nothing to support him besides the strength of his own genius. There is something so wild and yet so solemn in the speeches of his ghosts, fairies, witches and the like imaginary persons, that we cannot forbear thinking them natural, though we have no rule by which to judge of them, and must confess, if there are such beings in the world, it looks highly probable they should talk and act as he has represented them.

There is another sort of imaginary beings, that we sometimes meet with among the poets, when the author represents any passion, appetite, virtue or vice, under a visible shape, and makes it a person or an actor in his poem. Of this nature are the descriptions of hunger and envy in Ovid, of fame in Virgil, and of sin and death in Milton. We find a whole creation of the like shadowy persons in Spencer, who had an admirable talent in representations of this kind. I have discoursed of these emblematical persons in former papers, and shall therefore only mention them in this place. Thus we see how many ways poetry addresses it self to the imagination as it has not only the whole circle of nature for its province, but makes new worlds of its own, shews us persons who are not to be found in being, and represents even the faculties of the soul, with her several virtues and vices, in a sensible shape and character.

I shall, in my two following papers, consider in general, how other kinds of writing are qualified to please the imagination; with which I intend to conclude this essay.

No. 420 Wednesday, July 2, 1712

——*Quocunque volent animum auditoris agunto.*——Hor.

As the writers in poetry and fiction borrow their several materials from outward objects, and join them together at their own pleasure, there are others who are obliged to follow nature more closely, and to take entire scenes out of her. Such are historians, natural philosophers, travelers, geographers, and, in a word, all who describe visible objects of a real existence.

It is the most agreeable talent of an historian to be able to draw up his armies and fight his battles in proper expressions, to set before our eyes the divisions, cabals and jealousies of great men, and to lead us step by step into the several actions and events of his history. We love to see the subject unfolding it self by just degrees, and breaking upon us insensibly, that so we may be kept in a pleasing suspense, and have time given us to raise our expectations, and to side with one of the parties concerned in the relation. I confess this shews more the art than the veracity of the historian, but I am only to speak of him as he is qualified to please the imagination. And in this respect Livy has, perhaps, excelled all who went before him, or have written since his time. He describes every thing in so lively a manner, that his whole history is an admirable picture, and touches on such proper circumstances in every story, that this reader becomes a kind of spectator, and feels in himself all the variety of passions which are correspondent to the several parts of the relation.

But among this set of writers, there are none who more gratify and enlarge the imagination, than the authors of the new philosophy, whether we consider their theories of the earth or heavens, the discoveries they have made by glasses, or any other of their contemplations on nature. We are not a little pleased to find every green leaf swarm with millions of animals, that at their largest growth are not visible to the naked eye. There is something very engaging to the fancy, as well as to our reason, in the treatises of metals, minerals, plants, and meteors. But when we survey the whole earth at once, and the several planets that lie within its neighborhood, we are filled with a pleasing astonishment, to see so many worlds hanging one above another, and sliding round their axles in such an amazing pomp and solemnity. If, after this, we contemplate those wide fields of ether, that reach in height as far as from Saturn to the fixed stars, and run abroad almost to an infinitude, our imagination finds its capacity filled with so immense a prospect, and puts it self upon the stretch to comprehend it. But if we yet rise higher, and consider the fixed stars as so many vast oceans of flame, that are each of them attended with a different set of planets, and still discover new firmaments and new lights, that are sunk farther in those unfathomable depths of ether, so as not to be seen by the strongest of our telescopes, we are lost in such a labyrinth of suns and worlds, and confounded with the immensity and magnificence of nature.

Nothing is more pleasant to the fancy, than to enlarge it self, by degrees, in its contemplation of the various proportions which its several objects bear to each other, when it compares the body of man to the bulk of the whole earth, the earth to the circle it describes round the sun, that circle to the sphere of the fixed stars, the sphere of the fixed stars to the circuit of the whole creation, the whole creation it self to the infinite space that is every where diffused about it; or when the imagination works downward, and considers the bulk of a human body, in respect of an animal a hundred times less than a mite, the particular limbs of such an animal, the different springs which actuate the limbs, the spirits which set these springs a going, and the proportionable minuteness of these several parts, before they have arrived at their full growth and perfection. But if, after all this, we take the least particle of these animal spirits, and consider its capacity of being wrought into a world, that shall contain within those narrow dimensions a heaven and earth, stars and planets, and every different species of living creatures, in the same analogy and proportion they bear to each other in our own universe; such a speculation, by reason of its nicety, appears ridiculous to those who have not turned their thoughts that way, though at the same time it is founded on no less than the evidence of a demonstration. Nay, we might yet carry it farther, and discover in the smallest particle of this little world a new inexhausted fund of matter, capable of being spun out into another universe.

I have dwelt the longer on this subject, because I think it may shew us the proper limits, as well as the defectiveness, of our imagination; how it is confined to a very small quantity of space, and immediately stopped in its operations, when it endeavors to take in any thing that is very great, or very little. Let a man try to conceive the different bulk of an animal, which is twenty, from another which is a hundred times less than a mite, or to compare, in his thoughts, a length of a thousand diameters of the earth, with that of a million, and he will quickly find that he has no different measures in his mind, adjusted to such extraordinary degrees of grandeur or minuteness. The understanding, indeed, opens an infinite space on every side of us, but the imagination after a few faint efforts, is immediately at a stand, and finds her self swallowed up in the immensity of the void that surrounds it. Our reason can pursue a particle of matter through an infinite variety of divisions, but the fancy soon loses sight of it, and feels in it self a kind of chasm, that wants to be filled with matter of a more sensible bulk. We can neither widen, nor contract the faculty to the dimensions of either extreme: The object is too big for our capacity, when we would comprehend the circumference of a world, and dwindles into nothing, when we endeavor after the idea of an atom.

It is possible this defect of imagination may not be in the soul it self, but as it acts in conjunction with the body, perhaps there may not be room in the brain for such a variety of impressions, or the animal spirits may be incapable of figuring them in such a manner, as is necessary to excite so very large or very minute ideas. However it be, we may well suppose that beings of a higher nature very much excel us in this respect, as it is probable the soul of man will be infinitely more perfect hereafter in this faculty, as well as in all the rest; insomuch that, perhaps, the imagination will be able to keep pace with the understanding, and to form in it self distinct ideas of all the different modes and quantities of space.

No. 421 Thursday, July 3, 1712

Ignotis errare locis, ignota videre
Flumina gaudebat; studio minuente laborem.—Ovid.

The pleasures of the imagination are not wholly confined to such particular authors as are conversant in material objects, but are often to be met with among the polite masters of morality, criticism, and other speculations abstracted from matter, who, though they do not directly treat of the visible parts of nature, often draw from them their similitudes, metaphors, and allegories. By these allusions a truth in the understanding is as it were reflected by the imagination; we are able to see something like color and shape in a notion, and to discover a scheme of thoughts traced out upon matter. And here the mind receives a great deal of satisfaction, and has two of its faculties gratified at the same time, while the fancy is busy in copying after the understanding, and transcribing ideas out of the intellectual world into the material.

The great art of a writer shews it self in the choice of pleasing allusions, which are generally to be taken from the great or beautiful works of art or nature; for though whatever is new or uncommon is apt to delight the imagination, the chief design of an allusion being to illustrate and explain the passages of an author, it should be always borrowed from what is more known and common, than the passages which are to be explained.

Allegories, when well chosen, are like so many tracks of light in a discourse, that make every thing about them clear and beautiful. A noble metaphor, when it is placed to an advantage, casts a kind of glory round it, and darts a luster through a whole sentence; these different kinds of allusion are but so many different manners of similitude, and, that they may please the imagination, the likeness ought to be very exact, or very agreeable, as we love to see a picture where the resemblance is just, or the posture and air graceful. But we often find eminent writers very faulty in this respect; great scholars are apt to fetch their comparisons and allusions from the sciences in which they are most conversant, so that a man may see the compass of their learning in a treatise on the most indifferent subject. I have read a discourse upon love, which none but a profound chemist could understand, and have heard many a Sermon that should only have been preached before a congregation of Cartesians. On the contrary, your men of business usually have recourse to such instances as are too mean and familiar. They are for drawing the reader into a game of chess or tennis, or for leading him from shop to shop, in the cant of particular trades and employments. It is certain, there may be found an infinite variety of very agreeable allusions in both these kinds, but, for the generality, the most entertaining ones lie in the works of nature, which are obvious to all capacities, and more delightful than what is to be found in arts and sciences.

It is this talent of affecting the imagination, that gives an embellishment to good sense, and makes one man's compositions more agreeable than another's. It sets off all writings in general, but is the very life and highest perfection of poetry. Where it shines in an eminent degree, it has preserved several poems for many ages, that have nothing else to recommend them; and where all the other beauties are present, the work appears dry and insipid, if this single one be wanting. It has something in it like creation; it bestows a kind of existence, and draws up to the reader's view several objects which are not to be found in being. It makes additions to nature, and gives a greater variety to God's works. In a word, it is able to beautify and adorn the most illustrious scenes in the universe, or to fill the mind with more glorious shows and apparitions, than can be found in any part of it.

We have now discovered the several originals of those pleasures that gratify the fancy; and here, perhaps, it would not be very difficult to cast under their proper heads those contrary objects, which are apt to fill it with distaste and terror; for the imagination is as liable to pain as pleasure. When the brain is hurt by any accident, or the mind disordered by dreams or sickness, the fancy is over-run with wild dismal ideas, and terrified with a thousand hideous monsters of its own framing.

Eumenidum veluti demens videt agmina Pentheus,
Et solem geminum, & duplices se ostendere Thebas,
Aut Agamemnonius scenis agitatus Orestes,
Armatam facibus matrem & serpentibus atris
Cum fugit, ultricesque sedent in limine Dirae.—Virg.

There is not a sight in nature so mortifying as that of a distracted person, when his imagination is troubled, and his whole soul disordered and confused. Babylon in ruins is not so melancholy a spectacle. But to quit so disagreeable a subject, I shall only consider by way of conclusion, what an infinite advantage this faculty gives an almighty being over the soul of man, and how great a measure of happiness or misery we are capable of receiving from the imagination only.

We have already seen the influence that one man has over the fancy of another, and with what ease he conveys into it a variety of imagery; how great a power then may we suppose lodged in him, who knows all the ways of affecting the imagination, who can infuse what ideas he pleases, and fill those ideas with terror and delight to what degree he thinks fit? He can excite images in the mind without the help of words, and make scenes rise up before us and seem present to the eye, without the assistance of bodies or exterior objects. He can transport the imagination with such beautiful and glorious visions, as cannot possibly enter into our present conceptions, or haunt it with such ghastly specters and apparitions, as would make us hope for annihilation, and think existence no better than a curse. In short, he can so exquisitely ravish or torture the soul through this single faculty, as might suffice to make the whole heaven or hell of any finite being.

This essay on the pleasures of the imagination having been published in separate papers, I shall conclude it with a table of the principal contents of each paper.

The Contents

Paper I

The perfection of our sight above our other senses. The pleasures of the imagination arise originally from sight. The pleasures of the imagination divided under two heads. The pleasures of the imagination in some respects equal to those of the understanding. The extent of the pleasures of the imagination. The advantages a man receives from a relish of these pleasures. In what respect they are preferable to those of the understanding.

Paper II

Three sources of all the pleasures of the imagination, in our survey of outward objects. How what is great pleases the imagination. How what is new pleases the imagination. How what is beautiful in our own species, pleases the imagination. How what is beautiful in general pleases the imagination. What other accidental causes may contribute to the heightening of these pleasures.

Paper III

Why the necessary cause of our being pleased with what is great, new, or beautiful, unknown. Why the final cause more known and more useful. The final cause of our being pleased with what is great. The final cause of our being pleased with what is new. The final cause of our being pleased with what is beautiful in our own species. The final cause of our being pleased with what is beautiful in general.

Paper IV

The works of nature more pleasant to the imagination than those of art. The works of nature still more pleasant, the more they resemble those of art. The works of art more pleasant, the more they resemble those of nature. Our English plantations and gardens considered in the foregoing light.

Paper V

Of architecture as it affects the imagination. Greatness in architecture relates either to the bulk or to the manner. Greatness of bulk in the ancient oriental buildings. The ancient accounts of these buildings confirmed, 1. from the advantages, for raising such works, in the first ages of the world and in the eastern climates; 2. From several of them which are still extant. Instances how greatness of manner affects the imagination. A French author's observation on this subject. Why concave and convex figures give a greatness of manner to works of architecture. Every thing that pleases the imagination in architecture is either great, beautiful, or new.

Paper VI

The secondary pleasures of the imagination. The several sources of these pleasures, (statuary, painting, description and music) compared together. The final cause of our receiving pleasure from these several sources. Of descriptions in particular. The power of words over the imagination. Why one reader more pleased with descriptions than another.

Paper VII

How a whole set of ideas hang together, etc. A natural cause assigned for it. How to perfect the imagination of a writer. Who among the ancient poets had this faculty in its greatest perfection. Homer excelled in imagining what is great; Virgil in imagining what is beautiful; Ovid in imagining what is new. Our own country-man Milton, very perfect in all three respects.

Paper VIII

Why any thing that is unpleasant to behold, pleases the imagination when well described. Why the imagination receives a more exquisite pleasure from the description of what is great, new, or beautiful. The pleasure still heightened, if what is described raises passion in the mind. Disagreeable passions pleasing when raised by apt descriptions. Why terror and grief are pleasing to the mind when excited by descriptions. A particular advantage the writers in poetry and fiction have to please the imagination. What liberties are allowed them.

Paper IX

Of that kind of poetry which Mr. Dryden calls the fairy-way of writing. How a poet should be qualified for it. The pleasures of the imagination that arise from it. In this respect, why the moderns excel the ancients. Why the English excel the moderns. Who the best among the English. Of emblematical persons.

Paper X

What authors please the imagination who have nothing to do with fiction. How history pleases the imagination. How the authors of the new philosophy please the imagination. The bounds and defects of the imagination. Whether these defects are essential to the imagination.

Paper XI

How those please the imagination, who treat of subjects abstracted from matter, by allusions taken from it. What allusions most pleasing to the imagination. Great writers how faulty in this respect. Of the art of imagining in general. The imagination capable of pain as well as pleasure. In what degree the imagination is capable either of pain or pleasure.

CHAPTER 5

Francis Hutcheson*

Reflections Upon Laughter
1725

—— *Rapias in jus malis ridentem alienis.*—Hor.

TO HIBURNICUS.

There is scarce any thing that concerns human nature, which does not deserve to be inquired into: I send you some thoughts upon a very common subject, laughter; which you may publish, if you think they can be of any use, to help us to understand what so often happens in our own minds, and to know the use for which it is designed in the constitution of our nature.

Aristotle, in his *Art of Poetry*, has very justly explained the nature of one species of laughter, viz. the ridiculing of persons; the occasion or object of which he tells us, is
Ἁμάρτημα τι καὶ ἄισχος ἀνώδυιον καὶ οὐ φθαρτικόν

---

*Francis Hutcheson (1694-1746) was born in Ireland and educated at Glasgow. He returned to Ireland where he was licensed to preach by the Presbyterian Church of Ireland, though his moderate and humanistic sentiments were not approved by the church or his parishioners. He operated an academy and engaged in correspondences and periodical controversies, including one with Gilbert Burnet. In 1725, Hutcheson published *An Inquiry into the Original of Our Ideas of Beauty and Virtue* in which he undertook to advance the ideas of the Earl of Shaftesbury against the positions of Hobbes and Mandeville. This was followed in 1728 by *An Essay on the Nature and Conduct of the Passions and Affections.* His correspondence with Burnet was published in 1735. At the end of 1729, Hutcheson was elected to the faculty at Glasgow University where he lectured on natural religion, morals, jurisprudence, and government and published in Latin works on metaphysics and moral philosophy. He died in 1746 on a visit to his wife's family in Dublin. His son published his *System of Moral Philosophy* posthumously in 1754.

"Some mistake, or some turpitude, without grievous pain, and not very pernicious or destructive." But this he never intended as a general account of all sorts of laughter.

But Mr. Hobbes, who very much owes his character of a philosopher to his assuming positive solemn airs, which he uses most when he is going to assert some palpable absurdity, or some ill-natured nonsense, assures us, that "laughter is nothing else but sudden glory, arising from some sudden conception of some eminency in ourselves, by comparison with the infirmity of others, or with our own formerly: for men laugh at the follies of themselves past, when they come suddenly to remembrance, except they bring with them any present dishonor."

This notion the authors of the *Spectators*, No 47, have adopted from Mr. Hobbes. That bold author having carried on his inquiries, in a singular manner; without regard to authorities; and having fallen into a way of speaking, which was much more intelligible than that of the schoolmen, soon became agreeable to many free wits of his age. His grand view was to deduce all human actions from self-love: by some bad fortune he has over-looked everything which is generous or kind in mankind; and represents men in that light in which a thorough knave or coward beholds them, suspecting all friendship, love, or social affection, of hypocrisy, or selfish design or fear.

The learned world has often been told that Puffendorf had strongly imbibed Hobbes's principles, although he draws much better consequences from them; and this last author, as he is certainly much preferable to the generality of the schoolmen, in distinct intelligible reasoning, has been made the grand instructor in morals to all who have of late given themselves to that study: hence it is that the old notions of natural affections, and kind instincts, the *sensus communis*, the decorum, and *honestum*, are almost banished out of our books of morals; we must never hear of them in any of our lectures for fear of innate ideas: all must be interest, and some selfish view; laughter itself must be a joy from the same spring.

If Mr. Hobbes's notion be just, then, first, there can be no laughter on any occasion where we make no comparison of ourselves to others, or of our present state to a worse state, or where we do not observe some superiority of ourselves above some other thing: and again, it must follow, that every sudden appearance of superiority over another must excite laughter, when we attend to it. If both these conclusions be false, the notion from whence they are drawn must be so too.

First then, that laughter often arises without any imagined superiority of ourselves, may appear from one great fund of pleasantry, the parody, and burlesque allusion; which move laughter in those who may have the highest veneration for the writing alluded to, and also admire the wit of the person who makes the allusion. Thus many a profound admirer of the machinery in Homer and Virgil has laughed heartily at the interposition of Pallas, in *Hudibras*, to save the bold Talgol from the knight's pistol, presented to the outside of his skull:

But Pallas came in shape of rust,
and 'twixt the Spring and hammer thrust
Her Gorgon shield, which made the cock
Stand Stiff, as 'twere transform'd to stock.

And few, who read this, imagine themselves superior either to Homer or Butler; we indeed generally imagine ourselves superior in sense to the valorous knight, but not in this point, of firing rusty pistols. And pray, would any mortal have laughed, had the poet told, in a simple unadorned manner, that his knight attempted to shoot Talgol, but his pistol was so rusty that it would not give fire? and yet this would have given us the same ground of sudden glory from our superiority over the doughty knight.

Again, to what do we compare ourselves, or imagine ourselves superior, when we laugh at this fantastical imitation of the poetical imagery, and similitudes of the morning?

The sun, long since, had in the lap
Of Thetis taken out his nap;
And, like a lobster boil'd, the morn
From black to red began to turn.

Many an orthodox Scotch Presbyterian, which sect few accuse of disregard for the holy scriptures, has been put to it to preserve his gravity, upon hearing the application of Scripture made by his countryman Dr. Pitcairn, as he observed a crowd in the streets about a mason, who had fallen along with his scaffold, and was over-whelmed with the ruins of the chimney which he had been building, and which fell immediately after the fall of the poor mason; "Blessed are the dead which die in the Lord, for they rest from their labors, and their works follow them." And yet few imagine themselves superior either to the apostle or the doctor. Their superiority to the poor mason, I am sure, could never have raised such laughter, for this occurred to them before the doctor's consolation. In this case no opinion of superiority could have occasioned the laughter, unless we say, that people imagined themselves superior to the doctor in religion: but an imagined superiority to a doctor in religion, is not a matter so rare as to raise sudden joy; and with people who value religion, the impiety of another is no matter of laughter.

It is said, "That when men of wit make us laugh, it is by representing some oddness or infirmity in themselves, or others."[1] Thus allusions made on trifling occasions, to the most solemn figured speeches of great writers, contain such an obvious impropriety, that we imagine ourselves incapable of such mistakes as the alluder seemingly falls into; so that in this case too, there is an imagined superiority. But in answer to this, we may observe, that we often laugh at such allusions, when we are conscious, that the person who raises the laugh knows abundantly the justest propriety of speaking, and knows, at present, the oddness and impropriety of his own allusion as well as any in company; nay, laughs at it himself: we often admire his wit in such allusions, and study to imitate him in it, as far as we can. Now, what sudden sense of glory, or joy in our superiority, can arise from observing a quality in another, which we study to imitate, I cannot imagine. I doubt, if men compared themselves

[1]See the Spectator

with the alluder, whom they study to imitate, they would rather often grow grave or sorrowful.

Nay, farther, this is so far from truth, that imagined superiority moves our laughter, that one would imagine from some instances the very contrary: for if laughter arose from our imagined superiority, then, the more that any object appeared interior to us, the greater would be the jest; and the nearer any one came to an equality with us, or resemblance of our actions, the less we should be moved with laughter. But we see, on the contrary, that some ingenuity in dogs and monkeys, which comes near to some of our own arts, very often makes us merry; whereas their duller actions, in which they are much below us, are no matter of jest at all. Whence the author in the *Spectator* drew his observation, "That the actions of beasts, which move our laughter, bear a resemblance to a human blunder," I confess I cannot guess; I fear the very contrary is true, that their imitation of our grave wise actions would be fittest to raise mirth in the observer.

The second part of the argument, that opinion of superiority suddenly incited in us does not move laughter, seems the most obvious thing imaginable. If we observe an object in pain while we are at ease, we are in greater danger of weeping than laughing: and yet here is occasion for Hobbes's sudden joy. It must be a very merry state in which a fine gentleman is, when well dressed, in his coach, he passes our streets, where he will see so many ragged beggars, and porters and chairmen sweating at their labour, on every side of him. It is a great pity that we had not an infirmary or lazar-house to retire to in cloudy weather, to get an afternoon of laughter at these inferior objects: Strange! that none of our Hobbists banish all Canary birds and squirrels, and lap-dogs and pugs, and cats out of their houses, and substitute in their places asses, and owls, and snails, and oysters, to be merry upon. From these they might have higher joys of superiority, than from those with whom we now please ourselves. Pride, or an high opinion of ourselves, must be entirely inconsistent with gravity; emptiness must always make men solemn in their behavior; and conscious virtue and great abilities must always be upon the sneer. An orthodox believer, who is very sure that he is in the true way to salvation, must always be merry upon heretics, to whom he is so much superior in his own opinion; and no other passion but mirth should arise upon hearing of their heterodoxy. In general, all men of true sense, and reflection, and integrity, of great capacity for business, and penetration into the tempers and interests of men, must be the merriest little grigs imaginable; Democritus must be the sole leader of all the philosophers; and perpetual laughter must succeed into the place of the long beard,

> *————To be the grace*
> *Both of our wisdom and our face.*

It is pretty strange, that the authors whom we mentioned above, have never distinguished between the words laughter and ridicule: this last is but one particular species of the former when we are laughing at the follies of others; and in this species there may be some pretense to allege that some imagined superiority may occasion it; but then there are innumerable instances of laughter, where no person is ridiculed; nor does he who laughs compare himself to anything whatsoever. Thus how often do we laugh at some out-of-the-way description of natural objects, to which we never compare our state at all. I fancy few have ever read the *City Shower* without a strong disposition to laughter; and instead of imagining any superiority, are very sensible of a turn of wit in the author which they despair of imitating: thus what relation to our affairs has that smile in *Hudibras*,

> *Instead of trumpet and of drum,*
> *Which makes the warrior's stomach come,*
> *And whets men valour sharp, like beer*
> *By thunder turn'd to vinegar.*

The laughter is not here raised against either valor or martial music, but merely by the wild resemblance of a mean event.

And then farther, even in ridicule itself there must be something else than bare opinion to raise it, as may appear from this, that if any one would relate in the simplest manner these very weaknesses of others, their extravagant passions, their absurd opinions, upon which the man of wit would rally, should we here the best vouchers of all the facts alleged, we shall not be disposed to laughter by bare narration; or should one do a real important injury to another, by taking advantage of his weakness, or by some pernicious fraud let us see another's simplicity, this is no matter of laughter: and yet these important cheats do really discover our superiority over the person cheated, more than the trifling impostures of our humorists. The opinion of our superiority may raise a sedate joy in our minds, very different from laughter; but such a thought seldom arises in our minds in the hurry of a cheerful conversation among friends, where there is often an high mutual esteem. But we go to our closets often to spin out some fine conjectures about the principles of our actions, which no mortal is conscious of in himself during the action; thus the same authors above mentioned tell us, that the desire which we have to see tragical representations is, because of the secret pleasure we find in thinking ourselves secure from such evils; we know from what sect this notion was derived.

> *Quibus ipse malis liber es, quia cernere suave.*—Lucr.

This pleasure must indeed be a secret one, so very secret, that many a kind compassionate heart was never conscious of it, but felt itself in a continual state of horror and sorrow; our desiring such sights flows from a kind instinct of nature, a secret bond between us and our fellow-creatures.

> *Nature a imperio gemimus cum sunus adultae*
> *Virginis occurrit, vel terra clauditur insans.*
> ______________*Quis enim bonus*______________
> *Ulla aliena sibi credat mala.*   Juven.

TO THE AUTHOR OF THE DUBLIN JOURNAL

Humano capiti cervicem pictor equinam
Fungere si velit, et varias inducere plumas,
Undique conlatis membris, ut turpiter atrum
Desinat in piscem mulier formosa superne;
Spectatum admissi risum teneatis amici?

Hor.

Sir,

In my former letter, I attempted to shew that Mr. Hobbes's account of laughter was not just. I shall now endeavour to discover some other ground of that sensation, action, passion, or affection, I know not which of them a philosopher would call it.

The ingenious Mr. Addison, in his treatise of the pleasures of the imagination, has justly observed many sublimer sensations than those commonly mentioned among philosophers: he observes particularly, that we receive sensations of pleasure from those objects which are great, new, or beautiful; and on the contrary, that objects which are more narrow and confined, or deformed and irregular, give us disagreeable ideas. It is unquestionable, that we have a great number of perceptions, which one can scarcely reduce to any of the five senses, as they are commonly explained; such as either the ideas of grandeur, dignity, decency, beauty, harmony; or, on the other hand, of meanness, baseness, indecency, deformity; and that we apply these ideas not only to material objects, but to characters, abilities, actions.

It may be father observed, that by some strange associations of ideas made in our infancy, we have frequently come of these ideas recurring along with a great many objects, with which they have no other connection than what custom and education, or frequent allusions, give them, or at most, some very distant resemblance. The very affections of our minds are ascribed to inanimate objects; and some animals, perfect enough in their own kind, are made constant emblems of some vices or meanness: whereas other kinds are made emblems of the contrary qualities. For instances of these associations, partly from nature, partly from custom, we may take the following ones; sanctity in our churches, magnificence in public buildings, affection between the oak and ivy, the elm and vine; hospitality in a shade, a pleasant sensation of grandeur in the sky, the sea, and mountains, distinct from a bare apprehension or image of their extension; solemnity and horror in shady woods. An ass is the common emblem of stupidity and sloth, a swine of selfish luxury; an eagle of a great genius; a lion of intrepidity; an ant or bee of low industry, and prudent economy. Some inanimate objects have in like manner some accessory ideas of meanness, either for some natural reason, or oftener by mere chance and custom.

Now, the same ingenious author observes, in the *Spectator*, Vol. I. No. 62 that what we call a great genius, such as becomes a heroic poet, give us pleasure by filling the mind with great conceptions; and therefore they bring most of their similitudes and metaphors from objects of dignity and grandeur, where the resemblance is generally very obvious. This is not usually called wit, but something nobler. What we call grave wit, consists in bringing such resembling ideas together, as one could scarce have imagined had so exact a relation to each other; or when the resemblance is carried on through many more particulars than we could have at first expected: and this therefore gives the pleasure of surprise. In this serious wit, though we are not solicitous about the grandeur of the images, we must still beware of bringing in ideas of baseness or deformity, unless we are studying to represent an object as base and deformed. Now this sort of wit is seldom apt to move laughter, more than heroic poetry.

That then which seems generally the cause of laughter, is "the bringing together of images which have contrary additional ideas, as well as some resemblance in the principal idea: this contrast between ideas of grandeur, dignity, sanctity, perfection, and ideas of meanness, baseness, profanity, seems to be the very spirit of burlesque; and the greatest part of our raillery and jest is founded upon it."

We also find ourselves moved to laughter by an overstraining of wit, by bringing resemblances from subjects of a quite different kind from the subject to which they are compared. "When we see, instead of the easiness, and natural resemblance, which constitutes true wit, a forced straining of a likeness, our laughter is apt to arise; as also, when the only resemblance is not in the idea, but in the sound of the words." And this is the matter of laughter in the pun.

Let us see if this thought may not be confirmed in many instances. If any writing has obtained an high character for grandeur, sanctity, inspiration, or sublimity of thoughts, and boldness of images; the application of any known sentence of such writings to low, vulgar, or base subjects, never fails to divert the audience, and set them a-laughing. This fund of laughter the ancients had by allusions to Homer: of this the lives of some of the philosophers in Diogenes Laertius supply abundance of instances. Our late burlesque writers derive a great part of their pleasantry from their introducing, on the most trifling occasions, allusions to some of the bold schemes, or figures, or sentences, of the great poets, upon the most solemn subjects. *Hudibras* and *Don Quixote* will supply one with instances of this in almost every page. It were to be wished that the boldness of our age had never carried their ludicrous allusions to yet more venerable writings. We know that allusions to the phrases of holy writ have obtained to some gentlemen a character of wit, and often furnished laughter to their hearers, when their imaginations have been too barren to give any other entertainment. But I appeal to the religious themselves, if these allusions are not apt to move laughter, unless a more strong affection of the mind, a religious horror at the profanity of such allusions, prevents their allowing themselves the liberty of laughing at them. Now in this affair I fancy any one will acknowledge that an opinion of superiority is not at all the occasion of the laughter.

Again, any little accident to which we have joined the idea of meanness, befalling a person of great gravity, ability, dignity, is a matter of laughter, for the very same reason; thus the strange contortions of the body in a fall, the dirtying of a decent dress, the natural functions which we study to conceal from sight, are matter of laughter, when they occur to observation in persons of whom we have high ideas: nay, the very human form has the ideas of dignity so generally joined with it, that even in ordinary persons such mean accidents are matter of jest; but still the jest is increased by the dignity, gravity, or modesty of the person; which shews that it is this contrast, or opposition of ideas of dignity and meanness, which is the occasion of laughter.

We generally imagine in mankind some degree of wisdom above other animals, and have high ideas of them on this account. If then along with our notion of wisdom in our fellows, there occurs any instance of gross inadvertence, or great mistake; this is a great cause of laughter. Our countrymen are very subject to little trips of this kind, and furnish often some diversion to their neighbors, not only by mistakes in their speech, but in actions. Yet even this kind of laughter cannot well be said to arise from our sense of superiority. This alone may give a sedate joy, but not be a matter of laughter; since we shall find the same kind of laughter arising in us, where this opinion of superiority does not attend it: for if the most ingenious person in the world, whom the whole company esteems, should through inadvertent hearing, or any other mistake answer quite from the purpose the whole audience may laugh heartily, without the least abatement of their good opinion. Thus we know some very ingenious men have not in the least suffered in their characters by an extemporary pun, which raises the laugh very readily; whereas a premeditated pun, which diminishes our opinion of a writer, will seldom raise any laughter.

Again, the more violent passions, as fear, anger, sorrow, compassion, are generally looked upon as something great and solemn; the beholding of these passions in another strikes a man with gravity: now if these passions are artfully, or accidentally, raised upon a small or a fictitious occasion, they move the laughter of those who imagine the occasions to be small and contemptible, or who are conscious of the fraud: this is the occasion of the laugh in biting, as they call such deceptions.

According to this scheme, there must necessarily arise a great diversity in men's sentiments of the ridiculous in actions or characters, according as their ideas of dignity and wisdom are various. A truly wise man, who places the dignity of human nature in good affections and suitable actions, may be apt to laugh at those who employ their most solemn and strong affections about what, to the wise man, appears perhaps very useless or mean. The same solemnity of behaviour and keenness of passion, about a place or ceremony, which ordinary people only employ about the absolute necessaries of life, may make them laugh at their betters. When a gentleman of pleasure, who thinks that good fellowship and gallantry are the only valuable enjoyments of life, observes men, with great solemnity and earnestness, heaping up money, without using it, or encumbering themselves with purchases and mortgages, which the gay gentleman, with his paternal revenues, thinks very silly affairs, he may make himself very merry upon them: and the frugal man, in his turn, makes the same jest of the man of pleasure. The successful gamester, whom no disaster forces to lay aside the trifling ideas of an amusement in his play, may laugh to see the serious looks and passions of the gravest business arising in the loser, amidst the ideas of a recreation. There is indeed in these last cases an opinion of superiority in the laughter; but this is not the proper occasion of his laughter; otherwise I see not how we should ever meet with a composed countenance any where: men have their different relishes of life, most people prefer their own taste to that of others; but this moves no laughter, unless, in representing the pursuits of others, they do join together some whimsical image of opposite ideas.

In the more polite nations, there are certain modes of dress, behavior, ceremony, generally received by all the better sort, as they are commonly called: to these modes, ideas of decency, grandeur, and dignity are generally joined; hence men are fond of imitating the mode: and if in any polite assembly, a contrary dress, behavior, or ceremony appear, to which we have joined in our country the contrary ideas of meanness, rusticity, sullenness, a laugh does ordinarily arise, or a disposition to it, in those who have not the thorough good breeding, or reflection to restrain themselves, or break through these customary associations.

And hence we may see, that what is counted ridiculous in one age or nation, may not be so in another. We are apt to laugh at Homer, when he compares Ajax unwillingly retreating, to an ass driven out of a corn-field; or when he compares him to a boar: or Ulysses tossing all night without sleep through anxiety, to a pudding frying on the coals. Those three smiles have got low mean ideas joined to them with us, which it is very probable they had not in Greece in Homer's days; nay, as to one of them, the boar, it is well known that in some countries of Europe, where they have wild boars for hunting, even in our times, they have not these low sordid ideas joined to that animal, which we have in these kingdoms, who never see them but in their dirty sties, or on dunghills. This may teach us how impertinent a great many jests are, which are made upon the style of some other ancient writings, in ages when manners were very different from ours, though perhaps fully as rational, and every way as human and just.

TO THE AUTHOR OF THE DUBLIN JOURNAL

______________________Ridiculum acri
Fortius et melius magnas plerumque secat res.

Sir,

To treat this subject of laughter gravely, may subject the author to a censure, like to that which Longinus makes upon a prior treatise of the Sublime, because wrote in a manner very unsuitable to the subject. But yet it may be worth our pains to consider the effects of laughter, and the ends for which it was implanted in our nature, that thence we may know the proper use of it: which may be done in the following observations.

First, we may observe, that laughter, like many other dispositions of our mind, is necessarily pleasant to us, when it begins in the natural manner, from some perception in the mind of something ludicrous, and does not take its rise unnaturally from external motions in the body. Every one is conscious that a state of laughter is an easy and agreeable state, that the recurring or suggestion of ludicrous images tends to dispel fretfulness, anxiety, or sorrow, and to reduce the mind to an easy, happy state; as on the other hand, an easy and happy state is that in which we are most lively and acute in perceiving the ludicrous in objects: any thing, that gives us pleasure, puts us also in a fitness for laughter, when something ridiculous occurs; and ridiculous objects, occurring to a soured temper, will be apt to recover it to easiness. The implanting then a sense of the ridiculous, in our nature, was giving us an avenue to pleasure, and an easy remedy for discontent and sorrow.

Again, laughter, like other affections, is very contagious; our whole frame is so sociable, that one merry countenance may diffuse cheerfulness to many; nor are they all fools who are apt to laugh before they know the jest, however curiosity in wise men may restrain it, that their attention may be kept awake.

We are disposed by laughter to a good opinion of the person who raises it, if neither ourselves nor our friends are made the butt. Laughter is none of the smallest bonds of common friendships, though it be of less consequence in great heroic friendships.

If an object, action, or event, be truly great in every respect, it will have no natural relation or resemblance to any thing mean or base; and consequently, no mean idea can be joined to it with any natural resemblance. If we make some forced remote jests upon such subjects, they can never be pleasing to a man of sense and reflection, but raise contempt of the ridiculer, as void of just sense of those things which are truly great. As to any great and truly sublime sentiments, we may perhaps find that, by a playing upon words, they may be applied to a trifling or mean action, or object; but this application will not diminish our high idea of the great sentiment. He must be of a poor trifling temper who would lose his relish of the grandeur and beauty of that noble sentence of holy writ, mentioned in a former paper, from the doctor's application of it. Virgil Travesty may often come into an ingenious man's head, when he reads the original, and make him uneasy with impertinent interruptions; but will never diminish his admiration of Virgil. Who dislikes that line in Homer, by which Diogenes the Cynic answered a neighbor at an execution, who was inquiring into the cause of the criminal's condemnation? which had been the counterfeiting of the ancient purple.

Ἔλλαβε πορφύρεος θάνατος καὶ μοῖρα κραταιή.

Let any of our wits try their mettle in ridiculing the opinion of a good and wise mind governing the whole universe; let them try to ridicule integrity and honesty, gratitude, generosity, or the love of one's country, accompanied with wisdom. All their art will never diminish the admiration which we must have for such dispositions, where-ever we observe them pure and unmixed with any low views, or any folly in the exercise of them.

When in any object there is a mixture of what is truly great, along with something weak or mean, ridicule may, with a weak mind which cannot separate the great from the mean, bring the whole into disesteem, or make the whole appear weak or contemptible: but with a person of just discernment and reflection it will have no other effect, but to separate what is great from what is not so.

When any object either good or evil is aggravated and increased by the violence of our passions, or an enthusiastic admiration, or fear, the application of ridicule is the readiest way to bring down our high imaginations to a conformity to the real moment or importance of the affair. Ridicule gives our minds as it were a bend to the contrary side; so that upon reflection they may be more capable of settling in a just conformity to nature.

Laughter is received in a different manner by the person ridiculed, according as he who uses the ridicule evidences good-nature, friendship, and esteem of the person whom he laughs at; or the contrary.

The enormous crime or grievous calamity of another, is not of itself a subject which can be naturally turned into ridicule: the former raises horror in us, and hatred; and the latter pity. When laughter arises on such occasions, it is not excited by the guilt or the misery. To observe the contortions of the human body in the air, upon the blowing up of an enemy's ship, may rise laughter in those who do not reflect on the agony and distress of the sufferers; but the reflecting on this distress could never move laughter of itself. So some fantastic circumstances accompanying a crime may raise laughter; but a piece of cruel barbarity, or treacherous villainy, of itself, must raise very contrary passions. A jest is not ordinary in an impeachment of a criminal, or an invective oration: it rather diminishes than increases the abhorrence in the audience, and may justly raise contempt of the orator for an unnatural affection of wit. Jesting is still more unnatural in discourses designed to move compassion toward the distressed. A forced unnatural ridicule, on either of these occasions, must be apt to raise, in the guilty or the miserable, hatred against the laugher; since it must be supposed to flow from hatred in him toward the object of his ridicule, or from want of all compassion. The guilty will take laughter to be a triumph over him as contemptible; the miserable will interpret it as hardness of heart, and insensibility of the calamities of another. This is the natural effect of joining to either of these objects mean ludicrous ideas.

If smaller faults, such as are not inconsistent with a character in the main amiable, be set in a ridiculous light, the guilty are apt to be made sensible of their folly, more than by a bare grave admonition. In many of our faults, occasioned by too great violence of some passion, we get such enthusiastic apprehensions of some objects, as lead us to justify our conduct: the joining of opposite ideas or images allays this enthusiasm; and, if this be done with good nature, it may be the least offensive, and most effectual, reproof.

Ridicule upon the smallest faults, when it does not appear to flow from kindness, is apt to be extremely provoking; since the applying of mean ideas to our conduct discovers contempt of us in the ridiculer, and that he designs to make us contemptible to others.

Ridicule applied to those qualities or circumstances in one of our companions, which neither he nor the ridiculer thinks dishonorable, is agreeable to everyone; the butt himself is as well pleased as any in company.

Ridicule upon any small misfortune or injury, which we have received with sorrow or keen resentment, when it is applied by a third person, with appearance of good-nature, is exceeding useful to abate our concern or resentment, and to reconcile us to the person who injured us, if he does not persist in his injury.

From this consideration of the effects of laughter, it may be easy to see for what cause, or end, a sense of the ridiculous was implanted in human nature, and how it ought to be managed.

It is plainly of considerable moment in human society. It is often a great occasion of pleasure, and enlivens our conversation exceedingly, when it is conducted by good-nature. It spreads a pleasantry of temper over multitudes at once; and one merry easy mind may by this means diffuse a like disposition over all who are in company. There is nothing of which we are more communicative than of a good jest: and many a man, who is incapable of obliging us otherwise, can oblige us by his mirth, and really insinuate himself into our kind affections, and good wishes.

But this is not all the use of laughter. It is well known, that our passions of every kind lead us into wild enthusiastic apprehensions of their several objects. When any object seems great in comparison of ourselves, our minds are apt to run into a perfect veneration: when an object appears formidable, a weak mind will run into a panic, an unreasonable, impotent horror. Now in both these cases, by our sense of the ridiculous, we are made capable of relief from any pleasant, ingenious well-wisher, by more effectual means, than the most solemn, sedate reasoning. Nothing is so properly applied to the false grandeur, either of good or evil, as ridicule: nothing will sooner prevent our excessive admiration of mixed grandeur, or hinder our being led by that, which is, perhaps, really great in such an object, to imitate also and approve what is really mean.

I question not but the jest of Elijah upon the false deity, whom his countrymen had set up, has been very effectual to rectify their notions of the divine nature; as we find that like jests have been very seasonable in other nations. Baal, no doubt, had been represented as a great personage of unconquerable power: but how ridiculous does the image appear, when the prophet sets before them, at once, the poor ideas which must arise from such a limitation of nature as could be represented by their statues, and the high ideas of omniscience, and omnipotence, with which the people declared themselves possessed by their invocation. "Cry aloud, either he is talking, or pursuing, or he is on a journey, or he is asleep."

This engine of ridicule, no doubt, may be abused, and have a bad effect upon a weak mind; but with men of any reflection, there is little fear that it will ever be very pernicious. An attempt of ridicule before such men, upon a subject every way great, is sure to return upon the author of it. One might dare the boldest wit in company with men of sense, to make a jest upon a completely great action, or character. Let him try the story of Scipio and his fair captive, upon the taking of Cartagena; or the old story of Pylades and Orestes; I fancy he would sooner appear in a fool's coat himself, than he could put either of these characters in such a dress. The only danger is in objects of a mixed nature before people of little judgment, who, by jests upon the weak side, are sometimes led into neglect, or contempt, of that which is truly valuable in any character, institution, or office. And this may shew us the impertinence, and pernicious tendency of general undistinguished jests upon any character, or office, which has been too much over-rated. But, that ridicule may be abused, does not prove it useless, or unnecessary, more than a like possibility of abuse would prove all our senses and passions, impertinent or hurtful. Ridicule, like other edged tools, may do good in a wise man's hands, though fools may cut their fingers with it, or be injurious to an unwary by-stander.

The rules to avoid abuse of this kind of ridicule, are, first, "Either never to attempt ridicule upon what is every way great, whether it be any great being, character, or sentiments:" or, if our wit must sometimes run into allusions, on low occasions, to the expressions of great sentiments, "Let it not be in weak company, who have not a just discernment of true grandeur." And, secondly, concerning objects of a mixed nature, partly great, and partly mean, "Let us never turn the meanness into ridicule, without acknowledging what is truly great, and paying a just veneration to it." In this sort of jesting we ought to be cautious of our company.

Discit enim citius, meminitque libentius illud,
Quod quis deridet, quam quod probat et veneratur.
Hor.

Another valuable purpose of ridicule is with relation to smaller vices, which are often more effectually corrected by ridicule, than by grave admonition. Men have been laughed out of faults which a sermon could not reform; nay, there are many little indecencies which are improper to be mentioned in such solemn discourses. Now ridicule, with contempt or ill-nature, is indeed always irritating and offensive; but we may, by testifying a just esteem for the good qualities of the person ridiculed, and our concern for his interests, let him see that our ridicule of his weakness flows from love to him, and then we may hope for a good effect. This then is another necessary rule, "That along with our ridicule of smaller faults we should always join evidences of good-nature and esteem."

As to jests upon imperfections, which one cannot amend, I cannot see of what use they can be: men of sense cannot relish such jests; foolish trifling minds may by them be led to despise the truest merit, which is not exempted from the casual misfortunes of our mortal state. If these imperfections occur along with a vicious character, against which people should be alarmed and cautioned, it is below a wise man to raise aversions to bad men from their necessary infirmities, when they have a juster handle from their vicious dispositions.

I shall conclude this essay with the words of Father Malebranche, upon the last subject of laughter, the smaller misfortunes of others. That author amidst all his visions shews sometimes as fine sense as any of his neighbors.

"There is nothing more admirably contrived than those natural correspondences observable between the inclinations of men's minds and the motions of their bodies.—All this secret chain-work is a miracle, which can never sufficiently be admired or understood. Upon sense of some surprising evil, which appears too strong for one to overcome with his own strength, he raises, suppose, a loud cry: this cry, forced out by the disposition of our machine, pierces the ears of those who are near, and makes them understand it, let them be of what nation or quality soever: for it is the cry of all nations, and all conditions, as indeed it ought to be. It raises a commotion in their brain,—and makes them run to give succor without so much as knowing it. It soon obliges their will to desire, and their understanding to contrive, provided that it was just and according to the rules of society. For an indiscreet out-cry, made upon no occasion, or out of an idle fear, produces, in the assistants, indignation or laughter instead of pity.—That indiscreet cry naturally produces aversion, and desire of revenging the affront offered to nature, if he that made it without cause, did it willfully: but it ought only to produce the passion of derision, mingled with some compassion, without aversion or desire of revenge, if it were a fright, that is, a false appearance of a pressing exigency, which caused the clamor. For scoff or ridicule is necessary to re-assure and correct the man as fearful; and compassion to succor him as weak. It is impossible to conceive any thing better ordered."[2]

I am, Sir,

Your very humble Servant,

Philomedes.

Francis Hutcheson

An Inquiry Into the Original of our Ideas of Beauty and Virtue
1725

An Inquiry Concerning Beauty, Order, Etc.

Sect. I: *Concerning some powers of perception, distinct from what is generally understood by sensation.*

To make the following observations understood, it may be necessary to premise some definitions, and observations either universally acknowledged, or sufficiently proved by many writers both ancient and modern, concerning our perceptions, called sensations, and the actions of the mind consequent upon them.

Art. 1. Those ideas that are raised in the mind upon the presence of external objects, and their acting upon our bodies, are called sensations. We find that the mind in such cases is passive, and has not power directly to prevent the perception or idea or to vary it at its reception, as long as we continue our bodies in a state fit to be acted upon by the external object.

2. When two perceptions are entirely different from each other, or agree in nothing but the general idea of sensation, we call the powers of receiving those different perceptions, different senses. Thus seeing and hearing denote the different powers of receiving the ideas of colors and sounds. And although colors have vast differences among themselves, as also have sounds; yet there is a greater agreement about the most opposite colors, than between any color and a sound: Hence we call all colors perceptions of the same sense. All the several senses seem to have their

[2]Book IV, ch. 13.

distinct organs, except feeling, which is in some degree diffused over the whole body.

3. The mind has a power of compounding ideas that were received separately, of comparing their objects by means of the ideas, and of observing their relations and proportions; of enlarging and diminishing its ideas at pleasure, or in any certain ration, or degree; and of considering separately each of the simple ideas, which might perhaps have been impressed jointly in the sensation. This last operation we commonly call abstraction.

4. The ideas of substances are compounded of the various simple ideas jointly impressed, when they presented themselves to our senses. We define substances only by enumerating these sensible ideas: And such definitions may raise an idea clear enough of the substance in the mind of one who never immediately perceived the substance; provided he has separately received by his senses all the simple ideas that are in the composition of the complex one of the substance defined: But if he has not received any of these ideas, or wants the senses necessary for the perception of them, no definition can ever raise in him any idea of that sense in which he is deficient.

5. Many of our sensitive perceptions are pleasant, and many painful, immediately, and that without any knowledge of the cause of this pleasure or pain, or how the objects excite it, or are the occasions of it; or without seeing to what further advantage or detriment the use of such objects might tend: Nor would the most accurate knowledge of these things vary either the pleasure or pain of the perception, however it might give a rational pleasure distinct from the sensible; or might raise a distinct joy, from prospect of further advantage in the object, or aversion, from apprehension of evil.

6. Hence it follows, that when instruction, education, or prejudice of any kind raise any desire or aversion toward an object, this desire or aversion must be founded upon an opinion of some perfection, or some deficiency in those qualities for perception, of which we have the proper senses. Thus if beauty be desired by one who has not the sense of sight, the desire must be raised by some apprehended regularity of figure, sweetness of voice, smoothness or softness, or some other quality perceivable by the other senses, without relation to the ideas of color.

. . .

8. The only pleasure of sense, that our philosophers seem to consider, is that which accompanies the simple ideas of sensation: But there are vastly greater pleasures in those complex ideas of objects, which obtain the names of beautiful, regular, harmonious. Thus every one acknowledges he is more delighted with a fine face, a just picture, than with the view of any one color, were it as strong and lively as possible; and more pleased with a prospect of the sun rising among settled clouds and coloring their edges, with a starry hemisphere, a fine landscape, a regular building; than with a clear blue sky, a smooth sea, or a large open plain, not diversifyed by woods, hills, waters, buildings: And yet even these latter appearances are not quite simple. So in music, the pleasure of fine composition is incomparably greater than that of any one note, how sweet, full, or swelling soever.

9. Let it be observed, that in the following papers, the word beauty is taken for the idea raised in us, and a sense of beauty for our power of receiving this idea. Harmony also denotes our pleasant ideas arising from composition of sounds, and a good ear (as it is generally taken) a power of perceiving this pleasure. In the following sections, an attempt is made to discover what is the immediate occasion of these pleasant ideas, or what real quality in the objects ordinarily excites them.

10. It is of no consequence whether we call these ideas of beauty and harmony, perceptions of the external senses of seeing and hearing, or not. I should rather choose to call our power of perceiving these ideas, an *Internal sense*, were it only for the convenience of distinguishing them from other sensations of seeing and hearing, which men may have without perception of beauty and harmony. It is plain from experience, that many men have, in the common meaning, the senses of seeing and hearing perfect enough; they perceive all the simple ideas separately, and have their pleasures; they distinguish them from each other, such as one color from another, either quite different, or the stronger or fainter of the same color; they can tell in separate notes, the higher, lower, sharper or flatter, when separately sounded; in figures they discern the length, breadth, wideness, of each line, surface, angle; and may be as capable of hearing and seeing at great distances as any men whatsoever: And yet perhaps they shall relish no pleasure in musical compositions, in painting, architecture, natural landscape; or but a very weak one in comparison of what others enjoy from the same objects. This greater capacity of receiving such pleasant ideas we commonly call a fine genius or taste: In music we seem universally to acknowledge something like a distinct sense from the external one of hearing, and call it a good ear; and the like distinction we would probably acknowledge in other affairs, had we also got distinct names to denote these powers of perception by.

11. There will appear another reason perhaps afterwards, for calling this power of perceiving the ideas of beauty, an *Internal Sense*, from this, that in some other affairs, where our external senses are not much concerned, we discern a sort of beauty, very like, in many respects, to that observed in sensible objects, and accompanyed with like pleasure: Such is that beauty perceived in theorems, or universal truths, in general causes, and in some extensive principles of action.

12. Let every one here consider, how different we must suppose the perception to be, with which a poet is transported upon the prospect of any of those objects of natural beauty, which ravish us even in his description; from that cold lifeless conception which we imagine to be in a dull critic, or one of the virtuosi, without what we call a fine taste. This latter class of men may have greater perfection in that knowledge, which is derived from external sensation; they can tell all the specific differences of trees, herbs, minerals, metals; they know the form of every leaf, stalk, root, flower, and seed of all the species, about which the poet is often very ignorant: An yet the poet shall have a vastly more delightful perception of the whole; and not only the poet, but any man of fine taste. Our external sense may by measuring teach us all the proportions of architecture to the tenth of an inch, and the situation of every muscle in the human body; and a good memory may retain these; and yet there is still something further necessary, not only to make a compleat master in architecture, painting, or statuary, but even a tolerable judge in these works; or to receive the

highest pleasure in contemplating them. Since then there are such different powers of perception, where what are commonly called the external senses are the same; since the most accurate knowledge of what the external senses discover, often does not give the pleasure of beauty or harmony, which yet one of a good taste will enjoy at once without much knowledge; we may mostly use another name for these higher and more delightful perceptions of beauty and harmony, and call the power of receiving such impressions, an *Internal Sense*. The difference of the perceptions seems sufficient to vindicate the use of a different name.

13. This superior power of perception is justly called *a sense*, because of its affinity to the other senses in this, that pleasure does not arise from any knowledge of principles, proportions, causes, or of the usefulness of the object; but strikes us at first with the idea of beauty: nor does the most accurate knowledge increase this pleasure of beauty, however it may super-add a distinct rational pleasure from prospects of advantage, or from the increase of knowledge.

14. And further, the ideas of beauty and harmony, like other sensible ideas, are necessarily pleasant to us, as well as immediately so; neither can any resolution of our own, nor any prospect of advantage or disadvantage, vary the beauty or deformity of an object: For as in the external sensations, no view of interest will make an object grateful, nor detriment, distinct from immediate pain in the perception, make it disagreeable to the sense; so propose the whole world as a reward, or threaten the greatest evil, to make us approve a deformed object, or disapprove a beautiful one; dissimulation may be procured by rewards or threatenings, or we may in external conduct abstain from any pursuit of the beautiful, and pursue the deformed; but our sentiments of the forms, and our perceptions, would continue invariably the same.

15. Hence it plainly appears, that some objects are immediately the occasions of this pleasure of beauty, and that we have senses fitted for perceiving it; and that it is distinct from that joy which arises from self-love upon prospect of advantage: Nay, do not we often see convenience and use neglected to obtain beauty, without any other prospect of advantage in the beautiful form, than the suggesting the pleasant ideas of beauty? Now this shows us, that however we may pursue beautiful objects from self-love, with a view to obtain the pleasures of beauty, as in architecture, gardening, and many other affairs; yet there must be a sense of beauty, antecedent to prospects of this advantage, without which sense, these objects would not be thus advantageous, nor excite in us this pleasure which constitutes them advantageous. Our sense of beauty from objects, by which they are constituted good to us, is very distinct from our desire of them when they are thus constituted: Our desire of beauty may be counter-balanced by rewards or threatenings, but never our sense of it; even as fear of death, or love of life, may make us choose and desire a bitter potion, or neglect those meats which the sense of taste would recommend as pleasant; and yet no prospect of advantage, or fear of evil, can make that potion agreeable to the sense, or meats disagreeable to it, that were not so antecedently to this prospect. Just in the same manner as to the sense of beauty and harmony; that the pursuit of such objects is frequently neglected, from prospects of advantage, aversion to labor, or any other motive of self-love, does not prove that we have no sense of beauty, but only that our

desire of it may be counter-balanced by a stronger desire: So gold out-weighing silver, is never adduced as a proof that the latter is void of gravity.

. . .

17. Beauty is either original, or comparative; or if any like the terms better, absolute, or relative: Only let it be noted, that by absolute or original beauty, is not understood any quality supposed to be in the object, that should of itself be beautiful, without relation to any mind which perceives it: For beauty, like other names of sensible ideas, properly denotes the perception of some mind; so cold, heat, sweet, bitter, denote the sensations in our minds, to which perhaps there is not resemblance in the objects that excite these ideas in us, however we generally imagine that there is something in the object just like our perception. The ideas of beauty and harmony being excited upon our perception of some primary quality, and having relation to figure and time, may indeed have a nearer resemblance to objects, than these sensations that seem not so much any pictures of objects, as modifications of the perceiving mind; and yet were there no mind with a sense of beauty to contemplate objects, I see not how they could be called beautiful. We therefore by absolute beauty[1] understand only that beauty, which we perceive in objects without comparison to any thing external, of which the object is supposed an imitation, or picture; such as that beauty perceived from the works of nature, artificial forms, figures, theorems. Comparative or relative beauty is that which we perceive in objects, commonly considered as imitations or resemblances of something else.

. . .

Sect II: *Of Original or Absolute Beauty*

1. Since it is certain that we have ideas of beauty and harmony, let us examine what quality in objects excites these ideas, or is the occasion of them. And let it be here observed, that our inquiry is only about the qualities that are beautiful to men, or about the foundation of their sense of beauty; for, as was above hinted, beauty has always relation to the sense of some mind; and when we afterwards show how generally the objects that occur to us, are beautiful, we mean agreeable to the sense of men: for as there are not a few objects, which seem no way beautiful to men, so we see a variety of other animals who seem delighted with them; they may have senses otherwise constituted than those of men, and may have the ideas of beauty excited by objects of a quite different form. We see animals fitted for every place; and what to men appears rude and shapeless, or loathsome, may be to them a paradise.

2. That we may more distinctly discover the general foundation or occasion of the ideas of beauty among men, it will be necessary to considered it first in its simpler kinds, such as occurs to us in regular figures; and we may perhaps find that the same foundation extends to all the more complex species of it.

[1] This division of Beauty is taken from the different foundations of pleasure as to our sense of it, rather than from the objects themselves: for most of the following instances of relative beauty have also absolute beauty; and many of the instances of absolute beauty, have also relative beauty in some respect or other. But we may distinctly consider these two fountains of pleasure, uniformity in the object itself, and resemblance to some original.

3. Figures that excite in us the ideas of beauty, seem to be those in which there is *uniformity amidst variety*. There are many conceptions of objects that are agreeable upon other accounts, such as grandeur, novelty, sanctity, and some others, that shall be touched at afterwards.[2] But what we call beautiful in objects, to speak in the mathematical style, seems to be in a compound ratio of uniformity and variety; so that where the uniformity of bodies is equal, the beauty is as the variety; and where the variety is equal, the beauty is as the uniformity. This will be plain from examples.

First, the variety increases the beauty in equal uniformity. The beauty of an equilateral triangle is less than that of the square; which is less than that of a pentagon; and this again is surpassed by the hexagon. When indeed the number of sides is much increased, the proportion of them to the radius, or diameter of the figure, is so much lost to our observation, that the beauty does not always increase with the number of sides; and the want of parallelism in the sides of heptagons, and other figures of odd numbers, may also diminish their beauty. So in solids, the eicosohedron surpasses the dodecahedron, and this the octahedron, which is still more beautiful than the cube; and this again surpasses the regular pyramid: The obvious ground of this, is greater variety with equal uniformity.

The greater uniformity increases the beauty amidst equal variety, in these instances: an equilateral triangle, or even an isosceles, surpasses the scalenuum; a square surpasses the rhombus or lozenge, and this again the rhomboides, which yet is still more beautiful than the trapezium, or any figure with irregularly curved sides. So the regular solids vastly surpasses all other solids of equal number of plain surfaces: And the same is observable not only in the five perfectly regular solids, but in all those which have any considerable uniformity, as cylinders, prisms, pyramids, obelisks; which please every eye more than any rude figures, where there is not unity or resemblance among the parts.

. . .

5. It is the same foundation which we have for our sense of beauty in the works of nature; in every part of the world which we call beautiful, there is vast uniformity amidst almost infinite variety. Many parts of the universe seem not at all designed for the use of man; nay, it is but a very small spot with which we have any acquaintance. The figures and motions of the great bodies are not obvious to our senses, but found out by reasoning and reflection, upon many long observations; and yet as far as we can by sense discover, or by reasoning enlarge our knowledge, and extend our imagination, we generally find the structure, and order, and motion, agreeable to our sense of beauty. Every particular object in nature does not indeed appear beautiful to us; but there is a vast profusion of beauty over most of the objects which occur either to our senses or reasonings upon observation. . . .

. . .

14. But in all these instances of beauty let it be observed, that the pleasure is communicated to those who never reflected on this general foundation; and that all here alleged is this, that the pleasant sensation arises only from objects, in which

[2] See Sect 6, Art. 11, 12, 13.

there is uniformity amidst variety: We may have the sensation without knowing what is the occasion of it; as a man's taste may suggest ideas of sweets, acids, bitters, though he be ignorant of the forms of the small bodies, or their motions, which excite these perceptions in him.

. . .

Sect. III: *Of the Beauty of Theorems*

1. The beauty of theorems, or universal truths demonstrated, deserves a distinct consideration, because of a nature pretty different from the former kinds of beauty; and yet there is none in which we shall see such an amazing variety with uniformity: and hence arises a very great pleasure distinct from prospects on any further advantage.

2. For in one theorem we may find included, with the most exact agreement, an infinity of infinities: so that although the necessity of forming abstract ideas, and universal theorems, arises perhaps from the limitation of our minds, which cannot admit an infinite multitude of singular ideas or judgments at once, yet this power gives us an evidence of the largeness of the human capacity above our imagination. . . .

3. That we may the better discern this agreement, or unity of an infinity of objects in the general theorem, to be the foundation of the beauty or pleasure attending their discovery. let us compare our satisfaction in such discoveries, with the uneasy state of mind which we are in, when we can only measure lines, or surfaces, by a scale, or are making experiments which we can reduce to no general canon, but only heaping up a multitude of particular incoherent observations. Now each of these trials discovers a new truth, but with no pleasure or beauty, notwithstanding the variety, till we can discover some sort of unity, or reduce them to some general canon.

. . .

5. There is another beauty in propositions, which cannot be omitted; which is this, when one theorem shall contain a vast multitude of corollaries easily deducible from it. . . . It is easy to see how men are charmed with the beauty of such knowledge, besides its usefulness; and how this sets them upon deducing the properties of each figure from one genesis, and demonstrating the mechanic forces from one theorem of the composition of motion; even after they have sufficient knowledge and certainty in all these truths from distinct independent demonstrations. And this pleasure we enjoy even when we have no prospect of obtaining any other advantage in life from such manner of deduction, besides the immediate pleasure of contemplating the beauty, nor could love of fame excite us to such regular methods of deduction, were we not conscious that mankind are pleased with them immediately by this internal sense of beauty. . . .

6. This delight which accompanies sciences, or universal theorems, may really be called a kind of sensation; since it necessarily accompanies the discovery of any proposition, and is distinct from bare knowledge itself, being most violent at first, whereas the knowledge is uniformly the same. And however knowledge enlarges the mind, and makes us more capable of comprehensive views and projects in some kinds of business, whence advantage may also arise to us; yet we may leave it in the

breast of every student to determine, whether he has not often felt this pleasure without any such prospect of advantage from the discovery of his theorem. All that can thence be inferred is only this, that as in our external senses, so in our internal ones, the pleasant sensations generally arise from those objects which calm reason would have recommended, had we understood their use, and which might have engaged our pursuits from self-interest.

. . .

Sect. IV: *Of Relative or Comparative Beauty*

1. If the preceding thoughts concerning the foundation of absolute beauty be just, we may easily understand wherein relative beauty consists. All beauty is relative to the sense of some mind perceiving it; but what we call relative is that which is apprehended in any object, commonly considered as an imitation of some original: And this beauty is founded on a conformity, or a kind of unity between the original and the copy. The original may be either some object in nature, or some established idea; for if there be any known idea as a standard, and rules to fix this image or idea by, we may make a beautiful imitation. Thus a statuary, painter, or poet, may please us with an Hercules, if his piece retains that grandeur, and those marks of strength, and courage, which we imagine in that hero. And farther, to obtain comparative beauty alone, it is not necessary that there be any beauty in the original; the imitation of absolute beauty may indeed in the whole make a more lovely piece, and yet an exact imitation shall still be beautiful, though the original were entirely void of it: Thus the deformities of old age in a picture, the rudest rocks or mountains in a landscape, if well represented, shall have abundant beauty, though perhaps not so great as if the original were absolutely beautiful, and as well represented.

. . .

5. Concerning that kind of comparative beauty which has a necessary relation to some established idea, we may observe that some works of art acquire a distinct beauty by their correspondence to some universally supposed intention in the artificer, or the persons who employed him: and to obtain this beauty, some times they do not form their works so as to attain the highest perfection of original beauty separately considered; because a composition of this relative beauty, along with some degree of the original kind, may give more pleasure, than a more perfect original beauty separately. Thus we see that strict regularity in laying out gardens in parterres, vistas, parallel walks, is often neglected to obtain an imitation of nature even in some of its wildnesses. And we are more pleased with this imitation especially when the scene is large and spacious, than with the more confined exactness of regular work. So likewise in the monuments erected in honor of deceased heroes, although a cylinder, or prism, or regular solid, may have more original beauty than a very acute pyramid or obelisk, yet the latter pleases more, by answering better the supposed intentions of stability, and being conspicuous. For the same reason cubes, or square prisms, are generally chosen for the pedestals of statues, and not any of the more beautiful solids, which do not seem so secure from rolling. This may be the reason too why columns or pillars look best when made a little taper from the

middle, or a third from the bottom, that they may not seem top-heavy and in danger of falling.

6. The like reason may influence artists, in many other instances, to depart from the rules of original beauty, as above laid down. And yet this is not argument against our sense of beauty being founded as was above explained, on uniformity amidst variety, but only an evidence that our sense of beauty of the original kind may be varied and over balanced by another kind of beauty.

. . .

Sect. V: *Concerning our Reasonings about Design and Wisdom in the Cause, from the Beauty or Regularity of Effects.*

1. There seems to be no necessary connection of our pleasing ideas of beauty with the uniformity or regularity of the objects, from the nature of things, antecedently to some constitution of the author of our nature, which has made such forms pleasant to us. Other minds may possibly be so framed as to receive no pleasure from uniformity; and we actually find that the same regular forms do not seem equally to please all the animals known to us, as shall probably appear afterwards. Therefore let us make what is the must unfavorable supposition to the present argument possible; that the constitution of our sense so as to approve uniformity, is merely arbitrary in the author of our nature; and that there are an infinity of tastes or relishes of beauty possible; so that it would be impossible to throw together fifty or a hundred pebbles, which should not make an agreeable habitation for some animal or other, and appear beautiful to it. And then it is plain, that from the perception of beauty in any one effect, we should have no reason to conclude design in the cause: for a sense might be so constituted as to be pleased with such irregularity as may be the effect of an[3] undirected force. But then, as there are an infinity of forms possible into which any system may be reduced, an infinity of places in which animals may be situated, and an infinity of relishes or senses is supposed possible; that in the immense spaces any one animal should by chance be placed in a system agreeable to its taste, must be improbable as infinite to one at least: and much more unreasonable is it to expect from chance, that a multitude of animals agreeing in their sense of beauty should obtain agreeable places.

2. It is also certain that there is the same probability that in any one system of matter an undirected force may produce a regular form, as any one given irregular one, of the same degree of complication . . . and therefore supposing any one system agitated by undesigning force, it shall be infinitely more probable that it shall resolve itself into an irregular form than a regular; thus that a system of six parts upon agitation shall not obtain the form of a regular hexagon, is at least infinite to unity; and the more complex we make the system, the greater is the hazard, from a very

[3] This expression is taken from the Cartesian scheme, in which the author of nature is supposed to have designedly impressed a general force or *conatus ad motum* upon the mass of matter, without any direction whatsoever. This nonsensical notion did so much prevail, and men have so many confused conceptions of nature and chance, as real beings operating without wisdom or design, that it may be useful to shew that their very absurd *postulatum* is wholly insufficient, though it were granted them, to enforce the appearances in the regularity of the world. And this is what is attempted in the first fourteen articles of this section.

obvious reason. We see this confirmed by our constant experience, that regularity never arises from any undesigned force of ours; and from this we conclude, that wherever there is any regularity in the disposition of a system capable of many other positions, there must have been design in the cause; and the force of this evidence increases, according to the multiplicity of parts employed.

But this conclusion is too rash, unless some further proof be introduced; and what leads us into it is this. Men who have a sense of beauty in regularity, are led generally in all their arrangements of bodies to study some kind of regularity, and seldom ever design irregularity; and hence we judge the same of other beings too, that they study regularity, and presume upon intention in the cause wherever we see it, making irregularity always a presumption of want of design: Whereas if different senses of beauty be in other agents or if they have no sense of it at all, irregularity may as well be designed as regularity: and then let it be observed that in this case there is just the same reason to conclude design in the cause from any one irregular effect as from a regular one; for since there are an infinity of other forms possible as well as this irregular one produced, and since to such a being[4] void of a sense of beauty all forms are as to its own relish indifferent, and all agitated matter meeting must make some form or other, and all forms upon supposition that the force is applied by an agent void of a sense of beauty, would equally prove design; it is plain that no one form proves it more than another, or can prove it at all; except from a general metaphysical consideration, too subtle to be certain that there is no proper agent without design and intention, and that every effect flows from the intention of some cause.

. . .

Sect. VI: *Of the Universality of the Sense of Beauty among Men*

1. We before insinuated[5] that all beauty has a relation to some perceiving power; and consequently since we know not the variety of senses which may be among animals, there is no form of nature concerning which we can pronounce that it has no beauty; for it may still please some perceiving power. But our Inquiry is confined to men; and before we examine the universality of this sense of beauty, or agreement in approving uniformity, it may be proper to consider, if as the other senses which give us pleasure do also give us pain, so this sense of beauty does make some objects disagreeable to us, and the occasion of pain. That many objects give no pleasure to our sense is obvious, many are certainly void of beauty: but then there is

[4] There is a great difference between such a being as is here mentioned, and a being which has no intention for any reason whatsoever to produce one form more than another. This latter sort of being, as to the present argument, would be the same with chance, but not the former. For though a being has no sense of beauty, he may notwithstanding be capable of design, and of intention to produce regular forms; and the observation of greater regularity in any number of effects, than could be expected from undirected force, is a presumption of design and intention in the cause, even where the cause is supposed to have no sense of beauty in such forms, since perhaps he may have other reasons moving him to choose such forms. Thus supposing the Deity no way necessarily pleased with regularity, uniformity, or similarity in bodies, yet there may be reasons moving him to produce such objects, such as the pleasing his creatures, having given them a sense of beauty founded on those qualities. See the last paragraph of the last section.

[5] See above Sect 1, Art. 17. Sect 4, Art. 1.

no form which seems necessarily disagreeable of itself, when we dread no other evil from it, and compare it with nothing better of the kind. Many objects are naturally displeasing, and distasteful to our external senses, as well as others pleasing and agreeable; as smells, tastes, and some separate sounds: but for our sense of beauty, no decomposition of objects which give not unpleasant simple ideas, seems positively unpleasant or painful of itself, had we never observed any thing better of the kind. Deformity is only the absence of beauty, or deficient in the beauty expected in any species: Thus bad music pleases rustics who never heard any better, and the finest ear is not offended with tuning the instruments if it be not too tedious, where no harmony is expected; and yet much smaller dissonancy shall offend amidst the performance, where harmony is expected. A rude heap of stones is not way offensive to one who shall be displeased with irregularity in architecture, where beauty was expected. And had there been a species of that form which we call now ugly or deformed, and had we never seen or expected greater beauty, we should have received no disgust from it, although the pleasure would not have been so great in this form as in those we now admire. Our sense of beauty seems designed to give us positive pleasure, but not positive pain or disgust, any further than what arises from disappointment.

. . .

3. We shall see afterwards,[6] that association of ideas make objects pleasant, and delightful, which are not naturally apt to give any such pleasures; and the same way the casual conjunctions of ideas may give a disgust, where there is nothing disagreeable in the form itself. And this is the occasion of many fantastic aversions to figures of some animals, and to some other forms: Thus swine, serpents of all kinds, and some insects really beautiful enough, are beheld with aversion by many people, who have got some accidental ideas associated to them. And for distastes of this kind, there is no other account can be given.

4. But as to the universal agreement of mankind in their sense of beauty from uniformity amidst variety, we must consult experience; and as we allow all men reason, since all men are capable of understanding simple arguments, though few are capable of complex demonstrations; so in this case it must be sufficient to prove this sense of beauty universal, if all men are better pleased with uniformity in the simpler instances than the contrary, even when there is no advantage observed attending it; and likewise if all men according as their capacity enlarges, so as to receive and compare more complex ideas, do further extend their delight in uniformity, and are pleased with its more complex kinds, both original and relative. . . .

. . .

11. The association of ideas above hinted at,[7] is one great cause of the apparent diversity of fancies in the sense of beauty, as well as in the external senses; and often makes men have an aversion to objects of beauty, and a liking of others void of it, but under different conceptions than those of beauty or deformity. And here it may

[6] See below, Art. 11, 12 of this section.

[7] See above, Art. 3 of this section.

not be improper to give some instances of some of these associations. The beauty of trees, their cool shades, and their aptness to conceal from observation, have made groves and woods the usual retreat to those who love solitude, especially to the religious, the pensive, the melancholy, and the amorous. And do not we find that we have so joined the ideas of these dispositions of mind with those external objects, that they always recur to us along with them? The cunning of the heathen priests might make such obscure places the scene of the fictitious appearances of their deities; and hence we join ideas of something divine to them. We know the like effect in the ideas of our churches, from the perpetual use of them only in religious exercises. The faint light in Gothic buildings has had the same association of a very foreign idea, which our poet shews in his epithet:

——A Dim religious Light.[8]

In like manner it is known, that often all the circumstances of actions or places, or dresses of persons, or voice or song, which have occurred at any time together, when we were strongly affected by any passion, will be so connected that any one of these will make all the rest recur. And this is often the occasion both of great pleasure and pain, delight and aversion to many objects, which of themselves might have been perfectly indifferent to us; but these approbations, or distastes are remote from the ideas of beauty, being plainly different ideas.

. . .

Sect. VII: *Of the Power of Custom, Education, and Example, as to our Internal Senses.*

1. Custom, education, and example are so often alleged in this affair, as the occasion of our relish for beautiful objects, and for our approbation of, or delight in a certain conduct in life in a moral sense, that it is necessary to examine these three particularly, to make it appear "that there is a natural power of perception, or sense of beauty in objects, antecedent to all custom, education, or example."

2. Custom, as distinct from the other two, operates in this manner. As to actions, it only gives a disposition to the mind or body more easily to perform those actions which have been frequently repeated, but never leads us to apprehend them under any other view than what we were capable of apprehending them under at first; nor gives us any new power of perception about them. . . . Custom makes us more capable of retaining and comparing complex ideas, so as to discern more complicated uniformity, which escapes the observation of novices in any art; but all this presupposes a natural sense of beauty in uniformity: for had there been nothing in forms which was constituted necessarily the occasion of pleasure to our senses, no repetition of indifferent ideas as to pleasure or pain, beauty or deformity, could ever have made them grow pleasing or displeasing.

3. The effect of education is this, that thereby we receive many speculative opinions, sometimes true and sometimes false; and are often led to believe that

[8] Milt. Il Penseroso.

objects may be naturally apt to give pleasure or pain to our external senses, when in reality the object has no such qualities: and further, by education there are some strong associations of ideas, without any reason, by mere accidents sometimes, as well as by design, which it is very hard for us ever to break asunder. . . . Thus education and custom may influence our internal senses, where they are antecedently, by enlarging the capacity of our minds to retain and compare the parts of complex compositions: and if the finest objects are presented to us, we grow conscious of a pleasure far superior to what common performances excite. But all this presupposes our sense of beauty to be natural. Instruction in anatomy, observation of nature, and of those airs of the countenance and attitudes of body, which accompany any sentiment, action or passion, may enable us to know where there is a just imitation; but why should an exact imitation please upon observation, if we had not naturally a sense of beauty in it, more than the observing the situation of fifty or a hundred pebbles thrown at random? and should we repeat our attention to them ever so often, we shall never dream of their growing beautiful.

. . .

5. Example seems to operate in this manner. We are conscious that we act very much for pleasure, or private good; and hence are led to imagine that others do so too: hence we conclude there must be some perfection in the objects which we see other pursue, and evil in those which we observe them constantly shunning. Or, the example of others may serve to us as so many trials to remove the apprehension of evil in objects which we had an aversion to. But all this is done upon an apprehension of qualities perceivable by the senses which we have; for no example will induce the blind or deaf to pursue objects as colored or sonorous; nor could example any more engage us to pursue objects as beautiful or harmonious, had we no sense of beauty or harmony naturally.

Example may make us without examination conclude, that our countrymen have obtained the perfection of beauty in their works, or that there is less beauty in the orders of architecture or painting used in other nations, and so content our selves with very imperfect forms. And often fear of contempt as void of taste or genius, makes us join in approving the performances of the reputed masters in our country, and restrains those who have naturally a fine genius, or the internal senses very acute, from studying to obtain the greatest perfection: it makes also those of a bad taste pretend a perception of ideas of beauty when they do not perceive them: but all this presupposes some natural power of receiving ideas of beauty and harmony. Nor can example effect any thing further, unless it be to lead men to pursue objects by implicit faith, for some perfection which the pursuer is conscious he does not know, or which perhaps is some very different quality from the idea perceived by those of a good taste in such affairs.

Sect. VIII: *Of the Importance of the Internal Senses in Life, and the Final Causes of them.*

1. The busy part of mankind may look upon these things as airy dreams of an inflamed imagination, which a wise man should despise, who rationally pursues more solid possessions independent on fancy: but a little reflection will convince us,

"that the gratifications of our internal senses are as natural, real, and satisfying enjoyments as any sensible pleasure whatsoever;" and "that they are the chief ends for which we commonly pursue wealth and power." . . . In short, the only use of a great fortune, above a very small one (except in good offices and moral pleasures) must be to supply us with the pleasures of beauty, order, and harmony. . . .

. . .

4. But then, beside this consideration of interest, there does not appear to be any necessary connection, antecedently to the constitution of the author of nature, between the regular forms, actions, theorems, and that sudden sensible pleasure excited in us upon observation of them, even when we do not reflect upon the advantage mentioned in the former proposition. And possibly the deity could have formed us so as to have received no pleasure from such objects, or connected pleasure to those of a quite contrary nature. We have a tolerable presumption of this in the beauties of various animals; they give some small pleasure indeed to every one who views them, but then every one in its own species seems vastly more delighted with their peculiar beauties, than with the beauties of a different species, which seldom raise any desire but among animals of the same species with the one admired: this makes it probable, that the pleasure is not the necessary result of the form it self, otherwise it would equally affect all apprehensions in what species soever. This present constitution is much more adapted to preserve the regularity of the universe, and is probably not the effect of necessity but choice in the Supreme Agent who constituted our senses.

5. . . . This we may probably say, that since the divine goodness, for the reasons above mentioned, has constituted our sense of beauty as it is at present, the same goodness might determine the great architect to adorn this vast theater in that manner which should be agreeable to the spectators, and that part which is exposed to the observation of men, so as to be pleasant to them; especially if we suppose that he designed to discover himself to them as wise and good, as well as powerful; for thus he has given them greater evidences, through the whole earth, of his art, wisdom, design, and bounty, than they can possibly have for the reason, and counsel, and good will of their fellow creatures, with whom they converse with full persuasion of this in their common affairs.

As to the operations of the Deity by general laws, there is a further reason from a sense still superior to these already considered, even that of virtue, or the beauty of action, which is the foundation of our greatest happiness: for were there no general laws fixed in the course of nature, there could be no prudence or design in men, no rational expectation of effects from causes, no schemes of action projected, nor any regular execution. If then according to the frame of our nature, our greatest happiness must depend upon our actions, as it may perhaps be made appear it does, "the universe must be governed, not by particular wills, but by general laws, upon which we can found our expectations, and project our schemes of action."

CHAPTER 6

James Harris*

Three Treatises
1744

Concerning Art: A Dialogue

To the Right Honorable
The Earl of Shaftesbury

My Lord,
The following is a conversation in its kind somewhat uncommon, and for this reason I have remembered it more minutely than I could imagine. Should the same peculiarity prove a reason to amuse your Lordship, I shall think myself well rewarded in the labor of reciting. If not, you are candid enough to accept of the intention, and to think there is some merit even in the sincerity of my endeavors. To make no longer preface, the fact was as follows.

A friend from a distant country having by chance made me a visit, we were tempted by the serenity of a cheerful morning in the spring, to walk from Salisbury to see Lord Pembroke's at Wilton. The beauties of gardening, architecture, painting, and sculpture belonging to that seat, were the subject of great entertainment to my friend; nor was I, for my own part, less delighted than he was, to find that our walk had so well answered his expectations. We had given a large scope to our curiosity, when we left the seat, and leisurely began our return towards home.

*James Harris (1709-1780) was the eldest son of James Harris and Lady Elizabeth Ashley Cooper, the sister of the third earl of Shaftsbury. He was independently wealthy and settled in the family home in Salisbury where he served as magistrate. He subsequently served as Member of Parliament for Christ Church and as a Lord of the Admiralty and Treasury. He had a deep interest in the classics based on genuine learning. Boswell refers to him as "an eminent Grecian" (1773/I-462), and Johnson says of him that "Harris is a sound sullen scholar; he does not like interlopers. Harris, however is a prig, and a bad prig." The latter remark puzzled Boswell.

And here, my Lord, in passing over a few pleasant fields, commenced the conversation which I am to tell you, and which fell at first, as was natural, on the many curious works, which had afforded us both so elegant an amusement. This led us insensibly to discoursing upon ART, for we both agreed, that whatever we had been admiring of fair and beautiful, could all be referred to no other cause. And here, I well remember, I called upon my friend to give me his opinion upon the meaning of the word ART: a word it was (I told him) in the mouth of every one; but that nevertheless, as to its precise and definite idea, this might still be a secret; that so it was in fact with a thousand words beside, all no less common, and equally familiar, and yet all of them equally vague and undetermined. To this he answered, that as to the precise and definite idea of art, it was a question of some difficulty, and not so soon to be resolved; that, however, he could not conceive a more likely method of coming to know it, than by considering those several particulars, to each of which we gave the name. It is hardly probable, said he, that music, painting, medicine, poetry, agriculture, and so many more should be all called by one common name, if there was not something in each, which was common to all. It should seem so, replied I.

What then, said he, shall we pronounce this to be? At this, I remember, I was under some sort of hesitation. Have courage, cried my friend, perhaps the case is not so desperate. Let me ask you — is medicine the cause of any thing? Yes surely, said I, of health. And agriculture, of what? Of the plentiful growth of grain. And poetry, of what? Of plays and satires, and odes, and the like.

And is not the same true, said he, of music, of statuary, of architecture, and, in short, of every art whatever? I confess said I, it seems so. Suppose then, said he, we should say, it was common to every art to be a cause—should we err? I replied, I thought not. Let this then, said he, be remembered, that all art is cause. I promised him it should.

But how then, continued he, if all art be cause, is it also true, that all cause is art? At this again I could not help hesitating. You have heard, sad he, without doubt, of that painter famed in story, who being to paint the foam of a horse, and not succeeding to his mind, threw at the picture in resentment a sponge bedaubed with colors, and produced a foam the most natural imaginable. Now, what say you to this fact? Shall we pronounce art to have been the cause?

By no means, said I. What, said he, if instead of chance, his hand had been guided by mere compulsion, himself dissenting and averse to the violence? Even here, replied I, nothing could have been referred to his art. But what, continued he, if instead of a casual throw, or involuntary compulsion, he had willingly and designedly directed his pencil, and so produced that foam, which story says he failed in?—would not art here have been the cause? I replied, in this case, I thought it would. It should seem then, said he, that art implies not only cause, but the additional requisite of intention, reason, volition, and consciousness; so that not every cause is art, but only voluntary or intentional cause. So, said I, it appears.

And shall we then, added he, pronounce every intentional cause to be art? I see no reason, said I, why not. Consider, said he; hunger this morning prompted you to eat. You were then the cause, and that too the intentional cause, of consuming certain foods; and yet will you refer this consumption to art? Did you chew by art? Did you swallow by art?

No certainly, said I. So by opening your eyes, said he, you are the intentional cause of seeing, and by stretching your hand, the intentional cause of feeling, and yet will you affirm, that these things proceed from art? I should be wrong, said I, if I did: For what art can there be in doing, what everyone is able to do by mere will, and a sort of uninstructed instinct? You say right, replied he, and the reason is manifest: were it otherwise, we should make all mankind universal artists in every single action of their lives. And what can be a greater absurdity than this? I confessed that the absurdity appeared to be evident. But if nothing then, continued he, which we do by compulsion, or without intending it be art; and not even what we do intentionally, if it proceed from mere will and uninstructed instinct; what is it we have left remaining where art may be found conversant? or can it indeed possibly be in any thing else, than in that which we do by use, practice, experience and the like, all which are born with no one, but are all acquired afterward by advances unperceived. I can think, said I, of nothing else. Let therefore the words *habit* and *habitual*, said he, represent this requisite, and let us say, that art is not only a cause, but an intentional cause; and not only an intentional cause, but an intentional cause founded in habit, or, in other words, an habitual cause. You appear, said I, to argue rightly.

But if art, said he, be what we have now asserted, something learnt and acquired; if it be also a thing intentional or voluntary, and not governed either by chance or blind necessity—if this, I say, be the case, then mark the consequences.

And what, said I, are they? The first, said he, is that no events, in what we call the natural world, must be referred to art; such as tides, winds, vegetation, gravitation, attraction, and the like. For these all happen by stated laws; by a curious necessity, which is not to be withstood, and where the nearer and immediate causes appear to be wholly unconscious. I confess, said I, it seems so. In the next place, continued he, we must exclude all those admired works of the animal world, which, for their beauty and order, we metaphorically call artificial. The spider's web, the bee's comb, the beaver's house, and the swallow's nest, must all be referred to another source—for who can say, these every learnt to be thus ingenious? or, that they were ignorant by nature, and knowing only by education? None, surely, replied I. But we have still, said he, a higher consideration. And what, said I, is that? It is, answered he, this—not even the divine power, which gave form to all things, then acted by art, when it gave that form. For how, continued he, can that intelligence, which has all perfection ever in energy, be supposed to have any power, not original by its nature? how can it ever have anything to learn, when it knows all from the beginning; or, being perfect and complete, admit of what is additional and secondary? I should think, said I, it were impossible. If so, said he, then art can never be numbered among its attributes: for all art is something learnt, something secondary and acquired, and never original to any being, which possesses it. So the fact, said I, has been established.

If this therefore, continued he, be true; if art belong not either to the divine nature, the brute nature, or the inanimate nature,—to what nature shall we say it does belong? I know not, said I, unless it be to the human. Your are right said he; for every nature else you perceive is either too excellent to want it, or too base to be capable of it. Beside, except the human, what other nature is there left? Or where else can we find any of the arts already instanced, or indeed whatever others we may now fancy to enumerate? Who are statuaries, but men? Who pilots, who musicians? This seems, replied I, to be the fact.

Let us then, continued he, say, not only that art is a cause, but that it is man becoming a cause; and not only man, but man intending to do what is going to be done, and doing it also by habit; so that its whole idea, as far as we have hitherto conceived it, is—man becoming a cause, intentional and habitual. I confess, said I, it has appeared so.

And thus, said he, have you had exhibited to you a sketch of art. You must remember however, it is but a sketch: there is still something wanting to make it a finished piece. I begged to know what that was. In order to that, replied he, I cannot do better, than remind you of a passage in your admired Horace. It is concerning Alsenus; who (if you remember) he tells us, though his tools were laid aside, and his shop shut up, was still an artist as much as ever.—

—Alsenus vaser omni
Abjecto instrumento Artis clausaq, taberna,
Sutor erat—

I remember, said I, the passage, but to what purpose is it quoted? Only, replied he, to shew you, that I should not be without precedent, were I to affirm it not absolutely necessary to the being of art, that it should be man actually becoming a cause; but that it was enough, if he had the power or capacity of so becoming. Why then, said I, did you not settle it so at first? Because, replied he, faculties, powers, capacities (call them as you will) are in themselves, abstract from action, but obscure and hidden things. On the contrary energies and operations lie open to the senses, and cannot but be observed, even whether we will or no. And hence therefore, when first we treated of art, we chose to treat of it, as of a thing only in energy. Now we better comprehend it, we have ventured somewhat farther. Repeat then, said I, if you please, the alteration, which you have made. At first, answered he, we reasoned upon art, as if it was only man actually becoming a cause intentional and habitual. Now we say it is a power in man of becoming such cause; and that though he be not actually in the exercise of such a power. I told him, his amendment appeared to be just.

There is too another alteration, added he, which, for the sake of accuracy, is equally wanting; and that is with respect to the epithet, intentional or voluntary. And what, said I, is that? We have agreed it, replied he, to be necessary, that all art should be under the guidance of intention or volition, so that no man acting by compulsion, or by chance, should be called an artist. We have. Now though this, said he, be true, yet it is not sufficient. We must limit this intention or volition to a peculiar kind. For were every little fancy, which we may work up into habit, a sufficient foundation to constitute an art, we should make art one of the lowest and most despicable of things. The meanest trick of a common Juggler might, in such case, entitle a man to the character of an artist. I confessed, that without some limitation, this might be the consequence. But how limit intentions to a kind or species? What think you, replied he, if we were to do it, by the number and dignity of the precepts, which go to the directing of our intentions? You must explain, said I; for your meaning is obscure. Are there not precepts, replied he, in agriculture, about ploughing and sowing? Are there not precepts in architecture, about orders and proportions? are there not the same in medicine, in navigation, and the rest? There are.

And what is your opinion of these several precepts? Are they arbitrary and capricious; or rational and steady? Are they the inventions of a day; or well-approved by long experience? I told him, I should consider them for the most part as rational, steady, and well-approved by long experience. And what continued he, shall we say to their number? are they few? Or are they not rather so numerous, that in every particular art, scarce any comprehend them all, but the several artists themselves; and they only by length of time, with due attendance and application? I replied, it seemed so. Suppose then we were to pronounce, that to every art there was a system of such various and well-approved precepts: should we err? No certainly. And suppose we should say, that the intention of every artist, in his several art, was directed by such a system: would you allow this? Surely. And will not this limiting of intentions to such only, as are so directed, sufficiently distinguish art from any thing else which may resemble it?—in other words, is it likely, under this distinction, to be confounded with other habits of a trifling, capricious and inferior kind? I replied, I thought not.

Let us then see, said he, and collect all that we have said, together. We have already agreed, that the power of acting after a certain manner is sufficient to constitute art, without the actually operating agreeably to that power. And we have now farther held the intentions of every artist to be directed by a system of various and well-approved precepts. Besides all this, we settled it before, that all art was founded in habit; and was peculiar to man; and was seen by becoming the cause of some effect. It should seem then, that the whole idea of art was this—An habitual power in man of becoming the cause of some effect, according to a system of various and well-approved precepts.

I replied, that his account appeared to be probable and just.

§2. And now then, continued he, as we have gone thus far, and have settled between us what we believe art to be; shall we go a little farther, or is your patience at an end?

Oh! no, replied I, not if any thing be left. We have walked so leisurely, that much remains of our way; and I can think of no method, how we may better amuse ourselves.

My friend upon this proceeded with saying, that if art were a cause, (as we had agreed it was) it must be the cause of something. Allow it, said I. And if it be the cause of something, it must have a subject to operate on. For every agent has need of some patient; the smith of his iron, the carpenter of his wood, the statuary of his marble, and the pilot of his ship. I answered, it was true. If then, said he, the subjects of particular arts be thus evident: What idea shall we form of that universal subject, which is common to all art? At this question, it must be confessed, I was a little embarrassed.

This induced him to ask me, how many sorts of subjects I allowed of? Here I could not help hesitating again. There is nothing, continued he, so difficult in the question. You must needs perceive, that all natures whatever can be but either contingent or necessary. This may be, replied I; but even yet I do not comprehend you. Not comprehend me! said he; then answer me a question: can you conceive any medium between motion and no-motion, between change and no-change?

I replied, I could not. If not, can you conceive any thing in the whole order of being, which must not be either liable to these, or not liable? Nothing.

Call those things therefore, said he, which are liable to change and motion, contingent natures; and those, which are not liable, necessary natures: and thus you have a division, in which all things are included. We have so, said I.

In which therefore, said he, of these natures shall we seek for this common subject of art? To this, I told him, I was unable to answer. Reflect, said he, a little. We have found art to be a cause.

We have. And is it not essential to every cause to operate? Or can it be a cause, and be the cause of nothing? Impossible.

Wherever therefore there is cause, there is necessarily implied some operation.

There is. And can there possibly be operation, without motion and change?

There cannot. But change and motion must needs be incompatible with what is necessary and immutable. They must. So therefore is cause. It must.

And so therefore art. It must.

Truth therefore, said he, and knowledge; principles and demonstrations; the general and intellectual essences of things; in short, the whole immutable and necessary nature is no part of it reducible to a subject of art. It seems so, said I.

If therefore art, said he, have nothing to do with the steady, abstract, and necessary nature, it can have only to do with the transient, the particular, and contingent one. It is true, said I; for there is no other left. And shall we then say, replied he, it has to do with all contingent natures existing in the universe?

For aught, replied I, which to me appears contrary. What think you, said he, of those contingents of higher order? Such as the grand planetary system; the succession of the seasons; the regular and uniform course of all superior natures in the universe? has art any ability to intermeddle here? No certainly, said I.

These superior contingent then, which move without interruption, are, it seems, above it. They are. And shall we say the same of those of lower sort; those, whose course we see often interrupted; those, which the strength and cunning of man are able to influence and control? Give instances, said I, of what you mean. I mean, said he, earth, water, air, fire; sonnets, trees; animals; men themselves. Are these contingents within the reach of art, or has art here no influence? I should think, said I, a very great one.

If this, continued he, be true, it should seem that the common or universal subject of art was—all those contingent natures, which lie within the reach of the human powers to influence. I acknowledge, said I, it appears so.

Thus far then, said he, we have advanced with tolerable success. We have gained some idea of art, and some idea of its subject. Our inquiry, on the whole, has informed us, that art—an habitual power in man of becoming a certain cause—and that its subject is—every such contingent nature, which lies within the reach of the human powers to influence.

§3. It is true, said I, this appears to have been the result of our inquiry, and a full and ample one its seems to have been. A long one, replied he, if you please, but not a full and ample one. Can anything, said I, be wanting, after what you have said already. Certainly, replied he, a great deal. We have talked much indeed of art, considered as a cause; and much of the subject, on which it operated; but what moves these operations to commence, and where it is they end, these are topics, which we have as yet little thought of. I begged him then, that we might now consider them.

He was willing, he said, for his part, and immediately went on by asking, what I thought was the beginning of art? I mean, said he, by beginning, that cause for the sake of which it operates, and which being supposed away, men would be never moved to follow it. To this, I told him, I was unable to answer. You will not think it, said he, so difficult, when you have a little more considered. Reflect with ourselves—was it not the absence of health, which excited men to cultivate the art of medicine? I replied, it was.

What then, said he, if the human body had been so far perfect and self-sufficient, as never to have felt the vicissitudes of well and ill: would not then this art have been wholly unknown? I replied, I though it would. And what, said he, if we extend this perfection a degree farther, and suppose the body not only thus healthful, but withal so robust, as to have felt no uneasiness from all inclemencies of weather: would not then the arts of building also and clothing have been as useless, as that of medicine? I replied, it seemed they would. But what, said he, if we bound not this perfection of ours even here? what if we suppose, that not only things merely necessary, but that those also conducive to elegance and enjoyment were of course all implied in the constitution of human nature; that they were all steady, constant, and independent from without, and as inseparable from our being, as perspiring, or circulation: in such case, would not the arts of music, painting, and poetry, with every other art passing under the denomination of elegant, have been as useless, as we have held those others of medicine, clothing, and architecture? I replied, it seemed they would. It was then the absence of Joys, elegancies, and amusements from our constitution, as left by nature, which induced us to seek them in these arts of elegance and entertainment.

It was. And what, said he, are Joys, elegancies, amusements, health, robustness, with those several other objects of desire, whose absence leads to art, but so many different names of that complex being called good, under its various, and multiform, and popular appearances? I replied, it seemed so.

If this then, said he, be granted, it should seem that the beginning or principle of art was the absence of something thought good, because it has appeared that it is for the sake of some such absent good that every art operates; and because, if we suppose no such absence to have been, we should never have known any art. I confess, said I, it seems so.

But how then, continued he? if it be true that all art implies such principle, it is reciprocally true, that every such principle should imply art? I see no reason, said I, why not.

Consider, said he. It might be though a good by some perhaps, to be as strong as those horses, which are ploughing yonder field; to be as tall as those elms, and of a nature as durable.—yet would the absence of goods, like these, lead to art? Or is it not absurd to suppose, there should be an art of impossibilities? Absurd, said I, certainly. If so, said he, when we define the beginning or principle of art, it is not enough to call it the absence of something thought good, unless we add, that the good be a good possible; a thing attainable by men; a thing relative to human life, and consistent with human nature: or does not this also appear a requisite? I replied, I thought it did.

But still, continued he—is it a sufficient motive to art, that the good desired should be attainable? In other words, does every absence of good attainable lead to art, or is our account still too loose, and in need of stricter determination? Of none, said I, which appears to me. Reflect, said he; there are some the possible goods so obvious and easy, that every man, in an ordinary state of common natural perfection, is able to acquire them, without labor or application. Your will hardly deny but that a fair apple, tempting to eat, may be gathered; or a clear spring, tempting to drink, may be drank at, by the mere suggestions of will and uninstructed instinct. I granted they might.

It would be therefore impertinent, said he, to suppose that goods, like these, should lead to art, because art would be superfluous, and in no respect necessary. Indeed, said I, it seems so.

If therefore, said he, neither impossibles lead to art, because of such there can be no art; nor things easily possible, because in such nature can do without art: what is it we have left, to which we may refer it? Or can it indeed be to any other than to that middle class of things, which, however possible, are still not so easy, but to be beyond the powers of will, and instinct uninstructed? I replied, is seemed so. That there are many such things, said he, is evident past doubt. For what man would pay artists so largely for their arts, were he enabled by nature to obtain whatever he desired? Or who would study to be skilled in arts, were nature's original powers to be of themselves alone sufficient? I told him, it was not likely.

It should seem then, said he, according to this reasoning, that the beginning, motive, or principle of art; that cause, which first moves it to action, and, for the sake of which its several operations are exerted, is—the want or absence of something appearing good; relative to human life, and attainable by man, but superior to his natural and uninstructed faculties. I replied, I could not deny, but that the account appeared probable.

§4. Let this then, said he, suffice, as to the beginning of art. But how shall we describe its end? What is it we shall pronounce this? My answer, I replied, must be the same as often already; which was indeed, that I could not resolve the question. It should seem, said he, not so difficult, now we have discovered what beginning is. For if beginning and end are contraries and opposed, it is but to invert, as it were, the notion of beginning, and we gain of course the notion of end. I asked him, in what manner? Thus, said he, the beginning of art has been held to be something, which, if supposed away, men would be never moved to apply to art. By inversion therefore the end of art must be something, which, while supposed away, men will never cease applying to art; because, were they to cease, while the end was wanting, they would cease with imperfection, and their performance would be incomplete. To this I answered, that the account, however true, was by far too general, to give me much intelligence.

He replied, if it was, he would endeavor to be more particular. And what, continued he, should we say, that every art, according to its genius, will of course be accomplished either in some energy, or in some work; that, besides these two, it can be accomplished in nothing else; and consequently that one of these must of necessity be its end? I could not here but answer him with a smile, that the matter was now much obscurer than ever. I find then, said he, it is proper we should be more explicit in our inquiries, and deduce our reasonings from some clearer point of view. I told him, it was quite necessary, if he intended to be intelligible.

Thus then, said he. You will grant, that every art, being a cause, must be productive of some effect; for instance, music, of a tune; dancing, of a dance; architecture, of a palace; and sculpture, of a statue. It is allowed, said I. You will grant also, said he, that in these productions they are all accomplished and ended: or, in other words, that as music produces a tune, so it is ended and accomplished in a tune; and as sculpture produces a statue, so it is ended and accomplished in a statue. It is admitted, said I. Now these productions, continued he, if you will examine, are not like units or mathematical points; but, on the contrary, all consist of a certain number of parts, from whose accurate order is derived their beauty and perfection. For example; notes, ranged after such a manner, make a tune in music; and limbs, ranged after such a manner, make a statue or a picture. I replied, they did. If then the production, continued he, of every art thus consists of certain parts, it will follow, that these parts will be either co-existent, or not; and if not co-existent, replied he, as in a statue, where arms, legs, body, and head all subsist together at one individual instant: successive, as in a tune or dance, where there is no such co-existence, but where some parts are every passing away, and others are ever succeeding them.

Can anything be said to exist, said I, whose parts are every passing away? Surely, replied he, or how else exist years and seasons, months and days, with their common parent, time itself?—or indeed what is human life, but a compound of parts thus fleeting; a compound of various and multiform actions, which succeed each other in a certain order? The fact, said I, appears so.

This then, continued he, being the case, and there being this difference in productions, call every production, the parts of which exist successively, and whose nature hath its being or essence in a transition, call it, what it really is, a motion or an energy—thus a tune and a dance are energies; thus riding and sailing are energies; and so is elocution, and so is life itself. On the contrary, call every production, whose parts exist all at once, and whose nature depends not on a transition for its essence, call it a WORK, or thing done, and not an energy or operation.—thus a house is a work, a statue is a work, and so is a ship, and so a picture. I seem, said I, to comprehend you.

If then there be no productions, said he, but must be of parts, either co-existent or successive; and the one of these be, as you perceive, a work, and the other be an energy; it will follow, there will be no production, but will be either a work or an energy. There will not, said I. But every art, said he, you have granted, is accomplished and ended in what it produces? I replied, I had. And there are no productions, but works or energies? None.

It will follow then, said he, that every art will be accomplished and ended in a work or energy.

To this I answered, that his reasoning I could not impeach; but that still the distinction of a work and energy was what I did not comprehend. There are several circumstances, said he, which will serve sufficiently to make it clear. I begged he would mention some.

Thus then, said he—when the production of any art is an energy, then this perfection of the art can be only perceived during that energy. For instance, the perfection of a musician is only known, while he continues playing. But when the production if any art is a work, then is not the perfection visible during the energy, but only after it. Thus the perfection of the statuary is not seen during his energies as a statuary, but when his energies are over, when no stroke of the chisel is wanting, but the statue is left as the result of all. It is true, said I.

Again, continued he,—in consequence of this, where the production is an energy, there the production is of necessity co-eval with the artist. For how should the energy survive the man; the playing remain, when the musician is dead? but where the production is a work, then is there no such necessity. The work may well remain, when the artist is forgotten; there being no more reason, that the statue and the artist should be co-eval, than the man and the rude marble, before it received a regular figure. You seem now, said I, to have explained yourself.

If then, said he, work and energy be made intelligible terms, you cannot but perceive the truth of what we before asserted—that every art, according to its genius, must needs be accomplished in one of these; that, except in these two, it can be accomplished in nothing else; and consequently that one of these must of necessity be its end. I answered, that the reasoning appeared justly deduced. So much then, replied he, for the ending or accomplishment of art; and so much also for a long, and I fear, an intricate disquisition.

§5. He had no sooner said this, than I was beginning to applaud him; especially on his having treated a subject so copiously, started, as it were, by chance, and without any apparent preparation. But I had not gone far, before he interrupted me, by saying, that as to my praises they were more than he deserved; that he could pretend to no great merit for having been, as I called it, so copious, when he had so often before thought, on what at present we had been talking. In short, says he, to tell you a secret, I have been a long time amusing myself, in forming an essay upon this subject. I could not here forbear reproaching him, for having hitherto concealed his intentions. My reproaches produced a sort of amicable controversy, which at length ended in his offering, that, to make me some amends, he would now recite me (if I pleased) a small fragment of the piece; a fragment, which he had happened accidentally to have about him. The proposal, on my part, was willingly accepted, and without farther delay, the papers were produced.

As to the performance itself, it must be confessed, in point of style, it was somewhat high and florid, perhaps even bordering upon an excess. At the time however of recital, this gave me less offense, because it seemed, as it were, to palliate the dryness of what had passed before, and in some sort to supply the place of an epilogue to our conference. Not however to anticipate, he began reading as follows:

"Oh art! thou distinguishing attribute and honor of human kind! Who art not only able to imitate nature in her graces, but (what is more) even to adorn her with graces of thy own. Possessed of thee, the meanest genius grows deserving, and has a just demand for a portion of our esteem. Devoid of thee, the brightest of our kind lie lost and useless, and are but poorly distinguished from the most despicable and base. When we inhabited forests in common with brutes, nor otherwise known from them than by the figure of our species; thou taughtest us to assert the sovereignty of our nature, and to assume that empire for which providence intended us. Thousands of utilities owe their birth to thee; thousands of elegancies, pleasures, and Joys, without which life itself would be but an insipid possession.

Wide and extensive is the reach of thy dominion. No element is there either so violent or so subtle, so yielding or so sluggish, as by the powers of its nature to be superior to they direction. Thou dreadest not the fierce impetuosity of fire, but compellest its violence to be both obedient and useful. By it thou softened the stubborn tribe of minerals, so as to be formed and molded into shapes innumerable. Hence weapons, armor, coin; and previous to these, and other thy works and energies, hence all those various tools and instruments, which empower thee to proceed to farther ends more excellent. Nor is the subtle air less obedient to thy power, whether thou willest it to be a minister to our pleasure, or utility. At thy commandment it giveth birth to sounds, which charm the soul with all the powers of harmony. Under thy instruction it moves the ship o'er seas, while that yielding element, where otherwise we sink, even water itself is by thee taught to bear us; the vast ocean to promote that intercourse of nations, which ignorance would imagine it was destined to intercept. To say how thy influence is seen on earth, would be to teach the meanest, what he knows already. Suffice it but to mention fields of arable and pasture; lawns of groves, and gardens, and plantations; cottages, villages, castles, towns; palaces, temples, and spacious cities.

Nor does thy empire end in subjects: thus inanimate. Its power also extends through the various race of animals, who either patiently submit to become thy slaves, or are sure to find thee an irresistible foe. The faithful dog, the patient ox, the generous horse, and the mighty elephant, are content all to receive their instructions from thee, and readily to lend their natural instincts or strength, to perform those offices, which thy occasions call for. If there be found any species, which are serviceable when dead, thou suggestest the means to investigate and take them. If any be so savage, as to refuse being tamed; or of natures fierce enough, to venture an attack; thou teachest us to scorn their brutal rage; to meet, repel, pursue, and conquer.

And such, O art! is thy amazing influence, when through art employed only on these inferior subjects; on natures inanimate, or at best irrational. But when e'er thou choosest a subject more noble, and settest to the cultivating of mind itself, then it is thou becomest truly amiable and divine; the ever-flowing source of those sublimer beauties, of which no subject but mind alone is capable. Then it is thou art enabled to exhibit to mankind the admired tribe of poets and of orators; the sacred train of patriots and of heroes; the godlike list of philosophers and legislators; the forms of virtuous and equal polities, where private welfare is made the same with public; where crowds themselves prove disinterested and brave, and virtue is made a national and popular characteristic.

Hail! Sacred source of all these wonders! Thyself instruct me to praise thee worthily, through whom whate'er we do, is done with elegance and beauty; without whom, what we do, is ever graceless and deformed.—venerable power! By what name shall I address thee? Shall I call thee ornament of mind; or art thou more truly mind itself?—It is mind thou art, most perfect mind; not rude, untaught, but fair and polished; in such thou dwellest, of such thou art the form; nor is it a thing more possible to separate thee from such, than it would be to separate thee from thy own existence."—

My good friend was now arrived to a very exalted pitch, and was pursuing his panegyric with great warmth and fluency; when we entered the suburbs, our walk being near finished. The people, as we went along, began to look at us with surprise; which I, who was less engaged, having leisure to observe, thought it was proper to admonish my friend, that he should give over. He immediately ceased reading; put his papers up; and thanked me for stopping him at so seasonable a time.

§6. What remained of our discourse passed off with less rapture, and was indeed no more, than a kind of short recapitulation.

He observed to me, that our inquiries had furnished out an answer to four different questions. For thus, said he, if it be asked us, what art is? we have to answer, it is—an habitual power in man, of becoming the cause of some effect, according to a system of various and well approved precepts. If it be asked us, on what subject art operates? we can answer, on a contingent, which is within the reach of the human power to influence. If it be asked us, for what reason, for the sake of what, art operates? we may reply, for the sake of some absent good, relative to human life, and attainable by man, but superior to his natural and uninstructed faculties. Lastly, if it be asked, where it is the operations of art end? we may say, either in some energy, or in some work.

He added, that if he were not afraid of the imputation of pedantry, he could be almost tempted to say, that we had been considering art, with respect to those four causes, so celebrated once among professors in the schools. By these, upon inquiry, I found that he meant certain causes, called the efficient, the material, the final, and the formal.

But here, without farther explaining, he begged for the present that we might conclude, being sufficiently, as he said, fatigued with the length of what had passed already. The request was reasonable I could not but own, and thus ended our conversation, and soon after it our walk.

Treatise the Second
A Discourse on Music, Painting, and Poetry

Chap. I.

Introduction.—Design and distribution of the whole.—Preparation for the following chapters.

All arts have this in common, that they respect human life. Some contribute to its necessities, as medicine and agriculture; others to its elegance, as music, painting, and poetry.

Now, with respect to these two different species, the necessary arts seem to have been prior in time; if it be probable that men consulted how to live and to support themselves, before they began to deliberate how to render life agreeable. Nor is this indeed unconfirmed by fact, there being no nation known so barbarous and ignorant, as where the rudiments of these necessary arts are not in some degree cultivated. And hence possibly they may appear to be more excellent and worthy, as having claim to a preference, derived from their seniority.

The arts however of elegance cannot be said to want pretensions, if it be true, that nature framed us for something more than mere existence. Nay, farther,[1] if well-being be clearly preferable to mere-being, and this without it be but a thing contemptible, they may have reason perhaps to aspire even to a superiority. But enough of this, to come to our purpose.

§2. The design of this discourse is to treat of music, painting, and poetry; to consider in what they agree, and in what they differ; and which upon the whole, is more excellent than the other two.

In entering upon this inquiry, it is first to be observed, that the mind is made conscious of the natural world and its affections, and of other minds and their

, [1] Ὀυ τὸ ζῆν περὶ πλέιζου ποιητέον
Ἀλλὰ τὸ εὖ ζῆν. Plat. in Critone.

affections, by the several organs of the senses.[a] By the same organs, these arts exhibit to the end imitations, and imitate either parts or affections of this natural world, or else the passions, energies, and other affections of minds. There is this difference however between these arts and nature; that nature passes to the percipient through all the senses; whereas these arts use only two of them, that of seeing and that of hearing. And hence it is that the sensible objects or media, through which[b] they imitate, can be such only, as these two senses are framed capable of perceiving; and these media are motion, sound, color, and figure.

Painting, having the eye for its organ, cannot be conceived to imitate, but through the media of visible objects. And farther, its mode of imitating being always motionless, there must be subtracted from these the medium of motion. It remains then, that color and figure are the only media, through which painting imitates.

Music, passing to the mind through the organ of the ear, can imitate only by sounds and motions.

Poetry, having the ear also for its organ, as far as words are considered to be no more than mere sounds, can go no farther in imitating, than may be performed by sound and motion. But then, as these its sounds stand by[2] compact for the various ideas, with which the mind is fraught, it is enabled by this means to imitate, as far as language can express and that it is evident will, in a manner, include all things.

Now from hence may be seen, how these arts agree, and how they differ.

They agree, by being all mimetic, or imitative.

They differ, as they imitate by different media; painting by figure and color; music, by sound and motion; painting and music, by media which are natural; poetry, for the greatest part, by a medium which is artificial.[c]

§3. As to that art, which upon the whole is most excellent of the three; it must be observed, that among these various media of imitating, some will naturally be more accurate, some less; some will best imitate one subject; some, another. Again, among

[a]To explain some future observations, it will be proper here to remark, that the mind from these materials thus brought together, and from its own operations on them, and in consequence of them, becomes fraught with ideas——and that many minds so fraught, by a sort of compact assigning to each idea some sound to be its mark or symbol, were the first inventors and founders of language. See Vol. II or *Hermes*, Lib. iii, cap. 3.4.

[b]To prevent confusion it must be observed, that in all these arts there is a difference between the sensible media, thro' which they imitate, and the subjects imitated. The sensible media, thro' which they imitate, must be always relative to that sense, by which the particular art applies to the mind; but the subject imitated may be foreign to that sense, and beyond the power of its perception. Painting, for instance, (as is shewn in this chapter) has no sensible media, thro' which it operates, except colour and figure. But as to subjects, it may have motions, sounds, moral affections and actions; none of which are either colors or figures, but which however are all capable of being imitated thro' them. See chapter the second, notes (b), (c), (d).

[2]see note (a).

[c]A figure painted, or a composition of musical sounds have always a natural relation to that, of which they are intended to be the resemblance. But a description in words has rarely any such natural relation to the several ideas, of which those words are the symbols. None therefore understand the description, but those who speak the language. On the contrary, musical and picture-imitations are intelligible to all men.

Why it is said that poetry is not universally, but only for the greater part artificial, see below, Chapter the Third, where what natural force it has, is examined and estimated.

the number of subjects there will be naturally also a difference, as to the merit and demerit. There will be some sublime, and some low; some copious, and some short; some pathetic, and others void of passion; some formed to instruct, and other not capable of it.

Now, from these two circumstances; that is to say, from the accuracy of the imitation, and the merit of the subject imitated, the question concerning which art is most excellent, must be tried and determined.

This however cannot be done, without a detail of particulars, that so there may be formed, on every part, just and accurate comparisons.

To begin therefore with painting.

Chapter II

On the subjects which painting imitates.—On the subjects which music imitates.—comparison of music and painting.

The fittest subjects for painting, are all such things and incidents, as are[3] peculiarly characterized by figure and color.

Of this kind are the whole mass[a] of things inanimate and vegetable; such as flowers, fruits, buildings, landscapes—the various tribes of animal figures; such as birds, beasts, herds, flocks—the motions and sounds peculiar to each animal species, when accompanied with configuration, which are obvious and remarkable[b]—the human body in all its appearances (as male, female; young, old; handsome, ugly;) and in all its attitudes, (as laying, sitting, standing, etc.—the natural sounds peculiar to the human species, (such as crying, laughing, hollowing, etc.)[c]—all energies, passions, and affections of the soul, being in any degree more intense or violent than ordinary[d]—all actions and events, whose integrity or wholeness

[3]p. 178.

[a]The reason is, that those things are almost wholly known to us by their color and figure. Besides, they are as motionless, for the most part, in nature, as in the imitation.

[b]Instances of this kind are the flying of birds, the galloping of horses, the roaring of lions, the crowing of cocks. And the reason is, that though to paint motion or sound be impossible, yet the motions and sounds here mentioned having an immediate and natural connection with a cerain visible configuration of the parts; the mind, from a prospect of this configuration, conceives insensibly that which is concomitant; and hence it is that, by a sort of fallacy, the sounds and motions appear to be painted also. On the contrary, not so in such motions, as the swimming of many kinds of fish; or in such sounds, as the purring of a cat; because here is no such special configuration to be perceived.—Homer, in his shield describing the picture of a bull seized by two lions, says of the bull — ὁ δὲ μάκρα μεμυκὼς Ἕλκετο—he, bellowing loudly, was draged along. Where Eustathius, in commenting on this bellowing, says, ὡς ἐδήλου τῷ χῆμα τι, as he (the bull) made manifest (in the picture) by his figure or attitude. Eust. in j. Σ. p. 1224.

[c]The reason is of the same kind, as that given in the note immediately preceding; and by the same rule, the observation must be confined to natural sounds only. In language, few of the speakers know the configuration, which attend it.

[d]The reason is still of the same kind, viz. from their visible effects on the body. They naturally produce either to the countenance a particular redness or paleness; or a particular modification of its muscles; or else to the limbs, a particular attitude. Now all these effects are solely referable to color and figure, the two grand sensible media, peculiar to painting. See Raphael's cartoons of St. Paul at Athens, and of his striking the sorcerer Elymas blind: see also the crucifixion of Polycrates, and the sufferings of the consul Regulus, both by Salvator Rosa.

depends upon a short and self-evident succession of incidents[e]—or if the succession be extended, then such actions at least, whose incidents are all along, during that succession, similar[f]—all actions, which being qualified as above, open themselves into a large variety of circumstances concurring all in the same point of time.[g]—all actions which are known, and known universally, rather than actions newly invented or known but to a few.[h]

And thus much as to the subjects of painting.

§2. In music, the fittest subjects of imitation are all such things and incidents, as are most eminently[4] characterized by motion and sound.

Motion may be either slow or swift, even or uneven, broken or continuous—sound may be either soft or loud, high or low. Wherever therefore any of the species of motion or sound may be found in an eminent (not a moderate or mean) degree, there will be room for musical imitation.

Thus, in the natural or inanimate world, music may imitate the glidings, murmurings, tossing, roarings, and other accidents of water, as perceived in fountains, cataracts, rivers, seas, etc.—the same thunder—the same winds, as well the stormy as the gentle.—In the animal world, it may imitate the voice of some animals, but chiefly that of singing birds—it may also faintly copy some of their motions.—in the

[e]For of necessity every picture is a *punctum temporis* or instant.

[f]Such, for instance, as a storm at sea; whose incidents of vision may be nearly all included in foaming waves, a dark sky, ships out of their erect posture, and men hanging upon the ropes—or as a battle; which from beginning to end presents nothing else, than blood, fire, smoke, and disorder. Now such events may be well imitated all at once: For how long soever they last, they are but repetitions of the same—Nicias, the painter, recommended much the same subjects, viz. a sea-fight or a land-battle of cavalry. His reasons too are much the same with those mentioned in note (g). He concludes with a maxim, (little regarded by his successors, however important,) that the subject itself is as much a part of the painter's art, as the poet's fable is a part of poetry. See Demetrius Phal. p. 53. Edit. Ox.

[g]For painting is not bounded in extension, as it is in duration. Besides, it seems true in every species of composition, that, as far as perplexity and confusion may be avoided, the wholeness of the piece may be preserved clear and intelligible; the more ample the magnitude, and the greater the variety, the greater also, in proportion, the beauty and perfection. Noble instances of this are the pictures above-mentioned in note (d). See Aristot. Poet. cap. 7. ὁ δε καθ' αὐτὴν [την] φύσιν τοῦ πραγμάτος. ὅρος, ἀεί μὲν, &c. See also *Characteristics*, V.I.p. 143. and Bossu, V. I. Cap. 16. *L'achille d'homere est si grand*, etc.

[h]The reason is, that a picture being (as has been said) but a point or instant, in a story well known the spectator's memory will supply the previous and the subsequent. But this cannot be done where such knowledge is wanting. And therefore it may be justly questioned, whether the most celebrated subjects, borrowed by painting from history, would have been any of them intelligible through the medium of painting only, supposing history to have been silent, and to have given no additional information.

It may be here added, that Horace, conformably to this reasoning, recommends even to poetic imitation a known story, before an unknown.

—— tuque
Rectius Iliacum carmen deducis in aelus,
Quam si proferres ignota, indictaque primus.
Art. Poet. v. 128

And indeed as the being understood to others, either hearers or spectators, seems to be a common requisite to all mimetic arts whatever; (for to those, who understand them not, they are in fact no mimetic arts) it follows, that perspecuity must be essential to them all; and that no prudent artist would neglect, if it were possible, any just advantage to obtain this end. Now there can be no advantage greater, than the notoriety of the subject imitated.

[4]p. 178.

human kind, it can also imitate some motions and sounds[k] ; and of sounds those most perfectly, which are expressive of grief and anguish.[l]

And thus much as to the subjects, which music imitates.

§3. It remains then, that we compare these two arts together. And here indeed, as to musical imitation in general, it must be confessed that — as it can, from its genius, imitate only sounds and motions—as there are not many motions either in the animal or in the inanimate world, which are exclusively peculiar even to any species and scarcely any to an individual—as there are no natural sounds, which characterize at least lower than a species (for the natural sounds of individual are in every species the same)—farther, as music does but imperfectly imitate even these sounds and motions[m]—on the contrary, as figures, postures of figures, and colors characterize not only every sensible species, but even every individual; and for the most part also the various[5] energies and passions of every individual—and farther, as painting is able, with the highest accuracy and exactness, to imitate all these colors and figures; and while musical imitation pretends at most to no more, than the raising of ideas similar, itself aspires to raise ideas the very same—in a word, as painting, in respect of its subjects, is equal to the noblest part of imitation, the imitating regular actions consisting of a whole and parts; and of such imitation, music is utterly incapable—from all this it must be confessed, that musical imitation is greatly below that of painting, and at best it is but an imperfect awing.

As to the efficacy therefore of MUSIC, it must be derived from another source, which must be left for the present, to be considered hereafter.[6]

There remains to be mentioned imitation by poetry.

Chap. III

On the subjects which poetry imitates, but imitates only through natural media, or mere sounds—Comparison of poetry in this capacity, first with painting, then with music.

Poetic imitation includes every thing in it, which is performed either by picture-imitation or musical; for its materials are words, and words are symbols[7] by compact of all ideas.

Farther as words, beside their being symbols by compact, are also sounds variously distinguished by their aptness to be rapidly or slowly pronounced, and by

[k]As the shouts of a multitude, in the coronation anthem of *God Save the King*, etc.

[l]The reason is, that this species of musical imitation most nearly approaches nature. For grief, in most animals, declares itself by sounds, which are not unlike to long notes in the chromatic system. Of this kind is the chorus of Baal's priests in the oratorio of Deborah, *Doleful tidings, how ye wound*, etc.

[m]The reason is from the dissimilitude between the sounds and motions of nature, and those of music. Musical sounds are all produced from even vibrations, most natural from uneven; musical motions are chiefly definite in their measure, most natural are indefinite.

[5]see note (d) of this chapter.

[6]ch. vi.

[7]see note (a) chap. I.

the respective prevalence of mutes, liquids, or vowels in the composition; it will follow that, beside their compact-relation, they will have likewise a natural relation to all such things, between which and themselves there is any natural resemblance. Thus, for instance, there is natural resemblance between all sorts of harsh and grating sounds. There is therefore (exclusive of its signification) a natural relation between the sound of a vile hautboy, and of that verse in Virgil,[8]

Stridenti miserum stipula disperdere Carmen.

or of the other in Milton.

Grate on their scrannel pipes of wretched straw.[9]

So also between the smooth swift glidings of a river, and that of that verse in Horace,[10]

——*at ille*
Labiture, & labetur in omne volubilis aevum.

And thus in part even poetic imitation has its foundation in nature. But then this imitation goes not far; and taken without the meaning derived to the sounds from compact, is but little intelligible, however perfect and elaborate.

§2. If therefore poetry be compared with painting, in respect of this its merely natural and in artificial resemblance, it may be justly said that—in as much as of this sort of resemblance, poetry (like music) has no other sources, than those two of sound and motion—in as much as it often wants these sources themselves (for numbers of words neither have, nor can have any resemblance to those ideas, of which they are the symbols)—in as much as natural sounds and motions, which poetry thus imitates, are themselves but[11] loose and indefinite accidents of those subjects, to which they belong, and consequently do but loosely and indefinitely characterize them—lastly, in as much as poetic sounds and motions do but faintly resemble those of nature, which are themselves confessed to be so imperfect and vague—from all this it will follow (as it has already followed of music) that—poetic imitation founded in mere natural resemblance is much inferior to that of painting, and at best but very imperfect.

§3. As to the preference, which such poetic imitation may claim before musical, or musical imitation before that; the merits on each side may appear perhaps equal. They both fetch their imitations from sound and motion. Now music seems to imitate nature better as to motion, and POETRY as to sound. The reason is, that in motions

[8]Ecl. 3. Ver. 27.
[9]in his *Lycidas.*
[10]Epist. 2. l.r. ver. 42,43.
[11]p. 181.

music[a] has a greater variety; and in sounds, those of poetry approach nearer to nature.[b]

Chap. IV

On the subjects which poetry imitates, not by mere sounds or natural media, but by words significant; the subjects at the same time being such, to which the genius of each of the other two arts is most perfectly adapted—its comparison in these subjects, first with painting, then with music.

The mimetic art of poetry has been hitherto considered, as fetching its imitation from mere natural resemblance. In this it has been shewn much inferior to painting, and nearly equal to music.

It remains to be considered, what its merits are, when it imitates not by mere natural sound, but by sound significant; by words, the compact symbols of all kinds of ideas. From hence depends its genuine force. And here, as it is able to find sounds expressive of every idea, so is there no subject either of picture-imitation, or musical, to which it does not aspire; all things and incidents whatever being, in a manner, to be described by words.

Whether therefore poetry, in this its proper sphere, be equal to its imitation of the other two arts, is the question at present, which comes in order to be discussed.

Now as subjects are infinite, and the other two arts are not equally adapted to imitate all; it is proposed, first to compare poetry with them in such subjects, to which they are most perfectly adapted.

§2. To begin therefore with painting. A subject, in which the power of this art may be most fully exerted, (whether it be taken from the inanimate, or the animal, or the moral world) must be a subject, which is principally and eminently characterized by certain colors, figures, and postures of figures—whose comprehension depends not on a succession of events; or at least, if on a succession, on a short and self-evident one—which admits a large variety of such circumstances, as all concur in the same individual point of time, and relate all to one principle action.

As to such a subject therefore—in as much as poetry is forced to pass through the medium of compact, while painting applies immediately through the medium of nature; the one being understood to all, the other to the speakers of a certain language[12] only—in as much as natural operations must needs be more affecting, than artificial—in as much as painting helps our own rude ideas by its own, which are consummate and wrought up to the perfection of art; while poetry can raise no

[a]Music has no less than five different lengths of notes in ordinary use, reckoning from the semi-brief to the semi-quaver; all which may be infinitely compounded, even in any one time, or measure—Poetry, on the other hand, has but two lengths or quantities, a long syllable and a short, (which is its half) and all the variety of verse arises from such feet and metres, as these two species of syllables, by being compounded, can be made to produce.

[b]Musical sounds are produced by even vibrations, which scarcely any natural sounds are—on the contrary, words are the products of uneven vibration, and so are most natural sounds—add to this, that words are far more numerous, than musical sounds. So that poetry, as to imitation by sound, seems to exceed music, not only in nearness of resemblance, but even in variety also.

[12]note (c) p. 179.

other[a] than what every mind is furnished with before—in as much as painting shews all the minute and various concurrent circumstances of the event in the same individual point of time, as they appear in nature; while poetry is forced to want this circumstance of intelligibility, by being ever obliged to enter into some degree of detail—in as much as this detail creates often the dilemma of either becoming tedious, to be clear; or if not tedious, then obscure—lastly, in as much as all imitations more similar, more immediate, and more intelligible, are preferable to those which are less so; and for the reasons above, the imitations of poetry are less similar, less immediate, and less intelligible than those of painting—from all this it will follow, that—in all subjects, where painting can fully exert itself, the imitations of painting are superior to those of poetry, and consequently in all such subjects that painting has the preference.

§3. And now to compare poetry with music, allowing to music the same advantage of a well-adapted subject, which has already been allowed to painting in the comparison just preceding.

What such a subject is, has already been described.[13] and as to preference, it must be confessed, that—in as much as musical imitations, though natural, aspire not to raise the same ideas,[14] but only ideas similar and analogous; while poetic imitation, though artificial, raises ideas the very same—in as much as the definite and certain is ever preferable to the indefinite and uncertain; and that more especially in imitations, where the principal[b] delight is in recognizing the thing

[a]When we read in Milton of Eve, that

Grace was in all her steps, heav'n in her eye,
In ev'ry gesture dignity and love;

we have an image not of that Eve, which Milton conceived, but of such an Eve only, as every one by his own proper genius, is able to represent, from reflecting on those ideas, which he has annexed to these several sounds. The greater part, in the mean time, have never perhaps bestowed one accurate thought upon what grace, heaven, love, and dignity mean; or even enriched the mind with ideas of beauty, or asked whence they are to be acquired, and by what proportions they are constituted. On the contrary, when we view EVE as painted by an able painter, we labor under no such difficulty; because we have exhibited before us the better conception of an artist, the genuine ideas of perhaps a Titian or a Raphael.

[13]see chap. ii, §2.

[14]p. 181.

[b]That there is an eminent delight in this very recognition itself, abstract from any thing pleasing in the subject recognized, is evident from hence—that, in all the mimetic arts, we can be highly charmed with imitations, at whose originals in nature we are shocked and terrified. Such, for instance, as dead bodies, wild beasts, and the like.

The cause, assigned for this, seems to be of the following kind. We have a Joy, not only in the sanity and perfection, but also in the just and natural energies of our several limbs and faculties. And hence, among others, the Joy in reasoning, as being the energy of that principal faculty, our intellect or understanding. This Joy extends, not only to the wise, but to the multitude. For all men have an aversion to ignorance and error; and in some degree, however moderate, are glad to learn and to inform themselves.

Hence therefore the delight, arising from these imitations; as we are enabled, in each of them, to exercise the reasoning faculty; and, by comparing the copy with the archetype in our minds, to infer that this is such a thing; and that, another; a fact remarkable among children, even in their first and earliest days.

Τὸ, τε γὰρ μεμεῖσθαι, σύμφυτον τοῖς ἀνθρώποις ἐκ παίδων ἐστι, καί τούτω δικφέρουσι τῶ ν ἄλλων ζώων, ὅτι μιμητικώτατον ἐστὶ, κὰι τὰς μαθήσεις ποιεῖται διὰ μεμήσεως τὰς πρώτας καὶ τὸ χαίρειν τοῖς μιμήμασι μάντας. Σημεῖον δὲ τούτου τὸ συμζᾶινον ἐπὶ τῶν ἔργον. Ἅ γὰρ αὐτὰ λυπηρῶς ὁρῶμεν τέτων τὰς εἰκόνας τὰς μάλιστα ἠκριβωμένας, χαίρομεν θεωροῦντες, οἷον θηρίων τε μορφὰς τῶν ἀγριωτάτων, καὶ νεκρῶν. Ἄιτίον δὲ καὶ τούτου, ὅτι μανθάνειν οὐ μόνοῦ τοῖς φιλοσόφοις ἥδιοτον, ἀλλά καὶ τοῖς ἄλλοις ὁμοιως ἀλλ' ἐπὶ βραχὺ κοινωνοῦ σις ἄυτου. Διὰ γὰρ τοῦτο χαίρουσι τὰς εἰκόνας ὁρῶντες, ὅτι συμδαίνει θεωροῦντας μανθάνειν καὶ συλλογίζεσθαι, τί ἕκασ τον οἷον, ὅτι οὗτοδ εκεῖνος. Arist. Poet. c. 4.

imitated—it will follow from hence that—even in subjects the best adapted to musical imitation, the imitation of poetry will be still more excellent.

Chap. V.

On the subjects which poetry imitates by words significant, being at the same time subjects not adapted to the genius of either of the other arts—The nature of those subjects—The abilities of poetry to imitate them—Comparison of poetry in these subjects, first with painting, then with music.

The mimetic art of poetry has now been considered in two views—first, as imitating by mere natural media; and in this it has been placed on a level with music, but much inferior to painting—it has been since considered as imitating through sounds significant by compact, and that in such subjects respectively, where painting and music have the fullest power to exert themselves. Here to painting it has been held inferior, but to music it has been preferred.

It remains to be considered—what other subjects poetry has left, to which the genius of the other two arts is less perfectly adapted—how far poetry is able to imitate them—and whether from the perfection of its imitation, and the nature of the subjects themselves, it ought to be called no more than equal to its sister arts; or whether, on the whole, it should not rather be called superior.

§2. To begin, in the first place, by comparing it with painting.

The subjects of poetry, to which the genius of painting is not adapted, are—all actions, whose whole[a] is of so lengthened a duration, that no point of time, in any part of that whole, can be given fit for painting; neither in its beginning, which will teach what is subsequent; nor in it end, which will teach what is previous; nor in its middle, which will declare both the previous and the subsequent.—Also all subjects so framed, as to lay open the internal constitution of man, and give us an insight into characters, manners, passions, and sentiments.[b]

The merit of these subjects is obvious. They must necessarily of all be the most affecting; the most improving; and such of which the mind has the strongest comprehension.

[a]For a just and accurate description of wholeness and unity, see Arist. poet. ch. 7 & 8. and Bossu, his best interpreter, in his treatise on the epic poem, B. ii. ch. 9, 10, 11.

[b]For a description of character, see note (d) p. 187.

As for manners, it may be said in general, that a certain system of them makes a character; and that as these systems, by being differently compounded, make each a different character, so is it that one man truly differs from another.

Passions are obvious: pity, fear, anger, etc.

Sentiments are discoverable in all those things, which are the proper business and end of speech or discourse. The chief branches of this end are to assert and prove; to solve and refute; to express or excite passions; to amplify incidents, and to diminish them. It is in these things therefore, that we must look for sentiment. See Arist. Poet. c. 19. — ἐστί δὲ κατὰ τὴν Διάνοιαν ταῦτα, ὅσι ὑπὸ τοῦ λόγου δεῖ παρασκευασθῆαι. Μέρη δὲ τόυτων, τό, τε αποδεικνυναι, καὶ τὸ λύειν, καὶ τὸ πάθη παρασκευαζειν,—καὶ ἔτι μέγεθος, καὶ σμικρότητα.

For as to the affecting part—if it be true, that all events more or less affect us, as the subjects, which they respect, are more or less nearly related to us; then surely those events must needs be most affecting, to whose subjects we are of all the most intimately related. Now such is the relation, which we bear to mankind; and men and human actions are the subjects, here proposed for imitation.

As to improvements—there can be none surely (to man at least) so great, as that which is derived from a just and decent representation of human manners, and sentiments. For what can more contribute to give us that master-knowledge,[c] without which all other knowledge will prove of little or no utility?

As to our comprehension—there is nothing certainly, of which we have so strong ideas, as of that which happens in the moral or human world. For as to the internal part, or active principle of the vegetable, we know it but obscurely; because there we can discover neither passion, nor sensation. In the animal world indeed that principle is more seen, and that from the passions and sensations which there declare themselves. Yet all still rests upon the mere evidence of sense; upon the force only of external and unassisted experience. But in the moral or human world, as we have a medium of knowledge far more accurate than this; so from hence it is, that we can comprehend accordingly.

With regard therefore to the various events which happen here, and the various causes, by which they are produced—in other words, of all characters, manners, human passions, and sentiments; besides the evidence of sense, we have the highest evidence additional, in having an express consciousness of something familiar within; of something homogeneous in the recesses of our own minds; in that, which constitutes to each of us his true and real self.

These therefore being the subjects, not adapted to the genius of painting, it comes next to be considered, how far poetry can imitate them.

[c]ΓΗΩΘΙ ΣΑΓΤΟΝ Ἔστιν οὖν τραγωδία μίμησις πράξεως σπουδαίας και τελείας—δι' ἐλεόυ καὶ φόβου περαίνουσα τὴν τῶν ποιούτων παθημάτων κάθαρσιν. But farther, besides obtaining this moral science from the contemplation of human life; an end common both to epic, tragic, and comic poetry; there is a peculiar end to tragedy, that of eradicating the passions of pity and fear. *Greek text* arist. poet. c. 6, tragedy is the imitation of an action important and perfect, through pity and fear working the purgation of such-like passions.

There are none, it is evident so devoid of these two passions, as those perpetually conversant, where the occasions of them are most frequent; such, for instance, as the military men, the professors of medicine, chirugery, and the like. Their minds, by this intercourse, become as it were callous; gaining an apathy by experience, which no theory can every teach them.

Now that, which is wrought in these men by the real disasters of life, may be supposed wrought in others by the fictions of tragedy; yet with this happy circumstance in favor of tragedy, that, without the disasters being real, it can obtain the same end.

It must however, for all this, be confessed, that an effect of this kind cannot reasonably be expected, except among nations, like the Athenians of old, who lived in a perpetual attendance upon these theatrical representations. For it is not a single or occasional application to these passions, but a constant and uninterrupted, by which alone they may be lessened or removed.

It would be improper to conclude this note, without observing, that the philosopher in this place by pity means not philanthropy, natural affection, a readiness to relieve others in their calamities and distress; but, by pity, he means that senseless effeminate consternation, which seizes weak minds, on the sudden prospect of any thing disastrous; which, in its more violent effects, is seen in shriekings, swoonings, etc. a passions, so far from laudable, or from operating to the good of others, that it is certain to deprive the party, who labors under its influence, of all capacity to do the least good office.

And here, that it has abilities clearly equal, cannot be doubted; as it has that for the medium of its imitation, through which nature declares herself in the same subjects. For the sentiments in real life are only known by men's discourse.[15] And the characters, manners, and passions of men being the prompters to what they say; it must needs follow, that their discourse will be a constant specimen of those characters, manners, and passions.

Format enim natura prius nos intus ad on men
Fortunarum habitum; juvat, aut impellit ad iram:
Post effert animi motus, interprete lingua.[16]

Not only therefore language is an adequate medium of imitation, but in sentiments it is the only medium; and in manners and passions there is no other, which can exhibit them to us after that clear, precise, and definite way, as they in nature stand allotted to the various sorts of men, and are found to constitute the several characters of each.[d]

§3. To compare therefore poetry, in these subjects, with painting—in as much as no subjects of painting are wholly[17] superior to poetry; while subjects, here described, far exceed the power of painting—in as much as they are of all subjects the most affecting[18], and improving, and such of which we have the strongest comprehension—further, in as much as poetry can most accurately[19] imitate them—in as much as, besides all imitation, there is a charm in poetry, arising from its very

[15] p. 185, note (b).

[16] Hor. De Arte Poet. vers. 108.

[d] It is true indeed that (besides what is done by poetry) there is some idea of character, which even painting can communicate. Thus there is no doubt, but that such a countenance may be found by painters for Aeneas, as would convey upon view a mild, human, and yet a brave disposition. But then this idea would be vague and general. It would be concluded, only in the gross, that the hero was good. As to that system of qualities peculiar to Aeneas only, and which alone properly constitutes his true and real character, this would still remain a secret, and be no way discoverable. For how deduce it from the mere lineaments of a countenance? Or, if it were deducible, how few spectators would there be found so sagacious? It is here therefore, that recourse must be had, not to painting, but to poetry. So accurate a conception of character can be gathered only from a succession of various, and yet consistent actions; a succession, enabling us to conjecture, what the person of the drama will do in the future, from what already he has done in the past. Now to such an imitation, poetry only is equal; because it is not bounded, like painting, to short, and, as it were, instant events, but may imitate subjects of any duration whatever. See Arist. Poet. cap. 6. Ἔστι δὲ ἦθος μὲν τὸ τοιοῦτον, ὅ δηλοῖ τὴν προκρέσιν ὁποῖα τις ἐστὶν, ἐν οἷς οὐκ ἔζι δῆλον, ἐι προαιρεῖται ἤ θεύγει ὁ λέγων. See also the ingenious and learned Bossu, book 4, ch. 4.

[17] p. 178, 183.

[18] p. 185, etc.

[19] p. 187, etc. [above]

numbers[e] ; whereas painting has pretense to no charm, except that of imitation only—lastly, (which will soon be shewn[20]) in as much as poetry is able to associate music, as a most powerful ally; of which assistance, painting is utterly incapable—from all this it may be fairly concluded, that—poetry is not only equal, but that it is in fact far superior to its sister art of painting.

§4. But if it exceed painting in subjects, to which painting is not adapted; no doubt will it exceed music in subjects to [which] music [is] not adapted. For here it has been preferred[21], even in those subjects, which have been held adapted the best of all.

§5. Poetry is therefore, on the whole, much superior to either of the other mimetic arts; it having been shewn to be equally excellent in the accuracy[22] of its imitation; and to imitate subjects, which far surpass, as well in utility[23], as in dignity[24].

Chap. VI

On music considered not as an imitation, but as deriving its efficacy from another source.—On its joint operation by this means with poetry—An objection to music solved.—The advantage arising to it, as well as to poetry, from their being united.—Conclusion.

In the above discourse, music has been mentioned as an ally[25] to poetry. It has also been said to derive its efficacy[26] from another source, than imitation. It remains therefore, that these things be explained.

[e]That there is a charm in poetry, arising from its numbers only, may be made evident from the five or six first lines of the *Paradise Lost*; where, without any pomp of phrase, sublimity of sentiment, or the least degree of imitation, every reader must find himself to be sensibly delighted; and that, only from the graceful and simple cadence of the numbers, and artful variation of the saesura or pause, so essential to the harmony of every good poem.

An English heroic verse consists of ten semipeds, or half-feet. Now in the lines above-mentioned the pauses are varied upon differnt semipeds in the order which follows; as may be seen by any, who will be at the pains to examine

Paradise Lost, B. I.

verse 1		semiped 7
——— 2		——— 6
——— 3	has its pause	——— 6
——— 4	fall upon	——— 5
——— 5		——— 3
——— 6		——— 4

[20]chap. vi.
[21]ch iv. §3.
[22]p. 187.
[23]p. 186.
[24]see p. 185 and p. 180, note g. See also p. 179.
[25]p. 188 [above].
[26]p. 181.

Now, in order to this, it is first to be observed, that there are various affections, which may be raised by the power of music. There are sounds to make us cheerful, or sad; martial, or tender; and so of almost every other affection, which we feel.

It is also further observable, that there is a reciprocal operation between our affections, and our ideas; so that, by a sort of natural sympathy, certain ideas necessarily tend to raise in us certain affections; and those affections, by a sort of counter-operation, to raise the same ideas. Thus ideas derived from funerals, torture, murders, and the like, naturally generate the affection of melancholy. And when, by any physical causes, that affection happens to prevail, it is, that ideas, derived from external causes, have at different times, upon the same person, so different an effect. If they happen to suit the affections, which prevail within, then is their impression most sensible, and their effect most lasting. If the contrary be true, then is the effect contrary. Thus, for instance, a funeral will much more affect the same man, if he see it when melancholy, than if he see it when cheerful.

Now this being premised, it will follow, that whatever happens to be the affection or disposition of mind, which ought naturally to result from the genius of any poem, the same probably it will be in the power of some species of music to excite. But whenever the proper affection prevails, it has been allowed that then all kindred ideas, derived from external causes, make the most sensible impressions. The ideas therefore of poetry must needs make the most sensible impression, when the affections[a], peculiar to them, are already excited by the music. For here a double force is made co-operate to one end. A poet, thus assisted, finds not an audience in a temper, averse to the genius of his poem, or perhaps at best under a cool indifference; but by the preludes, the symphonies, and concurrent operation of the music in all its parts, roused into those very affections, which he would most desire.

An audience, so disposed, not only embraces with pleasure the ideas of the poet, when exhibited; but, in a manner, even anticipates them in their several imaginations. The superstitious have not a more previous tendency to be frightened at the sight of specters, or a lover to fall into raptures at the sight of his mistress; than a mind, thus tempered by the power of music, to enjoy all ideas, which are suitable to that temper.

And hence the genuine charm of music, and the wonders which it works, through its great professors.[b] a power which consists not in imitations, and the raising ideas; but in the raising affections, to which ideas may correspond. There are few to be found so insensible, I may even say so inhumane, as when good poetry is justly set to music, not in some degree to feel the force of so amiable an union. But to the muses friends it is a force irresistible, and penetrates into the deepest recesses of the soul.

[a]Quintilian elegantly, and exactly apposite to this reasoning, says of music—*Namque etc. voce etc. modulatione grandia elate, jucunda dulciter, morderata leniter canit, totaque arte consentit cum corum, quae dicuntur, affectibus.* Inst. orator. 1. I. cap. 10.

[b]Such, above all, is George Frederick Handel; whose genius, having been cultivated by continued exercise, and being itself far the sublimist and most universal now known, has justly placed him without an equal, or a second. This transient testimony could not be denied so excellent an artist, from whom this treatise has borrowed such eminent examples, to justify its assertions in what it has offered concerning music.

—— pectus inaniter angit,
Irritat, mulcet, falsis terroribus implet.[27]

§2. Now this is that source, from whence music was said[28] formerly to derive its greatest efficacy. And here indeed, not in imitation,[c] ought it to be chiefly cultivated. On this account also it has been called a powerful ally[29] to poetry. And farther, it is by the help of this reasoning, that the objection is solved, which is raised against the singing of poetry (as in opera's, oratorio's, etc.) from the want of probability and resemblance to nature. To one indeed, who has no musical ear, this objection may have weight. It may even perplex a lover of music, if it happen to surprise him in his hours of indifference. But when he is feeling the charm of poetry so accompanied, let him be angry (if he can) with that, which serves only to interest him more feelingly in the subject, and support him in a stronger and more earnest attention; which enforces, by its aid, the several ideas of the poem, and gives them to his imagination with unusual strength and grandeur. He cannot surely but confess, that he is a gainer in the exchange, when he barters the want of a single probability, that of pronunciation (a thing merely arbitrary and every where different) for a noble heightening of affections which are suitable to the occasion, and enable him to enter into the subject with double energy and enjoyment.

§3. From what has been said it is evident, that these two arts can never be so powerful singly, as when they are properly united. For poetry, when alone, must be necessarily forced to waste many of its richest ideas, in the mere raising of affections, when, to have been properly relished, it should have found those affections in their highest energy. And music, when alone, can only raise affections, which soon languish and decay, if not maintained and fed by the nutritive images of poetry. Yet must it be remembered, in this union, that poetry ever have the precedence; its utility,[30] as well as dignity, being by far the more considerable.

§4. And thus much, for the present as to music,[31] painting, and poetry, the circumstances, in which they agree, and in which they differ; and the preference, due to one of them above the other two.

[27]Horat. Epist. I. 1. 2. vers. 211.
[28]p. 181.
[c]For the narrow extent and little efficacy of music, considered as mimetic or imitative art, see ch. ii, §3.
[29]p. 188.
[30]ch. v. §2. p. 185.
[31]p. 178.

CHAPTER 7

John Baillie*

An Essay on the Sublime
1744

Sec. I.

We are now, Palemon, to treat of that kind of writing, which of all others is the truly excellent and great manner, and which is peculiar to a genius noble, lofty, comprehensive. You will easily know I mean the sublime, and perhaps may tell me the talk is difficult; I acknowledge it, especially when I consider that we have already a great author upon the subject, who has received the approbation of ages, and who, in the opinion of most, has exhausted it.—Yet I have something to plead as my apology for my presumption, for such I believe it may be reckoned, although not by you, yet by one, *qui redit ad fastos, et virtutem aestimat annis.*

Not withstanding Longinus entitles his treatise, *A Treatise Upon the Sublime*, yet whoever considers the full extent of the work, will perceive the author does not confine himself to the bare explanation of any one certain and particular manner in writing. Some part of his treatise regards the figurative style, some the pathetic, and indeed some part regards what I think is properly called the sublime.—However, the

*Although Dr. John Baillie's *Essay* evidently attracted some notice when it was published, and it is frequently cited in current work on the eighteenth century, he is a somewhat shadowy figure. He does not appear in the *Dictionary of National Biography*. Samuel Monk says of him "Ralph Strauss records the publication by Dodsley of his play, *The Married Coquet*, on April 8, 1747, and of the Essay on April 20 of the same year. See *Robert Dodsley* (London and New York, 1910), p. 333. The *Biographica Dramatica* states the he was one of the 'physicians to St. George's Hospital, and also physician to the English army in Flanders. He died of a spotted fever in Ghent, in December, 1743.' See D. E. Baker, *Biographica Dramtica*, etc. (Dublin, 1787), I, 9. The date of his death seems to be correct, since it agrees with the appearance of Baillie's name in the list of deaths in 'The Monthly Chronologer,' *The London Magazine* (January, 1747), p. 49." See Samuel H. Monk, *The Sublime* (Ann Arbor: University of Michigan Press, 1960), n. 26, pp. 72-73.

bulk of the performance relates more to the perfection of writing in general, than to any particular kind or species.

As every different manner of writing has its peculiar character, it must likewise have its different principles, and to treat of them separately must undoubtedly be the clearer method. Besides, Longinus has entirely passed over the inquiry of what the sublime is, as a thing perfectly well known and is principally intent upon giving rules to arrive at the elevated turn and manner. That the sublime no sooner presents itself than we are affected by it, I readily acknowledge; but that we generally form accurate and distinct ideas upon this subject, is by no means true; and although in itself perfectly distinct from either the pathetic, or figurative manner, yet it is often confounded with both. The genuine work therefore of criticism is to define the limits of each kind of writing, and to prescribe their proper distinctions. Without this there can be no legitimate performance, which is the just conformity to the laws or rules of that manner of writing in which the piece is designed. But the manner must be defined before the rules can be established; and we must know, for example, what history is before we can know how it differs from novel and romance, and before we can judge how it ought to be conducted.

Hence it seems, that rules for the sublime should most naturally result from an inquiry what the sublime is; and if this is an inquiry which Longinus has entirely passed over, there is still room for further speculation. But as the sublime in writing is no more than a description of the sublime in nature, and as it were painting to the imagination what nature herself offers to the senses, I shall begin with an inquiry into the sublime of natural objects, which I shall afterwards apply to writing.

Few are so insensible, as not to be struck even at first view with what is truly sublime; and every person upon seeing a grand object is affected with something which as it were extends his very being, and expands it to a kind of immensity. Thus in viewing the heavens, how is the soul elevated; and stretching itself to larger scenes and more extended prospects, in a noble enthusiasm of grandeur quits the narrow earth, darts from planet to planet, and takes in worlds at one view! Hence comes the name of sublime to every thing which thus raises the mind to fits of greatness, and disposes it to soar above her mother earth; hence arises that exultation and pride which the mind ever feels from the consciousness of its own vastness.—That object only can be justly called sublime, which in some degree disposes the mind to this enlargement of itself, and gives her a lofty conception of her own powers.

This exalted sensation, then, will always determine us to a right judgment; for wherever we feel the elevated disposition, there we are sure the sublime must be. But notwithstanding we acknowledge its presence, we are frequently ignorant what it is in objects which constitutes the grand, and gives them this power of expanding the mind. We often confess the sublime as we do the deity; it fills and dilates our soul without being able to penetrate into its nature, and define its essence. Yet however true this may be in many instances, a diligent inquiry may overcome the difficulty; and from an examination of particulars, we may come at such general principles, as shall enable us universally to define the sublime of every natural object.

We know by experience, that nothing produces this elevation equal to large prospects, vast extended views, mountains, the heavens, and an immense ocean.—But what in these objects affects us? For we can view, without being the least exalted, a little brook, although as smooth a surface, nay, clearer stream than the Nile or Danube; but can we behold these vast rivers, or rather, the vaster ocean, without feeling an elevated pleasure? A flowery vale, or the verdure of a hill, may charm; but to fill the soul, and raise it to the sublime sensations, the earth must rise into an Alp, or Pyrrhenean, and mountains piled upon mountains, reach to the very heavens.—May not also the clearness of the sky, and its agreeable azure, be viewed through a crevice without the least admiration? But when a flood of light bursts in, and the vast heavens are on every side widely extended to the eye, it is then the soul enlarges, and would stretch herself out to the immense expanse. It is not, therefore, the vastness of these objects which elevates us, and shall we not by looking a little narrowly into the mind be convinced that large objects only are fitted to raise this exaltedness?

The soul naturally supposes herself present to all the objects she perceives, and has lower or higher conceptions of her own excellency, as this extensiveness of her being is more or less limited. An universal presence is one of the sublime attributes of the Deity; then how much greater an existence must the soul imagine herself when contemplating the heavens she takes in the mighty orbs of the planets, and is present to a universe, than when shrunk into the narrow space of a room, and how much nearer advancing to the perfections of the universal presence?—This extending her being, raises in her a noble pride, and upon such occasions no wonder she conceives (as Longinus observes) something greater of herself. But as a consciousness of her own vastness is what pleases, so nothing can raise this consciousness but a vastness in the objects about which she is employed.—For whatever the essence of the soul may be, it is the reflections arising from sensations only which makes her acquainted with herself, and know her faculties. Vast objects occasion vast sensations, and vast sensations give the mind a higher idea of her own powers—small scenes (except from association, which I shall hereafter consider) have never this effect; the beauty of them may please, and the variety be agreeable, but the soul is never filled by them.

Sect. II.

Thus far, Palemon, we have proceeded in a kind of investigation; we have first inquired what disposition of mind was created by grand objects, the sublime of nature; this we found to be an effort of the soul to extend its being, and hence an exultation, from a consciousness of its own vastness: We then in particular and confessed instances examined what it was in objects raised this disposition, which we afterwards found to be their magnitude, and this likewise in a more universal manner from the very nature of our minds.

Yet notwithstanding we have demonstrated that the vastness of the object constitutes the sublime, to render the sublime perfect, two things are requisite; a certain degree of uniformity, and that by long custom the objects do not become familiar to the imagination.

From reason, as well as from experience, we may be convinced how requisite uniformity is; for when the object is uniform, by seeing part, the least glimpse gives a full and complete idea of the whole, and thus at once may be distinctly conveyed the vastest sensation. On the contrary, where this uniformity is wanting, the mind must run from object to object, and never get a full and complete prospect. Thus instead of having one large and grand idea, a thousand little ones are shuffled in. Here the magnitude of the scene is entirely broke, and consequently the noble pride and sublime sensation destroyed.—For what a different conception must the soul have of herself, when with the greatest facility she can view the greatest objects, and when with pain she must hurry from part to part, and with difficulty acquire even an incomplete view? But as uniformity contributes much to the mind's receiving a grand idea of the object itself, so likewise does it greatly flatter that conscious pride I have already mentioned. Where an object is vast, and at the same time uniform, there is to the imagination no limit of its vastness, and the mind runs out into infinity, continually creating as it were from the pattern. Thus when the eye loses the vast ocean, the imagination having nothing to arrest it, catches up the scene and extends the prospect to immensity, which it could by no means do, were the uniform surface broke by innumerable little islands scattered up and down, and the mind thus led into the consideration of the various parts; for this adverting to dissimilar parts ever destroys the creative power of the imagination. However beautiful the hemisphere may be when curled over with little silver-tinged clouds, and the blue sky every where breaking through, yet the prospect is not near so grand as when in a vast and uniform heaven there is nothing to stop the eye, or limit the imagination. You will here, Palemon, object the evening heavens diversified by numberless stars, than which I grant nothing can be more sublime; but I believe your acuteness will no sooner start than resolve the difficulty. We who have considered the fixed stars as so many suns, the centers of systems, and know the planets, like our earth, move in vast orbits, how must our imagination, stretching to myriads of worlds, measure an immense space between each revolving planet? It will not be here improper to observe, that a solemn sedateness generally attends a sublime turn; for although the pathetic may be often joined with it, yet of itself the sublime rather composes, than agitates the mind; which being filled with one large, simple, and uniform idea, becomes (if I may use the expression) one simple, grand sensation.

Uncommoness, though it does not constitute the sublime of natural objects, very much heightens its effect upon the mind: For as great part of the elevation raised by vast and grand prospects, is owing to the mind's finding herself in the exercise of more enlarged powers, and hence judging higher of herself, custom makes this familiar, and she no longer admires her own perfection. It is here, as in all other things, variety is wanting; and indeed could there be a continual shifting of scenes, something of the admiration might be kept up, and even of that opinion the soul conceives of herself. But we are in a world too limited for such a change of prospects; a large mountain, the ocean, a rainbow, the heavens, and some few more of the like kind, yield all the variety we can here enjoy. The grandeur of the heavens seldom affects us, it is our daily object, and two or three days at sea would sink all that elevated pleasure we feel upon viewing a vast ocean; yet, upon particular occasions, both the one and the other of these objects will raise the mind, how much soever accustomed to them—and this is when by any circumstance the imagination is set to work, and by its creative power the object is rendered new.—Thus in a clear evening heaven, each star awakens the imagination to new creation, and the whole firmament is extended out into systems of worlds; nay, perhaps, it is even true, that wherever the mind adverts to the vastness of the object, there she always feels the sublime sensation; but from long custom the object being made familiar, although before her, she does not advert to it.—As kings themselves forget their dignity, till roused by the ensigns of power, they re-assume their grandeur. Admiration, a passion always attending the sublime, arises from uncommonness, and constantly decays as the object becomes more and more familiar.

An attempt to determine the greatness requisite to constitute the sublime of objects, would be vain and fruitless; upon the other hand, there is no affirming, that an object, although truly grand, will equally affect all minds; some are naturally fitted to consider things in the most enlarged views; others as naturally dissect great objects themselves, and by a diminutive genius render what is truly magnificent, little, and mean; for no object is so grand, but is attended with some trifling circumstance, upon which a little mind will surely fix; the universe has its cockle-shells, and its butterflies, the ardent pursuits of childish geniuses. Not that even great minds do not sometimes unbend, and amuse themselves with baubles; nay, they are not at all times equally fitted to receive sublime impressions; for when the soul flags and is depressed, the vastest object is uncapable of raising her. But at other times, when the blood moves brisk, the pulse beats high, and the soul has lofty conceptions of herself, she sublimes every thing about her, or to speak more truly, snatches herself away from the minute of things, and throws herself into grand prospects, and the magnificence of nature.

From all this it is evident how different are the degrees of greatness, fitted to raise this passion: First, the Nile within his banks; then when he swelling overflows them, and widely extends himself over the whole country; but above all, when the eye loses itself in the immense ocean, or the imagination in infinite space and the unbounded system of things.

Sect. III.

These, then, are the general principles, nor am I aware how many objections will be made against them. Is there not a sublime in painting, in music, in architecture, but above all, in virtue?—Yet are there large objects, or is there anything immense in Prodicus's Hercules, whose judgment or resolution is universally allowed noble and sublime?—Here we must own the difficult part of our task begins; yet if the principles we have laid down be applied even to such things as seemingly contradict them, it will be no small confirmation of their soundness and truth. We shall therefore consider the sublime of the passions, the sublime of science, and of the arts, such as architecture, music, and painting, and the sublime of such objects as arise merely from association.

In searching into the sublime of the passions, it is not my intent to re-examine the disposition we feel upon viewing the grand and magnificent; but to inquire into those affections, which when they appear in another, are ever deemed great, and affect the person who contemplates them with an elevated turn of mind. For the sublime of the passions must influence the mind in the same manner as the sublime of natural objects, and must produce the same exaltedness of disposition.—Were not their effect upon the mind, the same exaltedness of disposition;—they would with impropriety, bear the same name, and could by no means be the subject of this inquiry.

Although names are at first arbitrarily imposed, yet things of like nature ought ever to be classed under like appellations; and nothing brings greater confusion into knowledge than giving like names to things of unlike nature. Language abounds with too many inaccuracies of this kind, and hence arises the vast difficulty in adjusting and defining the proper limits to many things. Beauty attributed to ten thousand dissimilar objects has never yet, nor ever can be universally defined; for definition is the selecting of such common properties in objects as ever exist with the objects, and constitute their very nature, and thus regards a class, or arrangement of things similar, under the same head or appellation. Mathematicians, when they define a circle, disregarding the greatness or smallness, pitch upon a common property peculiar to the figure, by which they define and reduce all figures with this property under the same head. But if many things of different nature go by the same name, no one definition can be applicable to them. Beauty, indeed, when applied to figure and proportion, may be and has been defined, because here it regards a class. Thus when we call regular figures beautiful, and irregular ones deformed, we find the common property of uniformity amidst variety constitutes the beauty of the first, and the want of this uniformness, the ugliness or deformity of the latter.

But not to digress too far. It is equally incumbent upon the philosopher and critic to prevent names from being confounded, and to refer each thing to its proper class, if such there be; therefore when I treat of the sublime, I treat of a certain order of things, which from a similitude either in themselves, or their effects, are arranged under one head, and constitute a class or species. And let the name of sublime be ever so frequently applied to a thing, yet if it bears no relation to this class, either in itself, or its effect, it is falsely so called, and is not the business of this present inquiry. I have been the more particular, Palemon, upon this point, because I know how often the word sublime is improperly used.

Such affections, then, or passions, as produce in the person who contemplates them an exalted and sublime disposition, can alone with propriety be called sublime: But affections which are only felt by him in whose breast they are, can never be the immediate object of another's knowledge; and when we contemplate passions out of ourselves, we know them only at a kind of second hand. But as no affection can subsist without its proper object, the cause or motive of the affection; we must argue from the cause to the effect, and judge and determine of the passion merely from a consideration of its object.—What one person, in whose breast they are, knows immediately and by sensation, another can only know mediately and by induction; and therefore in considering the sublime of the passions, their objects only can be the proper subject for examination, the objects alone being really what affects the person who would contemplate the passions—And thus we judge of the courage of a person, by his steadiness in braving dangers; of his piety, by the just adoration he pays to the supreme being; and of his humanity, by his deportment to his fellow-creatures. He himself can only know the affection as it exists in his own breast.

Now, if the objects of such passions as are universally allowed sublime, be themselves vast and extended, the principles I have already laid down will be as equally applicable to the sublime of the passions, as to the sublime of inanimate objects; and we shall find that loftiness of mind and elevated turn, which we feel upon contemplating any of these affections, to arise from the imagination being immediately thrown into large prospects, and extended scenes of action.

The affections unexceptionably sublime, are heroism, or desire of conquest, such as in an Alexander or a Caesar; love of one's country; of mankind in general, or universal benevolence; a desire of fame and immortality: Nor has the contempt of death, power, or of honor, a less title to be numbered amongst the sublime affections.

Heroism, or pursuit of conquest, generally arises either from a desire of power, or passion for fame; or from both. Power and fame, therefore, are the objects of this affection, which let us separately consider.

It is not every power which is the ambition of a hero, nor every power which carries the idea of sublime. A Caligula commanding armies to fill their helmets with cockle-shells, is a power mean and contemptible, although ever so absolute; but suppose an Alexander laying level towns, depopulating countries, and ravaging the whole world, how does the sublime rise, nay though mankind be the sacrifice to his ambition! The same may be said of power when it regards strength; for the greatest strength, even that of the giants or *terra filii*, if only employed in grinding the hardest adamant to powder, or in reducing the solidest gold to dust, has nothing sublime or grand.—But consider them in their fabulous history rooting up mountains and piling Ossa upon Olympus, then is their strength attended with the sublime. Thus our idea of power is more or less sublime, as the power itself is more or less extended. The absolute authority of a master over his slaves, is a power nothing grand; yet the same authority in a prince is sublime.—But why? From his sway extending to multitudes, and from nations bowing to his commands. But it is in the almighty that this sublime is completed, who with a nod can shatter to pieces the foundations of a universe, as with a word he called it into being.

I cannot here pass over (although more properly belonging to the sublime of writing) the passage in Moses.—"God said, let there be light, and there was light." The sublime of this passage consists in the idea it gives us of the power of the almighty; but his power with regard to what? A vastly diffused being, unlimited as his own essence.—And hence the idea becomes so exalted. Let there be earth, and there was earth, surely would come infinitely short of the other, as the object or power presents itself to us infinitely more limited. From all this, I think I may fairly conclude, that the sublime of power is from its object being vast and immense.

I need say little upon the head of fame. To be praised not only by the present generation, but through the revolving circle of ages down to latest posterity, is stretching our expectations and our ideas to an immensity; and from this the sublime of the passion itself arises; for although the approbation of a worthy man ought to bear more weight than the undistinguishing applause of thousands, yet the desire of such a single approbation, however virtuous, has nothing great or sublime in it. Thus, if it be true of any one passion, that the vastness of its object constitutes the sublime, it is most strictly so of this; and whatever is the motive of heroism, whether desire of power, or of fame, or of both, the sublime of the affection is the greatness of its object.

As to the love of our country, or rather universal benevolence, which like the sun every where diffuses itself, who can have any idea of it, without taking into his view large societies, numberless nations, all mankind reaching from pole to pole, from the rising to the setting-sun? And this is the sublime of benevolence, extending itself to the remotest of humankind. But how would the sublime sink, if in this large scene the imagination should fix upon a narrow object, a child, a parent, or a mistress! Indeed, love to any of the individuals, nay, to all of them, when considered as individuals, and one by one, has nothing of exalted; it is when we love them collectively, when we love them in vast bodies stretching over large countries, that we feel the sublime rise.

The affection of a parent to a child, although more intense, perhaps, than any other, yet has nothing great in it; nay, I will venture to affirm, not even friendship itself, without it be accidental; as all the passions, by apt connection may exist with the sublime.

Thus when friendship prompts a man to sacrifice honors, wealth, and power, to despise the greatness of the world and brave death, it then becomes truly great; nor need I, Palemon, cloy you with the repeated reasons.

Hence the object of the passion only, not the intenseness of it, renders it great and noble; and hence a contempt of riches, of honors, power, and empire, may be justly reckoned amongst the grand affections. But perhaps it may be asked, how the contempt of that can be great, the desire of which I have already allowed so; or if it be true, that the contempt is great, how can I reconcile my former assertion to what Longinus affirms; to wit,—nothing is great, the contempt of which is great—as riches, dignities, honors, and empire.

Sect. IV.

Here, Palemon, I must observe that the sublime, and virtue, are quite different things; the decorum of actions, distinct from the exalted. Honors, dignities, and empire, in their own nature partake nothing of virtue; but that they do of the grand, I think I have plainly shewn. Now in a moral sense it is certainly true, if in any circumstance the contempt of these things is great (by which Longinus can surely mean no more than becoming or virtuous,) in the same circumstance the desire of them can never be great; but if he understands the word great in its true and genuine sense, I cannot see why the desire, as well as the contempt of them may not be truly grand: For as the object is the same in both cases, and as it is the object which renders the affection sublime, in both cases there must be a sublime. And the passion of Caesar to conquest and empire, is no less sublime, than the stoic apathy of the philosopher (if such there ever was, or ever shall be,) who should reject them; though we might allow in the latter a more virtuous and laudable affection.

When virtue is at any time sublime, it is not that she is the same as the sublime, but that she associates with it, and from this association each acquires new charms: Virtue becomes more commanding, the sublime more engaging. When Hercules rejecting the proffered luxury of palaces, and pomp of courts, prefers virtue, traverses the earth in the pursuit of honor, and thinks the whole world scene little enough of action, how does the virtuous greatness of his soul charm and strike us with a sublime admiration! Had he only preferred an honest retirement to rosy garlands, banquet, song, and dance, the enticements of the alluring goddess, where would have been the sublime? Indeed his resolution would have been even then still virtuous.

A just order of affections, where no one desire, by a dissonance and jarring with the rest, breaks the harmony of the passions, is what constitutes the beauty and becomingness of character; and if virtue be the pursuit of our greatest happiness in the good of society, this becomingness is virtue herself: For proportioned affections render us most happy in ourselves, and most beneficial to mankind; and a virtuous passion or appetite is such as the satisfying of it neither necessarily produces disturbance in the affections, nor disorder in society.—I say, necessarily;—For often by accident the most virtuous affection is attended with bad consequences; but this is not equally true of the sublime passions.—Desire of fame, honors, or empire, often creates the greatest tumult in the affections, and the greatest mischief to mankind.

Thus most of the sublime passions, when virtuous, are so by association and accident; and although the indications of elevated souls, yet are not always of virtuous. The hero who insults mankind, and ravages the earth merely for power and fame, is but an immense monster, and as such only ought to be gazed at; he may indeed, by a mild use of conquest, gild over the cruelty of his actions, but can never render them solidly good.—Yet such is the force of the sublime, that even these men, who in one light can be esteemed no other than the butchers of human race, yet when considered as braving dangers, conquering kingdoms, and spreading the terror of their name to the rest of mankind, and become almost the objects of worship. But there is a sublime which is always virtuous, and where the virtue as well as sublime increases with the object; I mean that of love; first to the particular community whereof we are members; then to our native country; to mankind in general; and last to the universal genius. When once the soul can be raised to this noble enthusiasm, and can make an infinitely great being the object of her love, and as it were take him into her affections, it is then she feels the greatest sublime possible, and conceives something infinitely grand of herself; honors, dignity, and empire are objects truly little and mean to a mind thus united with divinity.

Contempt of death is neither always virtuous, nor always sublime; the wretch who, intoxicated with liquor, braves death at a gallows, shews neither a virtuous nor a great soul; but a Cato, who will not barter the real dignity of character for all the false honors a cajoling Caesar can heap upon him, and who in cool deliberation, rather than drag a life in the slavery of vile submission, and mean adulations, chooses to die with liberty and his country, evinces, in the action, the grandeur and virtue of a Roman soul. In these circumstances, the contempt of death is both laudable and sublime; the fear of it, mean and despicable. Cato, in giving up life, had in view immortality and everlasting liberty, the sublime enjoyment of the almighty; whilst the orator, who basely courted life in mean flatteries to a tyrant, had in prospect nothing but the contracted space of a few years spent in abject slavery: And yet this, perhaps, was more pardonable in the orator than it would have been in the patriot. For besides the beauty of virtue in general, there is likewise a decorum or becomingness belonging to character.—The easy manners of an Atticus can allow many things which would be deformed in the inflexible virtue of a Cato. The good-natured Atticus had the humanness, not the dignity of character to support; roughness and cruelty would have defaced and deformed his character, not compliance and submission. But for the rigid Roman to have lived quietly under tyranny, would have been such a breach of character, such a depravity in his manners, that he must have preferred a thousand deaths before it.—For to see the stubborn oak bow to every blast, is unnatural, however agreeable it may be to see the yielding corn wave to the breeze.

I think now, Palemon, I have considered most, if not all the sublime passions, and have shewn that the greatness of the object makes the sublime of the affections. This we shall find true, should we yet in another manner render the passions the objects of our senses. Allegory has already clothed most of them in human form, and should we attempt in the ancient way of fable to draw the sublime affections of their objects in emblematical portraitures, what a giant would heroism appear! Liberty, perhaps, like the deity, is too vast a being to be circumscribed by form; but fame has been already pictured to us, and pictured as a being of immense greatness:—*Ingrediturq; solo, et caput inter nubila condit.*—Nor does power deserve a less size: But how would benevolence, spreading out her downy wings wide as the arched heavens, kindly brood over the world! In short, if we do these passions justice, we ought to paint them in all the grandeur and majesty Homer does his Neptune, under whose vast strides, forests and mountains trembled.

Before I conclude this subject, I must observe, that all the passions of the human mind may exist each with the other, and hence it frequently happens that the sublime affections are blended with those of a quite contrary nature. There ever enters in the description of storms (as I have already observed) some small degree of dread, and this dread may be so heightened (when a person is actually in one) as entirely to destroy the sublime. By this means an object in itself grand may by association lose most if not all it's effect. Yet, Palemon, it seems strange that a being so simple, so much one as the mind, should at the same time feel joy and grief, pleasure and pain, in short, be the subject of contradictions; or can it be true that the mind can feel pleasure and pain at the same instant? or rather, do not they succeed each other by such infinitely quick vicissitudes, as to appear instantaneous; as a lighted globe, moving in quick revolutions, seems one continued circle of fire?—but which every way the mind perceives, it is certain to common observation, the most different passions and sensations possess the mind at the same time. The prick of a pin will give pain, while the most delicious food is flattering the palate, or the highest perfumes the smell. The sublime dilates and elevates the soul, fear sinks and contracts it; yet both are felt upon viewing what is great and awful. And we cannot conceive a deity armed with thunder without being struck with a sublime terror; but if we regard him as infinite source of happiness, the benign dispenser of benefits, it is not then the dreadful, but the joyous sublime we feel. From these associations there arises different kinds of sublime, where yet the sublime is the predominant; and from these associations, likewise, results a greater beauty to it.—The fine blue of the heavens yields a more delightfully sublime prospect, than had they been of a dusky obscure color. These connections, however, often occasion not only a confusion of terms, but even of ideas; nor indeed is it always so easy to separate our sensations. The grand may be so blended with the pathetic and warm, in the description of battles, as difficultly to be divided, and consequently the complex sensation arising from thence as difficultly resolved. By this means the pathetic is often mistaken for the sublime; but whoever considers the different nature of the two, will upon all occasions easily distinguish them.

The sublime, when it exists simple and unmixed, by filling the mind with one vast and uniform idea, affects it with a solemn sedateness; by this means the soul itself becomes, as it were, one simple grand sensation. Thus the sublime not hurrying us from object to object, rather composes than agitates, whilst the very essence of the pathetic conflicts in an agitation of the passions, which is ever effected by crowding into the thoughts a thousand different objects, and hurrying the mind into various scenes.

Sect. V.

Before I proceed to examine the sublime in arts and sciences, it will not perhaps be entirely useless to observe, that objects in general delight from two sources; either because naturally fitted to please, from a certain harmony and disposition of their parts, or because long associated with objects really agreeable; and thus, though in themselves there be nothing at first delightful, they at last become so. Perhaps of this kind of association the fondness which a lover conceives even to the imperfections of his mistress, may not be the worst instance; a cast of the eye, a lisp, or any other little blemish, shall by a fond lover quickly be deified into a beauty, and receive more adoration than the real beautiful and charming.

Hence we see the powerful force of connection. Nor does this only happen in the whimsical imagination of a fond lover; the gravest philosophers also owe great part of their pleasure to this stealing of beauty from one object to deck and adorn another: For by daily experience we know, when certain pleasures have been raised in the mind by certain objects, from an association of this kind, the very same pleasure shall be raised, though the objects themselves which first occasioned them are not so much as painted in the imagination; and it is from this source that the beauty and delight of metaphor flows. Who ever thought of the rosy blush of his mistress, without feeling something like that agreeable sensation which the rose itself excites, not only by its color, but even by its fragrance?

But to return to our present purpose; we may hence perceive, that objects which in themselves are not great and immense, if long connected with such, will often produce an exaltedness of mind; and this seems partly to be the case in architecture. The face of a fine building shall give a greater loftiness to the soul, than an object vastly more extended; neither indeed does the size of any building seem to rise to that largeness as constitutes the sublime: Whence, therefore, it is, that it raises this passion?—One of the reasons certainly is, we have always found such buildings connected with great riches, power, and grandeur; and though the mind may not reflect on these connections, yet from what I before mentioned, the passion occasioned by these things may exist in the mind without the idea of the things themselves. Should the buildings be perfectly plain, without any manner of ornaments, though vastly large, as those in Edinburgh, they would not at all elevate the soul; for in these buildings we have found no necessary connection with power and grandeur. But besides this, with columns there is always connected the imagination of strength and durableness; and these working together, may very well give a sublimity to the mind. However, I am apt to think, we sometimes imagine a greater sublime in objects than what there really is. Thus in a fine building, the proportion of the parts, their aptitude, and a thousand other circumstances, which form the beauty of the structure, afford a refined delight, much different from the exalted disposition already mentioned; and may not two or three different pleasures existing in the mind at the same time, by a kind of reverberating on each other, increase the intenseness of each, as a parcel of diamonds, when artfully set, by a reciprocal reflection of their rays, strike the eye with redoubled luster? What, indeed, is poetry, but the art of throwing a number of agreeable images together, whence each of them yields a greater delight than they possibly could separately.—There might be something likewise said from the variety of the parts, and yet so uniform as not to distract the imagination.—If a great crowd of ideas can be distinctly conveyed into a small portion of the mind, something of the pride of the sublime will be raised in her; for if she can take in so great a variety, and yet have room for so much more, she certainly must feel something exalted. That the uniformity does contribute to give this turn of mind, is plain by observing those buildings which abound in little and trifling ornaments, where every thing is broke into miniature.—Here, though the bulk of the building be vastly large, no very great ideas are conveyed.

The sublime of painting consists mostly in finely representing the sublime of the passions, such as the tablature of Hercules; and what a greatness of mind he shews in Hercules!—Behold what large scenes of action virtue points out to him in choosing them! The indolence of pleasure affords no such vast prospects.—The whole world was a scene little enough for his enlarged soul. Landscape painting may likewise partake of the sublime; such as representing mountains, etc. which shews how little objects by an apt connection may affect us with this passion: For the space of a yard of canvass, by only representing the figure and color of a mountain, shall fill the mind with nearly as great an idea as the mountain itself.

I know so little of music, that I will not pretend to determine the sublime of it. This I know;—all grave sounds, where the notes are long, exalt my mind much more than any other kind; and that wind-instruments are the most fitted to elevate; such as the hautboy, the trumpet, and organ:—For, as Pope has it,

"In more lengthen'd notes and flow,
"Deep, majestic, solemn organs blow."

In all acute sounds, the vibrations are short and quick; on the contrary, in the grave. And may not long sounds be to the ear what extended prospects are to the eye? Here also connection takes great place; the most fantastic jig of a bagpipe shall elevate a highlander more than the most solemn music; for to such they have been ever accustomed even in their martial engagements.

Whatever outward appearance the sublime of the mind assumes, that appearance likewise acquires a name similar to that turn of soul, as lofty, majestic, etc. And indeed whatever conveys to us the imagination of such a disposition in another, affects us also with the like passion. For example; a grave and sedate gesture, especially in princes, we call majestic and noble; and it even gives a small degree of loftiness to the spectator himself: For, as I before hinted, the true sublime of the mind is grave and composed, which in gesture can only be expressed by a grave and composed gate. Should a prince frisk about in short and quick motions, it would take away very much from the imagination of his possessing a great and elevated soul. And this also may be something the case in music; it being inconsistent with a sedate mind to run through all the quick notes and short turns of a jig. Though after all, I believe the pathetic in music is frequently taken for the sublime; and not only here, but even in other cases. Nor, indeed, is it always so easy to separate our sensations: The grand may be so blended with the pathetic and warm, (viz. in the description of a battle) as difficultly to be divided and consequently the complex sensation arising from thence as difficultly resolved. Hence not only comes a confusion of terms, but even of ideas. With a great storm, when the swelling waves rise in mountains to the skies, and the black clouds thicken from all quarters of the heavens, there is always joined the apprehension of danger, which puts the passions into a hurry: Here the complex sensation is generally esteemed the sublime; but from what I have already said it will appear, that the vastness only of the objects produces it, by no means the agitation of the passions, which, if nicely considered, has rather fear than the sublime for its cause. After this manner the sublime may be connected with any one passion, and from such connections different kinds of sublime will arise; I mean in a lax way of speaking; and indeed, from the different ways of blending it in objects, our pleasure may be greatly increased. Thus, the fine blue of the heavens makes the sublime itself yield a greater delight, and for the reason I before hinted.

Had I time, I would consider something of the sublime in sciences. But I shall only observe, that in mathematics it is the universal theorems, and the vast similarity in the properties of infinite curves. And in studying the sciences, it is the mark of a truly great mind not to dwell on the minutiae of things, but rather to consider their universal relations: Studies which seem dry, become exalted and agreeable, by such a management.

I shall end with this one remark, that the eyes and ears are the only inlets to the sublime. Taste, smell, nor touch convey nothing that is great and exalted; and this may be some farther confirmation that large objects only constitute the sublime.

CHAPTER 8

Samuel Johnson*

The Rambler
1751

No. 121. Tuesday, 14 May 1751

O imitatores, servum pecus!

Horace, Epistles, 1.19.19

Away, ye imitators, servile herd!

Elphinston.

I have been informed by a letter, from one of the universities, that among the youth from whom the next swarm of reasoners is to learn philosophy, and the next flight of beauties to hear elegies and sonnets, there are many, who, instead of endeavoring by books and meditation to form their own opinions, content themselves with the secondary knowledge, which a convenient bench in a coffeehouse can supply; and, without any examination or distinction, adopt the criticisms and remarks, which happen to drop from those, who have risen, by merit or fortune, to reputation and authority.

These humble retailers of knowledge my correspondent stigmatizes with the name of Echoes; and seems desirous, that they should be made ashamed of lazy submission, and animated to attempts after new discoveries, and original sentiments.

---

*Samuel Johnson (1709-1784) was the son of a Litchfield bookseller. He attended Pembroke College, Oxford, but was forced for lack of funds to leave without a degree. He was for a time a schoolmaster whose pupil David Garrick, the actor, preceded him to London where Johnson embarked on his remarkable literary career. He was critic, lexicographer, poet, playwright, and journalist as well as the leading member of "The Club," an informal literary circle that included Garrick, Oliver Goldsmith, Joshua Reynolds, James Boswell, and Edmund Burke. Johnson dominated literary London in the second half of the century until his death. Boswell's *Life of Johnson* gives us a detailed picture of Johnson's life after their meeting in 1763.

It is very natural for young men to be vehement, acrimonious, and severe. For, as they seldom comprehend at once all the consequences of a position, or perceive the difficulties by which cooler and more experienced reasoners are restrained from confidence, they form their conclusions with great precipitance. Seeing nothing that can darken or embarrass the question, they expect to find their own opinion universally prevalent, and are inclined to impute uncertainty and hesitation to want of honesty, rather than of knowledge. I may, perhaps, therefore be reproached by my lively correspondent, when it shall be found, that I have no inclination to persecute these collectors of fortuitous knowledge with the severity required; yet, as I am now too old to be much pained by hasty censure, I shall not be afraid of taking into protection those whom I think condemned without a sufficient knowledge of their cause.

He that adopts the sentiments of another, whom he has reason to believe wiser than himself, is only to be blamed, when he claims the honors which are not due but to the author, and endeavors to deceive the world into praise and veneration; for, to learn, is the proper business of youth; and whether we increase our knowledge by books, or by conversation, we are equally indebted to foreign assistance.

The greater part of students are not born with abilities to construct systems, or advance knowledge; nor can have any hope beyond that of becoming intelligent hearers in the schools of art, of being able to comprehend what others discover, and to remember what others teach. Even those to whom Providence has allotted greater strength of understanding, can expect only to improve a single science. In every other part of learning, they must be content to follow opinions, which they are not able to examine; and, even in that which they claim as peculiarly their own, can seldom add more than some small particle of knowledge, to the hereditary stock devolved to them from ancient times, the collective labor of a thousand intellects.

In science, which being fixed and limited, admits of no other variety than such as arises from new methods of distribution, or new arts of illustration, the necessity of following the traces of our predecessors is indisputably evident; but there appears no reason, why imagination should be subject to the same restraint. It might be conceived, that of those who profess to forsake the narrow paths of truth every one may deviate towards a different point, since though rectitude is uniform and fixed, obliquity may be infinitely diversified. The roads of science are narrow, so that they who travel them must either follow or meet one another; but in the boundless regions of possibility, which fiction claims for her dominion, there are surely a thousand recesses unexplored, a thousand flowers unplucked, a thousand fountains unexhausted, combinations of imagery yet unobserved, and races of ideal inhabitants not hitherto described.

Yet, whatever hope may persuade, or reason evince, experience can boast of very few additions to ancient fable. The wars of Troy, and the travels of Ulysses, have furnished almost all succeeding poets with incidents, characters, and sentiments. The Romans are confessed to have attempted little more than to display in their own tongue the inventions of the Greeks. There is, in all their writings, such a perpetual recurrence of allusions to the tales of the fabulous age, that they must be confessed often to want that power of giving pleasure which novelty supplies; nor can we wonder, that they excelled so much in the graces of diction, when we consider how rarely they were employed in search of new thoughts.

The warmest admirers of the great Mantuan poet can extol him for little more than the skill with which he has, by making his hero both a traveler and a warrior, united the beauties of the *Iliad* and *Odyssey* in one composition: yet his judgment was perhaps sometimes overborne by his avarice of the Homeric treasurers; and, for fear of suffering a sparkling ornament to be lost, he has inserted it where it cannot shine with its original splendor.

When Ulysses visited the infernal regions, he found, among the heroes that perished at Troy, his competitor Ajax, who, when the arms of Achilles were adjudged to Ulysses, died by his own hand in the madness of disappointment. He still appeared to resent, as on earth, his loss and disgrace. Ulysses endeavored to pacify him with praises and submission; but Ajax walked away without reply. This passage has always been considered as eminently beautiful; because Ajax, the haughty chief, the unlettered soldier, of unshaken courage, of immovable consistency, but without the power of recommending his own virtues by eloquence, or enforcing his assertions by any other argument than the sword, had no way of making his anger known, but by gloomy sullenness, and dumb ferocity. His hatred of a man whom he conceived to have defeated him only by volubility of tongue, was therefore naturally shewn by silence more contemptuous and piercing than any words that so rude an orator could have found, and by which he gave his enemy no opportunity of exerting the only power in which he was superior.

When Aeneas is sent by Virgil to the shades, he meets Dido the queen of Carthage, whom his perfidy had hurried to the grave; he accosts her with tenderness and excuses; but the lady turns away like Ajax in mute disdain. She turns away like Ajax, but she resembles him in none of those qualities which give either dignity or propriety to silence. She might, without any departure from the tenor of her conduct, have burst out like other injured women into clamor, reproach, and denunciation; but Virgil had his imagination full of Ajax, and therefore could not prevail on himself to teach Dido any other mode of resentment.

If Virgil could be thus seduced by imitation, there will be little hope, that common wits should escape; and accordingly we find, that besides the universal and acknowledged practice of copying the ancients, there has prevailed in every age a particular species of fiction. At one time all truth was conveyed in allegory; at another, nothing was seen but in a vision; at one period, all the poets followed sheep, and every event produced a pastoral; at another they busied themselves wholly in giving directions to a painter.

It is indeed easy to conceive why any fashion should become popular, by which idleness is favored, and imbecility assisted; but surely no man of genius can much applaud himself for repeating a tale with which the audience is already tired, and which could bring no honor to any but its inventor.

There are, I think, two schemes of writing, on which the laborious wits of the present time employ their faculties. One is the adaptation of sense to all the rhymes which our language can supply to some word, that makes the burden of the stanza; but this, as it has been only used in a kind of amorous burlesque, can scarcely be censured with much acrimony. The other is the imitation of Spenser, which, by the influence of some men of learning and genius, seems likely to gain upon the age, and therefore deserves to be more attentively considered.

To imitate the fictions and sentiments of Spenser can incur no reproach, for allegory is perhaps one of the most pleasing vehicles of instruction. But I am very far from extending the same respect to his diction or his stanza. His style was in his own time allowed to be vicious, so darkened with old words and peculiarities of phrase, and so remote from common use, that Jonson boldly pronounces him "to have written no language." His stanza is at once difficult and unpleasing; tiresome to the ear by its uniformity, and to the attention by its length. It was at first formed in imitation of the Italian poets, without due regard to the genius of our language. The Italians have little variety of termination, and were forced to contrive such a stanza as might admit the greatest number of similar rhymes; but our words end with so much diversity, that it is seldom convenient for us to bring more than two of the same sound together. If it be justly observed by Milton, that rhyme obliges poets to express their thoughts in improper terms, these improprieties must always be multiplied, as the difficulty of rhyme is increased by long concatenations.

The imitators of Spenser are indeed not very rigid censors of themselves, for they seem to conclude, that when they have disfigured their lines with a few obsolete syllables, they have accomplished their design, without considering that they ought not only to admit old words, but to avoid new. The laws of imitation are broken by every word introduced since the time of Spenser, as the character of Hector is violated by quoting Aristotle in the play. It would indeed be difficult to exclude from a long poem all modern phrases, though it is easy to sprinkle it with gleanings of antiquity. Perhaps, however, the style of Spenser might by long labor be justly copied; but life is surely given us for higher purposes than to gather what our ancestors have wisely thrown away, and to learn what is of no value, but because it has been forgotten.

CHAPTER 9

William Hogarth*

Analysis of Beauty, Written with a View of Fixing the Fluctuating Ideas of Taste 1753

Introduction

I now offer to the public a short essay, accompanied with two explanatory prints, in which I shall endeavor to shew what the principles are in nature, by which we are directed to call the forms of some bodies beautiful, others ugly; some graceful, and others the reverse; by considering more minutely than has hitherto been done, the nature of those lines, and their different combinations, which serve to raise in the mind the ideas of all the variety of forms imaginable. At first, perhaps, the whole design, as well as the prints, may seem rather intended to trifle and confound, than to entertain and inform: but I am persuaded that when the examples in nature, referred to in this essay, are duly considered and examined upon the principles laid down in it, it will be thought worthy of a careful and attentive perusal: and the prints themselves too will, I make no doubt, be examined as attentively, when it is found, that almost every figure in them (how oddly soever they may seem to be grouped together) is referred to singly in the essay, in order to affix the reader's imagination, when the original examples in art, or nature, are not themselves before him.

And in this light I hope my prints will be considered, and that the figures referred to in them will never be imagined to be placed there by me as examples themselves, of beauty or grace, but only to point out to the reader what sorts of

*William Hogarth (1697-1764) was the son of a London schoolmaster. He was trained as an engraver, but began his career as a painter. His reputation was made as a satirist and moralist by his series of engravings of *The Harlot's Progress* and then *The Rake's Progress*. He continued to work as a painter and engraver until his death. He also was instrumental in securing the first copyright protection in England for artist's work.

objects he is to look for and examine in nature, or in the works of the greatest masters. My figures, therefore, are to be considered in the same light, with those a mathematician makes with his pen, which may convey the idea of his demonstration, though not a line in them is either perfectly straight, or of that peculiar curvature he is treating of. Nay, so far was I from aiming at grace, that I purposely chose to be least accurate, where most beauty might be expected, that no stress might be laid on the figures to the prejudice of the work itself. For I must confess, I have but little hopes of having a favorable attention given to my design in general, by those who have already had a more fashionable introduction into the mysteries of the arts of painting, and sculpture. Much less do I expect, or in truth desire, the countenance of that set of people, who have an interest in exploding any kind of doctrine, that may teach us to see with our own eyes.

It may be needless to observe, that some of the last-mentioned, are not only the dependents on, but often the only instructors and leaders of the former; but in what light they are so considered abroad, may be partly seen by a burlesque representation of them, taken from a print published by Mr. Pond, designed by Cavr. Ghezzi at Rome. [Fig. 1. T. p. I].*

To those, then, whose judgments are unprejudiced, this little work is submitted with most pleasure; because it is from such that I have hitherto received the most obligations, and now have reason to expect most candor.

Therefore I would fain have such of my readers be assured, that however they may have been awed, and over-born by pompous terms of art, hard names, and the parade of seemingly magnificent collections of pictures and statues; they are in a much fairer way, ladies, as well as gentlemen, of gaining a perfect knowledge of the elegant and beautiful in artificial, as well as natural forms, by considering them in a systematical, but at the same time familiar way, than those who have been prepossessed by dogmatic rules, taken from the performances of art only: nay, I will venture to say, sooner, and more rationally, than even a tolerable painter, who has imbibed the same prejudices.

The more prevailing the notion may be, that painters and connoisseurs are the only competent judges of things of this sort; the more it becomes necessary to clear up and confirm, as much as possible, what has only been asserted in the foregoing paragraph: that no one may be deterred, by the want of such previous knowledge, from entering into this enquiry.

The reason why gentlemen, who have been inquisitive after knowledge in pictures, have their eyes less qualified for our purpose, than others, is because their thoughts have been entirely and continually employed and encumbered with considering and retaining the various *manners* in which pictures are painted, the histories, names, and characters of the masters, together with many other little circumstances belonging to the mechanical part of the art; and little or no time has been given for perfecting the ideas they ought to have in their minds, of the objects themselves in nature: for by having thus espoused and adopted their first notions

*The references in brackets are to Hogarth's illustrative plates. Thus, figure 1 at the top, plate I. — editor.

Plate I.

Plate II.

from nothing but *imitations,* and becoming too often as bigoted to their faults, as their beauties, they at length, in a manner, totally neglect, or at least disregard the works of nature, merely because they do not tally with what their minds are so strongly prepossessed with.

Were not this a true state of the case, many a reputed capital picture, that now adorns the cabinets of the curious in all countries, would long ago have been committed to the flames: nor would it have been possible for the Venus and Cupid, represented by the figure [Under Fig. 49. T. p. I] to have made its way into the principal apartment of a palace.

It is also evident that the painter's eye may not be a bit better fitted to receive these new impressions, who is in like manner too much captivated with the works of art; for he also is apt to pursue the shadow, and drop the substance. This mistake happens chiefly to those who go to Rome for the accomplishment of their studies, as they naturally will, without the utmost care, take the infectious turn of the connoisseur, instead of the painter: and in proportion as they turn by those means bad proficients in their own arts, they become the more considerable in that of a connoisseur. As a confirmation of this seeming paradox, it has ever been observed at all auctions of pictures, that the very worst painters sit as the most profound judges, and are trusted only, I suppose, on account of their *disinterestedness.*

I apprehend a good deal of this will look more like resentment, and a design to invalidate the objections of such as are not likely to set the faults of this work in the most favorable light; than merely for the encouragement, as was said above, of such of my readers, as are neither painters, nor connoisseurs: and I will be ingenuous enough to confess something of this may be true; but, at the same time, I cannot allow that this alone would have been a sufficient motive to have made me risk giving offense to any; had not another consideration, besides that already alleged, of more consequence to the purpose in hand, made it necessary. I mean the setting forth, in the strongest colors, the surprising alterations objects seemingly undergo through the prepossessions and prejudices contracted by the mind.—Fallacies, strongly to be guarded against by such as would learn to see objects truly!

Although the instances already given are pretty flagrant, yet it is certainly true, (as a farther confirmation of this, and for the consolation of those, who may be a little piqued at what has been said) that painters of every condition are stronger instances of the almost unavoidable power of prejudice, than any people whatever.

What are all the manners, as they are called, of even the greatest masters, which are known to differ so much from one another, and all of them from nature, but so many strong proofs of their inviolable attachment to falsehood, converted into established truth in their own eyes, by self-opinion? Rubens would, in all probability, have been as much disgusted at the dry manner of Poussin, as Poussin was at the extravagant of Rubens. The prejudices of inferior proficients in favor of the imperfections of their own performances, is still more amazing.—Their eyes are so quick in discerning the faults of others, at the same time they are so totally blind to their own! Indeed it would be well for us all, if one of Gulliver's flappers could be placed at our elbows to remind us at every stroke how much prejudice and self-opinion perverts our sight.

From what has been said, I hope it appears that those, who have no bias of any kind, either from their own practice, or the lessons of others, are fittest to examine into the truth of the principles laid down in the following pages. But as every one may not have had an opportunity of being sufficiently acquainted with the instances, that have been given: I will offer one of a familiar kind, which may be a hint for their observing a thousand more. How gradually does the eye grow reconciled even to a disagreeable dress, as it becomes more and more the fashion, and how soon return to its dislike of it, when it is left off, and a new one has taken possession of the mind?—so vague is taste, when it has no solid principles for its foundation!

Notwithstanding I have told you my design of considering minutely the variety of lines, which serve to raise the ideas of bodies in the mind, and which are undoubtedly to be considered as drawn on the surfaces only of solid or opaque bodies: yet the endeavoring to conceive, as accurate an idea as is possible, of the inside of those surfaces, if I may be allowed the expression, will be a great assistance to us in the pursuance of our present enquiry.

In order to my being well understood, let every object under our consideration, be imagined to have its inward contents scooped out so nicely, as to have nothing of it left but a thin shell, exactly corresponding both in its inner and outer surface, to the shape of the object itself: and let us likewise suppose this thin shell to be made up of very fine threads, closely connected together, and equally perceptible, whether the eye is supposed to observe them from without, or within; and we shall find the ideas of the two surfaces of this shell will naturally coincide. The very word, shell, makes us seem to see both surfaces alike.

The use of this conceit, as it may be called by some, will be seen to be very great, in the process of this work: and the oftener we think of objects in this shell-like manner, we shall facilitate and strengthen our conception of any particular part of the surface of an object we are viewing, by acquiring thereby a more perfect knowledge of the whole, to which it belongs: because the imagination will naturally enter into the vacant space within this shell, and there at once, as from a center, view the whole form within, and mark the opposite corresponding parts so strongly, as to retain the idea of the whole, and make us masters of the meaning of every view of the object, as we walk round it, and view it from without.

Thus the most perfect idea we can possibly acquire of a sphere, is by conceiving an infinite number of straight rays of equal lengths, issuing from the center, as from the eye, spreading every way alike; and circumscribed or wound about at their other extremities with close connected circular threads, or lines, forming a true spherical shell.

But in the common way of taking the view of any opaque object, that part of its surface, which fronts the eye, is apt to occupy the mind alone, and the opposite, nay even every other part of it whatever, is left unthought of at that time: and the least motion we make to reconnoiter any other side of the object, confounds our first idea, for want of the connection of the two ideas, which the complete knowledge of the whole would naturally have given us, if we had considered it in the other way before.

Another advantage of considering objects thus merely as shells composed of lines, is, that by these means we obtain the true and full idea of what is called the outlines of a figure, which has been confined within too narrow limits, by taking it only from drawings on paper; for in the example of the sphere given above, every one of the imaginary circular threads has a right to be considered as an out-line of the sphere, as well as those which divide the half, that is seen, from that which is not seen; and if the eye be supposed to move regularly round it, these threads will each of them as regularly succeed one another in the office of out-lines, (in the narrow and limited sense of the word:) and the instant any one of these threads, during this motion of the eye, comes into sight on one side, its opposite thread is lost, and disappears on the other. He who will thus take the pains of acquiring perfect ideas of the distances, bearings, and oppositions of several material points and lines in the surfaces of even the most irregular figures, will gradually arrive at the knack of recalling them into his mind when the objects themselves are not before him: and they will be as strong and perfect as those of the most plain and regular forms, such as cubes and spheres; and will be of infinite service to those who invent and draw from fancy, as well as enable those to be more correct who draw from the life.

In this manner, therefore, I would desire the reader to assist his imagination as much as possible, in considering every object, as if his eye were placed within it. As straight lines are easily conceived, the difficulty of following this method in the most simple and regular forms will be less than may be first imagined; and its use in the more compounded will be greater: as will be more fully shewn when we come to speak of composition.

But as fig. 2. L. p. I may be of singular use to young designers in the study of the human form, the most complex and beautiful of all, in shewing them a mechanical way of gaining the opposite points in its surface, which never can be seen in one and the same view; it will be proper to explain the design of it in this place, as it may at the same time add some weight to what has been already said.

It represents the trunk of a figure cast in soft wax, with one wire passed perpendicularly through its center, another perpendicularly to the first, going in before and coming out in the middle of the back, and as many more as may be thought necessary, parallel to and at equal distances from these, and each other; as is marked by the several dots in the figure.—Let these wires be so loose as to be taken out at pleasure, but not before all the parts of them, which appear out of the wax, are carefully painted close up to the wax, of a different color from those, that lie within it. By these means the horizontal and perpendicular *contents* of these parts of the body (by which I mean the distances of opposite points in the surface of these parts) through which the wires have passed, may be exactly known and compared with each other; and the little holes, where the wires have pierced the wax, remaining on its surface, will mark out the corresponding opposite points on the external muscles of the body; as well as assist and guide us to a readier conception of all the intervening parts. These points may be marked upon a marble figure with calibers properly used.

The known method, many years made use of, for the more exactly and expeditiously reducing drawings from large pictures, for engravings; or for enlarging designs, for painting ceilings and cupolas, (by striking lines perpendicular to each other, so as to make an equal number of squares on the paper designed for the copy, that hath been first made on the original; by which means, the situation of every part of the picture is mechanically seen, and easily transferred) may truly be said to be somewhat of the same kind with what has been here proposed, but that one is done upon a flat surface, the other upon a solid; and that the new scheme differs in its application, and may be of a much more useful and extensive nature than the old one.

But it is time now to have done with the introduction: and I shall proceed to consider the fundamental principles, which are generally allowed to give elegance and beauty, when duly blended together, to compositions of all kinds whatever; and point out to my readers, the particular force of each, in those compositions in nature and art, which seem most to please and entertain the eye, and give that grace and beauty, which is the subject of this enquiry. The principles I mean, are fitness, variety, uniformity, simplicity, intricacy, and quantity;—all which Cooperate in the production of beauty, mutually correcting and restraining each other occasionally.

Chapter I
Of Fitness

Fitness of the parts to the design for which every individual thing is formed, either by art or nature, is first to be considered, as it is of the greatest consequence to the beauty of the whole. This is so evident, that even the sense of seeing, the great inlet of beauty, is itself so strongly biased by it, that if the mind, on account of this kind of value in a form, esteem it beautiful, though on all other considerations it be not so; the eye grows insensible of its want of beauty, and even begins to be pleased, especially after it has been a considerable time acquainted with it.

It is well known on the other hand, that forms of great elegance often disgust the eye by being improperly applied. Thus twisted columns are undoubtedly ornamental; but as they convey an idea of weakness, they always displease, when they are improperly made use of as supports to any thing that is bulky, or appears heavy.

The bulks and proportions of objects are governed by fitness and propriety. It is this that has established the size and proportion of chairs, tables, and all sorts of utensils and furniture. It is this that has fixed the dimensions of pillars, arches, &c. for the support of great weight, and so regulated all the orders in architecture, as well as the sizes of windows and doors, &c. Thus though a building were ever so large, the steps of the stairs, the seats in the windows must be continued of their usual heights, or they would lose their beauty with their fitness: and in ship-building the dimensions of every part are confined and regulated by fitness for sailing. When a vessel sails well, the sailors always call her a beauty; the two ideas have such a connection!

The general dimensions of the parts of the human body are adapted thus to the uses they are designed for. The trunk is the most capacious on account of the quantity of its contents, and the thigh is larger than the leg, because it has both the leg and foot to move, the leg only the foot, &c.

Fitness of parts also constitutes and distinguishes in a great measure the characteristics of objects; as for example, the race-horse differs as much in quality, or character, from the war-horse, as to its figure, as the Hercules from the Mercury.

The race-horse, having all its parts of such dimensions as best fit the purposes of speed, acquires on that account a consistent character of one sort of beauty. To illustrate this, suppose the beautiful head and gracefully-turned neck of the war-horse were placed on the shoulders of the race-horse, instead of his own awkward straight one: it would disgust, and deform, instead of adding beauty; because the judgment would condemn it as unfit.

The Hercules, by Glicon [Fig. 3. p. I], hath all its parts finely fitted for the purposes of the utmost strength, the texture of the human form will bear. The back, breast and shoulders have huge bones, and muscles adequate to the supposed active strength of its upper parts; but as less strength was required for the lower parts, the judicious sculptor, contrary to all modern rule of enlarging every part in proportion, lessened the size of the muscles gradually down towards the feet; and for the same reason made the neck larger in circumference than any part of the head [Fig. 4. p. I]; otherwise the figure would have been burdened with an unnecessary weight, which would have been a draw-back from his strength, and in consequence of that, from its characteristic beauty.

These seeming faults, which shew the superior anatomical knowledge as well as judgment of the ancients, are not to be found in the leaden imitations of it near Hyde-Park. These saturnine genius's imagined they knew how to correct such apparent disproportions.

These few examples may be sufficient to give an idea of what I mean, (and would have understood) by the beauty of fitness, or propriety.

Chapter II
Of Variety

How great a share variety has in producing beauty may be seen in the ornamental part of nature.

The shapes and colors of plants, flowers, leaves, the paintings in butterflies wings, shells, &c. seem of little other intended use, than that of entertaining the eye with the pleasure of variety.

All the senses delight in it, and equally are averse to sameness. The ear is as much offended with one even continued note, as the eye is with being fixed to a point, or to the view of a dead wall.

Yet when the eye is glutted with a succession of variety, it finds relief in a certain degree of sameness; and even plain space becomes agreeable, and properly introduced, and contrasted with variety, adds to it more variety.

I mean here, and every where indeed, a composed variety; for variety uncomposed, and without design, is confusion and deformity.

Observe, that a gradual lessening is a kind of varying that gives beauty. The pyramid diminishing from its basis to its point, and the scroll or *voluta*, gradually lessening to its center, are beautiful forms. So also objects that only seem to do so, though in fact they do not, have equal beauty: thus perspective views, and particularly those of buildings, are always pleasing to the eye.

The little ship, between figure 47 and 88 [R. plate I], supposed moving along the shore even with the eye, might have its top and bottom bounded by two lines at equal distances all the way, as A; but if the ship puts out to sea, these lines at top and bottom would seem to vary and meet each other by degrees, as B, in the point C, which is in the line where the sky and water meets, called the horizon. Thus much of the manner of perspectives adding beauty, by seemingly varying otherwise unvaried forms, I thought, might be acceptable to those, who have not learnt perspective.

Chapter III
Of Uniformity; Regularity; or Symmetry

It may be imagined that the greatest part of the effects of beauty results from the symmetry of parts in the objects, which is beautiful: but I am very well persuaded, this prevailing notion will soon appear to have little or no foundation.

It may indeed have properties of greater consequence, such as propriety, correctness, and use; and yet but little serve the purposes of pleasing the eye, merely on the score of beauty.

We have, indeed, in our nature a love of imitation from our infancy, and the eye is often entertained, as well as surprised, with mimicry, and delighted with the exactness of counterparts: but then this always gives way to its superior love of variety, and soon grows tiresome.

If the uniformity of figures, parts, or lines were truly the chief cause of beauty, the more exactly uniform their appearances were kept, the more pleasure the eye would receive: but this is so far from being the case, that when the mind has been once satisfied, that the parts answer one another, with so exact an uniformity, as to preserve to the whole the character of fitness to stand, to move, to sink, to Swim, to fly, &c. without losing the balance: the eye is rejoiced to see the object turned, and shifted, so as to vary these uniform appearances.

Thus the profile of most objects, as well as faces, are rather more pleasing than their full fronts.

Whence it is clear, the pleasure does not arise from seeing the exact resemblance, which one side bears the other, but from the knowledge that they do so on account of fitness, with design, and for use. For when the head of a fine woman is turned a little to one side, which takes off from the exact similarity of the two halves of the face, and somewhat reclining, so varying still more from the straight and parallel lines of a formal front face: it is always looked upon as most pleasing. This is accordingly said to be a graceful air of the head.

It is a constant rule in composition in painting to avoid regularity. When we view a building, or any other objects in life, we have it in our power, by shifting the ground, to take that view of it which pleases us best; and in consequence of this, the painter if he is left to his choice, takes it on the angle rather than in front, as most agreeable to the eye; because the regularity of the lines is taken away by their running into perspective, without losing the idea of fitness: and when he is of necessity obliged to give the front of a building, with all its equalities and parallelisms, he generally breaks (as it is termed) such disagreeable appearances, by throwing a tree before it, or the shadow of an imaginary cloud, or some other object that may answer the same purpose of adding variety, which is the same with taking away uniformity.

If uniform objects were agreeable, why is there such care taken to contrast, and vary all the limbs of a statue?

The picture of Henry the Eighth [Fig. 72. p. 2], would be preferable to the finely contrasted figures of Guido or Correggio; and the Antinous's easy sway [Fig. 6. p. I], must submit to the stiff and straight figure of the dancing master [Fig. 7. p. I]; and the uniform out-lines of the muscles in the figure taken from Albert Durer's book of proportions [Fig. 55. p. I], would have more taste in them than those in the famous part of an antique figure from which Michael Angelo acquired so much of his skill in grace [Fig. 54. p. I]

In short, whatever appears to be fit, and proper to answer great purposes, ever satisfies the mind, and pleases on that account. Uniformity is of this kind. We find it necessary, in some degree, to give the idea of rest and motion, without the possibility of falling. But when any such purposes can be as well effected by more irregular parts, the eye is always better pleased on the account of variety.

How pleasingly is the idea of firmness in standing conveyed to the eye by the three elegant claws of a table, the three feet of a tea-lamp, or the celebrated tripod of the ancients?

Thus you see regularity, uniformity, or symmetry, please only as they serve to give the idea of fitness.

. . .

Chapter IX
Of Composition with the Wavy Line

There is scarce a room in any house whatever, where one does not see the waving-line employed in some way or other. How inelegant would the shapes of all our moveables be without it? how very plain and unornamental the moldings of cornices, and chimney-pieces, without the variety introduced by the *ogee* member, which is entirely composed of waving-lines.

Though all sorts of waving-lines are ornamental, when properly applied; yet, strictly speaking, there is but one precise line, properly to be called *the line of beauty,* which in the scale of them [Fig. 49. T. p. I] is number 4: the lines 5, 6, 7, by their bulging too much in their curvature becoming gross and clumsy; and, on the contrary, 3, 2, I, as they straighten, becoming mean and poor; as will appear in the next figure [50. T. p. I] where they are applied to the legs of chairs.

A still more perfect idea of the effects of the precise waving-line, and of those lines that deviate from it, may be conceived by the row of stays, figure 53. B. p. I, where number 4 is composed of precise waving-lines, and is therefore the best shaped stay. Every whale-bone of a good stay must be made to bend in this manner: for the whole stay, when put close together behind, is truly a shell of well-varied contents, and its surface of course a fine form; so that if a line, or the lace were to be drawn, or brought from the top of the lacing of the stay behind, round the body, and down to the bottom peak of the stomacher it would form such a perfect, precise, serpentine-line, as has been shewn, round the cone, figure 26 in plate I.—For this reason all ornaments obliquely contrasting the body in this manner, as the ribbons worn by the knights of the garter, are both genteel and graceful. The numbers 5, 6, 7, and 3, 2, 1, are deviations into stiffness and meanness on one hand, and clumsiness and deformity on the other. The reasons for which disagreeable effects, after what has been already said, will be evident to the meanest capacity.

It may be worth our notice however, that the stay, number 2, would better fit a well-shaped man than number 4; and that number 4, would better fit a well-formed woman, than number 2; and when on considering them, merely as to their forms, and comparing them together as you would do two vases, it has been shewn by our principles, how much finer and more beautiful number 4 is, than number 2: does not this in our determination enhance the merit of these principles, as it proves at the same time how much the form of a woman's body surpasses in beauty that of a man?

From the examples that have been given, enough may be gathered to carry on our observations from them to any other objects that may chance to come in our way, either animate or inanimate; so that we may not only lineally account for the ugliness of the toad, the hog, the bear and the spider, which are totally void of this waving-line, but also for the different degrees of beauty belonging to those objects that possess it.

Chapter X
Of Compositions With The Serpentine Line

The very great difficulty there is in describing this line, either in words, or by the pencil (as was hinted before, when I first mentioned it) will make it necessary for me to proceed very slowly in what I have to say in this chapter, and to beg the reader's patience whilst I lead him step by step into the knowledge of what I think the sublime in form, so remarkably displayed in the human body; in which, I believe, when he is once acquainted with the idea of them, he will find this species of lines to be principally concerned.

First, then, let him consider fig. 56. B. p. 2, which represents a straight horn, with its contents, and he will find, as it varies like the cone, it is a form of some beauty, merely on that account.

Next let him observe in what manner, and in what degree the beauty of this horn is increased, in fig. 57. B. p. 2, where it is supposed to be bent two different ways.

And lastly, let him attend to the vast increase of beauty, even to grace and elegance, in the same horn, fig. 58. B. p. 2, where it is supposed to have been twisted round, at the same time, that it was bent two different ways, (as in the last figure.)

In the first of these figures, the dotted line down the middle expresses the straight lines of which it is composed; which, without the assistance of curve lines, or light and shade, would hardly shew it to have contents.

The same is true of the second, though by the bending of the horn, the straight dotted line is changed into the beautiful waving-line.

But in the last, this dotted line, by the twisting as well as the bending of the horn, is changed from the waving into the serpentine-line; which, as it dips out of sight behind the horn in the middle, and returns again at the smaller end, not only gives play to the imagination, and delights the eye, on that account; but informs it likewise of the quantity and variety of the contents.

I have chosen this simple example, as the easiest way of giving a plain and general idea of the peculiar qualities of these serpentine-lines, and the advantages of bringing them into compositions, where the contents you are to express, admit of grace and elegance.

And I beg the same things may be understood of these serpentine-lines, that I have said before of the waving-lines. For as among the vast variety of waving-lines that may be conceived, there is but one that truly deserves the name of *the line of beauty,* so there is only one precise serpentine-line that I call *the line of grace.* Yet, even when they are made too bulging, or too tapering, though they certainly lose of their beauty and grace, they do not become so wholly void of it, as not to be of excellent service in compositions, where beauty and grace are not particularly designed to be expressed in their greatest perfection.

Though I have distinguished these lines so particularly as to give them the titles of *the lines of beauty and grace,* I mean that the use and application of them should still be confined by the principles I have laid down for composition in general; and that they should be judiciously mixed and combined with one another, and even with those I may term *plain* lines, (in opposition to these) as the subject in hand requires. Thus the cornucopia, fig. 59. B. p. 2, is twisted and bent after the same manner, as the last figure of the horn; but more ornamented, and with a greater number of other lines of the same twisted kind, winding round it with as quick returns as those of a screw.

This sort of form may be seen with yet more variations, (and therefore more beautiful) in the goat's horn, from which, in all probability, the ancients originally took the extreme elegant forms they have given their cornucopias.

There is another way of considering this last figure of the horn I would recommend to my reader, in order to give him a clearer idea of the use both of the waving and serpentine-lines in composition.

This is to imagine the horn, thus bent and twisted, to be cut length-ways by a very fine saw into two equal parts; and to observe one of these in the same position the whole horn is represented in; and these two observations will naturally occur to him. First, that the edge of the saw must run from one end to the other of the horn in the line of beauty; so that the edges of this half of the horn will have a beautiful shape: and, secondly, that wherever the dotted serpentine line on the surface of the whole horn dips behind, and is lost to the eye, it immediately comes into sight on the hollow surface of the divided horn.

The use I shall make of these observations will appear very considerable in the application of them to the human form, which we are next to attempt.

It will be sufficient, therefore, at present only to observe, first, that the whole horn acquires a beauty by its being thus gently bent two different ways; secondly, that whatever lines are drawn on its external surface become graceful, as they must all of them, from the twist that is given the horn, partake in some degree or other, of the shape of the serpentine-line: and, lastly, when the horn is split, and the inner, as well as the outward surface of its shell-like form is exposed, the eye is peculiarly entertained and relieved in the pursuit of these serpentine-lines, as in their twistings their concavities and convexities are alternately offered to its view. Hollow forms, therefore, composed of such lines are extremely beautiful and pleasing to the eye; in many cases more so, than those of solid bodies.

Almost all the muscles, and bones, of which the human form is composed, have more, or less of these kind of twists in them; and give in a less degree, the same kind of appearance to the parts which cover them, and are the immediate object of the eye: and for this reason it is that I have been so particular in describing these forms of the bent, and twisted, and ornamented horn.

There is scarce a straight bone in the whole body. Almost all of them are not only bent different ways, but have a kind of twist, which in some of them is very graceful; and the muscles annexed to them, though they are of various shapes, appropriated to their particular uses, generally have their component fibers running in these serpentine-lines, surrounding and conforming themselves to the varied shape of the bones they belong to: more especially in the limbs. Anatomists are so satisfied of this, that they take a pleasure in distinguishing their several beauties. I shall only instance in the thigh-bone, and those about the hips.

The thigh-bone fig. 62, R. p. 2, has the waving and twisted turn of the horn, 58: but the beautiful bones adjoining, called the offa innominata [Fig. 60. B. p. 2], have, with greater variety, the same turns and twists of that horn when it is cut; and its inner and outward surfaces are exposed to the eye.

How ornamental these bones appear, when the prejudice we conceive against them, as being part of a skeleton, is taken off; by adding a little foliage to them, may be seen in fig. 61. B. p. 2—such shell-like winding forms, mixed with foliage, twisting about them, are made use of in all ornaments; a kind of composition calculated merely to please the eye. Divest these of their serpentine twinings and they immediately lose all grace, and return to the poor gothic taste they were in an hundred years ago [Fig. 63. B. p. 2].

Fig. 64. R. p. 2 is meant to represent the manner, in which most of the muscles, (those of the limbs in particular) are twisted round the bones, and conform themselves to their length and shape; but with no anatomical exactness. As to the running of their fibers, some anatomists have compared them to skeins of thread, loose in the middle, and tight at each end, which, when they are thus considered as twisted contrary ways round the bone, gives the strongest idea possible of a composition of serpentine-lines.

Of these fine winding forms then are the muscles and bones of the human body composed, and which, by their varied situations with each other, become more intricately pleasing, and form a continued waving of winding forms from one into the other, as may be best seen by examining a good anatomical figure, part of which you have here represented, in the muscular leg and thigh, fig. 65. p. I: which shews the serpentine forms and varied situations of the muscles, as they appear when the skin is taken off. It was drawn from a plaster of paris figure cast off nature, the original of which was prepared for the mold by Cowper, the famous anatomist. In this last figure, as the skin is taken off the parts are too distinctly traced by the eye, for that intricate delicacy which is necessary to the utmost beauty; yet the winding figures of the muscles, with the variety of their situations, must always be allowed elegant forms: however, they lose in the imagination some of the beauty, which they really have, by the idea of their being flayed; nevertheless, by what has already been shewn both of them and the bones, the human frame hath more of its parts composed of serpentine-lines than any other objects in nature; which is a proof both of its superior beauty to all others, and, at the same time, that its beauty proceeds from those lines: for although they may be required sometimes to be bulging in their twists, as in the thick swelling muscles of the Hercules, yet elegance and greatness of taste is still preserved; but when these lines lose so much of their twists as to become almost straight, all elegance of taste vanishes.

Thus fig. 66. p. 1, was also taken from nature, and drawn in the same position, but treated in a more dry, stiff, and what the painters call, *sticky manner,* than the nature of flesh is ever capable of appearing in, unless when its moisture is dried away: it must be allowed, that the parts of this figure are of as right dimensions, and as truly situated, as in the former; it wants only the true twist of the lines to give it taste.

To prove this further, and to put the mean effect of these plain or unvaried lines in a stronger light, see fig. 67. p. I, where, by the uniform, unvaried shapes and situation of the muscles, without so much as a waving-line in them, it becomes so wooden a form, that he that can fashion the leg of a joint-stool may carve this figure as well as the best sculptor. In the same manner, divest one of the best antique statues of all its serpentine winding parts, and it becomes from an exquisite piece of art, a figure of such ordinary lines and unvaried contents, that a common stone-mason or carpenter, with the help of his rule, calipers, and compasses, might carve out an exact imitation of it: and were it not for these lines a turner, in his lathe, might turn a much finer neck than that of the Grecian Venus, as according to the common notion of a beautiful neck, it would be more truly round. For the same reason, legs much swollen with disease, are as easy to imitate as a post, having lost their *drawing,* as the painters call it; that is, having their serpentine-lines all effaced, by the skin's being equally puffed up, as figure 68. p.1.

If in comparing these three figures one with another, the reader, notwithstanding the prejudice his imagination may have conceived against them, as anatomical figures, has been enabled only to perceive that one of them is not so disagreeable as the others; he will easily be led to see further, that this tendency to beauty in one, is not owing to any greater degree of exactness in the proportions of its parts, but merely to the more pleasing turns, and intertwistings of the lines, which compose its external form; for in all the three figures the same proportions have been observed, and, on that account, they have all an equal claim to beauty.

And if he pursues this anatomical enquiry but a very little further, just to form a true idea of the elegant use that is made of the skin and fat beneath it, to conceal from the eye all that is hard and disagreeable, and at the same time to preserve to it whatever is necessary in the shapes of the parts beneath, to give grace and beauty to the whole limb: he will find himself insensibly led into the principles of that grace and beauty which is to be found in well-turned limbs, in fine, elegant, healthy life, or in those of the best antique statues; as well as into the reason why his eye has so often unknowingly been pleased and delighted with them.

Thus, in all other parts of the body, as well as these, wherever, for the sake of the necessary motion of the parts, with proper strength and agility, the insertions of the muscles are too hard and sudden, their swellings too bold, or the hollows between them too deep, for their out-lines to be beautiful; nature most judiciously softens these hardnesses, and plumps up these vacancies with a proper supply of fat, and covers the whole with the soft, smooth, springy, and, in delicate life, almost transparent skin, which, conforming itself to the external shape of all the parts beneath, expresses to the eye the idea of its contents with the utmost delicacy of beauty and grace.

The skin, therefore, thus tenderly embracing, and gently conforming itself to the varied shapes of every one of the outward muscles of the body, softened underneath by the fat, where, otherwise, the same hard lines and furrows would appear, as we find come on with age in the face, and with labor, in the limbs, is evidently a shell-like surface (to keep up the idea I set out with) formed with the utmost delicacy in nature; and therefore the most proper subject of the study of every one, who desires to imitate the works of nature, as a master should do, or to judge of the performances of others as a real connoisseur ought.

I cannot be too long, I think, on this subject, as so much will be found to depend upon it; and therefore shall endeavor to give a clear idea of the different effect such anatomical figures have on the eye, from what the same parts have, when covered by the fat and skin; by supposing a small wire (that has lost its spring and so will retain every shape it is twisted into) to be held fast to the out-side of the hip (fig. 65, pl. 1) and thence brought down the other side of the thigh obliquely over the calf of the leg, down to the outward ankle (all the while pressed so close as to touch and conform itself to the shape of every muscle it passes over) and then to be taken off. If this wire be now examined it will be found that the general uninterrupted flowing twist, which the winding round the limbs would otherwise have given to it, is broke into little better than so many separate plain curves, by the sharp indentures it every where has received on being closely pressed in between the muscles.

Suppose, in the next place, such a wire was in the same manner twisted round a living well-shaped leg and thigh, or those of a fine statue; when you take it off you will find no such sharp indentures, nor any of those regular *engravings* (as the heralds express it) which displeased the eye before. On the contrary, you will see how gradually the changes in its shape are produced; how imperceptibly the different curvatures run into each other, and how easily the eye glides along the varied wavings of its sweep. To enforce this still further, if a line was to be drawn by a pencil exactly where these wires have been supposed to pass, the point of the pencil, in the muscular leg and thigh, would perpetually meet with stops and rubs, whilst in the others it would flow from muscle to muscle along the elastic skin, as pleasantly as the lightest skiff dances over the gentlest wave.

This idea of the wire, retaining thus the shape of the parts it passes over, seems of so much consequence, that I would by no means have it forgot; as it may properly be considered as one of the threads (or outlines) of the shell (or external surface) of the human form: and the frequently recurring to it will assist the imagination in its conceptions of those parts of it, whose shapes are most intricately varied: for the same sort of observations may be made, with equal justice, on the shapes of ever so many such wires twisted in the same manner in ever so many directions over every part of a well made man, woman, or statue.

And if the reader will follow in his imagination the most exquisite turns of the chisel in the hands of a master, when he is putting the finishing touches to a statue; he will soon be led to understand what it is the real judges expect from the hand of such a master, which the Italians call, the little more, Il poco piu, and which in reality distinguishes the original master-pieces at Rome from even the best copies of them.

An example or two will sufficiently explain what is here meant; for as these exquisite turns are to be found, in some degree of beauty or other, all over the whole surface of the body and limbs: we may by taking any one part of a fine figure, (though so small a one that only a few muscles are expressed in it) explain the manner in which so much beauty and grace has been given to them, as to convince a skillful artist, almost at sight, that it must have been the work of a master.

I have chosen, for this purpose, a small piece of the body of a statue, fig. 76. T. p. 2, representing part of the left side under the arm, together with a little of the breast, (including a very particular muscle, which, from the likeness its edges bear to the teeth of a saw, is, if considered by itself, void of beauty) as most proper to the point in hand, because this its regular shape more peculiarly requires the skill of the artist to give it a little more variety than it generally has, even in nature.

First, then, I will give you a representation of this part of the body, from an anatomical figure 77. T. p. 2, to show what a sameness there is in the shapes of all the teeth-like insertions of this muscle; and how regularly the fibers, which compose it, follow the almost parallel outlines of the ribs they partly cover.

From what has been said before of the use of the natural covering of the skin, &c. the next figure 78. T. p. 2 will easily be understood to mean so tame a representation of the same part of the body, that though the hard and stiff appearance of the edges of this muscle is taken off by that covering, yet enough of its regularity and sameness remains to render it disagreeable.

Now as regularity and sameness, according to our doctrine, is want of elegance and true taste, we shall endeavor in the next place to show how this very part (in which the muscles take so very regular a form) may be brought to have as much variety as any other part of the body whatever. In order to do this, though some alteration must be made in almost every part of it, yet it should be so inconsiderable in each, that no remarkable change may appear in the shape and situation of any.

Thus, let the parts marked 1, 2, 3, 4, (which appear so exactly similar in shape, and parallel in situation in the muscular figure 77) and not much mended in fig. 78, be first varied in their sizes, but not gradually from the uppermost to the lowest, as in fig. 79. T. p.2, nor alternately one long and one short, as in fig. 80. T. p. 2, for in either of these cases there would still remain too great a formality. We should therefore endeavor, in the next place, to vary them every way in our power, without losing entirely the true idea of the parts themselves. Suppose them then to have changed their situations a little, and slipped beside each other irregularly, (some how as is represented in fig. 81. T. p. 2, merely with regard to their situation) and the external appearance of the whole piece of the body, now under our consideration, will assume the more varied and pleasing form, represented in fig. 76; easily to be discerned by comparing the three figures 76, 77, 78, one with another; and it will as easily be seen, that were lines to be drawn, or wires to be bent, over these muscles, from one to the other, and so on to the adjoining parts; they would have a continued waving slow, let them pass in any direction whatever.

The unskillful, in drawing these parts after the life, as their regularities are much more easily seen and copied than their fine variations, seldom fail of making them more regular and poor than they really appear even in a consumptive person.

The difference will appear evident by comparing fig. 78, purposely drawn in this tasteless manner, with fig. 76. But will be more perfectly understood by examining this part in the Torso of Michael Angelo [Fig. 54. p. I], whence this figure was taken.

Note, there are casts of a small copy of that famous trunk of a body to be had at almost every plaster-figure makers, wherein what has been here described may be sufficiently seen, not only in the part which figure 76 was taken from, but all over that curious piece of antiquity.

I must here again press my reader to a particular attention to the windings of these superficial lines, even in their passing over every joint, what alterations soever may be made in the surface of the skin by the various bendings of the limbs: and though the space allowed for it, just in the joints, be ever so small, and consequently the lines ever so short, the application of this principle of varying these lines, as far as their lengths will admit of, will be found to have its effect as gracefully as in the more lengthened muscles of the body.

It should be observed in the fingers, where the joints are but short, and the tendons straight; and where beauty seems to submit, in some degree, to use, yet not so much but you trace in a full-grown taper finger, these little winding lines among the wrinkles, or in (what is more pretty because more simple) the dimples of the knuckles. As we always distinguish things best by seeing their reverse set in opposition with them; if fig. 82. T. p. 2, by the straightness of its lines, shews fig. 83. T. p. 2, to have some little taste in it, though it is so slightly sketched; the difference will more evidently appear when you in like manner compare a straight coarse finger in common life with the taper dimpled one of a fine lady.

There is an elegant degree of plumpness peculiar to the skin of the softer sex, that occasions these delicate dimplings in all their other joints, as well as these of the fingers; which so perfectly distinguishes them from those even of a graceful man; and which, assisted by the more softened shapes of the muscles underneath, presents to the eye all the varieties in the whole figure of the body, with gentler and fewer parts more sweetly connected together, and with such a fine simplicity as will always give the turn of the female frame, represented in the Venus [Fig. 13. p. I], the preference to that of the Apollo [Fig. 12. p. I].

Now whoever can conceive lines thus constantly flowing, and delicately varying over every part of the body even to the fingers ends, and will call to his remembrance what led us to this last description of what the Italians call, Il poco piu *(the little more* that is expected from the hand of a master) will, in my mind, want very little more than what his own observation on the works of art and nature will lead him to, to acquire a true idea of the word *Taste,* when applied to form; however inexplicable this word may hitherto have been imagined.

We have all along had recourse chiefly to the works of the ancients, not because the moderns have not produced some as excellent; but because the works of the former are more generally known: nor would we have it thought, that either of them have ever yet come up to the utmost beauty of nature. Who but a bigot, even to the antiques, will say that he has not seen faces and necks, hands and arms in living women, that even the Grecian Venus doth but coarsely imitate?

And what sufficient reason can be given why the same may not be said of the rest of the body?

CHAPTER 10

David Hume*

Of the Delicacy of Taste and Passion
1741

Some people are subject to a certain delicacy of passion, which makes them extremely sensible to all the accidents of life, and gives them a lively joy upon every prosperous event, as well as a piercing grief, when they meet with misfortunes and adversity. Favors and good offices easily engage their friendship; while the smallest injury provokes their resentment. Any honor or mark of distinction elevates them above measure; but they are as sensibly touched with contempt. People of this character have, no doubt, more lively enjoyments, as well as more pungent sorrows, than men of cool and sedate tempers: But, I believe, when everything is balanced, there is no one, who would not rather be of the latter character, where he entirely

---

*David Hume (1711-1776) was a major figure in the Scottish Enlightenment. Hume was educated in the law, but he was drawn to books and philosophy at an early age. In 1729, he underwent a mental crisis, the nature of which remains a matter of conjecture. It produced both a mental depression and a remarkable physical change from being lean and raw-boned to quite heavy in a short period. He sought to escape from his depressed mental state first by turning to business in Bristol, and then by withdrawing to France where he wrote *A Treatise of Human Nature.* It was written while Hume was still in his twenties and published in 1739-1740. Hume held a number of positions as a tutor, military lawyer, and diplomatic secretary before his *History of England* established his reputation as one of the leading intellectuals and popular writers of the mid-eighteenth century and allowed him to live and write in Edinburgh and occasionally in London. Hume's reputation was that of a skeptic and atheist. He was widely attacked by the religious establishment of his day. He held a post for a time as librarian to the advocates (lawyers) library in Edinburgh, but he was denied appointment to the university by ecclesiastical opposition. Hume managed to disarm all but the most conservative of his opponents by his personal manner, however. His last major work, *Dialogues Concerning Natural Religion*, could not be published until after his death because of its skepticism about revealed religion. Boswell was appalled that Hume, even facing death, retained his skeptical positions and seemed unaffected by fear of dying.

master of his own disposition. Good or ill fortune is very little at our disposal: And when a person, that has this sensibility of temper, meets with any misfortune, his sorrow or resentment takes entire possession of him, and deprives him of all relish in the common occurrences of life; the right enjoyment of which forms the chief part of our happiness. Great pleasures are much less frequent than great pains; so that a sensible temper must meet with fewer trials in the former way than in the latter. Not to mention, that men of such lively passions are apt to be transported beyond all bounds of prudence and discretion, and to take false steps in the conduct of life, which are often irretrievable.

There is a delicacy of taste observable in some men, which very much resembles this delicacy of passion, and produces the same sensibility to beauty and deformity of every kind, as that does to prosperity and adversity, obligations and injuries. When you present a poem or a picture to a man possessed of this talent, the delicacy of his feeling makes him be sensibly touched with every part of it; nor are the masterly strokes perceived with more exquisite relish and satisfaction, than the negligences or absurdities with disgust and uneasiness. A polite and judicious conversation affords him the highest entertainment; rudeness or impertinence is as great a punishment to him. In short, delicacy of taste has the same effect as delicacy of passion: It enlarges the sphere both of our happiness and misery, and makes us sensible to pains as well as pleasures, which escape the rest of mankind.

I believe, however, every one will agree with me, that, notwithstanding this resemblance, delicacy of taste is as much to be desired and cultivated as delicacy of passion is to be lamented, and to be remedied, if possible. The good or ill accidents of life are very little at our disposal; but we are pretty much masters what books we shall read, what diversions we shall partake of, and what company we shall keep. Philosophers have endeavored to render happiness entirely independent of everything external. That degree of perfection is impossible to be attained: But every wise man will endeavor to place his happiness on such objects chiefly as depend upon himself: and that is not to be attained so much by any other means as by this delicacy of sentiment. When a man is possessed of that talent, he is more happy by what pleases his taste, than by what gratifies his appetites, and receives more enjoyment from a poem or a piece of reasoning than the most expensive luxury can afford.

Whatever connection there may be originally between these two species of delicacy, I am persuaded, that nothing is so proper to cure us of this delicacy of passion, as the cultivating of that higher and more refined taste, which enables us to judge of the characters of men, of compositions of genius and of the productions of the nobler arts. A greater or less relish for those obvious beauties, which strike the senses, depends entirely upon the greater or less sensibility of the temper: But with regard to the sciences and liberal arts, a fine taste is, in some measure, the same with strong sense, or at least depends so much upon it, that they are inseparable. In order to judge aright of a composition of genius, there are so many views to be taken in, so many circumstances to be compared, and such a knowledge of human nature requisite, that no man, who is not possessed of the soundest judgment, will ever make a tolerable critic in such performances. And this is a new reason for cultivating a relish in the liberal arts. Our judgment will strengthen by this exercise: We shall form juster notions of life: Many things, which please or afflict others, will appear to us too frivolous to engage our attention: And we shall lose by degrees that sensibility and delicacy of passion, which is so incommodious.

But perhaps I have gone too far in saying, that a cultivated taste for the polite arts extinguishes the passions, and renders us indifferent to those objects, which are so fondly pursued by the rest of mankind. On farther reflection, I find that it rather improves our sensibility for all the tender and agreeable passions; at the same time that it renders the mind incapable of the rougher and more boisterous emotions.

Ingenuas didicisse fideliter artes,
Emollit mores, nec sinit esse feros.

For this, I think there may be assigned two very natural reasons. In the *first* place, nothing is so improving to the temper as the study of the beauties, either of poetry, eloquence, music, or painting. They give a certain elegance of sentiment to which the rest of mankind are strangers. The emotions which they excite are soft and tender. They draw off the mind from the hurry of business and interest; cherish reflection; dispose to tranquillity; and produce an agreeable melancholy, which, of all dispositions of the mind, is the best suited to love and friendship.

In the *second* place, a delicacy of taste is favorable to love and friendship, by confining our choice to few people, and making us indifferent to the company and conversation of the greater part of men. You will seldom find, that mere men of the world, whatever strong sense they may be endowed with, are very nice in distinguishing characters, or in marking those insensible differences and gradations, which make one man preferable to another. Any one, that has competent sense, is sufficient for their entertainment: They talk to him, of their pleasure and affairs, with the same frankness that they would to another; and finding many, who are fit to supply his place, they never feel any vacancy or want in his absence. But to make use of the allusion of a celebrated French[1] author, the judgment may be compared to a clock or watch, where the most ordinary machine is sufficient to tell the hours; but the most elaborate alone can point out the minutes and seconds, and distinguish the smallest differences of time. One that has well digested his knowledge both of books and men, has little enjoyment but in the company of a few select companions. He feels too sensibly, how much all the rest of mankind fall short of the notions which he has entertained. And, his affections being thus confined within a narrow circle, no wonder he carries them further, than if they were more general and undistinguished. The gaiety and frolic of a bottle companion improves with him into a solid friendship: And the ardors of a youthful appetite become an elegant passion.

[1]Mons. Fontenelle, *Pluralité des Mondes,* Soir. 6.

David Hume

Of the Standard of Taste
1757

The great variety of Taste, as well as of opinion, which prevails in the world, is too obvious not to have fallen under every one's observation. Men of the most confined knowledge are able to remark a difference of taste in the narrow circle of their acquaintance, even where the persons have been educated under the same government, and have early imbibed the same prejudices. But those, who can enlarge their view to contemplate distant nations and remote ages, are still more surprized at the great inconsistency and contrariety. We are apt to call *barbarous* whatever departs widely from our own taste and apprehension: But soon find the epithet of reproach retorted on us. And the highest arrogance and self-conceit is at last startled, on observing an equal assurance on all sides, and scruples, amidst such a contest of sentiment, to pronounce positively in its own favour.

As this variety of taste is obvious to the most careless enquirer; so will it be found, on examination, to be still greater in reality than in appearance. The sentiments of men often differ with regard to beauty and deformity of all kinds, even while their general discourse is the same. There are certain terms in every language, which import blame, and others praise; and all men, who use the same tongue, must agree in their application of them. Every voice is united in applauding elegance, propriety, simplicity, spirit in writing; and in blaming fustian, affectation, coldness, and a false brilliancy: But when critics come to particulars, this seeming unanimity vanishes; and it is found, that they had affixed a very different meaning to their expressions. In all matters of opinion and science, the case is opposite: The difference among men is there oftener found to lie in generals than in particulars; and to be less in reality than in appearance. An explanation of the terms commonly ends the controversy; and the disputants are surprized to find, that they had been quarreling, while at bottom they agreed in their judgment.

Those who found morality on sentiment, more than on reason, are inclined to comprehend ethics under the former observation, and to maintain, that, in all questions which regard conduct and manners, the difference among men is really greater than at first sight it appears. It is indeed obvious, that writers of all nations and all ages concur in applauding justice, humanity, magnanimity, prudence, veracity; and in blaming the opposite qualities. Even poets and other authors, whose compositions are chiefly calculated to please the imagination, are yet found, from Homer down to Fenelon, to inculcate the same moral percepts, and to bestow their applause and blame on the same virtues and vices. This great unanimity is usually ascribed to the influence of plain reason; which, in all these cases, maintains similar sentiments in all men, and prevents those controversies, to which the abstract science are so much exposed. So far as the unanimity is real, this account may be admitted as satisfactory: But we must also allow that some part of the seeming harmony in morals may be accounted for from the very nature of language. The word *virtue*, with its equivalent in every tongue, implies praise; as that of *vice* does blame: And no one, without the most obvious and grossest impropriety, could affix reproach to a term, which in general acceptation is understood in a good sense; or bestow applause, where the idiom requires disapprobation. Homer's general percepts, where he delivers any such, will never be controverted; but it is obvious, that, when he draws particular pictures of manners and represents heroism in Achilles and prudence in Ulysses, he intermixes a much greater degree of ferocity in the former, and of cunning and fraud in the latter, than Fenelon would admit of. The sage Ulysses in the Greek poet seems to delight in lies and fictions, and often employs them without any necessity or even advantage: But his more scrupulous son, in the French epic writer, exposes himself to the most imminent perils, rather than depart from the most exact line of truth and veracity.

The admirers and followers of the Alcoran insist on the excellent moral percepts interspersed throughout that wild and absurd performance. But it is to be supposed, that the Arabic words, which correspond to the English, equity, justice, temperance, meekness, charity, were such as, from the constant use of that tongue, must always be taken in a good sense; and it would have argued the greatest ignorance, not of morals, but of language, to have mentioned them with any epithets, besides those of applause and approbation. But would we know, whether the pretended prophet had really attained a just sentiment of morals? Let us attend to his narration; and we shall soon find, that he bestows praise on such instances of treachery, inhumanity, cruelty, revenge, bigotry, as are utterly incompatible with civilized society. No steady rule of right seems there to be attended to; and every action is blamed or praised, so far only as it is beneficial or hurtful to the true believers.

The merit of delivering true general percepts in ethics is indeed very small. Whoever recommends any moral virtues, really does no more than is implied in the terms themselves. That people, who invented the word *charity*, and used it in a good sense, inculcated more clearly and much more efficaciously, the precept, *be charitable*, than any pretended legislator or prophet, who should insert such a *maxim* in his writings. Of all expressions, those, which, together with their other meaning, imply a degree either of blame or approbation, are the least liable to be perverted or mistaken.

It is natural for us to seek a *Standard of Taste*; a rule, by which the various sentiments of men may be reconciled; at least, a decision, afforded, confirming one sentiment, and condemning another.

There is a species of philosophy, which cuts off all hopes of success in such an attempt, and represents the impossibility of ever attaining any standard of taste. The difference, it is said, is very wide between judgment and sentiment. All sentiment is right; because sentiment has a reference to nothing beyond itself, and is always real, wherever a man is conscious of it. But all determinations of the understanding are not right; because they have a reference to something beyond themselves, to wit, real matter of fact; and are not always conformable to that standard. Among a thousand different opinions which different men may entertain of the same subject, there is one, and but one, that is just and true; and the only difficulty is to fix and ascertain it. On the contrary, a thousand different sentiments, excited by the same object, are all right: Because no sentiment represents what is really in the object. It only marks a certain conformity or relation between the object and the organs or faculties of the mind; and if that conformity did not really exist, the sentiment could never possibly have being. Beauty is no quality in things themselves: It exists merely in the mind which contemplates them; and each mind perceives a different beauty. One person may even perceive deformity, where another is sensible of beauty; and every individual ought to acquiesce in his own sentiment, without pretending to regulate those of others. To seek the real beauty, or real deformity, is as fruitless an enquiry, as to pretend to ascertain the real sweet or real bitter. According to the disposition of the organs, the same object may be both sweet and bitter; and the proverb has justly determined it to be fruitless to dispute concerning tastes. It is very natural, and even quite necessary, to extend this axiom to mental, as well as bodily taste; and thus common sense, which is so often at variance with philosophy, especially with the sceptical kind, is found, in one instance at least, to agree in pronouncing the same decision.

But though this axiom, by passing into a proverb, seems to have attained the sanction of common sense; there is certainly a species of common sense which opposes it, at least serves to modify and restrain it. Whoever would assert an equality of genius and elegance between Ogilby and Milton, or Bunyan and Addison, would be thought to defend no less an extravagance, than if he had maintained a mole-hill to be as high as Teneriffe, or a pond as extensive as the ocean. Though there may be found persons, who give the preference to the former authors; no one pays attention to such a taste; and we pronounce with scruple the sentiment of these pretended critics to be absurd and ridiculous. The principle of the natural equality of tastes is then totally forgot and while we admit it on some occasions, where the objects seem near an equality, it appears an extravagant paradox, or rather a palpable absurdity, where objects so disproportioned are compared together.

It is evident that none of the rules of composition are fixed by reasonings *a priori*, or can be esteemed abstract conclusions of the understanding, from comparing those habitudes and relations of ideas which are eternal and immutable. Their foundation is the same with that of all the practical sciences, experience; nor are they any thing but general observations, concerning what has been universally found to please in all countries and in all ages. Many of the beauties of poetry and even of eloquence are founded on falsehood and fiction, on hyperboles, metaphors, and an abuse or perversion of terms from their natural meaning. To check the sallies of the imagination, and to reduce every expression to geometrical truth and exactness, would be the most contrary to the laws of criticism; because it would produce a work, which, by universal experience, has been found the most insipid and disagreeable. But though poetry can never submit to exact truth, it must be confined by rules of art, discovered to the author either by genius or observation. If some negligent or irregular writers have pleased, they have not pleased by their transgressions of rule or order, but in spite of these transgressions: They have possessed other beauties, which were conformable to just criticism; and the force of these beauties has been able to overpower censure, and give the mind a satisfaction superior to the disgust arising from the blemishes. Ariosto pleases; but not by his monstrous and improbable fictions, by his bizarre mixture of the serious and comic styles, by the want of coherence in his stories, or by the continual interruptions of his narration. He charms by the force and clearness of his expression, by the readiness and variety of his inventions, and by his natural pictures of the passions, especially those of the gay and amorous kind: And however his faults may diminish our satisfaction, they are not able entirely to destroy it. Did our pleasure really arise from those parts of his poem, which we denominate faults, this would be no objection to criticism in general: It would only be an objection to those particular rules of criticism, which would establish such circumstances to be faults, and would represent them as universally blameable. If they are found to please, they cannot be faults, let the pleasure, which they produce, be ever so unexpected and unaccountable.

But though all the general rules of art are founded only on experience and on the observation of the common sentiments of human nature, we must not imagine, that, on every occasion, the feelings of men will be conformable to the rules. Those finer emotions of the mind are of a very tender and delicate nature, and require the concurrence of many favourable circumstances to make them play with facility and exactness, according to their general and established principles. The least exterior hindrance to such small springs, or the least internal disorder, disturbs their motion, and confounds the operation of the whole machine. When we would make an experiment of this nature, and would try the force of any beauty or deformity, we must choose with care a proper time and place, and bring the fancy to a suitable situation and disposition. A perfect serenity of mind, a recollection of thought, a due attention to the object; if any of these circumstances be wanting, our experiment will be fallacious, and we shall be unable to judge of the catholic and universal beauty. The relation, which nature has placed between the form and the sentiment, will at least be more obscure; and it will require greater accuracy to trace and discern it. We shall be able to ascertain its influence not so much from the operation of each particular beauty, as from the durable admiration, which attends those works, that have survived all the caprices of mode and fashion, all the mistakes of ignorance and envy.

The same Homer, who pleased at Athens and Rome two thousand years ago, is still admired at Paris and London. All the changes of climate, government, religion, and language, have not been able to obscure his glory. Authority or prejudice may give a temporary vogue to a bad poet or orator; but his reputation will never be durable or general. When his compositions are examined by posterity or by foreigners, the enchantment is dissipated, and his faults appear in their true colors. On the contrary, a real genius, the longer his works endure, and the more wide they are spread, the more sincere is the admiration which he meets with. Envy and jealousy have too much place in a narrow circle; and even familiar acquaintance with his person may diminish the applause due to his performances: But when these obstructions are removed, the beauties, which are naturally fitted to excite agreeable sentiments, immediately display their energy; and while the world endures, they maintain their authority over the minds of men.

It appears then, that, amidst all the variety and caprice of taste, there are certain general principles of approbation or blame, whose influence a careful eye may trace in all operations of the mind. Some particular forms or qualities, from the original structure of the internal fabric, are calculated to please, and others to displease; and if they fail of their effect in any particular instance, it is from some apparent defect or imperfection in the organ. A man in a fever would not insist on his palate as able to decide concerning flavours; nor would one, affected with the jaundice, pretend to give a verdict with regard to colors. In each creature, there is a sound and a defective state; and the former alone can be supposed to afford us a true standard of taste and sentiment. If, in the sound state of the organ, there be an entire or a considerable uniformity of sentiment among men, we may thence derive an idea of the perfect beauty; in like manner as the appearance of objects in day-light, to the eye of a man in health, is denominated their true and real color, even while color is allowed to be merely a phantasm of the senses.

Many and frequent are the defects in the internal organs, which prevent or weaken the influence of those general principles, on which depends our sentiment of beauty or deformity. Though some objects, by the structure of the mind, be naturally calculated to give pleasure, it is not to be expected, that in every individual the pleasure will be equally felt. Particular incidents and situations occur, which either throw a false light on the objects, or hinder the true from conveying to the imagination the proper sentiment and perception.

One obvious cause, why many feel not the proper sentiment of beauty, is the want of that *delicacy* of imagination, which is requisite to convey a sensibility of those finer emotions. This delicacy every one pretends to: Every one talks of it; and would reduce every kind of taste or sentiment to its standard. But as our intention in this essay is to mingle some light of the understanding with the feelings of sentiment, it will be proper to give a more accurate definition of delicacy, than has hitherto been attempted. And not to draw our philosophy from too profound a source, we shall have recourse to a noted story in Don Quixote.

It is a good reason, says Sancho to the squire with the great nose, that I pretend to have a judgment in wine: This is a quality hereditary in our family. Two of my Kinsmen were once called to give their opinion of a hogshead, which was supposed to be excellent, being old and of a good vintage. One of them tastes it, considers it; and after mature reflection pronounces the wine to be good, were it not for a small taste of leather, which he perceived in it. The other, after using the same precautions, gives also his verdict in favour of the wine; but with the reserve of a taste of iron, which he could easily distinguish. You cannot imagine how much they were both ridiculed for their judgment. But who laughed in the end? On emptying the hogshead, there was found at the bottom, an old key with a leathern thong tied to it.

The great resemblance between mental and bodily taste will easily teach us to apply this story. Though it be certain, that beauty and deformity, more than sweet and bitter, are not qualities in objects, but belong entirely to the sentiment, internal or external; it must be allowed, that there are certain qualities in objects, which are fitted by nature to produce those particular feelings. Now as these qualities may be found in a small degree, or may be mixed and confounded with each other, it often happens, that the taste is not affected with such minute qualities, or is not able to distinguish all the particular flavors, amidst the disorder, in which they are presented. Where the organs are so fine, as to allow nothing to escape them; and at the same time so exact as to perceive every ingredient in the composition: This we call delicacy of taste, whether we employ these terms in the literal or metaphorical sense. Here then the general rules of beauty are of use; being drawn from established models, and from the observation of what pleases or displeases, when presented singly and in a high degree: And if the same qualities, in a continued composition and in a smaller degree, affect not the organs with a sensible delight or uneasiness, we exclude the person from all pretensions to this delicacy. To produce these general rules or avowed patterns of composition is like finding the key with the leathern thong; which justified the verdict of Sancho's kinsmen, and confounded those pretended judges who had condemned them. Though the hogshead had never been emptied, the taste of the one was still equally delicate, and that of the other equally dull and languid: But it would have been more difficult to have proved the superiority of the former, to the conviction of every by-stander. In like manner, though the beauties of writing had never been methodized, or reduced to general principles; though no excellent models had ever been acknowledged; the different degrees of taste would still have subsisted, and the judgment of one man been preferable to that of another; but it would not have been so easy to silence the bad critic, who might always insist upon his particular sentiment, and refuse to submit to his antagonist. But when we show him an avowed principle of art; when we illustrate this principle by examples, whose operation, from his own particular taste, he acknowledges to be conformable to the principle; when we prove, that the same principle may be applied to the present case, where he did not perceive or feel its influence: He must conclude, upon the whole, that the faults lies in himself, and that he wants the delicacy, which is requisite to make him sensible of every beauty and every blemish, in any composition or discourse.

It is acknowledged to be the perfection of every sense or faculty, to perceive with exactness its most minute objects, and allow nothing to escape its notice and observation. The smaller the objects are, which become sensible to the eye, the finer is that organ, and the more elaborate its make and composition. A good palate is not tried by strong flavors; but by a mixture of small ingredients, where we are still sensible of each part, notwithstanding its minuteness and its confusion with the rest. In like manner, a quick and acute perception of beauty and deformity must be the perfection of our mental taste; nor can a man be satisfied with himself while he suspects, that any excellence or blemish in a discourse has passed him unobserved. In this case, the perfection of the man, and the perfection of the sense or feeling, are found to be united. A very delicate palate, on many occasions, may be a great inconvenience both to a man himself and to his friends: But a delicate taste of wit or beauty must always be a desirable quality; because it is the source of all the finest and most innocent enjoyments, of which human nature is susceptible. In this decision the sentiments of all mankind are agreed. Whenever you can ascertain a delicacy of taste, it is sure to meet with approbation; and the best way of ascertaining it is to appeal to those models and principles, which have been established by the uniform consent and experience of nations and ages.

But though there be naturally a wide difference in point of delicacy between one person and another, nothing tends further to increase and improve this talent, than *practice* in a particular art, and the frequent survey or contemplation of a particular species of beauty. When objects of any kind are first presented to the eye or imagination, the sentiment, which attends them, is obscure and confused; and the mind is, in a great measure, incapable of pronouncing concerning their merits or defects. The taste cannot perceive the several excellences of the performance; much less distinguish the particular character of each excellency, and ascertain its quality and degree. If it pronounce the whole in general to be beautiful or deformed, it is the utmost that can be expected; and even this judgment, a person, so unpractised, will be apt to deliver with great hesitation and reserve. But allow him to acquire experience in those objects, his feeling becomes more exact and nice: He not only perceives the beauties and defects of each part, but marks the distinguishing species of each quality, and assigns it suitable praise or blame. A clear and distinct sentiment attends him through the whole survey of the objects; and he discerns that very degree and kind of approbation or displeasure, which each part is naturally fitted to produce. The mist dissipates, which seemed formerly to hang over the object: The organ acquires greater perfection in its operations; and can pronounce, without danger of mistake, concerning the merits of every performance. In a word, the same address and dexterity, which practice gives to the execution of any work, is also acquired by the same means, in the judging of it.

So advantageous is practice to the discernment of beauty, that, before we can give judgment on any work of importance, it will even be requisite, that that very individual performance be more than once perused by us, and be surveyed in different lights with attention and deliberation. There is a flutter or hurry of thought which attends the first perusal of any piece, and which confounds the genuine sentiment of beauty. The relation of the parts is not discerned: The true characters of style are little distinguished: The several perfections and defects seem wrapped up in a species of confusion, and present themselves indistinctly to the imagination. Not to mention, that there is a species of beauty, which, as it is florid and superficial, pleases at first; but being found incompatible with a just expression either of reason or passion, soon palls upon the taste, and is then rejected with disdain, at least rated at a much lower value.

It is impossible to continue in the practice of contemplating any order of beauty, without being frequently obliged to form *comparisons* between the several species and degrees of excellence, and estimating their proportion to each other. A man, who has had no opportunity of comparing the different kinds of beauty, is indeed totally unqualified to pronounce an opinion with regard to any object presented to him. By comparison alone we fix the epithets of praise or blame, and learn how to assign the due degree of each. The coarsest daubing contains a certain lustre of colors and exactness of imitation, which are so far beauties, and would affect the mind of a peasant or Indian with the highest admiration. The most vulgar ballads are not entirely destitute of harmony or nature; and none but a person, familiarized to superior beauties, would pronounce their numbers harsh, or narration uninteresting. A great inferiority of beauty gives pain to a person conversant in the highest excellence of the kind, and is for that reason pronounced a deformity: As the most finished object, with which we are acquainted, is naturally supposed to have reached the pinnacle of perfection, and to be entitled to the highest applause. One accustomed to see, and examine, and weigh the several performances, admired in different ages and nations, can only rate the merits of a work exhibited to his view, and assign its proper rank among the productions of genius.

But to enable a critic the more fully to execute this undertaking, he must preserve his mind free from all *prejudice*, and allow nothing to enter into his consideration, but the very object which is submitted to his examination. We may observe, that every work of art, in order to produce its due effect on the mind, must be surveyed in a certain point of view, and cannot be fully relished by persons, whose situation, real or imaginary, is not conformable to that which is required by the performance. An orator addresses himself to a particular audience, and must have a regard to their particular genius, interests, opinions, passions, and prejudices; otherwise he hopes in vain to govern their resolutions, and inflame their affections. Should they even have entertained some prepossessions against him, however unreasonable, he must not overlook this disadvantage; but, before he enters upon the subject, must endeavour to conciliate their affection, and acquire their good graces. A critic of a different age or nation, who should peruse this discourse, must have all these circumstances in his eye, and must place himself in the same situation as the audience, in order to form a true judgment of the oration. In like manner, when any work is addressed to the public, though I should have a friendship or enmity with the author, I must depart from this situation; and considering myself as a man in general, forget, if possible, my individual being and my peculiar circumstances. A person influenced by prejudice, complies not with this condition; but obstinately maintains his natural position, without placing himself in that point of view, which the performance supposes. If the work be addressed to persons of a different age or nation, he makes no allowance for their peculiar views and prejudices; but, full of the manners of his own age and country, rashly condemns what seemed admirable in the eyes of those for whom alone the discourse was calculated. If the work be executed for the public, he never sufficiently enlarges his comprehension, or forgets his interest as a friend or enemy, as a rival or commentator. By this means, his sentiments are perverted; not have the same beauties and blemishes the same influence upon him, as if he had imposed a proper violence on his imagination, and had forgotten himself for a moment. So far his taste evidently departs from the true standard; and of consequence loses all credit and authority.

It is well known, that in all questions, submitted to the understanding, prejudice is destructive of sound judgment, and perverts all operations of the intellectual faculties: It is no less contrary to good taste; nor has it less influence to corrupt our sentiment of beauty. It belongs to *good sense* to check its influence in both cases; and in this respect, as well as in many others, reason, if not an essential part of taste, is at least requisite to the operations of this latter faculty. In all the nobler productions of genius, there is a mutual relation and correspondence of parts; nor can either the beauties or blemishes be perceived by him, whose thought is not capacious enough to comprehend all those parts, and compare them with each other, in order to perceive the consistence and uniformity of the whole. Every work of art has also a certain end or purpose, for which it is calculated; and is to be deemed more or less perfect, as it is more or less fitted to attain this end. The object of eloquence is to persuade, of history to instruct, of poetry to please by means of the passions and the imagination. These ends we must carry constantly in our view, when we peruse any performance; and we must be able to judge how far the means employed are adapted to their respective purposes. Besides, every kind of composition, even the most poetical, is nothing but a chain of propositions and reasonings; not always, indeed, the justest and most exact, but still plausible and specious, however disguised by the coloring of the imagination. The persons introduced in tragedy and epic poetry, must be represented as reasoning, and thinking, and concluding, and acting, suitably to their character and circumstances; and without judgment, as well as taste and invention, a poet can never hope to succeed in so delicate an undertaking. Not to mention, that the same excellence of faculties which contributes to the improvement of reason, the same clearness of conception, the same exactness of distinction, the same vivacity of apprehension, are essential to the operations of true taste, and are its infallible concomitants. It seldom, or never happens, that a man of sense, who has experience in any art, cannot judge of its beauty; and it is no less rare to meet with a man who has a just taste without a sound understanding.

Thus, though the principles of taste be universal, and, nearly, if not entirely the same in all men; yet few are qualified to give judgment on any work of art, or establish their own sentiment as the standard of beauty. The organs of internal sensation are seldom so perfect as to allow the general principles their full play, and produce a feeling correspondent to those principles. They either labor under some defect, or are vitiated by some disorder; and by that means, excite a sentiment, which may be pronounced erroneous. When the critic has no delicacy, he judges without any distinction, and is only affected by the grosser and more palpable qualities of the object: The finer touches pass unnoticed and disregarded. Where he is not aided by practice, his verdict is attended with confusion and hesitation. Where no comparison has been employed, the most frivolous beauties, such as rather merit the name of defects, are the object of his admiration. Where he lies under the influence of prejudice, all his natural sentiments are perverted. Where good sense is wanting, he is not qualified to discern the beauties of design and reasoning, which are the highest and most excellent. Under some or other of these imperfections, the generality of men labor; and hence a true judge in the finer arts is observed, even during the most polished ages, to be so rare a character: Strong sense, united to delicate sentiment, improved by practice, perfected by comparison, and cleared of all prejudice, can alone entitle critics to this valuable character; and the joint verdict of such, wherever they are to be found, is the true standard of taste and beauty.

But where are such critics to be found? By what marks are they to be known? How distinguish them from pretenders? These questions are embarrassing; and seem to throw us back into the same uncertainty, from which, during the course of this essay, we have endeavored to extricate ourselves.

But if we consider the matter aright, these are questions of fact, not of sentiment. Whether any particular person be endowed with good sense and a delicate imagination, free from prejudice, may often be the subject of dispute, and be liable to great discussion and enquiry: But that such a character is valuable and estimable will be agreed in by all mankind. Where these doubts occur, men can do no more than in other disputable questions, which are submitted to the understanding: They must produce the best arguments, that their invention suggests to them; they must acknowledge a true and decisive standard to exist somewhere, to wit, real existence and matter of fact; and they must have indulgence to such as differ from them in their appeals to this standard. It is sufficient for our present purpose, if we have proved, that the taste of all individuals is not upon an equal footing, and that some men in general, however difficult to be particularly pitched upon, will be acknowledged by universal sentiment to have a preference above others.

But in reality the difficulty of finding, even in particulars, the standard of taste, is not so great as it is represented. Though in speculation, we may readily avow a certain criterion in science and deny it in sentiment, the matter is found in practice to be much more hard to ascertain in the former case than in the latter. Theories of abstract philosophy, systems of profound theology, have prevailed during one age: In a successive period, these have been universally exploded: Their absurdity has been detected: Other theories and systems have supplied their place, which again gave place to their successors: And nothing has been experienced more liable to the revolutions of chance and fashion than these pretended decisions of science. The case is not the same with the beauties of eloquence and poetry. Just expressions of passion and nature are sure, after a little time, to gain public applause, which they maintain for ever. Aristotle, and Plato, and Epicurus, and Descartes, may successively yield to each other: But Terence and Virgil maintain an universal, undisputed empire over the minds of men. The abstract philosophy of Cicero has lost its credit: The vehemence of his oratory is still the objects of our admiration.

Though men of delicate taste be rare, they are easily to be distinguished in society, by the soundness of their understanding and the superiority of their faculties above the rest of mankind. The ascendant, which they acquire, gives a prevalence to that lively approbation, with which they receive any productions of genius, and renders it generally predominant. Many men, when left to themselves, have but a faint and dubious perception of beauty, who yet are capable of relishing any fine stroke, which is pointed out to them. Every convert to the admiration of the real poet or orator is the cause of some new conversion. And though prejudices may prevail for a time, they never unite in celebrating any rival to the true genius, but yield at last to the force of nature and just sentiment. Thus, though a civilized nation may easily be mistaken in the choice of their admired philosopher, they never have been found long to err, in their affection for a favorite epic or tragic author.

But notwithstanding all our endeavors to fix a standard of taste, and reconcile the discordant apprehensions of men, there still remain two sources of variation, which are not sufficient indeed to confound all the boundaries of beauty and deformity, but will often serve to produce a difference in the degrees of our approbation or blame. The one is the different humors of particular men; the other, the particular manners and opinions of our age and country. The general principles of taste are uniform in human nature: Where men vary in their judgments, some defect or perversion in the faculties may commonly be remarked; proceeding either from prejudice, from want of practice, or want of delicacy; and there is just reason for approving one taste, and condemning another. But where there is such a diversity in the internal frame or external situation as is entirely blameless on both sides, and leaves no room to give one the preference above the other; in that case a certain degree of diversity in judgment is unavoidable, and we seek in vain for a standard, by which we can reconcile the contrary sentiments.

A young man, whose passions are warm, will be more sensibly touched with wise, philosophical reflections concerning the conduct of life and moderation of the passions. At twenty, Ovid may be the favourite author; Horace at forty; and perhaps Tacitus at fifty. Vainly would we, in such cases, endeavor to enter into the sentiments of others, and divest ourselves of those propensities, which are natural to us. We choose our favorite author as we do our friend, from a conformity of humor and disposition. Mirth or passion, sentiment or reflection; whichever of these most predominates in our temper, it gives us a peculiar sympathy with the writer who resembles us.

One person is more pleased with the sublime; another with the tender; a third with raillery. One has a strong sensibility to blemishes, and is extremely studious of correctness: Another has a more lively feeling of beauties, and pardons twenty absurdities and defects for one elevated or pathetic stroke. The ear of man is entirely turned towards conciseness and energy; that man is delighted with a copious, rich, and harmonious expression. Simplicity is affected by one; ornament by another. Comedy, tragedy, satire, odes, have each its partisans, who prefer that particular species of writing to all others. It is plainly an error in a critic, to confine his approbation to one species or style of writing, and condemn all the rest. But it is almost impossible not to feel a predilection for that which suits our particular turn and disposition. Such preferences are innocent and unavoidable, and can never reasonably be the object of dispute, because there is no standard, by which they can be decided.

For a like reason, we are more pleased, in the course of our reading, with pictures and characters, that resembles objects which are found in our own age or country, than with those which describe a different set of customs. It is not without some effort, that we reconcile ourselves to the man, who can boast of great constancy and uniformity in this particular. Whatever speculative errors may be found in the polite writings of any age or country, they detract but little from the value of those compositions. There needs but a certain turn of thought or imagination to make us enter into all the opinions, which then prevailed, and relish the sentiments or conclusions derived from them. But a very violent effort is requisite to change our judgment of manners, and excite sentiments of approbation or blame, love or hatred, different from those to which the mind from long custom has been familiarized. And where a man is confident of the rectitude of that moral standard, by which he judges, he is justly jealous of it, and will not pervert the sentiments of his heart for a moment, in complaisance to any writer whatsoever.

Of all speculative errors, those, which regard religion, are the most excusable in compositions of genius; nor is it ever permitted to judge of the civility or wisdom of any people, or even of single persons, by the grossness or refinement of their theological principles. The same good sense, that directs men in the ordinary occurrences of life, is not hearkened to in religious matters, which are supposed to be placed altogether above the cognizance of human reason. On this account, all the absurdities of the pagan system of theology must be overlooked by every critic, who would pretend to form a just notion of ancient poetry; and our posterity, in their turn, must have the same indulgence to their forefathers. No religious principles can ever be imputed as a fault to any poet, while they remain merely principles, and take not such strong possession of his heart, as to lay him under the imputation of *bigotry* or *superstition*. Where that happens, they confound the sentiments of morality, and alter the natural boundaries of vice and virtue. They are therefore eternal blemishes, according to the principle above mentioned; nor are the prejudices and false opinions of the age sufficient to justify them.

It is essential to the Roman catholic religion to inspire a violent hatred of every other worship, and to represent all pagans, mahometans, and heretics as the objects of divine wrath and vengeance. Such sentiments, though they are in reality very blameable, are considered as virtues by the zealots of that communion, and are represented in their tragedies and epic poems as a kind of divine heroism. This bigotry has disfigured two very fine tragedies of the French theatre, *Polieucte* and *Athalia*; where an intemperate zeal for particular modes of worship is set off with all the pomp imaginable, and forms the predominant character of the heroes. "What is this," says the sublime Joad to Josabet, finding her in discourse with Mathan, the priest of Baal. "Does the daughter of David speak to this traitor? Are you not afraid, lest the earth should open and pour forth flames to devour you both? Or lest these holy walls should fall and crush you together? What is his purpose? Why comes that enemy of God hither to poison the air, which we breathe, with his horrid presence?" Such sentiments are received with great applause on the theatre of Paris; but at London the spectators would be full as much pleased to hear Achilles tell Agamemnon, that he was a dog in his forehead, and a deer in his heart, or Jupiter threaten Juno with a sound drubbing, if she will not be quiet.

Religious principles are also a blemish in any polite composition, when they rise up to superstition, and intrude themselves into every sentiment, however remote from any connection with religion. It is no excuse for the poet, that the customs of his country had burthened life with so many religious ceremonies and observances, that no part of it was exempt from that yoke. It must for ever be ridiculous in Petrarch to compare his mistress Laura, to Jesus Christ. Nor is it less ridiculous in that agreeable libertine, Boccace, very seriously to give thanks to God Almighty and the ladies, for their assistance in defending him against his enemies.

David Hume

Of Tragedy
1757

It seems an unaccountable pleasure, which the spectators of a well-written tragedy receive from sorrow, terror, anxiety, and other passions, that are in themselves disagreeable and uneasy. The more they are touched and affected, the more are they delighted with the spectacle; and as soon as the uneasy passions cease to operate, the piece is at an end. One scene of full joy and contentment and security is the utmost, that any composition of this kind can bear; and it is sure always to be the concluding one. If, in the texture of the piece, there be interwoven any scenes of satisfaction, they afford only faint gleams of pleasure, which are thrown in by way of variety, and in order to plunge the actors into deeper distress, by means of that contrast and disappointment. The whole art of the poet is employed, in rousing and supporting the compassion and indignation, the anxiety and resentment of his audience. They are pleased in proportion as they are afflicted, and never are so happy as when they employ tears, sobs, and cries to give vent to their sorrow, and relieve their heart, swollen with the tenderest sympathy and compassion.

The few critics who have had some tincture of philosophy, have remarked this singular phenomenon, and have endeavored to account for it.

L'Abbe Dubos, in his reflections on poetry and painting, asserts, that nothing is in general so disagreeable to the mind as the languid, listless taste of indolence, into which it falls upon the removal of all passion and occupation. To get rid of this painful situation, it seeks every amusement and pursuit; business, gaming, shews, executions; whatever will rouse the passions, and take its attention from itself. No matter what the passion is: Let it be disagreeable, afflicting, melancholy, disordered; it is still better than that insipid languor, which arises from perfect tranquillity and repose.

It is impossible not to admit this account, as being, at least in part, satisfactory. You may observe, when there are several tables of gaming, that all the company run to those, where the deepest play is, even though they find not there the best players. The view, or, at least, imagination of high passions, arising from great loss or gain, affects the spectator by sympathy, gives him some touches of the same passions, and serves him for a momentary entertainment. It makes the time pass the easier with him, and is some relief to that oppression, under which men commonly labor, when left entirely to their own thoughts and meditations.

We find that common liars always magnify, in their narrations, all kinds of danger, pain, distress, sickness, deaths, murders, and cruelties; as well as joy, beauty, mirth, and magnificence. It is an absurd secret, which they have for pleasing their company, fixing their attention, and attaching them to such marvelous relations, by the passions and emotions, which they excite.

There is, however, a difficulty in applying to the present subject, in its full extent, this solution, however ingenious and satisfactory it may appear. It is certain, that the same object of distress, which pleases in a tragedy, were it really set before us, would give the most unfeigned uneasiness; though it be then the most effectual cure to languor and indolence. Monsieur Fontenelle seems to have been sensible of this difficulty; and accordingly attempts another solution of the phenomenon; at least makes some addition to the theory above mentioned.[1]

"Pleasure and pain," says he, "which are two sentiments so different in themselves, differ not so much in their cause. From the instance of tickling, it appears, that the movement of pleasure, pushed a little too far, becomes pain; and that the movement of pain, a little moderated, becomes pleasure. Hence it proceeds, that there is such a thing as sorrow, soft and agreeable: It is a pain weakened and diminished. The heart likes naturally to be moved and affected. Melancholy objects suit it, and even disastrous and sorrowful, provided they are softened by some circumstance. It is certain, that, on the theater, the representation has almost the effect of reality; yet it has not altogether that effect. However we may be hurried away by the spectacle; whatever dominion the senses and imagination may usurp over the reason, there still lurks at the bottom a certain idea of falsehood in the whole of what we see. This idea, though weak and disguised, suffices to diminish the pain which we suffer from the misfortunes of those whom we love, and to reduce that affliction to such a pitch as converts it into a pleasure. We weep for the misfortune of a hero, to whom we are attached. In the same instant we comfort ourselves, by reflecting, that it is nothing but a fiction: And it is precisely that mixture of sentiments, which composes an agreeable sorrow, and tears that delight us. But as that affliction, which is caused by exterior and sensible objects, is stronger than the consolation which arises from an internal reflection, they are the effects and symptoms of sorrow, that ought to predominate in the composition."

This solution seems just and convincing; but perhaps it wants still some new addition, in order to make it answer fully the phenomenon, which we here examine. All the passions, excited by eloquence, are agreeable in the highest degree, as well as those which are moved by painting and the theater. The epilogues of Cicero are, on this account chiefly, the delight of every reader of taste; and it is difficult to read some of them without the deepest sympathy and sorrow. His merit as an orator, no doubt, depends much on his success in this particular. When he had raised tears in his judges and all his audience, they were then the most highly delighted, and expressed the greatest satisfaction with the pleader. The pathetic description of the butchery, made by Verres of the Siclian captains, is a masterpiece of this kind: But I believe none will affirm, that the being present at a melancholy scene of that nature would afford any entertainment. Neither is the sorrow here softened by fiction: For the audience were convinced of the reality of every circumstance. What is it then, which in this case raises a pleasure from the bosom of uneasiness, so to speak; and a pleasure, which still retains all the features and outward symptoms of distress and sorrow?

[1] *Reflexions sur la poetiqaue,* §36.

I answer: This extraordinary effect proceeds from that very eloquence, with which the melancholy scene is represented. The genius required to paint objects in a lively manner, the art employed in collecting all the pathetic circumstances, the judgment displayed in disposing them: the exercise, I say, of these noble talents, together with the force of expression, and beauty of oratorial numbers, diffuse the highest satisfaction on the audience, and excite the most delightful movements. By this means, the uneasiness of the melancholy passions is not only overpowered and effaced by something stronger of an opposite kind; but the whole impulse of those passions is converted into pleasure, and swells the delight which the eloquence raises in us. The same force of oratory, employed on an uninteresting subject, would not please half so much, or rather would appear altogether ridiculous; and the mind, being left in absolute calmness and indifference, would relish none of those beauties of imagination or expression, which, if joined to passion, give it such exquisite entertainment. The impulse or vehemence, arising from sorrow, compassion, indignation, receives a new direction from the sentiments of beauty. The latter, being the predominant emotion, seize the whole mind, and convert the former into themselves, at least tincture them so strongly as totally to alter their nature. And the soul, being, at the same time, roused by passion, and charmed by eloquence, feels on the whole a strong movement, which is altogether delightful.

The same principle takes place in tragedy; with this addition, that tragedy is an imitation; and imitation is always of itself agreeable. This circumstance serves still farther to smooth the motions of passion, and convert the whole feeling into one uniform and strong enjoyment. Objects of the greatest terror and distress please in painting, and please more than the most beautiful objects, that appear calm and indifferent.[2] The affection, rousing the mind, excites a large stock of spirit and vehemence; which is all transformed into pleasure by the force of the prevailing movement. It is thus the fiction of tragedy softens the passion, by an infusion of a new feeling, not merely by weakening or diminishing the sorrow. You may by degrees weaken a real sorrow, till it totally disappears; yet in none of its gradations will it ever give pleasure; except, perhaps by accident, to a man sunk under lethargic indolence, whom it rouses from that languid state.

To confirm this theory, it will be sufficient to produce other instances, where the subordinate movement is converted into the predominant, and gives force to it, though of a different, and even sometimes though of a contrary nature.

Novelty naturally rouses the mind, and attracts our attention; and the movements, which it causes, are always converted into any passion, belonging to the object, and join their force to it. Whether an event excite joy or sorrow, pride or shame, anger or good-will, it is sure to produce a stronger affection, when new or

[2] Painters make no scruple of representing distress and sorrow as well as any other passion: But they seem not to dwell so much on these melancholy affections as the poets, who, though they copy every motion of the human breast, yet pass quickly over the agreeable sentiments. A painter represents only one instant; and if that be passionate enough, it is sure to affect and delight the spectator: But nothing can furnish to the poet a variety of scenes and incidents and sentiments, except distress, terror, or anxiety. Complete joy and satisfaction is attended with security, and leaves no farther room for action.

unusual. And though novelty of itself be agreeable, it fortifies the painful, as well as agreeable passions.

Had you any intention to move a person extremely by the narration of any event, the best method of increasing its effect would be artfully to delay informing him of it, and first to excite his curiosity and impatience before you let him into the secret. This is the artifice practiced by Iago in the famous scene of Shakespeare; and every spectator is sensible, that Othello's jealousy acquires additional force from his preceding impatience, and that the subordinate passion is here readily transformed into the predominant one.

Difficulties increase passions of every kind; and by rousing our attention, and exciting our active powers, they produce an emotion, which nourishes the prevailing affection.

Parents commonly love that child most, whose sickly infirm frame of body has occasioned them the greatest pains, trouble, and anxiety in rearing him. The agreeable sentiment of affection here acquires force from sentiments of uneasiness.

Nothing endears so much a friend as sorrow for his death. The pleasure of his company has not so powerful an influence.

Jealousy is a painful passion; yet without some share of it, the agreeable affection of love has difficulty to subsist in its full force and violence. Absence is also a great source of complaint among lovers, and gives them the greatest uneasiness: Yet nothing is more favorable to their mutual passion than short intervals of that kind. And if long intervals often prove fatal, it is only because, through time, men are accustomed to them, and they cease to give uneasiness. Jealousy and absence in love compose the *dolce peccante* of the Italians, which they suppose so essential to all pleasure.

There is a fine observation of the elder Pliny, which illustrates the principle here insisted on. "It is very remarkable," says he, "that the last works of celebrated artists, which they left imperfect, are always the most prized, such as the Iris of Aristides, the Tyndarides of Nicomachus, the Medea of Timomachus, and the Venus of Apelles. These are valued even above their finished productions: The broken lineaments of the piece, and the half-formed idea of the painter are carefully studied; and our very grief for that curious hand, which had been stopped by death, is an additional increase to our pleasure."[3]

These instances (and many more might be collected) are sufficient to afford us some insight into the analogy of nature, and to show us, that the pleasure, which poets, orators, and musicians give us, by exciting grief, sorrow, indignation, compassion, is not so extraordinary or paradoxical, as it may at first sight appear. The force of imagination, the energy of expression, the power of numbers, the charms of imitation; all these are naturally, of themselves, delightful to the mind: And when the

[3] Illud vero perquam rarum ac memoria dignum, etiam suprema opera artificum, imperfectasque tabulas, sicut, Irin Aristidus, Tynaridas Nicomachi, Medeam Timomachi, & quam diximus Venerem Apellis, in majori admiratione esse quam perfecta. Quippe in iis lineamenta reliqua, ipsaeque cogitationes artificum spectantur, atque in lenocinio commendatitionis dolor est manus, cum id ageret, extinctae. Lib. xxxv. cap. 11.

object presented lays also hold of some affection, the pleasure still rises upon us, by the conversion of this subordinate movement into that which is predominant. The passion, though, perhaps, naturally, and when excited by the simple appearance of a real object, it may be painful; yet is so smoothed, and softened, and mollified, when raised by the finer arts, that it affords the highest entertainment.

To confirm this reasoning, we may observe, that if the movements of the imagination be not predominant above those of the passion, a contrary effect follows; and the former, being now subordinate, is converted into the latter, and still farther increases the pain and affliction of the sufferer.

Who could ever think of it as a good expedient for comforting an afflicted parent, to exaggerate, with all the force of elocution, the irreparable loss, which he has met with by the death of a favorite child? The more power of imagination and expression you here employ, the more you increase his despair and affliction.

The shame, confusion, and terror of Verres, no doubt, rose in proportion to the noble eloquence and vehemence of Cicero: So also did his pain and uneasiness. These former passions were too strong for the pleasure arising from the beauties of elocution; and operated, though from the same principle, yet in a contrary manner, to the sympathy, compassion, and indignation of the audience.

Lord Clarendon, when he approaches towards the catastrophe of the royal party, supposes, that his narration must then become infinitely disagreeable; and he hurries over the king's death, without giving us one circumstance of it. He considers it as too horrid a scene to be contemplated with any satisfaction, or even without the utmost pain and aversion. He himself, as well as the readers of that age, were too deeply concerned in the events, and felt a pain from subjects, which an historian and a reader of another age would regard as the most pathetic and most interesting, and, by consequence, the most agreeable.

An action, represented in tragedy, may be too bloody and atrocious. It may excite such movements of horror as will not soften into pleasure; and the greatest energy of expression, bestowed on descriptions of that nature, serves only to augment our uneasiness. Such is that action represented in the *Ambitious Stepmother*, where a venerable old man, raised to the height of fury and despair, rushes against a pillar, and striking his head upon it, besmears it all over with mingled brains and gore. The English theater abounds too much with such shocking images.

Even the common sentiments of compassion require to be softened by some agreeable affection, in order to give a thorough satisfaction to the audience. The mere suffering of plaintive virtue, under the triumphant tyranny and oppression of vice, forms a disagreeable spectacle, and is carefully avoided by all masters of the drama. In order to dismiss the audience with entire satisfaction and contentment, the virtue must either convert itself into a noble courageous despair, or the vice receive its proper punishment.

Most painters appear in this light to have been very unhappy in their subjects. As they wrought much for churches and convents, they have chiefly represented such horrible subjects as crucifixions and martyrdoms, where nothing appears but tortures, wounds, executions, and passive suffering without any action or affection. When they turned their pencil from this ghastly mythology, they had commonly recourse to Ovid, whose fictions, though passionate and agreeable, are scarcely natural or probable enough for painting.

The same inversion of that principle, which is here insisted on, displays itself in common life, as in the effects of oratory and poetry. Raise so the subordinate passion that it becomes the predominant, it swallows up that affection which it before nourished and increased. Too much jealousy extinguishes love: Too much difficulty renders us indifferent: Too much sickness and infirmity disgusts a selfish and unkind parent.

What so disagreeable as the dismal, gloomy, disastrous stories, with which melancholy people entertain their companions? The uneasy passion being there raised alone, unaccompanied with any spirit, genius, or eloquence, conveys a pure uneasiness, and is attended with nothing that can soften it into pleasure or satisfaction.

CHAPTER 11

Edmund Burke*

A Philosophical Enquiry into the Origin of Our Ideas of the Sublime and Beautiful 1757/1759

Introduction on Taste

On a superficial view, we may seem to differ very widely from each other in our reasonings, and no less in our pleasures: but notwithstanding this difference, which I think to be rather apparent than real, it is probable that the standard both of reason and taste is the same in all human creatures. For if there were not some principles of judgment as well as of sentiment common to all mankind, no hold could possibly be taken either on their reason or their passions, sufficient to maintain the ordinary correspondence of life. It appears indeed to be generally acknowledged, that with regard to truth and falsehood there is something fixed. We find people in their disputes continually appealing to certain tests and standards which are allowed on all sides, and are supposed to be established in our common nature. But there is not the same obvious concurrence in any uniform or settled principles which relate to taste. It is even commonly supposed that this delicate and aerial faculty, which seems too volatile to endure even the chains of a definition, cannot be properly tried by any

*Edmund Burke (1729-1797) was born in Dublin of a protestant father and catholic mother. He graduated from Trinity College, Dublin in 1748 and began the study of law in London before turning to writing. His only work on aesthetics was probably begun while he was still a student. In 1765 he became a Member of Parliament and secretary to the Whig politician, the Marquees of Rockingham. His political career saw him defend individual liberty against the crown and oppose Tory policy on Ireland and America, but he came to fear and thus to oppose disruption of the established order. His opposition to the French revolution made him a spokesman for politically conservative causes. With the exception of this work on the sublime and beautiful, his writings are primarily topical political speeches and pamphlets and works of political philosophy.

test, nor regulated by any standard. There is so continual a call for the exercise of the reasoning faculty, and it is so much strengthened by perpetual contention, that certain maxims of right reason seem to be tacitly settled amongst the most ignorant. The learned have improved on this rude science, and reduced those maxims into a system. If taste has not been so happily cultivated, it was not that the subject was barren, but that the laborers were few or negligent; for to say the truth, there are not the same interesting motives to impel us to fix the one, which urge us to ascertain the other. And after all, if men differ in their opinion concerning such matters, their difference is not attended with the same important consequences, else I make no doubt but that the logic of taste, if I may be allowed the expression, might very possibly be as well digested, and we might come to discuss matters of this nature with as much certainty, as those which seem more immediately within the province of mere reason. And indeed it is very necessary at the entrance into such an enquiry as our present, to make this point as clear as possible; for if taste has no fixed principles, if the imagination is not affected according to some invariable and certain laws, our labor is like to be employed to very little purpose as it must be judged an useless, if not an absurd undertaking, to lay down rules for caprice, and to set up for a legislator of whims and fancies.

The term *taste*, like all other figurative terms, is not extremely accurate: the thing which we understand by it, is far from a simple and determinate idea in the minds of most men, and it is therefore liable to uncertainty and confusion. I have no great opinion of a definition, the celebrated remedy for the cure of this disorder. For when we define, we seem in danger of circumscribing nature within the bounds of our own notions, which we often take up by hazard, or embrace on trust, or form out of a limited and partial consideration of the object before us, instead of extending our ideas to take in all that nature comprehends, according to her manner of combining. We are limited in our enquiry by the strict laws to which we have submitted at our setting out.

> *Circa vilem patulumque morabimur orbem*
> *Unde pudor proferre pedem vetat aut operis lex.*

A definition may be very exact, and yet go but a very little way towards informing us of the nature of the thing defined; but let the virtue of a definition be what it will, in the order of things, it seems rather to follow than to precede our enquiry, of which it ought to be considered as the result. It must be acknowledged that the methods of disquisition and teaching may be sometimes different, and on very good reason undoubtedly; but for my part, I am convinced that the method of teaching which approaches most nearly to the method of investigation, is incomparably the best; since not content with serving up a few barren and lifeless truths, it leads to the stock on which they grew; it tends to set the reader himself in the track of invention, and to direct him into those paths in which the author has made his own discoveries, if he should be so happy as to have made any that are valuable.

But to cut off all pretence for cavilling, I mean by the word taste no more than that faculty, or those faculties of the mind which are affected with, or which form a judgment of the works of imagination and the elegant arts. This is, I think, the most general idea of that word, and what is the least connected with any particular theory. And my point in this enquiry is to find whether there are any principles, on which the imagination is affected, so common to all, so grounded and certain, as to supply the means of reasoning satisfactorily about them. And such principles of taste, I fancy there are; however paradoxical it may seem to those, who on a superficial view imagine, that there is so great a diversity of tastes both in kind and degree, that nothing can be more indeterminate.

All the natural powers in man, which I know, that are conversant about external objects, are the Senses; the Imagination; and the Judgment. And first with regard to the senses. We do and we must suppose, that as the conformation of their organs are nearly, or altogether the same in all men, so the manner of perceiving external objects is in all men the same, or with little difference. We are satisfied that what appears to be light to one eye, appears light to another; that what seems sweet to one palate, is sweet to another; that what is dark and bitter to this man, is likewise dark and bitter to that; and we conclude in the same manner of great and little, hard and soft, hot and cold, rough and smooth; and indeed of all the natural qualities and affections of bodies. If we suffer ourselves to imagine, that their senses present to different men different images of things, this sceptical proceeding will make every sort of reasoning on every subject vain and frivolous, even that sceptical reasoning itself, which had persuaded us to entertain a doubt concerning the agreement of our perceptions. But as there will be very little doubt that bodies present similar images to the whole species, it must necessarily be allowed, that the pleasures and the pains which every object excites in one man, it must raise in all mankind, whilst it operates naturally, simply, and by its proper powers only; for if we deny this, we must imagine, that the same cause operating in the same manner, and on subjects of the same kind, will produce different effects, which would be highly absurd. Let us first consider this point in the sense of taste and the rather as the faculty in question has taken its name from that sense. All men are agreed to call vinegar sour, honey sweet, and aloes bitter and as they are all agreed in finding these qualities in those objects, they do not in the least differ concerning their effects with regard to pleasure and pain. They all concur in calling sweetness pleasant, and sourness and bitterness unpleasant. Here there is no diversity in their sentiments; and that there is not appears fully from the consent of all men in the metaphors which are taken from the sense of taste. A sour temper, bitter expressions, bitter curses, a bitter fate, are terms well and strongly understood by all. And we are altogether as well understood when we say, a sweet disposition, a sweet person, a sweet condition, and the like. It is confessed, that custom, and some other causes, have made many deviations from the natural pleasures or pains which belong to these several tastes; but then the power of distinguishing between the natural and the acquired relish remains to the very last. A man frequently comes to prefer the taste of tobacco to that of sugar, and the flavor of vinegar to that of milk; but this makes no confusion in tastes, whilst he is sensible that the tobacco and vinegar are not sweet, and whilst he knows that habit alone has reconciled his palate to these alien pleasures. Even with such a person we may speak, and with sufficient precision, concerning tastes. But should any man be found who declares, that to him tobacco has a taste like sugar, and that he cannot distinguish between milk and vinegar; or that tobacco and vinegar are sweet, milk bitter, and sugar sour, we immediately conclude that the organs of this man are out of order, and that his palate is utterly vitiated. We are as far from conferring with such a person upon tastes, as from reasoning concerning the relations of quantity with one who should deny that all the parts together were equal to the whole. We do not call a man of this kind wrong in his notions, but absolutely mad. Exceptions of this sort in either way, do not at all impeach our general rule, nor make us conclude that men have various principles concerning the relations of quantity, or the taste of things. So that when it is said, taste cannot be disputed, it can only mean, that no one can strictly answer what pleasure or pain some particular man may find from the taste of some particular thing. This indeed cannot be disputed; but we may dispute, and with sufficient clearness too, concerning the things which are naturally pleasing or disagreeable to the sense. But when we talk of any peculiar or acquired relish, then we must know the habits, the prejudices, or the distempers of this particular man, and we must draw our conclusion from those.

This agreement of mankind is not confined to the taste solely. The principle of pleasure derived from sight is the same in all. Light is more pleasing than darkness. Summer, when the earth is clad in green, when the heavens are serene and bright, is more agreeable than winter, when every thing makes a different appearance. I never remember that any thing beautiful, whether a man, a beast, a bird, or a plant, was ever shewn, though it were to an hundred people, that they did not all immediately agree that it was beautiful, though some might have thought that it fell short of their expectation, or that other things were still finer. I believe no man thinks a goose to be more beautiful than a swan, or imagines that what they call a Friezland hen excels a peacock. It must be observed too, that the pleasures of the sight are not near so complicated, and confused, and altered by unnatural habits and associations, as the pleasures of the taste are; because the pleasures of the sight more commonly acquiesce in themselves; and are not so often altered by considerations which are independent of the sight itself. But things do not spontaneously present themselves to the palate as they do to the sight; they are generally applied to it, either as food or as medicine; and from the qualities which they possess for nutritive or medicinal purposes, they often form the palate by degrees, and by force of these associations. Thus opium is pleasing to Turks, on account of the agreeable delirium it produces. Tobacco is the delight of Dutchmen, as it diffuses a torpor and pleasing stupefaction. Fermented spirits please our common people, because they banish care, and all consideration of future or present evils. All of these would lie absolutely neglected if their properties had originally gone no further than the taste; but all these, together with tea and coffee, and some other things, have past from the apothecary's shop to our tables, and were taken for health long before they were thought of for pleasure. The effect of the drug has made us use it frequently; and frequent use, combined with the agreeable effect, has made the taste itself at last agreeable. But this does not in the least perplex our reasoning; because we distinguish to the last the acquired from the natural relish. In describing the taste of an unknown fruit, you would scarcely say, that it had a sweet and pleasant flavor like tobacco, opium, or garlic, although you spoke to those who were in the constant use of these drugs, and had great pleasure in them. There is in all men a sufficient remembrance of the original natural causes of pleasure, to enable them to bring all things offered to their senses to that standard, and to regulate their feelings and opinions by it. Suppose one who had so vitiated his palate as to take more pleasure in the taste of opium than in that of butter or honey, to be presented with a bolus of squills; there is hardly any doubt but that he would prefer the butter or honey to this nauseous morsel, or to any other bitter drug to which he had not been accustomed; which proves that his palate was naturally like that of other men in all things, that it is still like the palate of other men in many things, and only vitiated in some particular points. For in judging of any new thing, even of a taste similar to that which he has been formed by habit to like, he finds his palate affected in the natural manner, and on the common principles. Thus the pleasure of all the senses, of the sight, and even of the taste, that most ambiguous of the senses, is the same in all, high and low, learned and unlearned.

Besides the ideas, with their annexed pains and pleasures, which are presented by the sense; the mind of man possesses a sort of creative power of its own; either in representing at pleasure the images of things in the order and manner in which they were received by the senses, or in combining those images in a new manner, and according to a different order. This power is called Imagination; and to this belongs whatever is called wit, fancy, invention, and the like. But it must be observed, that this power of the imagination is incapable of producing any thing absolutely new; it can only vary the disposition of those ideas which it has received from the senses. Now the imagination is the most extensive province of pleasure and pain, as it is the region of our fears and our hopes, and of all our passions that are connected with them; and whatever is calculated to affect the imagination with these commanding ideas, by force of any original natural impression, must have the same power pretty equally over all men. For since the imagination is only the representative of the senses, it can only be pleased or displeased with the images from the same principle on which the sense is pleased or displeased with the realities; and consequently there must be just as close an agreement in the imaginations as in the senses of men. A little attention will convince us that this must of necessity be the case.

But in the imagination, besides the pain or pleasure arising from the properties of the natural object, pleasure is perceived from the resemblance, which the imitation has to the original; the imagination, I conceive, can have no pleasure but what results from one or other of these causes. And these causes operate pretty uniformly upon all men, because they operate by principles in nature, and which are not derived from any particular habits or advantages. Mr. Locke very justly and finely observes of wit, that it is chiefly conversant in tracing resemblances; he remarks at the same time, that the business of judgment is rather in finding differences. It may perhaps appear, on this supposition, that there is no material distinction between the wit and the judgment, as they both seem to result from different operations of the same faculty of comparing. But in reality, whether they are or are not dependent on the same power of the mind, they differ so very materially in many respects, that a perfect union of wit and judgment is one of the rarest things in the world. When two distinct objects are unlike to each other, it is only what we expect; things are in their common way; and therefore they make no impression on the imagination: but when two distinct objects have a resemblance, we are struck, we attend to them, and we are pleased. The mind of man has naturally a far greater alacrity and satisfaction in tracing resemblances than in searching for differences; because by making resemblances we produce new images, we unite, we create, we enlarge our stock; but in making distinctions we offer no food at all to the imagination; the task itself is more severe and irksome, and what pleasure we derive from it is something of a negative and indirect nature. A piece of news is told me in the morning; this, merely as a piece of news, as a fact added to my stock, gives me some pleasure. In the evening I find there was nothing in it. What do I gain by this, but the dissatisfaction to find that I had been imposed upon? Hence it is, that men are much more naturally inclined to belief than to incredulity. And it is upon this principle, that the most ignorant and barbarous nations have frequently excelled in similitudes, comparisons, metaphors, and allegories, who have been weak and backward in distinguishing and sorting their ideas. And it is for a reason of this kind that Homer and the oriental writers, though very fond of similitudes, and though they often strike out such as are truly admirable, they seldom take care to have them exact; that is, they are taken with the general resemblance, they paint it strongly, and they take no notice of the difference which may be found between the things compared.

Now as the pleasure of resemblance is that which principally flatters the imagination, all men are nearly equal in this point, as far as their knowledge of the things represented or compared extends. The principle of this knowledge is very much accidental, as it depends upon experience and observation, and not on the strength or weakness of any natural faculty; and it is from this difference in knowledge that what we commonly, though with no great exactness, call a difference in taste proceeds. A man to whom sculpture is new, sees a barber's block, or some ordinary piece of statuary; he is immediately struck and pleased, because he sees something like an human figure; and entirely taken up with this likeness, he does not at all attend to its defects. No person, I believe, at the first time of seeing a piece of imitation ever did. Some time after, we suppose that this novice lights upon a more artificial work of the same nature; he now begins to look with contempt on what he admired at first; not that he admired it even then for its unlikeness to a man, but for that general though inaccurate resemblance which it bore to the human figure. What he admired at different times in these so different figures, is strictly the same; and though his knowledge is improved, his taste is not altered. Hitherto his mistake was from a want of knowledge in art, and this arose from his inexperience; but he may be still deficient from a want of knowledge in nature. For it is possible that the man in question may stop here, and that the masterpiece of a great hand may please him no more than the middling performance of a vulgar artist; and this not for want of better or higher relish, but because all men do not observe with sufficient accuracy on the human figure to enable them to judge properly of an imitation of it. And that the critical taste does not depend upon a superior principle in men, but upon superior knowledge, may appear from several instances. The story of the ancient painter and the shoemaker is very well known. The shoemaker set the painter right with regard to some mistakes he had made in the shoe of one of his figures, and which the painter, who had not made such accurate observations on shoes, and was content with a general resemblance, had never observed. But this was no impeachment to the taste of the painter, it only shewed some want of knowledge in the art of making shoes. Let us imagine, that an anatomist had come into the painter's working room. His piece is in general well done, the figure in question in a good attitude, and the parts well adjusted to their various movements; yet the anatomist, critical in his art, may observe the swell of some muscle not quite just in the peculiar action of the figure. Here the anatomist observes what the painter had not observed, and he passes by what the shoemaker had remarked. But a want of the last critical knowledge in anatomy no more reflected on the natural good taste of the painter, or of any common observer of his piece, than the want of an exact knowledge in the formation of a shoe. A fine piece of a decollated head of St. John the Baptist was shewn to a Turkish emperor; he praised many things, but he observed one defect; he observed that the skin did not shrink from the wounded part of the neck. The sultan on this occasion, though his observation was very just, discovered no more natural taste than the painter who executed this piece, or than a thousand European connoisseurs who probably never would have made the same observation. His Turkish majesty had indeed been well acquainted with that terrible spectacle, which the others could only have represented in their imagination. On the subject of their dislike there is a difference between all these people, arising from the different kinds and degrees of their knowledge; but there is something in common to the painter, the shoemaker, the anatomist, and the Turkish emperor, the pleasure arising from a natural object, so far as each perceives it justly imitated; the satisfaction in seeing an agreeable figure; the sympathy proceeding from a striking and affecting incident. So far as taste is natural, it is nearly common to all.

In poetry, and other pieces of imagination, the same parity may be observed. It is true, that one man is charmed with Don Bellianis, and reads Virgil coldly; whilst another is transported with the Eneid, and leaves Don Bellianis to children. These two men seem to have a taste very different from each other; but in fact they differ very little. In both these pieces, which inspire such opposite sentiments, a tale exciting admiration is told; both are full of action, both are passionate, in both are voyages, battles, triumphs, and continual changes of fortune. The admirer of Don Bellianis perhaps does not understand the refined language of the Eneid, who if it was degraded into the style of the *Pilgrim's Progress*, might feel it in all its energy, on the same principle which made him an admirer of Don Bellianis.

In his favourite author he is not shocked with the continual breaches of probability, the confusion of times, the offences against manners, the trampling upon geography; for he knows nothing of geography and chronology, and he has never examined the grounds of probability. He perhaps reads of a shipwreck on the coast of Bohemia; wholly taken up with so interesting an event, and only solicitous for the fate of his hero, he is not in the least troubled at this extravagant blunder. For why should he be shocked at a shipwreck on the coast of Bohemia, who does not know but that Bohemia may be an island in the Atlantic ocean? And after all, what reflection is this on the natural good taste of the person here supposed?

So far then as taste belongs to the imagination, its principle is the same in all men; there is no difference in the manner of their being affected, nor in the causes of the affection; but in the degree there is a difference, which arises from two causes principally; either from a greater degree of natural sensibility, or from a closer and longer attention to the object. To illustrate this by the procedure of the senses in which the same difference is found, let us suppose a very smooth marble table to be set before two men; they both perceive it to be smooth, and they are both pleased with it, because of this quality. So far they agree. But suppose another, and after that another table, the latter still smoother than the former, to be set before them. It is now very probable that these men, who are so agreed upon what is smooth, and in the pleasure from thence, will disagree when they come to settle which table has the advantage in point of polish. Here is indeed the great difference between tastes, when men come to compare the excess or diminution of things which are judged by degree and not by measure. Nor is it easy, when such a difference arises, to settle the point, if the excess or diminution be not glaring. If we differ in opinion about two quantities, we can have recourse to a common measure, which may decide the question with the utmost exactness; and this I take it is what gives mathematical knowledge a greater certainty than any other. But in things whose excess is not judged by greater or smaller, as smoothness and roughness, hardness and softness, darkness and light, the shades of colors, all these are very easily distinguished when the difference is any way considerable, but not when it is minute, for want of some common measures which perhaps may never come to be discovered. In these nice cases, supposing the acuteness of the sense equal, the greater attention and habit in such things will have the advantage. In the question about the tables, the marble polisher will unquestionably determine the most accurately. But notwithstanding this want of a common measure for settling many disputes relative to the senses and their representative the imagination, we find that the principles are the same in all, and that there is no disagreement until we come to examine into the preeminence or difference of things, which brings us within the province of the judgment.

So long as we are conversant with the sensible qualities of things, hardly any more than the imagination seems concerned; little more also than the imagination seems concerned when the passions are represented, because by the force of natural sympathy they are felt in all men without any recourse to reasoning, and their justness recognized in every breast. Love, grief, fear, anger, joy, all these passions have in their turns affected every mind; and they do not affect it in an arbitrary or casual manner, but upon certain, natural and uniform principles. But as many of the works of imagination are not confined to the representation of sensible objects, nor to efforts upon the passions, but extend themselves to the manners, the characters, the actions, and designs of men, their relations, their virtues and vices, they come within the province of the judgment, which is improved by attention and by the habit of reasoning. All these make a very considerable part of what are considered as the objects of taste; and Horace sends us to the schools of philosophy and the world for our instruction in them. Whatever certainty is to be acquired in morality and the science of life; just the same degree of certainty have we in what relates to them in works of imitation. Indeed it is for the most part in our skill in manners, and in the observances of time and place, and of decency in general, which is only to be learned in those schools to which Horace recommends us, that what is called taste by way of distinction, consists; and which is in reality no other than a more refined judgment. On the whole it appears to me, that what is called taste, in its most general acceptation, is not a simple idea, but is partly made up of a perception of the primary pleasures of sense, of the secondary pleasures of the imagination, and of the conclusions of the reasoning faculty, concerning the various relations of these, and concerning the human passions, manners and actions. All this is requisite to form taste, and the ground-work of all these is the same in the human mind; for as the senses are the great originals of all our ideas, and consequently of all our pleasures, if they are not uncertain and arbitrary, the whole ground-work of taste is common to all, and therefore there is a sufficient foundation for a conclusive reasoning on these matters.

Whilst we consider taste, merely according to its nature and species, we shall find its principles entirely uniform; but the degree in which these principles prevail in the several individuals of mankind, is altogether as different as the principles themselves are similar. For sensibility and judgment, which are the qualities that compose what we commonly call a *taste,* vary exceedingly in various people. From a defect in the former of these qualities, arises a want of taste; a weakness in the latter, constitutes a wrong or a bad one. There are some men formed with feelings so blunt, with tempers so cold and phlegmatic, that they can hardly be said to be awake during the whole course of their lives. Upon such persons, the most striking objects make but a faint and obscure impression. There are others so continually in the agitation of gross and merely sensual pleasures, or so occupied in the low drudgery of avarice, or so heated in the chace of honors and distinction, that their minds, which had been used continually to the storms of these violent and tempestuous passions, can hardly be put in motion by the delicate and refined play of the imagination. These men, though from a different cause, become as stupid and insensible as the former; but whenever either of these happen to be struck with any natural elegance or greatness, or with these qualities in any work of art, they are moved upon the same principle.

The cause of a wrong taste is a defect of judgment. And this may arise from a natural weakness of understanding (in whatever the strength of that faculty may consist) or, which is much more commonly the case, it may arise from a want of proper and well-directed exercise, which alone can make it strong and ready. Besides that ignorance, inattention, prejudice, rashness, levity, obstinacy, in short, all those passions, and all those vices which pervert the judgment in other matters, prejudice it no less in this its more refined and elegant province. These causes produce different opinions upon every thing which is an object of the understanding, without inducing us to suppose, that there are no settled, principles of reason. And indeed on the whole one may observe, that there is rather less difference upon matters of taste among mankind, than upon most of those which depend upon the naked reason; and that men are far better agreed on the excellence of a description in Virgil, than on the truth or falsehood of a theory of Aristotle.

A rectitude of judgment in the arts which may be called a good taste, does in a great measure depend upon sensibility; because if the mind has no bent to the pleasures of the imagination, it will never apply itself sufficiently to works of that species to acquire a competent knowledge in them. But, though a degree of sensibility is requisite to form a good judgment, yet a good judgment does not necessarily arise from a quick sensibility of pleasure; it frequently happens that a very poor judge, merely by force of a greater complexional sensibility, is more affected by a very poor piece, than the best judge by the most perfect; for as every thing new, extraordinary, grand, or passionate is well calculated to affect such a person, and that the faults do not affect him, his pleasure is more pure and unmixed; and as it is merely a pleasure of the imagination, it is much higher than any which is derived from a rectitude of the judgment; the judgment is for the greater part employed in throwing stumbling blocks in the way of the imagination, in dissipating the scenes of its enchantment, and in tying us down to the disagreeable yoke of our reason: for almost the only pleasure that men have in judging better than others, consists in a sort of conscious pride and superiority, which arises from thinking rightly; but then, this is an indirect pleasure, a pleasure which does not immediately result from the object which is under contemplation. In the morning of our days, when the senses are unworn and tender, when the whole man is awake in every part, and the gloss of novelty fresh upon all the objects that surround us, how lively at that time are our sensations, but how false and inaccurate the judgments we form of things? I despair of ever receiving the same degree of pleasure from the most excellent performances of genius which I felt at that age, from pieces which my present judgment regards as trifling and contemptible. Every trivial cause of pleasure is apt to affect the man of too sanguine a complexion: his appetite is too keen to suffer his taste to be delicate; and he is in all respects what Ovid says of himself in love,

> *Molle meum levibus cor est violabile telis,*
> *Et semper causa est, cur ego semper amem.*

One of this character can never be a refined judge; never what the comic poet calls *elegans formarum, spectator.* The excellence and force of a composition must always be imperfectly estimated from its effect on the minds of any, except we know the temper and character of those minds. The most powerful effects of poetry and music have been displayed, and perhaps are still displayed, where these arts are but in a very low and imperfect state. The rude hearer is affected by the principles which operate in these arts even in their rudest condition; and he is not skilful enough to perceive the defects. But as the arts advance towards their perfection, the science of criticism advances with equal pace, and the pleasure of judges is frequently interrupted by the faults which are discovered in the most finished compositions.

Before I leave this subject I cannot help taking notice of an opinion which many persons entertain, as if the taste were a separate faculty of the mind, and distinct from the judgment and imagination; a species of instinct by which we are struck naturally, and at the first glance, without any previous reasoning with the excellencies, or the defects of a composition. So far as the imagination and the passions are concerned, I believe it true, that the reason is little consulted; but where disposition, where decorum, where congruity are concerned, in short wherever the best taste differs from the worst, I am convinced that the understanding operates and nothing else; and its operation is in reality far from being always sudden, or when it is sudden, it is often far from being right. Men of the best taste by consideration, come frequently to change these early and precipitate judgments which the mind from its aversion to neutrality and doubt loves to form on the spot. It is known that the taste (whatever it is) is improved exactly as we improve our judgment, by extending our knowledge, by a steady attention to our object, and by frequent exercise. They who have not taken these methods, if their taste decides quickly, it is always uncertainly; and their quickness is owing to their presumption and rashness, and not to any sudden irradiation that in a moment dispels all darkness from their minds. But they who have cultivated that species of knowledge which makes the object of taste, by degrees and habitually attain not only a soundness, but a readiness of judgment, as men do by the same methods on all other occasions. At first they are obliged to spell, but at last they read with ease and with celerity: but this celerity of its operation is no proof, that the taste is a distinct faculty. Nobody I believe has attended the course of a discussion, which turned upon matters within the sphere of mere naked reason, but must have observed the extreme readiness with which the whole process of the argument is carried on, the grounds discovered, the objections raised and answered, and the conclusions drawn from premises, with a quickness altogether as great as the taste can be supposed to work *with;* and yet where nothing but plain reason either is or can be suspected to operate. To multiply principles for every different appearance, is useless, and unphilosophical too in a high degree.

This matter might be pursued much further; but it is not the extent of the subject which must prescribe our bounds, for what subject does not branch out to infinity? It is the nature of our particular scheme, and the single point of view in which we consider it, which ought to put a stop to our researches.

PART ONE

Section I
Novelty

The first and the simplest emotion which we discover in the human mind, is curiosity. By curiosity, I mean whatever desire we have for, or whatever pleasure we take in novelty. We see children perpetually running from place to place to hunt out something new; they catch with great eagerness, and with very little choice, at whatever comes before them; their attention is engaged by every thing, because every thing has, in that stage of life, the charm of novelty to recommend it. But as those things which engage us merely by their novelty, cannot attach us for any length of time, curiosity is the most superficial of all the affections; it changes its object perpetually; it has an appetite which is very sharp, but very easily satisfied; and it has always an appearance of giddiness, restlessness and anxiety. Curiosity from its nature is a very active principle; it quickly runs over the greatest part of its objects, and soon exhausts the variety which is commonly to be met with in nature; the same things make frequent returns, and they return with less and less of any agreeable effect. In short, the occurrences of life, by the time we come to know it a little, would be incapable of affecting the mind with any other sensations than those of loathing and weariness, if many things were not adapted to affect the mind by means of other powers besides novelty in them, and of other passions besides curiosity in ourselves. These powers and passions shall be considered in their place. But whatever these powers are, or upon what principle soever they affect the mind, it is absolutely necessary that they should not be exerted in those things which a daily and vulgar use have brought into a stale unaffecting familiarity. Some degree of novelty must be one of the materials in every instrument which works upon the mind; and curiosity blends itself more or less with all our passions.

Section II
Pain and Pleasure

It seems then necessary towards moving the passions of people advanced in life to any considerable degree, that the objects designed for that purpose, besides their being in some measure new, should be capable of exciting pain or pleasure from other causes. Pain and pleasure are simple ideas, incapable of definition. People are not liable to be mistaken in their feelings, but they are very frequently wrong in the names they give them, and in their reasonings about them. Many are of opinion, that pain arises necessarily from the removal of some pleasure; as they think pleasure does from the ceasing or diminution of some pain. For my part I am rather inclined to imagine, that pain and pleasure in their most simple and natural manner of affecting, are each of a positive nature, and by no means necessarily dependent on each other for their existence. The human mind is often, and I think it is for the most part, in a state neither of pain nor pleasure, which I call a state of indifference. When I am carried from this state into a state of actual pleasure, it does not appear necessary that I should pass through the medium of any sort of pain. If in such a state of indifference, or ease, or tranquillity, or call it what you please, you were to be suddenly entertained with a concert of music; or suppose some object of a fine shape, and bright lively colors to be presented before you; or imagine your smell is gratified with the fragrance of a rose; or if without any previous thirst you were to drink of some pleasant kind of wine; or to taste of some sweetmeat without being hungry; in all the several senses, of hearing, smelling, and tasting, you undoubtedly find a pleasure; yet if I enquire into the state of your mind previous to these gratifications, you will hardly tell me that they found you in any kind of pain; or having satisfied these several senses with their several pleasures, will you say that any pain has succeeded, though the pleasure is absolutely over? Suppose on the other hand, a man in the same state of indifference, to receive a violent blow, or to drink of some bitter potion, or to have his ears wounded with some harsh and grating sound; here is no removal of pleasure; and yet here is felt, in every sense which is affected, a pain very distinguishable. It may be said perhaps, that the pain in these cases had its use from the removal of the pleasure which the man enjoyed before, though that pleasure was of so low a degree as to be perceived only by the removal.

But this seems to me a subtilty, that is not discoverable in nature. For if previous to the pain, I do not feel any actual pleasure, I have no reason to judge that any such thing exists; since pleasure is only pleasure as it is felt. The same may be said of pain, and with equal reason. I can never persuade myself that pleasure and pain are mere relations, which can only exist as they are contrasted: but I think I can discern clearly that there are positive pains and pleasures, which do not at all depend upon each other. Nothing is more certain to my own feelings than this. There is nothing which I can distinguish in my mind with more clearness than the three states, of indifference, of pleasure, and of pain. Every one of these I can perceive without any sort of idea of its relation to any thing else. Caius is afflicted with a fit of the cholic; this man is actually in pain; stretch Caius upon the rack, he will feel a much greater pain; but does this pain of the rack arise from the removal of any pleasure? Or is the fit of the cholic a pleasure or a pain just as we are pleased to consider it?

Section III
The difference between the removal of PAIN and positive PLEASURE

We shall carry this proposition yet a step further. We shall venture to propose, that pain and pleasure are not only, not necessarily dependent for their existence on their mutual diminution or removal, but that, in reality, the diminution or ceasing of pleasure does not operate like positive pain; and that the removal or diminution of pain, in its effect has very little resemblance to positive pleasure.[1] The former of these propositions will, I believe, be much more readily allowed than the latter; because it is very evident that pleasure, when it has run its career, sets us down very nearly where it found us. Pleasure of every kind quickly satisfies; and when it is over, we relapse into indifference, or rather we fall into a soft tranquillity, which is tinged with the agreeable color of the former sensation. I own, it is not at first view so apparent, that the removal of a great pain does not resemble positive pleasure: but let us recollect in what state we have found our minds upon escaping some imminent danger, or on being released from the severity of some cruel pain. We have on such occasions found, if I am not much mistaken, the temper of our minds in a tenor very remote from that which attends the presence of positive pleasure; we have found them in a state of much sobriety, impressed with a sense of awe, in a sort of tranquillity shadowed with horror. The fashion of the countenance and the gesture of the body on such occasions is so correspondent to this state of mind, that any person, a stranger to the cause of the appearance, would rather judge us under some consternation, than in the enjoyment of any thing like positive pleasure.

[1] Mr. Locke [*Essay on Human Understanding,* 1. 2. c. 20. section 16] thinks that the removal or lessening of a pain is considered and operates as a pleasure, and the loss or diminishing of pleasure as a pain. It is this opinion which we consider here.

ὡς δ'ὅτ'ἂν ἄνδρ'ἄτη πυκινὴ, λάβη, ὅς τ'ενὶ πάτρη
φῶτα κατακτείνας ἄλλων ἐξίκετο δῆμον
ἀνδρὸς ἐς ἀφνειοῦ θάμβος δ'ἔχει εἰσοροωντας

Iliad. 24.3

As when a wretch, who conscious of his crime,
Pursued for murder from his native clime,
Just gains some frontier, breathless, pale, amaz'd;
All gaze, all wonder!

This striking appearance of the man whom Homer supposes to have just escaped an imminent danger, the sort of mixt passion of terror and surprize, with which he affects the spectators, paints very strongly the manner in which we find ourselves affected upon occasions any way similar. For when we have suffered from any violent emotion, the mind naturally continues in something like the same condition, after the cause which first produced it has ceased to operate. The tossing of the sea remains after the storm; and when this remain of horror has entirely subsided, all the passion, which the accident raised, subsides along with it; and the mind returns to its usual state of indifference. In short, pleasure (I mean any thing either in the inward sensation, or in the outward appearance like pleasure from a positive cause) has never, I imagine, its origin from the removal of pain or danger.

Section IV
Of Delight and Pleasure, as Opposed to Each Other

But shall we therefore say, that the removal of pain or its diminution is always simply painful? Or affirm that the cessation or the lessening of pleasure is always attended itself with a pleasure? By no means. What I advance is no more than this; first, that there are pleasures and pains of a positive and independent nature; and secondly, that the feeling which results from the ceasing or diminution of pain does not bear a sufficient resemblance to positive pleasure to have it considered as of the same nature, or to entitle it to be known by the same name; and thirdly, that upon the same principle the removal or qualification of pleasure has no resemblance to positive pain. It is certain that the former feeling (the removal or moderation of pain) has something in it far from distressing, or disagreeable in its nature. This feeling, in many cases so agreeable, but in all so different from positive pleasure, has no name which I know; but that hinders not its being a very real one, and very different from all others. (It is most certain, that every species of satisfaction or pleasure, how different soever in its manner of affecting, is of a positive nature in the mind of him who feels it. The affection is undoubtedly positive; but the cause may be, as in this case it certainly is, a sort of privation. And it is very reasonable that we should distinguish by some term two things so distinct in nature, as a pleasure that is. such simply, and without any relation, from that pleasure, which cannot exist without a relation, and that too a relation to pain. Very extraordinary it would be, if these affections, so distinguishable in their causes, so different in their effects, should be confounded with each other, because vulgar use has ranged them under the same general title.) Whenever I have occasion to speak of this species of relative pleasure, I call it *delight;* and I shall take the best care I can, to use that word in no other sense. I am satisfied the word is not commonly used in this appropriated signification; but I thought it better to take up a word already known, and to limit its signification, than to introduce a new one which would not perhaps incorporate so well with the language. I should never have presumed the least alteration in our words, if the nature of the language, framed for the purposes of business rather than those of philosophy, and the nature of my subject that leads me but of the common track of discourse, did not in a manner necessitate me to it. I shall make use of this liberty with all possible caution. As I make use of the word *delight* to express the sensation which accompanies the removal of pain or danger; so when I speak of positive pleasure, I shall for the most part call it simply *pleasure.*

. . .

Section VII
Of the Sublime

Whatever is fitted in any sort to excite the ideas of pain, and danger, that is to say, whatever is in any sort terrible, or is conversant about terrible objects, or operates in a manner analogous to terror, is a source of the *sublime;* that is, it is productive of the strongest emotion which the mind is capable of feeling. (I say the strongest emotion, because I am satisfied the ideas of pain are much more powerful than those which enter on the part of pleasure. Without all doubt, the torments which we may be made to suffer, are much greater in their effect on the body and mind, than any pleasures which the most learned voluptuary could suggest, or than the liveliest imagination, and the most sound and exquisitely sensible body could enjoy. Nay I am in great doubt, whether any man could be found who would earn a life of the most perfect satisfaction, at the price of ending it in the torments, which justice inflicted in a few hours on the late unfortunate regicide in France. But as pain is stronger in its operation than pleasure, so death is in general a much more affecting idea than pain; because there are very few pains, however exquisite, which are not preferred to death; nay, what generally makes pain itself, if I may say so, more painful, is, that it is considered as an emissary of this king of terrors.) When danger or pain press too nearly, they are incapable of giving any delight, and are simply terrible; but at certain distances, and with certain modifications, they may be, and they are delightful, as we every day experience. The cause of this I shall endeavour to investigate hereafter.

. . .

Section X
Of Beauty

The passion which belongs to generation, merely as such, is lust only; this is evident in brutes, whose passions are more unmixed, and which pursue their purposes more directly than ours. The only distinction they observe with regard to their mates, is that of sex. It is true, that they stick severally to their own species in preference to all others. But this preference, I imagine, does not arise from any sense of beauty which they find in their species, as Mr. Addison supposes, but from a law of some other kind to which they are subject; and this we may fairly conclude, from their apparent want of choice amongst those objects to which the barriers of their species have confined them. But man, who is a creature adapted to a greater variety and intricacy of relation, connects with the general passion, the idea of some social qualities, which direct and heighten the appetite which he has in common with all other animals; and as he is not designed like them to live at large, it is fit that he should have something to create a preference, and fix his choice; and this in general should be some sensible quality; as no other can so quickly, so powerfully, or so surely produce its effect. The object therefore of this mixed passion which we call love, is the beauty of the sex. Men are carried to the sex in general, as it is the sex, and by the common law of nature; but they are attached to particulars by personal beauty. I call beauty a social quality; for where women and men, and not only they, but when other animals give us a sense of joy and pleasure in beholding them, (and there are many that do so) they inspire us with sentiments of tenderness and affection towards their persons; we like to have them near us, and we enter willingly into a kind of relation with them, unless we should have strong reasons to the contrary. But to what end, in many cases, this was designed, I am unable to discover; for I see no greater reason for a connection between man and several animals who are attired in so engaging a manner, than between him and some others who entirely want this attraction, or possess it in a far weaker degree. But it is probable, that providence did not make even this distinction, but with a view to some great end, though we cannot perceive distinctly what it is, as his wisdom is not our wisdom, nor our ways his ways.

. . .

Section XVI
Imitation

The second passion belonging to society is imitation, or, if you will, a desire of imitating, and consequently a pleasure in it. This passion arises from much the same cause with sympathy. For as sympathy makes us take a concern in whatever men feel, so this affection prompts us to copy whatever they do; and consequently we have a pleasure in imitating, and in whatever belongs to imitation merely as it is such, without any intervention of the reasoning faculty, but solely from our natural constitution, which providence has framed in such a manner as to find either pleasure or delight according to the nature of the object, in whatever regards the purposes of our being. It is by imitation far more than by precept that we learn every thing; and what we learn thus we acquire not only more effectually, but more pleasantly. This forms our manners, our opinions, our lives. It is one of the strongest links of society; it is a species of mutual compliance which all men yield to each other, without constraint to themselves, and which is extremely flattering to all. Herein it is that painting and many other agreeable arts have laid one of the principal foundations of their power. And since by its influence on our manners and our passions it is of such great consequence, I shall here venture to lay down a rule, which may inform us with a good degree of certainty when we are to attribute the power of the arts, to imitation, or to our pleasure in the skill of the imitation merely, and when to sympathy, or some other cause in conjunction with it. When the object represented in poetry or painting is such, as we could have no desire of seeing in reality; then I may be sure that its power in poetry or painting is owing to the power of imitation, and to no cause operating in the thing itself. So it is with most of the pieces which the painters call still life. In these a cottage, a dunghill, the meanest and most ordinary utensils of the kitchen, are capable of giving us pleasure. But when the object of the painting or poem is such as we should run to see if real, let it affect us with what odd sort of sense it will, we may rely upon it, that the power of the poem or picture is more owing to the nature of the thing itself than to the mere effect of imitation, or to a consideration of the skill of the imitator however excellent. Aristotle has spoken so much and so solidly upon the force of imitation in his poetics, that it makes nay further discourse upon this subject the less necessary.

. . .

PART TWO

Section I
Of the Passion Caused by the Sublime

The passion caused by the great and sublime in nature, when those causes operate most powerfully, is astonishment; and astonishment is that state of the soul, in which all its motions are suspended, with some degree of horror.[2] In this case the mind is so entirely filled with its object, that it cannot entertain any other, nor by consequence reason on that object which employs it. Hence arises the great power of the sublime, that far from being produced by them, it anticipates our reasonings, and hurries us on by an irresistible force. Astonishment, as I have said, is the effect of the sublime in its highest degree; the inferior effects are admiration, reverence and respect.

Section II
Terror

No passion so effectually robs the mind of all its powers of acting and reasoning as fear.[3] For fear being an apprehension of pain or death, it operates in a manner that resembles actual pain. Whatever therefore is terrible, with regard to sight, is sublime too, whether this cause of terror, be endued with greatness of dimensions or not; for it is impossible to look on any thing as trifling, or contemptible, that may be dangerous. There are many animals, who though far from being large, are yet capable of raising ideas of the sublime, because they are considered as objects of

[2] Part 1, sections 3, 4, 7.

[3] Part 4, sections 3, 4, 5, 6.

terror. As serpents and poisonous animals of almost all kinds. And to things of great dimensions, if we annex an adventitious idea of terror, they become without comparison greater. A level plain of a vast extent on land, is certainly no mean idea; the prospect of such a plain may be as extensive as a prospect of the ocean; but can it ever fill the mind with any thing so great as the ocean itself? This is owing to several causes, but it is owing to none more than this, that the ocean is an object of no small terror. (Indeed terror is in all cases whatsoever, either more openly or latently the ruling principle of the sublime. Several languages bear a strong testimony to the affinity of these ideas. They frequently use the same word, to signify indifferently the modes of astonishment or admiration and those of terror. Θάμβοζ is in greek, either fear or wonder; δεινόζ is terrible or respectable; ἀιδέω, to reverence or to fear. *Vereor* in latin, is what αιδεω is in greek. The Romans used the verb *stupeo,* a term which strongly marks the state of an astonished mind, to express the effect either of simple fear, or of astonishment; the word *attonitus,* (thunderstruck) is equally expressive of the alliance of these ideas; and do not the French *etonnement,* and the English *astonishment* and *amazement,* point out as clearly the kindred emotions which attend fear and wonder? They who have a more general knowledge of languages, could produce, I make no doubt, many other and equally striking examples.)

Section III
Obscurity

To make any thing very terrible, obscurity[4] seems in general to be necessary. When we know the full extent of any danger, when we can accustom our eyes to it, a great deal of the apprehension vanishes. Every one will be sensible of this, who considers how greatly night adds to our dread, in all cases of danger, and how much the notions of ghosts and goblins, of which none can form clear ideas, affect minds, which give credit to the popular tales concerning such sorts of beings. Those despotic governments, which are founded on the passions of men, and principally upon the passion of fear, keep their chief as much as may be from the public eye. The policy has been the same in many cases of religion. Almost all the heathen temples were dark. Even in the barbarous temples of the Americans at this day, they keep their idol in a dark part of the hut, which is consecrated to his worship. For this purpose too the druids performed all their ceremonies in the bosom of the darkest woods, and in the shade of the oldest and most spreading oaks. No person seems better to have understood the secret of heightening, or of setting terrible things, if I may use the expression, in their strongest light by the force of a judicious obscurity, than Milton. His description of Death in the second book is admirably studied; it is astonishing with what a gloomy pomp, with what a significant and expressive uncertainty of strokes and coloring he has finished the portrait of the king of terrors.

[4] Part 4, sections 14, 15, 16.

The other shape,
If shape it might be called that shape had none
Distinguishable, in member, joint, or limb;
Or substance might be called that shadow seemed,
For each seemed either; black he stood as night;
Fierce as ten furies; terrible as hell;
And shook a deadly dart. What seemed his head
The likeness of a kingly crown had on.

In this description all is dark, uncertain, confused, terrible, and sublime to the last degree.

Section IV
Of the Difference Between Clearness and Obscurity with regard to the Passions

It is one thing to make an idea clear, and another to make it affecting to the imagination. If I make a drawing of a palace, or a temple, or a landscape, I present a very clear idea of those objects; but then (allowing for the effect of imitation which is something) my picture can at most affect only as the palace, temple, or landscape would have affected in the reality. On the other hand, the most lively and spirited verbal description I can give) raises a very obscure and imperfect idea of such objects; but then it is in my power to raise a stronger emotion by the description than I could do by the best painting. This experience constantly evinces. The proper manner of conveying the affections of the mind from one to another, is by words; there is a great insufficiency in all other methods of communication; and so far is a clearness of imagery from being absolutely necessary to an influence upon the passions, that they may be considerably operated upon without presenting any image at all, by certain sounds adapted to that purpose; of which we have a sufficient proof in the acknowledged and powerful effects of instrumental music. In reality a great clearness helps but little towards affecting the passions, as it is in some sort an enemy to all enthusiasms whatsoever.

Section V
The same Subject Continued

There are two verses in Horace's art of poetry that seem to contradict this opinion, for which reason I shall take a little more pains in clearing it up. The verses are,

Segnius inritant animos demissa per aurem
Quam qua sunt oculis subjecta fidelibus.

On this the abbe Du Bos founds a criticism, wherein he gives painting the preference to poetry in the article of moving the passions; principally on account of the greater *clearness* of the ideas it represents. I believe this excellent judge was led into this mistake (if it be a mistake) by his system, to which he found it more conformable than I imagine it will be found to experience. I know several who admire and love painting, and yet who regard the objects of their admiration in that art, with coolness enough, in comparison of that warmth with which they are animated by affecting pieces of poetry or rhetoric. Among the common sort of people, I never could perceive that painting had much influence on their passions. It is true that the best sorts of painting, as well as the best sorts of poetry, are not much understood in that sphere. But it is most certain, that their passions are very strongly roused by a fanatic preacher, or by the ballads of Chevy-Chase, or the children in the wood, and by other little popular poems and tales that are current in that rank of life. I do not know of any paintings, bad or good, that produce the same effect. So that poetry with all its obscurity, has a more general as well as a more powerful dominion over the passions than the other art. And I think there are reasons in nature why the obscure idea, when properly conveyed, should be more affecting than the clear. It is our ignorance of things that causes all our admiration, and chiefly excites our passions. Knowledge and acquaintance make the most striking causes affect but little. It is thus with the vulgar, and all men are as the vulgar in what they do not understand. The ideas of eternity, and infinity, are among the most affecting we have, and yet perhaps there is nothing of which we really understand so little, as of infinity and eternity. We do not any where meet a more sublime description than this justly celebrated one of Milton, wherein he gives the portrait of Satan with a dignity so suitable to the subject.

He above the rest
In shape and gesture proudly eminent
Stood like a tower; his form had yet not lost
All her original brightness, nor appeared
Less than archangel ruin'd, and th' excess
Of glory obscured: as when the sun new ris'n
Looks through the horizontal misty air
Shorn of his beams; or from behind the moon
In dim eclipse disastrous twilight sheds
On half the nations; and with fear of change
Perplexes monarchs.

Here is a very noble picture; and in what does this poetical picture consist? In images of a tower, an archangel, the sun rising through mists, or in an eclipse, the ruin of monarchs, and the revolutions of kingdoms. The mind is hurried out of itself, by a crowd of great and confused images; which affect because they are crowded and confused. For separate them, and you lose much of the greatness, and join them, and you infallibly lose the clearness. The images raised by poetry are always of this obscure kind; though in general the effects of poetry, are by no means to be attributed to the images it raises; which point we shall examine more at large hereafter.[5] But painting, when we have allowed for the pleasure of imitation, can

[5] Part 5

only affect simply by the images it presents; and even in painting a judicious obscurity in some things contributes to the effect of the picture; because the images in painting are exactly similar to those in nature; and in nature dark, confused, uncertain images have a greater power on the fancy to form the grander passions than those have which are more clear and determinate. But where and when this observation may be applied to practice, and how far it shall be extended, will be better deduced from the nature of the subject, and from the occasion, than from any rules that can be given.

I am sensible that this idea has met with opposition, and is likely still to be rejected by several. But let it be considered that hardly any thing can strike the mind with its greatness, which does not make some sort of approach towards infinity; which nothing can do whilst we are able to perceive its bounds; but to see an object distinctly, and to perceive its bounds, is one and the same thing. A clear idea is therefore another name for a little idea. There is a passage in the book of Job amazingly sublime, and this sublimity is principally due to the terrible uncertainty of the thing described. *In thoughts from the visions of the night, when deep sleep falleth upon men, fear came upon me and trembling, which made all my bones to shake. Then a spirit passed before my face. The hair of my flesh stood up. It stood still, but I could not discern the form thereof; an image was before mine eyes; there was silence; and I heard a voice,—Shall mortal man be more just than God?* We are first prepared with the utmost solemnity for the vision; we are first terrified, before we are let even into the obscure cause of our emotion; but when this grand cause of terror makes its appearance, what is it? is it not, wrapt up in the shades of its own incomprehensible darkness, more aweful, more striking, more terrible, than the liveliest description, than the clearest painting could possibly represent it? When painters have attempted to give us clear representations of these very fanciful and terrible ideas, they have I think almost always failed; insomuch that I have been at a loss, in all the pictures I have seen of hell, whether the painter did not intend something ludicrous. Several painters have handled a subject of this kind, with a view of assembling as many horrid phantoms as their imagination could suggest; but all the designs I have chanced to meet of the temptations of St. Anthony, were rather a sort of odd wild grotesques, than any thing capable of producing a serious passion. In all these subjects poetry is very happy. Its apparitions, its chimeras, its harpies, its allegorical figures, are grand and affecting; and though Virgil's Fame, and Homer's Discord, are obscure, they are magnificent figures. These figures in painting would be clear enough, but I fear they might become ridiculous.

. . .

PART THREE

Section I
Of Beauty

It is my design to consider beauty as distinguished from the sublime; and in the course of the enquiry, to examine how far it is consistent with it. But previous to this we must take a short review of the opinions already entertained of this quality; which I think are hardly to be reduced to any fixed principles; because men are used to talk of beauty in a figurative manner, that is to say, in a manner extremely uncertain, and indeterminate. By beauty I mean, that quality or those qualities in bodies by which they cause love, or some passion similar to it. (I confine this definition to the merely sensible qualities of things, for the sake of preserving the utmost simplicity in a subject which must always distract us, whenever we take in those various causes of sympathy which attach us to any persons or things from secondary considerations, and not from the direct force which they have merely on being viewed. I likewise distinguish love, by which I mean that satisfaction which arises to the mind upon contemplating any thing beautiful, of whatsoever nature it may be, from desire or lust; which is an energy of the mind, that hurries us on to the possession of certain objects, that do not affect us as they are beautiful, but by means altogether different. We shall have a strong desire for a woman of no remarkable beauty; whilst the greatest beauty in men, or in other animals, though it causes love, yet excites nothing at all of desire. Which shews that beauty, and the passion caused by beauty, which I call love, is different from desire, though desire may sometimes operate along with it; but it is to this latter that we must attribute those violent and tempestuous passions, and the consequent emotions of the body which attend what is called love in some of its ordinary acceptations, and not to the effects of beauty merely as it is such.)

. . .

Section XI
How far the Idea of Beauty may be Applied to Virtue

From what has been said in the foregoing section, we may easily see, how far the application of beauty to virtue may be made with propriety. The general application of this quality to virtue, has a strong tendency to confound our ideas of things; and it has given rise to an infinite deal of whimsical theory; as the affixing the name of beauty to proportion, congruity and perfection, as well as to qualities of things yet more remote from our natural ideas of it, and from one another, has tended to confound our ideas of beauty, and left us no standard or rule to judge by, that was not even more uncertain and fallacious than our own fancies. (This loose and inaccurate manner of speaking, has therefore misled us both in the theory of taste and of morals; and induced us to remove the science of our duties from their proper basis, (our reason, our relations, and our necessities,) to rest it upon foundations altogether visionary and unsubstantial.)

Section XII
The real cause of Beauty

Having endeavoured to shew what beauty is not, it remains that we should examine, at least with equal attention, in what it really consists. Beauty is a thing much too affecting not to depend upon some positive qualities. And, since it is no creature of our reason, since it strikes us without any reference to use, and even where no use at all can be discerned, since the order and method of nature is generally very different from our measures and proportions, we must conclude that beauty is, for the greater part, some quality in bodies, acting mechanically upon the human mind by the intervention of the senses. We ought therefore to consider attentively in what manner those sensible qualities are disposed, in such things as by experience we find beautiful, or which excite in us the passion of love, or some correspondent affection.

Section XIII
Beautiful Objects Small

The most obvious point that presents itself to us in examining any object, is its extent or quantity. And what degree of extent prevails in bodies, that are held beautiful, may be gathered from the usual manner of expression concerning it. I am told that in most languages, the objects of love are spoken of under diminutive epithets. It is so in all the languages of which I have any knowledge. In Greek the ιον, and other diminutive terms, are almost always the terms of affection and tenderness. These diminutives were commonly added by the Greeks to the names of persons with whom they conversed on terms of friendship and familiarity. Though the Romans were a people of less quick and delicate feelings, yet they naturally slid into the lessening termination upon the same occasions. Anciently in the English language the diminishing *ling* was added to the names of persons and things that were the objects of love. Some we retain still, as darling, (or little dear) and a few others. But to this day in ordinary conversation, it is usual to add the endearing name of *little* to every thing we love; the French and Italians make use of these affectionate diminutives even more than we. In the animal creation, out of our own species, it is the small we are inclined to be fond of; little birds, and some of the smaller kinds of beasts. A great beautiful thing, is a manner of expression scarcely ever used; but that of a great ugly thing, is very common. There is a wide difference between admiration and love. The sublime, which is the cause of the former, always dwells on great objects, and terrible; the latter on small ones, and pleasing; we submit to what we admire, but we love what submits to us; in one case we are forced, in the other we are flattered into compliance. In short, the ideas of the sublime and the beautiful stand on foundations so different, that it is hard, I had almost said impossible, to think of reconciling them in the same subject, without considerably lessening the effect of the one or the other upon the passions. So that attending to their quantity, beautiful objects are comparatively small.

Section XIV
Smoothness

The next property constantly observable in such objects is[6] Smoothness. A quality so essential to beauty, that I do not now recollect any thing beautiful that is not smooth. In trees and flowers, smooth leaves are beautiful; smooth slopes of earth in gardens; smooth streams in the landscape; smooth coats of birds and beasts in animal beauties; in fine women, smooth skins; and in several sorts of ornamental furniture, smooth and polished surfaces. A very considerable part of the effect of beauty is owing to this quality; indeed the most considerable. For take any beautiful object, and give it a broken and rugged surface, and however well formed it may be in other respects, it pleases no longer. Whereas let it want ever so many of the other constituents, if it wants not this, it becomes more pleasing than almost all the others without it. This seems to me so evident, that I am a good deal surprised, that none who have handled the subject have made any mention of the quality of smoothness in the enumeration of those that go to the forming of beauty. For indeed any ruggedness, any sudden projection, any sharp angle, is in the highest degree contrary to that idea.

Section XV
Gradual Variation

But as perfectly beautiful bodies are not composed of angular parts, so their parts never continue long in the same right line.[7] They vary their direction every moment, and they change under the eye by a deviation continually carrying on, but for whose beginning or end you will find it difficult to ascertain a point. The view of a beautiful bird will illustrate this observation. Here we see the head increasing insensibly to the middle, from whence it lessens gradually until it mixes with the neck; the neck loses itself in a larger swell, which continues to the middle of the body, when the whole decreases again to the tail; the tail takes a new direction; but it soon varies its new course; it blends again with the other parts; and the line is perpetually changing, above, below, upon every side. In this description I have before me the idea of a dove; it agrees very well with most of the conditions of beauty. It is smooth and downy; its parts are (to use that expression) melted into one another; you are presented with no sudden protuberance through the whole, and yet the whole is continually changing. Observe that part of a beautiful woman where she is perhaps the most beautiful, about the neck and breasts; the smoothness; the softness; the easy and insensible swell; the variety of the surface, which is never for the smallest space the same; the deceitful maze, through which the unsteady eye slides giddily, without knowing where to fix, or whither it is carried. Is not this a demonstration of that change of surface continual and yet hardly perceptible at any point which forms one

[6] Part 4, section 21.

[7] Part 4, section 23.

of the great constituents of beauty? (It gives me no small pleasure to find that I can strengthen my theory in this point, by the opinion of the very ingenious Mr. Hogarth; whose idea of the line of beauty I take in general to be extremely just. But the idea of variation, without attending so accurately to the manner of the variation, has led him to consider angular figures as beautiful; these figures, it is true, vary greatly; yet they vary in a sudden and broken manner; and I do not find any natural object which is angular, and at the same time beautiful. Indeed few natural objects are entirely angular. But I think those which approach the most nearly to it, are the ugliest. I must add too, that, so far as I could observe of nature, though the varied line is that alone in which complete beauty is found, yet there is no particular line which is always found in the most completely beautiful; and which is therefore beautiful in preference to all other lines. At least I never could observe it.)

Section XVI
Delicacy

An air of robustness and strength is very prejudicial to beauty. An appearance of delicacy, and even of fragility, is almost essential to it. Whoever examines the vegetable or animal creation, will find this observation to be founded in nature. It is not the oak, the ash, or the elm, or any of the robust trees of the forest, which we consider as beautiful; they are awful and majestic; they inspire a sort of reverence. It is the delicate myrtle, it is the orange, it is the almond, it is the jessamine, it is the vine, which we look on as vegetable beauties. It is the flowery species, so remarkable for its weakness and momentary duration, that gives us the liveliest idea of beauty, and elegance. Among animals; the greyhound is more beautiful than the mastiff; and the delicacy of a gennet, a barb, or an Arabian horse, is much more amiable than the strength and stability of some horses of war or carriage. I need here say little of the fair sex, where I believe the point will be easily allowed me. The beauty of women is considerably owing to their weakness, or delicacy, and is even enhanced by their timidity, a quality of mind analogous to it. I would not here be understood to say, that weakness betraying very bad health has any share in beauty; but the ill effect of this is not because it is weakness, but because the ill state of health which produces such weakness alters the other conditions of beauty; the parts in such a case collapse; the bright color, the *lumen purpureum juventae* is gone; and the fine variation is lost in wrinkles, sudden breaks, and right lines.

Section XVII
Beauty in Color

As to the colors usually found in beautiful bodies; it may be somewhat difficult to ascertain them, because in the several parts of nature, there is an infinite variety. However, even in this variety, we may mark out something on which to settle. First, the colors of beautiful bodies must not be dusky or muddy, but clean and fair. Secondly, they must not be of the strongest kind. Those which seem most appropriated to beauty, are the milder of every sort; light greens; soft blues; weak whites;

pink reds; and violets. Thirdly, if the colors be strong and vivid, they are always diversified, and the object is never of one strong color; there are almost always such a number of them (as in variegated flowers) that the strength and glare of each is considerably abated. In a fine complexion, there is not only some variety in the coloring, but the colors, neither the red nor the white are strong and glaring. Besides, they are mixed in such a manner, and with such gradations, that it is impossible to fix the bounds. On the same principle it is, that the dubious color in the necks and tails of peacocks, and about the heads of drakes, is so very agreeable. In reality, the beauty both of shape and coloring are as nearly related, as we can well suppose it possible for things of such different natures to be.

Section XVIII
Recapitulation

On the whole, the qualities of beauty, as they are merely sensible qualities, are the following. First, to be comparatively small. Secondly, to be smooth. Thirdly, to have a variety in the direction of the parts; but fourthly, to have those parts not angular, but melted as it were into each other. Fifthly, to be of a delicate frame, without any remarkable appearance of strength. Sixthly, to have its colors clear and bright; but not very strong and glaring. Seventhly, or if it should have any glaring color, to have it diversified with others. These are, I believe, the properties on which beauty depends; properties that operate by nature, and are less liable to be altered by caprice, or confounded by a diversity of tastes, than any others.

. . .

Section XXVII
The Sublime and Beautiful Compared

On closing this general view of beauty, it naturally occurs, that we should compare it with the sublime; and in this comparison there appears a remarkable contrast. For sublime objects are vast in their dimensions, beautiful ones comparatively small; beauty should be smooth, and polished; the great, rugged and negligent; beauty should shun the right line, yet deviate from it insensibly; the great in many cases loves the right line, and when it deviates, it often makes a strong deviation; beauty should not be obscure; the great ought to be dark and gloomy; beauty should be light and delicate; the great ought to be solid, and even massive. They are indeed ideas of a very different nature, one being founded on pain, the other on pleasure; and however they may vary afterwards from the direct nature of their causes, yet these causes keep up an eternal distinction between them, a distinction never to be forgotten by any whose business it is to affect the passions. (In the infinite variety of natural combinations we must expect to find the qualities of things the most remote imaginable from each other united in the same object. We must expect also to find combinations of the same kind in the works of art. But when we consider the power of an object upon our passions, we must know that when any thing is intended to affect the mind by the force of some predominant property, the affection produced is like to be the more uniform and perfect, if all the other properties or qualities of the object be of the same nature, and tending to the same design as the principal;

> *If black, and white blend, soften, and unite,*
> *A thousand ways, are there no black and white?*

If the qualities of the sublime and beautiful are sometimes found united, does this prove, that they are the same, does it prove, that they are any way allied, does it prove even that they are not opposite and contradictory? Black and white may soften, may blend, but they are not therefore the same. Nor when they are so softened and blended with each other, or with different colors, is the power of black as black, or of white as white, so strong as when each stands uniform and distinguished.)

The end of the Third Part.

PART FOUR

Section I
Of the efficient cause of the Sublime and Beautiful

When I say, I intend to enquire into the efficient cause sublimity and beauty, I would not be understood to say, that I can come to the ultimate cause. I do not pretend that I shall ever be able to explain, why certain affections of the body produce such a distinct emotion of mind, and no other; or why the body is at all affected by the mind, or the mind by the body. A little thought will shew this to be impossible. But I conceive, if we can discover what affections of the mind produce certain emotions of the body; and what distinct feelings and qualities of body shall produce certain determinate passions in the mind, and no others, I fancy a great deal will be done; something not unuseful towards a distinct knowledge of our passions, so far at least as we have them at present under our consideration. This is all, I believe, we can do. If we could advance a step farther, difficulties would still remain, as we should be still equally distant from the first cause. When Newton first discovered the property of attraction, and settled its laws, he found it served very well to explain several of the most remarkable phenomena in nature; but yet with reference to the general system of things, he could consider attraction but as an effect, whose cause at that time he did not attempt to trace. But when he afterwards began to account for it by a subtle elastic ether, this great man (if in so great a man it be not impious to discover any thing like a blemish) seemed to have quitted his usual cautious manner of philosophising; since, perhaps, allowing all that has been advanced on this subject to be sufficiently proved, I think it leaves us with as many difficulties as it found us. That great chain of causes, which linking one to another even to the throne of God himself, can never be unravelled by any industry of ours. When we go but one step beyond the immediately sensible qualities or things, we go out of our depth. All we do after, is but a faint struggle, that shews we are in an element which does not belong to us. So that when I speak of cause, and efficient cause, I only mean, certain affections of the mind, that cause certain changes in the body; or certain powers and properties in bodies, that work a change in the mind. As if I were to explain the motion of a body falling to the ground, I would say it was caused by gravity, and I would endeavour to shew after what manner this power operated, without attempting to shew why it operated in this manner; or if I were to explain the effects of bodies striking one another by the common laws of percussion, I should not endeavor to explain how motion itself is communicated.

Section II
Association

It is no small bar in the way of our enquiry into the cause of our passions, that the occasion of many of them are given, and that their governing motions are communicated at a time when we have not capacity to reflect on them; at a time of which all sort of memory is worn out of our minds. For besides such things as affect us in various manners according to their natural powers, there are associations made at that early season, which we find it very hard afterwards to distinguish from natural effects. Not to mention the unaccountable antipathies which we find in many persons, we all find it impossible to remember when a steep became more terrible than a plain; or fire or water more dreadful than a clod of earth; though all these are very probably either conclusions from experience, or, arising from the premonitions of others; and some of them impressed, in all likelihood, pretty late. But as it must be allowed that many things affect us after a certain manner, not by any natural powers they have for that purpose, but by association; so it would be absurd on the other hand, to say that all things affect us by association only; since some things must have been originally and naturally agreeable or disagreeable, from which the others derive their associated powers; and it would be, I fancy, to little purpose to look for the cause of our passions in association, until we fail of it in the natural properties of things.

. . .

Section V
How the Sublime is Produced

Having considered terror as producing an unnatural tension and certain violent emotions of the nerves; it easily follows, from what we have just said, that whatever is fitted to produce such a tension, must be productive of a passion similar to terror,[8]

[8] Part 2, section 2.

and consequently must be a source of the sublime, though it should have no idea of danger connected with it. So that little remains towards shewing the cause of the sublime, but to shew that the instances we have given of it in the second part, relate to such things, as are fitted by nature to produce this sort of tension, either by the primary operation of the mind or the body. With regard to such things as affect by the associated idea of danger, there can be no doubt but that they produce terror, and act by some modification of that passion, and that terror, when sufficiently violent, raises the emotions of the body just mentioned, can as little be doubted. But if the sublime is built on terror, or some passion like it, which has pain for its object; it is previously proper to enquire how any species of delight can be derived from a cause so apparently contrary to it. I say, *delight*, because, as I have often remarked, it is very evidently different in its cause, and in its own nature, from actual and positive pleasure.

Section VI
How Pain can be a Cause of delight

Providence has so ordered it, that a state of rest and inaction, however it may flatter our indolence, should be productive of many inconveniencies; that it should generate such disorders, as may force us to have recourse to some labor, as a thing absolutely requisite to make us pass our lives with tolerable satisfaction; for the nature of rest is to suffer all the parts of our bodies to fall into a relaxation, that not only disables the members from performing their functions, but takes away the vigorous tone of fibre which is requisite for carrying on the natural and necessary secretions. At the same time, that in this languid inactive state, the nerves are more liable to the most horrid convulsions, than when they are sufficiently braced and strengthened. Melancholy, dejection, despair, and often self-murder, is the consequence of the gloomy view we take of things in this relaxed state of body. The best remedy for all these evils is exercise or labor; and labor is a surmounting of difficulties, an exertion of the contracting power of the muscles; and as such resembles pain, which consists in tension or contraction, in every thing but degree. Labor is not only requisite to preserve the coarser organs in a state fit for their functions, but it is equally necessary to these finer and more delicate organs, on which, and by which, the imagination, and perhaps the other mental powers act. Since it is probable, that not only the inferior parts of the soul, as the passions are called, but the understanding itself makes use of some fine corporeal instruments in its operation; though what they are, and where they are, may be somewhat hard to settle: but that it does make use of such, appears from hence; that a long exercise of the mental powers induces a remarkable lassitude of the whole body; and on the other hand, that great bodily labor, or pain, weakens, and sometimes actually destroys the mental faculties. Now, as a due exercise is essential to the coarse muscular parts of the constitution, and that without this rousing they would become languid, and diseased, the very same rule holds with regard to those finer parts we have mentioned; to have them in proper order, they must be shaken and worked to a proper degree.

Section VII
Exercise Necessary for the Finer Organs

As common labor, which is a mode of pain, is the exercise of the grosser, a mode of terror is the exercise of the finer parts of the system; and if a certain mode of pain be of such a nature as to act upon the eye or the ear, as they are the most delicate organs, the affection approaches more nearly to that which has a mental cause. In all these cases, if the pain and terror are so modified as not to be actually noxious; if the pain is not carried to violence, and the terror is not conversant about the present destruction of the person, as these emotions clear the parts, whether fine, or gross, of a dangerous and troublesome incumbrance, they are capable of producing delight; not pleasure, but a sort of delightful horror, a sort of tranquillity tinged with terror; which as it belongs to self-preservation is one of the strongest of all the passions. Its object is the sublime.[9] Its highest degree I call *astonishment;* the subordinate degrees are awe, reverence, and respect, which by the very etymology of the words shew from what source they are derived, and how they stand distinguished from positive pleasure.

Section VIII

Why Things not Dangerous Produce a Passion like Terror

A mode of terror,[10] or of pain, is always the cause of the sublime. For terror, or associated danger, the foregoing explication is, I believe, sufficient. It will require something more trouble to shew, that such examples, as I have given of the sublime in the second part, are capable of producing a mode of pain, and of being thus allied to terror, and to be accounted for on the same principles. And first of such objects as are great in their dimensions. I speak of visual objects.

[9] Part 2, section 2.

[10] Part 1, section 7. Part 2, section 2.

CHAPTER 12

Alexander Gerard*

An Essay on Taste
1759

A fine taste is neither wholly the gift of *nature,* nor wholly the effect of art. It derives its origin from certain powers natural to the mind; but these powers cannot attain their full perfection, unless they be assisted by proper culture. Taste consists chiefly in the improvement of those principles which are commonly called *the powers of imagination,* and are considered by modern philosophers as *internal* or *reflex senses,*[1] supplying us with finer and more delicate perceptions, than any which

[1] Mr. Hutcheson was the first who considered the powers of imagination as so many senses. In his *Inquiry Concerning Beauty and Virtue,* and his *Essays on the Passions,* he calls them internal senses. In his later works, he terms them subsequent and reflex senses; subsequent, because they always suppose some previous perception of the objects about which they are employed; thus a perception of harmony presupposes our hearing certain sounds, and is totally distinct from merely hearing them, since many who enjoy the external sense of hearing in the greatest perfection, have no musical ear; reflex, because, in order to their exertion, the mind reflects upon, and takes notice of some circumstance or mode of the object that was perceived, besides those qualities which offered themselves to its attention at first view. Thus the perception of any object does not give us the pleasant sentiment of novelty, till we have reflected on this circumstance, that we never perceived it formerly. In the following essay, the terms internal sense and reflex sense are used promiscuously.

---

*Alexander Gerard (1728-1795) was successively professor of moral philosophy (1752) and professor of divinity (1759) at Marischal College and professor of divinity (1773) at King's College, Aberdeen. He was a leading member of the Aberdeen Philosophical Club. His works include a new plan of education for Marischal College and works on Divinity, but it is primarily for his *Essay on Taste* (1759) that he is known. In 1774, Gerard returned to the subject with *An Essay on Genius*. Gerard was associated with Thomas Reid (1710-1796) in the Philosophical Society until Reid's transfer to Glasgow in 1764. The work of David Hume (1711-1776) was a principle influence.

can be properly referred to our external organs. These are reducible to the following principles; the senses of novelty, of sublimity, of beauty, of imitation, of harmony, of ridicule, and of virtue. With the explication of these, we must, therefore, begin our inquiry into the nature of taste. We shall next endeavor to discover, how these senses cooperate in forming taste, what other powers of the mind are combined with them in their exertions, what constitutes that refinement and perfection of them which we term *good taste,* and by what means it is obtained. And, last of all, we shall, by a review of the principles, operation, and subject of taste, determine its genuine rank among our faculties, its proper province, and real importance.

. . .

Part One
Section III

Of the sense or taste of Beauty

Beautiful objects are of different kinds, and produce pleasure by means of different principles of human nature.

The first species of beauty is that of figure; and belongs to objects possessed of uniformity, variety, and proportion. Each of these qualities pleases in some degree; but all of them united give exquisite satisfaction.

Facility in the conception of an object if it be moderate, gives us pleasure: the mind thinks well of itself, when it is able to form its conception without pain or labor. This constitutes the value of perspicuity of thought and language; which is agreeable in opposition to obscurity as this occasions an uneasy search into the meaning of the parts, or the tendency of the whole, which requires greater labor than we are willing to bestow. Hence too it is that uniformity and simplicity become agreeable. Objects endued with these qualities enter easily into the mind: they do not distract our attention, or hurry us too fast from one scene to another: each part is distinctly and strongly conceived: the view of a part suggests the whole, and, impelling the mind to imagine the rest, produces a grateful exertion of its energy.

Accordingly, in all the beautiful works of nature, uniformity is preserved in the general appearance of the correspondent parts. And though a perfectly accurate regularity is avoided, both in natural effects and in the fine arts; yet so much of it must be retained, as to keep the variety from degenerating into perplexity and confusion. Regular figures are in general preferred to irregular; and such as have parallel sides to such as have not. Equality is requisite to the beauty of every piece of painting.[2] Even when a perfect similarity in the appearance of the counterparts seems

[2] Altera pars tabulae vacuo ne frigida campo,
Aut deserta fiet, dum pluribus altera formis
Fervida mole sua supremam exurgit ad oram.
Set tibi sie positis respondeat utraque rebus,
Ut si aliquid sursum se parte attollat in una,
Sic aliquid parte ex alia consurgat, et ambas
Aequiparet, geminas cumulando aequaliter oras.
Fresnoy, *De Art. Graph.* ver. 145.

to be studiously shunned, as in a side-view of a human face, the attitude of the body, or the profile of a building; yet still it must be so contrived, that though it does not exhibit a sensation, it may notwithstanding, according to the rules of perspective, suggest the idea of exact uniformity. To bestow simplicity upon a multitude of separate phenomena, the philosopher traces them up to common qualities, and general causes; and it is only when he has done so, that the beauty of science begins.[3]

But uniformity, when perfect and unmixed, is apt to pall upon the sense, to grow languid and to sink the mind into an uneasy state of indolence. It cannot therefore alone produce pleasure, either very high, or of very long duration. Variety is necessary to enliven it. Where this is wanting, uniformity degenerates into dull formality. Variety in some measure gratifies the sense of novelty, as our ideas vary in passing from the contemplation of one part to that of another. This transition puts the mind in action, and gives it employment, the consciousness of which is agreeable.[4]

In the works of nature we find variety studiously sought after; as in the uneven surface of the globe; the infinity of shapes and hues in the flowers that adorn it; the intricate windings of rivers; the wildnesses of nature, which we even set ourselves to copy by art; and in ten thousand other instances. To procure it, the architect enriches his buildings with ornaments of different forms. In all works of taste, too great uniformity is avoided by numberless graceful attitudes, by varying of members, and by contrasting the parts.[5]

Were the variety indeed boundless, the mind would be fatigued and pained with continual shifting from part to part, without the prospect of any end of its labor; it would be displeased and disgusted, when it found, that, after numberless efforts to conceive the object, the endless dissimilitude and perplexed composition of the parts still baffled its endeavors, and hindered it from perfecting its idea. A certain degree of uniformity must therefore be blended with the variety of objects; other-wise this

[3] Uniformity and simplicity are, strictly speaking, distinct ideas; the former implying the similarity of the correspondent parts; the latter, the fewness of unlike parts in the whole object. But as both please by the same principle, it was judged unnecessary precisely to distinguish them here.

[4] Intricacy, which often greatly contributes to beauty, may be considered as a species of variety; at least its agreeableness is derived from the same cause; and variety is most naturally combined with uniformity, intricacy with simplicity.

[5] Inque figuram cumulis non omnibus idem
Corporis inflexus, motusque; vel artubus omnes
conversis pariter non connitantur eodem;
Sed quaedam in diversa trahant contraria membra,
Transverseque aliis pugnent, et caetera frangant.
Fresnoy. *De Art. Graph.* ver 137.

So great is the power of variety in producing beauty, that an ingenius artist, who has lately analysed it, resolves almost the whole of it, not altogether without reason, into that principle, and defines the art of composing to be nothing else but "the art of varying well." He holds uniformity no further necessary, than it is requisite to convey the idea of rest or motion, without possibility of falling. But here he goes too far. It were easy to point out instances, where uniformity is studied, though it cannot have any degree of this effect: and he acknowledges that beauty resides only in a composed variety; which necessarily implies a mixture of uniformity. He indeed sufficiently proves, that uniformity is not the only, or the chief principle of perfect beauty. Yet it often by itself constitutes some degree of it; as in the straight and parallel sides of a canal.

variety, instead of producing moderate energy, would subject us to insurmountable toil, which would make our pleasure soon degenerate into pain.

These two qualities, by thus moderating the effects of one another, increase the pleasure resulting from each; giving the mind at once the opposite gratifications of facility and active exertion, mixed with, and mellowing one another.

Proportion consists not so much in relations of the parts precisely measurable, as in a general aptitude of the structure to the end proposed which experience enables us instantaneously to perceive, better than any artificial methods can determine it. Its influence on beauty is therefore derived from fitness,[6] a principle which will be illustrated presently.

A very small disproportion in any of the members of the human body produces deformity. The least deviation, in the productions of the fine arts, from the natural harmony of the parts, always occasions a blemishes.

There is another kind of proportion, at least not wholly dependent on utility, which is preserved in the appearances of things, when none of the parts are so small, in respect of one another, and of the whole, as to disappear through their smallness, while we contemplate the whole; and when none of them are so large, that, when we fix our view on them, we cannot distinctly perceive at the same time their relation to the whole, and to the other parts. Figures, the sides of which are very numerous, lose a great part of the beauty which would arise from this variety, by the want of proportion between the sides and the diameter. Works in the Gothic taste, crowded with minute ornaments, fall as much short of perfect beauty by their disproportion, as by their deviation from simplicity.

As nothing gives us greater pleasure than what leads us to form a lofty conception of our own faculties, so nothing is more disagreeable than what reminds us of their imperfection. On this account it is, that the want of this kind of proportion disgusts us. It leads us to entertain a low, and consequently ungrateful, opinion of our capacity, by rendering it impossible to form one entire distinct conception of the object. The variety of its parts may amuse us, and keep us from attempting to comprehend the whole; and then, especially if it be joined with uniformity, it will yield us some degree of pleasure, and constitute an inferior and imperfect species of beauty. But still proportion is necessary for perfecting the beauty and fully gratifying a correct and improved taste.

Thus the absence of any one of these ingredients, the want either of uniformity, of variety, or of proportion, diminishes the beauty of objects: but where all of them are in a great measure wanting, deformity must prevail. Figures may be desirable or valuable or other accounts; but without these qualities they cannot be beautiful.

There is another cause, besides those already mentioned, which contributes greatly to render each of these qualities, uniformity, variety, and proportion, agreeable, and to render the combination of them a source of high delight. It is, that they are all indications of design, wisdom, and contrivance; qualities of mind which we

[6] See Hogarth's *Analysis of Beauty*, chap. II.

never fail to survey with pleasure. When we behold uniformity in a work, we naturally conclude, that it could not be the effect of chance, and that it could scarce be formed without intention. When we behold variety in a work, we are sure that it could not proceed from undesigning, and merely mechanical causes and are disposed to suspect at least, that it is the production of a mind. But uniformity and variety artfully blended in the same object, by excluding both chance and mechanism, put it beyond doubt, that it springs from a mind; that design, and wisdom, and art, have been employed in uniting these opposite qualities so skillfully: we rest in the conclusion with perfect satisfaction; we take pleasure in conceiving the excellence of the cause, and by this the delight is heightened which we find in beholding the effect that suggests that excellence. Proportion of every kind is an additional evidence of the wisdom of the cause, and indicates a higher degree of wisdom; and therefore it is a source of further pleasure in contemplating the effect. Thus the qualities which constitute beauty of form, suggest design, and lead us to infer art and wisdom in the cause. The judgment is natural, immediate, and inevitable. We conceive this character of the cause with pleasure; and we ascribe this pleasure to the visible objects which led us to conceive, and to infer that character. This measure is in itself a species of admiration, and therefore akin to the sentiment of sublimity; but being occasioned by qualities in the object which produce a soft and tender sensation, it is modified by that sensation, and assumes its character; it renders it more intensely pleasant, but does not alter its nature: on the contrary, it is altered by it; it acquires that tenderness and softness which is peculiar to the perception of beauty, and which distinguishes it from the more elevated emotions of the soul.

Utility, or the fitness of things for answering their ends,[7] constitutes another species of beauty, distinct from that of figure. It is of so great importance, that though *convenience* is sometimes, in minuter instances, sacrificed to *regularity;* yet a great degree of inconvenience generally destroys all the pleasure which should have arisen from the symmetry and proportion of the parts. It is the peculiar excellence of nature's works, that, at least in the noblest of them, the most perfect fitness for their respective ends is united and rendered consistent with the greatest elegance of form.[8] We pay a very great regard to fitness and utility, in establishing the standard of beauty and proportion in the several kinds. And, though the most perfect art falls infinitely short of nature, in combining the useful with the regular, yet none of its productions is reckoned a masterpiece, in which these excellencies do not meet;[9] and to obtain utility, forms of inferior beauty are, for particular purposes, constantly preferred, even where beauty is far from being neglected. The cube, not any of the more varied polygons, is chosen for a pedestal, on account of its stability. Utility has determined, though with considerable latitude, the dimensions and general form of

[7] This, which is the principle of a distinct order of beauty, is confounded with uniformity, which is but one ingredient in that of figure, by Crousaz; *Traité du Beau,* passim.

[8] In plerisque rebus incredibiliter hoc natura est ipsa fabricata,—ut ea quae maximam utilitatem in se continerent, eadem haberent plurimum, vel dignitatis, vel saepe etiam venustatis. Cic. de Orat. lib. 3.

[9] Cic. ibid. ΧΕΝΟΦ. Απομνημ. β.ϛ γ.

most instruments and works, without adhering to which, the greatest profusion of ornament cannot render them beautiful in the kind. Unfitness renders ornaments displeasing when wrong applied, which, in their proper place, might be truly elegant. The splendor of a single figure in history painting will but augment its faultiness, if it takes off the eye from what ought to be the principal, and obstructs the effect which should be produced by the whole. In composition, the most refined reflections, the most elaborate descriptions, the warmest pathos, displease, if they break the unity, if they do not promote, much more if they retard the main design, to which all the parts should be subordinate.

Sed nunc non erat his locus——

The impropriety of their position wholly defaces their intrinsic beauty. In general, it is from the end and design of works of genius that their peculiar rules must be deduced: this directs the author in the choice, disposition, and embellishment of the parts: and by this the critic must regulate his judgment. It is from the relation which they bear to different ends, that narration, poetry, and eloquence, are subject to very different laws: and from the same source is derived the diversity of the rules belonging to the subordinate branches of each. Could fitness be dispensed with, a collection of fine sentiments and figures clothed in agreeable language, might fully gratify our taste, however unconnected they were with one another.

That we may comprehend the nature of that pleasure which is produced by fitness, it must be observed, that, whenever we discover in effects a greater degree of uniformity, or well adapted complication, than could be expected from the laws of chance; especially when we recognize a fitness for answering an important end; we then infer, not only intention, but art and skill in the cause: which implying mental excellence and perfection, the view of it gives a noble satisfaction; as, on the other hand, faultiness of contrivance, by suggesting imperfect skill, and want of genius, displeases us greatly. When therefore we see a work, it leads us by a natural association to conceive its end; prone to comparison, we examine the propriety of the parts in relation to this end; if any of them are prejudicial to it, we are disgusted with the want of skill which this imperfection betrays. Further, we dwell in imagination on the inconveniences which must arise from the unfitness of the structure; we form strong ideas of them, which produce almost the same uneasy sentiments and passions as if we actually experienced them; and by this mean they often obliterate all the pleasing impressions which the other qualities of the object might have caused. But when, on examination, the fitness of all the parts appears, the satisfaction with which we think on the skill and ingenuity thus displayed, communicates itself to the effect so closely connected with it by causation; and, besides, we sympathetically enter into a strong feeling of the delight which must attend the possession or use of what is so well designed and executed.

The beauty of colors is entirely distinct from both the former, and pleases us from principles wholly different. Colors being nothing else but various degrees and modifications of light, some of them are less hurtful to the organs of sight than others; and are, on that account, in some instances approved as beautiful.

Some colors again, by their splendor, afford a lively and vigorous sensation, which gratifies us, by producing a cheerful and vivacious disposition of mind in contemplating them.

But the beauty of colors is, in most instances, resolvable into association; those being approved, which, either by a natural resemblance, or by custom, or opinion, introduce and are connected with agreeable ideas of any sort; and those being disapproved, which have any way become related to disagreeable ones. The verdure of the fields is delightful, not only by being inoffensive to the eye, but chiefly by its suggesting the pleasant idea of fertility. Heath in bloom would form a carpet agreeable enough to sight, if we could separate from its appearance the idea of the barrenness of the mountains and wilds which it covers. In dress, colors are either beautiful or the contrary, according to the nature of the idea which they lead us to form of the station, sentiments, and character of the wearer.

In some cases, a particular dress, in consequence of established manners, suggests to the generality nearly the same idea. Where-ever this *general* connection takes place, it forms a kind of standard in dress, for persons in certain stations or professions. We come to perceive a propriety in conforming to it; and we are displeased with the indecency of deviating remarkably from it.

When the idea suggested by dress is different in different persons, so also is the relish for the color; what suggests to one a liveliness and vivacity of turn, gives another the idea of gaudiness and levity; the same dress may convey to some the idea of gravity and sedateness, to others that of dullness and austerity.

. . .

Part Four
Section V

That the Standard of Taste is to be found in general Principles

Thus, in whatever light we consider general or universal approbation, we find great difficulties in applying it as the sole or the immediate standard of excellence in works of taste; and all these difficulties seem to point to science, to criticism, or philosophy, as capable of supplying us with a standard more determinate, more accurate, and more easily applicable.[10] Indeed to such a standard, the general sense

[10]It is the professed design of D'Alembert's *Reflections on Taste*, to prove that philosophy justly claims authority as a standard in matters of taste, and to suggest some rules and cautions respecting the application of it. The ingenious author of *Elements of Criticism*, after having allowed general approbation all the weight which he thought that it could possess, concludes with referring to general principles of human nature, scientifically investigated, the principles that ought to govern the taste of individuals, as a standard in which he puts great confidence, as more unerring than any selection of the persons capable of judging; and with intimating that to lay a foundation for this branch of knowledge, that is in other words, to form such a standard, is the declared purpose of that work. Chap 25, at the end. This observation appears to me to be perfectly just and well founded, and will perhaps be both confirmed and illustrated by the remarks which I am now making.

of mankind leads them constantly to have recourse, however much they may in words seem to acquiesce in sentiment as ultimate. Every man whom we acknowledge to possess any degree of taste, not only approves or disapproves, but specifies what it precisely is that pleases or displeases him, what is the nature of the pleasure or the disgust which it excites, and what the manner in which it excites them. The very operation of taste, when in any measure improved, implies so much of judgment, reflection, and analysis, as plainly intimates how serviceable they may be in defining, vindicating, or correcting its sensations. When our judgment in a particular instance is called in question, we reckon it always allowable to support it by reasons; and our reasons are always deduced from principles more or less general; the authority of which in preference to mere sentiment, we therefore tacitly acknowledge by our using them. In every art there are some general rules of established authority, to which all readily appeal, and which all reverence as the fundamental laws by which the differences of individuals must be terminated. Were general approbation the only standard, so much as to point out beauties which have, by any means, failed of actually obtaining it, would be not only useless, but preposterous and absurd. Since then it is clear that general principles and rules have authority in matters of taste, it only remains to explain, in what manner they serve as the real and just standard of excellence or defect.

When we deny that general approbation is the proper or immediate standard, we are far from insinuating that it is of no account. It is of very great account. Though it be not itself the standard, it is the materials of which the standard must be composed: it is the block from which it must be hewed out: it is the principal of those ingredients from which it must be extracted. It holds the same place in this enquiry, that experiments and observations concerning the real phenomena of things, hold in physical investigations of the laws of the material world. It is from the experiments and observations, that all just conclusion concerning these laws must be deduced; it is only by examining and comparing them, that the laws of nature can be discovered: that cannot be truly a law of nature, which is contradictory to the phenomena; however plausible it may appear, however strongly supported by some of them, there must be an error in the reasoning by which it is inferred: such error may very readily be committed; many false hypotheses have been adopted in natural philosophy; but it will not follow, that we ought to rest satisfied with observing the phenomena, not attempting to investigate the laws according to which they are produced, or that these laws may not be traced out successfully by a more careful and skillful induction: when any general law is traced out, it accounts for phenomena which at first sight appear unaccountable; it reconciles such as appear discordant, and often shews that they proceed from the same principle differently modified; it answers many purposes which could not be answered by a mere collection of the experiments from which it is inferred. All this is directly and without difficulty applicable to our present subject. It is only from what actually pleases and displeases in works of imagination, that the true critic deduces his general principles and rules: it is on what has pleased or displeased universally that he lays the greatest stress; he founds his conclusion, not on his own feelings only, but on the common feelings of men; it is from the most excellent and admired performances in every art, that the rules of that art ought to be, and by judicious critics always have been taken: so far is he from despising sentiment, that he pays some regard to whatever has actually pleased or displeased any; he acknowledges that it has some sort of fitness to please or displease; and he examines whether it is owing to a natural or to a distempered state of the organ. His decisions, his general principles and rules claim no authority in opposition to the common sense of mankind; if they really oppose it, if they be irreconcilable to the unperverted sentiments of any individual, they are false, there is some mistake in the induction by which they were established. Men are necessarily fallible; many false principles and arbitrary rules of criticism have been proposed: but we cannot hence conclude, that we ought not to search for any principles or rules, or that it is impossible to find out such as are true and solid. Suppose that in forming general conclusions there is always a possibility of error, but that in acquiescing in clear and distinct sensations there is none; yet the former may in some instances have indubitable certainty, and may be applicable to many uses, for which the latter are insufficient: they may lead us to perceive how works whose qualities are in appearance contrary, come nevertheless all to give us pleasure; they may convince us that sentiments seemingly incompatible, excited in different persons by the same work or even the same part of a work, proceed from principles equally natural to man; it may enable us to reconcile the most dissimilar sentiments, to account for the most singular, to explain which are most conformable to the real constitution of human nature. This is all that can be expected from a standard of taste; and this, general principles only can perform. In a word, as it is not a mere comprehension of the separate phenomena of things, but a discernment of their common causes and laws that immediately serves to explain the operations and the course of nature; as it is the knowledge of the general principles of mechanics that best enables us to judge of the construction and merit of a complicated machine; so it is an acquaintance with the objects and the sources of our pleasures, not an undistinguishing attention to them as they affect the several individuals, that proximately contributes to ascertain the genuine excellence in the fine arts.

Not only is every work of taste complicated, containing lights, shades and blemishes; but almost every part of the work is in like manner complex, made up of something that pleases and something that is in itself indifferent. To separate these, to distinguish the excellence from what serves only as a vehicle for it, or from the fault which adheres closely to it, to point out what it precisely is in a passage, that gives us pleasure or disgust, is the lowest and simplest effort of criticism. It is a degree of reflection, an exercise of abstraction, which every man of tolerable acuteness of taste employs for himself: without it there could be no distinct perception, but only a blind, enthusiastic feeling. It cannot therefore be expected that by this alone, criticism should supply us with a very precise standard. Yet even by this, it gives a standard more accurate than mere sentiment. It enlightens us so far as to prevent our ascribing our pleasure or our disgust, to causes which have no share in the production of them. It prepares us for discerning and estimating passages in which there is the same excellence or the same fault, but differently accompanied. It leads us to form our judgment of a work, from its intrinsic qualities, not from any extraneous or unessential circumstances. It substitutes a determinate judgment, in the place of an indefinite, indiscriminate admiration. It defends us from the danger of being so much dazzled with shining beauties in a work, as to become insensible to gross deformities mingled with them, or perhaps to mistake them also for beauties. It is absolutely necessary, in order to our ascertaining the real degree of merit to which a work is entitled; confused consciousness of the feelings which it has anyhow excited, would be totally insufficient for this purpose.

All objects which produce the same species of pleasure, however different in other respects, have some qualities in common. It is by means of these qualities, that they produce this pleasure. It belongs to criticism to investigate and ascertain these qualities: and the discovery of them contributes in many ways, both to render our appreciation of excellence more easy and accurate, and to furnish principles for deciding between discordant appreciations. The qualities of an object, which gratify us, are more fixed and definite than the sensation which they excite. When we attempt to confine our attention to the latter, it as it were twinkles in the eye, and eludes a steady contemplation: but when we turn our view to the former, we can contemplate them at leisure, examine them on all sides, and determine their precise dimensions. We can compare them with the same qualities in other objects, decide which object possesses them in the highest degree, and infer which ought to give the highest pleasure. We can compare them with the sensation which they produce; examine whether it be exactly adequate to them, whether it be rendered more intense than they alone could have rendered it, by the operation of other qualities of a similar tendency, in this instance conjoined with it, or whether it be weakened by the conjunction of qualities of an opposite tendency. When we discern that an object which we approve, has the same general qualities with other objects which generally please, we are satisfied that our approbation is right; when we evince that it has them, we account for our approbation, we justify it, and are entitled to condemn the taste which disapproves that object, or is indifferent to it, as perverted or defective. Many of those qualities in objects, from which the pleasures of taste result, are capable of being measured with considerable accuracy. The degree of uniformity, for instance, of variety, of amplitude, of fitness for its end, which a particular object possesses, can generally be defined with tolerable precision. This gives a rule for assigning to each of them its own rank. Among beautiful objects, that is, the most beautiful, which has the highest degree of those qualities which are acknowledged to constitute beauty. Of grand objects, that is, the grandest, which possesses the greatest unbroken amplitude. Of descriptions of an object, that is, the finest, which impresses on the mind an image of its most characteristical and striking features. If a man's sentiments be not proportioned to the degrees of such qualities, which objects are acknowledged to possess, they must be so far wrong.

It is chiefly attention to the general qualities of objects which gratify taste, that enables us to perceive to what class the gratification belongs. The gratifications of taste agree in this, that they are all pleasant; they are likewise analogous in other respects: if we regard only our feelings, we cannot sufficiently distinguish them into kinds. But the quality, or the combination of qualities, which produces one gratification, is very different from that which produces another: by turning our view to it, we can decide with certainty, of what kind our pleasure is, and either correct or confute his opinion who, from indefinite feeling, would refer it to a different kind. If the object which pleases us, possess uniformity, variety, and proportion, we are sure that it is beautiful. If it possess amplitude along with simplicity, we know that it is grand. We can thus determine, whether different works gratify taste in the same way or in different ways. This is of great advantage in comparing them: if they please in the same way, our business is, to inquire which possesses the greatest degree of those qualities from which the pleasure results; if in different ways, we must estimate the moment of the several species of pleasure.

It is generally by a combination of different qualities, that any object gratifies taste. One object excels in one of these qualities, another object in another of them. In this case, there is a difficulty in determining which object deserves the preference; we cannot always say, which of these qualities gives separately the highest pleasure. The Grecian architecture excels in simplicity; this is unquestionably a source of pleasure: the Gothic has variety; this is likewise a source of pleasure: Which of them is most approveable? Of two sublime objects, one exceeds the other in magnitude, but falls as much below it in simplicity: How shall we determine, which is the most sublime? But this difficulty is not always insurmountable. It may happen, for instance, that one of the objects has more approveable qualities, the other no more: the Grecian architecture has proportion, the Gothic is destitute of it; the addition of this quality plainly turns the balance in favor of the former. Thus again, every work has its end and use: some qualities productive of pleasure, may by their situation be subservient to this; other qualities very pleasing in themselves, may by their position obstruct it: on this principle, we justly condemn very beautiful passages in a poem, and very beautiful figures in a picture, as blemishes, which take from the merit of the whole.

There are many combinations of qualities, each of which produces a distinct species of pleasure. A complete enumeration of these combinations would enable us to determine many questions concerning discordant sentiments. In particular, it would supply principles for a just estimate of all such sentiments as are of a complicated nature. It is in these that men are most apt to differ, and general principles to run counter to the feelings of individuals. A person who is equally attentive to all the pleasing qualities which are united in an object, and equally formed for relishing them all, will approve it more highly than another person who has overlooked some of these qualities, or is defective in that sense which is adapted to the perception of them. The former will prefer that object to one which has some of these qualities in greater perfection, but is destitute of the rest: the latter will give the contrary judgment. It is by analyzing the object, that the difference can be adjusted. One man sets a high value on a particular object; to justify this, he shews that it possesses a great degree of those qualities which produce a particular species of pleasure: another, who sets less value on it, acknowledging this, points out some blemishes which justly bring down its value: and by doing so, evinces that the former has given a wrong judgment through want of discernment sufficient for detecting these blemishes.—A full enumeration of all the qualities which are fit to gratify taste, would go far to banish contracted rules of criticism. Such rules have given the most plausible handle for calling in question the authority of general principles. When a thing is contrary to rule, and yet actually pleases, we conclude with reason that the rule is false. The qualities which it requires do actually please: but objects destitute of them, may likewise please by means of other qualities; of these the critic was not aware when he formed his rule: he did right in pronouncing that the former set of qualities are fit to gratify taste; but he did wrong in affirming, that they are absolutely necessary to its gratification: he mistook for a general canon, what is only one of the cases subordinate to that canon. That the regularity and the unities of the ancient drama, pointed out by Aristotle, are means of pleasing, is certain: the fault lies only in reckoning them essential. Shakespeare has given convincing evidence, that a dramatic work in which they are totally neglected, may yet have other qualities productive of very high gratification. Partial and confined principles of criticism in any art, arise only from our being unacquainted with, or not taking into the account, some class of qualities which constitute a real excellence in that art.

In a word, an analysis of the several combinations of qualities which are agreeable or disagreeable to taste, would enable us to compare and to fix the rank of all those objects which please by means of the same combination: the degree of these qualities, which belongs to each of them, can generally be ascertained with abundant accuracy; and every sentiment which is disporportioned to the acknowledged degree of pleasing qualities in its object, may confidently be condemned as wrong and perverted. The only difficulty would be, to decide between objects which, possessing different qualities, yield distinct species of pleasure. In this, attention to these qualities, it must be acknowledged, can give us no assistance. But this is a case in which it is seldom necessary to decide; there is often an impropriety in attempting it. To render objects capable of being compared, they must have something in common: it is only objects which have some quality in common, that can be compared in respect of the degree of it. When two pleasures are different in kind, it is not generally of importance, it is not always possible to determine which deserves the preference; it is sufficient to define the kind to which each belongs. Whether beauty of form, or harmony of sounds, whether the sublime or the pathetic, whether the witty or the humorous, give the highest pleasure, are questions which, with many similar ones, if it be difficult to answer, it is not perhaps altogether proper to propose. Yet there are general principles which may lead to the solution even of such questions. In order to discover them, let us turn our view from the external objects of our pleasures, to their internal causes.

The sources of all the sentiments of taste lie in the mind. The qualities of objects affect, in a certain manner, some principles of human nature, which by their operation, either singly or several in conjunction, produce gratification or disgust. It is the business of philosophical criticism, to investigate these principles: many of them have been pointed out in the course of our enquiry. Simplicity, for instance, occasions easiness of conception; novelty or variety, an effort to conceive; amplitude, an expansion of soul. This takes place in every individual, in numberless cases; he is therefore certain from his own experience, that it is conformable to the constitution of his nature. It is likewise to every man, [a] matter of experience, that some of these modes of conception are ordinarily pleasant, and others ordinarily painful. The experience with respect to both these points is extensive, various, and unequivocal;

for it occurs not only in matters of taste, but likewise in science, and in common life. When, therefore, taste is analyzed into its simple principles, these will serve as a criterion for distinguishing the genuine from the false sentiment: for if, in a particular instance, either an object acknowledged to have certain qualities, fails to produce the mode of conception generally correspondent to it; or that mode of conception, when confessedly produced, fails to give the pleasure or the pain which it used to give; it must be owing to some indisposition, distemper or perversion of soul. The person who labors under it, may have convincing evidence of this, not only from the general experience of mankind, but from his own. Often too the precise distemper of mind, which he has contracted, may be discovered; and his sentiments corrected, at least satisfactorily accounted for, even to himself.

When taste is analyzed into its simple principles, it will be found that, in its province as well as in that of the external senses, pleasure and pain border closely upon, and sometimes by an almost imperceptible gradation run into one another. Both facility and difficulty of conception, are pleasant when moderate; but both become painful when they exceed a certain degree, the former producing languor, and the latter fatigue. What expands or elevates the mind is agreeable, but an object may give uneasiness by straining its powers. It is no wonder then, that what gratifies one man, sometimes disgusts another: these contrary effects may proceed from the very same principle, in minds possessed of different degrees of vigor. To evince this, is in some measure to give an account of them; and whenever it can be ascertained, which is the degree that commonly belongs to mankind, this decides which is in the present case right sentiment, and which the wrong. If a person is in one instance disgusted with such an effort to conceive an object, as is commonly agreeable both to other men and to himself, it must be owing to a fit of sickly languor, of which he may be rendered as sensible, as of an accidental imbecility of body.

Different qualities in objects, may affect the same simple principles of human nature, and affect them in a manner nearly similar. To point out the principle thus affected, is to prove it natural and right, that these objects, however unlike or opposite in some respects, should be equally approved; and that either of them should attach the person who has attended to it alone. It is not necessary to proscribe either the correct fable, and regular sublime of the classical writer, or the wild fiction, and extravagant greatness of the oriental tale; however distant in degree their merit is, both have real merit; the gratification produced by both is in a great measure resolvable into the same ultimate principles of the mind, and is sufficiently accounted for by being resolved into them. Sentiments in appearance very dissimilar, are reconciled by being traced up to a simple principle common to all men; as the ascent of vapors and the descent of rain are shewn to be consistent by being explained from the very same law of gravitation. In taste, as in the material world, the phenomena are various and mutable; but the laws of nature, from which they proceed, are universal, uniform, and fixed.

The general principles and laws into which the sentiments of taste must be finally resolved, are numerous. One of them, however real and powerful, may in a particular situation be counteracted by another. A projectile force makes an heavy body fly upwards: it overbalances the effect of gravitation, but does not destroy the principle: the observation of it only suggests an enquiry concerning the nature of that force. In like manner, when a particular judgment in the fine arts, seems to be contradictory to a general law of human nature, it often amounts only to this, that the operation of this law is suspended by the opposition of another law equally authentic: and by the discovery and explication of the latter, that judgment is shewn to be natural, in the circumstances in which it is pronounced; and we are furnished with the means of determining, whether these circumstances indicate a sound or a diseased temperament, a free or a constrained exertion of the powers of taste.

If a person has attended only to some of those simple principles of human nature, which are the sources of our pleasures, he will be ready to fall into mistakes in explaining these pleasures. He will resolve every pleasure into one or other of the few principles with which he is acquainted; and a pleasure which cannot be referred to any of them, he will endeavor to discredit. Hence have arisen many of the critical rules which contradict sentiment and experience. Simplicity in any system, is an excellence; but an injudicious affection of simplicity has, in every species of philosophy, occasioned many ill-founded hypotheses. Genuine simplicity consists not merely in resolving phenomena into a few principles; but in rendering the principles, by a just induction, as general and comprehensive as possible. If any thing which actually pleases, cannot be accounted for from any general principle hitherto established, there must be some other real principle of human nature, yet unexplored, to which it ought to be referred. An investigation of all the immediate or proximate sources of the pleasures of taste, together with an analysis of these into the more ultimate principles of the mind, which give them power, is necessary for establishing general rules of real authority. And if all such principles were traced out, and the proper influence of each of them acknowledged, the result would be, a system of rules coinciding exactly with the natural, unperverted sentiments of individuals, and fit for discriminating them from such as are unnatural and vitiated.

Acquaintance with the general principles of taste, puts it in our power, in many cases, to compare pleasures different in kind, and to determine to which the preference is due. That one of these principles is the source of higher pleasure than another, may be proved by its influence in numberless situations of human life. We have experience every day, that moderate difficulty gives higher pleasure than facility; it is in activity that man finds his chief enjoyment. This leads us to conclude, that such pleasures of taste as are resolvable into a sense of difficulty, are superior to those which hold of facility. The conclusion is just; in all the fine arts, it is the work which draws out the powers of the mind, and gives them play, that excites our admiration. Again, an object which gratifies only one of these principles, must yield to an object which gratifies several of them at once. Beauty addresses itself to more mental principles than novelty; and it will be universally acknowledged to be a greater excellence. There is not perhaps any general character by which the lesser kinds of poetry can be more precisely distinguished from the higher than this, that they touch fewer principles of our nature, and occasion a more imperfect exertion of soul.

Thus, as in natural philosophy it is not collections of experiments and observations, but the general conclusions legitimately deduced from them, that amount to an explication of the course of nature; so in the fine arts it is not the several sentiments of individuals, but just conclusions deduced from them, concerning the qualities in objects which gratify taste, and the simple mental principles from whose operation the gratification is derived, that serve immediately for estimating excellence or faultiness. To assert this, is not to establish general rules, in opposition to sentiment; for they are wholly founded upon sentiment, and if they be just, cannot but be conformable to it. It is from it they derive their whole authority: but this hinders not that, after having been thus duly vested with authority, they may perform what it could not so well accomplish by itself. In every part of knowledge, general rules and principles give us great advantage for judging concerning particular phenomena. If none of the laws of matter were yet investigated, a great number of experiments, and each of them frequently repeated, would be necessary for establishing any one general conclusion with certainty: but after these laws have been ascertained, a certain conclusion conformable to them, may often be deduced from a single experiment carefully conducted; our very limited experience in this particular instance becomes unquestionable by borrowing the force of that extensive experience from which the known laws of nature have been already inferred. In like manner, when excellence in the fine arts has been traced up to its general principles, we are not obliged to wait the event of general approbation, before we can determine the rank to which a new performance is entitled; every man of true taste may determine it, by the feelings which it produces in himself, compared with, and authorized by, well established principles of criticism in the kind; when he determines it with assurance, he does not fondly *presume* that others will approve or disapprove, because he does; but he *foresees* that their judgment will coincide with his own, because he perceives that it is justified by those very principles to which the general judgment is in all other cases consonant.

To those who are destitute of taste, general principles and rules, however just, will not supply the want of it. Whenever they pretend to judge, they will go wrong: not because the principles and rules are useless, but because they are incapable of applying them to the present case. Though a person be acquainted with all the laws of motion, he cannot by them account for a phenomenon till he has first observed it: the phenomena of excellence or faultiness in any work of art, taste alone can lead us to perceive; if after this, general principles can give us assurance, whether our manner of perceiving them be right or wrong, singular or co-incident with that of others, it is all that is requisite for entitling them to be regarded as the proper and immediate standard of taste.

Submission to their authority in this extent can have no tendency to repress the sensibility, to abate the ardor, or to diminish the pleasures of taste. It by no means substitutes frigid discussion and analysis, in the place of warm and enrapturing sensations. It allows us to give full scope to every feeling which a work impresses on us; it even requires us to give scope to it, that we may form a genuine conception of its features. While sense is touched, reflection is in a great measure suspended, and general principles are little attended to even by those who are best acquainted with them. It is after sense has performed its office, it is after we have felt; it is when we come to review our feelings, when we find reason to suspect that they need to be corrected, or when we are inclined to justify them, that we recollect the general principles to which they ought to be conformable. With the fullest indulgence of sentiment, the application of these principles in this situation, cannot possibly interfere. But if the habit of examining our sentiments by them, should lead us to intermix attention to them, with the first exertions of sensation, this will not damp its vivacity, or cool its fervor. It will always improve the feelings, and heighten the gratification of a correct taste; by suggesting a view of their causes, it will add a new ingredient; by infusing a consciousness of their rectitude, it will encourage us to give up ourselves, with unrestrained confidence, to admiration and enjoyment. Sound principles of criticism can never betray us into the irksome task of disputing against our pleasant sentiments: they will generally enable us to approve, as well as to feel them; and when at any time they condemn them, it is only to prepare us for receiving more refined pleasures.

The investigation of general principles, and deference to them as the test and measure of excellence, far from extinguishing the fire, or confining the range of genius, will contribute most effectually to its elevation and enlargement. From a person who satisfies himself with observing and admiring a number of curious machines, the utmost that can be expected is, the production of a similar machine: it is only from him who, either by his natural sagacity, or by study, has acquired a comprehension of the general principles of mechanics, that we can expect the invention of new and dissimilar machines, or even any considerable improvement of the former. The same must happen in the fine arts. Any one work is necessarily confined to the prosecution of one end, to the production of one kind of gratification; and it can admit only one set of means for answering this purpose. The man who seeks for no other criterion of excellence, but what has always pleased, will naturally employ his attention on those works which have been distinguished by universal admiration, will think himself obliged to adhere to them as his models, will endeavor to produce the same effect by the same means, or by means as analogous as possible. If he have genius sufficient to preserve him from sinking into a servile copier, still he is no more than a successful imitator; whenever the originality of his own powers would carry him into a new track, his excursion is checked by the reflection, that this would be a deviation from the course which mankind have concurred in approving. "I have long been of opinion," says an elegant writer,[11] "that the moderns pay too blind a deference to the ancients; and though I have the highest veneration for several of their remains, yet I am inclined to think they have occasioned us the loss of some excellent originals. Whilst it is thought sufficient praise to be their followers, genius is checked in her flights, and many a fair track lies undiscovered in the boundless regions of imagination. Thus had Virgil trusted more to his native strength, the Romans, perhaps, might have seen an original epic in their language. But Homer was considered by that admired poet as the sacred object of his first and

[11]Fitzosborne's Lett. 5.

principal attention; and he seemed to think it the noblest triumph of genius, to be adorned with the spoils of that glorious chief." Knowledge of the ultimate sources of our pleasures, tends directly to overturn this tyranny of precedent, and to free genius from the fetters which it would put upon it. That knowledge may enable a person to perceive that ends may be aimed at, that modifications of pleasure may be conveyed, considerably different from those which have been attempted by preceding artists; but equally adapted to the natural principles of the mind, and equally enchanting: and will thus enrich the arts with a new species of composition. Or it may lead him to discover, that an end which has been often pursued, will be as successfully obtained by other means, as by those which have been hitherto employed; may prompt him to make trial of these; and thus introduce an agreeable variety of execution. In either case, it impels imagination to strike into an unbeaten road, which blind deference to what has been universally approved, would have deterred him from essaying. Whether by being enlightened with an uncommon comprehension of the manifold sources of human pleasures, or by being supported by an undaunted consciousness of his own abilities, Milton, it is certain, has with full success ventured on a mode of poetry, in so many respects unlike to any which had been exhibited before, that it has been made a question, whether it can properly be called heroic, or reduced to any species defined by critics. Perfectly acquainted with the ancient epics, exquisitely sensible to all its beauties, adhering to its principles so far as they are really catholic and indispensable, imitating it in the artificial structure of the fable, in the unity of the design, in the splendor of diction; he has boldly deserted it, in conceiving an action specifically different, in carrying it only by spiritual and supernatural agents, in displaying characters which never came within the reach of human experience, in directing the whole rather to fix the mind in astonishment, than to raise it into admiration.

If the observations by which we have endeavored to shew that principles of science form the most accurate standard of excellence in the fine arts, be well founded, they will justify our considering philosophical inquiries into the objects and the causes of our feelings, as of very great importance. They are not the amusements of the idle, or the entertainments of the speculative. They rest not in gratifying curiosity, by unveiling the inward springs of our sensations. They are of real and extensive utility. They both stimulate genius, and expand it. They contribute in many ways to the improvement of taste; they excite its attention, correct its deceptions, and add both light and assurance to its sentiments; and when the decisions of individuals differ, they often reconcile them, and almost always account for them, and determine which of them deserves the preference. The principles established by means of them, admit as indubitable certainty, and as great precision, as those of any science. If human imperfection allowed them to be rendered so general as to comprehend all the simple and ultimate causes of our gratifications, and human fallibility could be secure from error in the application of them, they would be sufficient for removing every difficulty, and resolving every question, concerning the merit of works of taste.

CHAPTER 13

Joseph Priestley*

A Course of Lectures on Oratory and Criticism 1759/1777

Lecture XI. Of Taste, and the Nature of Figurative Language

The third part into which the art of oratory is distributed, comprehends whatever is ornamental in a discourse or composition. The bare materials, and even the disposition of them in a discourse, are adapted to do little more than make an impression upon those persons who, of themselves, and from a regard to the nature and importance of the subject, will give their attention to it; whereas the subject of this last part is calculated to attract and engage the attention, by the grace and harmony of the style, the turn of thought, or the striking or pleasing manner in which sentiments are introduced and expressed. We have hitherto examined what we may call the bones, muscles, and nerves of a composition; we now come to the covering

---

*Joseph Priestley (1733-1804) was born into a Calvinist family but rejected Calvinism for a more moderate form of dissent. He advocated a tolerant, Socinian (Unitarian), and rational form of Protestant religion. He worked as a schoolmaster at a dissenting academy where he wrote his treatise on rhetoric that included his analysis of taste. It was written in 1759 but not published until 1777. Priestley became minister to a succession of dissenting congregations before being driven into retirement after his library and house were burned by a mob in Manchester. Priestley also had a substantial influence as an experimental scientist working on the nature of gases and combustion. He never rejected the "phlogiston" theory, which held that combustion required some special substance, but his experiments led him to identify oxygen as a separate gas from air. Finally, Priestley entered into the philosophical debates of his day, defending associationism and a Lockean view of ideas against the theories of Thomas Reid (1710-1796), James Beattie (1735-1802), James Oswald (d. 1793) and others and taking the side of toleration in ethical and political theory as well as in religious matters. He was honored by the revolutionary movement in France and eventually immigrated to the new United States where he died in western Pennsylvania.

of this body, to describe the external lineaments, the color, the complexion, and graceful attitude of it.

In treating of this part of my subject, I shall endeavor to lay open the sources of all the pleasures we receive from this most refined art, explaining what are the properties, or principles, in our frame which lay the mind open to its influences, as well as describe the various forms of expression which are found, by experience, to affect our minds in so agreeable a manner, and give examples of such forms of expression.

Whatever contributes to adorn a discourse, must either give life and beauty to the sentiment, or harmony to the diction. I shall consider each of these in their order. By ornament of thoughts, I mean that manner of introducing and presenting them to the mind which will give them the most favorable appearance. This, therefore, comprehends all the pleasures which may be said to be perceived by the mind; whereas, when I treat of the ornament of diction, I shall consider the language as affecting the ear only.

Whatever it be, in the sentiment or ideas, that makes a discourse to be read with pleasure, must either be interesting, by exciting those gross and more sensible feelings we call passions, or must awaken those more delicate sensations, which are generally called the pleasures of the imagination. Each of these kinds of feelings are, by some philosophers, referred to so many distinct reflex, or internal senses, as they call those faculties of the mind by which we perceive them; whereas, according to Dr. Hartley's theory, those sensations consist of nothing more than a congeries or combination of ideas and sensations, separately indistinguishable, but which were formerly associated either with the idea itself that excites them, or with some other idea, or circumstance, attending the introduction of them. It is this latter hypothesis that I adopt, and, by the help of it, I hope to be able to throw some new light on this curious subject.

An enumeration of the stronger passions of the human mind, which are roused by the powers of oratory, and the art of composition, I regard as foreign to my undertaking to attempt: but it may, with reason, be expected that I should describe those finer feelings which constitute the pleasures of the imagination, and which are seldom attended to in any delineations of human nature, as also some critical situations of mind respecting the passions and emotions in general, the knowledge of which is essential to criticism upon works of genius and imagination; and explain those forms of address which are adapted to gain assent. But, previous to this, I shall give some account of Taste, and of the difference between plain and figurative language.

An exquisite feeling of the finer sensations above mentioned, may be said to constitute a fine taste: but no person can be a complete judge of the merit of a composition unless he perfectly understand the subject of it, so as both clearly to distinguish the character of the design; as whether it be great or mean, new or common, etc. and also to judge how far the execution is adapted to the undertaking.

The well-known story of the shoemaker viewing the Venus of Apelles, may assist us to distinguish our ideas in this case. This artisan discovered no strong sense of pleasure upon the sight of so extraordinary an effect of human genius, and therefore could not be said to have taste, but he certainly was a very good judge of the proportions of the foot and of the shoe.

Judgment is universally acknowledged to be altogether acquired, and that taste, too, or the capacity of perceiving the pleasures of imagination, may also be acquired, to a very great degree, is evident from the actual acquirement of a variety of similar tastes, even late in life. Instances of this may be given in a taste for flowers, for gardening, and for architecture, which are hardly ever acquired very early in life.

It is hardly possible that any person who never attempted to sketch out an object himself, should have a high relish for the beauties of painting; but let any person be instructed in drawing, let him be much employed in viewing and examining a great variety of pictures, let him be led to converse much with painters, and other connoisseurs in that art; and I think one might pronounce, without any great apprehension of being mistaken, that he would, infallibly, not only acquire judgment in the productions of that art, and be able to distinguish a fine design and execution, but that he would have a relish for it, that what he approved he would admire, and that the view of it would affect him with a sensible pleasure. The same may be said with respect to music, poetry, and all the other fine arts.

Besides, it will appear very clearly, in our progress through this subject, that all the principles of taste in works of genius, the very sources from which all these fine pleasures are derived, are within the reach of all persons whatsoever; and that scarce any person can pass his life in cultivated society, where the fine arts flourish, without acquiring, in a greater or a less degree, a taste for some or other of them.

In fact, since all emotions excited by works of genius consist of such ideas and sensations as are capable of being associated with the perception of such works, nothing can be requisite to the acquisition of taste, but exposing the mind to a situation in which those associated ideas will be frequently presented to it. A great deal, however, depends upon the time of life, and other circumstances, in which such impressions are made upon the mind. Youth, especially, which is favorable to all impressions, is peculiarly favorable to these. But this circumstance makes a difference in degree only, and not in the nature of the thing. Some persons may also have acquired a dislike to these, as well as other studies; but as this dislike was produced by an early association of ideas, so it may be overcome by opposite associations. It must not be forgotten, also, that as our bodies in general differ with respect to their sensibility to impressions, so the texture of the brain, on which the mental faculties depend, must be subject to a similar difference.

I proposed in this place to shew in what figurative and ornamented style consists. In plain unadorned style every thing is called by its proper name, no more words are used than are apparently sufficient to express the sense, and the form and order of every part of the sentence are such as exactly express the real state of mind of him that uses it; not a question, for instance, being asked when the person who makes it is able to supply the answer. It is not enough to say, that plain unadorned style is that mode of expression which is the most natural: for style the most highly ornamented, and enlivened with the strongest figures, is as natural as the plain style, and occurs as naturally, without the precepts of art, and even without design, in proper circumstances.

Style may be said to be figurative when the literal interpretation, according to the usual sense of words, and the construction of them, would lead a person to mistake the sense; as, for instance, when anything is signified by a term which was not originally affixed to it; when the terms which are used to express any thing would, if interpreted literally, lead a person to imagine it was greater or less than it is; and when the form of the sentence is such as, when explained by the rules of grammar only, doth not truly express the state of mind of him that uses it.

Notwithstanding this, style that is merely figurative and ornamented, is far from being calculated to deceive. For whenever it is used, no other language, or mode of speech, could give so true an idea of the state of the speaker's mind, though it is confessed to be by no means literally expressive of that state. For instance, when Virgil calls the two Scipios, the Thunderbolts of War, he makes use of an ornamented and highly-figurative expression, not corresponding to his real sentiments; for he would never have replied in the affirmative, if he had been asked seriously whether he really imagined they were two thunderbolts; and yet no plainer terms, though more expressive of their true character, would have given his readers so clear an idea of the force and impetuosity which he meant to ascribe to those heroes.

Again, when the same excellent and correct poet says that Mount Aetna threw its fires as high as the stars, nobody taxes him with a designated falsehood; though his expressions be not literally true, and we are sure he could not but have been sensible of it himself at the time that he made use of them: but nothing short of an hyperbole could have given us a true image of the effort of his imagination, to express his idea of the very great height of those flames.

Lastly, when Aeneas, in the same poet, in the midst of the relation of his adventures, comes to mention Sicily, instead of saying, in so many words, that his father died there, addresses himself directly to his father, and exclaims, *Hic me, pater optime, sessium deseris*; do any of his readers imagine he really conceived his father to be within hearing? But no simple narration could sufficiently have expressed that strong regret, and tender affection, which the revival of his father's memory awakened in his mind. We naturally personify every thing that causes us much pleasure or pain, and a vivid recollection makes every thing seem present. Thus this direct address to the dead Anchises, though strictly speaking, without the least foundation, gives us the truest idea of the unfeigned grief of Aeneas, and of the affecting sense he had of his loss, and therefore lets us into the true state of his mind; not indeed, by a direct interpretation of his words, but in a more certain, though an indirect manner, by means of those circumstances which always accompany that state of mind.

Figurative speech, therefore, is indicative of a person's real feelings and state of mind, not by means of the words it consists of, considered as signs of separate ideas, and interpreted according to their common acceptation; but as circumstances naturally attending those feelings which compose any state of mind. Those figurative expressions, therefore, are scarce considered and attended to as words, but are viewed in the same light as attitudes, gestures, and looks, which are infinitely more expressive of sentiments and feelings than words can possibly be.

Since, however, the literal impropriety of figurative expressions is excused only on account of their being considered as indications of those feelings and sentiments which no words, literally interpreted, could describe, they should never be used but when the situation of the person who uses them is such as will render those feelings and sentiments natural. Otherwise, there being nothing left to excuse and cover the impropriety of the figure, the words present nothing but the naked absurdity, and the writer is detected, either in pretending to feelings that could have no existence, or in asserting what is apparently false and contradictory. This observation may be applied to every figure of speech; and as it is an observation of considerable consequence, it will be frequently repeated, and applied to the particular figures, when they come to be separately explained and illustrated.

LECTURE XII.

The Division of this Part of the Work into what affects the Passions, Judgment, and Imagination.

Of the Effect of Vivid Representation, the Use of the Present Tense in describing past Scenes, and of Particular Names and Circumstances.

Having considered the nature of taste, and of figurative language in general, I proceed to consider distinctly the several objects that offer themselves to our attention respecting the ornament that sentiment admits of. These, as they were before pointed out, are either some of the more remarkable and general affections of the stronger passions; those forms of address which are adapted to engage assent, or those finer feelings which constitute the pleasures of the imagination. Each of these three objects will engage our attention in the order in which they are here mentioned.

The first observation I shall make on the general affections of the passions, is, that they are engaged, and we feel ourselves interested, in proportion to the vividness of our ideas of those objects and circumstances which contribute to excite them. The genuine and proper use of the passions undoubtedly is to rouse men to just and vigorous action upon every emergency, without the slow intervention of reason. It is, therefore, wisely provided, that they should be raised by the immediate view and apprehension of the circumstances proper for their exertion. Being, therefore, blind and mechanical principles, they can only be connected with the view of suitable circumstances; so that, whenever these are presented, whether the passion would, in fact, be useful or not, it cannot fail to be excited, and to rise to its usual height.

This observation supplies us with a reason why our minds are as sensibly affected with scenes of past, or even of ideal distress, as with a mere relation of what is present and real. All the advantage that the latter circumstances united have, is, that they engage us to think more intensely of the case, which will consequently make the ideas more vivid, and the scene more interesting. But that scenes of ideal distress that are past, cannot but be allowed, when we consider, that even reason can plead nothing more in favor of the one than of the other; since the passion is equally unavailable in both cases. Why may I not, with reason, be as much interested in the adventures of Aeneas or Telemachus, as in those of Themistocles, Xenophon, or any of the heroes of Greece or Rome? If the one never had any existence, neither have the other any at present, which, with respect to the final causes of our passions, is the same thing.

The faithful historian, and the writer of romances, having the same access to the springs of the human passions, it is no wonder that the latter generally moves them more forcibly, since he hath the choice of every circumstance that contributes to raise them; whereas the former hath nothing in his power but the disposition of them, and is restricted even in that. I fancy, however, that no person of reading and observation can doubt of the fact, that more tears have been shed, and more intense joy hath been expressed in the perusal of novels, romances, and feigned tragedies, than in reading all the true histories in the world. Who ever, upon any occurrence in real history, ever felt what he must feel in reading *Clarissa*, *George Barnwell*, *Eliosa*, and many other well-contrived fictions. It is to no purpose to say to ourselves, "This is all a fiction, why am I thus affected?" if we read, and form an idea of the scenes there exhibited, we must feel in spite of ourselves. The thought of its being a fiction enables us to make but a feeble and ineffectual effort to repress our feelings, when the ideas which excite them are very strong and vivid. Some persons, however, may have acquired such an aversion to all works of fiction, that they cannot be prevailed upon to give that unprejudiced attention to them which this experiment requires.

CHAPTER 14

Daniel Webb*

An Inquiry into the Beauties of Painting and into the Merits of the Most Celebrated Painters, Ancient and Modern
1760

Dialogue I
General Plan of the Work

B. When you advanced the other day, in a circle of virtuoso's, that the ancients were, in painting, as in all the other polite arts, equal, if not superior, to the moderns; your assertion was received with an universal dislike. However different my sentiments were from yours at the time, I was yet persuaded, that you would not have given into so singular an opinion, without having good reasons to support it. I mentioned to you then my doubts, and you was so good as to promise me you would remove them.

A. I was not at all surprised at the dissatisfaction you remarked in those gentlemen; it is unpleasing to have an opinion brought into doubt, which we have looked upon all our lives as indisputable. You shall now be a judge of the grounds I had for my assertion. Had we no other object in view, but merely to determine the different merits of the artists, it would hardly be worth the labor; but, by examining the testimonies which we shall draw from the writings of the ancients, and comparing their ideas with the paintings of the moderns, we shall enlarge our conceptions, and improve our knowledge of the art itself.

---

*Daniel Webb (1719-1798) was born a Limerick in Ireland. His family was independently wealthy, and he resided chiefly in Bath where he wrote a series of essays on beauty and comparing painting, poetry, and music. He acquired some reputation as a gentleman/scholar and conversationalist but was dismissed by Johnson as of little consequence. He is representative of the polite scholarship of the well-to-do gentry.

B. This prospect which you have opened upon me, gives me a singular pleasure; for, after having read, with the utmost attention, the several authors on this subject, I cannot say, that I have received from them the instruction I expected.

A. This does not proceed from a want of capacity in them, but from a defect in their plans: they are, as you know, biographers; and, as the persons whose lives they write, are all of one profession, the continued repetition of the same thoughts, and of the same technical terms, tire and distract the reader. There is another objection to their manner of writing; their ideas, however just, are so scattered through the different parts of their works, that they are not easily reducible to any system. In the exposition of an art, as in the distribution of a picture, a loose dispersion of the objects, confounds both the eye and the understanding. But, these writers are subject to a still greater disadvantage; for, as the painters whose talents they describe, if we except a very few, excelled much more in the mechanic, than in the ideal part of painting, it throws the force of their observations on that point, with which we, who are but observers of the art, have the least to do.

B. Though I understand very well the terms mechanic and ideal, in their general acceptation, yet, I wish you would explain them, in their particular relation to the subject before us.

A. We may consider the imitative arts in two points of view; 1st, As imitations of such objects as are actually before the eye; secondly, As representations of those images which are formed by the fancy. The first, is the mechanic or executive part of the art; the second, the ideal or inventive. Tully[1] has justly distinguished those parts, when he observes, that the Jupiter of Phidias was not drawn from any pattern in nature, but from that idea of unexampled beauty, which the artist had formed in his mind. The great difference, observed among painters of any name, arises from their different excellencies in these two parts: those, whose chief merit is in the mechanic, will, like the Dutch painters, be servile copiers of the works of nature; but those, who give wholly into the ideal, without perfecting themselves in the mechanic, will produce sbozzo's,[2] not pictures: it is evident then, that the perfection of the art consists in an union of these two parts. Of all the moderns, Raphael seems to have come the nearest to this point. The next to him is, perhaps, Correggio. I have said, perhaps, because, though there is no great variety in his ideas, yet are they sometimes so happy, attended with such grace, and executed with such truth, that, as there is no one artist, whose paintings we see with more pleasure, so is there no one, whose impressions we receive more warmly, or remember longer; and this last is the test of perfect painting. But before I enter further into our subject, it may not be improper, to lay before you the method I propose to observe. First then, we will examine our capacity to judge of the imitative arts, which must be estimated, by their antiquity, their degree of credit with every polite nation, and, above all, by their

[1] Nec vero ille artifex, quum faceret lovis formam aut Minervae, contemplabatur aliquem e quo similitudinem duceret; sed ipsius in mente insidebat specie, pulchritudinis eximia quaedam, quam intuens, in enique defixus, ad illius similitudinem artem et manum dirigebat. In Bruto.

[2] The rough draught of a picture.

usefulness to society. I shall then divide painting, which is our principal object, into its four leading branches, namely, design, coloring, clear obscure, and composition. Concerning each of these, I shall endeavour to point out its different beauties and ends; how far ancients seem to have attained those ends; and of course, what light they must stand in, on a comparison with the moderns. One satisfaction you will have in this progress, that, almost every step we take, will be on classic ground; and, as all the testimonies I use, or lights I borrow, are from the best writers of antiquity, the vivacity and good sense in their remarks will at once entertain, and guide us in our pursuit. As the day is now too far spent to enter upon our subject, tomorrow, if you please, we will begin; and dedicate a morning to each of the divisions, in the order I just now stated them.

Dialogue II
Of our Capacity to judge of Painting

The learned, says Quintilian,[3] know the principles of an art, the illiterate its effects. He has, in those words, fixed the boundaries between taste and science. Were I to define the former, I should say, that taste[4] was a facility in the mind to be moved by what is excellent in an art; it is a feeling of the truth. But, science is to be informed of that truth, and of the means by which its effects are produced. It is easy to conceive, that, different as these principles may be in their setting out, they must often unite in their decisions: This agreement will occasion their being mistaken one for the other, which is the case, when it is affirmed, that no one but an artist can form a right judgment of sculpture or painting. This maxim may hold indeed with respect to the mechanic of an art, but not at all as to its effects; the evidence and force of which, are what determine both the value of the art, and merit of the artist. What Tully[5] observes of an excellent orator, may justly be said of an excellent painter; his superiority will be evident even to the least intelligent judges. But neither authority nor argument give a weight to our opinions, touching any art we treat of, equal to the illustrations and examples which they lend each other. Happily, the near affinity[6] that is observed between the polite arts, they being indeed all but different means of addressing the same passions, makes this, at once, the most effectual and ready method of conveying our ideas. I find in Dionysius Halicarnasseus[7] an observation on music much to my purpose. "I have learned," says he, "in theaters filled with a

[3] Docti rationem artis intelligunt, indocti voluptatem. Lib. ix.4.

[4] Many writers have opposed judgment to taste, as if they were distinct faculties of the mind; but this must be a mistake: The source of taste is feeling, so is it of judgment, which is nothing more than this same sensibility, improved by the study of its proper objects, and brought to a just point of certainty and correctness. Thus it is clear, that these are but different degrees of the same faculty, and that they are exercised wholly on our own ideas; but science is the remembrance or assemblage of the ideas of others; and hence it sometimes happens, that men the most remarkable for this kind of knowledge, are not equally so, for their sensibility.

[5] Id enim ipsum est summi oratoris, summum oratorem populo videri. In Bruto.

[6] Omnes artes, quae ad humanitaten perrinent, habent quoddam communie vinculum, et quasi cognatione inter se continentur. Cic. pro Archia poeta.

[7] Dion. Halicarn. De Struct. orat. sect. xi.

promiscuous and illiterate crowd, what a kind of natural correspondence we all have with melody, and the agreement of sounds: Having known the most admired and able musician to be hissed by the whole multitude, when he has struck a single string out of tune, to the disturbance of harmony; yet, put this same instrument into the hands of one of those simpletons, with orders to express that note, which he would exact from the artist, he cannot do it. Whence is this? The one is the effect of science, the lot but of a few; the other of feeling, which nature has bestowed on all." This applies itself to our present subject: The eye has its principle of correspondence with what is just, beautiful, and elegant: It acquires, like the ear, an habitual delicacy[8]; and answers, with the same fidelity and precision, to the finest impressions: Versed in the works of the best painters, it soon learns to distinguish true expressions from false, and grace from affectation; quickened by exercise, and confirmed by comparison, it outstrips reasoning, and feels in an instant that truth, which the other develops by degrees.

B. You have been describing, what Tully calls a learned, and we, I think, may terms a chaste eye. But, do you not, in this process, make the growth of taste to be little more than a sensitive vegetation, withdrawing it wholly from its dependency on science?

A. Let us observe its advances in poetry, as we have before in music: This too, will be the more decisive, as poetry is an union of the two powers of music and picture. In this, the imagination, on its first setting out, ever prefers extravagance to justness, or false beauties to true; it kindles at the flashes of Claudian, and flutters at the points of Statius; this is its childhood. As it grows in vigor, it refines in feeling, till, superior to its first attractions, it rests on the tender pathetic of Virgil; or the manly spirit of Lucretius. Exactly parallel to this, is the progress of the eye in painting; its first affections are always ill placed; it is enamored with the splendid impositions of Rubens, or the theatrical grace of Guido[9]; this lasts not long; it grows chaste in its pursuit; and slighting those false beauties, dwells on the native and mellow tints of Titian; on the unforced attitudes, and elegant simplicity of Raphael. Was this change, in both cases, the result of reasoning, or produced by a growing knowledge of the rules of each art, we should mark its advances, the contrary of which is almost ever the case, so that we are often surprised at this alternation in ourselves, and wonder, that the ideas and objects which affected us so warmly at first, should, in a short course of time, act so coldly upon us: Nay, some men there are, and those too very capable of judging in other matters, who never rise to this

[8] Consuetudo oculorum. Cic. liv. iv. Acad. quaest.

[9] The grace of Guido is rather technical than ideal; by the first is meant a certain flow of contour, invariably applied to every character, and on every occasion. Thus the daughter of Herodias receives the head of St. John, with the studied dignity of an actress; and the victorious St. Michael, treads on the body of his antagonist, with all the precision of a dancing master. By an ideal grace, I understand that particular image, which in the instant strikes a polite imagination, as peculiar to the action and character before it—Of this the Sancta Cecilia of Raphael, and the Magdalen in the St. Jerome of Correggio, are the happiest examples: The gracefulness in these figures is not only proper to their character, but gives a singular force and beauty to the expression. It was from this happiness, that the venustas of Apelles became proverbial; as, among us, any action that is singularly graceful, is termed Correggiesque.

change, but continue, to the last, under the influence of the same boyish and wanton imagination.

B. The greatest difficulty in your system, would be, to deduce the different degrees, as well as diversity of our tastes, from this same universal principle of feeling.

A. The first, I should think may be accounted for, from the different proportions of that sensibility, as bestowed on us by nature, or improved by ourselves: The second, from the diversity in our imaginations, in the direction given to them by education, and the constitutional or temporary flow of the animal spirits. But, as this is an inquiry quite beyond my reach, I shall leave it to those, who can trace the progress of our ideas, and can determine, and account for the various influences of outward objects on our senses. Instead of losing our time in such endless disquisitions, let us found our knowledge on facts, and pass from them to natural and useful conclusions. "The Lacedemonians," says Atheneus,[10] "are no where represented as being themselves musicians; yet, the purity of their taste in this art, is universally acknowledged: they having, at three different times, when it was corrupted and lost, restored and preserved it." The following observation by Tully, at the same time that it illustrates, receives authority from this fact.—"All men by a kind of tacit feeling, without art or science, distinguish, in both cases, what is right from what is wrong; and, as they evidently do so in painting and sculpture, so, etc. etc."[11] And again: "It is wonderful says he, that seeing the difference is so great between the knowing and the ignorant, in the practice of an art, that the difference should be so far from great, in their judgments concerning it."

B. You have, I think, fully established the principle you contend for, namely, that we have all within us the seeds of taste, and are capable, if we exercise our powers, of improving them into a sufficient knowledge of the polite arts. I am persuaded, that nothing is a greater hindrance to our advances in any art, than the high opinion we form of the judgment of its professors, and the proportionable diffidence of our own. I have rarely met with an artist, who was not an implict admirer of some particular school, or a slave to some favorite manner. They seldom, like gentlemen and scholars, rise to an unprejudiced and liberal contemplation of true beauty. The difficulties they find in the practice of their art, tie them down to the mechanic: at the same time, that self-love and vanity lead them into an admiration of those strokes of the pencil, which come the nearest to their own. I knew a painter at Rome, a man of sense too, who talked much more of Jacinto Brandi, than he did either of Correggio or Raphael.

[10] Atheneus, lib. xiii. Deipnosoph. c. 6.

[11] Omnes enim tacito quodam sensu, sine ulla arte aut raitione, qua sint in artibus ac rationibus recta ac parva dijudicant; idque cum faciunt in picturis et in signis, etc.

Mirabile elle plurimun in faciendo intersit inter doctum et rudem, quam non multum differat in judicaedo. De Oratore, lib iii.

CHAPTER 15

Henry Home, Lord Kames*

Elements of Criticism
1762

Chapter I.
Perceptions and Ideas in a Train.

A man while awake is sensible of a continued train of objects passing in his mind. It requires no activity on his part to carry on the train: nor has he power to vary it by calling up an object at will.[1] At the same time we learn from daily experience, that a train of thought is not merely casual. And if it depend not upon will, nor upon chance, we must try to evolve by what law it is governed. The subject is of importance in the science of human nature; and I promise beforehand, that it will be found of great importance in the fine arts.

[1] For how should this be done? What object is it that we are to call up? If this question can be answered, the object is already in the mind, and there is no occasion to exert the power. If the question cannot be answered, I next demand, how it is possible that a voluntary power can be exerted without any view of an object to exert it upon? We cannot form a conception of such a thing. This argument appears to me satisfactory: if it need confirmation, I urge experience. Whoever makes a trial will find, that objects are linked together in the mind, forming a connected chain; and that we have not the command of any object independent of the chain.

---

*Henry Home, Lord Kames (1696-1782) was the cousin of David Hume and a leading figure in the Scottish Enlightenment. He was never at university but was trained as a lawyer and was appointed judge of the Court of Sessions in 1752. His interests were widespread and included works on criticism and rhetoric as well as moral and legal philosophy. He opposed his friend, David Hume, on a number of points, but was grouped with him in the mind of his ecclesiastical opponents because he argued for a form of determinism that was thought irreligious. He also had a reputation as an agricultural reformer for his development of his estate at Blair Drummond.

It appears that the relations by which things are linked together, have a great influence in directing the train of thought; and we find by experience, that objects are connected in the mind precisely as they are externally. Beginning then with things external, we find that they are not more remarkable by their inherent properties than by their various relations. We cannot any where extend our view without perceiving things connected together by certain relations. One thing perceived to be a cause, is connected with its several effects; some things are connected by contiguity in time, others by contiguity in place; some are connected by resemblance, some by contrast; some go before, some follow. Not a single thing appears solitary, and altogether devoid of connection. The only difference is, that some are intimately connected, some more slightly; some near, some at a distance.

Experience as well as reason may satisfy us, that the train of mental perceptions is in a great measure regulated by the foregoing relations. Where a number of things are linked together, the idea of any one suggests the rest; and in this manner is a train of thoughts composed. Such is the law of succession; whether an original law, or whether directed by some latent principle, is doubtful; and probably will for ever remain so. This law, however, is not inviolable. It sometimes happens, though rarely, that an idea presents itself to the mind without any connection, so far at least as can be discovered.

But though we have not the absolute command of ideas, yet the will hath a considerable influence in directing the order of connected ideas. There are few things but what are connected with many others. By this means, when any thing becomes an object, whether in a direct survey, or ideally only, it generally suggests many of its connections. Among these a choice is afforded. We can insist upon one, rejecting others; and we can even insist upon what has the slightest connection. Where ideas are left to their natural course they are generally continued through the strongest connections. The mind extends its view to a son more readily than to a servant, and more readily to a neighbor than to one living at a distance. This order may be varied by will, but still within the limits of connected objects. In short, every train of ideas must be a chain, in which the particular ideas are linked to each other. We may vary the order of a natural train; but not so as to dissolve it altogether, by carrying on our thoughts in a loose manner without any connection. So far doth our power extend; and that power is sufficient for all useful purposes. To give us more power, would probably be detrimental instead of being salutary.

Will is not the only cause that prevents a train of thought from being continued through the strongest connections. Much depends on the present tone of mind; for a subject that accords with this tone is always welcome. Thus, in good spirits, a cheerful subject will be introduced by the slightest connection; and one that is melancholy, not less readily in low spirits. Again, an interesting subject is recalled, from time to time, by any connection indifferently, strong or weak. This is finely touched by Shakespeare, with relation to a rich cargo at sea.

> My wind, cooling my broth,
> Would blow me to an ague, when I thought
> What harm a wind too great might do at sea.

I should not see the sandy hour-glass run,
But I should think of shallows and of flats;
And see my wealthy Andrew dock'd in sand,
Vailing her high top lower than her ribs,
To kiss her burial. Should I go to church,
And see the holy edifice of stone,
And not bethink me straight of dangerous rocks?
Which touching but my gentle vessel's side,
Would scatter all the spices on the stream,
Enrobe the roaring waters with my silks,
And, in a word, but now worth this,
And now worth nothing.

Merchant of Venice, act I. sc. I.

Another cause clearly distinguishable from that now mentioned, hath also a considerable influence over the train of ideas. In some minds of a singular frame, thoughts and circumstances crowd upon each other by the slightest connection. I ascribe this to a defect in the faculty of discernment. A person who cannot accurately distinguish betwixt a slight connection and one that is more solid, is equally affected with both. Such a person must necessarily have a great command of ideas, because they are introduced by any relation indifferently; and the slighter relations, being without number, must furnish ideas without end. This doctrine is, in a lively manner, illustrated by Shakespeare.

Falstaff. What is the gross sum that I owe thee?

Hostess, Marry, if thou wert an honest man, thyself and thy money too. Thou didst swear to me on a parcel-gilt goblet, sitting in my Dolphin chamber, at the round table, by a sea-coal fire, on Wednesday in Whitsun-week, when the Prince broke thy head for likening him to a singing man of Windsor, thou didst swear to me then, as I was washing thy wound, to marry me, and make me my Lady thy wife. Canst thou deny it? Did not Goodwife Keech, the butcher's wife, come in then, and call me Gossip Quickly? Coming in to borrow a mess of vinegar; telling us she had a good dish of prawns; whereby thou didst desire to eat some; whereby I told thee they were ill for a green wound? And didst not thou, when she was gone down stairs, desire me to be no more so familiarity with such poor people, saying, that ere long they should call me Madam? And didst thou not kiss me, and bid me fetch thee thirty shillings? I put thee now to thy book-oath, deny it if thou canst.

Second part, Henry IV. act 2 sc. 2.

On the other hand, a man of accurate judgment cannot have a great flow of ideas. The slighter relations making no figure in his mind, have no power to introduce ideas. And hence it is, that accurate judgment is not friendly to declamation of copious eloquence. This reasoning is confirmed by experience; for it is a noted observation, That a great or comprehensive memory is seldom connected with a good judgment.

As an additional confirmation, I appeal to another noted observation, That wit and judgment are seldom united. Wit consists chiefly in joining things by distant and fanciful relations, which surprise because they are unexpected. Such relations being of the slightest kind, readily occur to that person only who makes every relation equally welcome. Wit, upon that account, is, in a good measure, incompatible with solid judgment; which, neglecting trivial relations, adheres to what are substantial and permanent. Thus memory and wit are often conjoined: solid judgment seldom with either.

The train of thought depends not entirely upon relations: another cause comes in for a share; and that is the sense of order and arrangement. To things of equal rank, where there is no room for a preference, order cannot be applied; and it must be indifferent in what manner they be surveyed, witness the sheep that make a flock, or the trees in a wood. But in things of unequal rank, order is a governing principle. Thus our tendency is, to view the principal subject before we descend to its accessories or ornaments, and the superior before the inferior or dependent. We are equally averse to enter into a minute consideration of constituent parts, till the thing be first surveyed as a whole. In passing from a part to the whole, and from an accessory to its principal, the connection is the same as in the opposite direction. But a sense of order aids the transition in the latter case, and a sense of disorder obstructs it in the former. It needs scarce be added, that in thinking or reflecting on any of these particulars, and in passing from one to another ideally, we are sensible of easiness or difficulty precisely as when they are set before our eyes.

Our sense of order is conspicuous with respect to natural operations; for it always coincides with the order of nature. Thinking upon a body in motion, we follow its natural course. The mind falls with a heavy body, descends with a river, and ascends with flame and smoke. In tracing out a family, we incline to begin at the founder, and to descend gradually to his latest posterity. On the contrary, musing on a lofty oak, we begin at the trunk, and mount from it to the branches. As to historical facts, we love to proceed in the order of time; or, which comes to the same, to proceed along the chain of causes and effects.

But though, in following out a historical chain, our bent is to proceed orderly from causes to their effects, we find not the same bent in matters of science. There we seem rather disposed to proceed from effects to their causes, and from particular propositions to those which are more general. Why this difference in matters that appear so nearly related? The cases are similar in appearance only, not in reality. In a historical chain, every event is particular, the effect of some former event, and the cause of others that follow. In such a chain, there is nothing to bias the mind from the order of nature. Widely different is the case of science, when we endeavor to trace out causes and their effects. Many experiments are commonly reduced under one cause; and again, many of these under some one still more general and comprehensive. In our progress from particular effects to general causes, and from particular propositions to the more comprehensive, we feel a gradual dilatation or expansion of mind, like what is felt in proceeding along an ascending series, which is extremely delightful. The pleasure here exceeds what arises from following the course of nature; and it is this pleasure which regulates our train of thought in the case now mentioned, and in others that are similar. These observations, by the way, furnish materials for instituting a comparison betwixt the synthetic and analytic methods of reasoning. The synthetic method descending regularly from principles to their consequences, is more agreeable to the strictness of order. But in following the opposite course in the analytic method, we have a sensible pleasure, like mounting upward, which is not felt in the other. The analytic method is more agreeable to the imagination. The other method will be preferred by those only who with rigidity adhere to order, and give no indulgence to natural emotions.[2]

It appears then that we are framed by nature to relish order and connection. When an object is introduced by a proper connection, we are conscious of a certain pleasure arising from that circumstance. Among objects of equal rank, the pleasure is proportioned to the degree of connection; but among unequal objects, where we require a certain order, the pleasure arises chiefly from an orderly arrangement. Of this one may be made sensible, in tracing objects contrary to the course of nature, or contrary to our sense of order. The mind proceeds with alacrity from a whole to its parts, and from a principal to its accessories; but in the contrary direction, it is sensible of a sort of retrograde motion, which is unpleasant. And here may be remarked the great influence of order upon the mind of man. Grandeur, which makes a deep impression, inclines us, in running over any series, to proceed from small to great, rather than from great to small. But order prevails over this tendency; and in passing from the whole to its parts, and from a subject to its ornaments, affords pleasure as well as facility, which are not felt in the opposite course. Elevation touches the mind not less than grandeur doth; and in raising the mind to elevated objects, there is a sensible pleasure. But the course of nature hath still a greater influence than elevation; and therefore the pleasure of falling with rain, and descending gradually with a river, prevails over that of mounting upward. Hence the agreeableness of smoke ascending in a calm morning. Elevation concurs with the course of nature, to make this object delightful.

I am extremely sensible of the disgust men generally have at abstract speculation; and for that reason I would avoid it altogether, were it possible in a work which professes to draw the rules of criticism from human nature, their true source. There is indeed no choice, other than to continue for some time in the same track, or to abandon the undertaking altogether. Candor obliges me to notify this to my readers, that such of them whose aversion to abstract speculation is invincible, may stop short here; for till principles be explained, I can promise no entertainment to those who shun thinking. But I flatter myself with a different taste in the bulk of readers. Some few, I imagine, will relish the abstract part for its own sake; and many for the useful purposes to which it may be applied. For encouraging the latter to proceed with alacrity, I assure them beforehand that the foregoing speculation leads to many important rules of criticism, which shall be unfolded in the course of this work. In the mean time, for instant satisfaction in part, they will be pleased to accept the following specimen.

[2] A train of perceptions or ideas, with respect to its uniformity and variety, is handled afterward, chapt. 9.

It is required in every work of art, that, like an organic system, the constituent parts be mutually connected, and bear each of them a relation to the whole, some more intimate, some less, according to their destination. Order is not less essential than connection; and when due regard is paid to these, we have a sense of just composition, and so far are pleased with the performance. Homer is defective in order and connection; and Pindar more remarkably. Regularity, order, and connection, are painful restraints on a bold and fertile imagination; and are not patiently submitted to, but after much culture and discipline. In Horace there is no fault more eminent than want of connection. Instances are without number. In the first fourteen lines of ode 7. lib. I. he mentions several towns and districts which by some were relished more than by others. In the remainder of the ode, Plancus is exhorted to drown his care in wine. Having narrowly escaped death by the fall of a tree, this poet[3] takes occasion properly to observe, that while we guard against some dangers, we are exposed to others we cannot foresee. He ends with displaying the power of music. The parts of ode 16. lib. 2. are so loosely connected as to disfigure a poem otherwise extremely beautiful. The 1st, 2d, 3d, 4th, 11th, 24th, 27th odes of the 3d book, lie open all of them to the same censure. The 1st satire, book I. is so deformed by want of unity and connection of parts, as upon the whole to be scarce agreeable. It commences with an important question, How it happens that persons who are so much satisfied with themselves, are generally so little with their condition? After illustrating the observation in a sprightly manner by several examples, the author, forgetting his subject, enters upon a declamation against avarice, which he pursues till the line 108. There he makes an apology for wandering, and promises to return to his subject. But avarice having got possession of his mind, he follows out that theme to the end, and never returns to the question proposed in the beginning.

In the *Georgics* of Virgil, though esteemed the most finished work of that author, the parts are ill connected, and the transitions far from being sweet and easy. In the first book[4] he deviates from his subject to give a description of the five zones. The want of connection here is remarkable, as well as in the description of the prodigies that accompanied the death of Caesar, with which the same book is concluded. A digression upon the praises of Italy in the second book,[5] is not more happily introduced. And in the midst of a declamation upon the pleasures of husbandry, that makes part of the same book[6] the author appears personally upon the stage without the slightest connection. The two prefaces of Sallust look as if they had been prefixed by some blunder to his two histories. They will suit any other history as well, or any subject as well as history. Even the members of these prefaces are but loosely connected. They look more like a number of maxims or observations than a connected discourse.

[3] Lib. 2. ode 13.

[4] Lin. 231.

[5] Lin. 136.

[6] Lin. 475.

An episode in a narrative poem being in effect an accessory, demands not that strict union with the principal subject which is requisite betwixt a whole and its constituent parts. The relation however of principal and accessory being pretty intimate, an episode loosely connected with the principal subject will never be graceful. I give for an example the descent of Aeneas into hell, which employs the sixth book of the *Aeneid.* The reader is not prepared for this important event. No cause is assigned, that can make it appear necessary or even natural, to suspend, for so long a time, the principal action in its most interesting period. To engage Aeneas to wander from his course in search of an adventure so extraordinary, the poet can find no better pretext, than the hero's longing to visit the ghost of his father recently dead. In the mean time the story is interrupted, and the reader loses his ardor. An episode so extremely beautiful is not at any rate to be dispensed with. It is pity however, that it doth not arise more naturally from the subject. I must observe that the same time, that full justice is done to this incident, by considering it to be an episode; for if it be a constituent part of the principal action, the connection ought to be still more intimate. The same objection lies against that elaborate description of Fame in the *Aeneid.*[7] Any other book of that heroic poem, or of any heroic poem, has as good a title to that description as the book where it is placed.

In a natural landscape, we every day perceive a multitude of objects connected by contiguity solely. Objects of sight make an impression so lively, as that a relation, even of the slightest kind, is relished. This however ought not to be imitated in description. Words are so far short of the eye in liveliness of impression, that in a description the connection of objects ought to be carefully studied, in order to make the deeper impression. For it is a known fact, the reason of which is suggested above, that it is easier by words to introduce into the mind a related object, than one which is not connected with the preceding train. In the following passage, different things are brought together without the slightest connection, if it be not what may be called verbal, i.e., taking the same word in different meanings.

> Surgamus: solet esse gravis cantantibus umbra.
> Juniperi gravis umbra: nocent et frugibus umbrae.
> Ite domum saturae, venit Hesperus, ite capellae.
>
> *Virg. Buc. 10. 75.*

The metaphorical or figurative appearance of an object, is no good cause for introducing that object in its real and natural appearance. A relation so slight can never be relished.

> Distrust in lovers is too warm a sun;
> But yet 'tis night in love when that is gone.
> And in those climes which most his scorching know,
> He makes the noblest fruits and metals grow.
>
> *Part 2. Conquest of Granada, act 3.*

[7] Lib. 4. lin. 173.

The relations among objects have a considerable influence in the gratification of our passions, and even in their production. But this subject is reserved to be treated in the chapter of emotions and passions.[8]

There is perhaps not another instance of a building so great erected upon a foundation so slight in appearance, as that which is erected upon the relations of objects and their arrangement. Relations make no capital figure in the mind: the bulk of them are transitory, and some extremely trivial. They are however the links that, uniting our perceptions into one connected chain, produce connection of action, because perceptions and actions have an intimate correspondence. But it is not sufficient for the conduct of life that our actions be linked together, however intimately: it is beside necessary that they proceed in a certain order; and this also is provided for by an original propensity. Thus order and connection, while they admit sufficient variety, introduce a method in the management of affairs. Without them our conduct would be fluctuating and desultory; and we would be hurried from thought to thought, and from action to action, entirely at the mercy of chance.

. . .

Chapter III.
Beauty

Having discoursed in general of emotions and passions, I proceed to a more narrow inspection of some particulars that serve to unfold the principles of the fine arts. It is the province of a writer upon ethics, to give a full enumeration of all the passions; and of each separately to assign the nature, the cause, the gratification, and the effect. But a treatise of ethics is not my province. I carry my view no farther than to the elements of criticism, in order to show that the fine arts are a subject of reasoning as well as of taste. An extensive work would be ill suited to a design so limited; and to keep within moderate bounds, the following plan may contribute. It has already been observed, that things are the causes of emotions, by means of their properties and attributes.[9] This furnisheth a hint for distribution. Instead of a painful and tedious examination of the several passions and emotions, I propose to confine my inquiries to such attributes, relations, and circumstances, as in the fine arts are chiefly employed to raise agreeable emotions. Attributes of single objects, as the most simple, shall take the lead; to be followed with particulars that depend on the relations of objects, and are not found in any one object singly considered. Dispatching next some coincident matters, I approach nearer to practice, by applying the principles unfolded in the foregoing parts of the work. This is a general view of the intended method; reserving however a privilege to vary it in particular instances, where a different method may be more commodious. I begin with beauty, the most noted of all the qualities that belong to single objects.

[8] Part I. sect. 4.

[9] Chap. 2, part I. sect. I. first note.

The term *beauty,* in its native signification, is appropriated to objects of sight. Objects of the other senses may be agreeable, such as the sounds of musical instruments, the smoothness and softness of some surfaces: but the agreeableness denominated *beauty* belongs to objects of sight.

Of all the objects of the external senses, an object of sight is the most complex. In the very simplest, color is perceived, figure, and length breadth and thickness. A tree is composed of a trunk, branches, and leaves. It has color, figure, size, and sometimes motion. By means of each of these particulars, separately considered, it appears beautiful: how much more so, when they enter all into one complex perception? The beauty of the human figure is extraordinary, being a composition of numberless beauties arising from the parts and qualities of the object, various colors, various motions, figure, size, etc.; all uniting in one complex perception, and striking the eye with combined force. Hence it is, that beauty, a quality so remarkable in visible objects, lends its name to express every thing that is eminently agreeable. Thus, by a figure of speech, we say a beautiful sound, a beautiful thought or expression, a beautiful theorem, a beautiful event, a beautiful discovery in art or science. But as figurative expression is not our present theme, this chapter is confined to beauty in its genuine signification.

It is natural to suppose, that a perception so various as that of beauty, comprehending sometimes many particulars, sometimes few, should occasion emotions equally various. And yet all the various emotions of beauty maintain one general character of sweetness and gaiety.

Considering attentively the beauty of visible objects, we discover two kinds. One may be termed *intrinsic* beauty, because it is discovered in a single object viewed apart without relation to any other object. The examples above given, are of that kind. The other may be termed *relative* beauty, being founded on the relation of objects. The former is a perception of sense merely; for to perceive the beauty of a spreading oak or of a flowing river, no more is required but singly an act of vision. The latter is accompanied with an act of understanding and reflection; for of a fine instrument or engine, we perceive not the relative beauty, until we be made acquainted with its use and destination. In a word, intrinsic beauty is ultimate: relative beauty is that of means relating to some good end or purpose. These different beauties agree in one capital circumstance, that both are equally perceived as spread upon the object. This will be readily admitted with respect to intrinsic beauty; but is not so obvious with respect to the other. The utility of the plough, for example, may make it an object of admiration or of desire; but why should utility make it appear beautiful? A principle mentioned above,[10] will explain this doubt. The beauty of the effect, by an early transition of ideas, is transferred to the cause, and is perceived as one of the qualities of the cause. Thus a subject void of intrinsic beauty, appears beautiful from its utility. An old Gothic tower that has no beauty in itself, appears beautiful, considered as proper to defend against an enemy. A dwelling-house void of all regularity, is however beautiful in the view of convenience; and the want of

[10]Chap. 2. part I sec. 4.

form or symmetry in a tree, will not prevent its appearing beautiful, if it be known to produce good fruit.

When these two beauties concur in any object, it appears delightful. Every member of the human body possesses both in a high degree. The slender make of a horse destined for running, pleases every taste; partly from symmetry, and partly from utility.

The beauty of utility, being proportioned accurately to the degree of utility, requires no illustration. But intrinsic beauty, so complex as I have said, cannot be handled distinctly without being analyzed into its constituent parts. If a tree be beautiful by means of its color, its figure, its size, its motion, it is in reality possessed of so many different beauties, which ought to be examined separately, in order to have a clear notion of the whole. The beauty of color is too familiar to need explanation. The beauty of figure requires an accurate discussion, for in it many circumstances are involved. When any portion of matter is viewed as a whole, the beauty of its figure arises from regularity and simplicity. Viewing the parts with relation to each other, uniformity, proportion, and order, contribute to its beauty. The beauty of motion deserves a chapter by itself; and another chapter is destined for grandeur, being distinguishable from beauty in a strict sense. For the definitions of regularity, uniformity, proportion, and order, if thought necessary, I remit my reader to the appendix at the end of the book. Upon simplicity I must make a few cursory observations, such as may be of use in examining the beauty of single objects.

A multitude of objects crowding into the mind at once, disturb the attention, and pass without making any impression, or any lasting impression. In a group, no single object makes the figure it would do apart, when it occupies the whole attention.[11] For the same reason, even a single object, when it divides the attention by the multiplicity of its parts, equals not, in strength of impression, a more simple object comprehended in a single view. Parts extremely complex must be considered in portions successively; and a number of impressions in succession, which cannot unite because not simultaneous, never touch the mind like one entire impression made as it were at one stroke. This justifies simplicity in works of art, as opposed to complicated circumstances and crowded ornaments. There is an additional reason for simplicity, in works that make an impression of dignity or elevation. The mind attached to beauties of a high rank, cannot descend to inferior beauties. And yet, notwithstanding these reasons, we find profuse decoration prevailing in works of art. But this is no argument against simplicity. For authors and architects who cannot reach the higher beauties, endeavor to supply their want of genius by dealing in those that are inferior. In all ages, the best writers and artists have been governed by a taste for simplicity.

These things premised, I proceed to examine the beauty of figure, as arising from the above-mentioned particulars, *viz.* regularity, uniformity, proportion, order, and simplicity. To exhaust this subject, would of itself require a large volume. I limit

[11]See the appendix, containing definitions and explanation of terms.

myself to a few cursory remarks, as matter for future disquisition. To inquire why an object, by means of the particulars mentioned, appears beautiful, would I am afraid be a vain attempt. It seems the most probable opinion, that the nature of man was originally framed with a relish for them, in order to answer wise and good purposes. The final causes have not hitherto been ascertained, though they are not probably beyond our reach. One thing is clear, that regularity, uniformity, order, and simplicity, contribute each of them to readiness of apprehension; and enable us to form more distinct images of objects, than can be done with the utmost attention where these particulars are not found. This final cause is, I acknowledge, too slight, to account satisfactorily for a taste that makes a figure so illustrious in the nature of man. That this branch of our constitution hath a purpose still more important, we have great reason to believe. With respect to proportion, I am still less successful. In several instances, accurate proportion is connected with utility. This in particular is the case of animals; for those that are the best proportioned, are the strongest and most active. But instances are still more numerous, where the proportions we relish the most, have no connection, so far as we see, with utility. Writers on architecture insist much upon the proportions of a column; and assign different proportions to the Doric, Ionic, and Corinthian. But no architect will maintain, that the most accurate proportions contribute more to use, than several that are less accurate and less agreeable. Neither will it be maintained, that the proportions assigned for the length breadth and height of rooms, tend to make them the more commodious. It appears then, so far as we can discover, that we have a taste for proportion independent altogether of utility. One thing indeed is certain, that any external object proportioned to our taste, is delightful. This furnishes a hint. May it not be thought a good final cause of proportion, that it contributes to our entertainment? The author of our nature has given many signal proofs, that this end is not below his care. And if so, why should we hesitate in assigning this as an additional final cause of regularity, and the other particulars above mentioned? We may be confirmed in this thought, by reflecting, that our taste, with respect to these, is not occasional or accidental, but uniform and universal, making an original branch of human nature.

One might fill a volume with the effects that are produced by the endless combinations of the principles of beauty. I have room only for a slight specimen, confined to the simplest figures. A circle and a square are each of them perfectly regular, being equally confined to a precise form, and admitting not the slightest variation. A square however is less beautiful than a circle, because it is less simple. A circle has parts as well as a square; but its parts not being distinct like those of a square, it makes one entire impression; whereas the attention is divided among the sides and angles of a square. The effect of simplicity may be illustrated by another example. A square, though not more regular than a hexagon or octagon, is more beautiful than either; for what other reason, than that a square is more simple, and the attention less divided? This reasoning will appear still more solid when we consider any regular polygon of very many sides; for of such figure the mind can never have any distinct perception. Simplicity thus contributes to beauty.

A square is more beautiful than a parallelogram. The former exceeds the latter in regularity and in uniformity of parts. But this holds with respect to intrinsic beauty only; for in many instances, utility comes in to cast the balance on the side of the parallelogram. This figure for the doors and windows of a dwelling-house, is preferred because of utility; and here we find the beauty of utility prevailing over that of regularity and uniformity.

A parallelogram again depends, for its beauty, on the proportion of its sides. The beauty is lost by a great inequality of sides. It is also lost, on the other hand, by the approximation toward equality. Proportion in this circumstance degenerates into imperfect uniformity; and the figure upon the whole appears an unsuccessful attempt toward a square.

An equilateral triangle yields not to a square in regularity nor in uniformity of parts, and it is more simple. But an equilateral triangle is less beautiful than a square, which must be owing to inferiority of order in the position of its parts. The sides of an equilateral triangle incline to each other in the same angle, which is the most perfect order they are susceptible of. But this order is obscure, and far from being so perfect as the parallelism of the sides of a square. Thus order contributes to the beauty of visible objects, not less than simplicity and regularity.

A parallelogram exceeds an equilateral triangle in the orderly disposition of its parts; but being inferior in uniformity and simplicity, it is less beautiful.

Uniformity is singular in one capital circumstance, that it is apt to disgust by excess. A number of things contrived for the same use, such as chairs spoons, etc. cannot be too uniform. But a scrupulous uniformity of parts in a large garden or field, is far from being agreeable. Uniformity among connected objects, belongs not to the present subject. It is handled in the chapter of uniformity and variety.

In all the works of nature, simplicity makes an illustrious figure. The works of the best artists are directed by it. Profuse ornament in painting, gardening, or architecture, as well as in dress and language, shows a mean or corrupted taste.

> Poets, like painters, thus unskill'd to trace
> The naked nature and the living grace,
> With gold and jewels cover ev'ry part,
> And hide with ornaments their want of art.
>
> *Pope's Essay on criticism.*

No one property recommends a machine more than its simplicity; not singly for better answering its purpose, but by appearing in itself more beautiful. Simplicity hath a capital effect in behaviour and manners; no other particular contributing more to gain esteem and love. The artificial and intricate manners of modern times, have little of dignity in them. General theorems, abstracting from their importance, are delightful by their simplicity, and by the easiness of their application to a variety of cases. We take equal delight in the laws of motion, which, with the greatest simplicity, are boundless in their influence.

A gradual progress from simplicity to complex forms and profuse ornament, seems to be the fate of all the fine arts; resembling behaviour, which from original candor and simplicity has degenerated into artificial refinements. At present, written productions are crowded with words, epithets, figures, etc. In music, sentiment is neglected, for the luxury of harmony, and for difficult movement which surprises in its execution. In *taste* properly so called, poignant sauces with complicated mixtures of different favors, prevail among people of condition. The French, accustomed to the artificial red on their women's cheeks, think the modest coloring of nature displayed on a fine face altogether insipid.

The same tendency appears in the progress of the arts among the ancients. Of this we have traces still remaining in architecture. Some vestige of the oldest Grecian buildings prove them to be of the Doric order. The Ionic succeeded, and seems to have been the favorite order, while architecture was in its height of glory. The Corinthian came next in vogue: and in Greece, the buildings of that order appear mostly to have been erected after the Romans got footing there. At last came the Composite with all its extravagances, where proportion is sacrificed to finery and crowded ornament.

But what taste is to prevail next? for fashion is in a continual flux, and taste must vary with it. After rich and profuse ornaments become familiar, simplicity appears by contrast lifeless and insipid. This would be an insurmountable obstruction, should any man of genius and taste endeavor to restore ancient simplicity.

In reviewing what is said above, I am under some apprehension of an objection, which, as it may possibly occur to the reader, ought to be obviated. A mountain, it will be observed, is an agreeable object, without so much as the appearance of regularity; and a chain of mountains still more agreeable, without being arranged in any order. But these facts considered in a proper light, afford not an objection. Regularity, order, and uniformity, are intimately connected with beauty; and in this view only, have I treated them. Every regular object, for example, must in respect of its regularity be beautiful. But I have not said, that regularity, order, and uniformity, are essential to beauty, so as that it cannot exist without them. The contrary appears in the beauty of color. Far less have I said, that an object cannot be agreeable in any respect independent of these qualities. Grandeur, as distinguished from beauty, requires very little regularity. This will appear more fully when that article is handled. In the mean time, to show the difference betwixt beauty and grandeur with respect to regularity, I shall give a few examples. Imagine a small body, let it be a globe, in a continual flux of figure, from the most perfect regularity till there remain no appearance of that quality. The beauty of this globe, depending on its regular figure, will gradually wear away with its regularity; and when it is no longer regular, it no longer will appear beautiful. The next example shall be of the same globe, gradually enlarging its sizes, but retaining its figure. In this body, we at first perceive the beauty of regularity only. But so soon as it begins to swell into a great size, it appears agreeable by its greatness, which joins with the beauty of regularity to make it a delightful object. In the last place, let it be imagined, that the figure as well as the quantity of matter are in a continual flux; and that the body, while it increases in size, becomes less and less regular, till it lose altogether the appearance of that quality. In this case, the beauty of regularity wearing off gradually, gives place to an agreeableness of a different sort, *viz.* that of greatness: and at last the emotion arising from greatness will be in perfection, when the beauty of regularity is gone. Hence it is, that in a large object the want of regularity is not much regarded by the spectator who is struck with its grandeur. A swelling eminence is agreeable, though not strictly regular. A towering hill is delightful, if it have but any distant resemblance of a cone. A small surface ought to be smooth; but in a wide-extended plain, considerable inequalities are overlooked. This observation holds equally in works of art. The slightest irregularity in a house of a moderate size hurts the eye; while the mind, struck with the grandeur of a superb edifice, which occupies it totally, cannot bear to descend to its irregularities unless extremely gross. In a large volume we pardon many defects that would make an epigram intolerable. In short, the observation holds in general, that beauty is connected with regularity in great objects as well as in small; but with a remarkable difference, that in passing from small to great, regularity is less and less required.

The distinction betwixt primary and secondary qualities in matter, seems now fully established. Heat and cold, though seeming to exist in bodies, are discovered to be effects caused by these bodies in a sensitive being. Color, which the eye represents as spread upon a substance, has no existence but in the mind of the spectator. Perceptions of this kind, which, by a delusion of sense, are attributed to external subjects, are termed *secondary qualities,* in contradistinction to figure, extension, solidity, which are primary qualities, and which are not separable, even in imagination, from the subjects they belong to. This suggests a curious inquiry, Whether beauty be a primary or only a secondary quality of objects? The question is easily determined with respect to the beauty of color; for if color be a secondary quality existing no where but in the mind of the spectator, its beauty must be of the same kind. This conclusion must also hold with respect to the beauty of utility, which is plainly a conception of the mind, arising not merely from sight, but from reflecting that the thing is fitted for some good end or purpose. The question is more intricate with respect to the beauty of regularity. If regularity be a primary quality, why not also its beauty? That this is not a good consequence, will appear from considering, that beauty, in its very conception, refers to a percipient; for an object is said to be beautiful, for no other reason but that it appears so to a spectator. The same piece of matter which to man appears beautiful, may possibly to another being appear ugly. Beauty therefore, which for its existence depends upon the percipient as much as upon the object perceived, cannot be an inherent property of either. What else then can it be, but a perception in the mind occasioned by certain objects? The same reasoning is applicable to the beauty of order, of uniformity, of grandeur. Accordingly, it may be pronounced in general, that beauty in no case whatever is a real quality of matter. And hence it is wittily observed by the poet, that beauty is not in the continence, but in the lover's eye. This reasoning is undoubtedly solid: and the only case of doubt or hesitation is, that we are taught a different lesson by sense. By a singular determination of nature, we perceive both beauty and color as belonging to the object; and, like figure or extension, as inherent properties. This mechanism is uncommon; and when nature, to fulfill her intention, chuseth any singular method of operation, we may be certain of some final cause that cannot be reached by ordinary means. It appears to me, that a perception of beauty in external objects is requisite to attach us to them. Doth not this mechanism, in the first place, greatly promote industry, by prompting a desire to possess things that are beautiful? Doth it not further join with utility, in prompting us to embellish our houses and enrich our fields? These however are but slight effects, compared with the connections which are formed among individuals in society by means of this singular mechanism. The qualifications of the head and heart, are undoubtedly the most solid and most permanent foundations of such connections. But as external beauty lies more in view, and is more obvious to the bulk of mankind than the qualities now mentioned, the sense of beauty possesses the more universal influence in forming these connections. At any rate, it concurs in any eminent degree with mental qualifications, to produce social intercourse, mutual good-will, and consequently mutual aid and support, which are the life of society.

It must not however be overlooked, that this sense doth not tend to advance the interests of society, but when in a due mean with respect to strength. Love in particular arising from a sense of beauty, loses, when excessive, its sociable character.[12] The appetite for gratification, prevailing over affection for the beloved object, is ungovernable; and tends violently to its end, regardless of the misery that must follow. Love in this state is no longer a sweet agreeable passion. It becomes painful like hunger or thirst; and produceth no happiness but in the instant of fruition. This discovery suggests a most important lesson, that moderation in our desire and appetites, which fits us for doing our duty, contributes at the same time the most so happiness. Even social passions, when moderate, are more pleasant than when they swell beyond proper bounds.

. . .

VOL. III

Chapt. XXV.

Standard of Taste.

That there is no disputing about "taste," meaning taste in its most extensive sense, is a saying so generally received as to have become a proverb. One thing indeed is evident, that if the proverb hold true with respect to any one external sense, it must hold true with respect to all. If the pleasures of the palate disdain a comparative trial and reject all criticism, the pleasures of touch, of smell, of sound, and even of sight, must be equally privileged. At this rate, a man is not within the reach of censure, even where, insensible to beauty, grandeur, or elegance, he prefers the Saracen's head upon a sign-post before the best tablature of Raphael, or a rude Gothic tower before the finest Grecian building: nor where he prefers the smell of a rotten carcass before that of the most odoriferous flower: nor jarring discords before the most exquisite harmony.

But we must not stop here. If the pleasure of external sense be exempted from criticism, why not every one of our pleasures, from whatever source derived? If taste in the proper sense of the word cannot be disputed, there is as little room for disputing it in its figurative sense. The proverb accordingly comprehends both; and

[12]See chap. 2. part I. sec. I.

in that large sense may be resolved into the following general proposition, That with respect to the sensitive part of our nature, by which some objects are agreeable some disagreeable, there is not such a thing as a *good* or *bad, a right* or *wrong;* that every man's taste is to himself an ultimate standard without appeal; and consequently that there is no ground of censure against any one, if such a one there be, who prefers Blackmore before Homer, selfishness before benevolence, or cowardice before magnanimity.

The proverb in the foregoing instances, is indeed carried very far. It seems difficult, however, to sap its foundation, or with success to attack it from any quarter. For in comparing the various tastes of individuals, it is not obvious what standard must be appealed to. Is not every man equally a judge of what is agreeable or disagreeable to himself. Doth it not seem odd, and perhaps absurd, that a man *ought not* to be pleased when he is, or that he *ought* to be pleased when he is not?

This reasoning may perplex, but, in contradiction to sense and feeling, will never afford conviction. A man of taste must necessarily feel the reasoning to be false, however unqualified to detect the fallacy. At the same time, though no man of taste will subscribe to the proverb as holding true in every case, no man will venture to affirm that it holds true in no case. Subjects there are undoubtedly, that we may like or dislike indifferently, without any imputation upon our taste. Were a philosopher to make scale for human pleasures with many divisions, in order that the value of each pleasure may be denoted by the place it occupies, he would not think of making divisions without end, but would rank together many pleasures arising perhaps from different objects, either as being equally valuable, or differing so imperceptibly as to make a separation unnecessary. Nature hath taken this course, so far as appears to the generality of mankind. There may be subdivisions without end; but we are only sensible of the grosser divisions, comprehending each of them many pleasures of various kinds. To these the proverb is applicable in the strictest sense; for with respect to pleasures of the same rank, what ground can there be for preferring one before another? If a preference in fact be given by any individual, it cannot be taste, but custom, imitation, or some peculiarity of mind.

Nature in her scale of pleasure, has been sparing of divisions: she hath wisely and benevolently filled every division with many pleasures; in order that individuals may be contented with their own lot, without envying the happiness of others: many hands must be employed to procure us the conveniences of life; and it is necessary that the different branches of business, whether more or less agreeable, be filled with hands. A taste too nice and delicate, would obstruct this plan; for it would crowd some employment, leaving others, not less useful, totally neglected. In our present condition, happy it is, that the plurality are not delicate in their choice. They fall in readily with the occupations, pleasures, food, and company, that fortune throws in their way; and if at first there be any displeasing circumstance, custom soon makes it easy.

The proverb will be admitted so far as it regards the particulars now explained. But when applied in general to every subject of taste, the difficulties to be encountered are insuperable. What shall we say, in particular, as to the difficulty that arises from human nature itself? Do we not talk of a good and a bad taste? of a right and a wrong taste? and upon that supposition, do we not, with great confidence, censure writers, painters, architects, and every one who deals in the fine arts? Are such criticisms absurd and void of foundation? Have the foregoing expressions, familiar in all languages and among all people, no sort of meaning? This can hardly be: what is universal must have a foundation in nature. If we can reach this foundation, the standard of taste will no longer be a secret.

All living creatures are by nature distributed into classes; the individuals of each, however diversified by slighter differences, having a wonderful uniformity in their capital parts internal and external. Each class is distinguishable from others by an external form, and not less distinguishable by an internal constitution, manifested by certain powers, feelings, desires, and actions, peculiar to the individuals of each class. Thus each class may be conceived to have a common nature, which, in framing the individuals belonging to the class, is taken for a model or standard.

Independent altogether of experience, men have a sense of conviction of a common nature or standard, not only in their own species, but in every species of animals. And hence it is a matter of wonder, to find any individual deviating from the common nature of the species, whether in its internal or external construction: a child born with an aversion to its mother's milk, is a matter of wonder, not less than if born without a mouth, or with more than one.[13]

With respect to this common nature or standard, we are so constituted as to conceive it to be *perfect* or *right;* and consequently that individuals *ought* to be made conformable to it. Every remarkable deviation accordingly from the standard, makes an impression upon us of imperfection, irregularity, or disorder: it is disagreeable and raises in us a painful emotion: monstrous births, exciting the curiosity of a philosopher, fail not at the same time to excite aversion in a high degree.

Lastly, we have a conviction, that the common nature of man is invariable not less than universal: we conceive that it hath no relation to time nor to place; but that it will be the same hereafter as at present, and as it was in time past; the same among all nations and in all corners of the earth. Nor are we deceived: giving allowance for the difference of culture and gradual refinement of manners, the fact corresponds to our conviction.

This conviction of a common nature or standard, and of its perfection, is the foundation of morality; and accounts clearly for that remarkable conception we have, of a right and a wrong taste in morals. It accounts not less clearly for the conception we have of a right and a wrong taste in the fine arts. A person who rejects objects generally agreeable, and delights in objects generally disagreeable, is condemned as a monster: we disapprove his taste as bad or wrong; and we have a clear conception that he deviates from the common standard. If man were so framed as not to have any notion of a common standard, the proverb mentioned in the beginning would hold universally, not only in the fine arts but in morals: upon that supposition, the taste of every man, with respect to both, would to himself be an ultimate

[13]See Essays on morality and natural religion, part I. essay 2. ch. I.

standard. But the conviction of a common standard being made a part of our nature, we intuitively conceive a taste to be right or good if conformable to the common standard, and wrong or bad if disconformable.

No particular concerning human nature is more universal, than the uneasiness a man feels when in matters of importance his opinions are rejected by others. Why should difference in opinion create uneasiness, more than difference in stature, in countenance, or in dress? The sense of a common standard is the only principle that can explain this mystery. Every man, generally speaking, taking it for granted that his opinions agree with the common sense of mankind, is therefore disgusted with those of a contrary opinion, not as differing from him, but as differing from the common standard. Hence in all disputes, we find the parties, each of them equally, appealing constantly to the common sense of mankind as the ultimate rule or standard. Were it not for this standard, of which the conviction is universal, I cannot discover the slightest foundation for rancor or animosity when persons differ in essential points more than in points purely indifferent. With respect to the latter, which are not supposed to be regulated by any standard, individuals are permitted to think for themselves with impunity. The same liberty is not indulged with respect to the former; for what reason, other than that the standard by which these are regulated, ought, as we judge, to produce an uniformity of opinion in all men? In a word, to this sense of a common standard must be wholly attributed the pleasure we take in those who espouse the same principles and opinions with ourselves, as well as the aversion we have at those who differ from us. In matters left indifferent by the standard, we find nothing of the same pleasure or pain. A bookish man, unless swayed by convenience, relisheth not the contemplative more than the active part of mankind: his friends and companions are chosen indifferently out of either class. A painter consorts with a poet or musician, as readily as with those of his own art; and one is not the more agreeable to me for loving beef, as I do, nor the less agreeable for preferring mutton.

I have said, that my disgust is raised, not by differing from me, but by differing from what I judge to be the common standard. This point, being of importance, ought to be firmly established. Men, it is true, are prone to flatter themselves, by taking it for granted, that their opinions and their taste are in all respects agreeable to the common standard. But there may be exceptions, and experience shows there are some. There are instances without number, or persons who cling to the grosser amusements of gaming, eating, drinking, without having any relish for more elegant pleasures, such, for example, as are afforded by the fine arts. Yet these very persons, taking the same language with the rest of mankind, pronounce in favor of the more elegant pleasures: they invariably approve those who have a more refined taste, and are ashamed of their own as low and sensual. It is in vain to think of giving a reason for this singular impartiality against self, other than the authority of the common standard. Every individual of the human species, the most groveling not excepted, hath a natural sense of the dignity of human nature.[14] Hence every man is esteemed

[14]See chap. II.

and respected in proportion to the dignity of his character, sentiments, and actions. And from the instances now given we discover, that the sense of the dignity of human nature is so vigorous, as even to prevail over self-partiality, and to make us despise our own taste compared with the more elevated taste of others.

In our sense of a common standard and in the pleasure individuals give us by their conformity to it, a curious final cause is discovered. An uniformity of taste and sentiment in matters of importance, forms an intimate connection among individuals, and is a great blessing in the social state. With respect to morals in particular, unhappy it would be for mankind did not this uniformity prevail: it is necessary that the actions of all men be uniform with respect to right and wrong; and in order to uniformity of action, it is necessary that all men think the same way in these particulars: if they differ through any irregular bias, the common sense of mankind is appealed to as the rule; and it is the province of judges, in matters especially of equity, to apply that rule. The same uniformity, it is yielded, is not so strictly necessary in other matters of taste: men, though connected in general as members of the same state, are, by birth, office, or occupation, separated and distinguished into different classes; and are thereby qualified for different amusements: variety of taste, so far, is no obstruction to the general connection. But with respect to the more capital pleasure, such as are best enjoyed in common, uniformity of taste is necessary for two great ends, first to connect individuals the more intimately in the social life, and next to advance these pleasures to their highest perfection. With respect to the first, if instead of a common taste, every man had a taste peculiar to himself, leading him to place his happiness upon things indifferent or perhaps disagreeable to others, these capital pleasure could not be enjoyed in common: every man would pursue his own happiness by flying from others; and instead of a natural tendency to union, remarkable in the human species, union would be our aversion: man would not be a consistent being: his interest would lead him to society, and his taste would draw him from it. The other end will be best explained by entering upon particulars. Uniformity of taste gives opportunity for sumptuous and elegant buildings, for fine gardens, and extensive embellishments, which please universally. Works of this nature could never have reached any degree of perfection, had every man a taste peculiar to himself: there could not be any suitable reward, either of profit or honor, to encourage men of genius to labor in such works. The same uniformity of taste is equally necessary to perfect the arts of music, sculpture, and painting, and to support the expense they require after they are brought to perfection. Nature is in every particular consistent with herself. We are formed by nature to have a high relish for the fine arts, which are a great source of happiness, and extremely friendly to virtue. We are, at the same time, formed with an uniformity of taste, to furnish proper objects for this high relish: if uniformity of taste did not prevail, the fine arts could never have made any figure.

Thus, upon a sense common to the species, is erected a standard of taste, which without hesitation is applied to the taste of every individual. This standard, ascertaining what actions are right what wrong, what proper what improper, hath enabled moralists to establish rules for our conduct from which no person is allowed to swerve. We have the same standard for ascertaining in all the fine arts, what is beautiful or ugly, high or low, proper or improper, proportioned or disproportioned. And here, as in morals, we justly condemn every taste that swerves from what is thus ascertained by the common standard.

The discovery of a rule or standard for trying the taste of individuals in the fine arts as well as in morals, is a considerable advance, but completes not our journey. We have a great way yet to travel. It is made out that there is a standard: but it is not made out, by what mean we shall prevent mistaking a false standard for that of nature. If from opinion and practice we endeavor to ascertain the standard of nature, we are betrayed into endless perplexities. Viewing this matter historically, nothing appears more various and more wavering than taste in the fine arts. If we judge by numbers, the Gothic taste of architecture will be preferred before that of Greece; and the Chinese taste probably before both. It would be endless, to recount the various tastes of gardening that have prevailed in different ages, and still prevail in different countries. Despising the modest coloring of nature, women of fashion in France daub their cheeks with a red powder. Nay, the unnatural swelling in the neck, a disease peculiar to the inhabitants of the Alps, is relished by that people. But we ought not to be discouraged by such untoward instances. For do we not find the like contradictions with respect to morals? was it not once held lawful, for a man to expose his infant children, and, when grown up, to sell them for slaves? was it not held equally lawful, to punish children for the crime of their parents? was not the murder of an enemy in cold blood an universal practice? what stronger instance can be given, than the abominable practice of human sacrifices, not less impious than immoral? Such aberrations from the rules of morality, prove only, that men, originally savage and brutish, acquire not rationality or any delicacy of taste, till they be long disciplined in society. To ascertain the rules of morality, we appeal not to the common sense of savages, but of men in their more perfect state: and we make the same appeal, in forming the rules that ought to govern the fine arts. In neither can we safely rely on a local or transitory taste; but on what is the most universal and the most lasting among polite nations.

In this very manner, a standard for morals has been established with a good deal of accuracy; and so well fitted for practice, that in the hand of able judges it is daily applied with general satisfaction. The standard of taste in the fine arts, is not yet brought to such perfection. And there is an obvious reason for its slower progress. The sense of a right and a wrong in action, is conspicuous in the breast of every individual, almost without exception. The sense of a right and a wrong in the fine arts, is more faint and wavering: it is by nature a tender plant, requiring much culture to bring it to maturity: in a barren soil it cannot live; and in any soil, without cultivation, it is weak and sickly. I talk chiefly with relation to its more refined objects: for some objects make such lively impressions of beauty, grandeur, and proportion, as without exception to command the general taste. There appears to me great contrivance, in distinguishing thus the moral sense from a taste in the fine arts. The former, as a rule of conduct and as a law we ought to obey, must be clear and authoritative. The latter is not entitled to the same authority, since it contributes to our pleasure and amusement only. Were it more strong and lively, it would usurp upon our duty, and call off the attention from matters of grater moment. Were it more clear and authoritative, it would banish all difference of taste: a refined taste would not form a character, nor be entitled to esteem. This would put an end to rivalship, and consequently to all improvement.

But to return to our subject. However languid and cloudy the common sense of mankind may be with respect to the fine arts, it is yet the only standard in these as well as in morals. And when the matter is attentively considered, this standard will be found less imperfect than it appears to be at first sight. In gathering the common sense of mankind upon morals, we may safely consult every individual. But with respect to the fine arts, our method must be different: a wary choice is necessary; for to collect votes indifferently, will certainly mislead us: those who depend for food on bodily labor, are totally void of taste; of such a taste at least as can be of use in the fine arts. This consideration bars the greater part of mankind; and of the remaining part, many have their taste corrupted to such a degree as to unqualify them altogether for voting. The common sense of mankind must then be confined to the few that fall not under these exceptions. But as such selection seems to throw matters again into uncertainty, we must be more explicit upon this branch of our subject.

Nothing tends more than voluptuousness to corrupt the whole internal frame, and to vitiate our taste, not only in the fine arts, but even in morals. It never fails, in course of time, to extinguish all the sympathetic affections, and to bring on a beastly selfishness which leaves nothing of man but the shape. About excluding persons of this stamp there will be no dispute. Let us next bring under trial, the opulent whose chief pleasure is expense. Riches, coveted by most men for the sake of superiority and to command respect, are generally bestowed upon costly furniture, numerous attendants, a princely dwelling, every thing superb and gorgeous, to amaze and humble all beholders. Simplicity, elegance, propriety, and every thing natural, sweet, or amiable, are despised or neglected; for these are not at the command of riches, and make no figure in the public eye. In a word, nothing is relished, but what serves to gratify pride, by an imagined exaltation of the possessor above those he reckons the vulgar. Such a tenor of life contracts the heart and makes every principle give way to self-interest. Benevolence and public spirit, with all their refined emotions, are little felt and less regarded. And if these be excluded, there can be no place for the faint and delicate emotions of the fine arts.

The exclusion of classes so many and various, reduce within a narrow compass those who are qualified to be judges in the fine arts. Many circumstances are necessary to form a judge of this sort: there must be a good natural taste: this taste must be improved by education, reflection, and experience: it must be preserved alive, by a regular course of life, by using the goods of fortune with moderation, and by following the dictates of improved nature which gives welcome to every rational pleasure without deviating into excess. This is the tenor of life which of all contributes the most to refinement of taste; and the same tenor of life contributes the most to happiness in general.

If there appear much uncertainty in a standard that requires so painful and intricate a selection, we may possibly be reconciled to it by the following consideration, That, with respect to the fine arts, there is less difference of taste than is commonly imagined. Nature hath marked all her works with indelible characters of high or low, plain or elegant, strong or weak. These, if at all perceived, are seldom misapprehended by any taste; and the same marks are equally perceptible in works of art. A defective taste is incurable; and it hurts none but the possessor, because it carries no authority to impose upon others. I know not if there be such a thing as a taste naturally bad or wrong; a taste, for example, that prefers a groveling pleasure before one that is high and elegant. Groveling pleasures are never preferred: they are only made welcome by those who know no better. Differences about objects of taste, it is true, are endless: but they generally concern trifles, or possibly matters of equal rank where the preference may be given either way with impunity. If, on any occasion, the dispute go deeper and persons differ where they ought not, a depraved taste will readily be discovered on one or other side, occasioned by imitation, custom, or corrupted manners, such as are described above.

If, after all that is said, the standard of taste be thought not yet sufficiently ascertained, there is still one resource in which I put great confidence. What I have in view, are the principles that constitute the sensitive part of our nature. By means of these principles, common to all men, a wonderful uniformity is preserved among the emotions and feelings of different individuals; the same object making upon every person the same impression; the same in kind, at least, if not in degree. There have been aberrations, as above observed, from these principles; but soon or late they always prevail, by restoring the wanderers to the right track. The uniformity of taste here accounted for, is the very thing that in other words is termed the common sense of mankind. And this discovery leads us to means for ascertaining the common sense of mankind or the standard of taste, more unerringly than the selection above insisted on. Every doubt with relation to this standard, occasioned by the practice of different nations and different times, may be cleared by applying to the principles that ought to govern the taste of every individual. In a word, a thorough acquaintance with these principles will enable us to form the standard of taste; and to lay a foundation for this valuable branch of knowledge, is the declared purpose of the present undertaking.

CHAPTER 16

Sir Joshua Reynolds*

The Idler
1759

No. 76. Saturday, 29 September 1759.
To The Idler

Sir,

I was much pleased with your ridicule of those shallow critics, whose judgment, though often right as far as it goes, yet reaches only to inferior beauties, and who, unable to comprehend the whole, judge only by parts, and from thence determine the merit of extensive works. But there is another kind of critic still worse, who judges by narrow rules, and those too often false, and which, though they should be true, and founded on nature, will lead him but a very little way towards the just estimation of the sublime beauties in works of genius; for whatever part of an art can be executed or criticized by rules, that part is no longer the work of genius, which implies excellence out of the reach of rules. For my own part, I profess myself an idler, and love to give my judgment, such as it is, from my immediate perceptions, without much fatigue of thinking; and I am of opinion, that if a man has not those

*Joshua Reynolds (1723-1792) was born in Devonshire, the son of a schoolmaster. He was influenced early by the painter Jonathan Richardson's theories and criticism, and at seventeen he was apprenticed to Richardson's student, the portrait painter, Thomas Hudson. In 1749, Reynolds went to Italy to study. He returned in 1752 and set up a household in London, where he rapidly achieved success as a painter and moved in the literary and artistic circles of the city. In 1762, he was one of the founding members of "The Club" along with Goldsmith, Garrick, and Johnson. He was also active in the founding of The Royal Academy in 1768 and became its first president. It was as president of the Royal Academy that Reynolds gave his *Discourses* annually. During most of his career, Reynolds was acknowledged as the leading painter in England. In 1789, he lost the sight of his left eye and was forced to give up painting. By 1791, he was nearly blind. He died in 1792, and his funeral at St. Paul's was virtually a state event.

perceptions right, it will be vain for him to endeavor to supply their place by rules; which may enable him to talk more learnedly, but not to distinguish more acutely. Another reason which has lessened my affection for the study of criticism is, that critics, so far as I have observed, debar themselves from receiving any pleasure from the polite arts, at the same time that they profess to love and admire them: for these rules being always uppermost, give them such a propensity to criticize, that instead of giving up the reins of their imagination into their author's hands, their frigid minds are employed in examining whether the performance be according to the rules of art.

To those who are resolved to be critics in spite of nature, and at the same time have no great disposition to much reading and study, I would recommend to them to assume the character of connoisseur, which may be purchased at a much cheaper rate than that of a critic in poetry. The remembrance of a few names of painters, with their general characters with a few rules of the Academy, which they may pick up among the painters, will go a great way towards making a very notable connoisseur.

With a gentleman of this cast, I visited last week the cartoons at Hampton-Court; he was just returned from Italy, a connoisseur of course, and of course his mouth full of nothing but the grace of Raffaelle, the purity of Domenichino, the learning of Poussin, the air of Guido, the greatness of taste of the Characches, and the sublimity and grand contorno of Michael Angelo; with all the rest of the cant of criticism, which he emitted with that volubility which generally those orators have who annex no ideas to their words.

As we were passing through the rooms, in our way to the gallery, I made him observe a whole length of Charles the first, by Van Dyke, as a perfect representation of the character as well as the figure of the man: he agreed it was very fine, but it wanted spirit and contrast, and had not the flowing line, without which a figure could not possibly be graceful. When we entered the gallery, I thought I could perceive him recollecting his rules by which he was to criticize Raffaelle. I shall pass over his observation of the boats being too little, and other criticisms of that kind, till we arrived at "St. Paul Preaching." "This," says he, "is esteemed the most excellent of all the cartoons; what nobleness, what dignity there is in that figure of St. Paul; and yet what an addition to that nobleness could Raffaelle have given, had the art of contrast been known in his time; but above all, the flowing line, which constitutes grace and beauty. You would not then have seen an upright figure standing equally on both legs, and both hands stretched forward in the same direction, and his drapery, to all appearance, without the least art of disposition." The following picture is the "Charge to Peter." "Here," says he, "are twelve upright figures; what a pity it is that Raffaelle was not acquainted with the pyramidal principle; he would then have contrived the figures in the middle to have been on higher ground, or the figures at the extremities stooping or lying, which would not only have formed the group into the shape of a pyramid, but likewise contrasted the standing figures. Indeed," added he, "I have often lamented that so great a genius as Raffaelle had not lived in this enlightened age, since the art has been reduced to principles, and had had his education in one of the modern academies; what glorious works might we then have expected from his divine pencil!"

I shall trouble you no longer with my friend's observations, which, I suppose, you are now able to continue by yourself. It is curious to observe, that at the same time that great admiration is pretended for a name of fixed reputation, objections are raised against those very qualities by which that great name was acquired.

Those critics are continually lamenting that Raffaelle had not the coloring and harmony of Rubens, or the light and shadow of Rembrant, without considering how much the gay harmony of the former, and affectation of the latter, would take from the dignity of Raffaelle; and yet Rubens had great harmony, and Rembrant understood light and shadow; but what may be an excellence in a lower class of painting, becomes a blemish in a higher; as the quick, sprightly turn, which is the life and beauty of epigrammatic compositions, would but ill suit with the majesty of heroic poetry.

To conclude; I would not be thought to infer from any thing that has been said, that rules are absolutely unnecessary, but to censure scrupulosity, a servile attention to minute exactness, which is sometimes inconsistent with higher excellency, and is lost in the blaze of expanded genius.

I do not know whether you will think painting a general subject. By inserting this letter, perhaps you will incur the censure a man would deserve, those business being to entertain a whole room, should turn his back to the company, and talk to a particular person.

I am, Sir, &c.

No. 79. Saturday, 20 October 1759.

TO THE IDLER.

SIR,

Your acceptance of a former letter on painting, gives me encouragement to offer a few more sketches on the same subject.

Amongst the painters, and the writers on painting, there is one maxim universally admitted and continually inculcated. "Imitate nature" is the invariable rule; but I know none who have explained in what manner this rule is to be understood; the consequence of which is, that every one takes it in the most obvious sense, that objects are represented naturally when they have such relief that they seem real. It may appear strange, perhaps, to hear this sense of the rule disputed; but it must be considered, that if the excellency of a painter consisted only in this kind of imitation, painting must lose its rank, and be no longer considered as a liberal art, and sister to poetry; this imitation being merely mechanical, in which the slowest intellect is always sure to succeed best; for the painter of genius cannot stoop to drudgery, in which the understanding has no part; and what pretense has the art to claim kindred with poetry, but by its powers over the imagination? To this power the painter of genius directs his aim; in this sense he studies nature, and often arrives at his end, even by being unnatural in the confined sense of the word.

The grand style of painting requires this minute attention to be carefully avoided, and must be kept as separate from it as the style of poetry from that of history. Poetical ornaments destroy that air of truth and plainness which ought to characterize history; but the very being of poetry consists in departing from this plain narration, and adopting every ornament that will warm the imagination. To desire to see the excellencies of each style united, to mingle the Dutch with the Italian school, is to join contrarieties which cannot subsist together, and which destroy the efficacy of each other. The Italian attends only to the invariable, the great and general ideas which are fixed and inherent in universal nature; the Dutch, on the contrary, to literal truth and a minute exactness in the detail, as I may say, of nature modified by accident. The attention to these petty peculiarities is the very cause of this naturalness so much admired in the Dutch pictures, which, if we suppose it to be a beauty, is certainly of a lower order, which ought to give place to a beauty of a superior kind, since one cannot be obtained but by departing from the other.

If my opinion was asked concerning the works of Michael Angelo, whether they would receive any advantage from possessing this mechanical merit, I should not scruple to say they would not only receive no advantage, but would lose, in a great measure, the effect which they now have on every mind susceptible of great and noble ideas. His works may be said to be all genius and soul, and why should they be loaded with heavy matter which can only counteract his purpose by retarding the progress of the imagination.

If this opinion should be thought one of the wild extravagances of enthusiasm, I shall only say, that those who censure it are not conversant in the works of the great masters. It is very difficult to determine the exact degree of enthusiasm that the arts of painting and poetry may admit. There may perhaps be too great an indulgence as well as too great a restraint of imagination; and if the one produces incoherent monsters, the other produces what is full as bad, lifeless insipidity. An intimate knowledge of the passions, and good sense, but not common sense, must at last determine its limits. It has been thought, and I believe with reason, that Michael Angelo sometimes transgressed those limits; and I think I have seen figures of him of which it was very difficult to determine whether they were in the highest degree sublime or extremely ridiculous. Such faults may be said to be the ebullitions of genius; but at least he had this merit, that he never was insipid, and whatever passion his works may excite, they will always escape contempt.

What I have had under consideration is the sublimest style, particularly that of Michael Angelo, the Homer of painting. Other kinds may admit of this naturalness, which of the lowest kind is the chief merit; but in painting, as in poetry, the highest style has the least of common nature.

One may very safely recommend a little more enthusiasm to the modern painters; too much is certainly not the vice of the present age. The Italians seem to have been continually declining in this respect from the time of Michael Angelo to that of Carlo Maratti, and from thence to the very bathos of insipidity to which they are now sunk; so that there is no need of remarking, that where I mentioned the Italian painters in opposition to the Dutch, I mean not the Moderns, but the heads of the old Roman and Bolognian schools; nor did I mean to include in my idea of an Italian painter, the Venetian school, which may be said to be the Dutch part of the Italian genius. I have only to add a word of advice to the painters, that however excellent they may be in painting naturally, they would not flatter themselves very much upon it; and to the connoisseurs, that when they see a cat or a fiddle painted so finely, that, as the phrase is, "It looks as if you could take it up," they would not for that reason immediately compare the painter to Raffaelle and Michael Angelo.

No. 82. Saturday, 10 November 1759.

TO THE IDLER

SIR,

Discoursing in my last letter on the different practice of the Italian and Dutch painters, I observed that "the Italian painter attends only to the invariable, the great and general ideas which are fixed and inherent in universal nature."

I was led into the subject of this letter by endeavoring to fix the original cause of this conduct of the Italian masters. If it can be proved that by this choice they selected the most beautiful part of the creation, it will shew how much their principles are founded on reason, and, at the same time, discover the origin of our ideas of beauty.

I suppose it will be easily granted, that no man can judge whether any animal be beautiful in its kind, or deformed, who has seen only one of that species; this is as conclusive in regard to the human figure; so that if a man, born blind, was to recover his sight, and the most beautiful woman was brought before him, he could not determine whether she was handsome or not; nor if the most beautiful and most deformed were produced could he any better determine to which he should give the preference, having seen only those two. To distinguish beauty, then, implies the having seen many individuals of that species. If it is asked how is more skill acquired by the observation of greater numbers? I answer that, in consequence of having seen many, the power is acquired, even without seeking after it, of distinguishing between accidental blemishes and excrescences which are continually varying the surface of nature's works, and the invariable general form which nature most frequently produces and always seems to intend in her productions.

Thus amongst the blades of grass or leaves of the same tree, though no two can be found exactly alike, yet the general form is invariable: a naturalist, before he chose one as a sample, would examine many, since if he took the first that occurred it might have, by accident or otherwise, such a form as that it would scarce be known to belong to that species; he selects, as the painter does, the most beautiful, that is, the most general form of nature.

Every species of the animal as well as the vegetable creation may be said to have a fixed or determinate form towards which nature is continually inclining, like various lines terminating in the center; or it may be compared to pendulums vibrating in different directions over one central point; and as they all cross the center, though only one passes through any other point, so it will be found that perfect beauty is oftener produced by nature than deformity; I don't mean than deformity in general, but than any one kind of deformity. To instance in a particular part of a feature; the line that forms the ridge of the nose is beautiful when it is straight; this then is the central form, which is oftener found than either concave, convex, or any other irregular form that shall be proposed. As we are then more accustomed to beauty than deformity, we may conclude that to be the reason why we approve and admire it, as we approve and admire customs and fashions of dress for no other reason than that we are used to them; so that though habit and custom cannot be said to be the cause of beauty, it is certainly the cause of our liking it; and I have no doubt but that if we were more used to deformity than beauty, deformity would then lose the idea now annexed to it, and take that of beauty; as if the whole world should agree, that "yes" and "no" should change their meanings; "yes" would then deny, and "no" would affirm.

Whoever undertakes to proceed further in this argument, and endeavors to fix a general criterion of beauty respecting different species, or to shew why one species is more beautiful than another, it will be required from him first to prove that one species is really more beautiful than another. That we prefer one to the other, and with very good reason, will be readily granted; but it does not follow from thence that we think it a more beautiful form; for we have no criterion of form by which to determine our judgment. He who says a swan is more beautiful than a dove, means little more than that he has more pleasure in seeing a swan than a dove, either from the stateliness of its motions or its being a more rare bird; and he who gives the preference to the dove, does it from some association of ideas of innocence that he always annexes to the dove; but if he pretends to defend the preference he gives to one or the other by endeavoring to prove that this more beautiful form proceeds from a particular gradation of magnitude, undulation of a curve, or direction of a line, or whatever other conceit of his imagination he shall fix on, as a criterion of form, he will be continually contradicting himself, and find at last that the great mother of nature will not be subjected to such narrow rules. Among the various reasons why we prefer one part of her works to another, the most general, I believe, is habit and custom; custom makes, in a certain sense, white black, and black white; it is custom alone determines our preference of the color of the Europeans to the Ethiopians, and they, for the same reason, prefer their own color to ours. I suppose no body will doubt, if one of their painters was to paint the goddess of beauty, but that he would present her black, with thick lips, flat nose, and woolly hair; and, it seems to me, he would act very unnaturally if he did not: for by what criterion will any one dispute the propriety of his idea? We, indeed, say, that the form and color of the European is preferable to that of the Ethiopian; but I know of no other reason we have for it, but that we are more accustomed to it. It is absurd to say, that beauty is possessed of attractive powers, which irresistibly seize the corresponding mind with love and admiration, since that argument is equally conclusive in favor of the white and the black philosopher.

The black and white nations must, in respect of beauty, be considered as of different species of the same kind; from one of which to the other, as I observed, no inference can be drawn.

Novelty is said to be one of the causes of beauty: that novelty is a very sufficient reason why we should admire, is not denied; but because it is uncommon, is it therefore beautiful? The beauty that is produced by color, as when we prefer one bird to another, though of the same form, on account of its color, has nothing to do with this argument, which reaches only to form. I have here considered the word beauty as being properly applied to form alone. There is a necessity of fixing this confined sense; for there can be no argument, if the sense of the word is extended to every thing that is approved. A rose may as well be said to be beautiful, because it has a fine smell, as a bird because of its color. When we apply the word beauty, we do not mean always by it a more beautiful form, but something valuable on account of its rarity, usefulness, color, or any other property. A horse is said to be a beautiful animal; but had a horse as few good qualities as a tortoise, I do not imagine that he would be then esteemed beautiful.

A fitness to the end proposed, is said to be another cause of beauty; but supposing we were proper judges of what form is the most proper in an animal to constitute strength or swiftness, we always determine concerning its beauty, before we exert our understanding to judge of its fitness.

From what has been said, it may be inferred, that the works of nature, if we compare one species with another, are all equally beautiful; and that preference is given from custom, or some association of ideas: and that in creatures of the same species, beauty is the medium or center of all its various forms.

To conclude, then, by way of corollary, if it has been provided that the painter, by attending to the invariable and general ideas of nature, produces beauty, he must, by regarding minute particularities, and accidental discriminations, deviate from the universal rule, and pollute his canvas with deformity.

Discourses on Art

Discourse Seven
1776

The reality of a standard of taste, as well as of corporeal beauty. Beside this immutable truth, there are secondary truths, which are variable, both requiring the attention of the artist, in proportion to their stability or their influence.

Gentlemen:

It has been my uniform endeavor, since I first addressed you from this place, to impress you strongly with one ruling idea. I wished you to be persuaded, that success in your art depends almost entirely on your own industry; but the industry which I principally recommended, is not the industry of the hands, but of the mind.

As our art is not a divine gift, so neither is it a mechanical trade. Its foundations are laid in solid science: and practice, though essential to perfection, can never attain that to which it aims, unless it works under the direction of principle.

Some writers upon art carry this point too far, and suppose that such a body of universal and profound learning is requisite, that the very enumeration of its kinds is enough to frighten a beginner. Vitruvius, after going through the many accomplishments of nature, and the many acquirements of learning, necessary to architect, proceeds with great gravity to assert that he ought to be well skilled in the civil law; that he may not be cheated in the title of the ground he builds on.

But without such exaggeration, we may go so far as to assert, that a painter stands in need of more knowledge than is to be picked off his pallet, or collected by looking on his model, whether it be in life or in picture. He can never be a great artist, who is grossly illiterate.

Every man whose business is description, ought to be tolerably conversant with the poets, in some language or other; that he may imbibe a poetical spirit, and enlarge his stock of ideas. He ought to acquire an habit of comparing and digesting his notions. He ought not to be wholly unacquainted with that part of philosophy which gives an insight into human nature, and relates to the manners, characters, passions, and affections. He ought to know *something* concerning the mind, as well as *a great deal* concerning the body of man. For this purpose, it is not necessary that he should go into such a compass of reading, as must, by distracting his attentions, disqualify him for the practical part of his profession, and make him sink the performer in the critic. Reading, if it can be made the favorite recreation of his leisure hours, will improve and enlarge his mind, without retarding his actual industry. What such partial and desultory reading cannot afford, may be supplied by the conversation of learned and ingenious men, which is the best of all substitutes for those who have not the means or opportunities of deep study. There are many such men in this age; and they will be pleased with communicating their ideas to artists, when they see them curious and docile, if they are treated with that respect and deference which is so justly their due. Into such society, young artists, if they make it the point of their ambition, will by degrees be admitted. There, without formal teaching, they will insensibly come to feel and reason like those they live with, and find a rational and systematic taste imperceptibly formed in their minds, which they will know how to reduce to a standard, by applying general truth to their own purposes, better perhaps than those to whom they owned the original sentiment.

Of these studies, and this conversation, the desire and legitimate offspring is a power of distinguishing right from wrong; which power applied to works of art, is denominated TASTE. Let me then, without further introduction, enter upon an examination, whether taste be so far beyond our reach, as to be unattainable by care; or be so very vague and capricious, that no care ought to be employed about it.

It has been the fate of arts to be enveloped in mysterious and incomprehensible language, as if it was thought necessary that even the terms should correspond to the idea entertained of the instability and uncertainty of the rules which they expressed.

To speak of genius and taste, as in any way connected with reason or common sense, would be, in the opinion of some towering talkers, to speak like a man who possessed neither; who had never felt that enthusiasm, or, to use their own inflated language, was never warmed by that Promethean fire, which animates the canvas and vivifies the marble.

If, in order to be intelligible, I appear to degrade art by bringing her down from her visionary situation in the clouds, it is only to give her a more solid mansion upon the earth. It is necessary that at some time or other we should see things as they really are, and not impose on ourselves by that false magnitude with which objects appear when viewed indistinctly as through a mist.

We will allow a poet to express his meaning, when his meaning is not well known to himself, with a certain degree of obscurity, as it is one source of the sublime. But when, in plain prose, we gravely talk of courting the Muse in shady bowers; waiting the call and inspiration of Genius, finding out where he inhabits, and where he is to be invoked with the greatest success; of attending to times and seasons when the imagination shoots with the greatest vigor, whether at the summer solstice or the vernal equinox; sagaciously observing how much the wild freedom and liberty of imagination is cramped by attention to established rules; and how this same imagination begins to grow dim in advanced age, smothered and deadened by too much judgment; when we talk such language, or entertain such sentiments as these, we generally rest contented with mere words, or at best entertain notions not only groundless but pernicious.

If all this means, what it is very possible was originally intended only to be meant, that in order to cultivate an art, a man secludes himself from the commerce of the world, and retires into the country at particular seasons: or at one time of the year his body is in better health, and consequently his mind fitter for the business of hard thinking than at another time; or that the mind may be fatigued and grow confused by long and unremitted application; this I can understand. I can likewise believe, that a man eminent when young for possessing poetical imagination, may, from having taken another road, so neglect its cultivation, as to show less of its powers in his latter life. But I am persuaded, that scarce a poet is to be found, from Homer down to Dryden, who preserved a sound mind in a sound body, and continued practicing his profession to the very last, whose latter works are not as replete with the fire of imagination, as those which were produced in his more youthful days.

To understand literally these metaphors, or ideas expressed in poetical language, seems to be equally absurd as to conclude, that because painters sometimes represent poets writing from the dictates of a little winged boy or genius, that this same genius did really inform him in a whisper what he was to write; and that he is himself but a mere machine, unconscious of the operations of his own mind.

Opinions generally received and floating in the world, whether true or false, we naturally adopt and make our own; they may be considered as a kind of inheritance to which we succeed and are tenants for life, and which we leave to our posterity very nearly in the condition in which we received it; it not being much in any one man's power either to impair or improve it. The greatest part of these opinions, like current coin in its circulation, we are used to take without weighing or examining; but by this inevitable inattention many adulterated pieces are received, which, when we seriously estimate our wealth, we must throw away. So the collector of popular opinions, when he embodies his knowledge, and forms a system, must separate those which are true from those which are only plausible. But it becomes more peculiarly a duty to the professors of art not to let any opinions relating to *that* art pass unexamined. The caution and circumspection required in such examination we shall presently have an opportunity of explaining.

Genius and taste, in their common acceptation, appear to be very nearly related; the difference lies only in this, that genius has superadded to it a habit or power of execution; or we may say, that taste, when this power is added, changes its name and is called genius. They both, in the popular opinion, pretend to an entire exemption from the restraint of rules. It is supposed that their powers are intuitive; that under the name of genius great works are produced, and under the name of taste an exact judgment is given, without our knowing why and without our being under the least obligation to reason, precept, or experience.

One can scarce state these opinions without exposing their absurdity; yet they are constantly in the mouths of men, and particularly of artists. They who have thought seriously on this subject, do not carry the point so far; yet I am persuaded, that even among those few who may be called thinkers, the prevalent opinion allows less than it ought to the powers of reason; and considers the principles of taste, which give all their authority to the rules of art, as more fluctuating, and as having less solid foundations, than we shall find, upon examination, they really have.

The common saying, that *tastes are not to be disputed*, owes its influence, and its general reception, to the same error which leads us to imagine this faculty of too high an original to submit to the authority of an earthly tribunal. It likewise corresponds with the notions of those who consider it as a mere phantom of the imagination, so devoid of substance as to elude all criticism.

We often appear to differ in sentiments from each other, merely from the inaccuracy of terms, as we are not obliged to speak always with critical exactness. Something of this too may arise from want of words in the language in which we speak, to express the more nice discriminations which a deep investigation discovers. A great deal however of this difference vanishes, when each opinion is tolerably explained and understood by constancy and precision in the use of terms.

We apply the term TASTE to that act of the mind by which we like or dislike, whatever be the subject. Our judgment upon an airy nothing, a fancy which has no foundation, is called by the same name which we give to our determination concerning those truths which refer to the most general and most unalterable principles of human nature; to the works which are only to be produced by the greatest efforts of the human understanding. However inconvenient this may be, we are obliged to take words as we find them; all we can do is to distinguish the THINGS to which they are applied.

We may let pass those things which are at once subjects of taste and sense, and which having as much certainty as the senses themselves, give no occasion to inquiry or dispute. The natural appetite or taste of the human mind is for TRUTH whether that truth results from the real agreement or equality of original ideas among themselves; from the agreement of the representation of any object with the thing represented; or from the correspondence of the several parts of any arrangement with each other. It is the very same taste which relishes a demonstration in geometry, that is pleased with the resemblance of a picture to an original, and touched with the harmony of music.

All these have unalterable and fixed foundations in nature, and are therefore equally investigated by reason, and known by study; some with more, some with less clearness, but all exactly in the same way. A picture that is unlike, is false. Disproportionate ordinance of parts is not right; because it cannot be true, until it ceases to be a contradiction to assert, that the parts have no relation to the whole. Coloring is true, when it is naturally adapted to the eye, from brightness, from softness, from harmony, from resemblance; because these agree with their object, NATURE, and therefore are true; as true as mathematical demonstration; but known to be true only to those who study these things.

But beside real, there is also apparent truth, or opinion, or prejudice. With regard to real truth, when it is known, the taste which conforms to it is, and must be, uniform. With regard to the second sort of truth, which may be called truth upon sufferance, or truth by courtesy, it is not fixed, but variable. However, whilst these opinions and prejudices, on which it is founded, continue, they operate as truth; and the art, whose office it is to please the mind, as well as instruct it, must direct itself according to opinion, or it will not attain its end.

In proportion as these prejudices are known to be generally diffused, or long received, the taste which conforms to them approaches nearer to certainty, and to a sort of resemblance to real science, even where opinions are found to be no better than prejudices. And since they deserve, on account of their duration and extent, to be considered as really true, they become capable of no small degree of stability and determination, by their permanent and uniform nature.

As these prejudices become more narrow, more local, more transitory, this secondary taste becomes more and more fantastical; recedes from real science; is less to be approved by reason, and less followed in practice; though in no case perhaps to be wholly neglected, where it does not stand, as it sometimes does, in direct defiance of the most respectable opinions received amongst mankind.

Having laid down these positions, I shall proceed with less method, because less will serve to explain and apply them.

We will take it for granted, that reason is something invariable, and fixed in the nature of things; and without endeavoring to go back to an account of first principles, which for ever will elude our search, we will conclude, that whatever goes under the name of taste, which we can fairly bring under the dominion of reason, must be considered as equally exempt from change. If therefore, in the course of this inquiry, we can show that there are rules for the conduct of the artist which are fixed and invariable, it follows of course, that the art of the connoisseur, or, in other words, taste, has likewise invariable principles.

Of the judgment which we make on the works of art, and the preference that we give to one class of art over another, if a reason be demanded, the question is perhaps evaded by answering, I judge from my taste; but it does not follow that a better answer cannot be given, though, for common gazers, this may be sufficient. Every man is not obliged to investigate the cause of his approbation or dislike.

The arts would lie open for ever to caprice and casualty, if those who are to judge of their excellencies had no settled principles by which they are to regulate their decisions, and the merit or defect of performances were to be determined by unguided fancy. And indeed we may venture to assert, that whatever speculative knowledge is necessary to the artist, is equally and indispensably necessary to the connoisseur.

The first idea that occurs in the consideration of what is fixed in art, or in taste, is that presiding principle of which I have so frequently spoken in former discourses, the general idea of nature. The beginning, the middle, and the end of every thing that is valuable in taste, is comprised in the knowledge of what is truly nature; for whatever notions are not conformable to those of nature, or universal opinion, must be considered as more or less capricious.

My notion of nature comprehends not only the forms which nature produces, but also the nature and internal fabric and organization, as I may call it, of the human mind and imagination. The terms beauty, or nature, which are general ideas, are but different modes of expressing the same thing, whether we apply these terms to statues, poetry, or pictures. Deformity is not nature, but an accidental deviation from her accustomed practice. This general idea therefore ought to be called Nature; and nothing else, correctly speaking, has a right to that name. But we are so far from speaking, in common conversation, with any such accuracy, that, on the contrary, when we criticize Rembrandt and other Dutch painters, who introduced into their historical pictures exact representations of individual objects with all their imperfections, we say, though it is not in a good taste, yet it is nature.

This misapplication of terms must be very often perplexing to the young student. Is not art, he may say, an imitation of nature? Must he not therefore who imitates her with the greatest fidelity be the best artist? By this mode of reasoning Rembrandt has a higher place than Raffaelle. But a very little reflection will serve to show us that these particularities cannot be nature: for how can that be the nature of man, in which no two individuals are the same?

It plainly appears, that as a work is conducted under the influence of general ideas, or partial, it is principally to be considered as the effect of a good or a bad taste.

As beauty therefore does not consist in taking what lies immediately before you, so neither, in our pursuit of taste, are those opinions which we first received and adopted, the best choice, or the most natural to the mind and imagination. In the infancy of our knowledge we seize with greediness the good that is within our reach; it is by after-consideration, and in consequence of discipline, that we refuse the present for a greater good at a distance. The nobility or elevation of all arts, like the excellency of virtue itself, consists in adopting this enlarged and comprehensive idea; and all criticism built upon the more confined view of what is natural, may properly be called shallow criticism, rather than false: its defect is, that the truth is not sufficiently extensive.

It has sometimes happened, that some of the greatest men in our art have been betrayed into errors by this confined mode of reasoning. Poussin, who, upon the whole may be produced as an artist strictly attentive to the most enlarged and extensive ideas of nature, from not having settled principles on this point, has, in one instance at least, I think, deserted truth for prejudice. He is said to have vindicated the conduct of Julio Romano for his inattention to the masses of light and shade, or grouping the figures in THE BATTLE OF CONSTANTINE, as if designedly neglected, the better to correspond with the hurry and confusion of a battle. Poussin's own conduct in many of his pictures, makes us more easily give credit to this report. That it was too much his own practice, THE SACRIFICE TO SILENUS, and THE TRIUMPH OF BACCHUS AND ARIADNE,[1] may be produced as instances; but this principle is still more apparent, and may be said to be even more ostentatiously displayed in his PERSEUS and MEDUSA'S HEAD.[2]

This is undoubtedly a subject of great bustle and tumult, and that the first effect of the picture may correspond to the subject, every principle of composition is violated; there is no principal figure, no principal light, no groups; every thing is dispersed, and in such a state of confusion, that the eye finds no repose any where. In consequence of the forbidding appearance, I remember turning from it with disgust, and should not have looked a second time, if I had not been called back to a closer inspection. I then indeed found, what we may expect always to find in the works of Poussin, correct drawing, forcible expression, and just character; in short all the excellencies which so much distinguish the works of this learned painter.

This conduct of Poussin I hold to be entirely improper to imitate. A picture should please at first sight, and appear to invite the spectator's attention: if on the contrary the general effect offends the eye, a second view is not always sought, whatever more substantial and intrinsic merit it may possess.

Perhaps no apology ought to be received for offenses committed against the vehicle (whether it be the organ of seeing, or of hearing,) by which our pleasures are conveyed to the mind. We must take care that the eye be not perplexed and distracted by a confusion of equal parts, or equal light and offended by an unharmonious mixture of colors, as we should guard against offending the ear by unharmonious sounds. We may venture to be more confident of the truth of this observation, since we find that Shakespeare, on a parallel occasion, has made Hamlet recommend to the players a precept of the same kind,—never to offend the ear by harsh sounds: *In the very torrent, tempest, and whirlwind of your passion,* says he, *you must acquire and beget a temperance that may give it smoothness.* And yet, at the same time, he very justly observes, *The end of playing, both at the first, and now was and is, to hold, as 't were, the mirror up to nature.* No one can deny, that violent passions will naturally emit harsh and disagreeable tones: yet this great poet and critic thought that this imitation of nature would cost too much, if purchased at the expense of disagreeable sensations, or, as he expressed it, of *splitting the ear.* The poet and actor, as well as the painter of genius who is well acquainted with all the variety and sources of pleasure in the mind and imagination has little regard or attention to common nature, or creeping, after common sense. By overleaping those narrow bounds, he more effectually seizes the whole mind, and more powerfully accomplishes his purpose. This success is ignorantly imagined to proceed from inattention to all rules,

[1] In the Cabinet of the Earl of Ashburnham.

[2] In the Cabinet of Sir Peter Burrel.

and a defiance of reason and judgment: whereas it is in truth acting according to the best rules in the justest reason.

He also thinks nature, in the narrow sense of the word, is alone to be followed, will produce but a scanty entertainment for the imagination: every thing is to be done with which it is natural for the mind to be pleased, whether it proceeds from simplicity or variety, uniformity or irregularity; whether the scenes are familiar or exotic; rude and wild, or enriched and cultivated; for it is natural for the mind to be pleased with all these in their turn. In short, whatever pleases has in it what is analogous to the mind, and is, therefore, in the highest and best sense of the word, natural.

It is the sense of nature or truth, which ought more particularly to be cultivated by the professors of art: and it may be observed, that many wise and learned men, who have accustomed their minds to admit nothing for truth but what can be proved by mathematical demonstration, have seldom any relish for those arts which address themselves to the fancy, the rectitude and truth of which is known by another kind of proof: and we may add, that the acquisition of this knowledge requires as much circumspection and sagacity, as is necessary to attain those truths which are more capable of demonstration. Reason must ultimately determine our choice on every occasion; but this reason may still be exerted ineffectually by applying to taste principles which though right as far as they go, yet do not reach the object. No man, for instance, can deny, that it seems at first view very reasonable, that a statue which is to carry down to posterity the resemblance of an individual, should be dressed in the fashion of the times, in the dress which he himself wore: this would certainly be true, if the dress were part of the man: but after a time, the dress is only an amusement for an antiquarian; and if it obstructs the general design of the piece, it is to be disregarded by the artist. Common sense must here give way to a higher sense. In the naked form, and in the disposition of the drapery, the difference between one artist and another is principally seen. But if he is compelled to exhibit the modern dress, the naked form is entirely hid, and the drapery is already disposed by the skill of the tailor. Were a Phidias to obey such absurd commands, he would please no more than an ordinary sculptor; since, in the inferior parts of every art, the learned and the ignorant are nearly upon a level.

These were probably among the reasons that induced the sculptor of that wonderful figure of Laocoon to exhibit him naked, notwithstanding he was surprised in the act of sacrificing to Apollo, and consequently ought to have been shown in his sacerdotal habits, if those greater reasons had not preponderated. Art is not yet in so high estimation with us, as to obtain so great a sacrifice as the ancients made, especially the Grecians; who suffered themselves to be represented naked, whether they were generals, lawgivers, or kings.

Under this head of balancing and choosing the greater reason, or of two evils taking the least, we may consider the conduct of Rubens in the Luxembourg gallery, where he has mixed allegorical figures with the representations of real personages, which must be acknowledged to be a fault; yet, if the artist considered himself as engaged to furnish this gallery with a rich, various, and splendid ornament, this could not be done, at least in an equal degree, without peopling the air and water with these allegorical figures: he therefore accomplished all that he purposed. In this case all lesser considerations, which tend to obstruct the great end of the work, must yield and give way.

The variety which portraits and modern dresses, mixed with allegorical figures, produce, is not to be slightly given up upon a punctilio of reason, when that reason deprives the art in a manner of its very existence. It must always be remembered that the business of a great painter is to produce a great picture; he must therefore take special care not to be cajoled by specious arguments out of his materials.

What has been so often said to the disadvantage of allegorical poetry, that it is tedious, and uninteresting, cannot with the same propriety be applied to painting, where the interest is of a different kind. If allegorical painting produces a greater variety of ideal beauty, a richer, a more various and delightful composition, and gives to the artist a greater opportunity of exhibiting his skill, all the interest he wishes for is accomplished, such a picture not only attracts, but fixes the attention.

If it be objected that Rubens judged ill at first in thinking it necessary to make his work so very ornamental, this puts the question upon new ground. It was his peculiar style; he could paint in no other; and he was selected for that work, probably because it was his style. Nobody will dispute but some of the best of the Roman or Bolognian schools would have produced a more learned and more noble work.

This leads us to another important province of taste, that of weighing the value of the different classes of the art, and of estimating them accordingly.

All arts have means within them of applying themselves with success both to the intellectual and sensitive part of our natures. It cannot be disputed, supposing both these means put in practice with equal abilities, to which we ought to give the preference; to him who represents the heroic arts and more dignified passions of man, or to him who, by the help of meretricious ornaments, however elegant and graceful, captivates the sensuality, as it may be called, of our taste. Thus the Roman and Bolognian schools are reasonably preferred to the Venetian, Flemish, or Dutch schools, as they address themselves to our best and noblest faculties.

Well-turned periods in eloquence, or harmony of numbers in poetry, which are in those arts what coloring is in painting, however highly we may esteem them, can never be considered as of equal importance with the art of unfolding truths that are useful to mankind, and which make us better or wiser. Nor can those works which remind us of the poverty and meanness of our nature, be considered as of equal rank with what excites ideas of grandeur, or raises and dignifies humanity; or, in the words of a late poet, which makes the beholder *learn to venerate himself as a man*.[3]

It is reason and good sense, therefore, which ranks and estimates every art, and every part of that art, according to its importance, from the painter of animated, down to inanimated nature. We will not allow a man, who shall prefer the inferior style, to say it is his taste; taste here has nothing or at least ought to have nothing, to do with the question. He wants not taste, but sense and soundness of judgment.

[3] Dr. Goldsmith

Indeed perfection in an inferior style may be reasonably preferred to mediocrity in the highest walks of art. A landscape of Claude Lorrain may be preferred to a history by Luca Giordano; but hence appears the necessity of the connoisseur's knowing in what consists the excellency of each class, in order to judge how near it approaches to perfection.

Even in works of the same kind, as in history-painting which is composed of various parts, excellence of an inferior species, carried to a very high degree; will make a work very valuable, and in some measure compensate for the absence of the higher kinds of merit. It is the duty of the connoisseur to know and esteem, as much as it may deserve, every part of painting: he will not then think even Bassano unworthy of his notice; who, though totally devoid of expression, sense, grace, or elegance, may be esteemed on account of his admirable taste of colors, which in his best works, are little inferior to those of Titian.

Since I have mentioned Bassano, we must do him likewise the justice to acknowledge, that though he did not aspire to the dignity of expressing the characters and passions of men yet, with respect to facility and truth in his manner of touching animals of all kinds, and giving them what painters call *their character*, few have excelled him.

To Bassano we may add Paul Veronese and Tintoret, for their entire inattention to what is justly thought the most essential part of our art, the expression of the passions. Not withstanding these glaring deficiencies, we justly esteem the works; but it must be remembered that they do not please *from* those defects, but from their great excellencies of another kind, and in spite of such transgressions. These excellencies, too, as far as they go, are founded in the truth of *general* nature; they tell the *truth,* though not *the whole truth.*

By these considerations, which can never be too frequently impressed, may be obviated two errors, which I observed to have been, formerly at least, the most prevalent, and to be most injurious to artists; that of thinking taste and genius to have nothing to do with reason, and that of taking particular living object for nature.

I shall now say something on that part of *taste,* which, as I have hinted to you before, does not belong so much to the external form of things, but is addressed to the mind, and depends on its original frame, or, to use the expression, the organization of the soul; I mean the imagination and the passions. The principles of these are as invariable as the former, and are to be known and reasoned upon in the same manner, by an appeal to common sense deciding upon the common feelings of mankind. This sense, and these feelings appear to me of equal authority, and equally conclusive. Now this appeal implies a general uniformity and agreement in the minds of men. It would be else an idle and vain endeavor to establish rules of art; it would be pursuing a phantom, to attempt to move affections with which we were entirely unacquainted. We have no reason to suspect there is a greater difference between our minds than between our forms; of which, though there are no two alike, yet there is a general similitude that goes through the whole race of mankind; and those who have cultivated their taste, can distinguish what is beautiful or deformed, or, in other words, what agrees with or deviates from the general idea of nature, in one case, well as in the other.

The internal fabric of our minds, as well as the external form of our bodies, being nearly uniform; it seems then to follow of course, that as the imagination is incapable of producing any thing originally of itself, and can only vary and combine those ideas with which it is furnished by means of the senses, there will be necessarily an agreement in the imaginations, as in the senses of men. There being this agreement, it follows, that in all cases, in our lightest amusement as well as in our most serious actions and engagements of life we must regulate our affections of every kind by that of others. The well-disciplined mind acknowledges this authority, and submits its own opinion to the public voice. It is from knowing what are the general feelings and passions of mankind, that we acquire a true idea of what imagination is; though it appears as if we had nothing to do but to consult our own particular sensations, and these were sufficient to ensure us from all error and mistake.

A knowledge of the disposition and character of the human mind can be acquired only by experience: a great deal will be learned, I admit, by a habit of examining what passes in our bosoms, what are our own motives of action, and of what kind of sentiments we are conscious on any occasion. We may suppose an uniformity, and conclude that the same effect will be produced by the same cause in the minds of others. This examination will contribute to suggest to us matters of inquiry; but we can never be sure that our own sentiments are true and right, till they are confirmed by more extensive observation. One man opposing another determines nothing; but a general union of minds, like a general combination of the forces of all mankind, makes a strength that is irresistible. In fact, as he who does not know himself, does not know others, so it may be said with equal truth, that he who does not know others, knows himself but very imperfectly.

A man who thinks he is guarding himself against prejudices by resisting the authority of others, leaves open every avenue to singularity, vanity, self-conceit, obstinacy, and many other vices, all tending to warp the judgment, and prevent the natural operation of his faculties. This submission to others is a deference which we owe, and indeed are forced involuntarily to pay. In fact, we never are satisfied with our opinions, whatever we may pretend, till they are ratified and confirmed by the suffrages of the rest of mankind. We dispute and wrangle for ever; we endeavor to get men to come to us, when we do not go to them.

He therefore who is acquainted with the works which have pleased different ages and different countries, and has formed his opinion on them, has more materials, and more means of knowing what is analogous to the mind of man, than he who is conversant only with the works of his own age or country. What has pleased, and continues to please, is likely to please again: hence are derived the rules of art, and on this immovable foundation they must ever stand.

This search and study of the history of the mind ought not to be confined to one art only. It is by the analogy that one art bears to another, that many things are ascertained, which either were but faintly seen, or, perhaps would not have been discovered at all, if the inventor had not received the first hints from the practices of a sister art on a similar occasion.[4] The frequent allusions which every man who treats of any art is obliged to make to others, in order to illustrate and confirm his principles, sufficiently show their near connection and inseparable relation.

All arts having the same general end, which is to please; and addressing themselves to the same faculties through the medium of the senses; it follows that their rules and principles must have a great affinity, as the different materials and the different organs or vehicles by which they pass to the mind, will permit them to retain.[5]

We may therefore conclude, that the real substance, as it may be called, of what goes under the name of taste, is fixed and established in the nature of things; that there are certain and regular causes by which the imagination and passions of men are affected; and that the knowledge of these causes is acquired by a laborious and diligent investigation of nature, and by the same slow progress as wisdom or knowledge of every kind, however instantaneous its operations may appear when thus acquired.

It has been often observed, that the good and virtuous man alone can acquire this true or just relish even of works of art. This opinion will not appear entirely without foundation, when we consider that the same habit of mind, which is acquired by our search after truth in the more serious duties of life, is only transferred to the pursuit of lighter amusements. The same disposition, the same desire to find something steady, substantial, and durable, on which the mind can lean as it were, and rest with safety, actuates us in both cases. The subject only is changed. We pursue the same method in our search after the idea of beauty and perfection of each; of virtue, by looking forwards beyond ourselves to society, and to the whole; of arts, by extending our views in the same manner to all ages and all times.

Every art, like our own, has in its composition fluctuating as well as fixed principles. It is an attentive inquiry into their difference that will enable us to determine how far we are influenced by custom and habit, and what is fixed in the nature of things.

To distinguish how much has solid foundation, we may have recourse to the same proof by which some hold that wit ought to be tried; whether it preserves itself when translated. That wit is false, which can subsist only in one language and that picture which pleases only one age or one nation, owes its reception to some local or accidental association of ideas.

We may apply this to every custom and habit of life. Thus the general principles of urbanity, politeness, or civility, have been the same in all nations; but the mode in which they are dressed, is continually varying. The general idea of showing respect is by making yourself less; but the manner, whether by bowing the body, kneeling,

[4] Nulla ars, non alterius artis, aut mater, aut propinqua est. Tertull. as cited by Junius.

[5] Omnes artes quae ad humanitatem pertinent, habent quoddam commune vinculum, et quasi cognatione inter se continentur. Cicero.

prostration, pulling off the upper part of our dress, or taking away the lower,[6] is a matter of custom.

Thus, in regard to ornaments,—it would be unjust to conclude that because they were at first arbitrarily contrived, they are therefore undeserving of our attention: on the contrary, he who neglects the cultivation of those ornaments, acts contrary to nature and reason. As life would be imperfect without its highest ornaments, the Arts, so these arts themselves would be imperfect without *their* ornaments. Though we by no means ought to rank these with positive and substantial beauties, yet it must be allowed, that knowledge of both is essentially requisite towards forming a complete, whole, and perfect taste. It is in reality from the ornaments, that arts receive their peculiar character and complexion; we may add, that in them we find the characteristical mark of a national taste; as by throwing up a feather in the air, we know which way the wind blows, better than by a more heavy matter.

The striking distinction between the works of the Roman, Bolognian, and Venetian schools, consists more in that general effect which is produced by colors, than in the more profound excellencies of the art; at least it is from thence that each is distinguished and known at first sight Thus it is the ornaments, rather than the proportions of architecture, which at the first glance distinguish the different orders from each other; the Doric is known by its triglyphs, the Ionic by its volutes, and the Corinthian by its acanthus.

What distinguishes oratory from a cold narration, is a more liberal, though chaste, use of those ornaments which go under the name of figurative and metaphorical expressions; and poetry distinguishes itself from oratory, by words and expressions still more ardent and glowing. What separates and distinguishes poetry, is more particularly the ornament of *verse:* it is this which gives it its character, and is an essential without which it cannot exist. Custom has appropriated different meter to different kinds of composition, in which the world is not perfectly agreed. In England the dispute is not yet settled, which is to be preferred, rhyme or blank verse. But however we disagree about what these metrical ornaments shall be, that some meter is essentially necessary, is universally acknowledged.

In poetry or eloquence, to determine how far figurative or metaphorical language may proceed, and when it begins to be affectation or beside the truth, must be determined by taste; though this taste, we must never forget, is regulated and formed by presiding feeling of mankind,—by those works which have approved themselves to all times and all persons. Thus, though eloquence has undoubtedly an essential and intrinsic excellence, and immovable principles common to all languages, founded in the nature of our passions and affections; yet it has its ornaments and modes of addresses, which are merely arbitrary. What is approved in the eastern nations as grand and majestic, would be considered by the Greeks and Romans as turgid and inflated; and they, in return, would be thought by the Orientals to express themselves in a cold and insipid manner.

[6] Put off thy shoes from off thy feet, for the place whereon thou standest is holy ground. Exodus, iii.5.

We may add likewise to the credit of ornaments, that it is by their means that Art itself accomplishes its purpose. Fresnoy calls coloring, which is one of the chief ornaments of painting, *lena sororis,* that which procures lovers and admirers to the more valuable excellencies of the art.

It appears to be the same right turn of mind which enables a man to acquire the *truth,* or the just idea of what is right, in the ornaments, as in the more stable principles of art. It has still the same center of perfection, though it is the center of a smaller circle.

To illustrate this by the fashion of dress, in which there is allowed to be a good or bad taste. The component parts of dress are continually changing from great to little, from short to long; but the general form still remains; it is still the same general dress, which is comparatively fixed, though on a very slender foundation; but it is on this which fashion must rest. He who invents with the most success, or dresses in the best taste, would probably, from the same sagacity employed to greater purposes, have discovered equal skill, or have formed the same correct taste, in the highest labors of art.

I have mentioned taste in dress, which is certainly one of the lowest subjects to which this word is applied; yet, as I have before observed, there is a right even here, however narrow its foundation, respecting the fashion of any nation. But we have still more slender means of determining to which of the different customs of different ages, or countries we ought to give the preference, since they seem to be all equally removed from nature. If an European when he has cut off his beard, and put false hair on his head, or bound up his own natural hair in regular hard knots, as unlike nature as he can possibly make it; and after having rendered them as immovable by the help of the fat of hogs, has covered the whole with flour, laid on by a machine, with the utmost regularity; if, when thus attired, he issues forth, and meets a Cherokee Indian, who has bestowed as much time at his toilet, and laid on with equal care yellow and red ocher on particular parts of his forehead or cheeks, as he judges most becoming; whoever of these two despises the other for this attention to the fashion of his country, which ever first feels himself provoked to laugh, is the barbarian.

All these fashions are very innocent; neither worth disquisition, nor any endeavor to alter them; as the charge would, in all probability, be equally distant from nature. The only circumstance against which indignation may reasonably be moved, is, where the operation is painful or destructive of health; such as some of the practices at Otaheite and the straight lacing of the English ladies; of the last of which practices, how destructive it must be to health and long life, the professor of anatomy took an opportunity of proving a few days since in this Academy.

It is in dress as in things of greater consequence. Fashions originate from those only who have the high and powerful advantages of rank, birth, and fortune. Many of the ornaments of art, those at least for which no reason can be given, are transmitted to us, are adopted, and acquire their consequence from the company in which we have been used to see them. As Greece and Rome are the fountains from whence have flowed all kinds of excellence, to that veneration which they have a right to claim for the pleasure and knowledge which they have afforded us, we voluntarily add our approbation of every ornament and every custom that belonged to them, even to the fashion of their dress. For it may be observed that, not satisfied with them in their own place, we make no difficulty of dressing statues of modern heroes or senators in the fashion of the Roman armor or peaceful robe; we go so far as hardly to bear a statue in any other drapery.

The figures of the great men of those nations have come down to us in sculpture. In sculpture remain almost all the excellent specimens of ancient art. We have so far associated personal dignity to the persons thus represented, and the truth of art to their manner of representation, that it is not in our power any longer to separate them. This is not so in painting; because having no excellent ancient portraits, that connection was never formed. Indeed we could no more venture to paint a general officer in a Roman military habit, than we could make a statue in the present uniform. But since we have no ancient portraits,—to show how ready we are to adopt those kind of prejudices, we make the best authority among the moderns serve the same purpose. The great variety of excellent portraits with which Van Dyck has enriched this nation, we are not content to admire for their real excellence, but extend our approbation even to the dress, which happened to be the fashion of that age. We all very well remember how common it was a few years ago for portraits to be drawn in this fantastic dress; and this custom is not yet entirely laid aside. By this means it must be acknowledged very ordinary pictures acquired something of the air and effect of the works of Van Dyck, and appeared therefore at first sight to be better pictures than they really were; they appeared so, however, to those only who had the means of making this association; and when made, it was irresistible. But this association is nature and refers to that secondary truth that comes from conformity to general prejudice and opinion; it is therefore not merely fantastical. Besides the prejudice which we have in favor of ancient dresses, there may be likewise other reasons for the effect which they produce; among which we may justly rank the simplicity of them, consisting of little more than one single piece of drapery, without those whimsical capricious forms by which all other dresses are embarrassed.

Thus, though it is from the prejudice we have in favor the ancients, who have taught us architecture, that we have adopted likewise their ornaments; and though we are satisfied that neither nature nor reason are the foundation of those beauties which we imagine we see in that art, yet if any one, persuaded of this truth, should therefore invent new orders of equal beauty, which we will suppose to be possible, they would not please; nor ought he to complain, since the old has that great advantage of having custom and prejudice on its side. In this case we leave what has every prejudice in its favor, to take that which will have no advantage over what we have left, but novelty: which soon destroys itself, and at any rate is but a weak antagonist against custom.

Ancient ornaments, having the right of possession, ought not to be removed, unless to make room for that which not only has higher pretensions, but such pretensions as will balance the evil and confusion which innovation always brings with it.

To this we may add, that even the durability of the materials will often contribute to give a superiority to one object over another. Ornaments in buildings, with which taste is principally concerned, are composed of materials which last longer than those of which dress is composed; the former therefore make higher pretensions to our favor and prejudice.

Some attention is surely due to what we can no more get rid of, than we can go out of ourselves. We are creatures of prejudice; we neither can nor ought to eradicate it; we must only regulate it by reason; which kind of regulation is indeed little more than obliging the lesser, the local and temporary prejudices, to give way to those which are more durable and lasting.

He, therefore, who in his practice of portrait-painting, wishes to dignify his subject, which we will suppose to be a lady, will not paint her in the modern dress, the familiarity of which alone is sufficient to destroy all dignity. He takes care that his work shall correspond to those ideas and that imagination which he knows will regulate the judgment of others; and therefore dresses his figure something with the general air of the antique for the sake of dignity, and preserves something of the modern for the sake of likeness. By this conduct his works correspond with those prejudices which we have in favor of what we continually see; and the relish of the antique simplicity corresponds with what we may call the more learned and scientific prejudice.

There was a statue made not long since of Voltaire, which the sculptor, not having that respect for the prejudices of mankind which he ought to have had, made entirely naked, and as meager and emaciated as the original is said to be. The consequence was what might have been expected: it remained in the sculptor's shop, though it was intended as a public ornament and a public honor to Voltaire, for it was procured at the expense of his contemporary wits and admirers.

Whoever would reform a nation, supposing a bad taste to prevail in it, will not accomplish his purpose by going directly against the stream of their prejudices. Men's minds must be prepared to receive what is new to them. Reformation is a work of time. A national taste, however wrong it may be, cannot be totally changed at once; we must yield a little to the prepossession which has taken hold on the mind, and we may then bring people to adopt what would offend them, if endeavored to be introduced by violence. When Battista Franco was employed, in conjunction with Titian, Paul Veronese and Tintoret, to adorn the library of St Mark, his work, Vasari says, gave less satisfaction than any of the others: the dry manner of the Roman school was very ill calculated to please eyes that had been accustomed to the luxuriancy, splendor, and richness of Venetian coloring. Had the Romans been the judges of this work, probably the determination would have been just contrary; for in the more noble parts of the art Battista Franco was perhaps not inferior to any of his rivals.

GENTLEMEN,

It has been the main scope and principal end of this discourse to demonstrate the reality of a standard in taste; as well as in corporeal beauty; that a false or depraved taste is a thing as well known, as easily discovered, as any thing that is deformed, misshapen, or wrong, in our form or outward make; and that this knowledge is derived from the uniformity or sentiments among mankind, from whence proceeds the knowledge of what are the general habits of nature; the result of which is an idea of perfect beauty.

If what has been advanced be true,—that beside this beauty or truth, which is formed on the uniform, eternal, and immutable laws of nature, and which of necessity can be but *one*; that beside this one immutable verity there are likewise what we have called apparent or secondary truths, proceeding from local and temporary prejudices, fancies, fashions or accidental connection of ideas; if it appears that these last have still the foundation, however slender, in the original fabric of our minds; it follows that all these truths or beauties deserve and require the attention of the artist, in proportion to their stability or duration, or as their influence is more or less extensive. And let me add, that as they ought not to pass their just bounds, so neither do they, in a well-regulated taste, at all prevent or weaken the influence of those general principles, which alone can give to art its true and permanent dignity.

To form this just taste is undoubtedly in your own power, but it is to reason and philosophy that you must have recourse; from them you must borrow the balance, by which is to be weighed and estimated the value of every pretension that intrudes itself on your notice.

The general objection which is made to the introduction of philosophy into the regions of taste, is, that it checks and restrains the flights of the imagination and gives that timidity which an over-carefulness not to err or act contrary to reason is likely to produce. It is not so. Fear is neither reason nor philosophy. The true spirit of philosophy, by giving knowledge, gives a manly confidence, and substitutes rational firmness in the place of vain presumption. A man of real taste is always a man of judgment in other respects; and those inventions which either disdain or shrink from reason, are generally, I fear, more like the dreams of a distempered brain, than the exalted enthusiasm of a sound and true genius. In the midst of the highest flights of fancy or imagination, reason ought to preside from first to last, though I admit her more powerful operation is upon reflection.

Let me add, that some of the greatest names of antiquity and those who have most distinguished themselves in works of genius and imagination, were equally eminent for their critical skill. Plato, Aristotle, Cicero, and Horace; and among the moderns, Boileau, Corneille, Pope, and Dryden, are at least instances of genius not being destroyed by attention or subjection to rules and science. I should hope therefore that the natural consequence of what has been said, would be, to excite in you a desire of knowing the principles and conduct of the great masters, of our art, and respect and veneration for them when known.

CHAPTER 17

James Beattie*

Essays on Poetry and Music, as They Affect the Mind 1762

Part I.
Poetry Considered with Respect to its Matter or Subject

When we affirm, that every art or contrivance which has a meaning must have an end, we only repeat an identical proposition: and when we say, that the essential or indispensable rules of an art are those that direct to the accomplishment of the end proposed by the artist, we repeat a definition whereof it would be captious to controvert the propriety. And therefore, before we can determine any thing in regard to the essential rules of this art, we must form an idea of its end or destination.

CHAPTER I.
Of the end of Poetical Composition.

That one end of Poetry, in its first institution, and in every period of its progress, must have been, to give pleasure, will hardly admit of any doubt. If men first employed it to express their adoration of superior and invisible beings, their gratitude to the benefactors of mankind, their admiration of moral, intellectual, or

*James Beattie (1735-1802) was the son of shopkeeper. He attended Marischal College, in Aberdeen where he studied philosophy under Alexander Gerard and classics. He was first a country schoolmaster, then usher at an Aberdeen school, and finally was installed as professor of moral philosophy and logic in Marischal College in 1760. He was also active in the Aberdeen Club with Gerard and Thomas Reid until the latter's departure for Glasgow. Beattie felt called upon to defend philosophy against what he saw as the attack of Hume, and his writings in defense of religion were popular. He remained interested in poetry and published poems as well as his critical essays. He declined positions in Edinburgh and in England to remain in Aberdeen where he died.

corporeal excellence, or, in general, their love of what was agreeable in their own species, or in other parts of Nature; they must be supposed to have endeavored to make their poetry pleasing; because, otherwise, it would have been unsuitable to the occasion that gave it birth, and to the sentiments it was intended to enliven. Or if, with Horace, we were to believe, that it was first used as a vehicle to convey into savage minds the principles of government and civility;[1] still we must allow, that one chief thing attended to in its composition must have been, to give it charms sufficient to engage the ear and captivate the heart of an unthinking audience. In latter times, the true poet, though in choosing materials he never lost sight of utility, yet in giving them form, (and it is the form chiefly that distinguishes poetry from other writings), has always made the entertainment of mankind his principal concern. Indeed, we cannot conceive, that, independently on this consideration, men would ever have applied themselves to arts so little necessary to life, and withal so difficult, as music, painting, and poetry. Certain it is, that a poem, containing the most important truths, would meet with a cold reception, if destitute of those graces of sound, invention, and language, whereof the sole end and aim is, to give pleasure.

But is it not the end of this art, to instruct, as well as to please? Verses, that give pleasure only, without profit,—what are they but chiming trifles? And if a poem were to please, and at the same time, instead of improving, to corrupt the mind, would it not deserve to be considered as a poison rendered doubly dangerous and detestable by its alluring qualities?—All this is true: and yet pleasure is undoubtedly the immediate aim of all those artifices by which poetry is distinguished from other compositions,—of the harmony, the rhythm, the ornamented language, the compact and diversified fable: for I believe it will be allowed, that a plain treatise, destitute of all these beauties, might be made to convey more instruction than any poem in the world. As writing is more excellent than painting, and speech than music, on account of its superior usefulness; so a discourse, containing profitable information even in a rude style, may be more excellent, because more useful, than any thing in Homer or Virgil: but such a discourse partakes no more of the nature of poetry, than language does of melody, or a manuscript of a picture; whereas an agreeable piece of writing may be poetical, though it yield little or no instruction. To instruct, is an end common to all good writing, to all poetry, all history, all sound philosophy. But of these last the principal end is to instruct; and if this single end be accomplished, the philosopher and the historian will be allowed to have acquitted themselves well: but the poet must do a great deal for the sake of pleasure only; and if he fail to please, he may indeed deserve praise on other accounts, but as a poet he has done nothing—But do not historians and philosophers, as well as poets, make it their study to please their readers? They generally do: but the former please, that they may instruct; the latter instruct, that they may the more effectually please. Pleasing,

[1] The honor of civilizing mankind, is by the poets ascribed to poetry, (*Hor. Ar. Poet. vers.* 391.); —by the orator, to oratory, (*Cicero, de Orat. lib. I.* § 33.); —and by others to philosophy, (*Cicero, de Orat. lib. I.* § 36-37.; and *Tusc. Quest. lib.* 5. § 5.)—It is probably a gradual thing, the effect of many co-operating causes; and proceeding rather from favorable accidents, or the special appointment of Heaven, than from the art and contrivance of men.

though uninstructive, poetry may gratify a light mind; and what tends even to corrupt the heart may gratify profligates: but the true poet addresses his work, not to the giddy, nor to the worthless, nor to any party, but to mankind; and, if he means to please the general taste, must often employ instruction as one of the arts that minister to this kind of pleasure.

The necessity of this arises from a circumstance in human nature, which is to man (as Erasmus in Pope's opinion was to the priesthood) "at once his glory and his shame"; namely, that the human mind, unless when debased by passion or prejudice, never fails to take the side of truth and virtue:—a sad reflection, when it leads us to consider the debasing influence of passion and prejudice; but a most comfortable one, when it directs our view to the original dignity and rectitude of the human soul. To favor virtue, and speak truth, and take pleasure in those who do so, is natural to man; to act otherwise, requires an effort, does violence to nature, and always implies some evil purpose in the agent. The first, like progressive motion, is easy and graceful; the last is unseemly and difficult, like walking side-ways, or backwards. The one is so common, that it is little attended to, and when it becomes the object of attention, is always considered as an energy suitable to moral and rational nature: the other has a strangeness in it, that provokes at once our surprise and disapprobation. And hence the virtuous character of the ancient chorus[2] was reconcilable, not only to probability, but to real matter of fact.—The dramatic poets of Greece rightly judged, that great persons, like those who appear in tragedy, engaged in any great action, are never without attendants or spectators, or those at least who observe their conduct, and make remarks upon it. And therefore, together with the persons principally concerned, they always introduced attendants or spectators on the stage, who, by the mouth of one of their number, joined occasionally in the dialogue, and were called the Chorus. That this artifice, though perhaps it might not suit the modern drama, had a happy effect in beautifying the poetry, illustrating the morality, and heightening the probability, of the ancient, is a point, which in my opinion admits of sufficient proof, and has in fact been fully proved by Mr. Mason, in his *Letters*, and admirably exemplified in his *Elfrida* and *Caractacus*; two poems that do honor to the English tongue, and to modern genius. But I do not now enter into any controversy on the subject: I speak of it with a view only to observe, that the propriety of the character assigned to the chorus is founded on that moral propensity above

[2] Aetoris partes chorus, officiumque virile
Defendat——————
Ille bonis faveatque, et consilietur amice,
Et regat iratos, et amet pacare tumentes;
Ille dapes laudet mensae brevis; ille salubrem
Justitiam, legesque, et apertis otia portis;
Ille tegat commissa, Deosque precetur et oret,
Ut redeat miseris; abeat fortuna superbis. *Hor. Ar. Poet. vers.* 195.

"Let the chorus, like the player, support a character, and let it act a manly part. Let it favor the good, and give friendly counsel, and restrain the angry, and love to compose the swellings of passion. Let it celebrate the praises of temperance, of salutary justice, of law, and of peace, with open gates: let it be faithful to its truth, and supplicate the Gods, and pray, that fortune may return to the afflicted, and forsake the haughty."

mentioned. For to introduce a company of unprejudiced persons, even of the vulgar, witnessing a great event, and yet not pitying the unfortunate, nor exclaiming against tyranny and injustice, nor rejoicing when the good are successful, nor wishing well to the worthy, would be to feign what seldom or never happens in real life; and what, therefore, in the improved state of things that poetry imitates, must never be supposed to happen.—Sentiments that betray a hard heart, a depraved understanding, unwarrantable pride, or any other moral or intellectual perversity, never fail to give offense, except where they appear to be introduced as examples for our improvement. Poetry, therefore, that is uninstructive, or immoral, cannot please those who retain any moral sensibility, or uprightness of judgment; and must consequently displease the greater part of any regular society of rational creatures. Great wickedness and great genius may have been united in the same person; but it may be doubted, whether corruption of heart and delicacy of taste be at all compatible.

Whenever a writer forgets himself so far, as to give us ground to suspect him even of momentary impiety or hard heartedness, we charge him in the same breath with want of conscience and want of taste; the former being generally, as well as justly, supposed to comprehend the latter.

. . . . . .

So true it is, that the bard who would captivate the heart must sing in unison to the voice of conscience!—and that instruction (taking the word in no unwarrantable latitude) is one of the means that must be employed to render poetry agreeable.

For by instruction I do not here understand merely the communication of moral and physical truth. Whatever tends to raise those human affections that are favorable to truth and virtue, or to repress the opposite passions, will always gratify and improve our moral and intellectual powers, and may properly enough be called *instructive.* All poetry, therefore, is entitled to this epithet, not only which imparts knowledge we had not before; but also which awakens our piety for the sufferings of our fellow-creatures; promotes a taste for the beauties of nature animated or inanimate; makes vice appear the object of indignation or ridicule; inculcates a sense of our dependence upon Heaven; fortifies our minds against the evils of life; or promotes the love of virtue and wisdom, either by delineating their native charms, or by setting before us in suitable colors the dreadful consequences of imprudent and immoral conduct. There are few good poems of length, that will not be found in one or more or perhaps in several of these respects, to promote the instruction of a reader of taste.

. . . . . .

But may not agreeable affections arise in the mind, which partake neither of vice nor of virtue; such as joy, and hope, and those emotions that accompany the contemplation of external beauty, or magnificence? And, if pastorals and songs, and Anacreontic odes, awaken these agreeable affections, may not such poems be pleasing, without being instructive? This may be, no doubt. And for this reason, among others, I take instruction to be only a secondary end of poetry. But it is only by short poems, as songs and pastorals, that these agreeable affections indifferent alike to vice and virtue, are excited, without any mixture of others. For moral sentiments are so prevalent in the human mind, that no affection can long subsist there, without intermingling with them, and being assimilated to their nature. Nor can a piece of real and pleasing poetry be extended to any great length, without operating, directly or indirectly, either on those affections that are friendly to virtue, or on those sympathies that quicken our moral sensibility, and prepare us for virtuous impressions. In fact, man's true happiness is derived from the moral part of his constitution; and therefore we cannot suppose, that any thing which affects not his moral part, should be lastingly and generally agreeable. We sympathize with the pleasure one takes in a feast, where there is friendship, and an interchange of good offices; but not with the satisfaction an epicure finds in devouring a solitary banquet. A short Anacreontic we may relish for its melody and sparkling images; but a long poem, in order to be pleasing, must not only charm the ear and the fancy, but also touch the heart and exercise the conscience.

Still perhaps it may be objected to these reasonings, that Horace, in a well-known verse,[3] declares the end of poetry to be twofold, to please, or to instruct; whereas we maintain, that the ultimate end of this art is to please; instruction being only one of the means (and not always a necessary one) by which that ultimate end is to be accomplished. This interpretation of Horace has indeed been admitted by some modern critics: but it is erroneous; for the passage, rightly understood, will not appear to contain anything inconsistent with the present doctrine. The author is there stating a comparison between the Greek and Roman writers, with a view to the poetry of the stage; and, after commending the former for their correctness, and for the liberal spirit wherewith they conducted their literary labors, and blaming his countrymen for their inaccuracy and avarice, he proceeds thus: "The ends proposed by our dramatic poets (or by poets in general) are, to please, to instruct, or to do both. When instruction is your aim, let your moral sentences be expressed with brevity, that they may be readily understood, and long remembered: where you mean to please, let your fictions be conformable to truth, or probability. The elder part of your audience (or readers) have no relish for poems that give pleasure only without instruction; nor the younger for such writings as give instruction without pleasure. He only can secure the universal suffrage in his favor, who blends the useful with the agreeable, and delights at the same time that he instructs the reader. Such are the works that bring money to the bookseller, that pass into foreign countries and perpetuate the author's name through a long succession of ages."[4]—Now, what is the meaning of all this? What, but that to the perfection of dramatic poetry (or, if you please, of poetry in general) both sound morals and beautiful fiction are requisite. But Horace never meant to say, that instruction, as well as pleasure, is necessary to give to any composition the poetical character: or he would not in another place have

[3] Aut prodesse volunt, aut delectare poetae.

[4] Hor. Ar. Poet. 333.—347.

celebrated, with so much affection and rapture, the melting strains of Sappho, and the playful genius of Anacreon;[5]—two authors transcendently sweet, but not remarkably instructive. We are sure, that pathos, and harmony, and elevated language, were, in Horace's opinion, essential to poetry;[6] and of these decorations no body will affirm, that instruction is the end, who considers that the most instructive books in the world are written in plain prose.

Let this therefore be established as a truth in criticism, That the end of poetry is, to please. Verses, if pleasing, may be poetical, though they convey little or no instruction; but verses, whose sole merit is, that they convey instruction, are not poetical. Instruction, however, especially in poems of length, is necessary to their perfection, because they would not be perfectly agreeable without it.

CHAP. II.
Of the Standard of Poetical Invention.

Homer's beautiful description of the heavens and earth, as they appear in a calm evening by the light of the moon and stars, concludes with this circumstance, "And the heart of the shepherd is glad."[7] Madame Dacier, from the turn she gives to the passage in her version, seems to think, and Pope, in order perhaps to make out his couplet, insinuates, that the gladness of the shepherd is owing to his sense of the utility of those luminaries. And this may in part be the case: but this is not in Homer; nor is it a necessary consideration. It is true, that, in contemplating the material universe, they who discern the causes and effects of things must be more rapturously entertained, than those who perceive nothing but shape and size, color and motion. Yet, in the mere outside of Nature's works, (if I may so express myself), there is a splendor and a magnificence to which even untutored minds cannot attend, without great delight.

Not that all peasants, or all philosophers, are equally susceptible of these charming impressions. It is strange to observe the callousness of some men, before whom all the glories of heaven and earth pass in daily succession, without touching their hearts, elevating their fancy, or leaving any durable remembrance. Even of those who pretend to sensibility, how many are there to whom the luster of the rising or setting sun; the sparkling concave of the midnight-sky; the mountain-forest tossing and roaring to the storm, or warbling with all the melodies of a summer evening; the sweet interchange of hill and dale, shade and sunshine, grove, lawn, and water, which an extensive landscape offers to the view; the scenery of the ocean, so lovely, so majestic, and so tremendous, and the many pleasing varieties of the animal and vegetable kingdom, could never afford so much real satisfaction, as the steams and noise of a ball-room, the insipid fiddling and squeaking of an opera, or the vexations and wranglings of a card-table!

[5] Hor. Carm. lib. 4. ode 9.

[6] Hor. Sat. lib. I. fat. 4. vers. 40.

[7] *Iliad*, b. δ. vers. 555.

But some minds there are of a different make; who, even in the early part of life, receive from the contemplation of Nature a species of delight which they would hardly exchange for any other; and who, as avarice and ambition are not the infirmities of that period, would, with equal sincerity and rapture, exclaim,

I care not, Fortune, what you me deny;
You cannot rob me of free Nature's grace;
You cannot shut the windows of the sky,
Through which Aurora shows her brightening face;
You cannot bar my constant feet to trace
The woods and lawns by living stream at eve[8] .—

Such minds have always in them the seeds of true taste, and frequently of imitative genius. At least, though their enthusiastic or visionary turn of mind (as the man of the world would call it) should not always incline them to practice poetry or painting, we need not scruple to affirm, that without some portion of this enthusiasm, no person ever became a true poet or painter. For he would imitate the works of Nature, must first accurately observe them; and accurate observation is to be expected from those only who take great pleasure in it.

To a mind thus disposed no part of creation is indifferent. In the crowded city, and howling wilderness; in the cultivated province, and solitary isle; in the flowery lawn, and craggy mountain; in the murmur of the rivulet, and in the uproar of the ocean; in the radiance of summer, and gloom of winter; in the thunder of heaven, and in the whisper of the breeze; he still finds something to rouse or to soothe his imagination, to draw forth his affections, or to employ his understanding. And from every mental energy that is not attended with pain, and even from some of those that are, as moderate terror and pity, a sound mind derives satisfaction; exercise being equally necessary to the body and the soul, and to both equally productive of health and pleasure.

This happy sensibility to the beauties of Nature should be cherished in young persons. It engages them to contemplate the Creator in his wonderful works; it purifies and harmonizes the soul, and prepares it for moral and intellectual discipline; it supplies an endless source of amusement; it contributes even to bodily health; and, as a strict analogy subsists between material and moral beauty, it leads the heart by an easy transition from the one to the other; and thus recommends virtue for its transcendent loveliness, and makes vice appear the object of contempt and abomination. An intimate acquaintance with the best descriptive poets, Spenser, Milton, and Thomson, but above all with the divine Georgic, joined to some practice in the art of drawing, will promote this amiable sensibility in early years; for then the face of Nature has novelty superadded to its other charms, the passions are not pre-engaged, the heart is free from care, and the imagination warm and romantic.

[8] Castle of Indolence.

But, not to insist longer on those ardent emotions that are peculiar to the enthusiastic disciple of Nature, may it not be affirmed of all men, without exception, or at least of all the enlightened part of mankind, that they are gratified by the contemplation of things natural, as opposed to unnatural? Monstrous sights please but for a moment, if they please at all; for they derive their charm from the beholder's amazement, which is quickly over. I have read indeed of a man of rank in Sicily,[9] who chooses to adorn his villa with pictures and statues of most unnatural deformity; but it is a singular instance: and one would not be much more surprised to hear of a person living without food, or growing fat by the use of poison. To say of any thing, that it is contrary to nature, denotes censure and disgust on the part of the speaker; as the epithet *natural* intimates an agreeable quality, and seems for the most part to imply, that a thing is as it ought to be, suitable to our own taste, and congenial with our own constitution. Think, with what sentiments we should peruse a poem, in which Nature was totally misrepresented, and principles of thought and of operation supposed to take place, repugnant to every thing we had seen or heard of:—in which, for example, avarice and coldness were ascribed to youth, and prodigality and passionate attachment to the old; in which men were made to act at random, sometimes according to character, and sometimes contrary to it; in which cruelty and envy were productive of love, and beneficence and kind affection of hatred; in which beauty was invariably the object of dislike, and ugliness of desire; in which society was rendered happy by atheism, and the promiscuous perpetration of crimes, and justice and fortitude were held in universal contempt. Or think, how we should relish a painting, where no regard was had to the proportions, colors, or any of the physical laws, of Nature:—where the ears and eyes of animals were placed in their shoulders; where the sky was green, and the grass crimson; where trees grew with their branches in the earth, and their roots in the air; where men were seen fighting after their heads were cut off, ships sailing on the land, lions entangled in cobwebs, sheep preying on dead carcasses, fishes sporting in the woods, and elephants walking on the sea. Could such figures and combinations give pleasure, or merit the appellation of sublime or beautiful? Should we hesitate to pronounce their author mad? And are the absurdities of madmen proper subjects either of amusement or of imitation to reasonable beings?

Let it be remarked too, that though we distinguish our internal powers by different names, because otherwise we could not speak of them so as to be understood, they are all but so many energies of the same individual mind; and therefore it is not to be supposed, that what contradicts any one leading faculty should yield permanent delight to the rest. That cannot be agreeable to reason, which conscience disapproves; nor can that gratify imagination, which is repugnant to reason.—Besides, belief and acquiescence of mind are pleasant, as distrust and disbelief are painful; and therefore, that only can give solid and general satisfaction, which has something of plausibility in it; something which we conceive it possible for a

[9] See Mr. Brydone's Tour in Sicily, letter 24.

rational being to believe. But no rational being can acquiesce in what is obviously contrary to nature, or implies palpable absurdity.

Poetry, therefore, and indeed every art whose end is to please, must be natural; and if so, must exhibit real matter of fact, or something like it; that is, in other words, must be, either according to truth, or according to verisimilitude.

And though every part of the material universe abounds in objects of pleasurable contemplation, yet nothing in nature so powerfully touches our hearts, or gives so great variety of exercise to our moral and intellectual faculties, as man. Human affairs and human feelings are universally interesting. There are many who have no great relish for the poetry that delineates only irrational or inanimate beings; but to that which exhibits the fortunes, the characters, and the conduct of men, there is hardly any person who does not listen with sympathy and delight. And hence, to imitate human action, is considered by Aristotle as essential to this art; and must be allowed to be essential to the most pleasing and most instructive part of it, I mean to epic and dramatic composition. Mere descriptions, however beautiful, and moral reflections, however just, become tiresome, where our passions are not occasionally awakened by some event that concerns our fellow-men. Do not all readers of taste receive peculiar pleasure from those little tales or episodes, with which Thomson's descriptive poem on the Seasons is here and there enlivened? and are they not sensible, that the thunder-storm would not have been half so interesting without the tale of the two lovers,[10] nor the harvest-scene, without that of Palemon and Lavinia;[11] nor the driving snows, without that exquisite picture of a man perishing among them?[12] It is much to be regretted, that Young did not employ the same artifice to animate his *Night-Thoughts*. Sentiments and descriptions may be regarded as the pilasters, carvings, gildings, and other decorations of the poetical fabric; but human actions are the columns and the rafters, that give it stability and elevation. Or, changing the metaphor, we may consider these as the soul which informs the lovely frame; while those are little more than the ornaments of the body.

Whether the pleasure we take in things natural, and our dislike to what is the reverse, be the effect of habit or of constitution, is not a material inquiry. There is nothing absurd in supposing, that between the soul, in its first formation, and the rest of nature, a mutual harmony and sympathy may have been established, which experience may indeed confirm, but no perverse habits could entirely subdue. As no sort of education could make man believe the contrary of a self-evident axiom, or reconcile him to a life of perfect solitude; so I should imagine, that our love of nature and regularity might still remain with us in some degree, though we had been born and bred in the Sicilian villa above mentioned, and never heard any thing applauded but what deserved censure, nor censured but what merited applause. Yet habit must be allowed to have a powerful influence over the sentiments and feelings of

[10]Summer, vers. 1171.

[11]Autumn, vers. 177.

[12]Winter, vers. 276.

mankind. Objects to which we have been long accustomed, we are apt to contract a fondness for; we conceive them readily, and contemplate them with pleasure; nor do we quit our old tracts of speculation or practice, without reluctance and pain. Hence in part arises our attachment to our own professions, our old acquaintance, our native soil, our homes, and to the very hills, streams, and rocks in our neighborhood. It would therefore be strange, if man, accustomed as he is from his earliest days to the regularity of nature, did not contract a liking to her productions, and principles of operation.

Yet we neither expect nor desire, that every human invention, where the end is only to please, should be an exact transcript of real existence. It is enough, that the mind acquiesce in it as probable, or plausible, or such as we think might happen without any direct opposition to the laws of Nature:—or, to speak more accurately, it is enough, that it be consistent, either, first, with general experience; or, secondly, with popular opinion; or, thirdly, that it be consistent with itself, and connected with probable circumstances.

First: If a human invention be consistent with general experience, we acquiesce in it as sufficiently probable. Particular experiences, however, there may be, so uncommon and so little expected, that we should not admit their probability, if we did not know them to be true. No man of sense believes, that he has any likelihood of being enriched by the discovery of hidden treasure; or thinks it probable, on purchasing a lottery-ticket, that he shall gain the first prize; and yet great wealth has actually been acquired by such good fortune. But we should look upon these as poor expedients in a play or romance for bringing about a happy catastrophe. We expect that fiction should be more consonant to the general tenor of human affairs; in a word, that not possibility, but probability, should be the standard of poetical invention.

Secondly: Fiction is admitted as conformable to this standard, when it accords with received opinions. These may be erroneous, but are not often apparently repugnant to nature. On this account, and because they are familiar to us from our infancy, the mind readily acquiesces in them, or at least yields them that degree of credit which is necessary to render them pleasing. Hence the fairies, ghosts, and witches of Shakespeare, are admitted as probable beings; and angels obtain a place in religious pictures, though we know that they do not now appear in the scenery of real life. Even when a popular opinion has long been exploded, and has become repugnant to universal belief, the fictions built upon it are still admitted as natural, because they were accounted such by the people to whom they were first addressed; whose sentiments and views of things we are willing to adopt, when, by the power of pleasing description, we are introduced into their scenes, and made acquainted with their manners. Hence we admit the theology of the ancient poets, their Elysium and Tartarus, Scylla and Charybdis, Cyclops and Circe, and the rest of those "beautiful wonders" (as Horace calls them) which were believed in the heroic ages; as well as the demons and enchantments of Tasso, which may be supposed to have obtained no small degree of credit among the Italians of the sixteenth century, and are suitable enough to the notions that prevailed universally in Europe not long before.[13] In fact, when Poetry is in other respects true; when it gives an accurate display of those parts of nature about which we know that men in all ages must have entertained the same opinion, I mean those appearances in the visible creation, and those feelings and workings of the human mind, which are obvious to all mankind;—when Poetry, I say, is thus far according to nature, we are very willing to be indulgent to what is fictitious in it, and to grant a temporary allowance to any system of fable which the author pleases to adopt; provided that he lay the scene in a distant country, or fix the date to a remote period. This is no unreasonable piece of compliance: we owe it both to the poet and to ourselves; for without it we should neither form a right estimate of his genius, nor receive from his works that pleasure which they were intended to impart. Let him, however, take care, that his system of fable be such, as his countrymen and contemporaries (to whom his work is immediately addressed) might be supposed capable of yielding their assent to; for otherwise we should not believe him to be in earnest: and let him connect it as much as he can with probable circumstances, and make it appear in a series of events consistent with itself.

For (thirdly) if this be the case, we shall admit his story as probable, or at least as natural, and consequently be interested in it, even though it be not warranted by general experience, and derive but slender authority from popular opinion. Calyban, in the Tempest, would have shocked the mind as an improbability, if we had not been made acquainted with his origin, and seen his character displayed in a series of consistent behaviour. But when we are told, that he sprung from a witch and a demon, a connection not contrary to the laws of Nature, as they were understood in Shakespeare's time, and find his manners conformable to his descent, we are easily reconciled to the fiction.

. . . . . .

CHAP. VI.
Remarks on Music.

SECT. I.

Of Imitation. Is Music an Imitative Art?

Man from his birth is prone to imitation, and takes great pleasure in it. At a time when he is too young to understand or attend to rules, he learns, by imitating others,

[13]In the fourteenth century, the common people of Italy believed, that the poet Dante actually went down to hell; that the *Inferno* was a true account of what he saw there; and that his sallow complexion, and stunted beard, (which seemed by its growth and color to have been too near the fire), were the consequence of his passing so much of his time in that hot and smoky region. *See Viccende della literatura del Sig. C. Denina, cap.* 4.—Sir John Mandeville's *Book of Travels,* written not long after, was not only ratified by the Pope, after having been compared with the *Mappa Mundi* of that time, but, what is more strange, seems to have been seriously believed by that adventurous knight himself, though a man of considerable learning, and no despicable taste. See the Conclusion of the Book.

to speak, and walk, and do many other things equally requisite to life and happiness. Most of the sports of children are imitative, and many of them dramatical. Mimicry occasions laughter; and a just imitation of human life upon the stage is highly delightful to persons of all ranks, conditions, and capacities.

Our natural propensity to imitation may in part account for the pleasure it yields: for that is always pleasing which gratifies natural propensity; nay, to please, and to gratify, are almost synonymous terms. Yet the peculiar charm of imitation may also be accounted for upon other principles. To compare a copy with the original, and trace out the particulars wherein they differ and wherein they resemble, is in itself a pleasing exercise to the mind; and, when accompanied with admiration of the object imitated, and of the genius of the imitator, conveys a most intense delight; which may be rendered still more intense by the agreeable qualities of the instrument of imitation,—by the beauty of the colors in painting, by the harmony of the language in poetry; and in music, by the sweetness, mellowness, pathos, and other pleasing varieties of vocal and instrumental sound. And if to all this there be added, the merit of a moral design, Imitation will then shine forth in her most amiable form, and the enraptured heart acknowledge her powers of pleasing to be irresistible.

Such is the delight we have in imitation, that what would in itself give neither pleasure nor pain, may become agreeable when well imitated. We see without emotion many faces, and other familiar objects; but a good picture even of a stone, or common plant, is not beheld with indifference. No wonder, then, that what is agreeable in itself, should, when surveyed through the medium of skillful imitation, be highly agreeable. A good portrait of a grim countenance is pleasing; but a portrait equally good of a beautiful one is still more so. Nay, though a man in a violent passion, a monstrous wild beast, or a body agonized with pain, be a most unpleasing spectacle, a picture, or poetical description of it, may be contemplated with delight;[14] the pleasure we take in the artist's ingenuity, joined to our consciousness that the object before us is not real, being more than sufficient to counterbalance every disagreeable feeling occasioned by the deformity of the figure.[15] Even human vices, infirmities, and misfortunes, when well represented on the stage, form a most interesting amusement. So great is the charm of imitation.

[14] Aristot. Poet. sect. 4; Gerard on Taste part I. sect. 4.

[15] Pictures, however, of great merit as imitations, and valuable for the morality of the design, may yet be too horrid to be contemplated with pleasure. A robber, who had broke into a repository of the dead, in order to plunder a corpse of some rich ornaments, is said to have been so affected with the hideous spectacle of morality which presented itself when he opened the coffin, that he slunk away, trembling and weeping, without being able to execute his purpose. [I] have met with an excellent print upon this subject; but was never able to look at it for half a minute together. Too many objects of the same character may be seen in Hogarth's *Progress of Cruelty*.—There is another class of shocking ideas, which poets have not always been sufficiently careful to avoid. Juvenal and Swift, and even Pope himself, have given us descriptions which it turns one's stomach to think of. And I must confess, that, notwithstanding the authority of Atterbury and Addision, and the general merit of the passage, I could never reconcile myself to some filthy ideas, which, to the unspeakable satisfaction of Mr. Voltaire, Milton has unwarily introduced in the famous allegory of Sin and Death.

That has been thought a very mysterious pleasure, which we take in witnessing tragical imitations of human action, even while they move us to pity and sorrow. Several causes seem to co-operate in producing it. 1. It gives an agreeable agitation to the mind, to be deeply interested in any event, that is not attended with real harm to ourselves or others. Nay, certain events of the most substantial distress would seem to give a gloomy entertainment to some minds: else why should men run so eagerly to see shipwrecks, executions, riots, and even battles, and fields of slaughter? But the distress upon the stage neither is, nor is believed to be, real; and therefore the agreeable exercise it may give to the mind is not allayed by any bitter reflections, but is rather heightened by this consideration, that the whole is imaginary. To those who mistake it for real, as children are said to do sometimes, it gives no pleasure, but intense pain. 2. Throughout the performance, we admire the genius of the poet, as it appears in the language and sentiments, in the right conduct of the fable, in diversifying and supporting the characters, and in devising incidents affecting in themselves, and conducive to the main design. 3. The ingenuity of the actors must be allowed to be a principal cause of the pleasure with which we witness either tragedy or comedy. A bad play well acted may please, and in fact often does; but a good play ill acted is intolerable. 4. We sympathize with the emotions of the audience, and this heightens our own. For I apprehend, that no person of sensibility would choose to be the sole spectator of a play, if he had it in his power to see it in company with a multitude. When we have read by ourselves a pleasing narrative, till it has lost every charm that novelty can bestow, we may renew its relish by reading it in company, and perhaps be even more entertained than at the first perusal. 5. The ornaments of the theatre, the music, the scenery, the splendor of the company, nay the very dress of the players, must be allowed to contribute something to our amusement: else why do managers expend so much money in decoration? And, lastly, let it be observed, that there is something very peculiar in the nature of pity. The pain, however exquisite, that accompanies this amiable affection, is such, that a man of a generous mind would not disqualify himself for it, even if he could: nor is the "luxury of woe," that we read of in poetry, a mere figure of speech, but a real sensation, wherewith every person of humanity is acquainted, by frequent experience. Pity produces a tenderness of heart very friendly to virtuous impressions. It inclines us to be circumspect and lowly, and sensible of the uncertainty of human things, and of our dependence upon the great Author of our being; while continued joy and prosperity harden the heart, and render men proud, irreligious, and inattentive: so that Solomon had good reason for affirming, that "by the sadness of the countenance the heart is made better." The exercise of pity, even towards imaginary sufferings, cannot fail to give pleasure, if attended, as it generally is, with the approbation of reason and conscience, declaring it to be a virtuous affection, productive of signal benefit to society, and peculiarly suitable to our condition, honorable to our nature, and amiable in the eyes of our fellow-creatures.[16]

[16]Since these remarks were written, Dr. Campbell has published a very accurate and ingenious dissertation on this subject. See his *Philosophy of Rhetoric*, vol. I.

Since Imitation is so plentiful a source of pleasure, we need not wonder, that the imitative arts of poetry and painting should have been greatly esteemed in every enlightened age. The imitation itself, which is the work of the artist, is agreeable; the thing imitated, which is nature, is also agreeable; and is not the same thing true of the instrument of imitation? Or does any one doubt, whether harmonious language be pleasing to the ear, or certain arrangements of color beautiful to the eye?

Shall I apply these, and the preceding reasonings, to the musical art also, which I have elsewhere called, and which is generally understood to be, imitative? Shall I say, that some melodies please, because they imitate nature, and that others, which do not imitate nature, are therefore unpleasing?—that an air expressive of devotion, for example, is agreeable, because it presents us with an imitation of those sounds by which devotion does naturally express itself?—Such an affirmation would hardly pass upon the reader; notwithstanding the plausibility it might seem to derive from that strict analogy which all the fine arts are supposed to bear to one another. He would ask, What is the natural sound of devotion? Where is it to be heard? When was it heard? What resemblance is there between Handel's *Te Deum* , and the tone of voice natural to a person expressing, by articulate sound, his veneration of the Divine Character and Providence?—In fact, I apprehend, that critics have erred a little in their determinations upon this subject, from an opinion, that Music, Painting, and Poetry, are all imitative arts. I hope at least I may say, without offense, that while this was my opinion, I was always conscious of some unaccountable confusion of thought, whenever I attempted to explain it in the way of detail to others.

But while I thus insinuate, that Music is not an imitative art, I mean no disrespect to Aristotle, who seems in the beginning of his Poetics to declare the contrary. It is not the whole, but the greater part of music, which that philosopher calls imitative; and I agree with him so far as to allow this property to some music, though not to all. But he speaks of the ancient music, and I of the modern; and to one who considers how very little we know of the former, it will not appear a contradiction to say, that the one might have been imitative, though the other is not.

Nor do I mean any disrespect to music, when I would strike it off the list of imitative arts. I allow it to be a fine art, and to have great influence on the human soul: I grant, that, by its power of raising a variety of agreeable emotions in the hearer, it proves its relation to poetry, and that it never appears to the best advantage but with poetry for its interpreter: and I am satisfied, that, though musical genius may subsist without poetical taste, and poetical genius without musical taste; yet these two talents united might accomplish nobler effects, than either could do singly. I acknowledge too, that the principles and essential rules of this art are as really founded in nature, as those of poetry and painting. But when I am asked, What part of nature is imitated in any good picture or poem, I find I can give a definite answer: whereas, when I am asked, What part of nature is imitated in Handel's *Water-Music*, for instance, or in Corelli's *Eighth Concerto*, or in any particular English song or Scotch tune, I find I can give no definite answer:—though no doubt I might say some plausible things; or perhaps, after much refinement, be able to show, that

Music may, by one shift or other, be made an imitative art, provided you allow me to give any meaning I please to the word *imitative*.

Music is imitative, when it readily puts one in mind of the thing imitated. If an explication be necessary, and if, after all, we find it difficult to recognize any exact similitude, I would not call such music an imitation of nature; but consider it as upon a footing, in point of likeness, with those pictures, wherein the action cannot be known but by a label proceeding from the mouth of the agent, nor the species of animals ascertained without a name written under it. But between imitation in music and imitation in painting, there is this one essential difference:—a bad picture is always a bad imitation of nature, and a good picture is necessarily a good imitation; but music may be exactly imitative, and yet intolerably bad; or not at all imitative, and yet perfectly good. I have heard, that the *Pastorale* in the eighth of Corelli's *Concertos* (which appears by the inscription to have been composed for the night of the Nativity) was intended for an imitation of the song of angels hovering above the fields of Bethlehem, and gradually soaring up to heaven. The music, however, is not such as would of itself convey this idea: and, even with the help of the commentary, it requires a lively fancy to connect the various movements and melodies of the piece with the motions and evolutions of the heavenly host; as sometimes flying off, and sometimes returning; singing sometimes in one quarter of the sky, and sometimes in another; now in one or two parts, and now in full chorus. It is not clear, that the author intended any imitation; and whether he did or not, is a matter of no consequence; for the music will continue to please when the tradition is no more remembered. The harmonies of this *Pastorale* are indeed so uncommon, and so ravishingly sweet, that it is almost impossible not to think of heaven when one hears them. I would not call them imitative; but I believe they are finer than any imitative music in the world.

Sounds in themselves can imitate nothing directly but sounds, nor in their motions any thing but motions. But the natural sounds and motions that music is allowed to imitate, are but few. For, first, they must all be consistent with the fundamental principles of the art, and not repugnant either to melody or to harmony. Now, the foundation of all true music, and the most perfect of all musical instruments, is the human voice; which is therefore the prototype of the musical scale, and a standard of musical sound. Noises, therefore, and inharmonious notes of every kind, which a good voice cannot utter without straining, ought to be excluded from this pleasing art: for it is impossible, that those vocal sounds which require any unnatural efforts, either of the finger or speaker, should ever give permanent gratification to the hearer. I say, permanent gratification; for I deny not, that the preternatural screams of an Italian singer may occasion surprise, and momentary amusement: but those screams are not music; they are admired, not for their propriety or pathos, but, like rope-dancing, and the eating of fire, merely because they are uncommon and difficult.—Besides, the end of all genuine music is, to introduce into the human mind certain affections, or susceptibilities of affection. Now, all the affections, over which music has any power, are of the agreeable kind. And therefore, in this art, no imitations of natural sound or motion, but such as tend to inspire agreeable affections, ought ever to find a place. The song of certain birds, the murmur of a stream, the shouts of multitudes, the tumult of a storm, the roar of thunder, or a chime of bells, are sounds connected with agreeable or sublime affections, and reconcilable both with melody and with harmony; and may therefore be imitated, when the artist has occasion for them: but the crowing of cocks, the barking of dogs, the mewing of cats, the grunting of swine, the gabbling of geese, the cackling of a hen, the braying of an ass, the creaking of a saw, or the rumbling of a cart-wheel, would render the best music ridiculous. The movement of a dance may be imitated, or the stately pace of an embattled legion; but the hobble of a trotting horse would be intolerable.

There is another sort of imitation by sound, which ought never to be heard, or seen, in music. To express the local elevation of objects by what we call high notes, and their depression of low or deep notes, has no more propriety in it, than any other pun. We call notes high or low, with respect of their situation in the written scale. There would have been no absurdity in expressing the highest notes by characters placed at the bottom of the scale or musical line, and the lowest notes by characters placed at the top of it, if custom or accident had so determined. And there is reason to think, that something like this actually obtained in the musical scale of the ancients. At least it is probable, that the deepest or gravest sound was called *Summa* by the Romans, and the shrillest or acutest *Ima*; which might be owing to the construction of their instruments; the string that sounded the former being perhaps highest in place, and that which sounded the latter lowest.—Yet some people would think a song faulty, if the word *heaven* was set to what we call a low note, or the word *hell* to what we call a high one.

All these sorts of illicit imitation have been practiced, and by those too from whom better things were expected. This abuse of a noble art did not escape the satire of Swift; who, though deaf to the charms of music, was not blind to the absurdity of musicians. He recommended it to Dr. Ecclin, an ingenious gentleman of Ireland, to compose a *Cantata* in ridicule of this puerile mimicry. Here we have motions imitated, which are the most inharmonious, and the least connected with human affections; as the trotting, ambling, and galloping, of Pegasus; and sounds the most unmusical, as crackling and sniveling, and rough roistering music roaring strains: the words high and deep have high and deep notes set to them; a series of short notes of equal lengths are introduced, to imitate shivering and shaking; an irregular rant of quick sounds, to express rambling; a sudden rise of the voice, from a low to a high pitch, to denote flying above the sky; a ridiculous run of chromatic divisions on the words *Celia dies*; with other droll contrivances of a like nature. In a word, Swift's Cantata alone may convince any person, that music uniformly imitative would be ridiculous.—I just observe in passing, that the satire of this piece is leveled, not at absurd imitation only, but also at some other musical improprieties; such as the idle repetition of the same words, the running of long extravagant divisions upon one syllable, and the setting of words to music that have no meaning.

If I were entitled to suggest any rules in this art, I would humbly propose, (and a great musician and ingenious writer seems to be of the same mind[17]), that no

[17] Avison on Musical Expression, p. 57.60. second edit.

imitation should ever be introduced into music purely instrumental. Of vocal melody the expression is, or ought to be, ascertained by the poetry; but the expression of the best instrumental music is ambiguous. In this, therefore, there is nothing to lead the mind of the hearer to recognize the imitation, which, though both legitimate and accurate, would run the risk of being overlooked and lost. If, again, it were so very exact, as to lead our thoughts instantly to the thing imitated, we should be apt to attend to the imitation only, so as to remain insensible to the general effect of the piece. In a word, I am inclined to think, that imitation in an instrumental concerto would produce either no effect, or a bad one. The same reasons would exclude it from instrumental solos; provided they were such as deserve to be called music:—if they be contrived only to show the dexterity of the performer, imitations, and all possible varieties of sound, may be thrown in *ad libitum*; any thing will do, that can astonish the audience; but to such fiddling or fingering I would no more give the honorable name of Music, than I would apply that of Poetry to Pope's "Fluttering spread thy purple pinions," or to Swift's *Ode on Ditton and Whiston*.

CHAPTER 18

Hugh Blair*

Lectures on Rhetoric and Belles Lettres
1783

Lecture II
Taste

The nature of the present undertaking leads me to begin with some inquires concerning taste, as it is this faculty which is always appealed to, in disquisitions concerning the merit of discourse in writing.

There are few subjects on which men talk more loosely and indistinctly than on taste; few which it is more difficult to explain with precision; and none which in this course of lectures will appear more dry or abstract. What I have to say on the subject, shall be in the following order. I shall first explain the nature of taste as a power or faculty in the human mind. I shall next consider, how far it is an improveable faculty. I shall show the sources of its improvement, and the characters of taste in its most perfect state. I shall then examine the various fluctuations to which it is liable and inquire whether there be any standard to which we can bring the different tastes of men, in order to distinguish the corrupted from the true.

---

*Hugh Blair (1718-1800) was born into a merchant family and studied at the university at Edinburgh. He entered the clergy and developed a reputation as a moderate divine and preacher. His sermons at St Giles High Kirk were said to be attended by all of Edinburgh society. In 1761 a chair of Rhetoric and Belles Lettres was founded for him at the university. He was fond of the theater and played cards, to the dismay of the evangelical clergy. He defended the authenticity of Ossian. His sermons were published to great success, and he was regarded as a literary arbiter in Edinburgh. He was known for his pride in his sermons, but was otherwise regarded as modest in company. His life seems to have been placid, successful, and relatively uneventful outside of his literary accomplishments.

Taste may be defined "The power of receiving pleasure from the beauties of nature and of art." The first question that occurs concerning it is, whether it is to be considered as an internal sense, or as an exertion of reason? Reason is a very general term; but if we understand by it, that power of the mind which in speculative matters discovers truth, and in practical matters judges of the fitness of means to an end, I apprehend the question may be easily answered. For nothing can be more clear, than that taste is not resolvable into any such operation of reason. It is not merely through a discovery of the understanding or a deduction of argument, that the mind receives pleasure from a beautiful prospect or a fine poem. Such objects often strike us intuitively, and make a strong impression, when we are unable to assign the reasons of our being pleased. They sometimes strike in the same manner the philosopher and the peasant; the boy and the man. Hence the faculty by which we relish such beauties, seems more nearly allied to a feeling of sense, than to a process of the understanding; and accordingly from an external sense it has borrowed its name; that sense by which we receive and distinguish the pleasures of food, having, in several languages given rise to the word taste, in the metaphorical meaning under which we now consider it. However, as in all subjects which regard the operations of the mind, the inaccurate use of words is to be carefully avoided, it must not be inferred from what I have said, that reason is entirely excluded from the exertions of taste. Though taste, beyond doubt, be ultimately founded on a certain natural and instinctive sensibility to beauty, yet reason, as I shall show hereafter, assists taste in many of its operations and serves to enlarge its power.[1]

Taste, in the sense in which I have explained it, is a faculty common in some degree to all men. Nothing that belongs to human nature is more general than the relish of beauty of one kind or other; of what is orderly, proportioned, grand, harmonious, new, or sprightly. In children, the rudiments of taste discover themselves very early in a thousand instances; in their fondness for regular bodies, their admiration of pictures and statues, and imitations of all kinds; and their strong attachment to whatever is new or marvelous. The most ignorant peasants are delighted with ballads and tales, and are struck with the beautiful appearance of nature in the earth and heavens. Even in the deserts of America, where human nature shows itself in its most uncultivated state, the savages have their ornaments of dress, their war and their death songs, their harangues and their orators. We must therefore conclude the principles of taste to be deeply founded in the human mind. It is no less

[1] See Dr. Gerard's *Essay on Taste*:—D'Alembert's Reflections on the use and abuse of Philosophy in matters which relate to Taste:—*Reflections Critiques sur la Poesic et sur la Peinture*, tome ii. ch. 22.31:—Elements of Criticism, chap. 25:—Mr. Hume's Essay on the Standard of Taste:—introduction to the *Essay on the Sublime and Beautiful.*

essential to man to have some discernment of beauty, than it is to possess the attributes of reason and of speech.[2]

But although none be wholly devoid of this faculty, yet the degrees in which it is possessed are widely different. In some men only the feeble glimmerings of taste appear; the beauties which they relish are of the coarsest kind; and of these they have but a weak and confused impression; while in others, taste rises to an acute discernment, and a lively enjoyment of the most refined beauties. In general, we may observe, that in the powers and pleasures of taste, there is a more remarkable inequality among men than is usually found in point of common sense, reason, and judgment. The constitution of our nature in this, as in all other respects, discovers admirable wisdom. In the distribution of those talents which are necessary for man's well-being, nature hath made less distinction among her children. But in the distribution of those which belong only to the ornamental part of life, she hath bestowed her favors with more frugality. She hath both sown the seeds more sparingly; and rendered a higher culture requisite for bringing them to perfection.

This inequality of taste among men is owing, without doubt, in part, to the different frame of their natures; to nicer organs, and finer internal powers, with which some are endowed beyond others. But, if it be owing in part to nature, it is owing to education and culture still more. The illustration of this leads to my next remark on this subject, that taste is a most improveable faculty, if there be any such in human nature; a remark which gives great encouragement to such a course of study as we are now proposing to pursue. Of the truth of this assertion we may easily be convinced, by only reflecting on that immense superiority which education and improvement give to civilized, above barbarous nations, in refinement of taste; and on the superiority which they give in the same nation to those who have studied the liberal arts, above the rude and untaught vulgar. The difference is so great, that there is perhaps no one particular in which these two classes of men are so far removed from each other, as in respect of the powers and the pleasures of taste: and assuredly for this difference no other general cause can be assigned, but culture and education. I shall now proceed to show what the means are by which taste becomes so remarkably susceptible of cultivation and progress.

[2] On the subject of taste, considered as a power or faculty of the mind, much less is to be found among the ancient, than among the modern rhetorical and critical writers. The following remarkable passage in Cicero serves, however, to show that his ideas on this subject agree perfectly with what has been said above. He is speaking of the beauties of style and numbers. "Illud autem nequis admirerur, quonam modo haec vulgus imperitorum in audiendo notet; cum in omni genere, tum in hoc ipso, magna quaedum est vis, incredibilisque naturae. Omnes enim tacito quodam sensu, sine ulla arte aut ratione, quae sint in artibus ac rationibus recta et prava dijudicant: idque cum faciunt in picturis, et in signis, et in aliis operibus, ad quorum intelligentiam a natura minus habent instrumenti, tum multo ostendunt magis in verborum, numerorum vecumque judicio; quod ea sunt in communibus infixa sensibus; neque earum rerum quenquam funditus natura voluit esse expertem." Cic. de Orat lib. iii. cap. 50. edit. Gruteri.—Quintilian seems to include taste (for which, in the sense which we now give to that word, the ancients appear to have had no distinct name) under what he calls judicium. "Locus de judicio, med quidem opinione adeo partibus hujus operis omnibus connectus ac mistus est, ut ne a sententiis quidem aut verbis saltem singulpossit separari, nec magis arte traditur quam gustus aut odor.—Ut contrario vitemus et communia, ne quid in cloquendo corruptum obsscurumque sit, referatur oportet ad sensus qui non docentur." Institnt. lib. vi. cap. 3. edit. Obrechti.

Reflect first upon that great law of our nature, that exercise is the chief source of improvement in all our faculties. This holds both in our bodily, and in our mental powers. It holds even in our external senses, although these be less the subject of cultivation than any of our other faculties. We see how acute the senses become in persons whose trade or business leads to nice exertions of them. Touch, for instance, becomes infinitely more exquisite in men whose employment requires them to examine the polish of bodies, than it is in others. They who deal in microscopical observations, or are accustomed to engrave on precious stones, acquire surprising accuracy of sight in discerning the minutest objects; and practice in attending to different flavors and tastes of liquors, wonderfully improves the power of distinguishing them, and of tracing their composition. Placing internal taste therefore on the footing of a simple sense, it cannot be doubted that frequent exercise, and curious attention to its proper objects, must greatly heighten its power. Of this we have one clear proof in that part of taste, which is called an ear for music. Experience every day shows, that nothing is more improvable. Only the simplest and plainest compositions are relished at first; use and practice extend our pleasure; teach us to relish finer melody, and by degrees enable us to enter into the intricate and compounded pleasures of harmony. So an eye for the beauties of painting is never all at once acquired. It is gradually formed by being conversant among pictures, and studying the works of the best masters.

Precisely in the same manner, with respect to the beauty of composition and discourse, attention to the most approved models, study of the best authors, comparisons of lower and higher degrees of the same beauties, operate towards the refinement of taste. When one is only beginning his acquaintance with works of genius, the sentiment which attends them is obscure and confused. He cannot point out the several excellencies or blemishes of a performance which he peruses; he is at a loss on what to rest his judgment: all that can be expected is, that he should tell in general whether he be pleased or not. But allow him more experience in works of this kind, and his taste becomes by degrees more exact and enlightened. He begins to perceive not only the character of the whole, but the beauties and defects of each part; and is able to describe the peculiar qualities which he praises or blames. The mist dissipates which seemed formerly to hang over the object; and he can at length pronounce firmly, and without hesitation; concerning it. Thus in taste, considered as mere sensibility, exercise opens a great source of improvement.

But although taste be ultimately founded on sensibility, it must not be considered as instinctive sensibility alone. Reason and good sense, as I before hinted, have so extensive an influence on all the operations and decisions of taste, that a thorough good taste may well be considered as a power compounded of natural sensibility to beauty, and of improved understanding. In order to be satisfied of this, let us observe, that the greater part of the productions of genius are no other than imitations of nature; representations of the characters, actions, or manners of men. The pleasure we receive from such imitations or representations is founded on mere taste: but to judge whether they be properly executed, belongs to the understanding, which compares the copy with the original.

In reading, for instance, such a poem as the *Aeneid*, a great part of our pleasure arises from the plan or story being well conducted, and all the parts joined together with probability and due connection; from the characters being taken from nature, the sentiments being suited to the characters, and the style to the sentiments. The pleasure which arises from a poem so conducted, is felt or enjoyed by taste as an internal sense; but the discovery of this conduct in the poem, is owing to reason; and the more that reason enables us to discover such propriety in the conduct, the greater will be our pleasure. We are pleased, through our natural sense of beauty. Reason shows us why, and upon what grounds, we are pleased. Wherever in works of taste, any resemblance to nature is aimed at; wherever there is any reference of parts to a whole, or of means to an end, as there is indeed in almost every writing and discourse, there the understanding must always have a great part to act.

Here then is a wide field for reason's exerting its powers in relation to the objects of taste, particularly with respect to composition, and works of genius; and hence arises a second and a very considerable source of the improvement of taste, from the application of reason and good sense to such productions of genius. Spurious beauties, such as unnatural characters, forced sentiments, affected style, may please for a little; but they please only because their opposition to nature and to good sense has not been examined, or attended to. Once show how nature might have been more justly imitated or represented; how the writer might have managed his subjects to greater advantage; the illusion will presently be dissipated, and these false beauties will please no more.

From these two sources then, first, the frequent exercise of taste, and next the application of good sense and reason to the objects of taste, taste as a power of the mind receives its improvement. In its perfect state, it is undoubtedly the result both of nature and of art. It supposes our natural sense of beauty to be refined by frequent attention to the most beautiful objects, and at the same time to be guided and improved by the light of the understanding.

I must be allowed to add, that as a sound head, so likewise a good heart, is a very material requisite to just taste. The moral beauties are not only themselves superior to all others, but they exert an influence, either more near, or more remote, on a great variety of other objects of taste. Wherever the affections, characters, or actions of men are concerned, (and these certainly afford the noblest subjects to genius,) there can be neither any just or affecting description of them, nor any thorough feeling of the beauty of that description, without our possessing the virtuous affections. He whose heart is indelicate or hard, he who has no admiration of what is truly noble or praise-worthy, nor the proper sympathetic sense of what is soft and tender, must have a very imperfect relish of the highest beauties of eloquence and poetry.

Delicacy of taste respects principally the perfection of that natural sensibility on which taste is founded. It implies those finer organs or powers which enable us to discover beauties that lie hid from a vulgar eye. One may have strong sensibility, and yet be deficient in delicate taste. He may be deeply impressed by such beauties as he perceives; but he perceives only what is in some degree course, what is bold and palpable; while chaster and simpler ornaments escape his notice. In this state, taste generally exists among rude and unrefined nations. But a person of delicate taste both feels strongly, and feels accurately. He sees distinctions and differences where others see none; the most latent beauty does not escape him, and he is sensible of the smallest blemish. Delicacy of taste is judged of by the same marks that we use in judging of the delicacy of an external sense. As the goodness of the palate is not tried by strong flavors, but by a mixture of ingredients, where, notwithstanding the confusion, we remain sensible of each; in like manner delicacy of internal taste appears, by a quick and lively sensibility to its finest, most compounded, or most latent objects.

Correctness of taste respects chiefly the improvement which that faculty receives through its connection with the understanding. A man of correct taste is one who is never imposed on by counterfeit beauties; who carries always in his mind that standard of good sense which he employs in judging of every thing. He estimates with propriety the comparative merit of the several beauties which he meets with in any work of genius; refers them to their proper classes; assigns the principles, as far as they can be traced, whence their power of pleasing flows; and is pleased himself precisely in that degree in which he ought, and no more.

It is true, that these two qualities of taste, delicacy and correctness, mutually imply each other. No taste can be exquisitely delicate without being correct; nor can be thoroughly correct without being delicate. But still a predominancy of one or other quality in the mixture is often visible. The power of delicacy is chiefly seen in discerning the true merit of a work; the power of correctness, in rejecting false pretensions to merit. Delicacy leans more to feeling; correctness, more to reason and judgment. The former is more the gift of nature; the latter, more the product of culture and art. Among the ancient critics, Longinus possessed most delicacy; Aristotle, most correctness. Among the moderns, Mr. Addison is a high example of delicate taste; Dean Swift, had he written on the subjects of criticism, would perhaps have afforded the example of a correct one.

Having viewed taste in its most improved and perfect state, I come next to consider its deviations from that state, the fluctuations and changes to which it is liable; and to inquire whether, in the midst of these, there be any means of distinguishing a true from a corrupted taste. This brings us to the most difficult part of our task. For it must be acknowledged, that no principle of the human mind is, in its operations, more fluctuating and capricious than taste. Its variations have been so great and frequent, as to create a suspicion with some, of its being merely arbitrary; grounded on no foundation, ascertainable by no standard, but wholly dependent on changing fancy; the consequence of which would be, that all studies or regular inquiries concerning the objects of taste were vain. In architecture, the Grecian models were long esteemed the most perfect. In succeeding ages, the Gothic architecture alone prevailed, and afterwards the Grecian taste revived in all its vigor, and engrossed the public admiration. In eloquence and poetry, the Asiatics at no time relished any thing but what was full of ornament, and splendid in a degree that we should denominate gaudy; whilst the Greeks admired only chaste and simple beauties, and despised the Asiatic ostentation. In our own country, how many writings that were greatly extolled two or three centuries ago, are now fallen into entire disrepute and oblivion! Without going back to remote instances, how very different is the taste of poetry which prevails in Great Britain now, from what prevailed there no longer ago than the rein of King Charles II, which the authors too of that time deemed an Augustan age: when nothing was in vogue but an affected brilliancy of wit; when the simple majesty of Milton was overlooked, and *Paradise Lost* almost entirely unknown; when Cowley's labored and unnatural conceits were admired as the very quintessence of genius; Waller's gay sprightliness was mistaken for the tender spirit of love poetry; and such writers as Suckling and Etheridge were held in esteem for dramatic composition?

The question is, what conclusion we are to form from such instances as these? Is there any thing that can be called a standard of taste, by appealing to which we may distinguish between a good and a bad taste? Or, is there in truth no such distinction? and are we to hold that, according to the proverb, there is no disputing of tastes; but that whatever pleases is right, for that reason that it does please? This is the question, and a very nice and subtle one it is, which we are now to discuss.

I begin by observing, that if there be no such thing as any standard of taste, this consequence must immediately follow, that all tastes are equally good; a position, which, though it may pass unnoticed in slight matters, and when we speak of the lesser differences among the tastes of men, yet when we apply it to the extremes, presently shows its absurdity. For is there any one who will seriously maintain that the taste of a Hottentot or a Laplander is as delicate and as correct as that of a Longinus or an Addison? or, that he can be charged with no defect or incapacity who thinks a common news writer as excellent an historian as Tacitus? As it would be held downright extravagance to talk in this manner, we are led unavoidably to this conclusion, that there is some foundation for the preference of one man's taste to that of another; or, that there is a good and a bad, a right and a wrong in taste, as in other things.

But to prevent mistakes on this subject, it is necessary to observe next, that the diversity of tastes which prevails among mankind, does not in every case infer corruption of taste, or oblige us to seek for some standard in order to determine who are in the right. The tastes of men may differ very considerably as to their objects, and yet none of them be wrong. One man relishes poetry most; another takes pleasure in nothing but history. One prefers comedy; another, tragedy. One admires the simple; another the ornamented style. The young are amused with gay and sprightly compositions. The elderly are more entertained with those of a graver cast. Some nations delight in bold pictures of manners, and strong representations of passion. Others incline to more correct and regular elegance both in description and sentiment. Though all differ, yet all pitch upon some one beauty which peculiarly suits their turn of mind; and therefore no one has a title to condemn the rest. It is not in matters of taste, as in questions of mere reason, where there is but one conclusion that can be true, and all the rest are erroneous. Truth, which is the object of reason, is one; beauty, which is the object of taste, is manifold. Taste, therefore, admits of latitude and diversity of objects, in sufficient consistency with goodness or justness of taste.

But then, to explain this matter thoroughly, I must observe farther, that this admissible diversity of tastes can only have place where the objects of taste are different. Where it is with respect to the same object that men disagree, when one condemns that as ugly, which another admires as highly beautiful; then it is no longer diversity, but direct opposition of taste that takes place; and therefore one must be in the right, and another in the wrong, unless that absurd paradox were allowed to hold, that all tastes are equally good and true. One man prefers Virgil to Homer. Suppose that I, on the other hand, admire Homer more than Virgil. I have as yet no reason to say that our tastes are contradictory. The other person is more struck with the elegance and tenderness which are the characteristics of Virgil; I, with the simplicity and fire of Homer. As long as neither of us deny that both Homer and Virgil have great beauties, our difference falls within the compass of that diversity of tastes, which I have showed to be natural and allowable. But if the other man shall assert that Homer has no beauties whatever; that he holds him to be a dull and spiritless writer, and that he would as soon peruse any old legend of knight-errantry as the *Iliad*; then I exclaim, that my antagonist either is void of all taste, or that his taste is corrupted in a miserable degree; and I appeal to whatever I think the standard of taste, to show him that he is in the wrong.

What that standard is to which, in such opposition of tastes, we are obliged to have recourse, remains to be traced. A standard properly signifies, that which is of such undoubted authority as to be the test of other things of the same kind. Thus a standard weight or measure, is that which is appointed by law to regulate all other measures and weights. Thus the court is said to be the standard of good breeding; and the scripture of theological truth.

When we say that nature is the standard of taste, we lay down a principle very true and just, as far as it can be applied. There is no doubt, that in all cases where an imitation is intended of some object that exists in nature, as in representing human characters or actions, conformity to nature affords a full and distinct criterion of what is truly beautiful. Reason hath in such cases full scope for exerting its authority; for approving or condemning; by comparing the copy with the original. But there are innumerable cases in which this rule cannot be at all applied; and conformity to nature, is an expression frequently used, without any distinct or determinate meaning. We must therefore search for somewhat that can be rendered more clear and precise, to be the standard of taste.

Taste, as I before explained it, is ultimately founded on an internal sense of beauty, which is natural to men, and which, in its application to particular objects, is capable of being guided and enlightened by reason. Now were there any one person who possessed in full perfection all the powers of human nature, whose internal senses were in every instance exquisite and just, and whose reason was unerring and sure, the determinations of such a person concerning beauty, would, beyond doubt, be a perfect standard for the taste of all others. Wherever their taste differed from his, it could be imputed only to some imperfection in their natural powers. But as there is no such living standard, no one person to whom all mankind will allow such submission to be due, what is there of sufficient authority to be the standard of the various and opposite tastes of men? Most certainly there is nothing but the taste, as far as it can be gathered, of human nature. That which men concur the most in admiring, must be held to be beautiful. His tasté must be esteemed just and true, which coincides with the general sentiments of men. In this standard we must rest. To the sense of mankind the ultimate appeal must ever lie, in all works of taste. If any one should maintain that sugar was bitter and tobacco was sweet, no reasonings could prevail to prove it. The taste of such a person would infallibly be held to be diseased, merely because it differed so widely from the taste of the species to which he belongs. In like manner, with regard to the objects of sentiment or internal taste, the common feelings of men carry the same authority, and have a title to regulate the taste of every individual.

But have we then, it will be said, no other criterion of what is beautiful, than the approbation of the majority? Must we collect the voices of others, before we form any judgment for ourselves, of what deserves applause in eloquence or poetry? By no means; there are principles of reason and sound judgment which can be applied to matters of taste, as well as to the subjects of science and philosophy. He who admires or censures any work of genius, is always ready, if his taste be in any degree improved, to assign some reasons for his decision. He appeals to principles, and points out the grounds on which he proceeds. Taste is a sort of compound power, in which the light of the understanding always mingles, more or less, with the feelings of sentiment.

But though reason can carry us a certain length in judging concerning works of taste, it is not to be forgotten that the ultimate conclusions to which our reasonings lead, refer at last to sense and perception. We may speculate and argue concerning propriety of conduct in a tragedy, or an epic poem. Just reasonings on the subject will correct the caprice of unenlightened taste, and establish principles for judging of what deserves praise. But, at the same time, these reasonings appeal always in the last resort, to feeling. The foundation upon which they rest, is what has been found from experience to please mankind universally. Upon this ground we prefer a simple and natural, to an artificial and affected style; a regular and well connected story, to loose and scattered narratives; a catastrophe which is tender and pathetic, to one which leaves us unmoved. It is from consulting out own imagination and heart, and from attending to the feelings of others, that any principles are formed which acquire authority in matters of taste.[3]

[3] The difference between the authors who found the standard of taste upon the common feelings of human nature ascertained by general approbation, and those who found it upon established principles which can be ascertained by reason, is more an apparent than a real difference. Like many other literary controversies, it turns chiefly on modes of expression. For they who lay the greatest stress on sentiment and feeling, make no scruple of applying argument and reason to matters of taste. They appeal, like other writers, to established principles, in judging of the excellencies of eloquence or poetry; and plainly show, that the general approbation to which they ultimately recur, is an approbation resulting from discussion as well as from sentiment. They, on the other hand, who, in order to vindicate taste from any suspicion of being arbitrary, maintain that it is ascertainable by the standard of reason, admit, nevertheless, that what pleases universally, must, on that account, be held to be truly beautiful; and that no rules or conclusions concerning objects of taste, can have any just authority, if they be found to contradict the general sentiments of men. These two systems, therefore, differ in reality very little from one another. Sentiment and reason enter into both; and by allowing to each of these powers its due place, both systems may be rendered consistent. Accordingly, it is in this light that I have endeavored to place the subject.

When we refer to the concurring sentiments of men as the ultimate taste of what is to be accounted beautiful in the arts, this is to be always understood of men placed in such situations as are favorable to the proper exertions of taste. Every one must perceive, that among rude and uncivilized nations, and during the ages of ignorance and darkness, any loose notions that are entertained concerning such subjects, carry no authority. In those states of society, taste has no materials on which to operate. It is either totally suppressed, or appears in its lower and most imperfect form. We refer to the sentiments of mankind in polished and flourishing nations; when arts are cultivated and manners refined; when works of genius are subjected to free discussion, and taste is improved by science and philosophy.

Even among nations, at such a period of society, I admit that accidental causes may occasionally warp the proper operations of taste; sometimes the taste of religion, sometimes the form of government, may for a while pervert; a licentious court may introduce a taste for false ornaments, and dissolute writings. The usage of one admired genius may procure approbation for his faults, and even render them fashionable. Sometimes envy may have power to bear down, for a little, productions of great merit; while popular humor, or party spirit, may, at other times, exalt to a high, though short-lived reputation, what little deserved it. But though such casual circumstances give the appearance of caprice to the judgments of taste, that appearance is easily corrected. In the course of time, the genuine taste of human nature never fails to disclose itself and to gain the ascendant over any fantastic and corrupted modes of taste which may chance to have been introduced. These may have currency for a while, and mislead superficial judges; but being subjected to examination, by degrees they pass away; while that alone remains which is founded on sound reason, and the native feelings of man.

I by no means pretend, that there is any standard of taste, to which, in every particular instance, we can resort for clear and immediate determination. Where, indeed, is such a standard to be found for deciding any of those great controversies in reason and philosophy, which perpetually divide mankind? In the present case, there was plainly no occasion for any such strict and absolute provision to be made. In order to judge of what is morally good or evil, of what man ought, or ought not in duty to do, it was fit that the means of clear and precise determination should be afforded us. But to ascertain in every case with the utmost exactness what is beautiful or elegant, was not at all necessary to the happiness of man. And therefore some diversity in feeling was here allowed to take place; and room was left for discussion and debate, concerning the degree of approbation to which any work of genius is entitled.

The conclusion, which it is sufficient for us to rest upon, is, that taste is far from being an arbitrary principle, which is subject to the fancy of every individual, and which admits of no criterion for determining whether it be false or true. Its foundation is the same in all human minds. It is built upon sentiments and perceptions which belong to our nature; and which, in general, operate with the same uniformity as our other intellectual principles. When these sentiments are perverted by ignorance and prejudice, they are capable of being rectified by reason. Their sound and natural state is ultimately determined, by comparing them with the general taste of mankind. Let men declaim as much as they please concerning the caprice and the uncertainty of taste, it is found, by experience, that there are beauties, which, if they be displayed in a proper light, have power to command lasting and general admiration. In every composition, what interests the imagination, and touches the heart, pleases all ages and all nations. There is a certain string to which, when properly struck, the human heart is so made as to answer.

Hence the universal testimony which the most improved nations of the earth have conspired, throughout a long tract of ages, to give to some few works of genius; such as the *Iliad* of Homer, and the *Aeneid* of Virgil. Hence the authority which such works have acquired, as standards in some degree of poetical composition; since from them we are enable to collect what the sense of mankind is, concerning those beauties which give them the highest pleasure, and which therefore poetry ought to exhibit. Authority of prejudice may, in one age or country, give a temporary reputation to an indifferent poet or a bad artist; but when foreigners, or when posterity examine his works, his faults are discerned, and the genuine taste of human nature appears. "Opinionum commenta delet dies; nature judicia confirmat." Time overthrows the illusions of opionion, but establishes the decisions of nature.

Lecture III.
Criticism, Genius, Pleasures of Taste, Sublimity in Objects.

Taste, criticism, and genius, are words currently employed, without distinct ideas annexed to them. In beginning a course of lectures where such words must often occur, it is necessary to ascertain their meaning with some precision. Having in the last lecture treated of taste, I proceed to explain the nature and foundation of criticism. True criticism is the application of taste and of good sense to the several fine arts. The object which it proposes is, to distinguish what is beautiful and what is faulty in every performance; from particular instances to ascend to general principles; and so to form rules or conclusions concerning the several kinds of beauty in works of genius.

The rules of criticism are not formed by any induction *a priori*, as it is called; that is, they are not formed by a train of abstract reasoning, independent of facts and observations. Criticism is an art founded wholly on experience; on the observations of such beauties as have come nearest to the standard which I before established; that is, of such beauties as have been found to please mankind most generally. For example: Aristotle's rules concerning the unity of action in dramatic and epic composition, were not rules first discovered by logical reasoning, and then applied to poetry; but they were drawn from the practice of Homer and Sophocles: they were founded upon observing the superior pleasure which we received from the relation of an action which is one and entire, beyond what we receive from the relation of scattered and unconnected facts. Such observations taking their rise at first from feeling and experience, were found on examination to be so consonant to reason and to the principles of human nature, as to pass into established rules, and to be conveniently applied for judging of the excellency of any performance. This is the most natural account of the origin of criticism.

A masterly genius, it is true, will of himself, untaught, compose in such a manner as shall be agreeable to the most material rules of criticism, for as these rules are founded in nature, nature will often suggest them in practice. Homer, it is more than probable, was acquainted with no systems of the art of poetry. Guided by genius alone, he composed in verse a regular story, which all posterity has admired. But this is no argument against the usefulness of criticism as an art. For as no human genius is perfect, there is no writer but may receive assistance from critical observations upon the beauties and faults of those who have gone before him. No observations or rules can indeed supply the defect of genius, or inspire it where it is wanting. But they may often direct it into its proper channel; they may correct its extravagances, and point out to it the most just and proper imitation of nature. Critical rules are designed chiefly to show the faults that ought to be avoided. To nature we must be indebted for the production of eminent beauties.

From what has been said, we are enabled to form a judgment concerning those complaints which it has long been fashionable for petty authors to make against critics and criticism. Critics have been represented as the great abridgers of the native liberty of genius; as the imposers of unnatural shackles and bonds upon writers, from those cruel persecution they must fly to the public, and implore its protection. Such supplicatory prefaces are not calculated to give very favorable ideas of the genius of the author. For every good writer will be pleased to have his work examined by the principles of sound understanding and true taste. The declamations against criticism commonly proceed upon this supposition, that critics are such as judge by rule, not by feeling; which is so far from being true, that they who judge after this manner are pedants, not critics. For all the rules of genuine criticism I have shown to be ultimately founded on feeling; and taste and feeling are necessary to guide us in the application of these rules to every particular instance. As there is nothing in which all sorts of persons more readily affect to be judges than in works of taste, there is no doubt that the number of incompetent critics will always be great. But this affords no more foundation for a general invective against criticism, than the number of bad philosophers or reasoners affords against reason and philosophy.

An objection more plausible may be formed against criticism, from the applause that some performances have received from the public, which, when accurately considered, are found to contradict the rules established by criticism. Now, according to the principles laid down in the last lecture, the public is the supreme judge to whom the last appeal must be made in every work of taste; as the standard of taste is founded on the sentiments that are natural and common to all men. But with respect to this, we are to observe, that the sense of the public is often too hastily judged of. The genuine public taste does not always appear in the first applause given upon the publication of any new work. There are both a great vulgar and a small, apt to be catched and dazzled by very superficial beauties, the admiration of which in a little time passes away; and sometimes a writer may acquire great temporary reputation merely by his compliance with the passions or prejudices, with the party-spirit or superstitious notions that may chance to rule for a time almost a whole nation. In such cases, though the public may seem to praise, true criticism may with reason condemn; and it will in progress of time gain the ascendant: for the judgment of true criticism, and the voice of the public, when once become unprejudiced and dispassionate, will ever coincide at last.

Instances, I admit, there are of some works that contain gross transgressions of the laws of criticism, acquiring, nevertheless, a general, and even a lasting admiration. Such are the plays of Shakespeare, which, considered as dramatic poems, are irregular in the highest degree. But then we are to remark, that they have gained the public admiration, not by their being irregular, not by their transgressions of the rules of art, but in spite of such transgressions. They possess other beauties which are conformable to just rules; and the force of these beauties has been so great as to overpower all censure, and to give the public a degree of satisfaction superior to the disgust arising from their blemishes. Shakespeare pleases, not by his bringing the transactions of many years into one play; not by his grotesque mixtures of tragedy and comedy in one piece, nor by the strained thoughts and affected witticisms, which he sometimes employs. These we consider as blemishes, and impute them to the grossness of the age in which he lived. But he pleases by his animated and masterly representations of characters, by the liveliness of his descriptions, the force of his sentiments, and his possessing, beyond all writers, the natural language of passion: Beauties which true criticism no less teaches us to place in the highest rank, than nature teaches us to feel.

I proceed next to explain the meaning of another term, which there will be frequent occasion to employ in these lectures; that is, *genius.*

Taste and genius are two words frequently joined together; and therefore by inaccurate thinkers, confounded. They signify, however, two quite different things. The difference between them can be clearly pointed out; and it is of importance to remember it. Taste consists in the power of judging; genius, in the power of executing. One may have a considerable degree of taste in poetry, eloquence, or any of the fine arts, who has little or hardly any genius for composition or execution in any of these arts: but genius cannot be found without including taste also. Genius, therefore, deserves to be considered as a higher power of the mind than taste. Genius always imports something inventive or creative; which does not rest in mere sensibility to beauty where it is perceived, but which can, moreover, produce new beauties, and exhibit them in such a manner as strongly to impress the minds of others. Refined taste forms a good critic; but genius is farther necessary to form the poet, or the orator.

It is proper also to observe, that genius is a word, which, in common acceptation, extends much farther than to the objects of taste. It is used to signify that talent or aptitude which we receive from nature, for excelling in any one thing whatever. Thus we speak of a genius for mathematics, as well as a genius for poetry; of a genius for war, for politics, or for any mechanical employment.

This talent or aptitude for excelling in some one particular, is, I have said, what we receive from nature. By art and study, no doubt, it may be greatly improved; but by them alone it cannot be acquired. As genius is a higher faculty than taste, it is ever, according to the usual frugality of nature, more limited in the sphere of its operations. It is not uncommon to meet with persons who have an excellent taste in several of the polite arts, such as music, poetry, painting, and eloquence, altogether:

but, to find one who is an excellent performer in all these arts, is much more rare; or rather, indeed, such an one is not to be looked for. A sort of universal genius, or one who is equally and indifferently turned towards several different professions and arts, is not likely to excel in any. Although there may be some few exceptions, yet in general it holds that when the bent of the mind is wholly directed towards some one object, exclusive in a manner of others, there is the fairest prospect of eminence in that, whatever it be. The rays must converge to a point, in order to glow intensely. This remark I here choose to make, on account of its great importance to young people; in leading them to examine with care, and to pursue with ardor, the current and pointing of nature towards those exertions of genius in which they are most likely to excel.

A genius for any of the fine arts, as I before observed, always supposes taste; and it is clear, that the improvement of taste will serve both to forward and to correct the operations of genius. In proportion as the taste of poet, or orator, becomes more refined with respect to the beauties of composition, it will certainly assist him to produce the more finished beauties in his work. Genius, however, in a poet or orator, may sometimes exist in a higher degree than taste; that is, genius may be bold and strong, when taste is neither very delicate, nor very correct. This is often the case in the infancy of arts; a period, when genius frequently exerts itself with great vigor, and executes with much warmth; while taste, which requires experience, and improves by slower degrees, hath not yet attained to its full growth. Homer and Shakespeare are proofs of what I now assert; in those admirable writings are found instances of rudeness and indelicacy, which the more refined taste of later writers, who had far inferior genius to them, would have taught them to avoid. As all human perfection is limited, this may very probably be the law of our nature, that it is not given to one man to execute with vigor and fire, and, at the same time, to attend to all the lesser and more refined grades that belong to the exact perfection of his work: while, on the other hand, a thorough taste for those inferior graces is for the most part, accompanied with a diminution of sublimity and force.

Having thus explained the nature of taste, the nature and importance of criticism, and the distinction between taste and genius; I am now to consider the sources of the pleasures of taste. Here opens a very extensive field; no less than all the pleasures of the imagination, as they are commonly called, whether afforded us by natural objects, or by the imitations and descriptions of them. But it is not necessary to the purpose of my lectures, that all these should be examined fully; the pleasure which we receive from discourse, or writing, being the main object of them. All that I propose is to give some openings into the pleasures of taste in general; and to insist more particularly upon sublimity and beauty.

We are far from having yet attained to any system concerning this subject. Mr. Addison was the first who attempted a regular inquiry, in his *Essay on the Pleasures of the Imagination*, published in the sixth volume of the *Spectator*. He has reduced these pleasures under three heads,—beauty, grandeur, and novelty. His speculations on this subject, if not exceedingly profound, are, however, very beautiful and entertaining; and he has the merit of having opened a track, which was before unbeaten. The advances made since his time in this curious part of philosophical criticism, are not very considerable; though some ingenious writers have pursued the subject. This is owing, doubtless, to that thinness and subtlety which are found to be properties of all the feelings of taste. They are engaging objects; but when we would lay firm hold of them, and subject them to a regular discussion, they are always ready to elude our grasp. It is difficult to make a full enumeration of the several objects that give pleasure to taste: it is more difficult to define all those which have been discovered, and to reduce them under proper classes; and, when we would go farther, and investigate the efficient causes of the pleasure which we receive from such objects, here, above all, we find ourselves at a loss. For instance; we all learn by experience, that certain figures of bodies appear to us more beautiful than others. On inquiring farther, we find that the regularity of some figures, and the graceful variety of others, are the foundation of the beauty which we discern in them; but when we attempt to go a step beyond this, and inquire what is the cause of regularity and variety producing in our minds the sensation of beauty, any reason we can assign is extremely imperfect. These first principles of internal sensation, nature seems to have covered with an impenetrable veil.

It is some comfort, however, that although the efficient cause be obscure, the final cause of those sensations lies in many cases more open: and, in entering on this subject, we cannot avoid taking notice of the strong impression which the powers of taste and imagination are calculated to give us of the benignity of our Creator. By endowing us with such powers, he hath widely enlarged the sphere of pleasure of human life; and those, too, of a kind the most pure and innocent. The necessary purposes of life might have been abundantly answered, though our senses of seeing and hearing had only served to distinguish external objects, without conveying to us any of those refined and delicate sensations of beauty and grandeur, with which we are now so much delighted. This additional embellishment and glory, which for promoting our entertainment, the Author of nature hath poured forth upon his works, is one striking testimony, among many others, of benevolence and goodness. This thought, which Mr. Addison first started, Dr. Akenside, in his poem on the Pleasures of the Imagination, has happily pursued.

> ....Not content
> With every food of life to nourish man,
> By Kind illusions of the wondering sense,
> Thou mak'st all nature beauty to his eye,
> Or music to his ear.

I shall begin with considering the pleasure which arises from sublimity or grandeur, which I propose to treat at some length; both, as this has a character more precise and distinctly marked than any other of the pleasures of the imagination, and as it coincides more directly with our main subject. For the greater distinctness I shall, first, treat of the grandeur or sublimity of external objects themselves, which will employ the rest of this lecture; and, afterwards, of the description of such objects, or, of what is called the sublime in writing, which shall be the subject of a following lecture. I distinguish these two things from one another, the grandeur of the objects themselves when they are presented to the eye, and the description of that grandeur in discourse or writing; though most critics, inaccurately I think, blend them together; and I consider grandeur and sublimity as terms synonymous, or nearly so. If there be any distinction between them, it arises from sublimity's expressing grandeur in its highest degree.[4]

It is not easy to describe, in words, the precise impression which great and sublime objects make upon us, when we behold them; but every one has a conception of it. It produces a sort of internal elevation and expansion; it raises the mind much above its ordinary state, and fills it with a degree of wonder and astonishment, which it cannot well express. The emotion is certainly delightful; but it is altogether of the serious kind; a degree of awfulness and solemnity, even approaching to severity, commonly attends it when at its height; very distinguishable from the more gay and brisk emotion raised by beautiful objects.

The simplest form of external grandeur appears in the vast and boundless prospects presented to us by nature; such as wide extended plains, to which the eye can see no limits; the firmament of heaven; or the boundless expanse of the ocean. All vastness produces the impression of sublimity. It is to be remarked, however, that space extended in length, makes not so strong an impression as height or depth. Though a boundless plain be a grand object, yet a high mountain, to which we look up, or an awful precipice or tower whence we look down on the objects which lie below, is still more so. The excessive grandeur of the firmament arises from its height joined to its boundless extent; and that of the ocean, not from its extent alone, but from the perpetual motion and irresistible force of that mass of waters. Wherever space is concerned, it is clear that amplitude or greatness of extent, in one dimension or other, is necessary to grandeur. Remove all bounds from any object, and you presently render it sublime. Hence infinite space, endless numbers, and eternal duration, fill the mind with great ideas.

From this some have imagined, that vastness, or amplitude of extent, is the foundation of all sublimity. But I cannot be of this opinion, because many objects appear sublime which have no relation to space at all. Such, for instance, is great loudness of sound. The burst of thunder or of cannon, the roaring of winds, the shouting of multitudes, the sound of vast cataracts of water, are all incontestably grand objects. "I heard the voice of a great multitude, as the sound of many waters, and of mighty thunderings, saying, Allelujah." In general we may observe, that great power and strength exerted, always raise sublime ideas; and perhaps the most copious source of these is derived from this quarter. Hence the grandeur of earthquakes and burning mountains; of great conflagrations; of the stormy ocean, and overflowing waters; of tempests of wind; of thunder and lightning; and of all the uncommon violence of the elements. Nothing is more

[4] See a Philosophical Inquiry into the Origin of our Ideas of the Sublime and Beautiful:—Dr. Gerard on Taste, section ii.:—Elements of Criticism, chap. iv.

sublime than mighty power and strength. A stream that runs within its banks, is a beautiful object, but when it rushes down with the impetuosity and noise of a torrent, it presently becomes a sublime one. From lions and other animals of strength, are drawn sublime comparisons in poets. A race-horse is looked upon with pleasure; but it is the war-horse, "whose neck is clothed with thunder," that carries grandeur in its idea. The engagement of two great armies, as it is the highest exertion of human might, combines a variety of sources of the sublime; and has accordingly been always considered as one of the most striking and magnificent spectacles that can be either presented to the eye, or exhibited to the imagination in description.

For the farther illustration of this subject, it is proper to remark, that all ideas of the solemn and awful kind, and even bordering on the terrible, tend greatly to assist the sublime; such as darkness, solitude, and silence. What are the scenes of nature that elevate the mind in the highest degree, and produce the sublime sensation? Not the gay landscape, the flowery field, or the flourishing city; but the hoary mountain, and the solitary lake; the aged forest, and the torrent falling over the rock. Hence, too, night-scenes are commonly the most sublime. The firmament when filled with stars, scattered in such vast numbers, and with such magnificent profusion, strikes the imagination with a more awful grandeur, than when we view it enlightened by all the splendor of the sun. The deep sound of a great bell, or the striking of a great clock, are at any time grand; but when heard amid the silence and stillness of the night, they become doubly so. Darkness is very commonly applied for adding sublimity to all our ideas of the Deity. "He maketh darkness his pavilion; he "dwelleth in the thick cloud." So Milton:

.............How oft, amidst
Thick clouds and dark, does heaven's all-ruling Sire
Choose to reside, his glory unobscur'd,
And with the majesty of darkness round
Circles his throne............ Book II.263.

Observe, with how much art Virgil has introduced all those ideas of silence, vacuity, and darkness, when he is going to introduce his hero to the infernal regions, and to disclose the secrets of the great deep.

Dii, quibus imperium est animarum, umbra que silentes,
Et Chaos, et Phlegethon, loca nocte silentia late,
Sit mihi fas audita loqui; sit numine vestro
Paudere res alta terra et caligine mersas.
Ibant obscuri, sola sub nocte, per umbram,
Perque domos Ditis vacuos, et inania regna;

Quale per incertam lunam, sub luce maligna
Est iter in Sylvis..........[5]

These passages I quote at present, not so much as instances of sublime writing, though in themselves they truly are so, as to show, by the effect of them, that the objects which they present to us, belong to the class of sublime ones.

Obscurity, we are farther to remark, is not unfavorable to the sublime. Though it render the object indistinct, the impression, however, may be great; for as an ingenious author has well observed, it is one thing to make an idea clear, and another to make it affecting to the imagination; and the imagination may be strongly affected, and, in fact, often is so, by objects of which we have no clear conception. Thus we see, that almost all the descriptions given us of the appearances of supernatural beings, carry some sublimity, though the conceptions which they afford us be confused and indistinct. Their sublimity arises from the ideas, which they always convey, of superior power and might, joined with an awful obscurity. We may see this fully exemplified in the following noble passage of the book of Job. "In thoughts from the visions of the night, when deep sleep falleth upon men, fear came upon me, and trembling, which made all my bones to shake. Then a spirit 'passed before my face; the hair of my flesh stood up: it stood still; but I could not discern the form thereof; an image was before mine eyes; there was silence; and I heard a voice—Shall mortal man be more just than God?"[6] (Job iv. 15.) No ideas, it is plain, are so sublime as those taken from the Supreme Being; the most unknown, but the greatest

[5] Ye subterranean gods, whose awful sway
The gliding ghost and silent shades obey:
O Choas, hear! and Phlegethon profound!
Whose solemn empire stretches wide around;
Give me, ye great tremendous powers! to tell
Of scenes and wonders in the depths of hell;
Give me your mighty secrets to display,
From those black realms of darkness to the day. PITT.

Obscure they went; through dreary shades that led
Along the waste dominions of the dead;
As wander travelers in woods by night,
By the moon's doubtful and malignant light. DRYDEN.

[6] The picture which Lucretius has drawn of the dominion of superstition over mankind, representing it as a portentous spectre showing its head from the clouds and dismaying the whole human race with its countenance, together with the magnanimity of Epicurus in raising himself up against it, carries all the grandeur of a sublime, obscure, and awful image.

Humana ante oculos foede cum vita jaceret
In terris, oppressa gravi sub religione,
Quae caput coeli regionibus ostendebat,
Horribili super aspectu mortalibus instans,
Primum Graius homo mortales tollere contra
Est oculos ausus..............LIB. I

of all objects; the infinity of whose nature, and the eternity of whose duration, joined with the omnipotence of his power, though they surpass our conceptions, yet exalt them to the highest. In general, all objects that are greatly raised above us, or far removed from us, either in space or in time, are apt to strike us as great. Our viewing them, as through the mist of distance or antiquity, is favorable to the impressions of their sublimity.

As obscurity so disorder too, is very compatible with grandeur; nay, frequently heightens it. Few things that are strictly regular and methodical, appear sublime. We see the limits on every side; we feel ourselves confined; there is no room for the mind's exerting any great effort. Exact proportion of parts, though it enters often into the beautiful, is much disregarded in the sublime. A great mass of rocks, thrown together by the hand of nature with wildness and confusion, strike the mind with more grandeur, than if they had been adjusted to one another with the most accurate symmetry.

In the feeble attempts, which human art can make towards producing grand objects, (feeble, I mean, in comparison with the powers of nature,) greatness of dimensions always constitutes a principal part. No pile of building can convey any idea of sublimity, unless it be ample and lofty. There is too, in architecture, what is called greatness of manner; which seems chiefly to arise, from presenting the object to us in one full point of view; so that it shall make its impression whole, entire, and undivided upon the mind. A Gothic cathedral raises ideas of grandeur in our minds, by its size, its height, its awful obscurity, its strength, its antiquity, and its durability.

There still remains to be mentioned one class of sublime objects, which may be called the moral, or sentimental sublime; arising from certain exertions of the human mind; from certain affections, and actions, of our fellow-creatures. These will be found to be all, or chiefly, of that class, which comes under the name of magnanimity or heroism: and they produce an effect extremely similar to what is produced by the view of grand objects in nature; filling the mind with admiration, and elevating it above itself. A noted instance of this, quoted by all the French critics, is the celebrated *Qu'il Mourut* of Corneille, in the tragedy of Horace. In the famous combat between the Horatii and the Curiatii, the old Horatius being informed that two of his sons are slain, and that the third had betaken himself to flight, at first will not believe the report; but being thoroughly assured of the fact, is fired with all the sentiments of high honor and indignation at this supposed unworthy behaviour of his surviving son. He is reminded, that his son stood alone against three, and asked what he wished him to have done? "To have died," he answers. In the same manner Porus, taken prisoner by Alexander, after gallant defense, and asked how he wished to be treated? answering, "Like a king;" and Caesar chiding the pilot who was afraid to set out with him in the storm, "Quid times? Caesarem vehis;" are good instances of this sentimental sublime. Wherever, in some critical and high situation, we behold a man uncommonly intrepid, and resting upon himself; superior to passion and to fear;

animated by some great principle to the contempt of popular opinion, of selfish interest, of dangers, or of death; there we are struck with a sense of the sublime.[7]

High virtue is the most natural and fertile source of this moral sublimity. However, on some occasions, where virtue either has no place, or is but imperfectly displayed, yet if extraordinary vigor and force of mind be discovered, we are not insensible to a degree of grandeur in the character; and from the splendid conqueror or the daring conspirator, whom we are far from approving, we cannot withhold our admiration.[8]

I have now enumerated a variety of instances, both in inanimate objects and in human life, wherein the sublime appears. In all these instances, the emotion raised in us is of the same kind, although the objects that produce the emotion be of widely different kinds. A question next arises, whether we are able to discover some one fundamental quality in which all these different objects agree, and which is the cause of their producing an emotion of the same nature in our minds? Various hypotheses have been formed concerning this; but, as far as appears to me, hitherto unsatisfactory. Some have imagined that amplitude, or great extent, joined with simplicity, is either immediately, or remotely, the fundamental quality of whatever is sublime; but we have seen that amplitude is confined to one species of sublime objects, and cannot, without violent straining be applied to them all. The author of *A*

[7] The sublime, in natural and in moral objects, is brought before us in one view, and compared together, in the following beautiful passage of Akenside's Pleasure of the Imagination:
Look then abroad through nature to the range
Of planets, suns, and adamantine spheres,
Wheeling, unshaken, thro' the void immense;
And speak, O man! does this capacious scene,
With half that kindling majesty dilate
Thy strong conception, as when Brutus rose,
Refulgent, from the stroke of Caesar's fate,
Amid the crowd of patriots; and his arm
Aloft extending, like eternal love,
When guilt brings down the thunder, call'd aloud
On Tully's name, and shook his crimson steel,
And bade the father of his country hail?
For, lo! the tyrant prostrate on the dust,
And Rome again is free. Book I.

[8] Silius Italicus has studied to give an august idea of Hannibal, by representing him as surrounded with all his victories, in the place of guards. One who had formed a design of assassinating him in the midst of a feast, is thus addressed:
Fallit te, mensas, inter quod credis inermem;
Tot bellis quaesita viro, tot coedibus, armat
Majestas aeterna ducem. Si adinoveris ora
Cannas et Trebiam ante oculos, Trasymenaque busta
Et Pauli stare ingentem miraberis umbram.
A thought somewhat of the same nature occurs in a French author: "Il se cache; mais sa reputation le decouvre; Il marche sans suite & sans equipage; mais chacun, dans son esprit, le met sur un char de triomphe. On compte en le voyant, les ennemis qu'il a vaincus, non pas les serviteurs qui le suivent. Tout seal qu'il est, on se figure, autour de lui, ses vertus, et ses victoires, qui l'accompagnent. Moins il est superbe, plus il devient venerable." Oraison funebre de M. de Turenne, par M. Flechier. Both these passages are splendid, rather than sublime. In the first, there is a want of justness in the thought: in the second, of simplicity in the expression.

Philosophical Inquiry into the Origin of our Ideas of the Sublime and Beautiful,[9] to whom we are indebted for several ingenious and original thoughts upon this subject, proposes a formal theory upon this foundation, that terror is the source of the sublime, and that no objects have this character, but such as produce impressions of pain and danger. It is indeed true, that many terrible objects are highly sublime; and that grandeur does not refuse an alliance with the idea of danger. But though this is very properly illustrated by the author, (many of whose sentiments on that head I have adopted,) yet he seems to stretch his theory too far, when he represents the sublime as consisting wholly in modes of danger, or of pain. For the proper sensation of sublimity appears to be distinguishable from the sensation of either of these; and on several occasions, to be entirely separated from them. In many grand objects, there is no coincidence with terror at all; as in the magnificent prospect of wide extended plains, and of the starry firmament; or in the moral dispositions and sentiments, which we view with high admiration; and in many painful and terrible objects also, it is clear there is no sort of grandeur. The amputation of a limb, or the bite of a snake, are exceedingly terrible; but are destitute of all claim whatever to sublimity. I am inclined to think, that mighty force or power, whether accompanied with terror or not, whether employed in protecting, or in alarming us, has a better title, than any thing that has yet been mentioned, to be the fundamental quality of the sublime; as, after the review which we have taken, there does not occur to me any sublime object, into the idea of which, power, strength, and force, either enter not directly, or are not at least intimately associated with the idea, by leading our thoughts to some astonishing power as concerned in the production of the object. However, I do not insist upon this as sufficient to found a general theory: it is enough, to have given this view of the nature and different kinds of sublime objects; by which I hope to have laid a proper foundation for discussing, with greater accuracy, the sublime in writing and composition.

Lecture IV
The Sublime in Writing

Having treated of grandeur or sublimity in external objects, the way seems now to be cleared, for treating, with more advantage, of the descriptions of such objects: or, of what is called the sublime in writing. Though I may appear early to enter on the consideration of this subject; yet, as the sublime is a species of writing which depends less than any other on the artificial embellishments of rhetoric, it may be examined with as much propriety here, as in any subsequent part of the lectures.

Many critical terms have unfortunately been employed in a sense too loose and vague; none more so, than that of the sublime. Every one is acquainted with the character of Caesar's *Commentaries*, and of the style in which they are written: a style remarkably pure, simple, and elegant; but the most remote from the sublime of any of the classical authors. Yet this author has a German critic, Johannes Gulielmus

[9] Mr. Burke.

Bergerus, who wrote no longer ago than the year 1720, pitched upon as the perfect model of the sublime, and has composed a quarto volume, entitled *De naturali pulchritudine Orationis*; the express intention of which is to show, that Caesar's *Commentaries* contain the most complete exemplification of all Longinus's rules relating to sublime writing. This I mention as a strong proof of the confused ideas which have prevailed, concerning this subject. The true sense of sublime writing, undoubtedly, is such a description of objects, or exhibition of sentiments, which are in themselves of a sublime nature, as shall give us strong impressions of them. But there is another very indefinite, and therefore very improper, sense, which has been too often put upon it; when it is applied to signify any remarkable and distinguishing excellency of composition; whether it raise in us the ideas of grandeur, or those of gentleness, elegance, or any other sort of beauty. In this sense, Caesar's *Commentaries* may, indeed, be termed sublime, and so may many sonnets, pastorals, and love elegies, as well as Homer's *Iliad*. But this evidently confounds the use of words, and marks no one species, or character, of composition whatever.

I am sorry to be obliged to observe, that the sublime is too often used in this last and improper sense, by the celebrated critic Longimus, in his treatise on this subject. He sets out, indeed, with describing it in its just and proper meaning; as something that elevates the mind above itself, and fills it with high conceptions, and a noble pride. But from this view of it he frequently departs; and substitutes in the place of it, whatever, in any strain of composition, pleases highly. Thus, many of the passages which he produces as instances of the sublime, are merely elegant, without having the most distant relation to proper sublimity; witness Sappho's famous ode, on which he descants at considerable length. He points outs five sources of the sublime. The first is boldness or grandeur in the thoughts; the second is, the pathetic; the third, the proper application of figures; the fourth, the use of tropes and beautiful expressions; the fifth, musical structure and arrangement of words. This is the plan of one who was writing a treatise of rhetoric, or of the beauties of writing in general; not of the sublime in particular. For of these five heads, only the two first have any peculiar relation to the sublime; boldness and grandeur in the thoughts, and in some instances the pathetic, or strong exertions of passion; the other three, tropes, figures, and musical arrangement, have no more relation to the sublime, than to other kinds of good writing; perhaps less to the sublime, than to any other species whatever; because it requires less the assistance of ornament. From this it appears, that clear and precise ideas on this head are not to be expected from that writer. I would not, however, be understood, as if I meant, by this censure, to represent his treatise as of small value. I know no critic, ancient or modern, that discovers a more lively relish of the beauties of fine writing, than Longinus; and he has also the merit of being himself an excellent, and in several passages, a truly sublime, writer. But as his work has been generally considered as a standard on this subject, it was incumbent on me to give my opinion concerning the benefit to be derived from it. It deserves to be consulted, not so much for distinct instruction concerning the sublime, as for excellent general ideas concerning the beauty in writing.

I return now to the proper and natural idea of the sublime in composition. The foundation of it must always be laid in the nature of the object described. Unless it be such an object as, if presented to our eyes, if exhibited to us in reality, would raise ideas of that elevating, that awful and magnificent kind, which we call sublime; the description, however finely drawn, is not entitled to come under this class. This excludes all objects that are merely beautiful, gay, or elegant. In the next place, the object must not only, in itself, be sublime, but it must be set before us in such a light as is most proper to give us a clear and full impression of it; it must be described with strength, with conciseness, and simplicity. This depends, principally, upon the lively impression which the poet, or orator, has of the object which he exhibits; and upon his being deeply affected, and warmed, by the sublime idea which he would convey. If his own feeling be languid, he can never inspire us with any strong emotion. Instances, which are extremely necessary on this subject, will clearly show the importance of all the requisites which I have just now mentioned.

It is, generally speaking, among the most ancient authors, that we are to look for the most striking instances of the sublime. I am inclined to think that the early ages of the world, and the rude unimproved state of society, are peculiarly favorable to the strong emotions of sublimity. The genius of men is then much turned to admiration and astonishment. Meeting with many objects, to them new and strange, their imagination is kept glowing, and their passions are often raised to the utmost. They think, and express themselves boldly, and without restraint. In the progress of society, the genius and manners of men undergo a change more favorable to accuracy, than to strength or sublimity.

. . .

Lecture V
Beauty, and other Pleasures of Taste

As sublimity constitutes a particular character of composition, and forms one of the highest excellences of eloquence and of poetry, it was proper to treat of it at some length. It will not be necessary to discuss so particularly all the other pleasure that arise from taste, as some of them have less relation to our main subject. On beauty only I shall make several observations, both as the subject is curious, and as it tends to improve taste, and to discover the foundation of several of the graces of description and of poetry.[10]

Beauty, next to sublimity, affords, beyond doubt, the highest pleasure to the imagination. The emotion which it raises, is very distinguishable from that of sublimity. It is of a calmer kind; more gentle and soothing; does not elevate the mind so much, but produces an agreeable serenity. Sublimity raises a feeling, too violent, as I showed, to be lasting; the pleasure arising from beauty admits of longer continuance. It extends also to a much greater variety of objects than sublimity; to a variety indeed so great, that the feelings which beautiful objects produce, differ considerably, not in

[10]See Hutchinson's Inquiry concerning Beauty and Virtue:—Gerard on Taste, chap. iii.:—Inquiry into the Origin of our Ideas of the Sublime and Beautiful:—Elelments of Criticism, chap. iii.:—Spectator, vol. vi.:—Essay on the Pleasures of Taste.

degree only, but also in kind, from one another. Hence, no word in the language is used in a more vague signification than beauty. It is applied to almost every external object that pleases the eye, or the ear; to a great number of the graces of writing; to many dispositions of the mind; nay, to several objects of mere abstract science. We talk currently of a beautiful tree or flower; a beautiful poem; a beautiful character; and a beautiful theorem in mathematics.

Hence we may easily perceive, that, among so great a variety of objects, to find out some one quality in which they all agree, and which is the foundation of that agreeable sensation they all raise, must be a very difficult, if not, more probably, a vain attempt. Objects denominated beautiful, are so different, as to please, not in virtue of any one quality common to them all, but by means of several different principles in human nature. The agreeable emotion which they all raise, is somewhat of the same nature; and therefore, has the common name of beauty given to it; but it is raised by different causes.

Hypotheses, however, have been framed by ingenious men, for assigning the fundamental quality of beauty in all objects. In particular, uniformity amidst variety has been insisted on as this fundamental quality. For the beauty of many figures, I admit that this accounts in a satisfactory manner. But when we endeavor to apply this principle to beautiful objects of some other kind, as to color, for instance, or emotion, we shall soon find that it has no place. And even in external figured objects it does not hold, that their beauty is in proportion to their mixture of variety with uniformity; seeing many please us as highly beautiful, which have almost no variety at all, and others, which are various to a degree of intricacy. Laying systems of this kind, therefore, aside, what I now propose is, to give an enumeration of several of those classes of objects in which beauty most remarkably appears; and to point out, as far as I can, the separate principles of beauty in each of them.

Color affords, perhaps, the simplest instance of beauty, and therefore the fittest to begin with. Here, neither variety, nor uniformity, nor any other principle that I know, can be assigned as the foundation of beauty. We can refer to it to no other cause but the structure of the eye, which determines us to receive certain modifications of the rays of light with more pleasure than others. And we see accordingly, that, as the organ of sensation varies in different persons, they have their different favorite colors. It is probable, that association of ideas has influence, in some cases, on the pleasure which we receive from colors. Green, for instance, may appear more beautiful, by being connected in our ideas with rural prospects and scenes; white, with innocence; blue with the serenity of the sky. Independent of associations of this kind, all that we can farther observe concerning colors is, that those chosen for beauty are, generally, delicate, rather than glaring. Such are those paintings with which nature hath ornamented some of her works, and which art strives in vain to imitate; as the feathers of several kinds of birds, the leaves of flowers, and the fine variation of colors exhibited by the sky at the rising and setting of the sun. These present to us the highest instances of the beauty of coloring; and have accordingly been the favorite subjects of poetical description in all countries.

From color we proceed to figure, which opens to us forms of beauty more complex and diversified. Regularity first occurs to be noticed as a source of beauty.

By a regular figure, is meant, one which we perceive to be formed according to some certain rule, and not left arbitrary, or loose, in the construction of its parts. Thus, a circle, a square, a triangle, or a hexagon, please the eye, by their regularity, as beautiful figures. We must not, however, conclude, that all figures please in proportion to their regularity; or that regularity is the sole, or the chief, foundation of beauty in figure. On the contrary, a certain graceful variety is found to be a much more powerful principle of beauty; and is therefore studied a great deal more than regularity, in all works that are designed merely to please the eye. I am, indeed, inclined to think, that regularity appears beautiful to us, chiefly, if not only, on account of its suggesting the ideas of fitness, propriety, and use, which have always a greater connection with orderly and proportioned forms, than with those which appear not constructed according to any certain rule. It is clear, that nature, who is undoubtedly the most graceful artist, hath, in all her ornamental works, pursued variety with an apparent neglect of regularity. Cabinets, doors, and windows, are made after a regular form, in cubes and parallelograms, with exact proportion of parts; and by being so formed they please the eye: for this good reason, that, being works of use, they are, by such figures, the better suited to the ends for which they were designed. But plants, flowers, and leaves, are full of variety and diversity. A straight canal is an insipid figure, in comparison of the meanders of rivers. Cones and pyramids are beautiful; but trees growing in their natural wilderness, are infinitely more beautiful than when trimmed into pyramids and cones. The apartments of a house must be regular in their disposition, for the conveniency of its inhabitants; but a garden which is designed merely for beauty, would be exceedingly disgusting, if it had as much uniformity and order in its parts as a dwelling-house.

Mr. Hogarth, in his *Analysis of Beauty*, has observed, that figures bounded by curve lines are, in general, more beautiful than those bounded by straight lines and angles. He pitches upon two lines, on which according to him, the beauty of figure principally depends; and he has illustrated and supported his doctrine, by a surprising number of instances. The one is the waving line, or a curve bending backwards and forwards, somewhat in the form of the letter S. This he calls the line of beauty; and shows how often it is found in shells, flowers, and such other ornamental works of nature; as is common also in the figures designed, by painters and sculptors, for the purpose of decoration. The other line, which he calls the line of grace, is the former waving curve, twisted round some solid body. The curling worm of a common jack is one of the instances he gives of it. Twisted pillars, and twisted horns, also exhibit it. In all the instances which he mentions, variety plainly appears to be so material a principle of beauty, that he seems not to err much when he defines the art of drawing pleasing forms, to be the art of varying well. For the curve line, so much the favorite of painters, derives, according to him, its chief advantage, from its perpetual bending and variation from the stiff regularity of the straight line.

Motion furnishes another source of beauty, distinct from figure. Motion of itself is pleasing; and bodies in motion are, *caeteris paribus*, preferred to those in rest. It is, however, only gentle motion that belongs to the beautiful; for when it is very swift, or very forcible, such as that of a torrent, it partakes of the sublime. The motion of a bird gliding through the air, is extremely beautiful; the swiftness with which lightning darts through the heavens, is magnificent and astonishing. And here, it is proper to observe, that the sensations of sublime and beautiful are not always distinguished by very distant boundaries; but are capable, in several instances, of approaching towards each other. Thus, a smooth running stream is one of the most beautiful objects in nature: as it swells gradually into a great river, the beautiful, by degrees, is lost in the sublime. A young tree is a beautiful object; a spreading ancient oak, is a venerable and grand one. The calmness of a fine morning is beautiful; the universal stillness of the evening is highly sublime. But to return to the beauty of motion, it will be found, I think, to hold very generally, that motion in a straight line is not so beautiful as in an undulating waving direction; and motion upwards is, commonly too, more agreeable than motion downwards. The easy curling motion of flame and smoke may be instanced, as an object singularly agreeable: and here Mr. Hogarth's waving line recurs upon us as a principle of beauty. That artist observes, very ingeniously, that all the common and necessary motions for the business of life, are performed by men in straight or plain lines: but that all the graceful and ornamental movements are made in waving lines: an observation not unworthy of being attended to, by all who study the grace of gesture and action.

Though color, figure, and motion, be separate principles of beauty; yet in many beautiful objects they all meet, and thereby render the beauty both greater, and more complex. Thus, in flowers, trees, animals, we are entertained at once with the delicacy of the color, with the gracefulness of the figure, and sometimes also with the motion of the object. Although each of these produce a separate agreeable sensation, yet they are of such a similar nature, as readily to mix and blend in one general perception of beauty, which we ascribe to the whole object as its cause: for beauty is all ways conceived by us, as something residing in the object which raises the pleasant sensation; a sort of glory which dwells upon, and invests it. Perhaps the most complete assemblage of beautiful objects that can any where be found, is presented by a rich natural landscape, where there is a sufficient variety of objects; fields in verdure, scattered trees and flowers, running water, and animals grazing. If to these be joined some of the productions of art, which suit such a scene: as a bridge with arches over a river, smoke rising from cottages in the midst of trees, and the distant view of a fine building seen by the rising sun; we then enjoy, in the highest perfection, that gay, cheerful, and placid sensation which characterizes beauty. To have an eye and a taste formed for catching the peculiar beauties of such scenes as these, is a necessary requisite for all who attempt poetical description.

The beauty of the human countenance is more complex than any that we have yet considered. It includes the beauty of color, arising from the delicate shades of the complexion; and the beauty of figure, arising from the lines which form the different features of the face. But the chief beauty of the countenance depends upon a mysterious expression, which it conveys, of the qualities of the mind; of good sense, or good humor; of sprightliness, candor, benevolence, sensibility, or other amiable dispositions. How it comes to pass that a certain conformation of features is connected in our idea with certain moral qualities; whether we are taught by instinct, or by experience, to form this connection, and to read the mind in the countenance, belongs not to us now to inquire, nor is indeed easy to resolve. The fact is certain, and acknowledged, that what gives the human countenance its most distinguishing beauty, is what is called its expression; or an image, which it is conceived to show of internal moral dispositions.

This leads us to observe, that there are certain qualities of the mind which, whether expressed in the countenance, or by words, or by actions, always raise in us a feeling similar to that of beauty. There are two great classes of moral qualities; one is of the high and the great virtues, which require extraordinary efforts, and turn upon dangers and sufferings; as heroism, magnanimity, contempt of pleasure, and contempt of death. These, as I have observed in a former lecture, excite in the spectator an emotion of sublimity and grandeur. The other class is generally of the social virtues, and such as are of a softer and gentler kind; as compassion, mildness, friendship, and generosity. These raise in the beholder a sensation of pleasure, so much akin to that produced by beautiful external objects, that, though of a more dignified nature, it may, without impropriety, be classed under the same head.

A species of beauty, distinct from any I have yet mentioned, arises from design of art; or in other words, from the perception of means being adapted to an end; or the parts of any thing being well fitted to answer the design of the whole. When, in considering the structure of a tree or a plant, we observe how all the parts, the roots, the stem, the bark, and the leaves, are suited to the growth and nutriment of the whole; much more when we survey all the parts and members of a living animal, or when we examine any of the curious works of art; such as a clock, a ship, or any nice machine; the pleasure which we have in the survey, is wholly founded on this sense of beauty. It is altogether different from the perception of beauty produced by color, figure, variety, or any of the causes for merely mentioned. When I look at a watch, for instance, the case of it, if finely engraved, and of curious workmanship, strikes me as beautiful in the former sense; bright color, exquisite polish, figures finely raised and turned. But when I examine the spring and the wheels, and praise the beauty of the internal machinery, my pleasure then arises wholly from the view of that admirable art, with which so many various and complicated parts are made to unite for one purpose.

This sense of beauty, in fitness and design, has an extensive influence over many of our ideas. It is the foundation of the beauty which we discover in the proportion of doors, windows, arches, pillars, and all the orders of architecture. Let the ornaments of a building be ever so fine and elegant in themselves, yet, if they interfere with this sense of fitness and design, they lose their beauty, and hurt the eye, like disagreeable objects. Twisted columns, for instance, are undoubtedly ornamental; but as they have an appearance of weakness, they always displease when they are made use of to support any part of a building that is massy, and that seems to require a more substantial prop. We cannot look upon any work whatever, without being led, by a natural association of ideas, to think of its end and design, and of course to examine the propriety of its parts, in relation to this design and end. When their propriety is clearly discerned, the work seems always to have some beauty; but when there is a total want of propriety, it never fails of appearing deformed. Our sense of fitness and design, therefore, is so powerful, and holds so high rank among our perceptions, as to regulate, in a great measure, our other ideas of beauty: an observation which I the rather make, as it is of the utmost importance, that all who study composition should carefully attend to it. For, in an epic poem, a history, an oration, or any work of genius, we always require, as we do in other works, a fitness, or adjustment of means to the end which the author is supposed to have in view. Let his descriptions be ever so rich, or his figures ever so elegant, yet, if they are out of place, if they are not proper parts of that whole, if they suit not the main design, they lose all their beauty, nay, from beauties they are converted into deformities. Such power has our sense of fitness and congruity, to produce a total transformation of an object whose appearance otherwise would have been beautiful.

After having mentioned so many various species of beauty, it now only remains to take notice of beauty as it is applied to writing or discourse; a term commonly used in a sense altogether loose and undetermined. For it is applied to all that pleases, either in style or sentiment, from whatever principle that pleases, either in style or sentiment, from whatever principle that pleasure flows; and a beautiful poem or oration means, in common language, no other than a good one, or one well composed. In this sense, it is plain, the word is altogether indefinite, and points at no particular species or kind of beauty. There is, however, another sense, somewhat more definite, in which beauty of writing characterizes a particular manner; when it is used to signify a certain grace and amenity in the turn either of style or sentiment for which some authors have been peculiarly distinguished. In this sense, it denotes a manner neither remarkably sublime, nor vehemently passionate, nor uncommonly sparkling; but such as raises in the reader an emotion of the gentle, placid kind, similar to what is raised by the contemplation of beautiful objects in nature; which neither lifts the mind very high, nor agitates it very much, but diffuses over the imagination an agreeable and pleasing serenity. Mr. Addison is a writer altogether of this character; and is one of the most proper and precise examples that can be given of it. Fenelon, the author of the *Adventures of Telemachus*, may be given as another example. Virgil too, though very capable of rising on occasions into the sublime, yet, in his general manner, is distinguished by the character of beauty and grace, rather than of sublimity. Among orators, Cicero has more of the beautiful than Demosthenes, whose genius led him wholly towards vehemence and strength.

This much is sufficient to have said upon the subject of beauty. We have traced it through a variety of forms; as next to sublimity, it is the most copious source of the pleasures of taste; and as the consideration of the different appearances, and principles of beauty, tends to the improvement of taste in many subjects.

But it is not only by appearing under the forms of sublime or beautiful, that objects delight the imagination. From several other principles also, they derive their power of giving it pleasure.

Novelty, for instance, has been mentioned by Mr. Addison, and by every writer on this subject. An object which has no merit to recommend it, except its being uncommon or new, by means of this quality alone, produces in the mind a vivid and an agreeable emotion. Hence that passion of curiosity, which prevails so generally among mankind. Objects and ideas which have been long familiar, make too faint an impression to give an agreeable exercise to our faculties. New and strange objects rouse the mind from its dormant state by giving it a quick and pleasing impulse.

Hence, in a great measure, the entertainment afforded us by fiction and romance. The emotion raised by novelty is of a more lively and pungent nature, than that produced by beauty; but much shorter in its continuance. For if the object have in itself no charms to hold our attention, the shining gloss thrown upon it by novelty soon wears off.

Besides novelty, imitation is another source of pleasure to taste. This gives rise to what Mr. Addison terms, the secondary pleasures of imagination; which form, doubtless, a very extensive class. For all imitation affords some pleasure; not only the imitation of beautiful or great objects, by recalling the original ideas of beauty or grandeur which such objects themselves exhibited; but even objects which have neither beauty nor grandeur, nay, some which are terrible or deformed, please us in a secondary or represented view.

The pleasures of melody and harmony belong also to taste: there is no agreeable sensation we receive either from beauty or sublimity, but what is capable of being heightened by the power of musical sound. Hence the delight of poetical numbers, and even of the more concealed and looser measures of prose. Wit, humor, and ridicule, likewise open a variety of pleasures of taste, quite distinct from any that we have yet considered.

At present it is not necessary to pursue any farther the subject of the pleasures of taste. I have opened some of the general principles; it is time now to make the application to our chief subject. If the question be put, to what class of those pleasures of taste which I have enumerated, that pleasure is to be referred which we receive from poetry, eloquence, or fine writing? My answer is, not to any one, but to them all. This singular advantage, writing and discourse possess, that they encompass so large and rich a field on all sides, and have power to exhibit, in great perfection, not a single set of objects only, but almost the whole of those which give pleasure to taste and imagination; whether that pleasure arise from sublimity, from beauty in its different forms, from design, and art, from moral sentiment, from novelty, from harmony, from wit, humor, and ridicule. To whichsoever of these the peculiar bent of a person's taste lies, from some writer or other, he has it always in his power to receive the gratification of it.

Now this high power which eloquence and poetry possess, of supplying taste and imagination with such a wide circle of pleasure, they derive altogether from their having a greater capacity of imitation and description than is possessed by any other art. Of all the means which human ingenuity has contrived for recalling the images of real objects, and awakening, by representation, similar emotions to those which are raised by the original, none is so full and extensive as that which is executed by words and writing. Through the assistance of this happy invention, there is nothing, either in the natural or moral world, but what can be represented and set before the mind, in colors very strong and lively. Hence it is usual among critical writers, to speak of discourse as the chief of all the imitative or mimetic arts; they compare it with painting and with sculpture, and in many respects prefer it justly before them.

This style was first introduced by Aristotle in his poetics; and, since this time, has acquired a general currency among modern authors. But as it is of consequence to introduce as much precision as possible into critical language, I must observe, that this manner of speaking is not accurate. Neither discourse in general, nor poetry in particular, can be called altogether imitative arts. We must distinguish betwixt imitation and description, which are ideas that should not be confounded. Imitation is performed by means of somewhat that has a natural likeness and resemblance to the thing imitated, and of consequence is understood by all: such as statues and pictures. Description, again, is the raising in the mind the conception of an object by means of some arbitrary or instituted symbols, understood only by those who agree in the institution of them; such are words and writing. Words have no natural resemblance to the ideas or objects which they are employed to signify; but a statue or a picture has a natural likeness to the original. And therefore imitation and description differ considerably in their nature from each other.

As far, indeed, as the poet introduces into his work persons actually speaking; and, by the words which he puts into their mouths, represents the discourse which they might be supposed to hold; so far his art may more accurately be called imitative; and this is the case in all dramatic composition. But, in narrative or descriptive works, it can with no propriety be called so. Who, for instance, would call Virgil's description of a tempest, in the first *Aeneid*, an imitation of a storm? If we heard of the imitation of a battle, we might naturally think of some mock fight, or representation of a battle on the stage, but would never apprehend, that it meant one of Homer's descriptions in the *Iliad.* I admit, at the same time, that imitation and description agree in their principal effect, of recalling, by external signs, the ideas of things which we do not see. But though in this they coincide, yet it should not be forgotten, that the terms themselves are not synonymous; that they import different means of effecting the same end; and of course make different impressions on the mind.[11]

[11]Though in the execution of particular parts, poetry is certainly descriptive rather than imitative, yet there is a qualified sense in which poetry, in the general, may be termed an imitative art. The subject of the poet (as Dr. Gerard has shown in the appendix to his *Essay on Taste*) is intended to be an imitation, not of things really existing, but of the course of nature: that is, a feigned representation of such events, or such scenes, as though they never had a being, yet might have existed; and which, therefore, by their probability, bear a resemblance to nature. It was probably in this sense, that Aristotle termed poetry a mimetic art. How far either the imitation or the description which poetry employs, is superior to the imitative powers of painting and music, is well shown by Mr. Harris, in his treatise on music, painting, and poetry. The chief advantage which poetry, or discourse in general, enjoys, is, that whereas, by the nature of his art, the painter is confined to the representation of a single moment, writing and discourse can trace a transaction through its whole progress. That moment, indeed, which the painter pitches upon for the subject of his picture, he may be said to exhibit with more advantage than the poet or orator; inasmuch as he sets before us, in one view, all the minute concurring circumstances of the event which happens in one individual point of time, as they appear in nature; while discourse is obliged to exhibit them in succession, and by means of a detail which is in danger of becoming tedious, in order to be clear; or, if not tedious, is in danger of being obscure. But to that point of time which he has chosen, the painter being entirely confined, he cannot exhibit various stages of the same action or event; and he is subject to this farther defect, that he can only exhibit objects as they appear to the eye, and can very imperfectly delineate characters and sentiments, which are the noblest subjects of imitation or description. The power of representing these with full advantage, gives a high superiority to discourse and writing, above all other imitative arts.

Whether we consider poetry in particular, and discourse in general, as imitative or descriptive; it is evident that their whole power, in recalling the impressions of real objects, is derived from the significancy of words. As their excellency flows altogether from this source, we must, in order to make way for further inquiries, begin at this fountain-head. I shall, therefore, in the next lecture enter upon the consideration of language: of the origin, the progress, and construction of which, I purpose to treat at some length.

CHAPTER 19

Archibald Alison*

Essay on the Nature and Principles of Taste
1790

Introduction

Taste is, in general, considered as that faculty of the human mind, by which we perceive and enjoy whatever is beautiful or sublime in the works of nature or art.

The perception of these qualities is attended with an emotion of pleasure, very distinguishable from every other pleasure of our nature, and which is accordingly distinguished by the name of the emotion of taste. The distinction of the objects of taste into the sublime and the beautiful, has produced a similar division of this emotion, into the emotion of sublimity and the emotion of beauty.

The qualities that produce these emotions are to be found in almost every class of the objects of human knowledge; and the emotions themselves afford one of the most extensive sources of human delight. They occur to us, amid every variety of external scenery, and among many diversities of disposition and affection in the mind of man. The most pleasing arts of human invention are altogether directed to their pursuit. And even the necessary arts are exalted into dignity, by the genius that can unite beauty with use. From the earliest period of society, to its last stage of improvement, they afford an innocent and elegant amusement to private life, at the same time that they increase the splendor of national character, and in the progress of nations, as well as of individuals, while they attract attention from the pleasures they bestow, they serve to exalt the human mind, from corporeal to intellectual pursuits.

---

*Archibald Alison (1757-1839) was born in Edinburgh but was educated at Balliol and ordained in the Church of England. He returned to Edinburgh in 1800 as an Anglican clergyman where he served until his death. His published works included collections of sermons, but he is best known for his *Essays on the Nature and Principles of Taste*. This work was published in 1790, the same year as Immanuel Kant's *Third Critique*, but it became popular only after a second edition appeared in 1811.

These qualities, however, though so important to human happiness, are not objects of immediate observation; and in the attempt to investigate them, various circumstances unite to perplex our research. They are often obscured under the number of qualities with which they are accidentally combined: They result often from peculiar combinations of the qualities of objects, or the relation of certain parts of objects to each other: They are still oftener, perhaps, dependent upon the state of our own minds, and vary in their effects with the disposition in which they happen to be observed. In all cases, while we feel the emotions they excite, we are ignorant of the causes by which they are produced; and when we seek to discover them, we have no other method of discovery, than that varied and patient experiment, by which, amid these complicated circumstances, we may gradually ascertain the peculiar qualities which, by the constitution of our nature, are permanently connected with the emotions we feel.

In the employment of this mode of investigation, there are two great objects of attention and inquiry, which seem to include all that is either necessary, or perhaps possible, for us to discover on the subject of taste.

These objects are,

I. To investigate the nature of those qualities that produce the emotions of taste, And,

II. To investigate the nature of that faculty, by which these emotions are received.

These investigations, however, are not to be considered only as objects of philosophical curiosity. They have an immediate relation to all the arts that are directed to the production either of the beautiful or the sublime; and they afford the only means by which the principles of these various arts can be ascertained. Without a just and accurate conception of the nature of these qualities, the artist must be unable to determine, whether the beauty he creates is temporary or permanent, whether adapted to the prejudices of his age, or the uniform constitution of the human mind; and whatever the science of criticism can afford for the improvement or correction of taste, must altogether depend on the laws of this faculty.

To both these inquiries, however, there is a preliminary investigation, which seems absolutely necessary, and without which every conclusion we form, must be either imperfect or vague. In the investigation of causes, the first and most important step, is the accurate examination of the effect to be explained. In the science of mind, however, as well as in that of body, there are few effects altogether simple, or in which accidental circumstances are not combined with the proper effect. Unless, therefore, by means of repeated experiment such accidental circumstances are accurately distinguished from the phenomena that permanently characterize the effect; we are under the necessity of including in the cause, the causes also of all the accidental circumstances with which the effect is accompanied.

With the emotions of taste, in almost every instance, many other accidental emotions of pleasure are united: the various simple pleasures that arise from other qualities of the object; the pleasure of agreeable sensation, in the case of material objects; and in all, that pleasure which, by the constitution of our nature; is annexed to the exercise of our faculties. Unless, therefore, we have previously acquired a distinct and accurate conception of that *peculiar* effect which is produced on our minds; when the emotions of taste are felt, and can precisely distinguish it from the effects that are produced by these accidental qualities, we must necessarily include in the causes of such emotions, those qualities also, which are the causes of the accidental pleasures with which this emotion is accompanied. The variety of systems that philosophers have adopted upon this subject, and the various emotions into which they have resolved the emotion of taste, while they afford a sufficient evidence of the numerous accidental pleasures that accompany these emotions, afford also a strong illustration of the necessity of previously ascertaining the nature of this effect, before we attempt to investigate its cause. With regard, therefore, to both these inquiries, the first and most important step is accurately to examine the nature of this emotion itself, and its distinction from every other emotion of pleasure; and our capacity of discovering either the nature of the qualities that produce the emotions of taste, or the nature of the faculty by which they are received, will be exactly proportioned to our accuracy in ascertaining the nature of the emotion itself.

When we look back to the history of these investigations, and to the theories which have been so liberally formed upon the subject, there is one fact that must necessarily strike us, *viz.* That all these theories have uniformly taken for granted the *simplicity* of this emotion; that they have considered it as an emotion too plain, and too commonly felt, to admit of any analysis; that they have as uniformly, therefore, referred it to some *one* principle or law of the human mind; and that they have therefore concluded, that the discovery of that *one* principle was the essential key by which all the pleasures of taste were to be resolved.

While they have assumed this fundamental principle, the various theories of philosophers may, and indeed must, be included in the two following classes of supposition.

I. The first class is that which resolves the emotion of taste directly into an original law of our nature; which supposes a sense, or senses, by which the qualities of beauty and sublimity are perceived and felt, as their appropriate objects; and concludes, therefore, that the genuine object of the arts of taste, is to discover, and to imitate, those qualities in every subject, which the prescription of nature has thus made essentially either beautiful or sublime.

To this first class of hypotheses belong almost all the theories of music, of architecture, and of sculpture; the theory of Mr. Hogarth, of the Abbé Winkelman, and perhaps, in its last result, also the theory of Sir Joshua Reynolds. It is the species of hypothesis which is naturally resorted to by all artists and amateurs, - by those, whose habits of thought lead them to attend more to the causes of their emotions, than to the nature of the emotions themselves.

II. The second class of hypotheses arises from the opposite view of the subject. It is that which resists the idea of any new or peculiar sense, distinct from the common principles of our nature; which supposes some *one* known and acknowledged principle or affection of mind, to be the foundation of all the emotions we receive from the objects of taste, and which resolves, therefore, all the various phenomena into some more general law of our intellectual or moral constitution. Of this kind are the hypotheses of M. Diderot, who attributes all our emotions of this kind to the perception of relation; of Mr. Hume, who resolves them into our sense of utility; of the venerable St. Austin, who, with nobler views, a thousand years ago, resolved them into the pleasure which belongs to the perception of order and design, &c. It is the species of hypothesis most natural to retired and philosophic minds; to those, whose habits have led them to attend more to the nature of the emotions they felt, than to the causes which produced them.

If the success of these long and varied inquiries has not corresponded to the genius of the philosophers who have pursued them, a suspicion may arise that there has been something faulty in the principle of their investigation; and that some fundamental assumption has been made which ought first to have been patiently and securely ascertained. It was this suspicion that first led to the following inquiries. It seemed to me that the simplicity of the emotion of taste, was a principle much too hastily adopted; and that the consequences which followed from it (under both these classes of hypotheses), were very little reconcilable with the most common experience of human feeling; and from the examination of this preliminary question, I was led gradually to conclusions which seemed not only to me, but to others, whose opinion I value far more than my own, of an importance not unworthy of being presented to the public. In doing this, I am conscious that I have entered upon a new and untrodden path; and I feel all my own weakness in pursuing it: yet I trust my readers will believe, that I should not have pursued it so long, if I were not convinced that it would finally terminate in views not only important to the arts of taste, but important also to the philosophy of the human mind.

The inquiries which follow, naturally divide themselves into the following parts; and are to be prosecuted in the following order.

I. I shall begin with an analysis of the effect which is produced upon the mind, when the emotions of beauty or sublimity are felt. I shall endeavor to show, that this effect is very different from the determination of a sense; that it is not in fact a simple, but a complex emotion; that it involves, in all cases, *1st*, the production of some simple emotion, or the exercise of some moral affection, and, *2dly*, the consequent excitement of a peculiar exercise of the imagination; that these concomitant effects are distinguishable, and, very often distinguished in our experience; and that the *peculiar* pleasure of the beautiful or the sublime is only felt when these two effects are conjoined, and the complex emotion produced.

The prosecution of this subject will lead to another inquiry of some difficulty and extent, *viz*. into the origin of the beauty and sublimity of the qualities of matter. To this subordinate inquiry I shall devote a separate essay. I shall endeavor to show, that all the phenomena are reducible to the same general principle, and that the qualities of matter are not beautiful or sublime in themselves, but as they are by various means, the signs or expressions of qualities capable of producing emotion.

II. From this examination of the effect I shall proceed, in the second part, to investigate the causes which are productive of it; or, in other words, the sources of the beautiful and the sublime in nature and art.

In the course of this investigation, I shall endeavor to show, 1st, that there is no single emotion into which these varied effects can be resolved; that on the contrary, every simple emotion, and therefore every object which is capable of producing any simple emotion, may be the foundation of the complex emotion of beauty or sublimity. But in the second place, that this complex emotion of beauty or sublimity is never produced, unless, beside the excitement of some simple emotion, the imagination also is excited, and the exercise of the two faculties combined in the general effect. The prosecution of the subject, will lead me to the principal object of the inquiry, to show what is that law of mind, according to which, in actual life, this exercise or employment of imagination is excited; and what are the means by which, in the different fine arts, the artist is able to awaken this important exercise of imagination, and to exalt objects of simple and common pleasure, into objects of beauty or sublimity.

In this part of the subject, there are two subordinate inquiries which will necessarily demand attention.

1. The qualities of sublimity and beauty, are discovered not only in pleasing or agreeable subjects, but frequently also in objects that are in themselves productive of pain; and some of the noblest productions of the fine arts are founded upon subjects of terror and distress. It will form, therefore, an obvious and important inquiry, to ascertain by what means this singular effect is produced in real nature, and by what means it may be produced in the compositions of art.

2. There is a distinction in the effects produced upon our minds by objects of taste; and this distinction, both in the emotions and their causes, has been expressed by the terms of sublimity and beauty. It will form, therefore, a second object of inquiry to ascertain the nature of this distinction, both with regard to these emotions and to the qualities that produce them.

III. From the preceding inquiries I shall proceed, in the last part, to investigate the nature of that faculty by which these emotions are perceived and felt. I shall endeavor to show, that it has no resemblance to a sense; that as, whenever it is employed, two distinct and independent powers of mind are employed, it is not to be considered as a separate and peculiar faculty, and that it is finally to be resolved into more general principles of our constitution. These speculations will probably lead to the important inquiry, whether there is any standard by which the perfection or imperfection of our sentiments upon these subjects may be determined; to some explanation of the means by which taste may be corrected or improved; and to some illustrations of the purposes which this peculiar constitution of our nature serves, in the increase of human happiness, and the exaltation of human character.

I feel it incumbent on me, however, to inform my readers, that I am to employ, in these inquiries, a different kind of evidence from what has usually been employed by writers upon these subjects, and that my illustrations will be derived, much less from the compositions of the fine arts, than from the appearances of common nature, and the experience of common men. If the fine arts are in reality arts of imitation, their principles are to be sought for in the subject which they imitate; and it is ever to be remembered, "That music, architecture, and painting, as well as poetry and oratory, are to deduce their laws and rules from the general sense and taste of mankind, and not from the principles of these arts themselves; in other words, that the taste is not to conform to the art, but the art to the taste."[1] In following this mode of illustration, while I am sensible that I render my book less amusing, I trust I may render it more useful. The most effectual method to check the empiricism, either of art or of science, is to multiply, as far as possible, the number of those who can observe, and judge; and (whatever may be the conclusions of my readers with regard to my own particular opinions), I shall not have occupied their attention in vain, if I can lead them to think and to feel for themselves; to employ the powers which are given them to the ends for which they were given; and, upon subjects where all men are entitled to judge, to disregard alike the abstract refinements of the philosopher who speculates in the closet, and the technical doctrines of the artist who dictates in the school.

Essay I
On the Nature of the emotions of Sublimity and beauty

Chapter I
Of the Effect produced upon the Imagination by Objects of Sublimity and beauty
Section I

The emotions of sublimity and beauty are uniformly ascribed, both in popular and in philosophical language, to the imagination. The fine arts are considered as the arts which are addressed to the imagination; and the pleasures they afford are described, by way of distinction, as the pleasures of the imagination. The nature of any person's taste is, in common life, generally determined by the nature or character of his imagination; and the expression of any deficiency in this power of mind, is considered as synonymous with the expression of a similar deficiency in point of taste.

Although, however, this connection is so generally acknowledged, it is not perhaps as generally understood in what it consists, or what is the nature of that effect which is produced upon the imagination by objects of sublimity and beauty. I shall endeavor, therefore, in the first place, to state what seems to me the nature of this effect, or, in what that exercise of imagination consists, which is so generally supposed to take place, when these emotions are felt.

When any object, either of sublimity or beauty, is presented to the mind, I believe every man is conscious of a train of thought being immediately awakened in his imagination, analogous to the character or expression of the original object. The simple perception of the object, we frequently find is insufficient to excite these emotions, unless, it is accompanied with this operation of mind,—unless, according to common expression, our imagination is seized, and our fancy busied in the pursuit of all those trains of thought which are allied to this character or expression.

Thus, when we feel either the beauty or sublimity of natural scenery,—the gay luster of a morning in spring or the mild radiance of a summer evening,—the savage

[1] Mr. Addison.

majesty of a wintry storm, or the wild magnificence of a tempestuous ocean,—we are conscious of a variety of images in our minds, very different from those which the objects themselves can present to the eye. Trains of pleasing or of solemn thought arise spontaneously within our minds; our hearts swell with emotions, of which the objects before us seem to afford no adequate cause; and we are never so much satiated with delight, as when, in recalling our attention, we are unable to trace either the progress or the connection of those thoughts, which have passed with so much rapidity through our imagination.

The effect of the different arts of taste is similar. The landscapes of Claude Lorraine, the music of Handel, the poetry of Milton, excite feeble emotions in our minds when our attention is confined to the qualities they present to our senses, or when it is to such qualities of their composition that we turn our regard. It is then, only, we feel the sublimity or beauty of their productions, when our imaginations are kindled by their power, when we lose ourselves amid the number of images that pass before our minds, and when we waken at last from this play of fancy, as from the charm of a romantic dream. The beautiful apostrophe of the Abbé de Lille upon the subject of gardening—

> N'avez-vous pas souvent, au lieux infrequentes,
> Rencontré tout-à-coup, ces aspects enchantés,
> Qui suspendent vos pas, dont l'image chérie
> Vous jette en une douce et longue reverie?

is equally applicable to every other composition of taste; and in the production of thought, seems to consist the effect which objects of sublimity and beauty have upon the imagination.

For the truth of this observation itself, I must finally appeal to the consciousness of the reader; but there are some very familiar considerations, which it may be useful to suggest, that seem very strongly to show the connection between this exercise of imagination, and the existence of the emotions of sublimity or beauty.

Section II

That unless this exercise of imagination is excited, the emotions of beauty or sublimity are unfelt, seems capable of illustration, from many instances of a very familiar kind.

I

If the mind is in such a state as to prevent this freedom of imagination, the emotion, whether of sublimity or beauty, is unperceived. In so far as the beauties of art or nature affect the external senses, their effect is the same upon every man who is in possession of these senses. But—to a man in pain or in grief, whose mind, by these means, is attentive only to one object or consideration, the same scene, or the same form, will produce no feeling of admiration, which, at other times, when his imagination was at liberty, would have produced it in its fullest perfection. Whatever is great or beautiful in the scenery of external nature, is almost constantly before us; and not a day passes, without presenting us with appearances, fitted both to harm, and to elevate our minds; yet it is in general with a heedless eye that we regard them, and only in particular moments, that we are sensible of their power. There is no man, for instance, who has not felt the beauty of sun set; yet every one can remember many instances, when this most striking scene had no effect at all upon his imagination; and when he has beheld all the magnificence with which nature generally distinguishes the close of day, without one sentiment of admiration or delight. There are times, in the same manner, when we can read the *Georgics*, or the *Season*s, with perfect indifference, and with no more emotion, than what we feel from the most uninteresting composition in prose; while in other moments, the first lines we meet with take possession of our imagination, and awaken in it such innumerable trains of imagery, as almost leave the fancy of the poet behind. In these, and similar cases of difference in our feelings, from the same objects, it will always be found, that the difference arises from the state of our imaginations; from our disposition to follow out the train of thought which such objects naturally produce, or our incapacity to do it, from some other idea, which has at that time taken possession of our minds, and renders us unable to attend to any thing else. That state of mind, every man must have felt, is most favorable to the emotions of taste, in which the imagination is free and unembarrassed, or, in which the attention is so little occupied by any private or particular object of thought, as to leave us open to all the impressions which the objects that are before us can produce. It is upon the vacant and the unemployed, accordingly, that the objects of taste make the strongest impression. It is in such hours alone, that we turn to the compositions of music, or of poetry, for amusement. The reasons of care, of grief, or of business, have other occupations, and destroy, for the time at least, our sensibility to the beautiful or the sublime, in the same proportion that they produce a state of mind unfavorable to the indulgence of imagination.

II

The same thing is observable in criticism. When we sit down to appreciate the value of a poem, or of a painting and attend minutely to the language or composition of the one, or to the coloring or design of the other, we feel no longer the delight which they at first produce. Our imagination in this employment is restrained, and, instead of yielding to its suggestions, we studiously endeavor to resist them, by fixing our attention upon minute and partial circumstances of the composition. How much this operation of mind tends to diminish our sense of its beauty, every one will feel, who attends to his own thoughts on such an occasion, or who will recollect how different was his state of mind, when he first felt the beauty either of the painting or the poem. It is this, chiefly, which makes it so difficult for young people, possessed of imagination, to judge of the merits of any poem or fable, and which induces them so often to give their approbation to compositions of little value. It is not that they are incapable of learning in what the merits of such compositions consist; for these principles of judgment are neither numerous nor abstruse. It is not that greater experience produces greater sensibility, for this everything contradicts; but it is, because everything, in that period of life, is able to excite their imaginations, and to move their hearts; because they judge of the composition, not by its merits, when compared with other works, or by its approach to any abstract or ideal standard, but by its effect in agitating their imaginations, and leading them into that fairy land in which the fancy of youth has so much delight to wander. It is their own imagination which has the charm which they attribute to the work that excites it; and the simplest tale, or the poorest novel, is, at that time, as capable of awakening it, as afterwards the eloquence of Virgil or Rousseau. All this, however, all this flow of imagination, in which youth and men of sensibility are so apt to indulge, and which so often brings them pleasure at the expense of their taste, the labor of criticism destroys. The mind, in such an employment, instead of being at liberty to follow whatever trains of imagery the composition before it can excite, is either fettered to the consideration of some of its minute and solitary parts; or pauses amid the rapidity of its conceptions, to make them the objects of its attention and review. In these operations, accordingly, the emotion, whether of beauty or sublimity, is lost; and if it is wished to be recalled, it can only be done by relaxing this vigor of attention, and resigning our selves again to the natural stream of our thoughts. The mathematician who investigates the demonstrations of the Newtonian philosophy, the painter who studies the designs of Raphael, the poet who reasons upon the measure of Milton, all, in such occupations lose the delight which these several productions can give; and, when they are willing to recover their emotion, must withdraw their attention from those minute considerations, and leave their fancy to expatiate, at will, amid all the great or pleasing conceptions which such productions of genius can raise.

III

The effect which is thus produced upon the mind by temporary exertions of attention, is also more permanently produced by the difference of original character; and the degree in which the emotions of sublimity or beauty are felt, is in general proportioned to the prevalence of those relations of thought in the mind, upon which this exercise of imagination depends. The principal relation which seems to take place in those trains of thought that are produced by objects of taste, is that of resemblance; the relation, of all others, the most loose and general, and which affords the greatest range of thought for our imagination to pursue. Wherever, accordingly, these emotions are felt, it will be found, not only that this is the relation which principally prevails among our ideas, but that the emotion itself is proportioned to the degree in which it prevails.

In the effect which is produced upon our minds, by the different appearances of natural scenery, it is easy to trace this progress of resembling thought, and to observe, how faithfully the conceptions which arise in our imaginations, correspond to the impressions which the characters of these seasons produce. What, for instance, is the impression we feel from the scenery of spring? The soft and gentle green with which the earth is spread, the feeble texture of the plants and flowers, the young of animals just entering into life, and the remains of winter yet lingering among the woods and hills,—all conspire to infuse into our minds somewhat of that fearful tenderness with which infancy is usually beheld. With such a sentiment, how innumerable are the ideas which present themselves to our imagination! ideas, it is apparent, by no means confined to the scene before our eyes or to the possible desolation which may yet await its infant beauty, but which almost involuntarily extend themselves to analogies with the life of man, and bring before us all those images of hope or fear, which, according to our peculiar situations, have the dominion of our heart!—The beauty of autumn is accompanied with a similar exercise of thought: The leaves begin then to drop from the trees; the flowers and shrubs, with which the fields were adorned in the summer months, decay; the woods and groves are silent; the sun himself seems gradually to withdraw his light, or to become enfeebled in his power.—Who is there, who, at this season, does not feel his mind impressed with a sentiment of melancholy? or who is able to resist that current of thought, which, from such appearance of decay, so naturally leads him to the solemn imagination of that inevitable fate, which is to bring on alike the decay of life, of empire, and of nature itself? In such cases of emotion, every man must have felt, that the character of the scene is no sooner impressed upon his mind, than various trains of correspondent imagery rise before his imagination; that, whatever may be the nature of the impression, the general tone of his thoughts partakes of this nature or character; and that his delight is proportioned to the degree in which this uniformity of character prevails.

The same effect, however, is not produced upon all men. There are many, whom the prospect of such appearances in nature excites to no exercise of fancy whatever, who, by their original constitution, are more disposed to the employment of attention, than of imagination; and who, in the objects that are presented to them, are more apt to observe their individual and distinguishing qualities, than those by which they are related to other objects of their knowledge. Upon the minds of such men, the relation of resemblance has little power; the efforts of their imagination, accordingly, are either feeble or slow; and the general character of their understandings is that of steady and precise, rather than that of enlarged and extensive thought. It is, I believe, consistent with general experience, that men of this description are little sensible to the emotions of sublimity or beauty; and they who have attended to the language of such men, when objects of this kind have been presented to them, must have perceived that the emotion they felt, was no greater than what they themselves have experienced in those cases where they have exerted a similar degree of attention, or when any other cause has restrained the usual exercise of their imagination. To the qualities which are productive of simple emotion, to the useful, the agreeable, the fitting, or the convenient in objects, they have the same sensibility with other men; but of the superior and more complex emotion of beauty, they seem to be either altogether unconscious, or to share in it only in proportion to the degree in which they can relax this severity of attention, and yield to the relation of resembling thought.

It is in the same manner, that the progress of life generally takes from men their sensibility to the objects of taste. The season in which these are felt in their fullest degree is in youth, when, according to common expression, the imagination is warm, or, in other words, when it is easily excited to that exertion upon which so much of the emotion of beauty depends. The business of life, in the greatest part of mankind, and the habits of more accurate thought, which are acquired by the few who reason and reflect, tend eventually to produce, in both, a stricter relation in the train of their thoughts, and greater attention to the objects of their consideration, than can either be expected, or can happen in youth. They become, by these means, not only less easily led to any exercise of imagination, but their associations become at the same time less consistent with the employment of it. The man of business, who has passed his life in studying the means of accumulating wealth, and the philosopher, whose years have been employed in the investigation of causes, have both not only acquired a constitution of mind very little fitted for the indulgence of imagination, but have acquired also associations of a very different kind from those which take place when imagination is employed. In the first of these characters, the prospect of any beautiful scene in nature would induce no other idea than that of its value. In the other, it would lead, only to speculations upon the causes of the beauty that was ascribed to it. In both, it would thus excite ideas, which could be the foundation of no exercise of imagination, because they required thought and attention. To a young mind, on the contrary, possessed of any sensibility, how many pleasing ideas would not such a prospect afford! Ideas of peace, and innocence; and rural joy, and all the unblemished delights of solitude and contemplation. In such trains of imagery, no labor of thought, or habits of attention are required; they rise spontaneously in the mind, upon the prospect of any object to which they bear the slightest resemblance; and they lead it almost insensibly along, in a kind of bewitching reverie, through all its store of pleasing or interesting conceptions. To the philosopher, or the man of business, the emotion of beauty, from such a scene, would be but feebly known; but by the young mind, which had such sensibility, it would be felt in all its warmth, and would produce an emotion of delight, which not only would be little comprehended by men of a severer or more thoughtful character, but which seems also to be very little dependent upon the object which excites it, and to be derived, in a great measure, from this exercise of mind.

In these familiar instances, it is obvious how much the emotions of taste are connected with this state or character of imagination; and how much those habits or employments of mind, which demand attention, or which limit it to the consideration of single objects, tend to diminish the sensibility of mankind to the emotions of sublimity or beauty.

Section III

There are many other instances equally familiar, which are sufficient to show, that whatever increases this exercise or employment of imagination increases also the emotion of beauty or sublimity.

I

This is very obviously the effect of all associations. There is no man who has not some interesting associations with particular scenes, or airs, or books, and who does not feel their beauty or sublimity enhanced to him by such connections. The view of the house where one was born, of the school where one was educated, and where the gay years of infancy were passed, is indifferent to no man. They recall so many images of past happiness and past affections,—they are connected with so many strong or interesting emotions, and lead altogether to so long a train of feelings and recollections, that there is hardly any scene which one ever beholds with so much rapture. There are songs also, that we have heard in our infancy, which, when brought to our remembrance in after years, raise emotions for which we cannot well account, and which, though perhaps very indifferent in themselves, still continue, from this association, and from the variety of conceptions which they kindle in our minds to be our favorites through life. The scenes which have been distinguished by the residence of any person whose memory we admire, produce a similar effect. "Movemur. enim, nescio quo pacto, locis ipsis, in quibus eorum, quos diligimus, aut admiramur adsunt vestigia." The scenes themselves may be little beautiful; but the delight with which we recollect the traces of their lives, blends itself insensibly with the emotions which the scenery excites; and the admiration which these recollections afford, seems to give a kind of sanctity to the place where they dwelt, and converts every thing into beauty which appears to have been connected with them. There are scenes, undoubtedly, more beautiful than Runnymede; yet, to those who recollect the great event which passed there, there is no scene, perhaps, which so strongly seizes upon the imagination; and although the emotions this recollection produces, are of a very different kind from those which the mere natural scenery can excite, yet they unite themselves so well with these inferior emotions, and spread so venerable a charm over the whole, that one can hardly persuade one's self, that the scene itself is not entitled to this admiration. The valley of Vaucluse is celebrated for its beauty; yet how much of it has been owing to its being the residence of Petrarch! . . .

Essay Two
Section VI
Conclusion of the Essay—of the Final Cause of the Constitution of Our Nature

The illustrations that have been offered in the course of this essay upon the origin of the sublimity and beauty of some of the principal qualities of matter, seem to afford sufficient evidence for the following conclusions:

I.—That each of these qualities is either from nature, from experience, or from accident, the sign of some quality capable of producing emotion, or the exercise of some moral affection. And,

II.—That when these associations are dissolved, or in other words, when the material qualities cease to be significant of the associated qualities, they cease also to produce the emotions, either of sublimity or beauty.

If these conclusions are admitted, it appears necessarily to follow, that the beauty and sublimity of such objects is to be ascribed, not to the material qualities themselves, but to the qualities they signify; and of consequence, that the qualities of matter are not to be considered as sublime or beautiful in themselves, but as being the signs or expressions of such qualities as, by the constitution of our nature, are fitted to produce pleasing or interesting emotion.

The opinion I have now stated coincides, in a great degree, with a doctrine that appears very early to have distinguished the Platonic school; which is to be traced, perhaps, (amid their dark and figurative language,) in all the philosophical systems of the East, and which has been maintained in this country, by several writers of eminence, by Lord Shaftesbury, Dr. Hutcheson, Dr. Aikenside, and Dr. Spence, but which has nowhere so finely and so philosophically been maintained as by Dr. Reid in his invaluable work *On the Intellectual Powers of Man*. The doctrine to which I allude, is, that matter is not beautiful in itself, but derives its beauty from the expression of mind.

As this doctrine, however, when stated in general terms, has somewhat of the air of paradox, I shall beg leave, in a few words, to explain in what sense I understand and adopt it, by enumerating what appears to me the principal classes of this expression, or the principal means by which the qualities of matter become significant to us of those qualities of mind which are destined to affect us with pleasing or interesting emotions.

The qualities of mind which are capable of producing emotion, are either its active, or its passive qualities; either its *powers* and capacities, as beneficence, wisdom, fortitude, innocence, etc. or its feelings and *affections*, as love, joy, hope, gratitude, purity, fidelity, innocence, etc. In the observation or belief of these qualities of mind, we are formed, by the original and moral constitution of our nature, to experience various and powerful emotions.

As it is only, however, through the medium of matter that, in the present condition of our being, the qualities of mind are known to us, the qualities of matter become necessarily expressive to us of all the qualities of mind they signify. They may be the signs, therefore, or expressions of these mental qualities, in the following ways:

I.—As the immediate signs of the powers or capacities of mind. It is thus, that all the works of human art or design, are directly significant to us of the wisdom, the invention, the taste, or the benevolence of the artist; and the works of nature, of the power, the wisdom, and the beneficence of the Divine artist.

II.—As the signs of all these affections, or dispositions of mind, which we love, or with which we are formed to sympathize. It is thus that the notes and motions of animals are expressive to us of their happiness and joy; that the tones of the human voice are significant of the various emotions by which it is animated; and that all the affections which we either have or admire in the human mind, are directly signified to us by the various appearances of the countenance and form.

These may be called the *direct* expressions of mind; and the material qualities which signify such power or affections, produce in us immediately the peculiar emotions which, by the laws of our nature, the mental qualities are fitted to produce. But besides these, there are other means by which the qualities of matter may be significant to us of the qualities of mind, *indirectly*, or by means of less universal and less permanent relations.

1. From experience, when peculiar forms or appearances of matter are considered as the means or instruments by which those feelings or affections of mind are produced with which we sympathize, or in which we are interested. It is thus that the productions of art are in so many various ways significant to us of the conveniences, the pleasures, or the happiness they bestow upon human life, and as the signs of happiness, affect us with the emotion this happiness itself is destined to produce. It is thus also, that the scenes of nature acquire such an accession of beauty, when we consider them as fitted, with such exquisite wisdom, for the habitation of so many classes of sentient being; and when they become thus expressive to us of all the varied happiness they produce, and contain, and conceal.

2. From analogy or resemblance; from that resemblance which has everywhere been felt between the qualities of matter and of mind, and by which the former becomes so powerfully expressive to us of the latter. It is thus, that the colors, the sounds, the forms, and above all, perhaps, the motions of inanimate objects, are so universally felt as resembling peculiar qualities or affections of mind, and when thus felt, are so productive of the analogous emotion; that the personification of matter is so strongly marked in every period of the history of human thought; and that the poet, while he gives life and animation to everything around him, is not displaying his own invention, but only obeying one of the most powerful laws which regulate the imagination of man.

3. From association (in the proper sense of that term) when by means of education, of fortune, or of accident, material objects are connected with pleasing or interesting qualities of mind; and from this connection become for ever afterwards expressive of them. It is thus that colors, forms, etc. derive their temporary beauty from fashion; that the objects which have been devoted to religion, to patriotism, or to honor, affect us with all the emotions of the qualities of which they become significant; that the beauty of natural scenery is so often exalted by the record of the events it has witnessed; and that, in every country, the scenes which have the deepest effect upon the admiration of the people, are those which have become sacred by the memory of ancient virtue, or ancient glory.

4. From *individual* association; when certain qualities or appearances of matter, are connected with our own private affections or remembrances; and when they give to these material qualities or appearances a character of interest which is solely the result of our own memory and affections.

Of the reality of these expressions I believe no person can doubt; and whoever will attend to the power and extent of their influence, will, I think, soon be persuaded, that they are sufficient to account for all the beauty or sublimity we discover in the qualities of matter.

The conclusion, therefore, in which I wish to rest is, that the beauty and sublimity which is felt in the various appearances of matter, are finally to be ascribed to their expression of mind; or to their being, either directly or indirectly, the signs of those qualities of mind which are fitted, by the constitution of our nature, to affect us with pleasing or interesting emotion. . . .

CHAPTER 20

William Gilpin*

Three Essays
1791

Essay I.

Disputes about beauty might perhaps be involved in less confusion, if a distinction were established, which certainly exists, between such objects as are beautiful, and such as are picturessque—between those, which please the eye in their natural state; and those, which please from some quality, capable of being illustrated by painting.

Ideas of beauty vary with objects, and with the eye of the spectator. The stone-mason sees beauties in a well-jointed wall, which escape the architect, who surveys the building under a different idea. And thus the painter, who compares his object with the rules of his art, sees it in a different light from the man of general taste, who surveys it only as simply beautiful.

As this difference therefore between the beautiful, and the picturesque appears really to exist, and must depend on some peculiar construction of the object; it may be worth while to examine, what that peculiar construction is. We inquire not into the general sources of beauty, either in nature, or in representation. This would lead into a nice, and scientific discussion, in which it is not our purpose to engage. The question simply is, What is that quality in objects, which particularly marks them as picturesque?

In examining the real object, we shall find, one source of beauty arises from that species of elegance, which we call smoothness, or neatness; for the terms are nearly synonymous. The higher the marble is polished, the brighter the silver is rubbed, and

*William Gilpin (1724-1804) was the brother of the painter Sawrey Gilpin. He was ordained in 1746 and served for a time as a curate and schoolmaster. During the long vacations, he went on sketching trips which led to his publishing his travel guides to the picturesque scenery of Britain. He also wrote biographies of religious figures including Latimer and Wycliff. He was appointed Vicar at Boldre in the New Forest where he earned a reputation as a benefactor of the poor. He founded a school at Boldre and arranged for its endowment. His religious catechism and published sermons were well received, and he did much to popularize the idea of domestic scenic touring.

the more the mahogany shines, the more each is considered as an object of beauty: as if the eye delighted in gliding smoothly over a surface.

In the class of larger objects the same idea prevails. In a pile of building we wish to see neatness in every part added to the elegance of the architecture. And if we examine a piece of improved pleasure-ground, every thing rough, and slovenly offends.

Mr. Burke, enumerating the properties of beauty, considers smoothness as one of the most essential. "A very considerable part of the effect of beauty, says he, is owing to this quality: indeed the most considerable: for take any beautiful object, and give it a broken, and rugged surface, and however well-formed it may be in other respects, it pleases no longer. Whereas, let it want ever so many of the other constituents, if it want not this, it becomes more pleasing, than almost all the others without it."[1] — How far Mr. Burke may be right in making smoothness the most considerable source of beauty, I rather doubt.[2] A considerable one it certainly is.

Thus then, we suppose, the matter stands with regard to beautiful objects in general. But in picturesque representation it seems somewhat odd, yet perhaps we shall find it equally true, that the reverse of this is the case; and that the ideas of neat and smooth, instead of being picturesque, in reality strip the object, in which they reside, of all pretensions to picturesque beauty.—Nay, farther, we do not scruple to assert, that roughness forms the most essential point of difference between the beautiful, and the picturesque; as it seems to be that particular quality, which makes objects chiefly pleasing in painting.—I use the general term roughness; but properly speaking roughness relates only to the surfaces of bodies: when we speak of their delineation, we use the word ruggedness. Both ideas however equally enter into the picturessque; and both are observable in the smaller, as well as in the larger parts of nature—in the outline, and bark of a tree, as in the rude summit, and craggy sides of a mountain.

Let us then examine our theory by an appeal to experience; and try how far these qualities enter into the idea of picturesque beauty; and how far they mark that difference among objects, which is the ground of our inquiry.

A piece of Palladian architecture may be elegant in the last degree. The proportion of its parts—the propriety of its ornaments—and the symmetry of the whole may be highly pleasing. But if we introduce it in a picture, it immediately becomes a formal object, and ceases to please. Should we wish to give it picturesque beauty, we must use the mallet instead of the chisel: we must beats down one half of it, deface

[1] Upon the sublime and beautiful [page 272, this volume].

[2] Mr. Burke is probably not very accurate in what he farther says on the connection between *beauty*, and *diminutives*.—Beauty excites love; and a loved object is generally characterized by diminutives. But it does not follow, that all objects characterized by diminutives, though they may be so because they are loved, are therefore beautiful. We often love them for their moral qualities; their affections; their gentleness; or their docility. Beauty, no doubt, awakens love; but also excites admiration, and respect. This combination forms the sentiment, which prevails, when we look at the Apollo of Belvidere, and the Niobe. No man of nice discernment would characterize these statues by diminutives.—There is then a beauty, between which and diminutives there is no relation; but which, on the contrary, excludes them: and in the description of figures, possessed of that species of beauty, we seek for terms, which recommend them more to our *admiration* than our *love*.

the other, and throw the mutilated members around in heaps. In short, from a smooth building we must turn it into a rough ruin. No painter, who had the choice of the two objects, would hesitate which to choose.

Again, why does an elegant piece of garden-ground make no figure on canvas? The shape is pleasing; the combination of the objects, harmonious; and the winding of the walk in the very line of beauty. All this is true; but the smoothness of the whole, though right, and as it should be in nature, offends in picture. Turn the lawn into a piece of broken ground: plant rugged oaks instead of flowering shrubs: break the edges of the walk: give it the rudeness of a road; make it with wheel-tracks; and scatter around a few stones, and brushwood; in a word, instead of making the whole smooth, make it rough; and you make it also picturesque. All the other ingredients of beauty it already possessed.

. . .

Animal life, as well as human, is, in general, beautiful both in nature, and on canvas. We admire the pampered horse, as a real object; the elegance of his form; the stateliness of his tread; the spirit of all his motions; and the glossiness of his coat. We admire him also in representation. But as an object of picturesque beauty, we admire more the worn-out cart-horse, the cow, the goat, or the ass; whose harder lines, and rougher coats, exhibit more the graces of the pencil. For the truth of this we may examine Berghem's pictures: we may examine the smart touch of Rosa of Tivoli. The lion with his rough mane; the bristly boar; and the ruffled plumage of the eagle,[3] are all objects of this kind. Smooth-coated animals could not produce so picturesque an effect.

[3] The idea of the *ruffled plumage of the eagle* is taken from the celebrated eagle of Pindar, in his first Pythian ode; which has exercised the pens of several poets; and is equally poetical, and picturesque. He is introduced as an instansce of the power of music. In Gray's ode on the progress of poesy we have the following picture of him.

Perching on the sceptered hand
Of Jove, thy magic lulls the feathered king
With ruffled plumes, and flagging wing:
Quenched in dark clouds of slumber lie
The terror of his beak, and lightening of his eye.

Akenside's picture of him, in his hymn to the Naiads, is rather a little stiffly painted.

—— With slackened wings,
While now the solemn concert breathes around,
Incumbent on the sceptre of his lord
Sleeps the stern eagle; by the numbered notes
Possessed; and satiate with the melting tone;
Sovereign of birds. ——

West's picture, especially the two last lines, is a very good one.

The bird's fierce monarch drops his vengeful ire.
Perched on the sceptre of th' Olympian king,
The thrilling power of harmony he feels
And indolently hangs his flagging wing;
While gentle sleep his closing eyelids seals,
And o'er his heaving limbs, in loose array,
To every balmy gale the ruffling feathers play.

But when the painter thus prefers the cart-horse, the cow, or the ass to other objects more beautiful in themselves, he does not certainly recommend his art to those, whose love of beauty makes them anxiously seek, by what means its fleeting forms may be fixed.

Suggestions of this kind are ungrateful. The art of painting allows you all you wish. You desire to have a beautiful object painted—your horse, for instance, led out of the stable in all his pampered beauty. The art of painting is ready to accommodate you. You have the beautiful form you admired in nature exactly transferred to canvas. Be then satisfied. The art of painting has given you what you wanted. It is no injury to the beauty of your Arabian, if the painter think he could have given the graces of his art more forcibly to your cart-horse.

But does it not depreciate his art, if he give up a beautiful form, for one less beautiful, merely because he can give it the graces of his art more forcibly— because its sharp lines afford him a greater facility of execution? Is the smart touch of a pencil the grand desideratum of painting? Does he discover nothing in picturesque objects, but qualities, which admit of being rendered with spirit?

I should not vindicate him, if he did. At the same time, a free execution is so very fascinating a part of painting, that we need not wonder, if the artist lay a great stress upon it.—It is not however entirely owing, as some imagine, to the difficulty of mastering an elegant line, that he prefers a rough one. In part indeed this may be the case; for if an elegant line be not delicately hit off, it is the most insipid of all lines: whereas in the description of a rough object, an error in delineation is not easily seen. However this is not the whole of the matter. A free, bold touch is in itself pleasing.[4] In elegant figures indeed there must be a delicate outline—at least a line true to nature: yet the surfaces even of such figures may be touched with freedom; and in the appendages of the composition there must be a mixture of rougher objects, or there will be a want of contrast. In landscape universally the rougher objects are admired; which give the freest scope to execution. If the pencil be timid, or hesitating, little beauty results. The execution then only is pleasing, when the hand firm, and yet decisive, freely touches the characteristic parts of each object.

If indeed, either in literary, or in picturesque composition you endeavor to draw the reader, or the spectator from the subject to the mode of executing it, your affectation[5] disgusts. At the same time, if some care, and pains be not bestowed on the execution, your slovenliness disgusts as much. Though perhaps the artist has

[4] A stroke may be called *free*, when there is no appearance of constraint. It is *bold*, when a part is given for the whole, which it cannot fail of suggesting. This is the laconism of genius. But sometimes it may be free, and yet suggest only how easily a line, which means nothing, may be executed. Such a stroke is not *bold*, but *impudent*.

[5] Language, like light, is a medium; and the true philosophic style, like light from a north-window, exhibits objects clearly, and distinctly, without soliciting attention to itself. In subjects of amusement indeed, language may gild somewhat more, and color with the dies of fancy: but where information is of more importance than entertainment, tho you cannot throw too *strong* a light, you should carefully avoid a *colored* one. The style of some writers resembles a bright light placed between the eye, and the thing to be looked at. The light shews itself; and hides the object: and, it must be allowed, the execution of some painters is as impertinent, as the style of such writers.

more to say, than the man of letters, for paying attention to his execution. A truth is a truth, whether delivered in the language of a philosopher, or of a peasant: and the intellect receives it as such. But the artist, who deals in lines, surfaces, and colors, which are in immediate address to the eye, conceives the very truth itself concerned in his mode of representing it. Guido's angel, and the angel on a sign-post, are very different beings; but the whole of the difference consists in an artful application of lines, surfaces, and colors.

It is not however merely for the sake of his execution, that the artist values a rough object. He finds it in many other respects accommodated to his art. In the first place, his composition requires it. If the history-painter threw all his draperies smooth over his figures; his groups, and combinations would be very awkward. And in landscape-painting smooth objects would produce no composition at all. In a mountain-scene what composition could arise from the corner of a smooth knoll coming forward on one side, intersected by a smooth knoll on the other; with a smooth plain perhaps in the middle, and a smooth mountain in the distance? The very idea is disgusting. Picturesque composition conflicts in uniting in one whole a variety of parts; and these parts can only be obtained from rough objects. If the smooth mountains, and plains were broken by different objects, the composition would be good, if we suppose the great lines of it were so before.

Variety too is equally necessary in his composition: so is contrast. Both these he finds in rough objects; and neither of them in smooth. Variety indeed, in some degree, he may find in the outline of a smooth object: but by no means enough to satisfy the eye, without including the surface also.

From rough objects also he seeks the effect of light and shade, which they are as well disposed to produce as they are the beauty of composition. One uniform light, or one uniform shade produces no effect. It is the various surfaces of objects, sometimes turning to the light in one way, and sometimes in another, that give the painter his choice of opportunities in massing, and graduating both his lights, and shades. The richness also of the light depends on the breaks, and little recesses, which it finds on the surfaces of bodies. What the painter calls richness on a surface, is only a variety of little parts; on which the light shining shews all its small inequalities, and roughnesses; or in the painter's language, enriches it.—The beauty also of catching lights arises from the roughness of objects. What the painter calls a catching light is a strong touch of light on some prominent part of a surface, while the rest is in shadow. A smooth surface hath no such prominences.

In coloring also, rough objects give the painter another advantage. Smooth bodies are commonly as uniform in their color, as they are in their surface. In glossy objects, though smooth, the coloring may sometimes vary. In general however it is otherwise; in the objects of landscape, particularly. The smooth side of a hill is generally of one uniform color; while the fractured rock presents its grey surface, adorned with patches of greensward running down its guttered sides; and the broken ground is every where varied with an ochrey tint, a grey gravel, or a leaden-colored clay: so that in fact the rich colors of the ground arise generally from its broken surface.

From such reasoning then we infer, that it is not merely for the sake of his execution that the painter prefers rough objects to smooth. The very essence of his art requires it.

As picturesque beauty therefore so greatly depends on rough objects, are we to exclude every idea of smoothness from mixing with it? Are we struck with no pleasing image, when the lake is spread upon the canvas; the *marmoreum aequor*, pure, limpid, smooth, as the polished mirror?

We acknowledge it to be picturesque: but we must at the same time recollect, that, in fact, the smoothness of the lake is more in reality, than in appearance. Were it spread upon the canvas in one simple hue, it would certainly be a dull, fatiguing object. But to the eye it appears broken by shades of various kinds; or by reflections from all the rough objects in its neighborhood.

It is thus too in other glossy bodies. Though the horse, in a rough state as we have just observed, or worn down with labor, is more adapted to the pencil, than when his sides shine with brushing, and high-feeding; yet in his latter state also he is certainly a picturesque object. But it is not his smooth, and shining coat, that makes him so. It is the apparent interruption of that smoothness by a variety of shades, and colors, which produces the effect. Such a play of muscles appears every where, through the fineness of his skin, gently swelling, and sinking into each other—he is all over so *lubricus aspici*, the reflections of light are so continually shifting upon him, and playing into each other, that the eye never considers the smoothness of the surface; but is amused with gliding up, and down, among those endless transitions, which in some degree, supply the room of roughness.

. . .

Having thus from a variety of examples endeavored to shew, that roughness either real, or apparent, forms an essential difference between the beautiful, and the picturesque; it may be expected, that we should point out the reason of this difference. It is obvious enough, why the painter prefers rough objects to smooth:[6] but it is not so obvious, why the quality of roughness should make an essential difference between objects of beauty, and objects suited to artificial representation.

To this question, we might answer, that the picturesque eye abhors art; and delights solely in nature: and that as art abounds with regularity, which is only another name for smoothness; and the images of nature with irregularity, which is only another name for roughness, we have here a solution of our question.

But is this solution satisfactory? I fear not. Though art often abounds with regularity, it does not follow, that all art must necessarily do so. The picturesque eye, it is true, finds it's chief object in nature; but it delights also in the images of art, if they are marked with the characteristics, which it requires. A painter's nature is whatever he imitates; whether the object be what is commonly called natural, or artificial. Is there a greater ornament of landscape, than the ruins of a castle? What

[6] See page 425, & c.

painter rejects it, because it is artificial?—What beautiful effects does Vandervelt produce from shipping? In the hands of such a master it furnishes almost as beautiful forms, as any in the whole circle of picturesque objects?—And what could the history-painter do, without his draperies to combine, contrast, and harmonize his figures? Unclothed, they could never be grouped. How could he tell his story, without arms; religious utensils; and the rich furniture of banquets? Many of these contribute greatly to embellish his pictures with pleasing shapes.

Shall we then seek the solution of our question in the great foundation of picturesque beauty? In the happy union of simplicity and variety; to which the rough ideas essentially contribute? An extended plain is a simple object. It is the continuation of only one uniform idea. But the mere simplicity of a plain produces no beauty. Break the surface of it, as you did your pleasure-ground; add trees, rocks, and declivities; that is, give it roughness, and you give it also variety. Thus by enriching the parts of a united whole with roughness, you obtain the combined idea of simplicity, and variety; from whence results the picturesque.—Is this a satisfactory answer to our question?

By no means. Simplicity and variety are sources of the beautiful, as well as of the picturesque. Why does the architect break the front of his pile with ornaments? Is it not to add variety to simplicity? Even the very black-smith acknowledges this principle by forming ringlets and bulbous circles on his tongs, and pokers. In nature it is the same; and your plain will just as much be improved in reality by breaking it, as upon canvas.—In a garden-scene the idea is different. There every object is of the neat, and elegant kind. What is otherwise, is inharmonious; and roughness would be disorder.

Shall we then change our ground; and seek an answer to our question in the nature of the art of painting? As it is an art strictly imitative, those objects will of course appear most advantageously to the picturesque eye which are the most easily imitated. The stronger the features are, the stronger will be the effect of imitation; and as rough objects have the strongest features, they will consequently, when represented, appear to most advantage.—Is this answer more satisfactory?

Very little, in truth. Every painter, knows that a smooth object may be as easily, and as well imitated, as a rough one.

Shall we then take an opposite ground, and say just the reverse (as men pressed with difficulties will say any thing) that painting is not an art strictly imitative, but rather deceptive—that by an assemblage of colors, and a peculiar art in spreading them, the painter gives a semblance of nature at a proper distance; which at hand, is quite another thing that those objects, which we call picturesque, are only such as are more adapted to this art—and that as this art is most concealed in rough touches, rough objects are of course the most picturesque.—Have we now attained a satisfactory account of the matter?

Just as much so, as before. Many painters of note did not use the rough stile of painting; and yet their pictures are as admirable, as the pictures of those, who did: nor are rough objects less picturesque on their canvas, than on the canvas of others: that is, they paint rough objects smoothly.

Thus foiled, should we in the true spirit of inquiry, persist; or honestly give up the cause, and own we cannot search out the source of this difference? I am afraid this is the truth, whatever airs of dogmatizing we may assume, inquiries into principles rarely end in satisfaction. Could we even gain satisfaction in our present question, new doubts would arise. The very first principles of our art would be questioned. Difficulties would start up *vestibulum ante ipsum*. We should be asked, What is beauty? What is taste?—Let us step aside a moment, and listen to the debates of the learned on these heads. They will at least shew us, that however we may with to fix principles, our inquiries are seldom satisfactory.

One philosopher will tell us, that taste is only the improvement of our own ideas. Every man has naturally his proportion of taste. The seeds of it are innate. All depends on cultivation.

Another philosopher following the analogy of nature, observes, that as all men's faces are different, we may well suppose their minds to be so likewise. He rejects the idea therefore of innate taste; and in the room of this makes utility the standard both of tastes, and beauty.

A third philosopher thinks the idea of utility as absurd, as the last did that of innate taste. What, cries he, can I not admire the beauty of a resplendent sun-set, till I have investigated the utility of that peculiar radiance in the atmosphere? He then wishes we had a little less philosophy among us, and a little more common sense. Common sense is despised like other common things: but, in his opinion, if we made common sense the criterion in matters of art, as well as science, we should be nearer the truth.

A fourth philosopher apprehends common sense to be our standard only in the ordinary affairs of life. The bounty of nature has furnished us with various other senses suited to the objects, among which we converse: and with regard to matters of taste, it has supplied us with what, he doubts not, we all feel within ourselves, a sense of beauty.

Pooh! says another learned inquirer, what is a sense of beauty? Sense is a vague idea, and so is beauty; and it is impossible that any thing determined can result from terms so inaccurate. But if we lay aside a sense of beauty, and adopt proportion, we shall all be right. Proportion is the great principle of taste, and beauty. We admit it both in lines, and colors; and indeed refer all our ideas of the elegant kind to its standard.

True, says an admirer of the antique; but this proportion must have a rule, or we gain nothing: and a rule of proportion there certainly is: but we may inquire after it in vain. The secret is lost. The ancients had it. They well knew the principles of beauty; and had that unerring rule, which in all things adjusted their taste. We see it even in their slightest vases. In their works, proportion, though varied through a thousand lines, is still the same; and if we could only discover their principles of proportion, we should have the *arcanum* of this science; and might settle all our disputes about taste with great ease.

Thus, in our inquiries into first principles we go on, without end, and without satisfaction. The human understanding is unequal to the search. In philosophy we inquire for them in vain—in physics—in metaphysics—in morals. Even in the polite arts, where the subject, one should imagine, is less recondite, the inquiry, we find, is equally vague. We are puzzled, and bewildered, but not informed: all is uncertainty; a strife of words; the old contest,

Empedocles, an Stertinii delliret acumen?

In a word, if a cause be sufficiently understood, it may suggest useful discoveries. But if it be not so (and where is our certainty in these disquisitions) it will unquestionably mislead.

End of the First Essay

CHAPTER 21

Uvedale Price*

An Essay on the Picturesque as Compared with the Sublime and Beautiful 1794

On the Picturesque, &c.

Chapter I

There is no country, I believe (if we except China) where the art of laying out grounds is so much cultivated as it now is in England. Formerly the embellishments of a place were confined to the garden, or a small space near the mansion; while the park, with all its timber and thickets, was left in a state of wealthy neglect: but now these embellishments extend over a whole district; and as they give a new and peculiar character to the general face of the country, it is well worth considering whether they give a natural and a beautiful one, and whether the present system of

*Uvedale Price (1747-1829) was the eldest son of a gentleman artist and musician in Herefordshire. His father illustrated the "Letter from an English Gentleman, giving an account of Glaciers" (Geneva, 1741). Uvedale came into a considerable fortune on the death of his father in 1761. He attended Eton and Christ Church Oxford, but left without a degree. He became friends with Charles James Fox, and they studied and traveled together in Italy, Switzerland, and France in 1767-68. Price then settled on his estate at Foxley where he began a program of improvements both agriculturally and aesthetically. Price lived the life of a country squire, serving as sheriff of Herefordshire in 1793. He opposed the systems of landscaping of Capability Brown and William Kent, arguing instead for natural and picturesque beauty, an interest that he shared with his neighbor, Richard Payne Knight. Price continued to publish and write about gardening and improvement of estates. He entertained Wordsworth, and he had an influence on Scott when the latter was planning his gardens at Abbotsford.

improving (to use a short though often an inaccurate term) is founded on any just principles of taste.

In order to examine this question, the first enquiry will naturally be, whether there is any standard to which works of this sort can be referred; any authority higher than that of the persons who have gained most reputation by those works? I think there is a standard; there are authorities of an infinitely higher kind; the authorities of those great artists who have most diligently studied the beauties of nature, both in their grandest and most general effects, and in their minutest detail; who have observed every variety of form and of color, have been able to select and combine, and then, by the magic of their art, to fix upon the canvas all these various beauties.

But, however highly I may think of the art of painting, compared with that of improving, nothing can be farther from my intention (and I wish to impress it in the strongest manner on the reader's mind) than to recommend the study of pictures in preference to that of nature, much less to the exclusion of it. Whoever studies art alone, will have a narrow pedantic manner of considering all objects, and of referring them solely to the minute and particular purposes of that art to which his attention has been particularly directed; this is what improvers have done: and if every thing is to be referred to art, at least let it be referred to one whose variety, compared to the monotony of what is called improvement, appears infinite, but which again falls as short of the boundless variety of the mistress of all art.

The use, therefore, of studying pictures is not merely to make us acquainted with the combinations and effects that are contained in them, but to guide us by means of those general heads (as they may be called) of composition, in our search of the numberless and untouched varieties and beauties of nature; for as he who studies art only will have a confined taste, so he who looks at nature only will have a vague and unsettled one; and in this more extended sense I should interpret the Italian proverb, "*Chi s'insegna, ha un pazzo per maestro*: He is a fool who does not profit by the experience of others."

We are therefore to profit by the experience contained in pictures, but not to content ourselves with that experience only; nor are we to consider even those of the highest class as absolute and infallible standards, but as the best and only ones we have; as compositions, which, like those of the great classical authors, have been consecrated by long uninterrupted admiration, and which therefore have a similar claim to influence our judgment, and to form our taste in all that is within their province. These are the reasons for studying copies of nature, though the original is before us, that we may not lose the benefit of what is of such great moment in all arts and sciences, the accumulated experience of past ages; and, with respect to the art of improving, we may look upon pictures as a set of experiments of the different ways in which trees, buildings, water, &c. may be disposed, grouped, and accompanied in the most beautiful and striking manner, and in every style, from the most simple and rural to the grandest and most ornamental: many of those objects, that are scarcely marked as they lie scattered over the face of nature, when brought together in the compass of a small space of canvas, are forcibly impressed upon the eye, which by that means learns how to separate, to select, and combine.

Who can doubt whether Shakespeare and Fielding had not infinitely more amusement from society, in all its various views, than common observers? I believe it can be as little doubted, but that the having read such authors must give any man (however acute his penetration) more enlarged views of human nature in general, as well as a more intimate acquaintance with particular characters, than he would have had from the observation of nature only; that many groups of characters, many combinations of incidents, which might otherwise have escaped his notice, would forcibly strike him, from the recollection of scenes and passages from such writers; that in all these cases the pleasure we receive from what passes in real life is rendered infinitely more poignant by a resemblance to what we have read or have seen on the stage. But will any man argue from thence that these characters and incidents have no intrinsic merit, but merely that which is derived from their having been made use of by great and admired authors? The parallel between this and the assistance which painting gives towards an accurate as well as a comprehensive view of nature is so obvious as hardly to require pointing out.

I am therefore persuaded that those men's minds will be the most amused (and perhaps not the least usefully employed) to whom "all the world's a stage," who remark wherever they go (and habit will give a rapid and unobserved facility in doing it) not only the characters of all individuals, but their effect on each other. Such an observer will not divide what passes into scenes and chapters, and be pleased with it in proportion as it will do for a novel or a play, but he will be pleased on the same principles as Shakespeare or Fielding would have been. This appears to me a true and exact statement of the mutual relation that painting and nature bear to each other.

Had the art of improving been cultivated for as long a time, and upon as settled principles, as that of painting, and were there extant various works of genius, which, like those of the other art, had stood the test of ages (though from the great change which the growth and decay of trees must produce in the original design of the artist, this is hardly possible) there would not be the same necessity of referring and comparing the works of reality to those of imitation; but as the case stands at present, the only models that approach to perfection, the only fixed and unchanging selections from the works of nature, united with those of art, are in the pictures and designs of the most eminent masters.

It may be objected, that there are many pleasing circumstances in nature, which, in painting, would appear flat and insipid, as there are others that have a striking effect in a picture, which yet in nature (by a common observer at least) would be unnoticed, or even disliked; but, however true this may be in particular instances, the great leading principles of the one art, as general composition—grouping the separate parts—harmony of tints—unity of character, are equally applicable to the other: I may add also, what is so very essential to the painter, though at first sight it seems hardly within the province of the improver—breadth and effect of light and shade.

Nothing can be more directly at war with all these principles (founded as they are in truth and nature) than the present system of laying out of grounds. A painter, or whoever views objects with a painter's eye,[1] looks with indifference, if not with disgust, at the clumps, the belts, the made water, and the eternal smoothness and sameness of a finished place; an improver, on the other hand, considers these as the most perfect embellishments, as the last finishing touches that nature can receive from art; and consequently must think the finest composition of Claude (and I mention him as the most ornamented of all the great masters) comparatively rude and imperfect; though he probably might allow, in Mr. Brown's phrase, that it had "capabilities."

...

Chapter II.

It seems to me, that the neglect, which prevails in the works of modern improvers, of all that is picturesque, is owing to their exclusive attention to high polish and flowing lines, the charms of which they are so engaged in contemplating, as to make them overlook two of the most fruitful sources of human pleasure; the first, that great and universal source of pleasure, variety, whose power is independent of beauty, but without which even beauty itself soon ceases to please; the other, intricacy, a quality which, though distinct from variety, is so connected and blended with it, that the one can hardly exist without the other.

According to the idea I have formed of it, intricacy in landscape might be defined, that disposition of objects which, by a partial and uncertain concealment, excites and nourishes curiosity.[2] Variety can hardly require a definition, though, from the practice of many layers-out of ground, one might suppose it did. Upon the whole, it appears to me, that as intricacy in the disposition, and variety in the forms, the tints, and the lights and shadows of objects, are the great characteristics of picturesque scenery; so monotony and baldness are the greatest defects of improved places.

Nothing would place this in so distinct a point of view as a comparison between some familiar scene in its natural and picturesque, and in what would be its improved state, according to the present principles of gardening. All painters, who have imitated the more confined scenes of nature, have been fond of making studies from old neglected bye roads and hollow ways; and, perhaps, there are few spots that, in so small a compass, have a greater variety of that sort of beauty called

[1] When I speak of a painter, I do not mean merely a professor, but any man (artist or not) of a liberal mind, with a strong feeling for nature as well as art, who has been in the habit of comparing both together.

A man of a narrow mind and little sensibility, in or out of a profession, is always a bad judge, and possibly (as that ingenious critic the Abbé du Bos has well explained) a worse judge for being an artist

[2] Many persons, who take little concern in the intricacy of oaks, beeches, and thorns, may feel the effects of partial concealment in more interesting objects, and may have experienced how differently the passions are moved by an open licentious display of beauties, and by the unguarded disorder which sometimes escapes the care of modesty, and which coquetry so successfully imitates:

Parte appar delle mamme acerbe & crude,
Parte altrui ne ricuopre invida veste;
Invida si, ma se aglie occhi il varco chiude,
L'amoroso pensier gia non s'arresta.

picturesque; but, I believe, the instances are very rare of painters, who have turned out volunteers into a gentleman's walk or drive, either when made between artificial banks, or when the natural sides or banks have been improved. I shall endeavor to examine from whence it happens, that a picturesque eye looks coldly on what is very generally admired, and discovers a thousand interesting objects where a common eye sees nothing but ruts and rubbish; and whether the pleasure of the one, and the indifference of the other, arise from the causes I have assigned.

. . .

Chapter III.

There are few words whose meaning has been less accurately determined than that of the word Picturesque.

In general, I believe, it is applied to every object, and every kind of scenery, which has been, or might be represented with good effect in painting, and that without any exclusion. But, considered as a separate character, it has never yet been accurately distinguished from the sublime and the beautiful; though as no one has ever pretended that they are synonymous, (for it is sometimes used in contradistinction to them) such a distinction must exist.

Mr. Gilpin, from whose very ingenious and extensive observations on this subject I have received great pleasure and instruction, has given his sanction to this common idea, by defining picturesque objects to be those "which please from some quality capable of being illustrated in painting,"[3] or, as he again defines it in his Letter to Sir Joshua Reynolds "such objects as are proper subjects for painting."[4] Both these definitions seems to me (what may perhaps appear a contradiction) at once too vague and too confined; for though we are not to expect any definition to be so accurate and comprehensive, as both to supply the place and stand the test of investigation, yet if it does not in some degree separate the thing defined from all others, it differs little from any general truth on the same subject. For instance, it is very true, that picturesque objects do please from some quality capable of being illustrated in painting; but so also does every object that is represented in painting if it pleases at all, otherwise it would not have been painted; and from hence we ought to conclude (what certainly is not meant) that all objects which please in pictures are therefore picturesque, for no distinction or exclusion is made. Were any other person to define picturesque objects to be those which please from some striking effect of form, color, or light and shadow, such a definition would indeed give but a very indistinct idea of the thing defined; but, though hardly more vague than the others, it would be much less confined, for it would not have an exclusive reference to art.

I hope to shew, in the course of this work, that the picturesque has a character not less separate and distinct than either the sublime or the beautiful, nor less

[3] Essay on Picturesque Beauty, page 1.

[4] End of Essay on picturesque Beauty, p. 36.

independent of the art of painting. It has indeed been pointed out and illustrated by that art, and is one of its most striking ornaments; but has not beauty been pointed out and illustrated by that art also?

> *Si Venerem Cous nunquam posuisset Apelles*
> *Mersa sub aequoreis illa lateret aquis.*

Examine the forms of those painters who lived before the age of Raphael, or in a country where the study of the antique (operating as it did at Rome on minds highly prepared for its influence) had not yet taught them to separate what is beautiful from the general mass; we might almost conclude that beauty did not then exist; yet those painters were capable of exact imitation, but not of selection. Examine *grandeur* of form in the same manner; look at the dry meager forms of A. Durer (a man of genius even in Raphael's estimation), of P. Perugino, A. Mantegna, &c. and compare them with those of M. Angelo and Raphael: Nature was not more dry and meager in Germany or Perugia than at Rome. — Compare the landscapes and back grounds of such artists with those of Titian; Nature was not changed, but a mind of a higher cast, and instructed by the experience of all who went before rejected minute detail, and pointed out, by means of such selections and such combinations, as were congenial to its own sublime conceptions, in what forms, in what colors, and in what effects, grandeur in landscape consisted. Can it then be doubted but, that grandeur and beauty have been pointed out and illustrated by painting as well as picturesqueness?[5] Yet, would it be a just definition of sublime or of beautiful objects to say, that they were such (and, let the words be taken in their most liberal construction) as pleased from some quality capable of being illustrated in painting, or that were proper subjects for that art? The ancients, indeed, not only referred beauty of form to painting, but even beauty of color; and the poet who could describe his mistress's complexion, by comparing it to the tints of Apelles's pictures, must have thought that beauty of every kind was highly illustrated by the art he referred to.

The principles of those two leading characters in nature, the sublime and the beautiful, have been fully illustrated and discriminated by a great master; but even when I first read that most original work, I felt that there were numberless objects which give great delight to the eye and yet differ as widely from the beautiful as from the sublime. The reflections I have since been led to make have convinced me that these objects form a distinct class, and belong to what may properly be called the picturesque.

That term (as we may judge from its etymology) is applied only to objects of sight, and that indeed in so confined a manner as to be supposed merely to have a reference to the art from which it is named. I am well convinced, however, that the name and reference only are limited and uncertain, and that the qualities which make objects picturesque are not only as distinct as those which make them beautiful or

[5] I have ventured to make use of this word, which I believe does not occur in any writer, from what appeared to me the necessity of having some one word to oppose to beauty and sublimity, in a work where they are so often compared.

sublime, but are equally extended to all our sensations, by whatever organs they are received; and that music (though it appears like a solecism) may be as truly picturesque, according to the general principles of picturesqueness, as it may be beautiful or sublime, according to those of beauty or sublimity.

There is, indeed, a general harmony and correspondence in all our sensations when they arise from similar causes, though they affect us by means of different senses; and these causes (as Mr. Burke has admirably explained[6]) can never be so clearly ascertained when we confine our observations to one sense only.

I must here observe (and I wish the reader to keep it in his mind) that the enquiry is not in what sense certain words are used in the best authors, still less what is their common and vulgar use and abuse; but whether there are certain qualities which uniformly produce the same effects in all visible objects, and, according to the same analogy, in objects of hearing and of all the other senses; and which qualities (though frequently blended and united with others in the same object or set of objects) may be separated from them, and assigned to the class to which they belong.

If it can be shewn that a character composed of these qualities, and distinct from all others, does prevail through all nature; if it can be traced in the different objects of art and of nature, and appears consistent throughout, it surely deserves a distinct title; but with respect to the real ground of enquiry, it matters little whether such a character, or the set of objects belonging to it, is called beautiful, sublime, or picturesque, or by any other name, or by no name at all.

Beauty is so much the most enchanting and popular quality, that it is often applied as the highest commendation to whatever gives us pleasure, or raises our admiration, be the cause what it will. Mr. Burke has pointed out many instances of these ill-judged applications, and of the confusion of ideas that result from them; but there is nothing more ill-judged, or more likely to create confusion (if we agree with Mr. Burke in his idea of beauty) than the joining of it to the picturesque, and calling the character by the title of Picturesque Beauty.[7]

In reality, the picturesque not only differs from the beautiful in those qualities Mr. Burke has so justly ascribed to it, but arises from qualities the most diametrically opposite.

According to Mr. Burke, one of the most essential qualities of beauty is smoothness; now, as the perfection of smoothness is absolute equality and uniformity of

[6] Sublime and Beautiful, page 236.

[7] Great part of what follows was written before I saw Mr. Gilpin's Essay on Picturesque Beauty. I had gained so much information on that subject from his other works, that I read it with great eagerness, on account of the interest I took in the subject itself, as well as from my opinion of the author. At first I thought my work had been anticipated; I was pleased however to find some of my ideas confirmed, and was in hopes of seeing many new lights struck out; but as I advanced, that distinction between the two characters, that line of separation which I thought would have been accurately marked out, became less and less visible, till at length the beautiful and the picturesque were more than ever mixed and incorporated together, the whole subject involved in doubt and obscurity, and a sort of anathema denounced against any one who should try to clear it up. Had I not advanced too far to think of retreating, I might possibly have been deterred by so absolute a veto from such authority; but I hope I shall not be thought presumptuous for having still continued my researches, though so diligent and acute an observer had given up the enquiry himself, and pronounced it hopeless.

surface, wherever that prevails there can be but little variety or intricacy; as, for instance, in smooth level banks, on a small, or in naked downs, on a large scale. Another essential quality of beauty is gradual variation; that is (to make use of Mr. Burke's expression) where the lines do not vary in a sudden and broken manner, and where there is no sudden protuberance. It requires but little reflection to perceive, that the exclusion of all but flowing lines cannot promote variety; and that sudden protuberances, and lines that cross each other in a sudden and broken manner, are among the most fruitful causes of intricacy.

I am therefore persuaded, that the two opposite qualities of roughness,[8] and of sudden variation, joined to that of irregularity, are the most efficient causes of the picturesque.

This, I think, will appear very clearly, if we take a view of those objects, both natural and artificial, that are allowed to be picturesque, and compare them with those which are as generally allowed to be beautiful.

. . .

Chapter IV.

Picturesqueness, therefore, appears to hold a station between beauty and sublimity; and on that account, perhaps is more frequently and more happily blended with them both than they are with each other. It is, however, perfectly distinct from either; and first, with respect to beauty, it is evident, from all that has been said, that they are founded on very opposite qualities; the one on smoothness,[9] the other on

[8] I have followed Mr. Gilpin's example in using roughness as a general term; he observes, however, that "properly speaking, roughness relates only to the surface of bodies; and that when we speak of their delineation we use the word ruggedness." In making roughness (in this general sense) a very principal distinction between the beautiful and picturesque, I believe I am supported by the general opinion of all who have considered the subject, as well as by Mr. Gilpin's authority. The authority is deservedly so high, that where in other points I have the misfortune to differ from him, his opinion will of course be preferred to mine, unless I can clearly shew that it is ill founded: I must therefore endeavor to shew in what respects it is ill-founded, as often as these points occur, and with the best of my abilities; for any thing short of victory is in this case a defeat.

I will first mention, in general, the difficulties into which so ingenious a writer has been led from losing sight of that genuine and universal distinction between the beautiful and the picturesque, which he himself had begun by establishing, and which separates their characters equally in nature and in art, and from confining himself to that unsatisfactory notion of a mere general reference to art only.

He has given it as his opinion, that "roughness forms the most essential point of difference between the beautiful and the picturesque, and seems to be that particular quality which makes objects chiefly please in painting." He therefore has thought it necessary, in some instances, to exclude smooth objects from painting, and to shew, in others, that what is smooth in reality is rough in appearance; so that when we fancy ourselves admiring the smoothness, we think we perceive (as in a calm lake) we are in fact admiring the roughness we have not observed. Of this I shall give instances in those places where they will most naturally present themselves.

[9] Baldness seems to be an exception, as there smoothness is picturesque, and not beautiful. It is, however, an exception, which, instead of weakening, confirms what I have said, and shews the constant opposition of the two characters, even where their causes appear to be confounded. Baldness is the smoothness of age and decay, not of youth, health, and freshness: it is picturesque from producing variety and peculiarity of character; from destroying the usual symmetry and regularity of the face, and substituting an uncertain instead of a certain boundary.

When a bald head is well plastered and flowered, and the boundary of the forehead distinctly marked in pomatum and powder, it has as little pretension to picturesqueness as to beauty.

roughness;—the one on gradual, the other on sudden variation;—the one on ideas of youth and freshness, the other on that of age, and even of decay.

But as most of the qualities of visible beauty (excepting color) are made known to us through the medium of another sense, the sight itself is hardly more to be attended to than the touch, in regard to all those sensations which are excited by beautiful forms; and the distinction between the beautiful and the picturesque will, perhaps, be most strongly pointed out by means of the latter sense. I am aware that this is liable to a gross and obvious ridicule; but for that reason none but gross and common-place minds will dwell upon it.

Mr. Burke has observed, that "men are carried to the sex, in general, as it is the sex, and by the common law of nature; but they are attached to particulars by personal *beauty*;"[10] he adds, "I call beauty a social quality; for where women and men, and not only they, but when other animals give us a sense of joy and pleasure in beholding them (and there are many that do so) they inspire us with sentiments of tenderness and affection towards their persons; we like to have them near us, and we enter willingly into a kind of relation with them."

These sentiments of tenderness and affection nature has taught us to express by caresses, by gentle pressure; these are the endearments we make use of (where sex is totally out of the question) to beautiful children, to beautiful animals, and even to things inanimate; and where the size and character (as in trees, buildings, &c.) excludes any such relation, still something of the same difference of sensation between them and rugged objects appears to subsist; that sensation however is diminished as the size of any beautiful object is increased; and as it approaches towards grandeur and magnificence, it recedes from loveliness.

As the eye borrows many of its sensations from the touch, so that again seems to borrow others from the sight. Soft, fresh, and beautiful colors, though "not sensible to feeling as to sight," give us an inclination to try their effect on the touch; whereas, if the color be not beautiful, that inclination, I believe, is always diminished, and, in objects merely picturesque, and void of all beauty, is rarely excited.[11]

These are the principal circumstances by which the picturesque is separated from the beautiful. It is equally distinct from the sublime; for though there are some qualities common to them both, yet they differ in many essential points, and proceed from very different causes. In the first place, greatness of dimension[12] is a powerful cause of the sublime; the picturesque has no connection with dimension of any kind (in which it differs from the beautiful also) and is as often found in the smallest as in the largest objects.—The sublime being founded on principles of awe and terror, never descends to any thing light or playful; the picturesque, whose characteristics

[10]Sublime and Beautiful, p. 66.

[11]I have read, indeed, in some fairy tale, of a country where age and wrinkles were loved and caressed, and youth and freshness neglected; but in real life, I fancy, the most picturesque old woman, however her admirer may ogle her on that account, is perfectly safe from his caresses.

[12]I would by no means lay too much stress on greatness of dimension; but what Mr. Burke has observed with regard to buildings, is true of many natural objects, such as rocks, cascades, &c.; where the scale is too diminutive, no greatness of manner will give them grandeur.

are intricacy and variety, is equally adapted to the grandest and to the gayest scenery.—Infinity is one of the most efficient causes of the sublime; the boundless ocean, for that reason, inspires awful sensations: to give it picturesqueness you must destroy that cause of its sublimity; for it is on the shape and disposition of its boundaries that the picturesque in great measure must depend.

. . .

It seems to me that mere unmixed ugliness does not arise from sharp angles, or from any sudden variation, but rather from that *want* of form, that unshapen lumpish appearance, which, perhaps, no one word exactly expresses; a quality that never can be mistaken for beauty, never can adorn it, and which is equally unconnected with the sublime and the picturesque. In Latin, *forma* is sometimes used singly for beauty, and seems to signify that beauty is form in its most exquisitely finished state, when the last touches of the master's hand have left nothing to add, nothing to diminish—such as we find in the most perfect Grecian sculpture. But were an artist to model, in any soft material, a head from the Venus or the Apollo, and then by way of experiment to make the nose longer or sharper—rising more suddenly towards the middle,—or strongly aquiline; were he to give a striking projection to the eyebrow,—or to break the outline of the face into angles,—though he would destroy beauty, yet he might create character, and something grand or picturesque might be produced by such a trial. But let him take the contrary method, let him clog and fill up all those nicely marked variations, of whose happy union and connection beauty is the result, and ugliness, and that only, must be the consequence. Were he afterwards to place warts and carbuncles on the nose, or any other unnatural wens and excrescencies on the face; were he to twist the mouth, or make the nose awry, or of an enormous size, he would then add deformity to ugliness.

Deformity is to ugliness what picturesqueness is to beauty; though distinct from it, and in many cases arising from opposite causes, it is often mistaken for it, often accompanies it, and greatly heightens its effect. Ugliness alone is merely disagreeable; when any striking deformity is added, it becomes hideous; when terror, sublime. All these are mixed in the

Monstrum horrendum, informe, ingens, cui lumen ademptum.

CHAPTER 22

Adam Smith*

Of the nature of that Imitation which Takes Place in What are Called the Imitative Arts
1795

Part I

The most perfect imitation of an object of any kind must in all cases, it is evident, be another object of the same kind, made as exactly as possible after the same model. What, for example, would be the most perfect imitation of the carpet which now lies before me? — Another carpet, certainly, wrought as exactly as possible after the same pattern. But, whatever might be the merit or beauty of this second carpet, it would not be supposed to derive any from the circumstance of its having been made in imitation of the first. This circumstance of its being not an original, but a copy, would even be considered as some diminution of that merit; a

*Adam Smith (1723-1790) was born at Kircaldy across the Firth of Forth from Edinburgh. He was a sickly child, and McCosh reports in *The Scottish Philosophy* that at three he was stolen by gypsies but was rescued quickly. He studied under Francis Hutcheson at Glasgow and then at Balliol College, Oxford before returning to Kircaldy and then moving to Edinburgh where he began to lecture on rhetoric and belles lettres. He was appointed professor of logic at Glasgow in 1751 and professor moral philosophy in 1752. In 1763 he resigned his professorship at Glasgow to accept the position of tutor to the young Duke of Buccleugh and his younger brother. Smith received both a salary and a pension for life. His position allowed him to travel in Europe, particularly in France, where his acquaintance with Hume secured him entry into the salons and intellectual circles. He returned to Scotland after the sudden death of the Duke's younger brother, where he lived with his mother and wrote *The Wealth of Nations*, which was published in 1776. In spite of the positions he takes in that work against tariffs, Smith was appointed commissioner of tariffs by Lord North. He remained in Edinburgh, where he was regarded as a genial eccentric, until his death. The *Philosophical Essays*, which include "Of the Nature of Imitation . . . ," were published posthumously.

greater or smaller, in proportion as the object was of a nature to lay claim to a greater or smaller degree of admiration. It would not much diminish the merit of a common carpet, because in such trifling objects, which at best can lay claim to so little beauty or merit of any kind, we do not always think it worth while to affect originality: it would diminish a good deal that of a carpet of very exquisite workmanship. In objects of still greater importance, this exact, or, as it would be called, this servile imitation, would be considered as the most unpardonable blemish. To build another St. Peter's, or St. Paul's church, of exactly the same dimensions, proportions, and ornaments with the present buildings at Rome, or London, would be supposed to argue such a miserable barrenness of genius and invention as would disgrace the most expensive magnificence.

The exact resemblance of the correspondent parts of the same object is frequently considered as a beauty, and the want of it as a deformity; as in the correspondent members of the human body, in the opposite wings of the same building, in the opposite trees of the same alley, in the correspondent compartments of the same piece of carpet-work, or of the same flower-garden, in the chairs or tables which stand in the correspondent parts of the same room, etc. But in objects of the same kind, which in other respects are regarded as altogether separate and unconnected, this exact resemblance is seldom considered as a beauty, nor the want of it as a deformity. A man, and in the same manner a horse, is handsome or ugly, each of them, on account of his own intrinsic beauty or deformity, without any regard to their resembling or not resembling, the one, another man, or the other, another horse. A set of coach-horses, indeed, is supposed to be handsomer when they are all exactly matched; but each horse is, in this case, considered not as a separated and unconnected object, or as a whole by himself, but as a part of another whole, to the other parts of which he ought to bear a certain correspondence: Separated from the set, he derives neither beauty from his resemblance, nor deformity from his unlikeness to the other horses which compose it.

Even in the correspondent parts of the same object, we frequently require no more than a resemblance in the general outline. If the inferior members of those correspondent parts are too minute to be seen distinctly, without a separate and distinct examination of each part by itself, as a separate and unconnected object, we should sometimes even be displeased if the resemblance was carried beyond this general outline. In the correspondent parts of a room we frequently hang pictures of the same size; those pictures, however, resemble one another in nothing but the frame, or, perhaps, in the general character of the subject: If the one is a landscape, the other is a landscape too; if the one represents a religious or a Bacchanalian subject, its companion represents another of the same kind. Nobody ever thought of repeating the same picture in each correspondent frame. The frame, and the general character of two or three pictures, is as much as the eye can comprehend at one view, or from one station. Each picture, in order to be seen distinctly, and understood thoroughly, must be viewed from a particular station, and examined by itself as a separate and unconnected object. In a hall or portico, adorned with statues, the niches, or perhaps the pedestals, may exactly resemble one another, but the statues are always different. Even the masks which are sometimes carried upon the different keystones of the same arcade, or of the correspondent doors and windows of the same front, though they may all resemble one another in the general outline, yet each of them has always its own peculiar features, and a grimace of its own. There are some Gothic buildings in which the correspondent windows resemble one another only in the general outline, and not in the smaller ornaments and subdivisions. These are different in each, and the architect had considered them as too minute to be seen distinctly, without a particular and separate examination of each window by itself, as a separate and unconnected object. A variety of this sort, however, I think, is not agreeable. In objects which are susceptible only of a certain inferior order of beauty, such as the frames of pictures, the niches or the pedestals of statues, etc. there seems frequently to be affectation in the study of variety, of which the merit is scarcely ever sufficient to compensate the want of that perspicuity and distinctness, of that easiness to be comprehended and remembered, which is the natural effect of exact uniformity. In a portico of the Corinthian or Ionic order, each column resembles every other, not only in the general outline, but in all the minutest ornaments; though some of them, in order to be seen distinctly, may require a separate and distinct examination in each column, and in the entablature of each intercolumnation. In the inlaid tables, which, according to the present fashion, are sometimes fixed in the correspondent parts of the same room, the pictures only are different in each. All the other more frivolous and fanciful ornaments are commonly, so far at least as I have observed the fashion, the same in them all. Those ornaments, however, in order to be seen distinctly, require a separate and distinct examination of each table.

The extraordinary resemblance of two natural objects, of twins, for example, is regarded as a curious circumstance; which, though it does not increase, yet does not diminish the beauty of either, considered as a separate and unconnected object. But the exact resemblance of two productions of art, seems to be always considered as some diminution of the merit of at least one of them; as it seems to prove, that one of them, at least, is a copy either of the other, or of some other original. One may say, even of the copy of a picture, that it derives its merit, not so much from its resemblance to the original, as from its resemblance to the object which the original was meant to resemble. The owner of the copy, so far from setting any high value upon its resemblance to the original, is often anxious to destroy any value or merit which it might derive from this circumstance. He is often anxious to persuade both himself and other people that it is not a copy, but an original, of which what passes for the original is only a copy. But, whatever merit a copy may derive from its resemblance to the original, an original can certainly derive none from the resemblance of its copy.

But though a production of art seldom derives any merit from its resemblance to another object of the same kind, it frequently derives a great deal from its resemblance to an object of a different kind, whether that object be a production of art or of nature. A painted cloth, the work of some laborious Dutch artist, so curiously shaded and colored as to represent the pile and softness of a woolen one, might derive some merit from its resemblance even to the sorry carpet which now lies before me. The copy might, and probably would, in this case, be of much greater value than the original. But if this carpet was represented as spread, either upon a floor or upon a table, and projecting from the back ground of the picture, with exact observation of perspective, and of light and shade, the merit of the imitation would be still greater.

In Painting, a plain surface of one kind is made to resemble, not only a plain surface of another, but all the three dimensions of a solid substance. In Statuary and Sculpture, a solid substance of one kind, is made to resemble a solid substance of another. The disparity between the object imitating, and the object imitated, is much greater in the one art than in the other; and the pleasure arising from the imitation seems to be greater in proportion as the disparity is greater.

In Painting, the imitation frequently pleases, though the original object be indifferent, or even offensive. In Statuary and Sculpture it is otherwise. The imitation seldom pleases, unless the original object be in a very high degree either great, or beautiful, or interesting. A butcher's stall, or a kitchen-dresser, with the objects which they commonly present, are not certainly the happiest subjects, even for Painting. They have, however, been represented with so much care and success by some Dutch masters, that it is impossible to view the pictures without some degree of pleasure. They would be most absurd subjects for Statuary or Sculpture, which are, however, capable of representing them. The picture of a very ugly or deformed man, such as Aesop, or Scarron, might not make a disagreeable piece of furniture. The statue certainly would. Even a vulgar ordinary man or woman, engaged in a vulgar ordinary action, like what we see with so much pleasure in the pictures of Rembrant, would be too mean a subject for Statuary. Jupiter, Hercules, and Apollo, Venus and Diana, the Nymphs and the Graces, Bacchus, Mercury, Antinous and Meleager, the miserable death of Laocoon, the melancholy fate of the children of Niobe, the Wrestlers, the fighting, the dying gladiator, the figures of gods and goddesses, of heroes and heroines, the most perfect forms of the human body, placed either in the noblest attitudes, or in the most interesting situations which the human imagination is capable of conceiving, are the proper, and therefore have always been the favorite subjects of Statuary: that art cannot, without degrading itself, stoop to represent any thing that is offensive, or mean, or even indifferent. Painting is not so disdainful; and, though capable of representing the noblest objects, it can, without forfeiting its title to please, submit to imitate those of a much more humble nature. The merit of the imitation alone, and without any merit in the imitated object, is capable of supporting the dignity of Painting: it cannot support that of Statuary. There would seem, therefore, to be more merit in the one species of imitation than in the other.

In Statuary, scarcely any drapery is agreeable. The best of the ancient statues were either altogether naked or almost naked; and those of which any considerable part of the body is covered, are represented as clothed in wet linen—a species of clothing which most certainly never was agreeable to the fashion of any country. This drapery too is drawn so tight, as to express beneath its narrow foldings the exact form and outline of any limb, and almost of every muscle of the body. The clothing which thus approached the nearest to no clothing at all, had, it seems, in the judgment of the great artists of antiquity, been that which was most suitable to Statuary. A great painter of the Roman school, who had formed his manner almost entirely upon the study of the ancient statues, imitated at first their drapery in his pictures; but he soon found that in Painting it had the air of meanness and poverty, as if the persons who wore it could scarce afford clothes enough to cover them; and that larger folds, and a looser and more flowing drapery, were more suitable to the nature of his art. In Painting, the imitation of so very inferior an object as a suit of clothes is capable of pleasing; and, in order to give this object all the magnificence of which it is capable, it is necessary that the folds should be large, loose, and flowing. It is not necessary in Painting that the exact form and outline of every limb, and almost of every muscle of the body, should be expressed beneath the folds of the drapery; it is sufficient if these are so disposed as to indicate in general the situation and attitude of the principal limbs. Painting, by the mere force and merit of its imitation, can venture, without the hazard of displeasing, to substitute, upon many occasions, the inferior in the room of the superior object, by making the one, in this manner, cover and entirely conceal a great part of the other. Statuary can seldom venture to do this, but with the utmost reserve and caution; and the same drapery, which is noble and magnificent in the one art, appears clumsy and awkward in the other. Some modern artists, however, have attempted to introduce into Statuary the drapery which is peculiar to Painting. It may not, perhaps upon every occasion, be quite so ridiculous as the marble periwigs in Westminister Abbey: but, if it does not always appear clumsy and awkward, it is at best always insipid and uninteresting.

It is not the want of coloring which hinders many things from pleasing in Statuary, which please in Painting; it is the want of that degree of disparity between the imitating and the imitated object, which is necessary, in order to render interesting the imitation of an object which is itself not interesting. Coloring, when added to Statuary, so far from increasing, destroys almost entirely the pleasure which we receive from the imitation; because it takes away the great source of that pleasure, the disparity between the imitating and the imitated object. That one solid and colored object should exactly resemble another solid and colored object, seems to be a matter of no great wonder or admiration. A painted statue, though it certainly may resemble a human figure much more exactly than any statue which is not painted, is generally acknowledged to be a disagreeable, and even an offensive object; and so far are we from being pleased with this superior likeness, that we are never satisfied with it; and, after viewing it again and again, we always find that it is not equal to what we are disposed to imagine it might have been: though it should seem to want scarce any thing but the life, we could not pardon it for thus wanting what it is altogether impossible it should have. The works of Mrs. Wright, a self-taught artist of great merit, are perhaps more perfect in this way than any thing I have ever seen. They do admirably well to be seen now and then as a show; but the best of them we should find, if brought home to our own house, and placed in a situation where it was to come often into view, would make instead of an ornamental, a most offensive piece of household furniture. Painted statues, accordingly, are universally reprobated, and we scarce ever meet with them. To color the eyes of statues is not altogether so uncommon: even this, however, is disapproved by all good judges. "I cannot bear it," (a gentleman used to say, of great knowledge and judgment in this art,) "I cannot bear it; I always want them to speak to me."

Artificial fruits and flowers sometimes imitate so exactly the natural objects which they represent, that they frequently deceive us. We soon grow weary of them, however; and, though they seem to want nothing but the freshness and the flavor of natural fruits and flowers, we cannot pardon them, in the same manner, for thus wanting what it is altogether impossible they should have. But we do not grow weary of a good flower and fruit painting. We do not grow weary of the foliage of the Corinthian capital, or the flowers which sometimes ornament the frieze of that order. Such imitations, however, never deceive us; their resemblance to the original objects is always much inferior to that of artificial fruits and flowers. Such as it is, however, we are contented with it; and, where there is such disparity between the imitating and the imitated objects, we find that it is as great as it can be, or as we expect that it should be. Paint that foliage and those flowers with the natural colors, and, instead of pleasing more, they will please much less. The resemblance, however, will be much greater; but the disparity between the imitating and the imitated objects will be so much less, that even this superior resemblance will not satisfy us. Where the disparity is very great, on the contrary, we are often contented with the most imperfect resemblance; with the very imperfect resemblance, for example, both as to figure and color, of fruits and flowers in shell-work.

It may be observed, however, that, though in Sculpture the imitation of flowers and foliage pleases as an ornament of architecture, as a part of the dress which is to set off the beauty of a different and a more important object, it would not please alone, or as a separate and unconnected object, in the same manner as a fruit and flower painting pleases. Flowers and foliage, how elegant and beautiful soever, are not sufficiently interesting; they have not dignity enough, if I may say so, to be proper subjects for a piece of Sculpture, which is to please alone, and not as the ornamental appendage of some other object.

In Tapestry and Needle-work, in the same manner as in Painting, a plain surface is sometimes made to represent all the three dimensions of a solid substance. But both the shuttle of the weaver, and the needle of the embroiderer, are instruments of imitation so much inferior to the pencil of the painter, that we are not surprised to find a proportionable inferiority in their productions. We have all more or less experience that they usually are much inferior; and, in appreciating a piece of Tapestry or Needle-work, we never compare the imitation of either with that of a good picture, for it never could stand that comparison, but with that of other pieces of Tapestry or Needle-work. We take into consideration, not only the disparity between the imitating and the imitated object, but the awkwardness of the instruments of imitation; and if it is as well as any thing that can be expected from these, if it is better than the greater part of what actually comes from them, we are often not only contented but highly pleased.

A good painter will often execute in a few days a subject which would employ the best tapestry-weaver for many years; though, in proportion to his time, therefore, the latter is always much worse paid than the former, yet his work in the end comes commonly much dearer to market. The great expense of good Tapestry, the circumstance which confines it to the palaces of princes and great lords, gives it, in the eyes of the greater part of people, an air of riches and magnificence, which contributes still further to compensate the imperfection of its imitation. In arts which address themselves, not to the prudent and the wise, but to the rich and the great, to the proud and the vain, we ought not to wonder if the appearance of great expense, of being what few people can purchase, of being one of the surest characteristics of great fortune, should often stand in the place of exquisite beauty, and contribute equally to recommend their productions. As the idea of expense seems often to embellish, so that of cheapness seems as frequently to tarnish the luster even of very agreeable objects. The difference between real and false jewels is what even the experienced eye of a jeweler can sometimes with difficulty distinguish. Let an unknown lady, however, come into a public assembly, with a head-dress which appears to be very richly adorned with diamonds, and let a jeweler only whisper in our ear that they are all false stones, not only the lady will immediately sink in our imagination from the rank of a princess to that of a very ordinary woman, but the head-dress, from an object of the most splendid magnificence, will at once become an impertinent piece of tawdry and tinsel finery.

It was some years ago the fashion to ornament a garden with yew and holly trees, clipped into the artificial shapes of pyramids, and columns, and vases, and obelisks. It is now the fashion to ridicule this taste as unnatural. The figure of a pyramid or obelisk, however, is not more unnatural to a yew-tree than to a block of porphyry or marble. When the yew-tree is presented to the eye in this artificial shape, the gardener does not mean that it should be understood to have grown in that shape: he means, first, to give it the same beauty of regular figure, which pleases so much in porphyry and marble; and, secondly, to imitate in a growing tree the ornaments of those precious materials: he means to make an object of one kind resemble another object of a very different kind; and to the original beauty of figure to join the relative beauty of imitation: but the disparity between the imitating and the imitated object is the foundation of the beauty of imitation. It is because the one object does not naturally resemble the other, that we are so much pleased with it, when by art it is made to do so. The shears of the gardener, it may be said, indeed, are very clumsy instruments of Sculpture. They are so, not doubt, when employed to imitate the figures of men, or even of animals. But in the simple and regular forms of pyramids, vases, and obelisks, even the shears of the gardener do well enough. Some allowance too is naturally made for the necessary imperfection of the instrument, in the same manner as in Tapestry and Needle-work. In short, the next time you have an opportunity of surveying those out-of-fashion ornaments, endeavor only to let yourself alone, and to restrain for a few minutes the foolish passion for playing the critic, and you will be sensible that they are not without some degree of beauty; that they give the air of neatness and correct culture at least to the whole garden; and that they are not unlike what the "retired leisure, that" (as Milton says) "in trim gardens takes his pleasure," might be amused with. What then, it may be said, has brought them into such universal disrepute among us? In a pyramid or obelisk of marble, we know that the materials are expensive, and that the labor which wrought them into that shape must have been still more so. In a pyramid or obelisk of yew, we know that the materials could cost very little, and the labor still less. The former are ennobled by their expense; the latter degraded by their cheapness. In the cabbage-garden of a tallow-chandler we may sometimes perhaps have seen as many columns and vases, and other ornaments in yew, as there are in marble and porphyry at Versailles: it is this vulgarity which has disgraced them. The rich and the great, the proud and the vain, will not admit into their gardens an ornament which the meanest of the people can have as well as they. The taste for these ornaments came originally from France; where, notwithstanding that inconstancy of fashion with which we sometimes reproach the natives of that country, it still continues in good repute. In France, the conditions of the inferior ranks of people is seldom so happy as it frequently is in England; and you will there seldom find even pyramids and obelisks of yew in the garden of a tallow-chandler. Such ornaments, not having in that country been degraded by their vulgarity, have not yet been excluded from the gardens of princes and great lords.

The works of the great masters in Statuary and Painting, it is to be observed, never produced their effect by deception. They never are, and it never is intended that they should be mistaken for the real objects which they represent. Painted Statuary may sometimes deceive an inattentive eye: proper Statuary never does. The little pieces of perspective in Painting, which it is intended should please by deception, represent always some very simple, as well as insignificant, object; a roll of paper, for example, or the steps of a staircase, in the dark corner of some passage or gallery. They are generally the works too of some very inferior artists. After being seen once, and producing the little surprise which it is meant they should excite, together with the mirth which commonly accompanies it, they never please more, but appear every after insipid and tiresome.

The proper pleasure which we derive from those two imitative arts, so far from being the effect of deception, is altogether incompatible with it. That pleasure is founded altogether upon our wonder at seeing an object of one kind represent so well an object of a very different kind, and upon our admiration of the art which surmounts so happily that disparity which Nature had established between them. The nobler works of Statuary and Painting appear to us a sort of wonderful phenomena of Nature, that they carry, as it were, their own explication along with them, and demonstrate, even to the eye, the way and manner in which they are produced. The eye, even of an unskillful spectator, immediately discerns, in some measure, how it is that a certain modification of figure in Statuary, and of brighter and darker colors in Painting, can represent, with so much truth and vivacity, the actions, passions, and behaviour of men, as well as a great variety of other objects. The pleasing wonder of ignorance is accompanied with the still more pleasing satisfaction of science. We wonder and are amazed at the effect; and we are pleased ourselves, and happy to find that we can comprehend, in some measure, how that wonderful effect is produced.

A good looking-glass represents the objects which are set before it with much more truth and vivacity than either Statuary or Painting. But, though the science of optics may explain to the understanding, the looking-glass itself does not at all demonstrate to the eye how this effect is brought about. It may excite the wonder of ignorance; and in a clown, who had never beheld a looking-glass before, I have seen that wonder rise almost to rapture and ecstasy; but it cannot give the satisfaction of science. In all looking-glasses the effects are produced by the same means, applied exactly in the same manner. In every different statue and picture the effects are produced; though by similar, yet not by the same means; and those means too are applied in a different manner in each. Every good statue and picture is a fresh wonder, which at the same time carries, in some measure, its own explication along with it. After a little use and experience, all looking-glasses cease to be wonders altogether; and even the ignorant become so familiar with them, as not to think that their effects require any explication. A looking-glass, besides, can represent only present objects; and, when the wonder is once fairly over, we choose, in all cases, rather to contemplate the substance than to gaze at the shadow. One's own face becomes then the most agreeable object which a looking-glass can represent to us, and the only object which we do not soon grow weary with looking at; it is the only present object of which we can see only the shadow: whether handsome or ugly, whether old or young, it is the face of a friend always, of which the features correspond exactly with whatever sentiment, emotion, or passion we may happen at that moment to feel.

In Statuary, the means by which the wonderful effect is brought about appear more simple and obvious than in Painting; where the disparity between the imitating and the imitated object being much greater, the art which can conquer that greater disparity appears evidently, and almost to the eye, to be founded upon a much deeper science, or upon principles much more abstruse and profound. Even in the meanest subjects we can often trace with pleasure the ingenious means by which Painting surmounts this disparity. But we cannot do this in Statuary, because the disparity not being so great, the means do not appear so ingenious. And it is upon this account, that in Painting we are often delighted with the representation of many things, which in Statuary would appear insipid, tiresome, and not worth the looking at.

It ought to be observed, however, that though in Statuary the art of imitation appears, in many respects, inferior to what it is in Painting, yet, in a room ornamented with both statues and pictures of nearly equal merit, we shall generally find that the statues draw off our eye from the pictures. There is generally but one, or little more than one, point of view from which a picture can be seen with advantage, and it always presents to the eye precisely the same object. There are many different points of view from which a statue may be seen with equal advantage, and from each it presents a different object. There is more variety in the pleasure which we receive from a good statue, than in that which we receive from a good picture; and one statue may frequently be the subject of many good pictures or drawings, all different from one another. The shadowy relief and projection of a picture, besides, is much flattened, and seems almost to vanish away altogether, when brought into comparison with the real and solid body which stands by it. How nearly soever these two arts may seem to be a-kin, they accord so very ill with one another, that their different productions ought, perhaps, scarce ever to be seen together.

Part II

After the pleasures which arise from the gratification of the bodily appetites, there seem to be none more natural to man than Music and Dancing. In the progress of art and improvement they are, perhaps, the first and earliest pleasure of his own invention; for those which arise from the gratification of the bodily appetites cannot be said to be of his own invention. No nation has yet been discovered so uncivilized as to be altogether without them. It seems even to be amongst the most barbarous nations that the use and practice of them is both most frequent and most universal, as among the Negroes of Africa and the savage tribes of America. In civilized nations, the inferior ranks of people have very little leisure, and the superior ranks have many other amusements; neither the one nor the other, therefore, can spend much of their time in Music and Dancing. Among savage nations, the great body of the people have frequently great intervals of leisure, and they have scarce any other amusement; they naturally, therefore, spend a great part of their time in almost the only one they have.

What the ancients called Rhythmus, what we call Time or Measure, is the connecting principle of those two arts; Music consisting in a succession of a certain sort of sounds, and Dancing in a succession of a certain sort of steps, gestures, and motions, regulated according to time or measure, and thereby formed into a sort of whole or system; which in the one art is called a song or tune, and in the other a dance; the time or measure of the dance corresponding always exactly with that of the song or tune which accompanies and directs it.[1]

The human voice, as it is always the best, so it would naturally be the first and earliest of all musical instruments: in singing, or in its first attempts towards singing, it would naturally employ sounds as similar as possible to those which it had been accustomed to; that is, it would employ words of some kind or other, pronouncing them only in time and measure, and generally with a more melodious tone than had been usual in common conversation. Those words, however, might not, and probably would not, for a long time have any meaning, but might resemble the syllables which we make use of in *sol-facing,* or the *derry-down-down* of our common ballads; and serve only to assist the voice in forming sounds proper to be modulated into melody, and to be lengthened or shortened according to the time and measure of the tune. This rude form of vocal Music, as it is by far the most simple and obvious, so it naturally would be the first and earliest.

In the succession of ages it could not fail to occur, that in the room of those unmeaning or musical words, if I may call them so, might be substituted words which expressed some sense or meaning, and of which the pronunciation might coincide as exactly with the time and measure of the tune, as that of the musical words had done before. Hence the origin of Verse or Poetry. The Verse would for a long time be rude and imperfect. When the meaning words fell short of the measure required, they would frequently be eked out with the unmeaning ones, as is sometimes done in our common ballads. When the public ear came to be so refined as to reject, in all serious Poetry, the unmeaning words altogether, there would still be a liberty assumed of altering and corrupting, upon many occasions, the pronunciation

[1] The author's observations on the affinity between music, dancing, and poetry, are annexed to the end of Part III of this Essay.

of the meaning ones, for the sake of accommodating them to the measure. The syllables which composed them would, for this purpose, sometimes be improperly lengthened, and sometimes improperly shortened; and though no unmeaning words were made use of, yet an unmeaning syllable would sometimes be stuck to the beginning, to the end, or into the middle of a word. All these expedients we find frequently employed in the verses even of Chaucer, the father of the English Poetry. Many ages might pass away before verse was commonly composed with such correctness, that the usual and proper pronunciation of the words alone, and without any other artifice, subjected the voice to the observation of a time and measure, of the same kind with the time and measure of Music.

The Verse would naturally express some sense which suited the grave or gay, the joyous or melancholy humor of the tune which it was sung to; being as it were blended and united with that tune, it would seem to give sense and meaning to what otherwise might not appear to have any, or at least any which could be clearly and distinctly understood, without the accompaniment of such an explication.

A pantomime dance may frequently answer the same purpose, and, by representing some adventure in love or war, may seem to give sense and meaning to a Music which might not otherwise appear to have any. It is more natural to mimic, by gestures and motions, the adventures of common life, than to express them in Verse or Poetry. The thought itself is more obvious, and the execution is much more easy. If this mimicry was accompanied by music, it would of its own accord, and almost without any intention of doing so, accommodate, in some measure, its different steps and movements to the time and measure of the tune; especially if the same person both sung the tune and performed the mimicry, as is said to be frequently the case among the savage nations of Africa and America. Pantomime Dancing might in this manner serve to give a distinct sense and meaning to Music many ages before the invention, or at least before the common use of Poetry. We hear little, accordingly, of the Poetry of the savage nations of Africa and America, but a great deal of their pantomime dances.

Poetry, however, is capable of expressing many things fully and distinctly, which Dancing either cannot represent at all, or can represent but obscurely and imperfectly; such as the reasonings and judgments of the understanding; the ideas, fancies, and suspicions of the imagination; the sentiments, emotions, and passions of the heart. In the power of expressing a meaning with clearness and distinctness, Dancing is superior to Music, and Poetry to Dancing.

Of those three Sister Arts, which originally, perhaps, went always together, and which at all times go frequently together, there are two which can subsist alone, and separate from their natural companions, and one which cannot. In the distinct observation of what the ancients called Rhythmus, of what we call Time and Measure, consists the essence both of Dancing and of Poetry or Verse; or the characteristical quality which distinguishes the former from all other motion and action, and the latter from all other discourse. But, concerning the proportion between those intervals and divisions of duration which constitute what is called time and measure, the ear, it would seem, can judge with much more precision than the eye; and Poetry, in the same manner as Music, addresses itself to the ear, whereas Dancing addresses itself to the eye. In Dancing, the rhythmus, the proper proportion, the time and measure of its motions, cannot distinctly be perceived, unless they are marked by the more distinct time and measure of Music. It is otherwise in Poetry; no accompaniment is necessary to mark the measure of good Verse. Music and Poetry, therefore, can each of them subsist alone; Dancing always requires the accompaniment of Music.

It is Instrumental Music which can best subsist apart, and separate from both Poetry and Dancing. Vocal Music, though it may, and frequently does, consist of notes which have no distinct sense or meaning, yet naturally calls for the support of Poetry. But "Music, married to immortal Verse," as Milton says, or even to words of any kind which have a distinct sense or meaning, is necessarily and essentially imitative. Whatever be the meaning of those words, though, like many of the songs of ancient Greece, as well as some of those of more modern times, they may express merely some maxims of prudence and morality, or may contain merely the simple narrative of some important event, yet even in such didactic and historical songs there will still be imitation; there will still be a thing of one kind, which by art is made to resemble a thing of a very different kind; there will still be Music imitating discourse; there will still be rhythmus and melody, shaped and fashioned into the form either of a good moral counsel, or of an amusing and interesting story.

In this first species of imitation, which being essential to, is therefore inseparable from, all such Vocal Music, there may, and there commonly is, added a second. The words may, and commonly do, express the situation of some particular person, and all the sentiments and passions which he feels from that situation. It is a joyous companion who gives vent to the gaiety and mirth with which wine, festivity, and good company inspire him. It is a lover who complains, or hopes, or fears, or despairs. It is a generous man who expresses either his gratitude for the favors, or his indignation at the injuries, which may have been done to him. It is a warrior who prepares himself to confront danger, and who provokes or defies his enemy. It is a person in prosperity who humbly returns thanks for the goodness, or one in affliction who with contrition implores the mercy and forgiveness, of that invisible Power to whom he looks up as the Director of all the events of human life. The situation may comprehend, not only one, but two, three, or more persons; it may excite in them all either similar or opposite sentiments; what is a subject of sorrow to one, being an occasion of joy and triumph to another; and they may all express, sometimes separately and sometimes together, the particular way in which each of them is affected, as in a duo, trio, or a chorus.

All this it may, and it frequently has been said is unnatural; nothing being more so, than to sing when we are anxious to persuade, or in earnest to express any very serious purpose. But it should be remembered, that to make a thing of one kind resemble another thing of a very different kind, is the very circumstance which, in all the Imitative Arts, constitutes the merits of imitation; and that to shape, and as it were to bend, the measure and the melody of Music, so as to imitate the tone and the language of counsel and conversation, the accent and the style of emotion and passion, is to make a thing of one kind resemble another thing of a very different kind.

The tone and the movements of Music, though naturally very different from those of conversation and passion, may, however, be so managed as to seem to resemble them. On account of the great disparity between the imitating and the imitated object, the mind in this, as in the other cases, cannot only be contented, but delighted, and even charmed and transported, with such an imperfect resemblance as can be had. Such imitative Music, therefore, when sung to words which explain and determine its meaning, may frequently appear to be a very perfect imitation. It is upon this account, that even the incomplete Music of a recitative seems to express sometimes all the sedateness and composure of serious but calm discourse, and sometimes all the exquisite sensibility of the most interesting passion. The more complete Music of an air is still superior, and, in the imitation of the more animated passions, has one great advantage over every sort of discourse, whether Prose or Poetry, which is not sung to Music. In a person who is either much depressed by grief or enlivened by joy, who is strongly affected either with love or hatred, with gratitude or resentment, with admiration or contempt, there is commonly one thought or idea which dwells upon his mind, which continually haunts him, which, when he has chased it away, immediately returns upon him, and which in company makes him absent and inattentive. He can think but of one object, and he cannot repeat to them that object so frequently as it recurs upon him. He takes refuge in solitude, where he can with freedom either indulge the ecstasy or give way to the agony of the agreeable or disagreeable passion which agitates him; and where he can repeat to himself, which he does sometimes mentally, and sometimes even aloud, and almost always in the same words, the particular thought which either delights or distresses him. Neither Prose nor Poetry can venture to imitate those almost endless repetitions of passion. They may describe them as I do now, but they dare not imitate them; they would become most insufferably tiresome if they did. The Music of a passionate air not only may, but frequently does, imitate them; and it never makes its way so directly or so irresistibly to the heart as when it does so. It is upon this account that the words of an air, especially of a passionate one, though they are seldom very long, yet are scarce ever sung straight on to the end, like those of a recitative; but are almost always broken into parts, which are transposed and repeated again and again, according to the fancy or judgment of the composer. It is by means of such repetitions only, that Music can exert those peculiar powers of imitation which distinguish it, and in which it excels all the other Imitative Arts. Poetry and Eloquence, it has accordingly been often observed, produced their effect always by a connected variety and succession of different thoughts and ideas: but Music frequently produces its effects by a repetition of the same idea; and the same sense expressed in the same, or nearly the same, combination of sounds though at first perhaps it may make scarce any impression upon us, yet, by being repeated again and again, it comes at last gradually, and by little and little to move, to agitate, and to transport us.

To these powers of imitating, Music naturally, or rather necessarily, joins the happiest choice in the objects of its imitation. The sentiments and passions which Music can best imitate are those which unite and bind men together in society; the social, the decent, the virtuous, the interesting and affecting, the amiable and agreeable, the awful and respectable, the noble, elevating, and commanding passions. Grief and distress are interesting and affecting; humanity and compassion, joy and admiration, are amiable and agreeable; devotion is awful and respectable; the generous contempt of danger, the honorable indignation at injustice, are noble, elevating, and commanding. But it is these and such like passions which Music is fittest for imitating, and which it in fact most frequently imitates. They are, if I may say so, all Musical Passions; their natural tones are all clear, distinct, and almost melodious; and they naturally express themselves in a language which is distinguished by pauses at regular, and almost equal, intervals; and which, upon that account, can more easily be adapted to the regular returns of the correspondent periods of a tune. The passions, on the contrary, which drive men from one another, the unsocial, the hateful, the indecent, the vicious passions, cannot easily be imitated by Music. The voice of furious anger, for example, is harsh and discordant; its periods are all irregular, sometimes very long and sometimes very short, and distinguished by no regular pauses. The obscure and almost inarticulate grumblings of black malice and envy, the screaming outcries of dastardly fear, the hideous growlings of brutal and implacable revenge, are all equally discordant. It is with difficulty that Music can imitate any of those passions, and the Music which does imitate them is not the most agreeable. A whole entertainment may consist, without any impropriety, of the imitation of the social and amiable passions. It would be a strange entertainment which consisted altogether in the imitation of the odious and the vicious. A single song expresses almost always some social, agreeable, or interesting passion. In an opera the unsocial and disagreeable are sometimes introduced, but it is rarely, and as discords are introduced into harmony, to set off by their contrast the superior beauty of the opposite passions. What Plato said of Virtue, that it was of all beauties the brightest, may with some sort of truth be said of the proper and natural objects of musical imitation. They are either the sentiments and passions, in the exercise of which consist both the glory and the happiness of human life, or they are those from which it derives its most delicious pleasures, and most enlivening joys; or, at the worst and the lowest, they are those by which it calls upon our indulgence and compassionate assistance to its unavoidable weaknesses, its distresses, and its misfortunes.

To the merit of its imitation and to that of its happy choice in the objects which it imitates, the great merits of Statuary and Painting, Music joins another peculiar and exquisite merit of its own. Statuary and Painting cannot be said to add any new beauties of their own to the beauties of Nature which they imitate; they may assembles a greater number of those beauties, and group them in a more agreeable manner than they are commonly, or perhaps ever, to be found in Nature. It may perhaps be true, what the artists are so very fond of telling us, that no woman ever equaled, in all the parts of her body the beauty of the Venus of Medicis, nor any man that of the Apollo of Belvidere. But they must allow, surely that there is no particular beauty in any part or feature of those two famous statues, which is not at least equaled, if not much excelled by what is to be found in many living subjects. But Music, by arranging, and as it were bending to its own time and measure, whatever sentiments and passions it expresses, not only assembles and groups, as well as

Statuary and Painting the different beauties of Nature which it imitates, but it clothes them besides, with a new and an exquisite beauty of its own; it clothes them with melody and harmony, which, like a transparent mantle, far from concealing any beauty, serve only to give a brighter color, a more enlivening luster, and a more engaging grace to every beauty which they enfold.

To these two different sorts of imitation,—to that general one, by which Music is made to resemble discourse, and to that particular one, by which it is made to express the sentiments and feelings with which a particular situation inspires a particular person,—there is frequently joined a third. The person who sings may join to this double imitation of the singer the additional imitation of the actor; and express, not only by the modulation and cadence of his voice, but by his countenance, by his attitudes, by his gestures, and by his motions, the sentiments and feelings of the person whose situation is painted in the song. Even in private company, though a song may sometimes perhaps be said to be well sung, it can never be said to be well performed, unless the singer does something of this kind; and there is no comparison between the effect of what is sung coldly from a music-book at the end of a harpsichord, and of what is not only sung, but acted with proper freedom, animation, and boldness. An opera actor does no more than this; and an imitation which is so pleasing, and which appears even so natural, in private society ought not to appear forced, unnatural, or disagreeable upon the stage.

In a good opera actor, not only the modulations and pauses of his voice, but every motion and gesture, every variation, either in the air of his head, or in the attitude of his body, correspond to the time and measure of Music: they correspond to the expression of the sentiment or passion which the Music imitates, and that expression necessarily corresponds to this time and measure. Music is as it were the soul which animates him, which informs every feature of his countenance, and even directs every movement of his eyes. Like the musical expression of a song, his action adds to the natural grace of the sentiment or action which it imitates, a new and peculiar grace of its own; the exquisite and engaging grace of those gestures and motions, of those airs and attitudes which are directed by the movement, by the time and measure of Music; this grace heightens and enlivens that expression. Nothing can be more deeply affecting than the interesting scenes of the serious opera, when to good Poetry and good Music, to the Poetry of Metastasio and the Music of Pergolese, is added the execution of a good actor. In the serious opera, indeed, the action is too often sacrificed to the Music; the castrati, who perform the principal parts, being always the most insipid and miserable actors. The sprightly airs of the comic opera are, in the same manner, in the highest degree enlivening and diverting. Though they do not make us laugh so loud as we sometimes do at the scenes of the common comedy, they make us smile more frequently; and the agreeable gaiety, the temperate joy, if I may call it so, with which they inspire us, is not only an elegant, but a most delicious pleasure. The deep distress and the great passions of tragedy are capable of producing some effect, though it should be but indifferently acted. It is not so with the lighter misfortunes and less affecting situations of comedy: unless it is at least tolerably acted, it is altogether insupportable. But the castrati are scarce ever tolerable actors; they are accordingly seldom admitted to play in the comic opera; which, being upon that account commonly better performed than the serious, appears to many people the better entertainment of the two.

The imitative powers of Instrumental are much inferior to those of Vocal Music; its melodious but unmeaning and inarticulate sounds cannot, like the articulations of the human voice, relate distinctly the circumstances of any particular story, or describe the different situations which those circumstances produced; or even express clearly, and so as to be understood by every hearer, the various sentiments and passions which the parties concerned felt from these situations: even its imitation of other sounds, the objects which it can certainly best imitate, is commonly so indistinct, that alone, and without any explication, it might not readily suggest to us what was the imitated object. The rocking of a cradle is supposed to be imitated in that concerto of Correlli, which is said to have been composed for the Nativity: but, unless we were told beforehand, it might not readily occur to us what it meant to imitate, or whether it meant to imitate any thing at all; and this imitation (which, though perhaps as successful as any other, is by no means the distinguished beauty of that admired composition) might only appear to us a singular and odd passage in Music. The ringing of bells and the singing of the lark and nightingale are imitated in the symphony of Instrumental Music which Mr. Handel has composed for the Allegro and Penseroso of Milton: these are not only sounds but musical sounds, and may therefore be supposed to be more within the compass of the powers of musical imitation. It is accordingly universally acknowledged, that in these imitations this great master has been remarkably successful; and yet, unless the verses of Milton explained the meaning of the Music, it might not even in this case readily occur to us what it meant to imitate, or whether it meant to imitate any thing at all. With the explication of the words, indeed, the imitation appears, what it certainly is, a very fine one; but without that explication it might perhaps appear only a singular passage, which had less connection either with what went before or with what came after it, than any other in the Music.

Instrumental Music is said sometimes to imitate motion; but in reality it only either imitates the particular sounds which accompany certain motions, or it produces sounds of which the time and measure bear some correspondence to the variations, to the pauses and interruptions, to the successive accelerations and retardations of the motion which it means to imitate: it is in this way that it sometimes attempts to express the march and array of an army, the confusion and hurry of a battle, etc. In all these cases, however, its imitation is so very indistinct, that without the accompaniment of some other art, to explain and interpret its meaning, it would be almost always unintelligible; and we could scarce ever know with certainty, either what it meant to imitate, or whether it meant to imitate any thing at all.

In the imitative arts, though it is by no means necessary that the imitating should so exactly resemble the imitated object, that the one should sometimes be mistaken for the other, it is, however, necessary that they should resemble at least so far, that the one should always readily suggest the other. It would be a strange picture which required an inscription at the foot to tell us, not only what particular person it meant to represent, but whether it meant to represent a man or a horse, or whether it meant to be a picture at all, and to represent any thing. The imitations of instrumental

Music may, in some respects, be said to resemble such pictures. There is, however, this very essential difference between them, that the picture would not be much mended by the inscription; whereas, by what may be considered as very little more than such an inscription, instrumental Music, though it cannot always even then, perhaps, be said properly to imitate, may, however, produce all the effects of the finest and most perfect imitation. In order to explain in what manner this is brought about, it will not be necessary to descend into any great depth of philosophical speculation.

That train of thoughts and ideas which is continually passing through the mind does not always move on with the same pace, if I may say so, or with the same order and connection. When we are gay and cheerful, its motion is brisker and more lively, our thoughts succeed one another more rapidly, and those which immediately follow one another seem frequently either to have but little connection, or to be connected rather by their opposition than by their mutual resemblance. As in this wanton and playful disposition of mind we hate to dwell long upon the same thought, so we do not much care to pursue resembling thoughts; and the variety of contrast is more agreeable to us than the sameness of resemblance. It is quite otherwise when we are melancholy and desponding; we then, frequently find ourselves haunted, as it were, by some thought which we would gladly chase away, but which constantly pursues us, and which admits no followers, attendants, or companions, but such as are of its own kindred and complexion. A slow succession of resembling or closely connected thoughts is the characteristic of this disposition of mind; a quick succession of thoughts, frequently contrasted and in general very slightly connected, is the characteristic of the other. What may be called the natural state of the mind, the state in which we are neither elated nor dejected, the state of sedateness, tranquillity, and composure, holds a sort of middle place between those two opposite extremes; our thoughts succeed one another more slowly, and with a more distinct connection, than in the one; more quickly, and with a greater variety, than in the other.

Acute sounds are naturally gay, sprightly, and enlivening; grave sounds solemn, awful, and melancholy. There seems too to be some natural connection between acuteness in tune and quickness in time or succession, as well as between gravity and slowness: an acute sound seems to fly off more quickly than a grave one: the treble is more cheerful than the bass; its notes likewise commonly succeed one another more rapidly. But instrumental Music, by a proper arrangement, by a quicker or slower succession of acute and grave, of resembling and contrasted sounds, can not only accommodate itself to the gay, the sedate, or the melancholy mood; but if the mind is so far vacant as not to be disturbed by any disorderly passion, it can, at least for the moment, and to a certain degree, produce every possible modification of each of those moods or dispositions. We all readily distinguish the cheerful, the gay, and the sprightly Music, from the melancholy, the plaintive, and the affecting; and both these from what holds a sort of middle place between them, the sedate, the tranquil, and the composing. And we are all sensible that, in the natural and ordinary state of the mind, Music can, by a sort of incantation, soothe and charm us into some degree of that particular mood or disposition which accords with its own character and temper. In a concert of instrumental Music the attention is engaged, with pleasure and delight, to listen to a combination of the most agreeable and melodious sounds, which follow one another, sometimes with a quicker, and sometimes with a slower succession; and in which those that immediately follow one another sometimes exactly or nearly resemble, and sometimes contrast with one another in tune, in time, and in order of arrangement. The mind being thus successively occupied by a train of objects, of which the nature, succession, and connection correspond, sometimes to the gay, sometimes to the tranquil, and sometimes to the melancholy mood or disposition, it is itself successively led into each of those moods or dispositions; and is thus brought into a sort of harmony or concord with the Music which so agreeably engages its attention.

It is not, however, by imitation properly, that instrumental Music produces this effect: instrumental Music does not imitate, as vocal Music, as Painting, or as Dancing would imitate, a gay, sedate, or a melancholy person; it does not tell us, as any of those other arts could tell us, a pleasant, a serious, or a melancholy story. It is not, as in vocal Music, in Painting, or in Dancing, by sympathy with the gaiety, the sedateness, or the melancholy and distress of some other person, that instrumental Music soothes us into each of these dispositions: it becomes itself a gay, sedate, or a melancholy object; and the mind naturally assumes the mood or disposition which at the time corresponds to the object which engages its attention. Whatever we feel from instrumental Music is an original, and not a sympathetic feeling: it is our own gaiety, sedateness, or melancholy; not the reflected disposition of another person.

When we follow the winding alleys of some happily situated and well laid out garden, we are presented with a succession of landscapes, which are sometimes gay, sometimes gloomy, and sometimes calm and serene; if the mind is in its natural state, it suits itself to the objects which successively present themselves, and varies in some degree its mood and present humor with every variation of the scene. It would be improper, however, to say that those scenes imitated the gay, the calm, or the melancholy mood of the mind; they may produce in their turn each of those moods, but they cannot imitate any of them. Instrumental Music, in the same manner, though it can excite all those different dispositions, cannot imitate any of them. There are no two things in nature more perfectly disparate than sound and sentiment; and it is impossible by any human power to fashion the one into any thing that bears any real resemblance to the other.

This power of exciting and varying the different moods and dispositions of the mind, which instrumental Music really possesses to a very considerable degree, has been the principal source of its reputation for those great imitative powers which have been ascribed to it. "Painting," says an Author, more capable of feeling strongly than of analyzing accurately, Mr. Rousseau of Geneva, "Painting, which presents its imitations, not to the imagination, but to the senses, and to only one of the senses, can represent nothing besides the objects of sight. Music, one might imagine, should be equally confined to those of hearing. It imitates, however, every thing, even those objects which are perceivable by sight only. By a delusion that seems almost inconceivable, it can, as it were, put the eye into the ear; and the greatest wonder, of an art which acts only by motion and succession, is, that it can imitate rest and repose. Night, Sleep, Solitude, and Silence are all within the compass of musical imitation.

Though all Nature should be asleep, the person who contemplates it is awake; and the art of the musician consists in substituting, in the room of an image of what is not the object of hearing, that of the movements which its presence would excite in the mind of the spectator."—That is, of the effects which it would produce upon his mood and disposition. "The musician" (continues the same Author) "will sometimes, not only agitate the waves of the sea, blow up the flames of a conflagration, make the rain fall, the rivulets flow and swell the torrents, but he will paint the horrors of a hideous desert, darken the walls of a subterraneous dungeon, calm the tempest, restore serenity and tranquillity to the air and the sky, and shed from the orchestra a new freshness over the groves and fields. He will not directly represent any of these objects, but he will excite in the mind the same movements which it would feel from seeing them."

Upon this very eloquent description of Mr. Rousseau I must observe, that without the accompaniment of the scenery and action of the opera, without the assistance either of the scene-painter or of the poet, or of both, the instrumental Music of the orchestra could produce none of the effects which are here ascribed to it; and we could never know, we could never even guess, which of the gay, melancholy, or tranquil objects above mentioned it meant to represent to us; or whether it meant to represent any of them, and not merely to entertain us with a concert of gay, melancholy, or tranquil Music; or, as the ancients called them, of the Diastaltic, of the Systaltic, or of the Middle Music. With that accompaniment, indeed, though it cannot always even then, perhaps, be said properly to imitate, yet by supporting the imitation of some other art, it may produce all the same effects upon us as if itself had imitated in the finest and most perfect manner. Whatever be the object or situation which the scene painter represents upon the theatre, the Music of the orchestra, by disposing the mind to the same sort of mood and temper which it would feel from the presence of that object, or from sympathy with the person who was placed in that situation, can greatly enhance the effect of that imitation: it can accommodate itself to every diversity of scene. The melancholy of the man who, upon some great occasion, only finds himself alone in the darkness, the silence and solitude of the night, is very different from that of one who, upon a like occasion, finds himself in the midst of some dreary and inhospitable desert; and even in this situation his feelings would not be the same as if he was shut up in a subterraneous dungeon. The different degrees of precision with which the Music of the orchestra can accommodate itself to each of those diversities, must depend upon the taste, the sensibility, the fancy and imagination of the composer: it may sometimes, perhaps, contribute to this precision, that it should imitate, as well as it can, the sounds which either naturally accompany, or which might be supposed to accompany, the particular objects represented. The Symphony in the French opera of *Alcyone*, which imitated the violence of the winds and the dashing of the waves, in the tempest which was to drown Coix, is much commended by contemporary writers. That in the opera of *Isse*, which imitated that murmuring in the leaves of the oaks of Dodona, which might be supposed to precede the miraculous pronunciation of the oracle: and that in the opera of *Amadis*, of which the dismal accents imitated the sounds which might be supposed to accompany the opening of the tomb of Ardan, before the apparition of the ghost of that warrior, are still more celebrated. Instrumental Music, however, without violating too much its own melody and harmony, can imitate but imperfectly the sounds of natural objects, of which the greater part have neither melody nor harmony. Great reserve, great discretion, and a very nice discernment are requisite, in order to introduce with propriety such imperfect imitations, either into Poetry or Music; when repeated too often, when continued too long, they appear to be what they really are, mere tricks, in which a very inferior artist, if he will only give himself the trouble to attend to them, can easily equal the greatest. I have seen a Latin translation of Mr. Pope's *Ode on St. Cecilia's Day*, which in this respect very much excelled the original. Such imitations are still easier in Music. Both in the one art and in the other, the difficulty is not in making them as well as they are capable of being made, but in knowing when and how far to make them at all: But to be able to accommodate the temper and character of the Music to every peculiarity of the scene and situation with such exact precision, that the one shall produce the very same effect upon the mind as the other, is not one of those tricks in which an inferior artist can easily equal the greatest; it is an art which requires all the judgment, knowledge, and invention of the most consummate master. It is upon this art, and not upon its imperfect imitation, either of real or imaginary sounds, that the great effects of instrumental Music depend; such imitations ought perhaps to be admitted only so far as they may sometimes contribute to ascertain the meaning, and thereby to enhance the effects of this art.

By endeavoring to extend the effects of scenery beyond what the nature of the thing will admit of, it has been much abused; and in the common, as well as in the musical drama, many imitations have been attempted, which, after the first and second time we have seen them, necessarily appear ridiculous: such are, the Thunder rumbling from the Mustard-bowl, and the Snow of Paper and thick Hail of Pease, so finely exposed by Mr. Pope. Such imitations resemble those of painted Statuary; they may surprise at first, but they disgust ever after, and appear evidently such simple and easy tricks as are fit only for the amusement of children and their nurses at a puppet-show. The thunder of either theatre ought certainly never to be louder than that which the orchestra is capable of producing; and their most dreadful tempests ought never to exceed what the scene painter is capable of representing. In such imitations there may be an art which merits some degree of esteem and admiration. In the other there can be none which merits any.

This abuse of scenery has both subsisted much longer, and been carried to a much greater degree of extravagance, in the musical than in the common drama. In France it has been long banished from the latter; but it still continues, not only to be tolerated, but to be admired and applauded in the former. In the French operas, not only thunder and lightning, storms and tempests, are commonly represented in the ridiculous manner above mentioned, but all the marvelous, all the supernatural of Epic Poetry, all the metamorphoses of Mythology, all the wonders of Witchcraft and Magic, every thing that is most unfit to be represented upon the stage, are every day exhibited with the most complete approbation and applause of that ingenious nation. The Music of the orchestra producing upon the audience nearly the same effect which a better and more artful imitation would produce, hinders them from feeling, at least in its full force, the ridicule of those childish and awkward imitations which necessarily abound in that extravagant scenery. And in reality such imitations, though no doubt ridiculous every where, yet certainly appear somewhat less so in the musical than they would in the common drama. The Italian opera, before it was reformed by Apostolo Zeno and Metastasio, was in this respect equally extravagant, and was upon that account the subject of the agreeable raillery of Mr. Addison in several different papers of the Spectator. Even since that reformation it still continues to be a rule, that the scene should change at least with every act; and the unity of place never was a more sacred law in the common drama, than the violation of it has become in the musical: the latter seems in reality to require both a more picturesque and a more varied scenery, than is at all necessary for the former. In an opera, as the Music supports the effects of the scenery, so the scenery often serves to determine the character, and to explain the meaning of the Music; it ought to vary therefore as that character varies. The pleasure of an opera, besides, is in its nature more a sensual pleasure, than that of a common comedy or tragedy; the latter produced their effect principally by means of the imagination: in the closet, accordingly, their effect is not much inferior to what it is upon the stage. But the effect of an opera is seldom very great in the closet; it addresses itself more to the external senses, and as it soothes the ear by its melody and harmony, so we feel that it ought to dazzle the eye with the splendor and variety of its scenery.

In an opera the instrumental Music of the orchestra supports the imitation both of the poet and of the actor, as well as of the scene painter. The overture disposes the mind to that mood which fits it for the opening of the piece. The Music between the acts keeps up the impression which the foregoing had made, and prepares us for that which the following is to make. When the orchestra interrupts, as it frequently does, either the recitative or the air, it is in order either to enforce the effect of what had gone before, or to put the mind in the mood which fits it for hearing what is to come after. Both in the recitatives and in the airs it accompanies and directs the voice, and often brings it back to the proper tone and modulation, when it is upon the point of wandering away from them; and the correctness of the best vocal Music is owing in a great measure to the guidance of instrumental; though in all these cases it supports the imitation of another art, yet in all of them it may be said rather to diminish than to increase the resemblance between the imitating and the imitated object. Nothing can be more unlike to what really passes in the world, than that persons engaged in the most interesting situations, both of public and private life, in sorrow, in disappointment, in distress, in despair, should, in all that they say and do, be constantly accompanied with a fine concert of instrumental Music. Were we to reflect upon it, such accompaniment must in all cases diminish the probability of the action, and render the representation still less like nature than it otherwise would be. It is not by imitation, therefore, that instrumental Music supports and enforces the imitations of the other arts; but it is by producing upon the mind, in consequence of other powers, the same sort of effect which the most exact imitation of nature, which the most perfect observation of probability, could produce. To produce this effect is, in such entertainments, the sole end and purpose of that imitation and observation. If it can be equally well produced by other means, this end and purpose may be equally well answered.

But if instrumental Music can seldom be said to be properly imitative, even when it is employed to support the imitation of some other art, it is commonly still less so when it is employed alone. Why should it embarrass its melody and harmony, or constrain its time and measure, by attempting an imitation which, without the accompaniment of some other art to explain and interpret its meaning, nobody is likely to understand? In the most approved instrumental Music, accordingly, in the overtures of Handel and the concertos of Correlli, there is little or no imitation, and where there is any, it is the source of but a very small part of the merit of those compositions. Without any imitation, instrumental Music can produce very considerable effects; though its powers over the heart and affections are, no doubt, much inferior to those of vocal Music, it has, however, considerable powers: by the sweetness of its sounds it awakens agreeably, and calls upon the attention; by their connection and affinity it naturally detains that attention, which follows easily a series of agreeable sounds which have all a certain relation both to a common, fundamental, or leading note, called the key note; and to a certain succession or combination of notes, called the song or composition. By means of this relation each foregoing sound seems to introduce, and as it were prepare the mind for the following: by its rythmus, by its time and measure, it disposes that succession of sounds into a certain arrangement, which renders the whole more easy to be comprehended and remembered. Time and measure are to instrumental Music what order and method are to discourse; they break it into proper parts and divisions, by which we are enabled both to remember better what is gone before, and frequently to foresee somewhat of what is to come after: we frequently foresee the return of a period which we know must correspond to another which we remember to have gone before; and, according to the saying of an ancient philosopher and musician, the enjoyment of Music arises partly from memory and partly from foresight. When the measure, after having been continued so long as to satisfy us, changes to another, that variety, which thus disappoints, becomes more agreeable to us than the uniformity which would have gratified our expectation: but without this order and method we could remember very little of what had gone before, and we could foresee still less of what was to come after; and the whole enjoyment of Music would be equal to little more than the effect of the particular sounds which rung in our ears at every particular instant. By means of this order and method it is, during the progress of the entertainment, equal to the effect of all that we remember, and of all that we foresee; and at the conclusion, to the combined and accumulated effect of all the different parts of which the whole was composed.

A well-composed concerto of instrumental Music, by the number and variety of the instruments, by the variety of the parts which are performed by them, and the perfect concord or correspondence of all these different parts; by the exact harmony or coincidence of all the different sounds which are heard at the same time, and by that happy variety of measure which regulates the succession of those which are heard at different times, presents an object so agreeable, so great, so various, and so interesting, that alone, and without suggesting any other object, either by imitation or otherwise, it can occupy, and as it were fill up, completely the whole capacity of the mind, so as to leave no part of its attention vacant for thinking of any thing else. In the contemplation of that immense variety of agreeable and melodious sounds, arranged and digested, both in their coincidence and in their succession, into so complete and regular and system, the mind in reality enjoys not only a very great sensual, but a very high intellectual, pleasure, not unlike that which it derives from the contemplation of a great system in any other science. A full concerto of such instrumental Music, not only does not require, but it does not admit of any accompaniment. A song or a dance, by demanding an attention which we have not to spare, would disturb, instead of heightening, the effect of the Music; they may often very properly succeed, but they cannot accompany it. That music seldom means to tell any particular story, or to imitate any particular event, or in general to suggest any particular object, distinct from that combination of sounds of which itself is composed. Its meaning, therefore, may be said to be complete in itself, and to require no interpreters to explain it. What is called the subject of such Music is merely, as has already been said, a certain leading combination of notes, to which it frequently returns, and to which all its digressions and variations bear a certain affinity. It is altogether different from what is called the subject of a poem or a picture, which is always something which is not either in the poem or in the picture, or something quite distinct from that combination, either of words on the one hand, or of colors on the other, of which they are respectively composed. The subject of a composition of instrumental Music is a part of that composition: the subject of a poem or picture is no part of either.

The effect of instrumental Music upon the mind has been called its expression. In the feeling it is frequently not unlike the effect of what is called the expression of Painting, and is sometimes equally interesting. But the effect of the expression of Painting arises always from the thought of something which, though distinctly and clearly suggested by the drawing and coloring of the picture, is altogether different from that drawing and coloring. It arises sometimes from sympathy with, sometimes from antipathy and aversion to, the sentiments, emotions, and passions which the countenance, the action, the air and attitude of the persons represented suggest. The melody and harmony of instrumental Music, on the contrary, do not distinctly and clearly suggest any thing that is different from that melody and harmony. Whatever effect it produces is the immediate effect of that melody and harmony, and not of something else which is signified and suggested by them: they in fact signify and suggest nothing. It may be proper to say that the complete art of painting, the complete merit of a picture, is composed of three distinct arts or merits; that of drawing, that of coloring, and that of expression. But to say, as Mr. Avision does, that the complete art of a musician, the complete merit of a piece of Music, is composed or made up of three distinct arts or merits, that of melody, that of harmony, and that of expression, is to say, that it is made up of melody and harmony, and of the immediate and necessary effect of melody and harmony: the division is by no means logical; expression in painting is not the necessary effect either of good drawing or of good coloring, or of both together; a picture may be both finely drawn and finely colored, and yet have very little expression: but that effect upon the mind which is called expression in Music, is the immediate and necessary effect of good melody. In the power of producing this effect consists the essential characteristic which distinguishes such melody from what is bad or indifferent. Harmony may enforce the effect of good melody, but without good melody the most skillful harmony can produce no effect which deserves the name of expression; it can do little more than fatigue and confound the ear. A painter may possess, in a very eminent degree, the talents of drawing and coloring, and yet possess that of expression in a very inferior degree. Such a painter, too, may have great merit. In the judgment of Du Piles, even the celebrated Titian was a painter of this kind. But to say that a musician possessed the talents of melody and harmony in a very eminent degree, and that of expression in a very inferior one, would be to say, that in his works the cause was not followed by its necessary and proportionable effect. A musician may be a very skillful harmonist and yet be defective in the talents of melody, air, and expression; his songs may be dull and without effect. Such a musician too may have a certain degree of merit, not unlike that of a man of great learning, who wants fancy, taste, and invention.

Instrumental Music, therefore, though it may, no doubt, be considered in some respects as an imitative art, is certainly less so than any other which merits that appellation; it can imitate but a few objects, and even these so imperfectly, that without the accompaniment of some other art, its imitation is scarce ever intelligible: imitation is by no means essential to it, and the principal effects which it is capable of producing arises from powers altogether different from those of imitation.

Part III

The imitative powers of Dancing are much superior to those of instrumental Music, and are at least equal, perhaps superior, to those of any other art. Like instrumental Music, however, it is not necessarily or essentially imitative, and it can produce very agreeable effects, without imitating any thing. In the greater part of our common dances there is little or no imitation, and they consist almost entirely of a succession of such steps, gestures, and motions, regulated by the time and measure of Music, as either display extraordinary grace or require extraordinary agility. Even some of our dances, which are said to have been originally imitative, have, in the way in which we practice them, almost ceased to be so. The minuet, in which the woman, after passing and repassing the man several times, first gives him up one hand, then the other, and then both hands, is said to have been originally a Moorish dance, which emblematically represented the passion of love. Many of my readers may have frequently danced this dance, and, in the opinion of all who saw them, with great grace and propriety, though neither they nor their spectators once thought of the allegorical meaning which it originally intended to express.

A certain measured, cadenced step, commonly called a dancing step, which keeps time with, and as it were beats the measure of, the Music which accompanies and directs it, is the essential characteristic which distinguishes a dance from every other sort of motion. When the dancer, moving with a step of this kind, and observing this time and measure, imitates either the ordinary or the more important actions of human life, he shapes and fashions, as it were, a thing of one kind, into the resemblance of another thing of a very different kind: his art conquers the disparity which Nature has placed between the imitating and the imitated object, and has upon that account some degree of that sort of merit which belongs to all the imitative arts. This disparity, indeed, is not so great as in some other of those arts, nor consequently the merit of the imitation which conquers it. Nobody would compare the merit of a good imitative dancer to that of a good painter or statuary. The dancer, however, may have a very considerable degree of merit, and his imitation perhaps may sometimes be capable of giving us as much pleasure as that of either of the other two artists. All the subjects, either of Statuary or of History Painting, are within the compass of his imitative powers; and in representing them, his art has even some advantage over both the other two. Statuary and History Painting can represent but a single instant of the action which they mean to imitate: the cause which prepared, the consequences which followed, the situation of that single instant are altogether beyond the compass of their imitation. A pantomime dance can represent distinctly those causes and consequences; it is not confined to the situation of a single instant; but, like Epic Poetry, it can represent all the events of a long story, and exhibit a long train and succession of connected and interesting situations. It is capable therefore of affecting us much more than either Statuary or Painting. The ancient Romans used to shed tears at the representations of their pantomimes, as we do at that of the most interesting tragedies; an effect which is altogether beyond the powers of Statuary or Painting.

The ancient Greeks appear to have been a nation of dancers, and both their common and their stage dances seem to have been all imitative. The stage dances of the ancient Romans appear to have been equally so. Among that grave people it was reckoned indecent to dance in private societies; and they could therefore have no common dances. Among both nations imitation seems to have been considered as essential to dancing.

It is quite otherwise in modern times: though we have pantomime dances upon the stage, yet the greater part even of our stage dances are not pantomime, and cannot well be said to imitate any thing. The greater part of our common dances either never were pantomime, or, with a very few exceptions, have almost all ceased to be so.

This remarkable difference of character between the ancient and the modern dances seems to be the natural effect of a correspondent difference in that of the Music, which has accompanied and directed both the one and the other.

In modern times we almost always dance to instrumental Music, which being itself not imitative, the greater part of the dances which it directs, and as it were inspires, have ceased to be so. In ancient times, on the contrary, they seem to have danced almost always to vocal Music; which being necessary and essentially imitative, their dances became so too. The ancients seem to have had little or nothing of what is properly called instrumental Music, or of Music composed not to be sung by the voice, but to be played upon instruments, and both their wind and their stringed instruments seem to have served only as an accompaniment and direction to the voice.

In the country it frequently happens that a company of young people take a fancy to dance, though they have neither fiddler nor piper to dance to. A lady undertakes to sing while the rest of the company dance: in most cases she sings the notes only, without the words, and then the voice being little more than a musical instrument, the dance is performed in the usual way, without any imitation. But if she sings the words, and if in those words there happens to be somewhat more than ordinary spirit and humor, immediately all the company, especially all the best dancers, and all those who dance most at their ease, become more or less pantomimes, and by their gestures and motions express, as well as they can, the meaning and story of the song. This would be still more the case, if the same person both danced and sung; a practice very common among the ancients: it requires good lungs and a vigorous constitution; but with these advantages and long practice, the very highest dances may be performed in this manner. I have seen a Negro dance to his own song, the war-dance of his own country, with such vehemence of action and expression, that the whole company, gentlemen as well as ladies, got up upon the chairs and tables, to be as much as possible out of the way of his furry. In the Greek language there are two verbs which both signify to dance; each of which has its proper derivatives, signifying a dance and a dancer. In the greater part of Greek authors, these two sets of words, like all others which are nearly synonymous, are frequently confounded, and used promiscuously. According to the best critics, however, in strict propriety, one of these verbs signifies to dance and sing at the same time, or to dance to one's own music. The other to dance without singing, or to dance to the music of other people. There is said to be a correspondent difference in the signification of their respective derivatives. In the choruses of the ancient Greek tragedies, consisting sometimes of more than fifty persons, some piped and some sung, but all danced, and danced to their own music.

[*The following Observations were found among Mr. Smith's Manuscripts, without any intimation whether they were intended as part of this, or of a different Essay. As they appeared too valuable to be suppressed, the Editors have availed themselves of their connection with the passage referred to in II.2 and have annexed them to this Essay.*]

Of the Affinity between Music, Dancing, and Poetry

In the second part of this Essay I have mentioned the connection between the two arts of *Music* and *Dancing* formed by the *Rythmus,* as the ancients termed it, or, as we call it, the tune or measure that equally regulates both.

It is not, however, every sort of step, gesture, or motion, of which the correspondence with the tune or measure of Music will constitute a Dance. It must be a step, gesture, or motion of a particular sort. In a good opera-actor, not only the modulations and pauses of his voice, but every motion and gesture, every variation, either in the air of his head or in the attitude of his body, correspond to the time and measure of Music. The best opera-actor, however, is not, according to the language of any country in Europe, understood to dance, yet in the performance of his part he generally makes use of what is called the stage step; but even this step is not understood to be a dancing step.

Though the eye of the most ordinary spectator readily distinguishes between what is called a dancing step and any other step, gesture, or motion, yet it may not perhaps be very easy to express what it is which constitutes this distinction. To ascertain exactly the precise limits at which the one species begins, and the other ends, or to give an accurate definition of this very frivolous matter, might perhaps require more thought and attention, than the very small importance of the subject may seem to deserve. Were I, however, to attempt to do this, I should observe, that though in performing any ordinary action—in walking, for example—from the one end of the room to the other, a person may show both grace and agility, yet if he betrays the least intention of showing either, he is sure of offending more or less, and we never fail to accuse him of some degree of vanity and affectation. In the performance of any such ordinary action, every person wishes to appear to be solely occupied about the proper purpose of the action: if he means to show either grace or agility, he is careful to conceal that meaning, and he is very seldom successful in doing so: he offends, however, just in proportion as he betrays it, and he almost always betrays it. In Dancing, on the contrary, every person professes, and avows, as it were, the intention of displaying some degree either of grace, or of agility, or of both. The display of one, or other, or both of these qualities, is in reality the proper purpose of the action; and there can never be any disagreeable vanity or affectation in following out the proper purpose of any action. When we say of any particular person, that he gives himself many affected airs and graces in Dancing, we mean either that he gives himself airs and graces which are unsuitable to the nature of the Dance, or that he executes awkwardly, perhaps exaggerates too much, (the most common fault in Dancing,) the airs and graces which are suitable to it. Every Dance is in reality a succession of airs and graces of some kind or other, and of airs and graces which, if I may say so, profess themselves to be such. The steps, gestures, and motions which, as it were, avow the intention of exhibiting a succession of such airs and graces, are the steps, gestures and motions which are peculiar to Dancing, and when these are performed to the time and measure of Music, they constitute what is properly called a Dance.

But though every sort of step, gesture, or motion, even though performed to the time and measure of Music, will not alone make a Dance, yet almost any sort of sound, provided it is repeated with a distinct rythmus, or according to a distinct time and measure, though without any variation as to gravity or acuteness, will make a sort of Music, no doubt indeed, an imperfect one. Drums, cymbals, and, so far as I have observed, all other instruments of percussion, have only one note; this note, however, when repeated with a certain rythmus, or according to a certain time and measure, and sometimes, in order to mark more distinctly that time and measure, with some little variation as to loudness and lowness, though without any as to acuteness and gravity, does certainly make a sort of Music which is frequently far from being disagreeable, and which even sometimes produces considerable effects. The simple note of such instruments, it is true, is generally a very clear, or what is called a melodious, sound. It does not however seem indispensably necessary that it should be so. The sound of the muffled drum, when it beats the dead march, is far from being either clear or melodious, and yet it certainly produces a species of Music, which is sometimes affecting. Even in the performance of the most humble of all artists, of the man who drums upon the table with his fingers, we may sometimes distinguish the measure, and perhaps a little of the humor, of some favorite song; and we must allow that even he makes some sort of Music. Without a proper step and motion, the observation of tune alone will not make a Dance; time alone, without tune, will make some sort of Music.

That exact observation of tune, or of the proper intervals of gravity and acuteness, which constitutes the great beauty of all perfect Music constitutes likewise its great difficulty. The time or measure of a song are simple matters, which even a course and unpracticed ear is capable of distinguishing and comprehending: but to distinguish and comprehend all the variations of the tune, and to conceive with precision, the exact proportion of every note, is what the finest and most cultivated ear is frequently no more than capable of performing. In the singing of the common people we may generally remark a distinct enough observation of time, but a very imperfect one of tune. To discover and to distinguish with precision the proper intervals of tune, must have been a work of long experience and much observation. In the theoretical treatises upon Music, what the authors have to say upon time is commonly discussed in a single chapter of no great length or difficulty. The theory of tune fills commonly all the rest of the volume, and has long ago become both an extensive and an abstruse science, which is often but imperfectly comprehended, even by intelligent artists. In the first rude efforts of uncivilized nations towards singing, the niceties of tune could be but little attended to: I have, upon this account, been frequently disposed to doubt of the great antiquity of those national songs, which it is pretended have been delivered down from age to age by a sort of oral tradition, without having been ever noted, or distinctly recorded for many successive generations. The measure, the humor of the song, might perhaps have been delivered down in this manner, but it seems scarcely possible that the precise notes of the tune should have been so preserved. The method of singing some of what we reckon our old Scotch songs, has undergone great alterations within the compass of my memory, and it may have undergone still greater before.

The distinction between the sounds or tones of singing and those of speaking seems to be of the same kind with that between the steps, gestures, and motions of Dancing, and those of any other ordinary action; though in speaking a person may show a very agreeable tone of voice, yet if he seems to intend to show it, if he appears to listen to the sound of his own voice, and as it were to tune it into a pleasing modulation, he never fails to offend, as guilty of a most disagreeable affectation. In speaking, as in every other ordinary action, we expect and require that the speaker should attend only to the proper purpose of the action, the clear and distinct expression of what he has to say. In singing, on the contrary, every person professes the intention to please by the tone and cadence of his voice; and he not only appears to be guilty of no disagreeable affectation in doing so, but we expect and require that he should do so. To please by the choice and arrangement of agreeable sounds is the proper purpose of all Music, vocal as well as instrumental;

and we always expect and require, that every person should attend to the proper purpose of whatever action he is performing. A person may appear to sing, as well as to dance, affectedly; he may endeavor to please by sounds and tones which are unsuitable to the nature of the song, or he may dwell too much on those which are suitable to it, or in some other way he may show an overweening conceit of his own abilities, beyond what seems to be warranted by his performance. The disagreeable affectation appears to consist always, not in attempting to please by a proper, but by some improper modulation of the voice. It was early discovered that the vibrations of chords or strings, which either in their lengths, or in their densities, or in their degrees of tension, bear a certain proportion to one another, produce sounds which correspond exactly, or, as the musicians say, are the unisons of those sounds or tones of the human voice which the ear approves of in singing. This discovery has enabled musicians to speak with distinctness and precision concerning the musical sounds or tones of the human voice; they can always precisely ascertain what are the particular sounds or tones which they mean, by ascertaining what are the proportions of the strings of which the vibrations produce the unisons of those sounds or tones. What are called the intervals; that is, the differences, in point of gravity and acuteness, between the sounds or tones of a singing voice, are much greater and more distinct than those of the speaking voice. Though the former, therefore, can be measured and appreciated by the proportions of chords or strings, the later cannot. The nicest instruments cannot express the extreme minuteness of these intervals. The heptamerede of Mr. Sauveur could express an interval so small as the seventh part of what is called a comma, the smallest interval that is admitted in modern Music. Yet even this instrument, we are informed by Mr. Duclos, could not express the minuteness of the intervals in the pronunciation of the Chinese language; of all the languages in the world, that of which the pronunciation is said to approach the nearest to singing, or in which the intervals are said to be the greatest.

As the sounds or tones of the singing voice, therefore, can be ascertained or appropriated, while those of the speaking voice cannot; the former are capable of being noted or recorded, while the latter are not.

Index

Aberdeen Philosophical Club, 279, 355
Absalom and Achitophel, 24
Achilles, 39, 41, 46, 207, 231, 241
Actium, 53
Addison, Joseph, **107-136**, 8, 16, 22, 24-27, 55, 107, 138, 140, 142, 232, 264, 378-379, 386-387, 400-401, 410, 461
  The Spectator, 8, 16, 26, 107, 137-138, 140, 142, 386, 395, 461
Aeneas, 39-41, 46-47, 52, 82, 109, 187, 207, 300, 302, 315
Aeneid, 41, 48, 51,124-125, 315, 377, 383, 402
Aesop, 52, 444
aesthetics, 1-2, 10-12, 16-18, 20-22, 27, 29, 30-31, 249
  apprehension, 8
  arguments, 7
  attitude, 2
  autonomy, 9
  distance, 22
  education, 30
  epistemology, 9
  experience, 10, 29, 30
  expression, 7, 11, 22, 31
  intuition, 19
  justification, 30
  modern, 1, 31
  movements, 31
  objects, 21
  passions, 9
  phenomena, 5
  philosophy, 6, 18
  picturesque, 431
  pleasure, 20-23, 30
[aesthetics]
  practice, 7
  predicates, 9, 26, 30
  questions, 6
  sentiment, 18
  significance, 23
  taste, 18, 19
  term, 1
  theories, 10, 14, 30
  thought, 7
  transcendent, 30
  vocabulary, 9
Agamemnon, 241
Ajax, 145, 207
Akenside, Mark, *Pleasure of the Imagination*, 387, 392, 417
Alberti, Leon Battisa, 36
Alcyone, 459
Alexander the Great, 68, 120, 197, 391
Alison, Archibald, **405-420**, 5, 18, 22, 30, 405
allegory, 10, 58, 132, 200, 207-208, 254, 269, 344-345, 367, 464
Alsenus, 168
Amadis, 459
Americans, 266
Anacreon, 360
Anacreontic odes, 358
Anchises, 46, 300
Antinous, 218, 444
Apelles, 36-37, 39, 43, 53, 76, 298, 306, 436
  Venus of, 245
Apollo, 39, 49, 225, 344, 440, 444, 454
  Apollo Belvedere, 422
Apollonius Tyanaeus, 36

appetites, 17, 77-79, 91, 93, 98, 130, 199, 228, 258, 259, 264, 323
animal, 18
bodily, 17, 449, 450
depraved, 44
for gratification, 323
for sensation, 31
moderate, 91
natural, 340
youthful, 229
Archemorus, 51
archetype, 184
architecture, 28, 75-76, 81, 86, 95, 118-121, 124-125, 135, 152, 153, 160, 162, 165-166, 169, 171, 173, 195, 202, 215, 289, 299, 319, 320-321, 328, 349, 351, 378, 391, 399, 407, 409, 422, 446
Greek, 321
Palladian, 422
Ariosto, Ludovico, 44, 77, 232
Aristides, *Iris* of, 245
Aristotle, 6-7, 15, 21, 23, 27, 35, 39, 43, 45, 111, 208, 239, 257, 353, 363, 378
De Anima, 14
causal structure, 25
dramatic unities, 13
empiricism, 9
epistemology, 21
imitation, 23, 24
Metaphysics, 23
Poetics, 12, 23, 43-44, 49, 137, 180, 185, 187, 265, 290, 367, 368, 383, 401-402
organization, 25
senses, 14-15
verbal form, 25
Ashburnham, Earl of, 343
association, 2-7, 22, 30, 71, 142, 145, 160-162, 193, 195, 199-201, 252, 276, 284-285, 297, 299, 336-337, 348, 351, 396, 399, 415-416, 418
Athalia, 241
Atheneus, 307
Avision, Mr., 463

Baal, 148, 181, 241
Babylon, 119, 133
Bacchus, 444
Bacon, Francis,112
Baier, Annette, *A Progress of Sentiments*, 17
Baillie, John, **191-204**, 13, 25, 27, 191
Bamboccio, Il (Pieter van Laer), 35
Barrell, John, *The Dark Side of Landscape*, 28, 30
Bassano, Jacopo, 346
Bath, 303
Baumgarten, A. G., 1-2, 8
Bays, Mr. in *The Rehearsal*, 129
Beattie, James, **355-372**, 17, 29, 355
beauties, 14, 35, 37-38, 53, 55-57, 76, 96, 108, 115-117, 123, 127, 133, 165, 205, 207, 212, 221, 228, 232-233, 236, 240, 286, 288, 295, 305-306, 317-318, 349, 351, 353, 356, 374-378, 380, 383-386, 398, 400, 421, 434, 454
and blemishes, 237
frivolous, 238
higher, 318, 375
inferior, 331
manly, 110
moral, 377
new, 109
of animals, 163, 272
of art, 229, 374, 411, 432
of an author, 108
of comedy, 56
of composition, 16, 386, 394
of design, 238
of elocution, 246
of eloquence, 377
of imagination, 244
of Italian Masters, 75
of a kind, 113, 114, 163
of nature, 37, 45, 128, 358, 361, 374, 384, 411, 432, 454-455
of painting, 24, 299, 303, 376
of poetry, 232, 239, 377, 383
of the stage, 41
of style and numbers, 375
of writing, 235
outward, 97
subaltern, 93
sublime, 176, 331
vegetable, 273
beauty, 5, 7-8, 21, 24-25, 35-37, 40, 46, 51, 74, 88-90, 94-97, 102-103,

[beauty]
110-111, 113, 122-123, 146, 150, 153-160, 162, 173, 176, 180, 193, 201-202, 209-210, 215-217, 219, 222, 224, 232-236, 238, 242, 263-264, 269-274, 279, 281-283, 288, 292, 303, 306, 316-323, 333, 335-337, 342, 351, 353, 362, 374-375, 377-380, 386-387, 394-401, 406, 409-412, 414, 416-418, 421-425, 427-428, 434, 436-443, 446-447, 454-455
absolute, 154, 157-158
and deformity, 160-161, 196, 232-233, 235, 239, 336
and desire, 153
and emotion, 21, 401, 405, 408-411, 413-416
and expression, 417, 420
and grace, 222-224, 332
and love, 270
and novelty, 337
and order, 320, 322
and pleasure, 20-21, 25, 112, 153-156, 158, 163, 217, 386, 395
and proportion, 282, 320
and truth, 95
apprehension of, 8
cause of, 217, 270, 336-337, 415
efficient, 275
characteristics of, 25
color, 273, 321
comparative, 124
conditions of, 273
constituents, 273
contemplation of, 307, 358
corporeal, 337, 352
criterion of, 336
definition of, 196
degrees of, 219
design, 399
effect of, 217, 422
external, 323, 358
feminine, 27
human, 35, 317, 398-399
idea of, 20-21, 25, 36, 137, 142, 152-155, 161-162, 184, 270, 273, 304, 335, 348, 353, 394, 399, 401, 421, 437
ideal, 24, 35-36, 39, 345, 454

[beauty]
impressions, 328
intrinsic, 284, 317-319, 442
kinds of, 236, 334, 383
line of, 218, 220, 225, 273, 397, 423
love of, 424
material, 361
moral, 95, 199-200, 361
no quality in things, 232, 234, 322
objects of, 411, 422, 426
of action, 163
of art and nature, 8
of color, 114, 116, 121, 273-274, 284-285, 318, 321-322, 337, 367, 396, 398-399, 418, 436
of composition and discourse, 376, 425
of fiction, 58
of figure, 318, 396-398, 447
of fitness, 216, 283, 382, 399
of form, 24, 219-220, 283, 290, 436, 440
of humor, 58
of imagination, 67
of imitation, 447, 456
of metaphor, 201
of motion, 318, 397-398
of music, 468
of nature, 10, 37, 49, 72, 89, 94, 112, 118, 152, 154, 161, 167, 216, 226, 410, 416, 418, 428, 458
of objects, 282, 317
of oratorial numbers, 244
of order, 322
of painting, 37, 46, 126, 280, 334, 336-337, 436
of poetry, 52
of regularity, 321, 322, 396
of science, 281
of shape, 274
of single objects, 318
of theorems, 152, 156
of tragedy, 46
of utility, 318, 320, 322, 405
of writing, 400
origin of, 408, 416, 421-422
original, 154, 447
perception of, 239, 283, 322
personal, 264, 439
picturesque, 422, 423, 426, 427, 431, 434, 435, 436, 437

[beauty]
principles of, 215, 319, 396-398, 400, 428
properties, 274
qualities of, 274, 283, 316, 322, 396, 407, 409, 438
relative, 154, 157, 317, 447
rules, 235
secondary quality, 24
sensation of, 387
sense of, 6-7, 21, 25, 151-156, 158-163, 215, 228, 264, 280, 323, 374, 376-377, 380, 399, 412, 428
sensibility to, 385
sentiment of, 74, 94, 230, 234, 236-237, 244, 298
sex, 264, 270, 273
smoothness, 272, 274, 437
social quality, 439
species, 115, 236, 280, 282, 283, 337, 400
standard of, 238, 283, 428
term, 21 317, 337, 342, 396, 422
theory of
Addison's, 24
Blair, 25
Burke, 27
classical, 7, 24, 25, 36
empiricist, 7, 8
Hogarth's, 282, 397
Hume's, 18, 22
Hutcheson's, 8
Kames's, 25
psychological, 25
rationalist, 8
transcendent, 30
universal, 233
use of, 1
visible, 439
Bellianis, Don, 255
Bellori, Giovanni Pietro, 34, 38, 41
Bergerus, Johannes Gulielmus, 394
Berkeley, Bishop, 10
Alciphron, 10
Blackmore, Richard, 324
Blair, Hugh, **373-404**, 9, 25, 373
Blunt, Anthony, 16
Boileau-Despreaux, Nicholas, 64, 66, 109, 353
Bossu, Rene, 40-41, 44, 109, 180, 185, 187
Boswell, James, 165, 205, 227
Brandi, Jacinto, 307
Brown, Lancelot (Capability), 28, 431, 434
Brutus, 35
Bruyere, Jean de La, 109
Brydone, Tour in Sicily, Patrick, 362
Buccleugh, Duke of, 441
Buckingham, Duke of, 56
Buckley, Mr., 56
Bunyan, John, 232, 255
Burke, Edmund, **249-278**, 9, 18, 22-23, 26-27, 205, 249, 393, 422, 437-439
Burlington, Duke of, 17
Burnet, Gilbert, 137
Burrel, Sir Peter, 343

Caesar, 197-198, 314, 391
Commentaries, 393-394
Caesar Augustus, 43, 51, 65, 109
Caligula, 197
Calvinism, 5-6, 297
Calyban, 365
Campbell, George, *Philosophy of Rhetoric*, 367
Capuchins, Church of the, 36
Caravaggio, Michaelangelo, 35
Carracci, 41, 75
Carthage, 41, 207
Castiglione, Baldassar, 36
castrati, 455
Catullus, 40
cause, 5, 12, 23, 63, 69, 72, 89-90, 95, 104, 116, 143-144, 146, 148, 150-151, 158-160, 166-173, 176, 184, 196, 203, 206, 217, 234, 239, 243, 251, 257-258, 262-265, 269-271, 275-277, 281-284, 310-312, 315-317, 334, 336, 341, 347, 367, 375, 387, 392, 396, 406-407, 411, 414, 428-429, 437, 464-465
efficient, 27, 115, 275-276, 387
final, 5-6, 25, 122, 134-135, 275, 319, 322, 327, 387, 416
first, 275, 335
formal, 23
habitual, 167-168
intentional, 166-168
just, 56, 101
mental, 278

[cause]
natural, 135
necessary, 115, 134
of beauty, 336-337, 398
of pleasure, 45
sublime, 277-278, 439-440
voluntary, 166
Charles the Fifth, 43
Charles the First, 332
Charles the Second, 56, 65-70
Chaucer, Geoffrey, 451
Cicero, 7, 9, 15, 35-36, 51, 108, 239, 243, 246, 283, 348, 353, 356, 375, 400
Circe, 364
Clarendon, Lord, 246
Clarissa, 302
Claude Lorrain, 28, 346, 411
Claudian, 306
Cleomenes, 36
The Club, 331
Coleridge, Samuel Taylor, 30
Collins, Anthony, 71
comedy, 13, 24, 38-39, 42, 44, 47, 52, 55-61, 65, 66, 67, 68, 69, 70, 240, 367, 379, 385, 455, 461
common sense, 21, 287, 326-330, 334, 343, 344, 346, 375
Cooper, Lady Elizabeth Ashley, 165
Copernican system, 48
Correlli, Arcangelo, *Eighth Concerto*, 368-369, 456, 462
Corinthian order, 321, 349, 446
Corneille, Pierre, 109, 353, 391
Correggio, Antonio Allegri, 34, 50, 218, 304, 306-307
Coryphaeus, 48
Cowley, Abraham, 65, 379
Cowper, William, 222
criticism, 2, 8, 13-14, 16, 55, 65, 132, 192, 232-233, 258, 267, 285, 287-290, 293-294, 297-298, 309, 313, 316, 320, 323, 325, 331-332, 340, 342, 360, 374, 378, 383-388, 395, 406, 412-413
critics, 1, 11, 25, 43, 59, 63, 76, 78, 81-82, 89, 152, 196, 228, 230, 232, 235, 237-238, 240-242, 284, 286-287, 290, 295, 331-332, 338, 368, 384-385, 388, 401, 447, 466
ancient, 109, 378, 394
[critics]
French, 43, 48, 391
German, 393
modern, 63, 109, 359, 394
painting, 333
poetry, 332, 343
professional, 31
rules, 384
Critique of Judgment, 18
Crousaz, Jean-Pierre, *Traité du Beau*, 283
Cumae, 41
Cupid, 37, 212
Curtius Rufus, Quintus, 41
Cyclops, 364
Cyllarus, 36

da Vinci, Leonardo, 36
Dacier, Madame, 48, 109, 360
D'Alembert, Jean, *Reflections on Taste*, 285, 374
Dancier, Andre, 44
Dante, Alighieri, 365
Davenant, Sir William, 42
Decii, 41
decorum, 74, 94, 96, 138, 198, 200, 258
delicacy, 17, 19, 37, 61, 222, 228, 234-236, 238, 240, 273, 306, 378, 398
definition of, 234
in nature, 223
of beauty, 223
of external sense, 378
of feeling, 228
of imagination, 234
of passion, 17-19, 227-229
of sentiment, 17, 228
of taste, 17-19, 227-229, 235, 328, 358, 377-378
delight, 44-45, 60, 69, 86, 92, 96, 111-114, 115, 133, 156, 160-161, 184, 201-203, 235, 244, 262-264, 277-278, 282-284, 363, 367, 405, 411-412, 413, 414, 415, 416, 458
Demetrius, 35
Democritus, 140
Demosthenes, 51, 400
Dennis, John, **55-70**; 8, 13, 31, 55, 70, 107
She Would If She Could, 65
Descartes, Rene, 1, 3, 7, 9, 13, 18, 124, 133, 158, 239

Diana, 444
Diderot, Denis, 407
Dido, 40, 46, 207
Diogenes the Cynic, 146
Dionysius Halicarnasseus, 305
disinterested, 176
  cases, 103
  disinterestedness, 2, 9, 13, 19, 30, 83, 212
  pleasure, 20
  word, 2
Dodsley, Robert, 191
Domenichino, 332
Domitian, 43
Don Quixote, 143, 234
Doric order, 321, 349
Dorset, Lord, 56
Dryden, John, **33-54**; 12, 24, 31, 33, 65, 128, 135, 339, 353, 390
  Absalom and Achitophel, 24
  Antony and Cleopatra, 49
  Montezuma, 46
  Spanish Fryar, 52
  Tyrannique Love, 50
  St. Catherine, 39
Du Bos, Abbe Jean-Baptiste, 12-13, 22, 242, 267, 434
Du Piles, Roger, 464
Duclos, Mr., 469
Durer, Albrecht, 218, 436

Ecclin, Dr., 370
Edinburgh University, 373, 441
efficient cause, 27, 115, 275-276, 387
Elijah, 148
Eliosa, 302
Elphinston, Lord, 205
Elysium, 364
empiricist, 1-3, 6-10, 12, 23
epic poetry, 6, 39-41, 44-45, 48-50, 185-186, 231, 238-239, 241, 294, 363, 381, 383, 400, 460, 465
Epicurus, 239, 390
Epistle to Burlington, 16
Erasmus, 357
Essay on Human Understanding, 262
Etheridge, Sir George, 379
Ethiopian, 336
Euripides, 43, 45, 49
Euryalus, 48
Evander, kingdom of, 41
Eve, 184
exemplar, 37, 74
expression
  theory of, 1, 7, 10, 30, 31, 38, 40, 49, 50, 60, 149, 233, 236, 239, 240, 244-246, 298, 306, 317, 343, 346, 370-371, 381, 398-399, 410, 417, 418, 455, 463-464, 466, 468
  of mind, 417, 420
  powers, 30
  music, 30
external sense, 21, 25, 152-153, 157, 160, 162, 279, 291, 317, 323, 374, 376, 378, 411, 461

faculty, 8, 15, 124, 132-135, 184, 235, 253, 362
  intellectual, 108
  natural, 254
  of discernment, 311
  of genius, 385
  of imagination, 25-26, 67, 110
  of reason, 8, 10, 184, 250, 257, 264
  of taste, 16, 18, 108-109, 237, 249, 251, 258-259, 305, 340, 373-375, 378, 405-407, 409
  of understanding, 257
Falstaff, 56, 57, 61, 62, 311
fancy, 25, 36-58, 64, 75-77, 79, 81, 83, 89-90, 92-93, 96-97, 109-112, 114-115, 117-118, 121, 123, 124, 126-133, 162, 168, 214, 233, 253, 269, 304, 340, 342, 344, 353, 359-360, 369, 378, 382, 410-413, 414, 424, 453, 459, 464
fear, 60, 127, 138, 144, 146, 153, 162, 185, 186, 200, 203, 207, 227, 256, 265-266, 269, 353, 390-391, 414, 454
Fenelon, Francois, 230-231
  Adventures of Telemachus, 400
Fenton, 57
Fielding, Henry, 433
final causes, 5-6, 23, 25, 115, 122, 134-135, 162, 302, 319, 322, 327, 387, 416

fine art, 2, 10, 12, 30, 280, 282, 287, 292-295, 299, 309, 316, 320, 325-329, 368, 383, 385, 386, 409-410
fitness, 4, 146, 215-218, 282-284, 287-288, 337, 374, 397, 399-400
  sense of, 399, 400
Fitzosborne, 294
Fontenelle, Bernard le Bovier de, 22, 227, 243
Ford, 57, 62
form, 12, 21, 23-24, 28, 30, 35-37, 73, 84, 103, 152, 158-160, 162, 167, 176, 209, 213, 217-220, 222, 226, 233, 268-269, 283, 299-300, 319, 320, 325, 336, 337, 344, 350, 351, 356, 390, 411, 432, 434, 436, 440
  Aristotelian, 9, 21, 25
  artificial, 154
  classical, 10-11
  cognitive, 21
  criterion, 336
  elegant, 215, 220, 222, 283
  external, 222, 346-347, 352, 388, 417
  formalism, 28
  human, 143, 200, 214, 216, 219, 220-221, 224, 444-445
  imagined, 35
  imitative, 367, 464
  irregular, 158
  logical, 8
  mental, 7, 27
  musical, 450
  natural, 35, 159, 210, 335, 337, 342, 424
  of beauty, 36, 153, 159, 202, 209, 215-216, 219, 221, 283, 290, 318, 336-337, 396-397, 400, 418, 424, 427, 439-440
  of emotion, 20
  of experience, 19
  of faces, 47
  of government, 382
  of judgment, 21
  of matter, 418
  of mind, 176, 418
  of pleasure, 21
  of reason, 18
  of the novel, 31
  of sublime, 400
  of tragedy, 39
[form]
  picturesque, 27, 435
  Platonic, 24, 34, 35
  pleasant, 158, 160-161, 225, 234, 397
  regular, 158-159, 163, 214, 224, 336, 397, 447
  serpentine, 221
  ugly, 160
Fox, Charles James, 431
Foxley, 431
Francis the First, 43
Franco, Battista, 352
Frazer, Dr., 56
Fresnoy, Charles du, 12, 33, 44, 46, 50, 280-281, 350
futurists, 27

Gainsborough, Thomas, 24
gardens, 27-28, 90, 92, 96, 116-119, 123, 124, 128, 134, 153, 157, 165, 175, 272, 299, 320, 327, 328, 397, 411, 423, 427, 431, 434, 442, 447, 448, 458
  Abbotsford, 431
  Gardens and the Picturesque, 28
Garrick, David, 205, 331
genius, 14, 25, 37, 43, 45, 47, 50, 73, 77-78, 86, 89, 91, 93, 96-97, 108-109, 118, 125, 129, 142, 152, 162, 173-175, 181, 183-186, 189, 191, 195, 199, 207-208, 216, 228, 232-233, 237, 239, 241, 244, 247, 258, 279, 284, 294-295, 298-299, 318, 321, 327, 331-335, 338-340, 343, 346, 353, 357, 358, 360-361, 365, 367-368, 376-379, 381-386, 395, 400, 405, 408, 413, 424, 433, 436, 442
George Barnwell, 302
George III, 24
Gerard, Alexander, **279-296**, 5, 9, 13, 20, 25, 279, 355, 367, 374, 388, 395
  Essay on Taste, 279, 402
Gilpin, Sawrey, 421
Gilpin, William, **421-430**, 25, 29, 31, 421, 435, 437, 438
Giordano, Luca, 346
Glasgow University, 279, 355, 441
Glycon, 36, 216

golden ratio, 25
Goldsmith, Oliver, 205, 331, 345
Gondibert, Sir William Davenant, 42
Gothic, 50, 77, 81
  architecture, 289, 317, 323, 378, 391, 443
  buildings, 161
  cathedral, 120
  manner, 49
  taste, 109, 221, 282, 328
grace, 5, 15, 65, 67, 72, 74-75, 78, 91, 94-95, 140, 184, 209-210, 215, 218-224, 297, 304, 306, 320, 332, 346, 361, 397, 398, 400, 455, 464, 467
  line of, 220
Graces, 444
grandeur, 92, 112, 120, 131, 142-143, 145, 146, 148-149, 155, 157, 190, 192, 194-195, 199-200, 202, 313, 318, 321-323, 328, 345, 386-394, 399, 401, 436, 439
Granville, Mr., 63
Gratian, Balthasar, 16, 19, 107
Gray, Thomas, 423
Guarini, Guarino, 50
Gulliver, 212

Hamlet, 343
Handel, George Friedrich, 189, 456, 462
  Te Deum, 368
  Water Music, 368
Hannibal, 392
harmonious, 70, 95, 103, 128, 151, 162, 240, 343, 368, 369, 370, 374, 423
harmony
  beauty, 25, 97
  to the eye, 96
  idea of, 142, 152, 154, 162
  mind, 96
  moral, 81, 230
  music, 30, 59, 75, 81, 160, 175, 236, 306, 321, 340, 370, 454-455, 458, 460-464
  nature, 12, 81, 95-96, 201, 282, 341, 363
  numerical, 25
  painting, 38, 333, 433
  passions, 199
  perception of, 279
  person, 96
[harmony]
  pleasure, 163, 376, 401
  poetry, 51, 85, 188, 345, 356, 360, 367, 423
  sense of, 25, 152-153, 162, 280, 437
  sound, 290, 298, 323, 369
  style, 297
Harris, James, **165-190**, 23, 165, 190, 402
Hartley, David, 4-5, 298
Hector, 40, 46, 52, 208
hedonism, 19, 20, 30
Helen, 35
Henry the Eighth, 218
Henry the Fourth, 56
Hercules, 37, 41, 157, 195, 199, 202, 215, 216, 222, 444
  of Farnese, 36
Hermes, 178
Herodias, 306
Hiburnicus, 137
Hippocrates, 43
Hobbes, Thomas, 2, 19-20, 137-138, 140, 142
Hogarth, William, **209-226**, 11, 25, 209, 273, 282, 398, 407
  Analysis of Beauty, 282, 397
  Progress of Cruelty, 367
Holbein, Hans, 34
Homer, 20, 37, 39-41, 45, 50, 52, 73, 111, 124-125, 135, 138-139, 143, 145-146, 179, 200, 207, 230, 231, 233, 254, 262, 269, 294, 314, 324, 334, 339, 356, 360, 380, 383, 384, 386, 394, 402
Horace, 43, 45, 50, 52, 64-65, 68, 70, 73, 88, 97, 103, 107, 109, 116-117, 123, 125, 128, 130, 137, 142, 149, 168, 180, 182, 240, 256, 257, 314, 353, 360, 364, 391
  Art of Poetry, 42, 46, 52, 141, 187, 205, 214, 223, 267, 356-357, 359
  Epistles, 55, 205
  Odes, 360
  Satires, 65, 244, 360
Hudibras, 138, 141, 143
Hudson, Thomas, 331
Hume, David, **227-248**, 5-11, 13, 17-23, 26, 227, 230, 242, 279, 309, 355, 374, 408, 441

[Hume, David]
Dialogues Concerning Natural Religion, 227
History of England, 227
Of Delicacy of Taste and Passion, 17, 18, 227
Of the Standard of Taste, 20
A Treatise of Human Nature, 18, 21, 227
Hunt, John Dixon, 28
Hutcheson, Francis, **137-164**, 4, 8-9, 19, 20-22, 25, 137, 150, 279, 417, 441
Essays on the Passions, 279
Inquiry Concerning Beauty, 279, 395
Hyde-Park, 216

idea, 3-5, 9, 21-22, 24-27, 30, 34-37, 95, 110, 113-115, 120-124, 132-133, 135, 142-145, 147, 150, 151-152, 157, 161, 166, 178, 181-184, 186-187, 189-190, 192, 194, 201, 203, 213-214, 218-219, 245, 250, 253-254, 261, 266, 270, 272, 281, 284-285, 298, 300-302, 305-307, 310, 311, 336, 338-339, 342, 367, 383, 399, 400, 402, 413-415, 428, 451, 453
abstract, 156
and judgment, 311
association, 3-5, 22, 142, 160-162, 215, 285, 298, 299, 309, 310-311, 313, 317, 336-337, 348, 353, 393, 396, 399, 457
clear, 266, 267, 269, 300, 390, 394
clear and distinct, 8
complex, 3, 17, 21, 25, 123, 151, 160, 161
confused, 394, 435, 437
correct, 350, 352
disagreeable, 124, 142, 425
distinct, 132
eternity, 268
from words, 126
gaudiness and levity, 285
gravity and sedateness, 285
high, elevated, great, 143-146, 148, 193-194, 197, 202, 334-335, 342, 345, 388-389, 391, 394, 395
imitation, 157

[idea]
in the mind, 116, 119, 202, 209, 210, 250, 311
innate, 4, 9, 138
Locke, John, 297
low, 143, 144-148, 367
moral, 398
obscure, 268
of an atom, 132
of art, 166, 169, 170, 171
of beauty, 8, 20, 36-37, 137, 142, 150, 152-155, 161-162, 184, 234, 249, 270-271, 273, 304, 335-336, 342, 348, 353, 388, 393, 395, 399, 401, 421-422, 428, 437
of character, 187
of color, 116, 150, 151
of danger, 277
of deformity, 36
of eloquence, 37
of falsehood, 243
of fitness, 218
of heroism, 82
of home, 96
of nature, 38, 45, 270, 337, 342, 347, 415
of objects, 111, 115, 122-123, 142, 154, 157, 213, 267, 270, 272, 301, 402, 422
of pain, 263
of a painter, 37
of perfection, 37-39, 72
of pleasantness, 127
of rest and motion, 218
of sensation, 150
of sense, 21, 151, 153-154, 156, 253, 257, 299, 347, 407, 428
of substance, 151
of taste, 162, 209
of terror, 266
of variety, 273
of weakness, 215
original, 340
perfection, 39-40, 143
picturesque, 422, 426, 427, 435, 439
Platonic, 34, 35
pleasant, 152, 158, 161, 189, 218, 285, 415
relation of, 232
representational, 21
rest or motion, 281

[idea]
simple, 5, 21-22, 151-152, 156, 160, 194, 257, 260
social, 264
sublime, 125, 197, 201, 249, 265, 271, 388-391, 393-395
true, 3
utility, 428
word, 21
Iliad, 40-41, 77, 124-125, 207, 262, 360, 380, 383, 394, 402
imagination, 7, 10, 14, 25-26, 30, 35-38, 42, 52-53, 58, 66-69, 72, 76, 84, 89, 92, 110-116, 118-136, 143, 147, 155-156, 162, 189, 190, 192-195, 197-198, 201-203, 206-207, 209, 213-214, 220, 222, 224, 232, 234, 236-238, 240, 242-246, 250-251, 253-256, 258, 263, 267, 269, 277, 284, 294-295, 298, 300-301, 306-307, 313-314, 322, 332, 334, 336, 339-340, 342, 344, 346-348, 352-353, 361-362, 381, 383, 389-390, 395, 400, 408-416, 418, 444, 447, 451, 458-459, 461
beauties of, 244
defects, 136
delicacy, 234, 239
faculty of, 25-26
force of, 245
pain, 136, 253
play of, 2, 257
pleasures of, 22, 26, 107, 110-114, 116-118, 121-122, 126, 130, 132, 134-136, 142, 230, 253, 257-258, 286, 298-299, 301, 343, 386-387, 392, 395, 400-401, 410
poetic, 339
polite, 306
power of, 121, 135, 246, 253, 279, 333, 387
taste, 256, 401
imitation, 462
theory of, 23-25, 29-30, 35, 157, 181, 184, 187, 264, 324, 402
Adam Smith, 25, 30
Aristotle, 23-24, 44, 265
art, 74, 178, 409
beauty, 157
divine, 83
[imitation]
effects, 427
Hume, 22
in children, 374
instruction, 264
language, 187
moral, 367
musical, 30, 180-185, 188-190, 365, 368-371
nature, 24, 179, 184, 212, 376, 380, 384, 402
objects, 24, 154, 157, 186, 188, 216, 304
painting, 24, 36, 181, 184, 236, 333, 369, 402, 436
passion, 45, 264
Plato, 24
pleasure, 23, 45, 61, 162, 184, 188, 217, 244, 245, 253-254, 264-265, 268, 365-368, 376, 386, 401
poetic, 139, 180-185, 187-188, 208
poetry, 402
power of, 265, 267
reality, 433
rules, 45, 157, 208, 265
senses, 280
Spenser, 208
tragedy, 186, 244, 367
truth, 44, 162, 179, 185, 222, 254, 256, 369, 370
Virgil, 207
imitation of nature, 14, 23, 24, 44, 61, 148, 157, 342-343, 369, 384, 461
Imlac, 26
impressions, 3, 5, 21, 69-70, 109, 116, 132, 153, 189, 195, 212, 253, 257, 284, 299, 304, 306, 313, 315, 318-319, 325, 328, 330, 359-360, 367, 374-375, 387-388, 390-391, 393-395, 400, 402-403, 412-414, 453, 461
association of, 5
intellectual soul, 21
interest, 44, 68, 88, 93, 98, 108, 138, 153, 163, 229, 237, 327, 345
national, 93
of princes, 68
private, 90, 93, 98, 100
public, 100, 103
self, 30, 87, 157, 329, 392

internal sense, 21, 24-26, 152-153, 156, 161-163, 238, 279, 298, 374, 377, 380
invention, 12, 42, 45, 50, 53, 122, 128, 169, 206, 233, 238-239, 251, 253, 294, 353, 356, 360, 364, 401, 405, 417-418, 442, 450-451, 460, 464
Ionic order, 321, 349
Isse, 459

James, Duke of York, 24
je ne sais quoi, 14, 72
Job, 269, 390
Johnson, Samuel, **205-208**, 10, 13-14, 26, 165, 205, 303, 331
  Rassalas, 26
Jonson, Ben, 61, 208
Joshua, 82
Jove, 36-37, 423
Juno, 37, 40, 241
Jupiter, 36, 39, 49, 119, 125, 241, 304, 444
Justice Shallow, 57
Juvenal, 367

Kames, Lord (Henry Home), **309-330**, 13, 20, 22-23, 25, 285, 309
Kant, Immanuel, 1-2, 9, 18-19, 30-31, 405
  Critique of Judgment, 18
  idealism, 30
Kent, William, 431
King's College, Aberdeen, 279
Kircaldy, 441
Kitcat Club, 107
Kivy, Peter, 10
Klein, Robert, 15
Knight, Richard Payne, 431
Koran, 231
Kristeller, P. O., 10

La Fontaine, Jean de, 109
Lacedemonia, 307
Landscape gardening, 27, 28
Laocoon, 344, 444
Latimer, William, 421
Laurentum, 41
Lausus, 46
Lawrence, Thomas, 24
laws of nature, 12, 49, 286, 291, 293, 353, 364-365
Leibniz, G. W. von, 1, 3, 7, 9
Lentulus, 39
Leo the Tenth, 43
Leonora, 52
Limerick, 303
line of beauty, 218, 220, 222, 225, 273, 397, 423
Livy, 41, 108, 130
Locke, John, 1, 3-8, 10, 12, 20, 25, 30, 71, 116, 253, 262, 297
logic, 8-9, 11, 25, 73, 87, 355, 441, 463
  classical, 11
  inferences, 11
  of taste, 250
  reasoning, 383
  rules, 11
Longinus, 9, 26-27, 109, 145, 191-193, 198, 378-379, 394
Lopez de Vega, Felix, 45
Lucan, 51
Lucretius, 110, 141
Lysippus, 35, 37, 120

Mandeville, Bernard, 137
Mandeville, Sir John, 365
mannerist painting, 16
Mantegna, Andrea, 436
Maratti, Carlo, 334
Marcellus, 51
Marischal College, 279, 355
Marlborough, Duke of, 55
Mason, William, 357
Massano, 36
Maximus Tyrius, 35
McCosh, James, 441
Medicean Venus, 36
Meleager, 444
Memnon, 37
Mercury, 444
Merry Wives of Windsor, 56
Metamorphosis, 125
metaphor, 9, 15-16, 18, 27, 34, 51-53, 108, 132, 142, 167, 201, 232, 251, 254, 315, 339, 349, 363, 374
Metastasio, 455
Michaelangelo, 34, 83, 125-126, 161, 218, 332, 334-335, 436

Milton, John, 130, 135, 182, 184, 208, 232, 266, 268, 295, 361, 367, 389, 411, 413, 447, 452, 456
Paradise Lost, 188, 379
mimesis, 178, 180, 183-185, 188, 190, 401, 402
Minerva of Athens, 36
Misenus, 51
modern(s), 2, 10, 36, 85, 86, 216, 320, 434, 465
aesthetic, 1, 31
and ancients, 5-7, 16, 43, 49-50, 56, 64, 67, 80, 83, 108-109, 118, 120, 135, 150, 208, 226, 294, 303, 305, 334, 351-353, 368, 375, 378, 394, 401, 452, 465
and classicism, 2, 3, 24
and empiricism, 7
and science,
authors, 84
critics, 359
drama, 357
dress, 344-345, 351-352
genius, 357
languages, 73
modernism, 1
moralists, 80
music, 469
painting, 304, 332, 334, 352, 445
philosophy, 116, 279
science, 3, 6, 10, 73, 116
Moliere, Jean Baptiste Poquelin, 61, 109
Monk, Samuel, 191
Montague, Charles, Earl of Halifax, 107
Montaigne, Michel de, 63
Montausier, Madame de, 61
Moses, 82
Mount Athos, 120
Moyle, Walter, 45
Muse, 74, 82-83, 189, 339
mythology, 460

natural law, 20
neo-classicism, 11
rules, 11, 12
neo-Platonism, 24, 27
Newton, Isaac, 1, 3, 4, 6-7, 9-10, 12, 275, 413
Nicias, 180
Nicomachus, *Tyndarides* of, 245
Niobe, 422, 444
Nisus, 48
Normanby, Marquees of, 40, 56, 59-60
novel, 25, 31, 77, 192, 302
Nugent, 13
Nymphs, 444

Octavia, 51
Oedipus, 39, 49
Of the Standard of Taste, **230-241**, 18
Ogilby, John, 232
Olympus, 197
Orestes, 133, 148
Ossa, 197
Oswald, James, 297
Othello, 245
Ovid, 36, 40, 114, 124-125, 130, 132, 135, 240, 247, 258

Pallas, 36, 39, 138
Paradise Lost, 125
Parrhasius, 43
passions, 4-5, 8-9, 11, 13, 17-19, 37, 42, 45-46, 49, 58-60, 67, 95, 98, 100-103, 126, 130, 135, 137, 141-142, 144, 147-148, 161-162, 178-179, 181, 185-187, 195-198, 200-203, 227-229, 233, 236-240, 242-249, 253, 256-258, 260, 262-264, 266, 267-271, 274-277, 279, 284, 298, 301-302, 305, 316, 334, 338, 343, 346-349, 357-358, 361, 363, 379, 384-385, 391, 394-395, 434, 447-449, 451-457, 463
active, 45
admiration, 195
agreeable, 229, 245, 323, 454
beauty, 270
calm, 21, 24
curiosity, 400
delicacy of, 17, 227-229
derision, 150
dignified, 345
disagreeable, 135
elegant, 229
fame, 197

[passions]
fear, 265-266
harmony, 199
hateful, 102
imitation, 264-265
jealousy, 245
love, 60, 96, 271, 464
lust, 263
melancholy, 244
mirth, 140, 240
musical, 454
natural, 27
painful, 26
self, 101-102
social, 323, 454
sublime, 27, 195-200, 202, 265, 276-278
superstition, 79
terror, 277-278
tragic, 79, 126, 186, 244, 455
uneasy, 242, 247
vicious, 454
violent, 144, 146-147, 257, 270, 343, 367
virtue, 199
pathetic, 179, 191-192, 194, 201, 203, 240, 243-244, 246, 290, 306, 381, 394
Patroclus, 52
Paul, St., 179, 332
Pembroke, Lord, 165
perfection, 40, 74, 123, 151, 162, 167, 171, 173, 180, 184, 194, 220, 228, 237, 270, 279, 284, 289, 321, 325, 327, 375, 386
human, 386
idea of, 37-39, 72, 143
of art, 6, 35-36, 43-44, 72, 75, 157, 174, 183, 258, 304, 327, 337, 346, 350, 398, 433
of beauty, 162
of character, 38, 58
of imagination, 123
of imitation, 185
of man, 107, 152, 171, 235
of music, 174
of nature, 94, 172
of numbers, 72
of painting, 43
of poetry, 39, 116, 125, 129, 133, 135, 359, 360
of proportion, 131
of sense, 134, 235, 279, 280, 380, 412
[perfection]
of the soul, 124
of statues, 174
of taste, 108-109, 235-236, 328, 377, 409
of tragedy, 48
of virtue, 348
of writing, 192, 401
Pergolese, Giovanni Batista, 455
Pericles, Prince of Tyre, 47
perspective, 6, 9, 11, 25, 103, 216-217, 281, 444, 448
Perugino, 436
Petrarch, 241, 416
Petronius, 52
Pharsalia, 51
Phidias, 35-37, 120, 304, 344
Philander, 95
Philostratus, 37-38, 43
picturesque, 9, 25-31, 421, 422-423, 426-427, 431, 434-440
beauty, 422-423, 427, 431, 435, 437, 440
composition, 424
eye, 426-427, 435
music, 437
object, 424, 426-427, 435-436, 439
poetry, 423
scenery, 421, 434, 461
tourists, 31
word, 435
Pilgrim's Progress, 255
Pindar, 423
Pitcairn, Dr., 139
Pity, 39, 46, 48-49, 72, 102, 126, 147, 150, 185-186, 315, 361, 367
Plato/Platonic, 23, 34, 37, 39, 239, 353, 454
beauty, 24
distinction between passion and appetite, 17
division of the mind, 18
emblem, 24
form, 24-25
imitation, 24
model, 24
participation, 27
Platonism, 24, 27
Republic, 17, 24
school of, 417
Timaeus, 35
pleasure of the fancy, 111

pleasure of the imagination, 22, 26, 107, 110-112, 114, 118, 121-122, 132, 134-135, 142, 257-258, 298, 301, 386-387, 392, 410
Pliny, 76, 245
Plutarch, 73
Polieucte, 241
Polycrates, 179
Pontormo, Jacopo, 15
Pope, Alexander, 3, 14, 16, 19, 202, 320, 353, 357, 360, 367, 371, 460
  Epistle to Burlington, 16
  Essay on Criticism, 55, 320
  Ode on St. Cecilia's Day, 460
Poussin, Nicholas, 42, 212, 332, 342-343
Praxiteles, 36
pre-Raphaelites, 30
Price, Uvedale, **431-440**, 27, 431
Priestley, Joseph, **297-302**, 2, 5, 19, 22-23, 297
Prometheus, 37
proportion, 9, 12-13, 25, 36, 38, 66-67, 74, 77, 81, 84, 92-99, 102-103, 108, 113-114, 120, 131, 151-153, 155, 169, 180, 184, 196, 199, 202, 212, 215-216, 218, 222, 232, 236, 242, 246, 270-271, 280, 282-283, 288-289, 299, 301, 307, 313, 318-321, 327-328, 337, 341, 349, 353, 362, 374, 386, 391, 396-397, 399, 407, 412-414, 422, 428, 433, 442, 446, 451-452, 464, 467-469
Protogenes, 37, 43, 53
psychological atomism, 30
Pufendorf, Samuel, Baron von, 138
Pylades, 148

Queen Charlotte, 24
Queen Elizabeth, 61
Quintilian, 9, 15, 189, 305, 375

Racine, 109
  Esther, 48
raillery, 86, 97, 143, 240, 461
Rand, Benjamin, 73
Raphael, 34, 36, 43-45, 75, 179, 184, 304, 306-307, 323, 332-333, 335, 342, 413, 436
Rassalas, 26
rational soul, 18
rationalist, 1, 8-11, 18
reflexive sense, 21
Rehearsal, The [George Villiers, 2nd Duke of Buckingham], 129
Regulus, 179
Reid, Thomas, 279, 297, 355
  On the Intellectual Powers of Man, 417
Rembrandt, 333, 342, 444
Reni, Guido, 36, 218, 306, 332, 425
Repton, Humphrey, 28
Republic, 17, 24
Reynolds, Joshua, **331-354**, 11-14, 24, 205, 331, 407, 435
rhetoric, 5, 9, 11-12, 15, 22, 25-27, 95, 268, 297, 309, 367, 373, 375, 393-394, 441
Richardson, Jonathon, 331
ridicule, 25, 86-87, 89, 96, 140-141, 146-150, 234, 280, 331, 358, 370, 401, 439, 447, 461
ridiculous, 88, 146
  objects, 146
  sense of, 58, 148
  sentiment of the, 144
Rochester, Lord, 53, 56
Rockingham, Marquees of, 249
romance (literary form), 77, 116, 128, 192, 302, 364, 401
Romano, Julio, 16, 342
romanticism, 10, 11, 26, 411
Rome, 6, 16, 36, 41, 75, 120, 210, 212, 224, 233, 302, 307, 350, 392, 436, 442
Rosa, Salvator, 28, 179, 423
roughness, 27, 251, 422-427, 438-439
Rousseau, Jean-Jacques, 10, 413, 458-459
Royal Academy, 331
Rubens, Peter Paul, 34, 212, 306, 333, 344-345
rules, 11-14, 75, 77, 82, 149, 232, 284, 326-327, 332
  for artists, 11
  for the audience, 11-12
  classical, 6, 12, 23, 43-44, 52, 76, 179
    Aristotle, 383
  common, 327
  critical, 11-14, 16, 89, 233, 286-287, 289-290, 292, 313, 331-332, 383-384
  dramatic, 8, 12, 45, 52, 383, 461

[rules]
empirical, 12, 13, 14, 20, 277, 287, 292, 293
and genius, 284, 331, 340, 353, 384
for gardens, 118
logical, 11-12
mechanical, 109
moral, 231, 327-328
musical, 368, 370
neo-classical, 11-12
of architecture, 118
of art, 12, 14, 39, 43, 45, 72, 210, 216, 232, 233, 286, 288, 306, 328, 331-333, 338, 340, 341, 343-344, 346-348, 355, 385, 421
of beauty, 158, 235, 270, 383, 385, 397, 428
of grammar, 300
of harmony, 81
of imitation, 45, 157, 222, 265, 333, 365
of nature, 12, 44, 233, 292, 333, 336, 368, 380, 383-384
of painting, 33, 44-46, 217, 269, 332-333, 337
of perspective, 281
of proportion, 428
of society, 150
of taste, 13, 16, 107, 109, 231, 250, 252, 285-286, 293, 328, 381, 384, 409
of tragedy, 43
poetic, 39, 41, 44, 45, 129, 339
time, 41
rhetorical, 27, 192, 232, 235
Longinus, 394
sublime, 192
Ruskin, John, 30

Sallust, 108, 314
Sappho, 394
Savil, Mr., 56
Schelling, Friedrich, 30
scholasticism
modes of expression, 1
speculaton, 2
Scipio, 41, 148, 300
Scornful Lady, 50
Scott, Walter, 431
Scottish Enlightenment, 227, 309
Scylla and Charybdis, 364
secondary quality, 24, 25, 322
Semiramis, 119
Seneca, 36
sense
beauty, 6-7, 21, 25, 151-156, 158-163, 215, 228, 264, 280, 323, 374, 376-377, 380, 399, 412, 428
external, 157
fitness, 399-400
harmony, 25, 152-153, 162, 280, 437
internal, 21, 24-26, 152-153, 156, 161-163, 238, 279, 298, 374, 377, 380
ridiculous, 58, 148
taste, 16, 24, 153, 251, 280, 340, 374
sensus communis, 138
sentiment, 7-8, 10-11, 13, 17-20, 26, 59, 70, 74, 81, 84, 94, 103-104, 144, 146, 149, 153, 162, 185-188, 205-206, 208, 229-241, 243-244, 249, 251, 255, 284-295, 297-298, 300-301, 303, 327, 338-340, 347, 352, 356, 358, 362-364, 367, 376-377, 379, 381-382, 385, 391, 393-394, 400, 402, 409, 412, 414, 422, 449, 451-452, 454-456, 458, 463
aesthetic, 18
delicacy, 17, 228
humanistic, 137
Hume's view, 11
in music, 320
moral, 17-19, 230-231, 241, 359, 401
of affection, 245, 264, 439
of compassion, 246
of melancholy, 414
of music, 453, 455
of sublimity, 283
of taste, 290-291, 384
of uneasiness, 245
pleasant, 279, 294
sentimentalism, 20, 24
Shaftesbury's view, 10
sublime, 146
serpentine
form, 221-222
line, 219-222
Shaftesbury, Anthony Ashley Cooper, Third Earl of, **71-106**; 6, 10-12, 16-19, 71, 73, 137, 190, 417
Advice to an Author, 17

Shakespeare, William, 14, 55, 57, 61, 70, 78, 129, 245, 290, 310-311, 343, 364-365, 385-386, 433
Sidley, Sir Charles, 56
simplicity, 9, 25, 73, 76, 80, 93, 110, 141, 215, 225, 230, 240, 270, 280-282, 289, 290, 292, 306, 318, 319-321, 329, 344, 351, 352, 380, 392, 395, 407, 408, 427
Slighted Maid, 49
Smith, Adam, **441-470**, 23-25, 30, 441, 466
smoothness, 25, 27-28, 121, 151, 182, 193, 223, 251, 256, 272, 274, 317, 322, 343, 398, 421-423, 425, 426-427, 434, 437-438
Socinian, 297
Socrates, 11, 109
soliloquy, 11, 76, 84-85, 95, 97
Sophocles, 39, 43, 45, 49, 383
Spectator, 8, 16, 26, 107, 137-138, 140, 142, 386, 395, 461
Spence, 417
Spenser, Edmund, 130, 208, 361
Sprat, Bishop, of Rochester, 65
St. Anthony, 269
St. Augustine, 21, 408
St. John the Baptist, 306
St. Mark, library of, 352
St. Michael, 306
St. Paul's, 331, 442
St. Peter's, 442
Statius, 51, 53, 306
Steele, Richard, 55, 107, 138
Strabo, 85
sublime, 2, 9, 13, 25-27, 73-74, 83, 103, 125, 142, 145-146, 176, 179, 191-203, 219, 240-241, 249, 263, 265-269, 271, 274-278, 289-291, 331, 334, 339, 362, 370, 374, 387-395, 397-398, 400, 405-408, 412, 417, 422, 431, 435-437, 439-440
  sublimity, 25-27, 30, 143, 188, 202, 269, 275, 280, 283, 332, 383, 387-395, 399-401, 405, 407-411, 413-418, 420, 436-438, 440
Suckling, Sir John, 379
Swift, Jonathan, 107, 221, 367, 370, 378
  Ode on Ditton and Whiston, 371
syllogism, 11-12
Sylvae, 51
symmetry, 38, 70, 74, 81, 94, 97, 111, 114, 217-218, 283, 318, 391, 422, 438

Tacitus, 108, 240, 379
Tasso, 364
taste, 1-2, 6-7, 9, 13-20, 24-25, 28-29, 44, 55-56, 63-66, 70, 73-78, 81-82, 85-86, 88-94, 97, 107-109, 121, 123, 133, 144, 152-153, 156, 158, 160, 162, 209, 213, 218, 222, 224-226, 228-230, 232-240, 242-243, 249-260, 274, 279, 280-282, 284-289, 291, 293-295, 297-299, 305-307, 313, 316, 318-321, 323-330, 332, 338, 340-342, 345-346, 348-350, 352-353, 358, 361-362, 365, 367, 373-388, 395, 398, 400-402, 406, 408-411, 417, 421, 428, 432, 447-448, 464
  a common, 327
  and color, 346
  and criticism, 383-384
  and dress, 350
  and genius, 152, 162, 321, 338, 340, 346, 368, 382-383, 385, 386
  and imagination, 387, 401, 459
  and judgment, 15-17, 75, 89
  and nature, 358
  and poetry, 379, 386
  and proportion, 319
  and reason, 9, 17-18, 249, 374, 377, 379, 381
  and religion, 382
  and rules, 13, 16, 107, 109, 231, 250, 252, 285-286, 293, 328, 381, 384, 409
  and sensibility, 377, 459
  and smell, 15, 203
  and touch, 15, 203
  Chinese, 328
  classical, 9, 14-15
  definition of, 374
  delicacy of, 17-19, 227-229, 235, 239, 258, 324, 328, 358, 377-378, 386
  diversity of, 379, 380
  emotions of, 18, 405-408, 412, 415

[taste]
faculty of, 16, 18, 251, 258-259, 373-375, 385, 405
Gothic, 221, 282, 328
Grecian, 378
innate, 428
internal, 376, 378, 381
internal sense, 377, 380
judgment of, 257, 299, 305, 329, 340-341
logic of, 250
mental, 235
metaphor of, 15-16, 18, 250, 374
in morals, 325
musical, 368, 376
national, 349, 352
nature of, 280, 301, 373, 386, 410
objects of, 256, 259, 288-289, 330, 342, 351, 377-381, 385, 405, 407, 409, 412-413, 415
in poetry, 379, 385
operations of, 382
pleasures of, 252-253, 288, 292, 294, 324, 357, 363, 375-376, 383, 386-387, 395, 400-401, 407, 413
powers of, 292, 377
principles of, 9, 238, 240, 249-252, 254, 256-257, 259, 279, 285-286, 291, 292-293, 299, 305, 330, 340-342, 344, 353, 374, 381-382, 384, 405, 428, 432
properties of, 387
public, 384
qualities of, 289-290, 293, 378, 406
refined, 385
sense of, 15-16, 24, 153, 251, 280, 340, 374
sentiments of, 290-291, 381-382
standard of, 13, 18-20, 86, 230, 231, 234, 238-239, 249, 285, 287, 294, 323-328, 330, 337, 352, 373-374, 379-382, 384, 428
subject of, 406
theory of, 5, 14, 270
uniformity of, 327, 330
variety of, 327
works of, 295
Tempest, 365
Terence, 239
terror, 126-127, 129, 133, 135, 199, 201, 242, 244, 246, 262-263, 265, 266,
[terror]
269, 276-278, 361, 393, 409, 423, 439-440
The Dark Side of Landscape, John Barrell, 28
Thebais, 51
theorem, 152, 154, 156-157, 163, 203, 317, 320, 396
Thomson, James, 361, 363
Seasons, 412
Timomachus, *Medea* of, 245
Tintoretto, 346, 352
Titian, 34, 44, 50, 184, 306, 346, 352, 436, 464
Toland, John, 71
Torismond, 52
Tower of Babel, 119
tragedy, 22, 24, 38-41, 43-48, 53, 70, 186, 238, 240, 242-244, 246, 357, 367, 379, 381, 385, 391, 455, 461
Treatise of Human Nature, 5, 18, 21, 227
Trojan, 47, 48, 52
tropes, 50-51, 394
Troy, 40-41, 52, 206, 207
Tully, 73, 304-307, 392
Turnus, 41, 46, 48, 52
Tuscany, 41

Ulysses, 145, 206-207, 231
uniformity amidst variety, 8-9, 21, 25, 155-156, 158, 160, 196, 280-283, 289, 313, 320, 344, 396, 437, 462
unities of time, place, and action, 109, 383, 461
Urban the Eighth, 36
utility, 25, 95, 175, 186, 188, 190, 282-283, 295, 317-320, 322-323, 356, 360, 408, 428

Van Dyck, Sir Anthony, 34, 332, 351
Vandervelt, 427
Vasari, 15, 352
Venus, 36, 39, 42, 74, 125, 212, 222, 225-226, 245, 298, 440, 444, 454
Medicean, 36
of Gnidus, 36
Veronese, Paolo, 346, 352
Verres, 243, 246

Versailles, 64, 448
Virgil, 34, 39-41, 44-45, 48, 50-53, 77, 109, 117-118, 124-127, 130, 133, 135, 138, 146, 182, 207, 239, 255, 257, 269, 294, 300, 306, 315, 356, 361, 380, 383, 389, 400, 402, 413
Georgics, 125, 314, 412
virtue, 4, 5, 8, 15, 17, 19, 25, 29, 38-39, 41, 44, 62, 71, 73-74, 80-81, 85, 91, 93, 95-98, 102, 104-105, 111, 130, 137, 140, 150, 163, 176, 195, 198-200, 202, 207, 230, 241, 246, 251, 256, 270, 279-280, 327, 342, 348, 357-359, 361, 392, 395, 399, 454
ancient, 6, 25, 418
moral, 30, 231, 241
public, 92
social, 74, 399
the word, 230
virtuoso, 73, 76, 86-87, 96, 303
Vitruvius, 95, 338
Voltaire, Francois Marie Aroet de, 352

Wall of China, 119
waving line, 218-220, 222, 397-398
Wealth of Nations, 441
Webb, Daniel, **303-308**, 7, 24, 303
Westminister Abbey, 445
Whichcote, Benjamin, 71
William III, 107
Winkelmann, Johan Joachim, 407
wit, 8, 58-60, 64, 71, 73, 79, 81-82, 86, 88-91, 96, 109-110, 122, 138-139, 141, 143, 147-149, 235, 253, 311-312, 348, 379
and comedy, 57-60
and humor, 8, 84, 401
and poetry, 82
human, 82
metaphysical, 10-11
satiric, 86
Wolff, Christian, 1
Wordsworth, William, 431
Wright, Mrs., 445
Wycherley, William, 60
Wycliff, William, 421

Xeuxis, 43

Young, Edward, *Night-Thoughts*, 363

Zerner, Henri, 15
Zeuxis, 35, 37, 50
Zuccaro, Federico, 15-16

For Product Safety Concerns and Information please contact our EU
representative GPSR@taylorandfrancis.com
Taylor & Francis Verlag GmbH, Kaufingerstraße 24, 80331 München, Germany

www.ingramcontent.com/pod-product-compliance
Ingram Content Group UK Ltd.
Pitfield, Milton Keynes, MK11 3LW, UK
UKHW021719240926
475702UK00029BA/1423
9780415772334